GEORGIOS DIMITROPOULOS /
ATHANASIOS GROMITSARIS / MARTIN SCHULTE (Hrsg.)

Staatsreform für ein besseres Europa
State Reform for a Better Europe

D1723678

Schriften zum Öffentlichen Recht

Band 1314

Staatsreform für ein besseres Europa
State Reform for a Better Europe

Herausgegeben von

Georgios Dimitropoulos
Athanasios Gromitsaris
Martin Schulte

Duncker & Humblot · Berlin

Gedruckt mit Unterstützung
der Alexander von Humboldt-Stiftung, Bonn

Bibliografische Information der Deutschen Nationalbibliothek

Die Deutsche Nationalbibliothek verzeichnet diese Publikation in
der Deutschen Nationalbibliografie; detaillierte bibliografische Daten
sind im Internet über http://dnb.d-nb.de abrufbar.

Fremddatenübernahme: Konrad Triltsch GmbH, Ochsenfurt
Druck: Meta Systems Publishing & Printservices GmbH, Wustermark
Printed in Germany

ISSN 0582-0200
ISBN 978-3-428-14858-5 (Print)
ISBN 978-3-428-54858-3 (E-Book)
ISBN 978-3-428-84858-4 (Print & E-Book)

Gedruckt auf alterungsbeständigem (säurefreiem) Papier
entsprechend ISO 9706 ∞

Internet: http://www.duncker-humblot.de

Vorwort

Die Beiträge dieses Bandes stellen die aktualisierte Dokumentation des in Athen und Sounion am 30./31. Mai 2013 stattgefundenen „Humboldt-Kollegs" zum Thema „Staatsreform für ein besseres Europa" dar. Sie befassen sich mit zwei einander bedingenden Aspekten der Euro- und Verschuldungskrise. Einerseits gibt es reformbedürftige Defizite im europäischen Integrationswerk. Andererseits gibt es einen Reformstau in den Mitgliedstaaten. Beide Aspekte verstärken sich gegenseitig und behindern nachhaltig die europäische Integration, die zusätzlich dadurch erschwert wird, dass alles Handeln in diesem Kontext schon sehr früh auf den Gesichtspunkt nationaler Divergenz gebracht wurde.

Die Tagungsbeiträge wollen zu adäquaten Problemstellungen führen. Diese können allerdings angesichts der Komplexität der Zusammenhänge nicht rein juristischer bzw. öffentlich-rechtlicher Natur sein. Vielmehr sollen komplexe Zusammenhänge durch wissenschaftlich kontrollierbare Begriffe und Instrumente und nicht allein mit Alltagstheorien und Erfahrungswissen erfasst werden: denn der öffentliche Sektor selbst erlebt seinen Alltag als eine Aufgabe im Spannungsfeld von Politisierung, Wirtschaftlichkeit und Stabilität. Vor dem Hintergrund der Mehrdimensionalität der Sachverhalte bewegt sich somit die Fragestellung im Überschneidungsbereich verschiedener Fachrichtungen. Erst eine Fachkombination von Verwaltungsrecht und Verwaltungswissenschaften kann die den verschiedenen Mitgliedstaaten der Europäischen Union zugrundeliegenden Verwaltungskulturen in ihrer öffentlich-rechtlichen Relevanz erfassen und rechtliche Fragestellungen entwickeln, die nicht lebensfremd sind.

Das Recht spielt bei der Staatsreform eine Doppelrolle. Einerseits verlangt das Verfassungs- und Verwaltungsrecht, dass sich ein Rechtsstaat nur mit rechtsstaatlichen Mitteln reformieren darf. Nicht alle Reformansätze sind daher rechtlich zulässig. Andererseits sind Rechtsdurchsetzung und Verfahrenseffizienz unverzichtbare Reformressourcen, die Vertrauen generieren und ein Land zu einem attraktiven Investitionsstandort machen können. Im Europa der Verschuldungskrise entwickeln sich ferner alle Lösungsansätze im Geltungsbereich der Schuldner/Gläubiger-Differenz. Den damit einhergehenden gegensätzlichen Strategien der Mitgliedstaaten und dem damit verbundenen moralischen Risiko versucht man mit der Entpolitisierung wichtiger Entscheidungen und Institutionen zu begegnen. Dies kann zwar dazu führen, dass politische und administrative Reformwiderstände erfolgreich überwunden werden. Die Schaffung entpolitisierter Instanzen erhöht aber zugleich das Demokratiedefizit. Gibt es Ersatzmechanismen, die hier juristisch, demokratietheoretisch und legitimatorisch einen Ausgleich schaffen können? Umgekehrt: Sind die Reformer selbst reformierbar? Sind sie imstande, von den ungewollten Nebenwirkungen ihres Handelns und den Rückbetroffenheiten, die sie selbst verursachen, zu lernen? Die Europa- und Staatsverschuldungskrise muss somit auch als eine Krise des Reformbegriffs thematisiert werden. Das bedeutet zugleich, dass ohne die Unterstützung der institutionellen Änderungen durch die jeweils betroffene Bevölkerung keinerlei Reformkonzept Aussicht auf Erfolg hat.

Die Realisierung des Humboldt-Kollegs verdankt sich der großzügigen Unterstützung der Alexander von Humboldt-Stiftung und des Deutschen Akademischen Austauschdienstes. Für die generöse Förderung der Veröffentlichung des Tagungsbandes sind wir der Alexander von Humboldt-Stiftung zu tiefem Dank verpflichtet. Herrn Prof. Spyridon Flogaitis und dem erfahrenen Verwaltungsstab der Organisation, die er leitet, der European Public Law Organisation (EPLO) danken wir für die tatkräftige Unterstützung in Athen und für die Zurverfügungstellung der Tagungsräume in Athen und Sounion. Dem geschäftsführenden Gesellschafter des Verlags Duncker & Humblot Herrn Dr. Florian R. Simon danken wir sehr herzlich für die Aufnahme des Bandes in das Veröffentlichungsprogramm des Verlags.

Dresden und Luxemburg, im November 2015

Georgios Dimitropoulos,
Athanasios Gromitsaris, Martin Schulte

Inhaltsverzeichnis

Erster Teil

Zur gegenseitigen Bedingtheit von Europäischer Integration und nationalen Reformen / On the Mutual Conditionality of the European Integration and National Reforms

Zweiter Teil

Krisenbewältigung und Gegenstand der Reform: Zur Reform als Krisenausweg / Crisis Management and Reform Agenda: On Reform as a Way Out of the Crisis

Dritter Teil

Der Staat im Spannungsfeld von Politisierung, Wirtschaftlichkeit und Stabilität / Facing the Challenges of the Public Sector: Party-Political Influence, Cost-Effectiveness and Stability

Begrüßung

Sehr geehrter Herr Botschafter der Bundesrepublik Deutschland,

Sehr geehrte Damen und Herren,

Ich heiße Sie an der European Public Law Organization willkommen, der internationalen Organisation, die unser Land der internationalen Gemeinschaft vorgestellt hat, mit dem Ziel, Forschung, Bildung, Ausbildung und den Aufbau von Institutionen in Griechenland, Europa und der ganzen Welt zu fördern.

Der heutige Tag ist sehr wichtig für uns, da die European Public Law Organization im Rahmen eines Humboldt-Kollegs zum ersten Mal eine institutionelle Partnerschaft mit zwei sehr wichtigen deutschen wissenschaftlichen Initiativen von internationaler Relevanz, der Alexander von Humboldt Stiftung und dem Deutschen Akademischen Austausch Dienst (DAAD), schafft. Die EPLO ist sehr stolz auf diese Kooperation und ich bin persönlich berührt. Ich bin mehrmals vom DAAD für die Vollendung meiner Promotion finanziell unterstützt worden, wobei ich auf der Grundlage der Unterstützung der Alexander von Humboldt Stiftung die Chance gehabt habe, drei unvergessliche Jahre in Heidelberg zu verbringen, wo ich die Monographie geschrieben habe, der ich meine (Voll-)Professur an der Universität von Athen verdanke, der Bildungseinrichtung, die die Tradition von Platon, Aristotelis, Libanios und so vielen anderen neu belebt hat.

Der griechische Staat wurde eigentlich von den Bayern errichtet, insbesondere vom Professor des französischen Öffentlichen Rechts an der Universität München und Mitglied der deutschen Verfassungsbewegung, Georg Ludwig von Maurer, mit der Unterstützung des stellvertretenden Mitglieds des Regentschaftsrates, Carl August von Abel. Maurer musste nach vierzehn Monaten unermüdlicher Versuche der Schaffung von Institutionen, die für die internationale Praxis seiner Zeit unvergleichbar gewesen sind, das Land verlassen und zurück nach München gehen. Nach vielen Jahren und kurz vor der Entthronung Ottos verfasste er ein zweites Buch mit seinen Erinnerungen und Beobachtungen; dieses Buch, das lange Zeit unbekannt und unveröffentlicht geblieben war, haben Frau Vassiliki Roustopani und ich herausgegeben. Die Wirklichkeit hat den anderen Geheimrat von König Ludwig, Friedrich von Tiersch, bestätigt, der die späteren Ereignisse in einem ebenfalls bis vor kurzem unbekannten Buch mit dem Titel „De la régence en Grece" vorhergesehen hatte, das Heinrich Scholler, Professor an der Universität München, und ich mitveröffentlicht haben.

Die bayerische Verwaltung des griechischen Staates mag zu einem Ende gekommen sein; die fruchtbare Beziehung zwischen der griechischen und der deutschen

Wissenschaft ist jedoch nie zu einem Ende gekommen, und auch heute noch ist die deutsche Sprache die am häufigsten gesprochene Sprache an der Juristischen Fakultät der Universität Athen. Diese Beziehung, die tief in den beiden Ländern verwurzelt ist, bringt uns heute alle zusammen, Deutsche und Griechen, um uns an Maurer und alle diejenigen zu erinnern, die sich mit Philhellenismus um dieses Land verdient gemacht haben, und um erneut den Grundstein für diese gute Beziehung im größeren Rahmen der Europäischen Union zu legen.

Sehr geehrter Herr Botschafter,

ich möchte noch einmal mein Gefühl der Ehre für Ihre heutige Präsenz unter uns zum Ausdruck bringen. Erlauben Sie mir gleichzeitig, die Gelegenheit nicht zu verpassen, Sie an den von der European Public Law Organization seit Jahren wiederholten Wunsch zu erinnern, dass Deutschland dem internationalen Gründungsvertrag der Organisation beitritt und in diesem Rahmen die entsprechende Rolle spielt.

Ich bedanke mich ganz herzlich bei Ihnen

Prof. Dr. Dr. Dr.h.c. Dr.h.c. *Spyridon Flogaitis*

Direktor der European Public Law Organization

Erster Teil

Zur gegenseitigen Bedingtheit von Europäischer Integration und nationalen Reformen / On the Mutual Conditionality of the European Integration and National Reforms

What Kind of State Does the EU Require?

By *Matthias Ruffert*

Initially, the European integration process does not formulate requirements for the internal structure and functioning of Member States, and all relevant theoretical approaches – federalism, constitutionalism, republicanism – about the (future) shape of the EU do not focus upon statehood. However, these theoretical foundations contain core concepts for governance within the Member States which are backed by positive obligations within the Treaties. The foundation of power in the Member States is interrelated to the law of the European Union by the concept of the common good developed in the idea of the office and in the values and aims of the EU, and so is the limitation of power by fundamental rights, the rule of law and democracy. This has also impacts on economic governance.

I. Introduction: The EU and the State

To ask for the requirements that the EU formulates for a (Member) State implies a paradox. Initially, the European integration process is not about States, but about overcoming their negative impact in the historical shape of nation States. Although the border-sweeping enthusiasm of the early 1950 s is apparently gone, the conservation of nation States as they were shaped in the 19th century is certainly not viable within the European Union.

The same applies to the political and legal concept of the State as coined before the beginning of the integration process. European integration theory is therefore in continuous search for alternative approaches. Just three of them – which are closely interlinked with each other – may be recalled:

- *Federalist* theories of European integration[1] are less searching for ways to build a European federal State in the sense of *Walter Hallstein's* "unvollendeter Bundesstaat" (unaccomplished federation)[2], but for a construction of Europe which underlines the federative elements in an environment of diversity. The "Staatenverbund" ("association of sovereign States")[3] created by the Bundesverfassungsge-

---

[1] Cf. only the seminal work by *R. Schütze*, From dual to cooperative federalism: the changing structure of European Law (OUP, 2009).

[2] *W. Hallstein*, Der unvollendete Bundesstaat (Econ, 1969).

[3] The concept is explained in the Court's English translation (highlighting by the Court) of its Lisbon judgment, (available at: http://www.bundesverfassungsgericht.de/entscheidungen/es20090630_2bve000208en.html) para 229.

richt in its Maastricht and Lisbon judgments belongs to these theoretical approaches as does the "Verfassungsverbund", a specific interpretation of multilevel constitutionalism established by *Ingolf Pernice*.[4]

– *Constitutionalism* generally is a theoretical perspective to analyse the European integration process.[5] The Treaties are seen as a constitution without a State, closely interlinked with constitutional provisions of the Member States. Again, we are faced with a concept for which statehood is of secondary importance, if important at all.

– More recently, some authors – whether lawyers or from other disciplines – are conceiving the European Union as a *Republic*[6]. The application of the republican idea which might appear somehow redundant at domestic level where democracy, the rule of law and the welfare State provide for many of the elements in what is deemed to be properly republican[7], at the supranational level brings along a series of traditional institutions for the well-being of the *res publica*. We shall see later that these institutions are very important to formulate and categorize the requirements that are at the core of this short contribution.

II. The (Re-)Discovery of the State

1. Reasons

If we are faced with a retreat of the State in theory – and also in practice if only the de-regulatory force of the internal market with its clear orientation towards private economic activity is considered[8] – it might appear confusing (or paradoxical) to look at requirements for States and their reform processes. However, in many fields of European Union law, the need for efficient Member States' governments has become apparent most recently: Can the EU operate an effective refugee policy respecting fundamental human rights without proper protection of its external borders and decent treatment of alien citizens within the Member States? How can a common eco-

---

[4] *I. Pernice*, 'The Treaty of Lisbon. Multilevel Constitutionalism in Action', (2009) 15 Columbia Journal of European Law 349–407.

[5] Cf. only: *A. von Bogdandy/J. Bast* (eds.), Principles of European Constitutional Law, 2nd edition (Hart, 2010).

[6] See most recently *R. Menasse*, Der Europäische Landbote: Die Wut der Bürger und der Friede Europas oder Warum die geschenkte Demokratie einer erkämpften weichen muß (Zsolnay, 1012), short version ('Es lebe die europäische Republik') in: Frankfurter Allgemeine Sonntagszeitung 24 March 2013, p. 24; and earlier *A. von Bogdandy*, ‚Konstitutionalisierung des europäischen öffentlichen Rechts in der europäischen Republik' (2005) 60 Juristenzeitung 529–540 at 533–537.

[7] Seminal contribution: *R. Gröschner*, 'Die Republik', in: J. Isensee/P. Kirchhof (eds.), Handbuch des Staatsrechts, Band II, Verfassungsstaat, 3rd ed. 2004, § 23.

[8] Overview: *M. Ruffert*, 'Zur Leistungsfähigkeit der Wirtschaftsverfassung' (2009), 134 Archiv des öffentlichen Rechts 197–239 at 229–233.

nomic policy be established in a currency union without well-working economic and fiscal institutions in the Member States? Is it not impossible to establish transnational governance if mutual trust into administrative structures of the Member States is disturbed?

The reason why we ask these questions today is not a legal, but a historical-political one. The Treaties are built around a reality of statehood and State governance which is rooted in the tradition of many of the Member States and which is so dominant that deviances might often have been overlooked. The questions just enumerated, however, show that a reflection of what kind of State the Union requires to build a federal, constitutional or republican superstructure on that basis is absolutely necessary. In doing so, we should try our best to avoid the transfer of particular domestic models to the Union as such but to take up the supranational theoretical approaches, to develop requirements out of them – and to show their realisation in positive EU law. This leads to a twofold analysis.

2. Core Concepts and Positive Obligations

a) Foundation of Power: The Common Good

aa) The Common Good

Taking up the European traditions of federalism, constitutionalism and republicanism, public power is first of all and above all founded to realise the common good. Politics in the European Union is ideally not to serve particular interests, a clientele or a class. This broad formulation might appear nearer to political philosophy than to constitutional law, but it has been moulded into clear and concrete legal institutions that may serve as tools and instruments to its fulfilment. The two most important of them shall be expounded here: the office ('Amt') and the values/aims of the Union.

bb) Office ('Amt')

The *office* ('Amt') is a neutral, though not un-political micro entity created for the common good and separate of its holder[9].

There is of course no explicit passage on this concept in the Treaties, but the idea of the office is virtually existent in European law. This is not only shown in the requirements for the holders of offices in the EU: The independence of the Commissioners, confirmed in the prohibition to "… engage in any other occupation, whether gainful or not." and in their duty to "… refrain from any action incompatible with their duties or the performance of their tasks.", all underlined by a respective solemn undertaking (Articles 17 (3) sub-section 3 sentence TEU, Article 245 TFEU)[10], can

---

[9] In detail: *Gröschner* (supra note 7), paras 62–68.
[10] Cf. also the Code of conduct for Commissioners, Doc. C (2011) 2904.

be named as well as the requirements for the office of a ECJ-judge, laid down in Article 254 – "... persons whose independence is beyond doubt and who possess the ability required for appointment to high judicial office." Generally: "In carrying out their missions, the institutions, bodies, offices and agencies of the Union shall have the support of an open, efficient and independent European administration." (Art. 298 (1) TFEU)[11]; the Staff Regulations (Article 336 TFEU) are enacted to that purpose[12]. What is more, the Member States' competences to create and maintain offices in the "public service" are explicitly recognised in Articles 45 (4) and 51 TFEU respectively.[13]

The dangers for the concept of office are as obvious as its political-philosophical and constitutional-legal foundations. The corruption reported in several Member States is a warning sign in this respect[14].

cc) Values and Aims

The formulation of *values* and *aims* of the EU as a polity, taking up the substantial orientation of the exercise of power rooted in European tradition.

The constitutional basis for such can be found right at the beginning of the TEU in Articles 2 and 3 TEU. It is useful to recall the text of Article 2 TEU which gives the Union a clear orientation in values: "The Union is founded on the values of respect for human dignity, freedom, democracy, equality, the rule of law and respect for human rights, including the rights of persons belonging to minorities."[15]

Article 3 TEU formulates and develops the EU's constitutional aims – "peace, its values and the well-being of its peoples." From that trifold aim-structure, only the third element ("well-being of its peoples") shall be taken up due to the fact that it contains the core economic aims and that it is within an economic context that the issue of 'state quality' is discussed in this volume.[16]

---

[11] Cf. *M. Ruffert*, in: C. Calliess/id. (eds.), EUV/AEUV-Kommentar (Beck, 4th ed. 2011), Article 298 AEUV, para 10.

[12] Last amendment: Regulation (EU, Euratom) No 1080/2010 of the European Parliament and of the Council of 24 November 2010 amending the Staff Regulations of Officials of the European Communities and the Conditions of Employment of Other Servants of those Communities, OJ L 311 p. 1.

[13] On this exception *T. Oppermann/C. D. Classen/M. Nettesheim*, Europarecht, (Beck, 5th ed. 2011), para 27/26–28.

[14] For the time being, the first EU-Anti-Curruption Report has not yet been published; cf. Commission Decision C(2011) 3673final of 6 June 2011. There is more information in the Evaluation and Compliance Reports of the GRECO (Groupe d'États contre la Corruption)-Reports within the Council of Europe; cf. http://www.coe.int/t/dghl/monitoring/greco/default_en.asp.

[15] On the value-orientation cf. *C. Calliess*, "Europa als Wertegemeinschaft – Integration und Identität durch europäisches Verfassungsrecht", (2004) 59 Juristenzeitung 1033–1045.

[16] The author owes many of the following arguments to the vivid discussion around the presentation in Athens.

The relevant aim is further concretised in Article 3 (3) 1st sub-paragraph, 2nd sentence TEU: The EU "... shall work for the sustainable development of Europe based on balanced economic growth and price stability, a highly competitive social market economy, aiming at full employment and social progress, and a high level of protection and improvement of the quality of the environment." Particularly a *highly competitive social market economy* requires effective government for the implementation of legal rules formulated at supranational level, for the following reasons:

To begin with, the current crisis that we are so intensively concerned with is by no means exclusively or even predominantly driven by external factors. One of the greatest problems in the factual perception of the crisis is the differentiation of its effects in the various Member States. Ireland and Spain had balanced public budgets before the crisis struck them; in Ireland, problems were obviously triggered by a too lenient policy in taxation and financial market regulation, in Spain by excessive developments in the real estate market[17]. Italy has been facing severe deficiencies in public governance for a long time, and so has Greece, where the external factors leading to the situation in late 2009/early 2010, i.e. the repercussions of the subprime crisis, were just the straw that broke the metaphorical camel's back[18]. A variety in reasons calls for a differentiated approach, and where internal causes are dominant, the requirements towards the respective Member State are more important than elsewhere. A highly competitive social market economy is apparently impossible without discipline in budgetary matters and an effective taxation system. The dangers for the latter need not be further expounded here.

What is more, the paradigmatic shift within the constitutional arrangements of the Economic and Monetary Union (EMU) since 2010 is putting even more responsibilities upon the Member States as it concentrates on political and administrative means of government rather than employing market forces for governing budgetary discipline.[19] Whether in the field of the administration of emergency measures (Troika and Task Force being extensively discussed in this volume), the intensification of centralised economic steering (as this is e.g. done in the Regulations on macro-economic governance that are part of the "Sixpack"[20]), the establishment of effective budgetary

---

[17] Contrary to what has been expressed as a singular view in the discussion, it is not EU action that caused the present high unemployment rate of young people in Spain, but the effects of the crash in the Spanish housing market.

[18] The internal problems of governance in Greece were most illustratively described in the presentations at the conference. Cf. in particular the contribution by *P. Karkatsoulis*, in this volume.

[19] This shift is explained in *M. Ruffert,* 'Mehr Europa – eine rechtswissenschaftliche Perspektive', (2013) 28 Zeitschrift für Gesetzgebung, pp. 1–20.

[20] Regulation (EU) No. 1176/2011 of the European Parliament and of the Council on the prevention and correction of macroeconomic imbalances, OJ 2011 L 306 p. 25, and Regulation (EU) No. 1174/2011 of the European Parliament and of the Council on enforcement action to correct excessive macroeconomic imbalances in the euro area, OJ 2011 L 306 p. 8.

control (which lie at the heart of the future of EMU[21]), the building of common banking supervision capacity (which is still rather controversial given the limited competence of the EU[22]) – in all these areas, capacity building at EU level, whether in the Commission, the ECB or in other institutions, must be accompanied by effective implementation capacity at Member State level. It shall not be overlooked that such implementation entails hardship in particular for those States that are subject to emergency measures, and in particular for the weakest members of society – the young, the unemployed, the poor etc. It would however be cynical to avoid a comparison of this hardship with what could have happened without any intervention of the EU and its Member States in March-May 2010 and the following time: the unprecedented default of a Member State (i.e. Greece) in its own currency (i.e. the Euro)[23].

b) Limitation of Power: The Sectoral State

Next to the foundation of power, it is also its limitation that can be rooted in the constitutional-republican (and federalist) concept as initially described. In this respect, the Treaties contain a series of indications that it is individual freedom, the rule of law and democracy to be at the heart of European integration – with a concomitant demand to the Member States and a sanctioning system for hard cases (Article 7 TEU)[24].

– The whole integration process is basically built on the four economic freedoms (persons, goods, capital, services) which submit State power under a requirement of rationality.[25]

---

[21] The most recent development is the adoption of the "Twopack": Regulation (EU) No 472/2013 of the European Parliament and of the Council of 21 May 2013 on the strengthening of economic and budgetary surveillance of Member States in the euro area experiencing or threatened with serious difficulties with respect to their financial stability, O.J. 2013 No. L 140, p. 1; Regulation (EU) No 473/2013 of the European Parliament and of the Council of 21 May 2013 on common provisions for monitoring and assessing draft budgetary plans and ensuring the correction of excessive deficit of the Member States in the euro area, O.J. 2013 No. L 140, p. 11.

[22] Cf. Doc. COM (2012) 511 final and the following deliberations.

[23] There were doubts in the discussion in Athens whether this obvious fact was common knowledge. The matter is discussed in *C. Herrmann*, 'Griechische Tragödie – der währungsverfassungsrechtliche Rahmen für die Rettung, den Austritt oder den Ausschluss von überschuldeten Staaten aus der Eurozone' (2010) Europäische Zeitschrift für Wirtschaftsrecht, pp. 413–418.

[24] On that system *K. Serini*, Sanktionen der Europäischen Union bei Verstoss eines Mitgliedstaats gegen das Demokratie- oder Rechtsstaatsprinzip (Duncker&Humblot, 2009).

[25] *M. Ruffert*, 'Sektorales Wirtschaftsrecht als Teil des europäischen Wirtschaftsrechts', in: id. (ed.), Europäisches Sektorales Wirtschaftsrecht – Enzyklopädie Europarecht, Vol. 5, (Nomos, 2013), para 1/9–13.

– Since the early 1970 s, a system of protection of fundamental rights has been developed by the ECJ[26] which was codified in the Charter of Fundamental Rights, formally binding since the entry into force of the Lisbon Treaty 2009[27]. The accession to the European Convention on Human Rights will provide an overarching level of protection.[28]

– The rule of law is a core value of the Union, and the protection of rights is institutionally enshrined in the ECJ, including its co-operative relationship with Member States' Courts (Articles 19 (1) TEU and 47 ChFR).

– "The functioning of the Union shall be founded on representative democracy." Democratic governance is not only laid down in this core sentence of Art. 10 (1) TEU, but also in the values of the Union and in its institutional construction. Member States must achieve democratic rule; the democratic accountability of the Members of the Council is expressly fixed.[29]

III. Summary and Outlook

When the EU was for the first time obliged to formulate conditions for accession following the lucky disruption of the iron curtain in the early 1990 s, the European Council did so in Copenhagen in 1993[30]. All Member States that are now subject to emergency measures were already Member States at that very time. The criteria are along the lines of the above theoretical description including its realisation in positive law, and they appear to lay down what had always been a matter of course in the States joined in European integration. This applies to the very fundamental criteria: stable institutions guaranteeing democracy, the rule of law, human rights and respect for and protection of minorities, but also for the ability to take on and implement effectively the obligations of membership, including adherence to the aims of political, economic and monetary union. Apparently, this already reveals core economic capacities of the States involved, which is further underlined in the criterion of a functioning market economy and the capacity to cope with competition and market forces in the EU. The central challenge now is to secure the fulfillment of the requirements after accession is completed.

---

[26] *D. Chalmers/G. Davies/G. Monti*, European Union Law (CUP, 2nd ed. 2010), at 232– 236.

[27] Consolidated text in OJ 2012 C 326 p. 391.

[28] The Draft Accession Agreement was finalised on 5 April 2013, COE Press release – DC041(2013).

[29] Cf. *M. Ruffert*, in: Calliess and id. (supra, n. 11), Article 10 TEU, para 7. Critically *R. A. Lorz*, 'Das Problem des demokratischen Defizits', in: Tsatsos (ed.), Die Unionsgrundordnung (Nomos, 2010) 331–355 at 341.

[30] Conclusions of the European Council, 21 to 22 June 1993, Dok. SN 180/1/93, p. 13.

What should be shown here, with reference to the theoretical foundations of European integration, the text of the Treaties and the current shift in economic governance, is that the requirements addressed to the Member States are not based on a simple import-export-relationship from one group of States (or even single State) to others (which would have no factual means to object), but that they are deeply rooted in European Union law and its well-based constitutional traditions. It is not the spectre of homogeneity that is haunting the EU, but the risk of failing to preserve these foundations.

Horizontalisierung von Governance und Reform in der Europäischen Union

Reform in der EU zwischen internationalen und supranationalen Governance-Strukturen

Von *Georgios Dimitropoulos*[1]

Einleitung

Die gegenwärtige Krise in Europa ist nicht nur das Ergebnis des Versagens der Finanzmärkte, sondern auch des Versagens von Politik und Recht.[2] Die Krise der politischen und rechtlichen Institutionen in der EU hat die europäischen Institutionen und die mitgliedstaatlichen Regierungen dazu geführt, zahlreiche Reformen vorzunehmen.[3]

Wenn die Debatte in der gegenwärtigen Phase der Entwicklung der EU die Reform von Institutionen betrifft, dann sollte darüber nachgedacht werden, was der richtige *locus* für Reformen ist. Reformen können auf der Ebene der europäischen Institutionen, auf der Ebene der Mitgliedstaaten oder auf der Ebene der Interaktion der Mitgliedstaaten mit den europäischen Institutionen vorgenommen werden. Die EU hat in den letzten zwanzig Jahren nachhaltig neue Governance-Strukturen geprägt, so dass eine besondere Beziehung zwischen Reformen auf der mitgliedstaatlichen und auf der europäischen Ebene entstanden ist. Auf der Grundlage neuer Governance-Strukturen entsteht nämlich eine gegenseitige Bedingtheit zwischen den Rechtsordnungen der Mitgliedstaaten und der Rechtsordnung der EU, die zu einer Bedingtheit der Reformen auf der einen Ebene bezüglich der anderen führt.

Im ersten Abschnitt beschreibt der Aufsatz die Evolution der Rechtsordnung der EU.[4] Diese Rechtsordnung kann als die Summe der mitgliedstaatlichen Rechtsordnungen und der Rechtsordnung der europäischen Institutionen begriffen werden. Es

---

[1] Dr. iur., LL.M. (Heidelberg), LL.M. (Yale); Senior Research Fellow, Max Planck Institute Luxembourg for International, European and Regulatory Procedural Law.

[2] Vgl. auch *Lene Hansen/Michael C. Williams*, The Myths of Europe: Legitimacy, Community and the „Crisis" of the EU, Journal of Common Market Studies 37 (2002), S. 233 ff.

[3] Siehe mit einer Bewertung aus rechtsstaatlicher Perspektive *Armin von Bogdanda/Michael Ioannidis*, Das systemische Defizit – Merkmale, Instrumente und Probleme am Beispiel der Rechtsstaatlichkeit und des neuen Rechtsstaatlichkeitsaufsichtsverfahrens, ZaöRV 74 (2014), S. 283 ff.

[4] Vgl. dazu den klassischen Aufsatz von *Joseph H. H. Weiler*, The Transformation of Europe, Yale Law Journal 100 (1991), S. 2403 ff.

werden die Entwicklung der Rechtsordnung der europäischen Ebene als eine klassische völkerrechtliche Ordnung, die Bildung der Autonomie dieser Rechtsordnung und die Harmonisierung der nationalen Rechtsordnungen auf der Grundlage der Vorgaben des *acquis communautaire* betrachtet. Der Staat nimmt jeweils unterschiedliche Rollen in der Entwicklung des Europäischen Rechts ein. In den letzten Jahren weist die Rechtsordnung der EU als Ganzes nochmals Charakteristika einer Völkerrechtsordnung auf. Das Verfahren der Wiedererscheinung von solchen Elementen in der Rechtsordnung der EU wird hier mit dem Begriff der „Horizontalisierung" beschrieben.

Die Horizontalisierung schlägt sich in bestimmten Governance-Strukturen nieder.[5] Beispiele von Funktionen und Bereichen horizontaler Governance im Europarecht werden im zweiten Abschnitt beschrieben. Das Ziel europäischer Governance ist es nicht mehr, große Strukturen auf der EU-Ebene oder gleiche nationale Rechtssysteme, sondern vielmehr nationale Systeme zu schaffen, die gleichwertig und kompatibel sind.

Diese Tendenzen beinhalten die Antwort auf die Frage, ob und wie eine Staatsreform Europa verbessern kann. Mit den aktuellen Reformdebatten und dem Trend einer Horizontalisierung kehrt der Staat noch einmal in den Vordergrund des Europarechts zurück. Im dritten Abschnitt wird gezeigt, dass Reformen auf der mitgliedstaatlichen Ebene erforderlich sind, wenn ebenfalls die europäische Ebene eventuell reformiert werden soll, und es werden erforderliche Reformen für ein besseres Europa vorgeschlagen. Auf der Grundlage der Idee der horizontalen Governance wird im vierten Abschnitt die Erscheinung eines „Rechts der Reformen" beschrieben.

---

[5] Vgl. auch *Paul James Cardwell*, The Changing Nature of European Regulatory Governance, in: David Levi-Faur (Hrsg.), Handbook on the Politics of Regulation, Cheltenham 2011, S. 536 (538). Diese Beschreibung basiert auf einem soziologischen Verständnis von Governance – da die Soziologie den gesellschaftlichen Wandel als eine der wichtigsten Fragen der Disziplin betrachtet – nicht als ein Instrument von Macht, sondern als Produkt der Gesellschaft. Siehe die Definition von Governance von *Hans-Heinrich Trute/Wolfgang Denkhaus/Doris Kühlers,* Governance in der Verwaltungsrechtswissenschaft, DV 37 (2004), S. 451 (463): „Hier ist es eben nicht mehr der nationale Gesetzgeber, der souverän die Meta-Regeln der Kooperation zwischen unterschiedlichen Ebenen und von Staat und Privaten gewährleistet. Er ist vielmehr in ein Geflecht mit anderen Akteuren eingebunden und hat es im Übrigen mit einer Verwaltung zu tun, die ihrerseits in ein Gefüge mit anderen nationalen und supranationalen Akteuren eingebunden ist und die die Wissensbestände in einem komplexen Prozess generiert, der zugleich darauf gerichtet ist, erst eine gemeinsame Problemsicht zu schaffen und damit dem Harmonisierungsziel gleichsam von der kognitiven Seite her näher zu kommen".

I. Horizontale Reform zwischen
internationalen und supranationalen Dimensionen

1. Die Evolution internationaler Rechtsordnungen

Im internationalen Rechtssystem gibt es ständige Strukturveränderungen, so dass von unterschiedlichen Paradigmen internationalen Zusammenwirkens gesprochen werden kann.[6] Traditionell gilt das Völkerrecht als das Recht der Koordination der staatlichen Interessen und der Sicherung koordinierten Existenz der Staaten.[7] Das Völkerrecht und die Völkerrechtsordnung haben sich mittlerweile aber weiterentwickelt. Ersteres dient nicht nur der Koordination staatlicher Interessenssphären, sondern allgemeiner der zwischenstaatlichen Kooperation. Es wird von einem Übergang vom traditionellen „Völkerrecht der Koexistenz" zum „Völkerrecht der Kooperation" gesprochen,[8] der sich hauptsächlich mit dem Anstieg der Zahl internationaler Organisationen nach dem Zweiten Weltkrieg und hauptsächlich in den letzten zwanzig Jahren vollzieht.[9]

Die Globalisierung führt zu einem weiteren Strukturwandel des internationalen Rechts und somit zur dritten Phase modernen internationalen Rechts. Einige internationale Regime gehen über die Institutionalisierung von Kooperation im Rahmen von internationalen Organisationen hinaus: Es bilden sich gemeinsame Werte einer internationalen Gemeinschaft.[10] So formen sich globale Güter, wie die Sicherung des

---

[6] Siehe allgemein dazu *Georgios Dimitropoulos*, Zertifizierung und Akkreditierung im Internationalen Verwaltungsverbund. Internationale Verbundverwaltung und gesellschaftliche Administration, Tübingen 2012, S. 299 ff.

[7] Siehe die klassische Entscheidung des StIGH im *Lotus*-Fall: The Lotus Case (France v. Turkey), PCIJ, Ser. A., No. 10, S. 18: „International law governs relations between independent states. The rules of law binding upon States therefore emanate from their own free will as expressed in conventions or by usages generally accepted as expressing principles of law and established in order to regulate the relations between these co-existing independent communities or with a view to the achievement of common aims. Restrictions upon the independence of States cannot be presumed".

[8] Grundlegend *Wolfgang Friedmann*, The Changing Structure of International Law, 1964, S. 60 ff.; vgl. auch *Rüdiger Wolfrum*, International Law of Cooperation, EPIL II (1995), S. 1242 ff.; *Abi-Saab*, Whither the International Community?, EJIL 9 (1998), S. 248 ff.; allgemein zur geschichtlichen Entwicklung modernen Völkerrechts siehe *Martti Koskenniemi*, From Apology to Utopia. The Structure of International Legal Argument, 2. Aufl., Cambridge 2005.

[9] Zum Paradigma der „internationalen Organisation" siehe *Jost Delbrück*, Von der Staatenordnung über die internationale institutionelle Kooperation zur „supraterritoral or global governance": Wandel des zwischenstaatlichen Völkerrechts zur Rechtsordnung des Menschen und der Völker?, in: Ulrich Bartosch/Jochen Wagner (Hrsg.), Weltinnenpolitik. Internationale Tagung anlässlich des 85. Geburtstags von Carl-Friedrich von Weizsäcker, Münster 1998, S. 55 (57 ff.). Zu den internationalen Organisationen als den institutionellen Rahmen zwischenstaatlicher Zusammenarbeit siehe *Klaus Dicke*, Effizienz und Effektivität internationaler Organisationen, Berlin 1994, S. 317, 324.

[10] Siehe *Andreas L. Paulus*, Die internationale Gemeinschaft im Völkerrecht. Eine Untersuchung zur Entwicklung des Völkerrechts im Zeitalter der Globalisierung, München 2001;

Friedens im Rahmen der UNO, der freie Handel mit Waren und Dienstleistungen[11] und der Umweltschutz[12] aus. Die Entwicklung gemeinsamer globaler Güter und Werte führt zu einem Zusammenarbeitsbedürfnis der internationalen Gemeinschaft als Ganzes zur Bewältigung globaler Probleme.[13] Jenseits der Staatenkooperation findet im Rahmen der *global governance* eine umfassendere Kooperation zwischen allen Akteuren der internationalen Gemeinschaft, einschließlich Staaten, internationalen Organisationen, der globalen Zivilgesellschaft und multinationalen Unternehmen, statt.[14] Es wird vom Übergang zum „Völkerrecht der global governance", zum „Recht der Globalisierung", zum „Internationalen Gemeinschaftsrecht" oder zum „Weltrecht" gesprochen.[15]

Rüdiger Wolfrum, Solidarity amongst States: An Emerging Structural Principle of International Law, in: Pierre-Marie Dupuy/ Bardo Fassbender/Malcolm N. Shaw/Karl-Peter Sommermann (Hrsg.), Völkerrecht als Wertordnung. Festschrift für Christian Tomuschat, Kehl 2006, S. 1087 (1087 f.).

[11] Vgl. *Christian Tietje*, Das Übereinkommen über technische Handelshemmnisse, in: Hans-Joachim Prieß/Georg M. Berrisch (Hrsg.), WTO-Handbuch, München 2003, B.I.5. Rn. 76.

[12] Vgl. *Charlotte Kreuter-Kirchhof*, Die Weiterentwicklung des internationalen Klimaschutzregimes, DVBl 120 (2005), S. 1552, S. 1560.

[13] *Rüdiger Wolfrum*, Solidarity amongst States: An Emerging Structural Principle of International Law, in: Pierre-Marie Dupuy/Bardo Fassbender/Malcolm N. Shaw/Karl-Peter Sommermann (Hrsg.), Völkerrecht als Wertordnung. Festschrift für Christian Tomuschat, Kehl 2006, S. 1087 (1087); vgl. auch *Christian Tietje*, Global Governance and Inter-Agency Co-operation in International Economic Law, Journal of World Trade 36 (2002), S. 501 (513). Aus ökonomischer Sicht und in Bezug auf die Produktion von globalen öffentlichen Gütern siehe *Inge Kaul/Isabelle Grundberg/Marc A. Stern* (Hrsg.), Global Public Goods. International Cooperation in the 21st Century – Published for the United Nations Development Programme (UNDP), New York u. a. 1999; *Scott Barrett*, Why cooperate? The Incentive to supply Global Public Goods, Oxford 2007.

[14] Siehe *Christian Tietje*, Global Governance and Inter-Agency Co-operation in International Economic Law, Journal of World Trade 36 (2002), S. 501 (504 und passim).

[15] Siehe respektiv *Jost Delbrück*, Von der Staatenordnung über die internationale institutionelle Kooperation zur „supraterritoral or global governance": Wandel des zwischenstaatlichen Völkerrechts zur Rechtsordnung des Menschen und der Völker?, in: Ulrich Bartosch/ Jochen Wagner (Hrsg.), Weltinnenpolitik. Internationale Tagung anlässlich des 85. Geburtstags von Carl-Friedrich von Weizsäcker, Münster 1998, S. 55 ff.; *Stephan Hobe*, Die Zukunft des Völkerrechts im Zeitalter der Globalisierung. Perspektiven der Völkerrechtsentwicklung im 21. Jahrhundert, AVR 37 (1999), S. 253 ff.; *Mehrdad Payandeh*, Internationales Gemeinschaftsrecht. Zur Herausbildung gemeinschaftsrechtlicher Strukturen im Völkerrecht der Globalisierung, Heidelberg u. a. 2010; *Angelika Emmerich-Fritsche*, Vom Völkerrecht zum Weltrecht, Berlin 2007; vgl. auch *Tiziano Balmelli/Julien Chaisse*, The Future of the World Trade Organization and the Changing Structure of the International Legal System, in: Julien Chaisse/Tiziano Balmelli (Hrsg.), Essays on the Future of the World Trade Organization, 2008, S. 1 (3): „from a law governing inter-State relations to a law governing international society"; ähnlich spricht für den Bereich des humanitären Völkerrechts *Thomas Vesting*, Die Staatsrechtslehre und die Veränderung ihres Gegenstandes, VVDStRL 63 (2004), S. 41 (52 ff.), von einem „Menschheitsrecht".

Joseph Weiler unterscheidet ebenfalls drei Entwicklungsphasen der internationalen Rechtsordnung: die Phase der „Transaktion" (*transaction*), in der der Bilateralismus in den internationalen Beziehungen herrscht; die Phase der „Gemeinschaft" (*community*), in der sich das Modell des Multilateralismus und des „International Law as Community" entwickelt; als Drittes die *Regulatory*-Phase, in deren Rahmen sich die *international governance* entwickelt.[16] *Weiler* spricht auf der Grundlage dieser Typologie von einer „Geologie des internationalen Rechts", um die Schichtung (*stratification*) statt eines Paradigmenwechsels der internationalen Rechtsordnung hervorzuheben: Die drei beschriebenen Transformationen der internationalen Rechtsordnung – vom Völkerrecht der Koordination über das Völkerrecht der Kooperation zum Weltrecht – sind mit einem „Zugewinn" (*accretion*)[17] an Formen, Strukturen und Prinzipien verbunden. Die unterschiedlichen Paradigmen koexistieren in der internationalen Rechtsordnung nach dem Verständnis der internationalen Rechtsordnung als eine „geologische Struktur".

Das Recht der Europäischen Union hat schon alle diese Entwicklungsphasen hinter sich und durchläuft noch eine weitere Phase.[18] Die Theorie der Geologie und die Idee des Zugewinns können die gegenwärtigen Entwicklungen der europäischen Rechtsordnung beschreiben.

2. Drei plus eins Entwicklungsschritte

a) Von der völkerrechtlichen zur autonomen Rechtsordnung

In der ersten Phase der Entwicklung der europäischen Rechtsordnung zeichnet sich eine Tendenz der Entfernung dieser Rechtsordnung vom Völkerrecht ab. Das geschieht mit deren schrittweiser Autonomisierung von den Rechtsordnungen der Mitgliedstaaten. Der Prozess der Autonomisierung einer europäischen Rechtsordnung mit unmittelbarer Anwendbarkeit und Geltungsvorrang gegenüber den mitgliedstaatlichen Rechtsordnungen war hauptsächlich ein Projekt des Gerichts der Europäischen Union und vollzieht sich mit den klassischen Entscheidungen *Costa/ Enel*, *Simmenthal* und hauptsächlich der bahnbrechenden Entscheidung *van Gend en Loos*.[19]

---

[16] Siehe *Joseph H. H. Weiler*, The Geology of International Law, ZaöRV 64 (2004), S. 547 ff.

[17] *Joseph H. H. Weiler*, The Geology of International Law, ZaöRV 64 (2004), S. 547 (549).

[18] Im Hinblick auf die Entstehung der damals neuartigen Europäischen Gemeinschaften sprach man an ihrem Beginn von einer dritten Kategorie des Völkerrechts, dem „Völkerrecht der Integration", im Rahmen dessen Rechtspflichten der Mitgliedstaaten zur Zusammenarbeit anerkannt waren; vgl. dazu *Francesco Capotorti* (Hrsg.), Du Droit International au Droit de l'Intégration. Liber Amicorum Pierre Pescatore, Baden-Baden 1987.

[19] EuGH v. 15. 7. 1964 – Rs. 6/64, Slg. 1964, 1251 –„Costa/Enel"; EuGH v. 9. 3. 1978 – Rs. 106/77, Slg. 1978, 629 – „Simnenthal"; EuGH v. 5. 2. 1963 – Rs. 26/62, Slg. 1963, 1 – „van Gend & Los".

Die zentrale Stellung des EuGH in dieser Entwicklung hat den Prozess der europäischen Integration zu einem Prozess einer „Integration durch Recht" gewandelt.[20]

b) Das Harmonisierungsbestreben

Die supranationale Vereinheitlichung trägt gleichzeitig zur transnationalen Vereinheitlichung der europäischen Rechtsordnungen bei. Die nationalen Rechtssysteme sollen in der zweiten Phase der hier beschriebenen Entwicklung größtmöglich aneinander angeglichen werden. Die Europäische Kommission steht hauptsächlich hinter dem Projekt der Harmonisierung nationaler Rechtsordnungen. Das Harmonisierungsprogramm war – und bleibt immer noch – sehr intensiv und hat zahlreiche Formen in unterschiedlichen Bereichen angenommen, wie z. B. die „Harmonisierung durch Standardisierung".[21] Das Harmonisierungsbestreben der nationalen Rechtsordnungen spiegelt sich auch in der verwaltungsrechtlichen Literatur der 1990er Jahre wider; als Europäisches Verwaltungsrecht war zu dieser Zeit das europäisierte nationale Recht zu verstehen.

Im Rahmen der geologischen Stratifizierung von Elementen unterschiedlicher Phasen des Europarechts passt sich die staatliche Souveränität an die Bedingungen einer autonomen europäischen Rechtsordnung an und sie überlebt in neuen Prinzipien. Im Europäischen Verwaltungsrecht gilt der sog. „Vorrang des mitgliedstaatlichen Vollzugs".[22] Neben diesem Kanon gibt es die „Unabhängigkeit in verfahrensrechtlicher und organisatorischer Hinsicht" der EU-Mitgliedstaaten bei dem Vollzug des Europarechts.[23] Diese Prinzipien finden gleichzeitig mit dem „Äquivalenz- und Effizienzgebot" als Ausdruck des Kooperationsprinzips im Europarecht eine weitere Anpassung an die Harmonisierungswelle.[24]

---

[20] *Mauro Cappelletti/Monica Seccombe/Joseph H. H. Weiler* (Hrsg.), Integration through Law. Europe and the American Federal Experience, Berlin, 1986; *Daniel Augenstein* (Hrsg.), „Integration through Law" Revisited. The Making of the European Polity, Surrey 2012.

[21] Siehe dazu *Georgios Dimitropoulos*, Zertifizierung und Akkreditierung im Internationalen Verwaltungsverbund. Internationale Verbundverwaltung und gesellschaftliche Administration, Tübingen 2012, S. 22 f., 81 f.

[22] Vgl. dazu *Eberhard Schmidt-Aßmann*, Verfassungsprinzipien für den Europäischen Verwaltungsverbund, in: Wolfgang Hoffmann-Riem/ders./Andreas Voßkuhle (Hrsg.), Grundlagen des Verwaltungsrechts, Band I: Methoden, Maßstäbe, Aufgaben, Organisation, München, 2. Aufl., 2012, § 5 Rn. 19 ff.

[23] Zu den Grundsätzen der institutionellen und verfahrensrechtlichen Autonomie siehe EuGH v. 11. 2. 1971 – Rs. 39/70, Slg. 1971, 49 (58) – „Norddeutsches Vieh- und Fleischkontor GmbH/Hauptzollamt Hamburg" und EuGH v. 15. 12. 1971 – v. Rs. 51–54/71, Slg. 1971, 1107 (1116) – „International Fruit Company NV".

[24] Zum heutigen *Status quo* des Äquivalenz- und Effektivitätsgrundsatzes siehe *Wolfgang Kahl*, Die Europäisierung des Verwaltungsrechts als Herausforderung an Systembildung und Kodifikationsidee, in: Peter Axer/Bernd Grzeszick/ders./Ute Mager/Ekkehart Reimer (Hrsg.), Das Europäische Verwaltungsrecht in der Konsolidierungsphase. Systembildung – Disziplinierung – Internationalisierung, DV, Beiheft 10, Berlin 2010, S. 39 (88 f.).

c) Die EU-Eigenverwaltung und der Europäische Verbund

Als dritte Phase der Entwicklung der europäischen Rechtsordnungen kann die Zunahme an Strukturen für die europäische Ebene beschrieben werden. Auch wenn der überwiegende Teil des Europarechts von nationalen Behörden vollzogen wird, gibt es inzwischen einen ausdifferenzierten Verwaltungsapparat der EU-Eigenverwaltung, der mit den Verwaltungen der Mitgliedstaaten in einem Verbund steht. Im Bereich der hauptsächlich seit den 1990er Jahren sich entwickelnden europäischen Eigenverwaltung wächst neben der Europäischen Kommission ein verwaltungsrechtlicher Unterbau mit zahlreichen Agenturen, Ausschüssen und Netzwerken.[25]

Die Intensivierung und Verrechtlichung der Beziehungen zwischen den Mitgliedstaaten und der EU sowie zwischen den Mitgliedstaaten untereinander hat zu der Entwicklung eines „Verfassungs- und Verwaltungsverbundes" geführt.[26] Der Begriff des Verbundes hat eine organisatorische Färbung und somit bietet der Verbund eine strukturelle Infrastruktur für unterschiedliche Phänomene europäischen Regierens und Verwaltens.

3. Die Geologie der EU-Rechtsordnung
und die neue Horizontalität im EU-Recht

Die Theorie der Geologie internationaler Rechtsordnungen eignet sich ebenfalls zur Beschreibung der neueren Entwicklungen der europäischen Rechtsordnung. Diese Rechtsordnung hat eine bestimmte geologische Struktur, die ihre geschichtliche Entwicklung widerspiegelt. Die neuesten Entwicklungen sind teilweise Wiedererscheinungen älterer Schichten, die sich den neuen Schichten und Entwicklungen anpassen. Die völkerrechtliche Schicht kehrt seit einigen Jahren in den Vordergrund zurück, indem eine gewisse Rückkehr des Staates in das EU-Recht ebenfalls stattfindet. Das geschieht sowohl auf der Ebene der Politik als auch des Rechts. Die Rück-

---

[25] *Paul James Cardwell*, The Changing Nature of European Regulatory Governance, in: David Levi-Faur (Hrsg.), Handbook on the Politics of Regulation, Cheltenham 2011, S. 536 (536).

[26] Siehe zum „Europäischen Verfassungsverbund" *Ingolf Pernice*, Die dritte Gewalt im europäischen Verfassungsverbund, EuR 31 (1996), S. 27 ff.; zum „Europäischen Verwaltungsverbund" siehe *Eberhard Schmidt-Aßmann/Bettina Schöndorf-Haubold* (Hrsg.), Der Europäische Verwaltungsverbund. Formen und Verfahren der Verwaltungszusammenarbeit in der EU, Tübingen 2005, S. 153 ff. Der Verbund ist teilweise das Ergebnis des Kanons des mitgliedstaatlichen Vollzugs; siehe *Hans Christian Röhl*, Verantwortung und Effizienz in der Mehrebenenverwaltung, DVBl 2006, S. 1070 (1072): „Weil die EG in großem Umfang auf die Durchsetzung des Gemeinschaftsrechts durch die mitgliedstaatliche Behörden vertraut, reagiert sie auf dieses Kohärenzbedürfnis mit der Installation eines Verwaltungsverbundes".

Das Konzept des Verfassungs- und Verwaltungsverbundes basiert auf der Idee eines vom Bundesverfassungsgericht entwickelten „Staatenverbundes"; siehe BVerfGE 89, 155 (181 ff.); bestätigt durch BVerfGE 123, 267 (348); siehe auch *Paul Kirchhof*, Der europäische Staatenverbund, in: von Bogdandy, Armin/Bast, Jürgen (Hrsg.): Europäisches Verfassungsrecht, 2. Aufl., Berlin 2009, S. 1009 ff.

kehr der völkerrechtlichen Schicht wird in diesem Aufsatz als „Horizontalisierung" beschrieben.

Im klassischen Völkerrecht geht es um die Koordination souverän gleicher Staaten. Die Eigenschaft dieser Interaktion ist die Horizontalität, d. h. die direkte Beziehung zwischen den Staaten.[27] Der Europäische Verbund hatte von Anfang an sowohl eine vertikale – zwischen den EU-Institutionen und den mitgliedstaatlichen Institutionen – als auch eine horizontale – zwischen den mitgliedstaatlichen Institutionen untereinander – Dimension.[28] In der gegenwärtigen Phase der Entwicklung der europäischen Integration kann eine Verstärkung der horizontalen Dimension des Europarechts erkannt werden.[29] Das führt zu einer weiteren Phase der Evolution der europäischen Rechtsordnung. Im Vergleich zu den früheren Phasen der Entwicklung der Rechtsordnung der EU spielt die staatliche Komponente eine wichtigere Rolle.

Die Wiederkehr des Staates ist das Ergebnis einer Veränderung der Governance-Strukturen der europäischen Rechtsordnung. Das geschieht aber teilweise unter ganz neuen Bedingungen für den Staat und für die gesamte Interaktion der Institutionen in der EU. Auch die neue Horizontalität hat eine gewisse Geologie. Nach der gegenwärtigen Praxis zeichnen sich zwei Wege der Horizontalität des Europäischen Rechts ab: Es gibt eine intergouvernementale Horizontalisierung und eine unionale Horizontalisierung. Die intergouvernementale Seite der Horizontalisierung ist hauptsächlich eine Reaktion der Mitgliedstaaten und der europäischen Institutionen auf die gegenwärtige finanzielle Krise. Sie kreiert zum Beispiel mit bilateralen Darlehen und Verträgen der Mitgliedstaaten der Eurozone auf der einen Seite mit Griechenland, Portugal und Irland auf der anderen sowie mit der Schaffung von Institutionen, wie die Europäische Finanzstabilisierungsfazilität (EFSF) und der Europäische Stabilitätsmechanismus (ESM), eine genuin völkerrechtliche Schicht des Europarechts.[30] Sie ist ein Relikt der traditionellen völkerrechtlichen Rolle des Staates in einem supranationalen Milieu. Die Horizontalisierung war aber schon vor der Finanzkrise präsent, und zwar in einer unionalen, supranationalen Form. Während die intergouver-

---

[27] Vgl. auch *Charles F. Sabel/Oliver Gerstenberg*, Constitutionalising an Overlapping Consensus: The ECJ and the Emergence of a Coordinate Constitutional Order, European Law Journal 16 (2010), S. 511 (550).

[28] Vgl. zum Ganzen *Eberhard Schmidt-Aßmann*, Europäische Verwaltung zwischen Kooperation und Hierarchie, in: FS Helmut Steinberger, 2002, S. 1375 ff.; *ders.*, Strukturen Europäischer Verwaltung und die Rolle des Verwaltungsrechts, in: FS Peter Häberle, 2004, S. 395 ff.

[29] Diese Tendenz wird durch die zunehmende Heranziehung der nationalen Identitätsklausel von Art. 4 Abs. 2 EUV bestätigt; vgl. dazu *Armin von Bogdandy/Stefan Schill*, Overcoming Absolute Primacy: Respect for National Identity under the Lisbon Treaty, Common Market Law Review 48 (2011), S. 1417 ff.

[30] Siehe, z. B., *Edoardo Chiti/Pedro Gustavo Teixeira*, The Constitutional Implications of the European Responses to the Financial and Public Debt Crisis, Common Market Law Review 50 (2013), S. 683 (insbes. 685 ff.). Einige völkerrechtliche Strukturen werden jedoch mittlerweile auf das unionale Recht übertragen.

nementale Variante die „archaische" Version der horizontalen Schicht darstellt, ist die unionale Horizontalität eine supranationale Variante davon.

Die neue Horizontalität im Sinne der unionalen Variante hat wesentlich andere Eigenschaften als die traditionelle völkerrechtliche Horizontalität: Erstens finden die Koordination und die Kooperation der Mitgliedstaaten in einem supranationalen rechtlichen Rahmen statt. Das Europarecht definiert die mitgliedstaatliche Interaktion. Zweitens wird die rechtliche Einrahmung institutionell verfestigt, indem die Koordination und die Kooperation unter der Führung von supranationalen Koordinations- und Kontrollinstanzen erfolgen. Diese führende Rolle wird hauptsächlich von der Europäischen Kommission, aber auch von einer Reihe von weiteren Instanzen wahrgenommen.[31] Drittens betrifft die supranationale Horizontalität die Koordination, Kooperation und Verkopplung von subnationalen Einheiten – und nicht mitgliedstaatlichen Regierungen –, und zwar ohne Mediatisierung der Regierungen. Aus diesem Grund müssen diese Instanzen (relativ) selbstständig und unabhängig von nationalen Interessen sein.[32] Diese Tendenz findet man mit großer Intensität im Bereich des Regulierungsrechts, wie z. B. in der Stromhandelsverordnung und Gasfernnetzzugangsverordnung, die den nationalen Regulierungsbehörden die Vollzugsverantwortung auferlegen – jedoch unter erheblicher Mitwirkung der Kommission.[33] Die EU-Dienstleistungsrichtlinie verwendet ein ähnliches Implementationsmodell.[34]

---

[31] Diese Funktion nimmt sehr oft die Form eines Monitorings der Implementation des Europaischen Rechts von den mitgliedstaatlichen Instanzen an; siehe dazu infra II. 1. c).

[32] Vgl. zur Selbstständigkeit in diesem Sinne *Thomas Groß*, Die öffentliche Verwaltung als normative Konstruktion, in: Hans-Heinrich Trute/ders./Hans Christian Röhl/Christoph Möllers (Hrsg.), Allgemeines Verwaltungsrecht – zur Tragfähigkeit eines Konzepts, Tübingen 2008, S. 349 (354 ff.); *Möllers*, Transnationale Behördenkooperation. Verfassungs- und völkerrechtliche Probleme transnationaler administrativer Standardsetzung, ZaöRV 65 (2005), S. 351 ff. Zur Unabhängigkeit nationaler Regulierungsbehörden siehe EuGH, Urteil vom 3. 12. 2009, JZ 2010, S. 195 ff. mit Anm. *K. F. Gärditz*, ebd., S. 198 ff.; zur Unabhängigkeit nationaler Datenschutzstellen siehe EuGH, Urteil vom 9. 3. 2010, EuZW 2010, S. 296 ff. mit Anm. *A. Roßnagel*, ebd., S. 299 ff.; siehe auch *Eberhard Schmidt-Aßmann*, Perspektiven der Europäisierung des Verwaltungsrechts, in: Peter Axer/Bernd Grzeszick/ders./Ute Mager/Ekkehart Reimer (Hrsg.), Das Europäische Verwaltungsrecht in der Konsolidierungsphase. Systembildung – Disziplinierung – Internationalisierung, DV, Beiheft 10, Berlin 2010, S. 263 (282); *Wolfgang Kahl*, Die Europäisierung des Verwaltungsrechts als Herausforderung an Systembildung und Kodifikationsidee, in: Peter Axer/Bernd Grzeszick/ders./Ute Mager/Ekkehart Reimer (Hrsg.), Das Europäische Verwaltungsrecht in der Konsolidierungsphase. Systembildung – Disziplinierung – Internationalisierung, DV, Beiheft 10, Berlin 2010, S. 39 (75 f. m. w. N.); *Matthias Ruffert*, Die neue Unabhängigkeit: Zur demokratischen Legitimation von Agenturen im europäischen Verwaltungsrecht, in: Peter-Christian Müller-Graff/Stefanie Schmahl/Vassilios Skouris (Hrsg.), Europäisches Recht zwischen Bewährung und Wandel. Festschrift für Dieter H. Scheuing, 2011, S. 399 (403 ff.).

[33] Siehe *Wolfgang Weiß*, Der Europäische Verwaltungsverbund. Grundfragen, Kennzeichen, Herausforderungen, Berlin 2010, S. 23 mit Fn. 8; *Gabrielle Britz*, Markt(er)öffnung durch Regulierung – Neue Regulierungsaufgaben nach den Energie-Beschleunigungsrichtlinien und der Stromhandelsverordnung, in: FS Zezwitsch, 2005, S. 374 (382).

[34] Zum Netzwerkcharakter der Verwaltungszusammenarbeit im Rahmen der Dienstleistungsrichtlinie (Richtlinie 2006/123/EG des Europäischen Parlaments und des Rates v.

Der Staat hat also eine teilweise getrennte Rolle gegenüber seiner Verwaltung. Somit entsteht ein „Dualismus von Behörde und Staat"[35]. Das führt zur Emergenz eines „Modells der zuständigen Behörde" für die Implementation des Europäischen Rechts.[36] In diesen Fällen bekommen die mitgliedstaatlichen Behörden – die auf der Grundlage des EU-Rechts zuständigen Behörden – ihr Mandat direkt vom EU-Recht und nicht von ihren Regierungen. Das Europäische Recht verändert die internen Strukturen der Mitgliedstaaten und stellt ihre Verfahrens- und Organisationsautonomie erneut in Frage.

Unterschiedliche Faktoren können die neue Horizontalisierungstendenz der Governance-Strukturen erklären. Mit den kontinuierlichen territorialen Erweiterungen sind die Diversität und Heterogenität in der EU extrem gewachsen. Weder das Modell des klassischen Völkerrechts, das der Harmonisierung der internen Strukturen der Mitgliedstaaten noch das der direkten Implementation durch supranationale Instanzen ist geeignet für einen Markt von über 500 Millionen Menschen und einen öffentlichen Sektor von 28 Mitgliedstaaten.[37] „One-size-fits-all"-Governance und Regulierung kann einer vielfältigen Union nicht mehr gerecht werden. Außerdem ist es unmöglich, die Anwendung des Europarechts in allen Mitgliedstaaten, Regionen und für jeden einzelnen Bürger zu kontrollieren. Als letzter Faktor könnte ebenfalls die tiefgreifendere Demokratisierung europäischer Gesellschaften erwähnt werden.

Die geologische Stratifizierung war ebenfalls im Rahmen der älteren Entwicklungsphasen präsent. Der Kanon des mitgliedstaatlichen Vollzugs sowie die organisatorische und verfahrensrechtliche Autonomie des Europäischen Verwaltungs- und Prozessrechts sind völkerrechtliche Weiterbelebungen staatlicher Souveränität während der Autonomisierungsphase der europäischen Rechtsordnung und der Harmo-

---

12. 12. 2006 über Dienstleistungen im Binnenmarkt, ABl. EU 2006 Nr. L 376, S. 36) siehe *Matthias Ruffert*, Von der Europäisierung des Verwaltungsrechts zum Europäischen Verwaltungsverbund, DÖV 2007, S. 761 (764 f.); siehe ebenfalls *Wolfram Cremer*, Umsetzung der Dienstleistungsrichtlinie in Deutschland – Verfassungsrechtliche Grenzen für die Installierung der Kammern als Einheitliche Ansprechpartner, EuZW 19 (2008), S. 655 ff.; *Peter M. Huber*, Die Kammern im Europäischen Verwaltungsverbund, in: Winfried Kluth (Hrsg.), Jahrbuch des Kammer- und Berufsrechts, 2007, 2008, S. 14; *Matthias Ruffert*, Europäische Amtshilfe im Rahmen der Berufsaufsicht durch Kammern, ebd., S. 28 ff.; zur Dienstleistungsrichtlinie als Kodifikations- und Systematisierungsvorbild siehe *Wolfgang Kahl*, Die Europäisierung des Verwaltungsrechts als Herausforderung an Systembildung und Kodifikationsidee, in: Peter Axer/Bernd Grzeszick/ders./Ute Mager/Ekkehart Reimer (Hrsg.), Das Europäische Verwaltungsrecht in der Konsolidierungsphase. Systembildung – Disziplinierung – Internationalisierung, DV, Beiheft 10, Berlin 2010, S. 39 (77 ff.).

[35] *Wolfgang Weiß*, Der Europäische Verwaltungsverbund. Grundfragen, Kennzeichen, Herausforderungen, Berlin 2010, S. 125 m. w. N.

[36] Man könnte ebenfalls allgemeiner von einem „Modell der benannten Stelle" (*designated body*) sprechen. Sehr oft sind diese Stellen als staatliche Stellen vorgeschrieben; vgl. z. B. Art. 4 Abs. 2 *lit.* iii) VO 1093/2010.

[37] Vgl. auch *Giandomenico Majone*, Europe as the Would-Be World Power. The EU at Fifty, Cambridge University Press, Cambridge 2009, S. 186.

nisierungsphase der mitgliedstaatlichen Rechtsordnungen. Die Idee der Autonomie der europäischen Rechtsordnung kehrt mit den Entscheidungen des EuGH zu den *targeted sanctions* des Sicherheitsrates zurück; dieses Mal gegenüber ihrer externen Umwelt.[38] Sehr charakteristisch für das Zusammenspiel der Schichten in den Jahren der Entwicklung der europäischen Rechtsordnung ist ebenfalls die sehr starke Präsenz des Modells der gegenseitigen Anerkennung (von Produkten, Zulassungen, Emissionsberechtigungen, Gerichtsentscheidungen usw.) trotz der sehr verbreiteten Anwendung des Modells der Harmonisierung in den europäischen Legislativakten.[39] Die Gleichwertigkeit der nationalen Rechtsordnungen und ihrer rechtlichen Produkte mit Anerkennungspflichten für sie in den anderen Mitgliedstaaten bleibt sehr wichtig als Governance-Modell in unterschiedlichen Bereichen der EU-Politiken.[40] Somit wird ein Kompromiss von Harmonisierung und Respekt für die Unterschiedlichkeit nationaler Rechtsordnungen erreicht.[41] In der gegenwärtigen Entwicklungsphase der EU zeichnet sich stärker die Tendenz ab, dass die europäische Integration nicht als Harmonisierung der Organisationsstrukturen der Mitgliedstaaten, sondern eher als Integration in Form von Gleichwertigkeit und Kompatibilität der Rechtsordnungen erfolgt.

---

[38] Vgl. EuGH v. 3. 9. 2008 – v. Rs. C-402/05 P und C-415/05 P, Slg. 2008, I-6351 – „Kadi/ Rat und Kommission"; vgl. dazu *Kämmerer*, Das Urteil des Europäischen Gerichtshofs im Fall „Kadi", EuR 44 (2009), S. 114 ff. Die Entscheidung des EuGH in der Sache „Kadi" führt die Rechtsprechung des EuGH in Richtung einer Staatswerdung der EU konsequent weiter (gemeint sind z. B. folgende Entscheidungen: EuGH v. 5. 2. 1963 – Rs. 26/62, Slg. 1963, 1 – „van Gend & Los"; EuGH v. 15. 7. 1964 – Rs. 6/64, Slg. 1964, 1251 –„Costa/Enel"). Mit der „Kadi"-Entscheidung erweitert sich diese Rechtsprechung im Hinblick auf das Verhältnis der EU zu ihrer Außenwelt.

[39] Das Funktionieren des Binnenmarktes wurde durch die *Cassis-de-Dijon*-Rechtsprechung des EuGH gewährleistet. Mit dem Urteil EuGH v. 20. 2. 1979 – Rs. 120/78, Slg. 1979, I-649 –„Rewe/Bundesmonopolverwaltung für Branntwein" entwickelte 1979 der EuGH den Grundsatz der Gleichwertigkeit und gegenseitigen Anerkennung nationaler Regelungen. Danach ist ein Produkt prinzipiell in allen Mitgliedstaaten der Gemeinschaft verkehrsfähig, wenn es nach dem sog. Herkunftslandprinzip in einem Mitgliedstaat rechtmäßig hergestellt und in Verkehr gebracht worden ist; vgl. z. B. *Sedemund*, „Cassis de Dijon" und das neue Harmonisierungskonzept der Kommission, in: Schwarze (Hrsg.), Der Gemeinsame Markt, Baden-Baden 1987, S. 37 ff. Allgemein zur gegenseitigen Anerkennung siehe *Sascha Michaels*, Anerkennungspflichten im Wirtschaftsverwaltungsrecht der Europäischen Gemeinschaft und der Bundesrepublik Deutschland. Zwecke des Internationalen Verwaltungsrechts, Berlin 2004.

[40] Vgl. *Hans Christian Röhl*, Akkreditierung und Zertifizierung im Produktsicherheitsrecht. Zur Entwicklung einer neuen Europäischen Verwaltungsstruktur, Berlin u. a. 2000, S. 29.

[41] Zur Beziehung zwischen Harmonisierung und Gleichwertigkeit siehe ebenfalls *Sidney Shapiro*, International Trade Agreements, Regulatory Protection, and Public Accountability, Administrative Law Review 54 (2002), S. 435 (insbes. 453 ff.).

II. Horizontale Funktionen und Bereiche

Horizontale Governance-Strukturen treten zunehmend anstelle von Governance durch EU-Organe auf. Einige Governance-Mechanismen dieser neuen Entwicklungsphase des Europäischen Rechts in den Bereichen Regelsetzung, Implementation und Monitoring werden in diesem Abschnitt beschrieben (*infra* II. 1.),[42] wobei noch konkrete Beispiele horizontaler Governance präsentiert werden (*infra* II. 2.).

1. Horizontale Funktionen

a) Regelsetzung

Horizontale Governance-Strukturen finden sich sowohl im Bereich der Unionsverwaltung als auch im Bereich der EU-Eigenverwaltung. Einige Gremien der EU-Ebene, wie Agenturen, Ausschüsse und Netzwerke, sind horizontale Governance-Formen, obwohl sie der europäischen EU-Eigenverwaltung angehören. Ihre interne Organisation macht sie in der Regel zu hybriden Organen.

Die Unabhängigkeit der nationalen Verwaltungsinstanzen von der zentralen nationalen Verwaltung wird durch eine Zunahme ihrer Abhängigkeit von der supranationalen Verwaltung kompensiert: Agenturen, Netzwerke, Erfahrungsaustauschkreise, Zusammenschlüsse und Gruppen zur Abstimmung der Implementationsprozesse und Agenturen formieren sich als EU-Organe oder Quasi-Organe. Diese Entwicklung kann als „Externalisierung"[43], „Dezentralisierung" oder „Ausgliederung"[44] beschrieben werden. Es handelt sich um „Gremien horizontaler Kooperation"[45], d. h. um horizontale europäische Gremien. Manchmal handelt es sich um „informelle Foren"[46], d. h. um Netzwerke wie das *European Competition Network* (ECN);[47] selbst die Agenturen sind aber in der Regel intern als Netzwerke von Repräsentanten der zuständigen nationalen Behörden strukturiert.[48]

Sie verwalten lose und auf einem horizontalen Weg bestimmte Governance-Bereiche. Diese Gremien erarbeiten auf der europäischen Ebene Standards für das ge-

---

[42] Siehe zu einer ähnlichen Typologie *Georgios Dimitropoulos*, Global Administrative Order. Towards a Typology of Administrative Levels and Functions in the Global Legal Order, European Review of Public Law 23 (2011), S. 433 ff.

[43] Siehe dazu *Michael H. Koch*, Die Externalisierungspolitik der Kommission, Baden-Baden 2004.

[44] Zur Ausgliederungspolitik der Kommission siehe *Wolfgang Weiß*, Der Europäische Verwaltungsverbund. Grundfragen, Kennzeichen, Herausforderungen, Berlin 2010, S. 63 ff.

[45] *Matthias Ruffert*, Von der Europäisierung des Verwaltungsrechts zum Europäischen Verwaltungsverbund, DÖV 60 (2007), S. 761 (765).

[46] *Felix Arndt*, Vollzugssteuerung im Regulierungsverbund, DV 39 (2006), S. 100 (105 ff.).

[47] Siehe *KOM*, Bekanntmachung der Kommission über die Zusammenarbeit innerhalb des Netzes der Wettbewerbsbehörden (2004/C 101/03), ABl. EU 2004 Nr. C 101, S. 43.

[48] *Johannes Saurer*, Supranational Governance and Networked Accountability Structures: Member State Oversight of EU Agencies, European Journal of Risk Regulation 2011, S. 51 ff.

meinsame Handeln der nationalen Behörden, die nachher von den Behörden auf der nationalen Ebene implementiert werden.[49] Die Regelsetzung und somit auch die Implementationspraxis werden also weder hierarchisch noch von einer Stelle unilateral bestimmt.[50] Die europäische Rechtsanwendung auf den Einzelfall erfolgt nach einem kooperativen Vorgang.[51] Die Entscheidungsfindung im Rahmen von Agenturen, Ausschüssen und Netzwerken ist also horizontal.

Die Horizontalisierung im Bereich der Regelsetzung erfolgt gleichzeitig im Hinblick auf private Regelsetzungsakteure. Die europäischen Normungsorganisationen werden zunehmend für die Unterstützung der europäischen Gesetzgebungstätigkeit eingesetzt, indem die Standards zum Zweck der Ergänzung des normativen Inhalts von Richtlinien und Verordnungen bearbeitet werden. Eine neue Form *gesellschaftlicher Administration* entsteht, die als Gleiche neben die „normale" Verwaltung tritt.[52]

b) Implementation

Die gegenwärtige Krise in Europa ist ebenfalls eine Implementationskrise. Die nationalen Verwaltungs- und Gerichtsapparate sind so überfordert, dass sie nicht mehr in der Lage sind, die europäischen Regeln zu implementieren. Das Implementationsmodell der EU war in der Regel immer dezentral-horizontal.[53] Das erklärt sich aus der völkerrechtlichen Abstammung des Europarechts. Nach einer langen Phase der Bildung EU-eigenverwaltungsrechtlicher Strukturen entwickeln sich neue Verbundstrukturen horizontaler Governance, die der Verbesserung der Implementationspraxis in den Mitgliedstaaten dienen sollen.

Nach einer Phase der Entwicklung der Eigenverwaltung der EU, die sich mehr auf die Regelsetzung konzentriert hat, kommt die effektive Durchsetzung der Regelwerke in den Mittelpunkt der europäischen Gesetzgebung. Viele neue Implementationsformen liegen in einem Bereich zwischen zentralem und dezentralem Vollzug bzw.

---

[49] Zur Regelsetzung der Agenturen *Edoardo Chiti*, European Agencies' Rulemaking: Powers, Procedures and Assessment, European Law Journal 19 (2013), S. 93.

[50] *Matthias Ruffert*, Völkerrechtliche Impulse und Rahmen des Europäischen Verfassungsrechts, in: Michael Fehling/ders. (Hrsg.): Regulierungsrecht, Tübingen 2010, § 3 Rn. 3: „So richtet sich das supranationale und nationale Recht vielfach ohne den Zwang einer Vorrangrelation an inter- und transnationalen Regelungskomplexen aus. Umgekehrt beziehen die inter-, trans- und supranationale Ebene zentrale Prinzipien, Institute und Strukturen aus nationalrechtlichen Entwicklungen".

[51] Vgl. auch *Herwig C. H. Hofmann*, Decision-Making in EU Administrative Law – The Problem of Composite Procedures, Administrative Law Review 61 (2009), S. 199 ff.

[52] Siehe dazu *Georgios Dimitropoulos*, Zertifizierung und Akkreditierung im Internationalen Verwaltungsverbund. Internationale Verbundverwaltung und gesellschaftliche Administration, Tübingen 2012.

[53] Siehe am Beispiel des Energierechts *Wolfgang Weiß*, Der Europäische Verwaltungsverbund. Grundfragen, Kennzeichen, Herausforderungen, Berlin 2010, S. 126.

zwischen EU-Eigenverwaltungsrecht und Unionsverwaltungsrecht.[54] Im Bereich zum Beispiel der Sicherheit und Nachhaltigkeit von Produkten wird das Mehrebenensystem umgangen, indem die Implementationsstruktur verändert wird. Nach dem Implementationsmodell der benannten Stelle erfolgt eine mitgliedstaatliche Implementation von supranationalen Kompetenzen. Der Logik des Trennungsprinzips entsprechend sollte der Mechanismus der Kontrolle des Marktzugangs entweder dezentral von den mitgliedstaatlichen Verwaltungen oder zentral von der EU-Administration organisiert werden. Der europäische Gesetzgeber hat aber ein neues System des Vollzugs entwickelt. Die Durchsetzung der Richtlinien und der Normen ist den notifizierten Zertifizierungsstellen als speziell dazu befugten Stellen überlassen, die weder zentrale noch dezentrale Verwaltungsträger darstellen.[55] Die Gesamtheit privater Zertifizierungsstellen bildet eine neue genuin europäische Verwaltungsstruktur als Teil der europäischen Verwaltung. Der europäische Gesetzgeber ergänzt die überkommene Verwaltungsorganisation um neue Strukturen.[56] Mit dieser Verwaltungsstruktur erlangt die obere Ebene einen direkten Zugriff auf die Unionsbürger und kontrolliert den Marktzugang der Produkte. Das EU-Recht hat einen verlängerten Arm für seinen Vollzug in den Mitgliedstaaten entwickelt, der nicht mitgliedstaatlicher Natur ist. Die notifizierten Stellen bilden einen dekonzentrierten Teil der EU-Eigenverwaltung. Die Neuartigkeit erscheint in der *Dekonzentrierung des direkten Vollzugs* und in der Ausübung dieses Vollzugs mit den Mitteln des Privatrechts. Beim Einsatz der notifizierten Stellen handelt es sich demzufolge um eine Zuweisung und Neuverteilung von Unionskompetenzen, die von national stationierten Instanzen wahrgenommen werden, und nicht um eine Delegation seitens der EU.[57]

c) Monitoring

Eine neuere Tendenz der Ausformung horizontaler Governance-Strukturen zeigt sich im Bereich des Monitorings. Zunehmend nimmt horizontales Monitoring die

---

[54] Zum System der Vollziehung des Unionsrechts (zentraler/direkter/gemeinschaftseigener Vollzug – dezentraler/indirekter/mitgliedstaatlicher Vollzug) siehe statt vieler *Ehlers*, in: Erichsen/ders. (Hrsg.), Allgemeines Verwaltungsrecht, 14. Aufl., 2010, § 4 Rn. 31 ff.

[55] *Hans Christian Röhl*, Ausgewählte Verwaltungsverfahren, GVwR II, § 30 Rn. 66, ordnet sie im Rahmen der „gemeinschaftsweit tätigen mitgliedstaatlichen Verwaltung" als „private Gemeinschaftsverwaltung" ein.

[56] *Hans Christian Röhl*, Konformitätsbewertung im Europäischen Produktsicherheitsrecht, in: Eberhard Schmidt-Aßmann/Bettina Schöndorf-Haubold (Hrsg.), Der Europäische Verwaltungsverbund. Formen und Verfahren der Verwaltungszusammenarbeit in der EU, Tübingen 2005, S. 153 (169, 175); *Ute Mager*, Die europäische Verwaltung zwischen Hierarchie und Netzwerk, in: Hans-Heinrich Trute/Thomas Groß/Hans Christian Röhl/Christoph Möllers (Hrsg.), Allgemeines Verwaltungsrecht – zur Tragfähigkeit eines Konzepts, Tübingen 2008, S. 369 (380): „ganz andere Form dezentralisierter Verwaltung".

[57] *Hans Christian Röhl*, Konformitätsbewertung im Europäischen Produktsicherheitsrecht, in: Eberhard Schmidt-Aßmann/Bettina Schöndorf-Haubold (Hrsg.), Der Europäische Verwaltungsverbund. Formen und Verfahren der Verwaltungszusammenarbeit in der EU, Tübingen 2005, S. 153 (168 f.).

Stelle der hierarchischen Aufsicht ein. Das hat oft die Form einer Beurteilung unter Gleichrangigen (*peer reviews*). *Peer reviews* sind nicht kontradiktorische und nicht konfrontative Monitoring-Systeme, die die Konformität des mitgliedstaatlichen Rechts mit dem entsprechenden EU-Recht überprüfen. Sie werden von Repräsentanten von mitgliedstaatlichen Instanzen unter Leitung eines europäischen Organs durchgeführt. Nach der Organisation for Economic Co-operation and Development werden die *peer reviews* wie folgt definiert:[58]

> „Peer review can be described as the systematic examination and assessment of the performance of a State by other States, with the ultimate goal of helping the reviewed State improve its policy making, adopt best practices, and comply with established standards and principles. The examination is conducted on a non-adversarial basis, and it relies heavily on mutual trust among the States involved in the review, as well as their shared confidence in the process. When peer review is undertaken in the framework of an international organization – as is usually the case – the Secretariat of the organization also plays an important role in supporting and stimulating the process. With these elements in place, peer review tends to create, through this reciprocal evaluation process, a system of mutual accountability."

Die EU benutzt dieses System in unterschiedlichen Bereichen, wie z. B. bei der Open Method of Coordination (OMC),[59] bei der Akkreditierung[60] und bei dem neuen krisenbedingten Finanzregime.[61] Die europäischen *Peer-review*-Verfahren haben folgende verfahrensrechtliche Charakteristika: 1) Ein *peer review team* von Repräsentanten unterschiedlicher mitgliedstaatlicher Rechtsordnungen wird aufgestellt. 2) Das Team sammelt Informationen über die Rechtslage in der zu untersuchenden Rechtsordnung und führt ein *on-site visit* durch. 3) In der dritten Phase wird ein *Peer-review*-Bericht mit einer Beschreibung der Rechtslage im Mitgliedstaat, einer Bewertung der Befunde und Verbesserungsvorschlägen verfasst.

Bekanntere Formen horizontaler Überwachung findet man bei der Marktüberwachung von Produktgefahren.[62] Mit der Verordnung 765/2008 schafft der europäische Gesetzgeber einen horizontalen Rahmen für die Marktüberwachung aller europäisch harmonisierten Produkte.[63] Die Marktüberwachung ist eine polizeirechtliche Tätig-

---

[58] *OECD*, Peer Review. An OECD Tool for Co-Operation and Change, SG/LEG (2002) 1, Paris 2003, S. 7. *Peer reviews* werden jenseits der EU auch in unterschiedlichen regionalen und internationalen Organisationen, wie z. B. im Rahmen der Afrikanischen Union (New Partnership for Africa's Development African Peer Review Mechanism – NEPAD APRM) und der Financial Action Task Force (FATF mutual evaluations programme) durchgeführt.

[59] Siehe *infra* II. 2. a).

[60] Siehe Art. 10 Verordnung 765/2008.

[61] Siehe Verordnung 1093/2010 (EBA); Verordnung 1094/2010 (EIOA); Verordnung 1095/2010 (ESMA); alle drei veröffentlicht im ABl. EU Nr. L 331 am 15. Dezember 2010.

[62] Die Marktüberwachung wird oft als „Marktaufsicht" bezeichnet; vgl. *KOM*, Leitfaden für die Umsetzung der nach dem Neuen Konzept und dem Gesamtkonzept verfassten Richtlinien, S. 53 ff.

[63] Art. 15 Verordnung 765/2008 und Anhang I Art. R31 ff. Beschluss 768/2008. Art. 15 Verordnung 765/2008 schließt von der Marktüberwachung die Bereiche der Lebens- und

keit, die hauptsächlich in die Zuständigkeit der Nationalstaaten fällt.[64] Mit der VO 765/2008 und dem Beschluss 768/2008 werden die Anforderungen an die Marktüberwachungsbehörden sowie die Verwaltungszusammenarbeit weitgehend harmonisiert.[65] Die Marktüberwachung soll auf einem Marktüberwachungsprogramm der nationalen Marktüberwachungsbehörden basieren.[66] Die Verordnung sieht zahlreiche Kooperationspflichten zwischen den mitgliedstaatlichen Marktüberwachungsbehörden, zwischen Mitgliedstaaten und der EU-Eigenverwaltung[67] sowie zwischen den nationalen Marktüberwachungsbehörden und den Zollbehörden vor.[68] Außerdem fördert die Kommission durch die Generaldirektion Unternehmen und Industrie den Einsatz von Netzwerken von Marktüberwachungsbehörden.[69] Diese Netzwerke sollen ein Diskussionsforum für die nationalen Experten darstellen, um kooperativ praktische Lösungen für die Implementierung der Marktüberwachung zu finden. Die Verwaltungskooperation wird von zahlreichen Pflichten zum Informationsaus-

---

Futtermittel, der lebenden Pflanzen und Tiere und die Erzeugnisse menschlichen Ursprungs aus, für die speziellere Regelungen gelten; vgl. *Arun Kapoor/Thomas Klindt*, „New Legislative Framework" im EU-Produktsicherheitsrecht, EuZW 19 (2008), S. 649 ff. (652 f.). Lediglich die Marktüberwachung von Produkten, die unter Harmonisierungsvorschriften der Union fallen, ist vorgesehen; siehe Art. 15 Abs. 1 Verordnung 765/2008; vgl. schon *KOM*, Leitfaden für die Umsetzung der nach dem neuen Konzept und dem Gesamtkonzept verfaßten Richtlinien, 2000, S. 19.

[64] Die Marktüberwachung soll sicherstellen, dass unter die Harmonisierungsvorschriften der Union fallende Produkte, die bei bestimmungsgemäßer oder vernünftiger Verwendung und ordnungsgemäßer Installation oder Wartung die Anforderungen des Unionsrechts nicht erfüllen, vom Markt genommen werden bzw. ihre Bereitstellung auf dem Markt untersagt oder eingeschränkt wird und dass die Öffentlichkeit und die europäische Verwaltung informiert werden; vgl. Art. 15 Abs. 2 sowie zu den einzelnen Maßnahmen Art. 19 ff. Verordnung 765/ 2008 und Anhang I Art. R31 ff. Beschluss 768/2008.

[65] In der allgemeinen Produktsicherheitsrichtlinie 2001/95/EG sind ebenfalls harmonisierte Marktüberwachungsanforderungen vorgesehen, die den Bestimmungen der Verordnung 765/ 2008/EG vorgehen, wobei die Verordnung 765/2008 die Regelungslücke bezüglich der Vereinheitlichung der nicht von der allgemeinen Produktsicherheits-RL abgedeckten Produkte schließt; siehe *Arun Kapoor/Thomas Klindt*, „New Legislative Framework" im EU-Produktsicherheitsrecht, EuZW 19 (2008), S. 649 ff. (652).

[66] Art. 18 Abs. 5 Verordnung 765/2008.

[67] Art. 18 Abs. 1, 24 Verordnung 765/2008; Art. 18 der Verordnung sieht weiter Organisationspflichten für die nationalen Marktüberwachungsbehörden vor.

[68] Siehe Art. 27–29 Verordnung 765/2008. Außerdem regelt Art. 26 Verordnung 765/2008 die Zusammenarbeit im Hinblick auf den Informationsaustausch und die technische Unterstützung mit den zuständigen Stellen von Drittstaaten.

[69] Vgl. Art. 25 Abs. 1 Verordnung 765/2008; *Administrative Co-operation (AdCo) Groups of Market Surveillance Experts* existieren im Bereich mehrerer Richtlinien; Querschnittsthemen der Marktüberwachung werden ebenfalls von den *Senior Officials Group on Standardisation and Conformity Assessment Policy* (SOGS) behandelt. Siehe auch die sog. Market Surveillance Operations Group (MSOG – Arbeitsgruppe Marktüberwachung): Sie erarbeitet Leitfäden für die praktische Umsetzung der Marktüberwachung. Die Kommission fungiert als Gastgeber für die MSOG und unterstützt sie im Rahmen ihrer Haushaltsmöglichkeiten; vgl. *KOM*, Mitteilung der Kommission an den Rat und das Europäische Parlament über Medizinprodukte, KOM (2003) 386 endg., 2. 7. 2003, S. 17 f.

tausch zwischen allen beteiligten Akteuren begleitet.[70] Somit entsteht eine horizontale Marktüberwachungsverwaltung in der EU.

2. Beispiele horizontalisierter Bereiche

Horizontalisierte Governance-Strukturen können in unterschiedlichen Politikbereichen gefunden werden. In einem der am weitesten entwickelten Bereiche, dem Wettbewerbsrecht, ist die Horizontalisierung mit der Verordnung 1/2003 schon seit 2003 vollzogen worden.[71] Im Finanzrecht, das gegenwärtig eine intensive Zentralisierung und Harmonisierung wegen der Finanzkrise erfährt, sind schon *peer reviews* für das Monitoring der Implementation des Europäischen Rechts eingeführt worden.

Drei Beispiele horizontaler Governance-Strukturen sollen näher beschrieben werden: die Open Method of Coordination (OMC), die Governance von Produkten und die Governance der Justiz.

a) Open Method of Coordination

Einen großen Schritt in Richtung der Horizontalisierung von Governance in der EU stellt die „Offene Koordinierungsmethode" (*Open Method of Coordination* – OMC) dar.[72] Sie wurde im Jahr 2000 beim Europäischen Rat von Lissabon als Governance-Modus eingeführt. Die OMC wird in Bereichen verwendet, in denen es Implementationsschwierigkeiten gibt, sowie in – im Hinblick auf die nationale Souveränität – sensiblen Bereichen.[73] Die Methode dient der Verbesserung der Implementierung von Entscheidungen in komplexen Politikbereichen. Die Implementation soll durch die Entwicklung von nationalen Politiken durch die Mitgliedstaaten und somit durch die Verstärkung der Eigenverantwortung der Mitgliedstaaten bei der Implementation von EU-Recht erfolgen. Dadurch entsteht auch die Horizontalisierung. Das soll in einem bestimmten Rahmen erfolgen, was im Einführungsdokument der OMC wie folgt beschrieben wird:[74]

---

[70] Vgl. Art. 22, 23, 24 Verordnung 765/2008.

[71] Siehe *José Rivas/Margot Horspool*, Modernisation and Decentralisation of EC Competition Law. The Hague 2000.

[72] Siehe allgemein dazu *Paul Craig/Gráinne de Búrca*, EU Law, 5. Aufl., OUP, Oxford 2011, S. 163 ff.; *Gráinne de Búrca*, The Constitutional Challenge of New Governance in the European Union, European Law Review 28 (2003), S. 814 ff.

[73] *Paul James Cardwell*, The Changing Nature of European Regulatory Governance, in: David Levi-Faur (Hrsg.), Handbook on the Politics of Regulation, Cheltenham 2011, S. 536 (543).

[74] *Europäischer Rat*, Schlussfolgerungen des Vorsitzes, Lissabon, 23. und 24. März 2000 (Hervorhebungen hinzugefügt).

„PRAKTISCHE UMSETZUNG DER BESCHLÜSSE: EINE KOHÄRENTERE
UND SYSTEMATISCHERE VORGEHENSWEISE
[...]

Anwendung eines neuen offenen Koordinierungsverfahrens

37. Dieses strategische Ziel wird sich durch die Anwendung eines neuen offenen Koordinierungsverfahrens als eines Mittels für die Verbreitung der bewährten Praktiken und die Herstellung einer größeren Konvergenz in bezug auf die wichtigsten Ziele der EU leichter verwirklichen lassen. Diese Verfahrensweise, die den Mitgliedstaaten eine Hilfe bei der schrittweisen Entwicklung *ihrer eigenen Politiken* sein soll, umfaßt folgendes:

– Festlegung von Leitlinien für die Union mit einem jeweils genauen Zeitplan für die Verwirklichung der von ihnen gesetzten kurz-, mittel- und langfristigen Ziele;

– gegebenenfalls Festlegung quantitativer und qualitativer Indikatoren und Benchmarks im Vergleich zu den Besten der Welt, die auf die *in den einzelnen Mitgliedstaaten und Bereichen bestehenden Bedürfnisse zugeschnitten* sind, als Mittel für den Vergleich der bewährten Praktiken;

– Umsetzung dieser europäischen Leitlinien in die nationale und regionale Politik durch Vorgabe konkreter Ziele und den Erlaß entsprechender Maßnahmen *unter Berücksichtigung der nationalen und regionalen Unterschiede*;

– regelmäßige Überwachung, Bewertung und *gegenseitige Prüfung* im Rahmen eines Prozesses, bei dem *alle Seiten voneinander lernen.*

38. Im Einklang mit dem Subsidiaritätsprinzip wird nach einem *völlig dezentralen Ansatz* vorgegangen werden, so daß die Union, die Mitgliedstaaten, die regionalen und lokalen Ebenen sowie die Sozialpartner und die Bürgergesellschaft im Rahmen unterschiedlicher Formen von Partnerschaften aktiv mitwirken. Die Europäische Kommission wird in Zusammenarbeit mit den verschiedenen Anbietern und Nutzern, wie den Sozialpartnern, den Unternehmen und den NRO ein Benchmarking der bewährten Praktiken zur Gestaltung des Wandels erstellen."

b) Die Governance von Produkten

aa) Produktsicherheit

Das Marktzugangsregime für Produkte in der EU ist nicht einheitlich, da für verschiedene Produktkategorien verschiedene Produktzugangsbedingungen gelten.[75] Obwohl das klassische Europarecht überwiegend die Belange der Warenverkehrsfreiheit gefördert hat,[76] während das nationale Verwaltungsrecht die Belange des

---

[75] Siehe zu der Einteilung der EU-Produktzugangsregime – ohne jedoch eine Einteilung des Zertifizierungssystems – *Gernot Sydow*, Verwaltungskooperation in der Europäischen Union, 2004, S. 118 ff.; siehe auch *Langner/Klindt*, in: Dauses (Hrsg.), Hdb. EU-Wirtschaftsrecht, 2011, C. VI. Rn. 1.

[76] Ähnlich *Eberhard Schmidt-Aßmann*, Verfassungsprinzipien für den Europäischen Verwaltungsverbund, in: Wolfgang Hoffmann-Riem/ders./Andreas Voßkuhle (Hrsg.), Grundlagen des Verwaltungsrechts, Band I: Methoden, Maßstäbe, Aufgaben, Organisation, München, 2. Aufl., 2012, § 5 Rn. 95 ff.

Schutzes von Sicherheit und Gesundheit der Bürger zu wahren suchte,[77] muss die den Binnenmarkt regulierende europäische Verwaltung beide Belange zur Geltung bringen.[78] Das Produktsicherheitsrecht ist also zu einem Hauptgebiet der unionalen Harmonisierungspolitik im Rahmen der Verwirklichung des Binnenmarktziels geworden.[79] Diese Harmonisierungspolitik nimmt zunehmend die Form der Entwicklung horizontaler Governance-Strukturen an.

Zur Schaffung eines gemeinsamen Rechtsrahmens für die Vermarktung von Produkten hat die EU den Neuen Rechtsetzungsrahmen (*New Legislative Framework* – NLF)[80] eingeführt. Mit diesem neuen Maßnahmenpaket bringt die Kommission die sog. alte und Neue Konzeption zur Gewährleistung der Produktsicherheit unter ein gemeinsames Dach und schafft einen übergeordneten und umfassenden Rahmen für alle Produktsektoren, wobei zugleich der existierende EU-Rechtsrahmen für den Warenverkehr und die Produktsicherheit vereinfacht und vereinheitlicht wird.[81] Die Vereinheitlichung soll durch die Verwendung des sog. „Systems der Zertifizierung und Akkreditierung" oder des „Systems der Konformitätsbewertung" stattfinden, das sich in Zukunft unter dem NLF als das europäische Hauptsystem für den Marktzugang profiliert. Es wird für eine sehr große Zahl von Produkten verschiedener Kate-

---

[77] Ähnlich *Uwe Kage*, Das Medizinproduktegesetz. Staatliche Risikosteuerung unter dem Einfluss europäischer Harmonisierung, Berlin u. a. 2005, S. 70 ff.

[78] Neben marktwirtschaftlichen Zielen verfolgt die EU im Rahmen des Binnenmarktes (Art. 3 Abs. 3 EUV, Art. 26 und 27 AEUV) weitere Ziele und Belange wie die Nachhaltigkeit, den Verbraucherschutz und weitere soziale Belange (vgl. Art. 3 Abs. 3 AEUV).

[79] *Florian Schumann*, Bauelemente des europäischen Produktsicherheitsrechts, Baden-Baden 2006, S. 36.

[80] Der NLF wurde im ABl. EU Nr. L 218 am 13. August 2008 veröffentlicht. Er besteht aus drei Rechtsakten: 1) Verordnung (EG) Nr. 764/2008 des Europäischen Parlaments und des Rates vom 9. Juli 2008 zur Festlegung von Verfahren im Zusammenhang mit der Anwendung bestimmter nationaler technischer Vorschriften für Produkte, die in einem anderen Mitgliedstaat rechtmäßig in den Verkehr gebracht worden sind, und zur Aufhebung der Entscheidung Nr. 3052/95/EG; 2) Verordnung (EG) Nr. 765/2008 des Europäischen Parlaments und des Rates vom 9. Juli 2008 über die Vorschriften für die Akkreditierung und Marktüberwachung im Zusammenhang mit der Vermarktung von Produkten und zur Aufhebung der Verordnung (EWG) Nr. 339/93 des Rates; 3) Beschluss Nr. 768/2008/EG des Europäischen Parlaments und des Rates vom 9. Juli 2008 über einen gemeinsamen Rechtsrahmen für die Vermarktung von Produkten und zur Aufhebung des Beschlusses 93/465/EWG des Rates. Der NLF stellt seinerseits einen Bestandteil des *New Internal Market Package for Goods* (sog. „*Goods Package*") dar. In seiner Entschließung vom 10. November 2003 (3) ABl. C 282 vom 25. 11. 2003, S. 3, erkannte der Rat die Bedeutung des Neuen Konzepts als zweckmäßiges und effizientes Rechtsetzungsmodell an, das technologische Innovation ermöglicht und die Wettbewerbsfähigkeit der europäischen Industrie stärkt, und er bekräftigte zudem, dass seine Grundsätze auf weitere Bereiche angewendet werden sollten, wobei er gleichzeitig darauf hinwies, dass ein präziserer Rahmen für die Konformitätsbewertung, Akkreditierung und Marktüberwachung zu schaffen sei.

[81] Der NLF geht mit einer doppelten Erweiterung des Produktrechts einher: Er erweitert die Neue Konzeption und das Globale Konzept auf nicht industrielle Produkte und zielt auf die Verwirklichung nicht nur der technischen Produktsicherheit, sondern auch weiterer Schutzziele, wie Umwelt- und Verbraucherschutz.

gorien benutzt, ohne dass sich eine ganz genaue Systematik bei der Auswahl der Produktkategorien seitens der Kommission erkennen lässt. Darunter fallen unterschiedliche Produktbereiche wie Medizinprodukte, Spielzeug, Druckgeräte, Fahrstühle und Baustoffe. Als relevantes Kriterium kommt auf jeden Fall die Erwägung in Betracht, dass diese Produkte weder einer hoheitlichen Prüfung unterzogen werden müssen noch dem freien Markt überlassen werden können.[82]

Auf der Grundlage des Neuen und des Globalen Konzepts sieht der NLF ein Regulierungssystem vor, das in drei unterschiedliche Regulierungsebenen untergliedert ist.[83] Die Regelsetzung stellt die erste Regulierungsebene dar, die Zertifizierung mit der mit ihr einhergehenden Akkreditierung stellt die zweite und die Marktüberwachung die dritte Ebene dar. Zertifizierung und teilweise zunehmend auch Akkreditierung sind dabei zwingende Erfordernisse für den Zugang eines Produkts zum europäischen Binnenmarkt. Die Zertifizierung betrifft die Sicherheit eines Produkts und die Akkreditierung die Kompetenz der Zertifizierungsstelle. Das Gesamtsystem ist durch ein kompliziertes Zusammenspiel zwischen Wirtschaftsakteuren, Zertifizierern, Akkreditierern, den Mitgliedstaaten, der Kommission und gegebenenfalls

---

[82] Eine Bestandsaufnahme der Produkte, die unter das Regelungsmuster der Neuen Konzeption fallen, findet sich bei *Holger Tobias Weiß*, Die rechtliche Gewährleistung der Produktsicherheit, Baden-Baden 2008, S. 265 ff.
Art. 2 Beschluss 768/2008 sieht Abweichungsmöglichkeiten von den allgemeinen Grundsätzen und Musterbestimmungen vor; spezifische Anpassungen finden sich im Bereich der Medizinprodukte; vgl. auch Erwägungsgründe 4, 5 und 6 Beschluss 768/2008. Beispiele von abweichenden Bereichen sind: Fahrzeuge – mit Ausnahmen im Eisenbahnsektor –, Lebens- und Futtermittel, Tabakerzeugnisse, Kosmetika, Arzneimittel, Chemikalien, genetisch veränderte Organismen (GVO). Die Regelung kann auf der Grundlage der Besonderheiten des jeweiligen Sektors spezifisch angepasst werden und insbesondere, wenn ein umfassendes Rechtssystem für die Vermarktung bestimmter Produktkategorien bereits besteht, kann davon abgewichen werden. Spezifische Anpassungen des Konformitätsbewertungssystems finden sich in Kategorien mit erhöhtem Risikopotential, wie Medizinprodukte. Umfassende Rechtssysteme für den Marktzugang finden sich im Arzneimittelrecht sowie im Futtermittel- und Lebensmittelrecht. In manchen Sektoren, wie z. B. die Lebensmittel, spielt jedoch die akkreditierte Zertifizierung eine sekundäre Rolle im Rahmen der Marktzugangskontrolle; sie ist eine Nebenpflicht; bei den Lebensmitteln gibt es ebenfalls Konformitätsbewertungssysteme, die nicht auf Sicherheit, sondern auf Qualität ausgerichtet sind; vgl. dazu *KOM*, Grünbuch zur Qualität von Agrarerzeugnissen: Produktnormen, Bewirtschaftungsauflagen und Qualitätsregelungen, KOM (2008) 641 endg., 15. 10. 2008, S. 4 f., sowie weiter unten im Text.
[83] Zu den drei Regulierungsbereichen siehe *Hans Christian Röhl*, Akkreditierung und Zertifizierung im Produktsicherheitsrecht. Zur Entwicklung einer neuen Europäischen Verwaltungsstruktur, Berlin 2000, S. 4 ff.; *ders.*, Konformitätsbewertung im Europäischen Produktsicherheitsrecht, in: Eberhard Schmidt-Aßmann/Bettina Schöndorf-Haubold (Hrsg.), Der Europäische Verwaltungsverbund. Formen und Verfahren der Verwaltungszusammenarbeit in der EU, Tübingen 2005, S. 153 (155 ff.); *ders./Yvonne Schreiber*, Konformitätsbewertung in Deutschland. Vorgelegt im Rahmen des Projekts Nr. 54/03 für das Bundesministerium für Wirtschaft und Technologie, Konstanz 2006, S. 49 ff.

europäischen Agenturen geprägt.[84] Die zentrale Koordinierungsrolle nimmt die Kommission wahr.

Der neue Rechtsrahmen besteht aus drei komplementären Rechtstexten. Der *sui generis*-Beschluss 768/2008 bildet einen horizontalen Rahmen für zukünftige Rechtsvorschriften zur Harmonisierung der Bedingungen der Vermarktung von Produkten sowie einen Bezugspunkt für geltende Rechtsvorschriften; der Beschluss richtet sich somit an die EU-Legislative für zukünftige Verwendung mit dem Ziel der Erreichung der Homogenität der sektoriellen Richtlinien.[85] Während sich der Beschluss 768/2008 mit schon geregelten Materien befasst, deckt die VO 765/2008 bisher nicht geregelte Rechtsmaterien ab.[86] Es wird ein übergeordneter Rahmen an Regelungen und Grundsätzen für die Akkreditierung und die Marktüberwachung festgelegt,[87] wobei dadurch die fehlenden Teile des Gesamtsystems des EU-Produktsicherheitsrechts ergänzt werden. Die Verordnung 764/2008 schließlich baut auf dem seit Langem in der Rechtsprechung des EuGH bekannten Prinzip der gegenseitigen Anerkennung auf und novelliert den Rahmen für die gegenseitige Anerkennung im nicht harmonisierten Bereich.[88]

Der NLF bildet den dritten legislativen Schritt im Europäisierungsprozess des Produktsicherheitsrechts. Zur Schaffung eines einheitlichen Marktes mit Produkten spielte zunächst die vom EuGH entwickelte gegenseitige Anerkennung der nationalen technischen Vorschriften die wichtigste Rolle. Entgegenstehende Erfordernisse des nationalen Gemeinwohls bilden aber ein Hindernis für dieses Konzept. Die Handelshemmnisse wurden weiter durch eine durch den EU-Gesetzgeber vorangetriebene Harmonisierung der mitgliedstaatlichen technischen Vorschriften abgebaut. Diese basierte auf den Harmonisierungsansätzen der Neuen Konzeption und des Globalen Konzepts.

---

[84] Im Rahmen des Gesamtsystems sind für das *pre-market assessment* die privaten Akteure (Wirtschaftsakteure und Zertifizierer) verantwortlich, während für die *post-market control* die staatlichen Akteure (Mitgliedstaaten und Kommission) die Verantwortung tragen. Die Akkreditierer haben eine eigene Stellung zwischen den privat agierenden Akteuren und den Mitgliedstaaten. So ergibt sich ein komplexes Interdependenzverhältnis; vgl. allgemein zu den Qualitätssicherungsverfahren *Andreas Voßkuhle*, Strukturen und Bauformen neuer Verfahren, in: Wolfgang Hoffmann-Riem/Eberhard Schmidt-Aßmann (Hrsg.), Verwaltungsverfahren und Verwaltungsverfahrensgesetz, Baden-Baden 2002, S. 277 (309 f.).

[85] *Robert Kovar*, Le Législateur Communautaire encadre le Régime de la Mise des Produits dans le Marché Intérieur, Revue Trimestrielle de Droit Européen 44 (2008), S. 289 (294).

[86] *Jörg Windmann*, Der Verifikateur und der Aufsichtsbeamte als zentrale Elemente des Sachverständigen-Vollzugsmodells im Technikrecht, DÖV 63 (2010), S. 396 (398).

[87] Siehe dazu *Arun Kapoor/Thomas Klindt*, „New Legislative Framework" im EU-Produktsicherheitsrecht, EuZW 19 (2008), S. 649 ff. (649 f.).

[88] *Andreas M. Haak/Oliver Klöck*, Warenverkehrsfreiheit gebietet Zulassung nicht prüffähiger Produkte, EuZW 21 (2010), S. 53 (56 f.). Die Verordnung für die gegenseitige Anerkennung umfasst zahlreiche Produkte nicht harmonisierter Produktkategorien, darunter unterschiedliche Typen von Nahrungsmitteln, wie z. B. Brot und Pasta, aber auch Bücher, Textilien, Möbel, Fahrräder, Leitern und Edelmetalle.

Die Neue Konzeption diente der Harmonisierung der materiellen Anforderungen der Produktsicherheit zur Vermarktung der Produkte.[89] Zum Vorantreiben der Harmonisierung gibt es unterschiedliche Möglichkeiten.[90] Nach der alten Konzeption des EU-Produktsicherheitsrechts waren die EU-Produktrichtlinien mit Detailregelungen beladen. Die Schwierigkeiten der alten Konzeption[91] zusammen mit dem Bedürfnis der Vollendung des Binnenmarktes bis Ende 1992 auf der Grundlage der Einheitlichen Europäischen Akte führten zum Aufkommen neuer Harmonisierungsmethoden.[92] Mit der innovativen „Neuen Konzeption auf dem Gebiet der technischen Harmonisierung und der Normung" wurde Ende der 1980er Jahre eine horizontale Harmonisierung des Produktzugangsregimes angestrebt.[93] Während nach dem alten Konzept bei der Harmonisierung je nach Produkt *ad hoc* entschieden worden war, versuchte die Neue Konzeption das Produktzugangsregime zu vereinheitlichen. Der *ad hoc* und sektorielle Charakter der Richtlinien wurde gewahrt, es wurden aber allgemeine Grundsätze festgelegt, an denen sich die zukünftige Richtliniengebung orientieren musste.[94] Die Neue Konzeption schrieb eine neue Art der Harmonisierung vor: Es wurde keine Detailharmonisierung, sondern eine Mindestharmonisierung angestrebt, indem nur die Mindestanforderungen an die Produkte festgelegt wurden, die als „grundlegende/wesentliche Anforderungen" in den Richtlinien niedergelegt waren.[95] Sie wurden von privaten Normungsorganisationen durch „harmo-

---

[89] Vgl. *KOM*, Grünbuch zur Qualität von Agrarerzeugnissen: Produktnormen, Bewirtschaftungsauflagen und Qualitätsregelungen, KOM(2008) 641 endgültig, 15. 10. 2008, S. 20: „In der EU reichen Zertifizierungsregelungen von der Einhaltung verbindlicher Produktionsvorschriften bis zu zusätzlichen Auflagen im Hinblick auf Umwelt- und Tierschutz, organoleptische Merkmale, Arbeitnehmerschutz, fairen Handel, Klimaschutz, ethische, religiöse oder kulturelle Erwägungen, Anbauverfahren und den Ursprung".

[90] Vgl. *Arun Kapoor/Thomas Klindt*, „New Legislative Framework" im EU-Produktsicherheitsrecht, EuZW 19 (2008), S. 649 ff. (649 f.).

[91] Zu den Schwächen der alten Konzeption der Vollharmonisierung siehe *Thomas Klindt*, Der „new approach" im Produktrecht des europäischen Binnenmarktes: Vermutungswirkung technischer Normung, EuZW 13 (2002), S. 133 (133 f.); *Jörissen*, Produktbezogener Umweltschutz und technische Normen, 1997, S. 13 f.

[92] Einheitliche Europäische Akte vom 17. 2. 1986, ABl. EG Nr. L 169, 29. 6. 1987; die ersten Ansätze der neuen Harmonisierungskonzeption legte die Kommission mit dem 1985 veröffentlichten „Weißbuch zur Vollendung des Binnenmarktes" (*KOM*, Vollendung des Binnenmarktes, Weißbuch der Kommission an den Europäischen Rat, KOM 85 (310) endg., 14. 6. 1985) vor.

[93] *KOM*, Entschließung des Rates vom 7. Mai 1985 über eine neue Konzeption auf dem Gebiet der technischen Harmonisierung und der Normung, ABl. EG Nr. C 136, 4. 6. 1985, S. 1 ff.

[94] Instrument dieser Harmonisierung sind die auf der Grundlage von Art. 114 AEUV erlassenen Richtlinien; nach *Udo Di Fabio*, Produktharmonisierung durch Normung und Selbstüberwachung, Köln 1996, S. 14, handelt es sich um eine pflichtige Rechtsgrundlage; siehe dazu auch *Günter Breulmann*, Normung und Rechtsangleichung in der Europäischen Wirtschaftsgemeinschaft, Berlin 1993, S. 76 ff.; beide beziehen sich auf den EGV.

[95] Art. 3 Abs. 1 Beschluss 768/2008. Im Beschluss werden außer der Gesundheit und der Sicherheit ebenfalls der Verbraucherschutz, der Umweltschutz und der faire Wettbewerb im

nisierte technische Normen" für jeden einzelnen Bereich konkretisiert. Zur Unterstützung der europäischen Gesetzgebung werden in immer mehr Bereichen Normen gesetzt. Die europäischen Normungsgremien arbeiten die Europäischen Normen (EN) aus. Zuständig für den Erlass von Konformitätsbewertungsnormen[96] sind das CEN[97] und das CENELEC[98]. Die europäischen Konformitätsbewertungsnormen sind eine Übertragung der internationalen Normen und sie gelten in Europa als EN ISO/IEC 17000 ff.

Die Neue Konzeption wurde vom „Gesamtkonzept für die Konformitätsbewertung" ergänzt.[99] Das Globale Konzept (oder Gesamtkonzept) war ein Harmonisierungskonzept der verfahrensrechtlichen Anforderungen für den Marktzugang der Produkte, mit welchem die Konformitätsbewertung in die EU-Produktsicherheit eingeführt worden war.[100] Unter Konformitätsbewertung ist sowohl die Zertifizierung als auch die Akkreditierung zu verstehen. Die Zertifizierung wird nicht für sämtliche Marktzugangskontrollen, sondern für bestimmte Produktkategorien, für gesonderte Fälle und anhand bestimmter Kriterien eingesetzt. Sie stellt eine Kontrolle der Übereinstimmung eines Produkts mit den wesentlichen Sicherheitsanforderungen für den Marktzugang dieses Produkts dar,[101] deren Unterscheidungskriterium im Hinblick auf andere Konformitätsbewertungsformen die Durchführung der Konformitätsbewertung durch eine dritte Stelle darstellt.[102] Die Zertifizierungsverfahren sind im Beschluss 768/2008 festgelegt.[103]

Gemeinschaftsmarkt als nicht abschließende Gründe des öffentlichen Interesses erwähnt; vgl. Art. 3 Abs. 1 Unterabs. 2 Beschluss 768/2008.

[96] Ausführlich zur Europäischen Normung siehe *Thomas Zubke-von Thünen*, Technische Normung in Europa, Berlin 1999; *Stefan Wiesendahl*, Technische Normung in der Europäischen Union, 2007; *Michael Winkelmüller/Katharina-Johanna Müller*, Reform der EU-Normung, EuZW 21 (2010), S. 681.

[97] Comité Europeén de Normalisation.

[98] Comité Europeén de Normalisation Electrotechnique.

[99] Vgl. *KOM*, Mitteilung der Kommission, Ein Globales Konzept für Zertifizierung und Prüfwesen. Instrument zur Gewährleistung der Qualität bei Industrieerzeugnissen, KOM/89/209 end., Syn. 208, ABl. Nr. C 267, 19. 10. 1989, S. 3 ff.; vom Rat angenommen durch: *Rat der EU*, Entschließung des Rates vom 21. Dezember 1989 zu einem Gesamtkonzept für die Konformitätsbewertung, ABl. EG Nr. C 010, 16. 1. 1990 S. 1 f.; trotz der vom Rat verwendeten Terminologie eines „Gesamtkonzepts" hat sich die Bezeichnung „Globales Konzept" durchgesetzt.

[100] Siehe dazu *Jan O. Merten*, Private Entscheidungsträger und Europäisierung der Verwaltungsrechtsdogmatik, Berlin 2005, S. 23 f. m. w. N.

[101] Vgl. auch *Jan O. Merten*, Private Entscheidungsträger und Europäisierung der Verwaltungsrechtsdogmatik, Berlin 2005, S. 53 m. w. N.; *Hermann Pünder*, Zertifizierung und Akkreditierung, ZHR 170 (2006), S. 567 (570).

[102] Es handelt sich um die in der Wirtschaft vor der Neuen Konzeption und den ISO-Normen entwickelte sog. *third party certification*; Befund bei *Udo Di Fabio*, Produktharmonisierung durch Normung und Selbstüberwachung, Köln 1996, S. 25. Nach der Terminologie des NLF und der ISO-Normen ist der Begriff „Zertifizierung" für die Konformitätsbewertung durch eine dritte Stelle vorbehalten.

Die Zertifizierung ist in der Regel eine private Tätigkeit, die von privaten, europaweit tätigen privatrechtsförmig organisierten Dienstleistungsanbietern betrieben wird.[104] Diese Zertifizierungsstellen werden im EU-Produktsicherheitsrecht als notifizierte Konformitätsbewertungsstellen bezeichnet.[105] In einigen Ländern sind jedoch auch Zertifizierungsstellen zu finden, die eine enge Beziehung zum Staat aufweisen.[106] Das Rechtsverhältnis zwischen einer Zertifizierungsstelle und einem Hersteller wird privatrechtlich ausgestaltet:[107] Die Zertifizierungsstelle nimmt ihre Tätigkeit nach Auftrag des Herstellers oder dessen Bevollmächtigten im Rahmen eines zivilrechtlichen Werk- oder Dienstleistungsvertrages wahr. Der restliche Inhalt des Vertrages ist zwingend in den Anhängen der Richtlinien geregelt. Die Stellen sind also privatrechtlich Handelnde, auch wenn staatliche Behörden notifiziert worden sind.[108]

---

[103] Ein Novum des EU-Produktsicherheitsrechts stellt die Durchführung eines Teils des Konformitätsbewertungsverfahrens durch *akkreditierte interne Stellen* dar; vgl. Art. 4 Abs. 5 *lit.* c und Anhang I Art. R21 Beschluss 768/2008.

[104] *Hans Christian Röhl*, Konformitätsbewertung im Europäischen Produktsicherheitsrecht, in: Eberhard Schmidt-Aßmann/Bettina Schöndorf-Haubold (Hrsg.), Der Europäische Verwaltungsverbund. Formen und Verfahren der Verwaltungszusammenarbeit in der EU, Tübingen 2005, S. 153 (159, 175); *ders.*, Akkreditierung und Zertifizierung im Produktsicherheitsrecht. Zur Entwicklung einer neuen Europäischen Verwaltungsstruktur, Berlin 2000, S. 23; *Jan O. Merten*, Private Entscheidungsträger und Europäisierung der Verwaltungsrechtsdogmatik, Berlin 2005, S. 122 f.; *Kurt-Christian Scheel*, „Benannte Stellen": Beliehene als Instrument für die Verwirklichung des Binnenmarktes, DVBl 114 (1999), S. 442 (445). Der Beschluss ist neutral formuliert, so dass unter seine Bestimmungen sowohl private als auch staatliche Stellen fallen können.

[105] Im NLF ist eine terminologische Verschiebung der Bekanntmachung der Konformitätsbewertungsstelle gegenüber der Kommission zu erkennen. Im neuen Maßnahmenpaket ist die Rede von „Notifizierung" und von „notifizierten Stellen" statt von „Benennung" und „benannten Stellen". Die deutschen Begriffe werden also sprachlich und akustisch den englischen Begriffen *notification* sowie *notified bodies* angepasst. Die Begriffe „notifiziert" und „benannt" werden als Synonyme verwendet.

[106] Auf der Grundlage des öffentlichen Rechts organisierte notifizierte Stellen erwecken Bedenken bezüglich der Vereinbarkeit mit der europäisch ausgerichteten Natur des Systems; siehe *Hans Christian Röhl*, Akkreditierung und Zertifizierung im Produktsicherheitsrecht. Zur Entwicklung einer neuen Europäischen Verwaltungsstruktur, Berlin 2000, S. 22 f., 88; diese Auffassung erscheint jedoch nicht in seinem späteren Aufsatz über dasselbe Thema: *Hans Christian Röhl*, Konformitätsbewertung im Europäischen Produktsicherheitsrecht, in: Eberhard Schmidt-Aßmann/Bettina Schöndorf-Haubold (Hrsg.), Der Europäische Verwaltungsverbund. Formen und Verfahren der Verwaltungszusammenarbeit in der EU, Tübingen 2005, S. 153 ff.; anders *Jan O. Merten*, Private Entscheidungsträger und Europäisierung der Verwaltungsrechtsdogmatik, Berlin 2005, S. 122.

[107] *Jan O. Merten*, Private Entscheidungsträger und Europäisierung der Verwaltungsrechtsdogmatik, Berlin 2005, S. 146.

[108] *Hans Christian Röhl*, Akkreditierung und Zertifizierung im Produktsicherheitsrecht. Zur Entwicklung einer neuen Europäischen Verwaltungsstruktur, Berlin 2000, S. 25; anders *Jürgen Niebling*, Rechtsfragen der Zertifizierung und Akkreditierung, WiB 1995, S. 737 (741 f.).

Die größte Innovation der Neuen und der Globalen Konzeption, die vom NLF weitergeführt wird, ist die Administratifizierung der auf dem Markt bereits bestehenden Konformitätsbewertungsstelle. Das hat zur Entstehung einer neuen europäischen Verwaltungsstruktur geführt.[109] Werden die Drittprüfer einbezogen, steht ihnen die Befugnis der zwingenden Vermarktungskontrolle zu. Diese Stelle entscheidet europaweit abschließend und bindend über den Marktzugang. Mit der Erteilung oder Verweigerung der Vermarktungsbescheinigung wird den Herstellern der Marktzugang eröffnet oder verschlossen. Den notifizierten Stellen kommen demzufolge genuin europäische Verwaltungsaufgaben zu, da sie für ein rein europäisches Vollzugskonzept eingesetzt werden. Trotz der privatrechtlichen Ausgestaltung der notifizierten Stellen sind sie aus einer funktionellen Betrachtungsweise Teil der Verwaltung und stellen Implementationsorgane des Europarechts dar.[110] Die Einbeziehung der Konformitätsbewertungsstelle in die Produktsicherheit kompensiert den Mangel an systematischen staatlichen Produktzugangskontrollen.[111] Somit entsteht eine Zertifizierungsinfrastruktur, die als Gleiche der staatlichen verwaltungsrechtlichen Infrastruktur gegenübersteht. Es handelt sich um eine weitere Form der gesellschaftlichen Verwaltung, die horizontal gleichberechtigt neben der staatlichen Verwaltung steht.[112]

Seit dem 1. Januar 2010 wird das gemeineuropäische Modell der Akkreditierung durch die Verordnung 765/2008 weiter vereinheitlicht.[113] Die Verordnung 765/2008 stellt einen „Akkreditierungskodex" für die in der EU tätigen Akkreditierungsstellen dar. Der NLF schafft ebenfalls eine horizontale Akkreditierungsverwaltung. Die Ak-

---

[109] Siehe dazu grundlegend *Hans Christian Röhl*, Akkreditierung und Zertifizierung im Produktsicherheitsrecht. Zur Entwicklung einer neuen Europäischen Verwaltungsstruktur, Berlin 2000; zusammenfassend und weiterbringend *ders.*, Konformitätsbewertung im Europäischen Produktsicherheitsrecht, in: Eberhard Schmidt-Aßmann/Bettina Schöndorf-Haubold (Hrsg.), Der Europäische Verwaltungsverbund. Formen und Verfahren der Verwaltungszusammenarbeit in der EU, Tübingen 2005, S. 153 ff.

[110] *Martin Eifert*, Regulierungsstrategien, in: GVwR I, § 19 Rn. 82 ff.; *Wolfgang Hoffmann-Riem*, Eigenständigkeit der Verwaltung, GVwR I, § 10 Rn. 53; ähnlich *Kurt-Christian Scheel*, „Benannte Stellen": Beliehene als Instrument für die Verwirklichung des Binnenmarktes, DVBl 114 (1999), S. 442 (445). Dieser Teil der Literatur spricht ebenfalls über die Ausübung hoheitlicher Gewalt seitens der notifizierten Stellen. Das ist insofern ungenau, als dass die notifizierten Stellen einen neuen Typus von Verwaltung darstellen; sie sind nämlich eine Form von gesellschaftlicher Administration (vgl. dazu *infra* 3. Kap. B). Die Befugnisse der notifizierten Stellen haben einen verminderten Inhalt im Vergleich zu denen der Stellen des traditionellen administrativen Apparats; vorsichtiger in dieser Hinsicht *Andreas Voßkuhle*, Strukturen und Bauformen neuer Verfahren, in: Wolfgang Hoffmann-Riem/Eberhard Schmidt-Aßmann (Hrsg.), Verwaltungsverfahren und Verwaltungsverfahrensgesetz, 2002, S. 277 (313).

[111] Siehe *Kurt-Christian Scheel*, „Benannte Stellen": Beliehene als Instrument für die Verwirklichung des Binnenmarktes, DVBl 114 (1999), S. 442 (445).

[112] Siehe *supra* II. 1. a).

[113] Vgl. auch *Jörg Windmann*, Der Verifikateur und der Aufsichtsbeamte als zentrale Elemente des Sachverständigen-Vollzugsmodells im Technikrecht, DÖV 63 (2010), S. 396 (398). Die Grundlage der Akkreditierung in Europa bildet die Normenreihe EN ISO 17000 ff. Die einzige Ausnahme stellte bis zum 1. 1. 2010 Deutschland dar.

kreditierung ist Teil des umfassenden und einheitlichen Systems der Konformitätsbewertung[114] und dient der Gewährleistung der Kompetenz der Zertifizierungsstelle.[115] Der NLF verbindet ausdrücklich die Akkreditierung mit der Zertifizierung, obwohl die Akkreditierung keine Pflicht der notifizierten Konformitätsbewertungsstellen darstellt.[116] Die Verordnung 765/2008 geht über die Zwecke der Produktsicherheit hinaus, indem sie das System der Akkreditierung umfassend und unabhängig
von der Produktbezogenheit der Akkreditierung regelt. Der Anwendungsbereich
der Verordnung ist also deutlich weiter als das bisher harmonisierte Binnenmarkt-
recht.[117]

Mit der Verordnung 765/2008 greift die EU direkt in die nationalen Verwaltungen
ein. Die wesentliche Reform der Verordnung besteht in der Pflicht zur Errichtung
einer nationalen Akkreditierungsstelle. Gemäß Art. 4 Abs. 1 Verordnung 765/
2008 muss jeder Mitgliedstaat eine einzige Akkreditierungsstelle benennen.[118]
Art. 4 Abs. 5 derselben Verordnung legt fest, dass die Akkreditierung entweder
von einer Behörde selbst oder von einer beliehenen Stelle durchgeführt wird[119],
und insofern ist die Akkreditierung eine Dienstleistung, die als *hoheitliche Tätigkeit*
erbracht wird. Die Anforderungen an die nationalen Akkreditierungsstellen werden
ausführlich in der Verordnung geregelt.[120]

---

[114] Siehe Erwägungsgrund 8 Verordnung 765/2008.

[115] In Übertragung der Definition der EN ISO-Normen legt diese Verordnung eine Definition der Akkreditierung zugrunde; siehe Art. 2 Nr. 10 Verordnung 765/2008: Akkreditierung
ist die „Bestätigung durch eine nationale Akkreditierungsstelle, dass eine Konformitätsbewertungsstelle die in harmonisierten Normen festgelegten Anforderungen und, gegebenenfalls, zusätzliche Anforderungen, einschließlich solcher in relevanten sektoralen Akkrediti-
erungssystemen, erfüllt, um eine spezielle Konformitätsbewertungstätigkeit durchzuführen";
siehe auch Erwägungsgründe 9, 15 derselben Verordnung.

[116] *De lege ferenda* und zur Vermeidung von Inkonsistenzen und Überlappungen mit der
mit der Notifizierung einhergehenden Bewertung hätte der EU-Gesetzgeber die Akkrediti-
rung als eine pflichtige Voraussetzung im Rahmen der EU-Produktsicherheit vorsehen müssen.

[117] *Arun Kapoor/Thomas Klindt*, Die Reform des Akkreditierungswesens im Europäischen
Produktsicherheitsrecht, EuZW 20 (2009), S. 134 (137); siehe auch *Langner/Klindt*, in:
Dauses (Hrsg.), Hdb. EU-Wirtschaftsrecht, 2011, C. VI. Rn. 30; a. A. *Schorn*, Akkredi-
tierungsgesetz oder Diskreditierungsgesetz?, MPJ 15 (2008), S. 155 (158), der darauf hinweist,
dass aus kompetenziellen Gründen die Harmonisierung des Akkreditierungswesens nur im
Bereich der Harmonisierungsrichtlinien der Produktsicherheit geschieht.
Mit der Verordnung wird die strikte Unterscheidung zwischen einem obligatorischen, d. h.
dem geregelten, und einem freiwilligen, d. h. dem nicht geregelten, Bereich abgeschafft; vgl.
Art. 3 Verordnung 765/2008.

[118] Nach Art. 4 Abs. 2 Verordnung 765/2008 darf der Mitgliedstaat auf eine Akkrediti-
rungsstelle oder auf bestimmte Akkreditierungsdienstleistungen verzichten, wenn es wirt-
schaftlich nicht sinnvoll oder tragfähig ist und er auf die nationale Akkreditierungsstelle eines
anderen Mitgliedstaates zurückgreifen darf.

[119] Art. 4 Abs. 5 Verordnung 765/2008.

[120] Siehe Art. 8 und 4 Verordnung 765/2008.

Die nationalen Akkreditierungsstellen bestehen aber nicht unabhängig voneinander in der EU, sondern sie sind horizontal miteinander verbunden. Mit der Verordnung 765/2008 wird eine horizontale Verwaltungsstruktur errichtet, die die Kompetenz der Konformitätsbewertungsstellen sicherstellen soll. Die horizontale Akkreditierungsverwaltung hat unterschiedliche Ausprägungen. Erstens entfaltet der Akkreditierungsbescheid, der einen nationalen Verwaltungsakt darstellt, transnationale Wirkung. Die europäische transnationale Verwaltung der Akkreditierungsstellen beschränkt sich aber nicht auf die grenzüberschreitende Wirkung der Akkreditierungsakte, sondern verfügt auch über die Möglichkeit grenzüberschreitender Akkreditierungen.[121] Für die Gewährleistung des Funktionierens der transnationalen EU-Verwaltungsstruktur sind ebenfalls umfangreiche Informationspflichten der Akkreditierungsstellen vorgesehen.[122] Gemäß Art. 11 Abs. 2 Verordnung 765/2008 sind die nationalen Behörden verpflichtet, die Gleichwertigkeit der von den Akkreditierungsstellen erbrachten Dienstleistungen anzuerkennen, was zu einer Anerkennung der Akkreditierungsurkunden mit Vermutungswirkung sowie der Anerkennung von durch Konformitätsbewertungsstellen, die durch nationale Akkreditierungsstellen akkreditiert wurden, ausgestellten Bestätigungen führt.

Die horizontale Zusammenarbeit der nationalen Akkreditierungsstellen wird auch institutionell verfestigt. Die Akkreditierungsstellen sammeln sich auf der europäischen Ebene in der Europäischen Kooperation für die Akkreditierung (*European Cooperation for Accreditation* – EA). Art. 4 Abs. 10 VO 765/2008 sieht eine Pflichtmitgliedschaft aller nationalen Akkreditierungsstellen in der EA vor.

bb) Nachhaltigkeit von Produkten

Ähnliche Systeme wie bei der Produktsicherheit finden sich ebenfalls im Bereich der Governance der Nachhaltigkeit von Produkten. Die verfolgte Strategie der EU bezieht sich auf einen integrierten Ansatz für die Unterstützung nachhaltiger Verbrauchs- und Produktionsmuster sowie für die Förderung der nachhaltigen Industriepolitik.[123] Unter den Maßnahmen für die Implementierung der Nachhaltigkeitspolitik der EU befindet sich ebenfalls die Einführung der Konformitätsbewertung und des Zertifizierungs- und Akkreditierungssystems. In diesem Rahmen wurde das freiwil-

---

[121] Siehe Art. 7 Abs. 1 Unterabs. 1 Verordnung 765/2008.

[122] Vgl. Art. 12 Verordnung 765/2008.

[123] Siehe Präambel, Art. 3 Abs. 3, 5 EUV sowie Art. 11 AEUV. Siehe ebenfalls *KOM*, Mitteilung der Kommission an das Europäische Parlament, den Rat, den Europäischen Wirtschafts- und Sozialausschuss und den Ausschuss der Regionen über den Aktionsplan für Nachhaltigkeit in Produktion und Verbrauch und für eine nachhaltige Industriepolitik, SEK (2008) 2110, SEK (2008) 2111, KOM (2008) 397 endg., 16. 7. 2008, insbes. S. 12; vgl. auch *KOM*, Mitteilung der Kommission an das Europäische Parlament, den Rat, den Europäischen Wirtschafts- und Sozialausschuss und den Ausschuss der Regionen. Förderung einer nachhaltigen Entwicklung durch die EU-Politik: Überprüfung der EU-Strategie für nachhaltige Entwicklung 2009, KOM (2009) 400 endg., den 24. 7. 2009, S. 3.

lige Gemeinschaftssystem für das Umweltmanagement und die Umweltbetriebsprüfung (EMAS) überarbeitet.[124]

Im Rahmen des integrierten Ansatzes finden sich ebenfalls Maßnahmen zur Förderung einer nachhaltigen Produktpolitik,[125] deren Ziel es ist, die Umweltauswirkungen eines Produkts während seines gesamten Lebenszyklus zu minimieren. Der Erfolg des Modells der Neuen Konzeption hat die Kommission dazu veranlasst, das oben beschriebene horizontale Modell auf umweltrelevante Konstruktionsanforderungen auszuweiten.[126] Die durch die Existenz unterschiedlicher nationaler Umweltanforderungen, die Hindernisse für den EU-Handel darstellen, bedingte Harmonisierung erfolgt für einige Produktkategorien im Rahmen eines pflichtigen Ökodesigns von Produkten. Mit der Richtlinie 2009/125 wird die pflichtige umweltgerechte Gestaltung energieverbrauchsrelevanter Produkte vorgeschrieben.[127] Wegen der Heterogenität der Produktkategorien unterliegen nicht alle energieverbrauchsrelevanten Produkte den Pflichten aus der Richtlinie 2009/125, sondern nur diejenigen, die von einer Durchführungsmaßnahme erfasst werden.

Seit 2006 entwickelt die Kommission eine Gesamtstrategie für Agrar- und Ernährungserzeugnisse in der EU.[128] Diese geht über die Sicherheit der Erzeugnisse hinaus

---

[124] Verordnung (EG) Nr. 1221/2009 des Europäischen Parlaments und des Rates vom 25. November 2009 über die freiwillige Teilnahme von Organisationen an einem Gemeinschaftssystem für Umweltmanagement und Umweltbetriebsprüfung und zur Aufhebung der Verordnung (EG) Nr. 761/2001 sowie der Beschlüsse der Kommission 2001/681/EG und 2006/193/EG, ABl. EU Nr. L 342, 22. 12. 2009.

[125] *Juliane Jörissen*, Produktbezogener Umweltschutz und technische Normen. Zur rechtlichen und politischen Gestaltbarkeit der europäischen Normung, Köln u. a. 1997, S. 8: „produktintegrierter Umweltschutz"; siehe auch *Henning Lustermann*, Klimaschutz durch integrierte Produktpolitik, NVwZ 26 (2007), S. 895.

[126] *Thomas Klindt*, Die CE-Kennzeichnung als umweltbezogene Produktaussage – Ökologisierung des technischen Sicherheitsrechts?, ZUR 2001, S. 321 ff.; *Henning Lustermann*, Klimaschutz durch integrierte Produktpolitik, NVwZ 26 (2007), S. 895 (896).

[127] Richtlinie 2009/125/EG des Europäischen Parlaments und des Rates vom 21. Oktober 2009 zur Schaffung eines Rahmens für die Festlegung von Anforderungen an die umweltgerechte Gestaltung energieverbrauchsrelevanter Produkte (Neufassung), ABl. EU Nr. L 285, 31. 10. 2009. Diese Richtlinie erstreckt den Geltungsbereich der pflichtigen umweltgerechten Gestaltung auf alle energieverbrauchsrelevanten Produkte, der bis zu ihrem Inkrafttreten nur energiebetriebene Produkte betraf; vgl. Richtlinie 2005/32/EG des Europäischen Parlaments und des Rates vom 6. 7. 2005 zur Schaffung eines Rahmens für die Festlegung von Anforderungen an die umweltgerechte Gestaltung energiebetriebener Produkte und zur Änderung der Richtlinie 92/42/EWG des Rates sowie der Richtlinien 96/57/EG und 2000/55/EG des Europäischen Parlaments und des Rates (ABl. EG Nr. L 191, S. 29); siehe dazu *Henning Lustermann*, Klimaschutz durch integrierte Produktpolitik, NVwZ 26 (2007), S. 895 ff.

[128] Vgl. *KOM*, Mitteilung der Kommission an das Europäische Parlament, den Rat, den Europäischen Wirtschafts- und Sozialausschuss und den Ausschuss der Regionen über die Qualitätspolitik für Agrarerzeugnisse, SEC (2009) 670, SEC (2009) 671, KOM (2009) 234 endg., 28. 5. 2009; angenommen vom Rat durch *Rat der EU*, Schlussfolgerungen des Rates zur Mitteilung der Kommission über die Qualitätspolitik für Agrarerzeugnisse, 16. 6. 2009 (18. 06.); vgl. schon *KOM*, Grünbuch zur Qualität von Agrarerzeugnissen: Produktnormen, Bewirtschaftungsauflagen und Qualitätsregelungen, KOM (2008) 641 endg., 15. 10. 2008.

und erfasst die besonderen und unverwechselbaren Eigenschaften der Waren der landwirtschaftlichen Erzeuger und Lebensmittelhersteller. Im Mittelpunkt steht also die Qualität dieser Erzeugnisse, wobei als Qualitätsmerkmale Eigenschaften des Erzeugnisses oder der Produktionsverfahren zu verstehen sind. Es gibt vier Regelungen zur Qualitätssicherung dieser Erzeugnisse, die mit einem Zertifizierungs- und Akkreditierungsmechanismus verbunden sind. Diese Qualitätspolitik erstreckt sich auf besondere Qualitätsmerkmale von Agrarerzeugnissen mit der Einführung folgender Gütezeichen: *geschützte Ursprungsbezeichnung* (g. U.), *geschützte geografische Angabe* (g. g. A.) und *garantiert traditionelle Spezialität* (g. t. S.); hinzu treten die Produkte aus Regionen in *äußerster Randlage* der EU.[129]

Seit den 1990er Jahren zielt eine Reihe von Maßnahmen, insbesondere im Rahmen der Gemeinsamen Agrarpolitik (GAP), auf die Förderung der biologischen/ökologischen Landwirtschaft (*organic farming*).[130] Das System der Konformitätsbewertung gilt ebenfalls bei der Regelung der ökologischen/biologischen Produktion in der EU. Detaillierte Regeln zum ökologisch/biologisch kontrollierten Anbau, zur Verarbeitung, zum Vertrieb, zur Kennzeichnung und zu Kontrollmechanismen sind im Rahmen der Verordnung 834/2007 berücksichtigt worden, die einen unionalen Rechtsrahmen für die biologische/ökologische Produktion und die biologischen/ökologischen Erzeugnisse etabliert. Die technischen Details werden von der Kommission in Durchführungsverordnungen festgelegt. Die VO 834/2007 stellt eine

---

[129] Zu den ersten beiden Kennzeichnungen siehe Verordnung (EG) Nr. 510/2006 des Rates vom 20. März 2006 zum Schutz von geografischen Angaben und Ursprungsbezeichnungen für Agrarerzeugnisse und Lebensmittel, ABl. EU Nr. L 93/12, 31. 3. 2006; zu den geografischen Herkunftsangaben unter dieser Verordnung vgl. *Knaak*, Geographische Herkunftsangaben, in: Sosnitza (Hrsg.), Aktuelle Entwicklungen im deutschen und europäischen Lebensmittelrecht, 2007, S. 113 ff. Zur dritten Kennzeichnung siehe Verordnung (EG) Nr. 509/2006 des Rates vom 20. März 2006 über die garantiert traditionellen Spezialitäten bei Agrarerzeugnissen und Lebensmitteln, ABl. EU Nr. L 93/1, 31. 3. 2006. Die Erzeugnisse der beiden ersten Kategorien weisen einen Bezug zu einem bestimmten geografischen Territorium, das dem Erzeugnis seine spezifischen Qualitätsmerkmale verleiht, auf, wobei bei der dritten Kategorie die Qualität nur die Produktionsmethode ausmacht. Deswegen sind sie in getrennten Verordnungen geregelt. Während zwischen den beiden ersten Kategorien ein Unterschied bezüglich des Grades besteht, besteht zwischen den beiden ersten und der dritten ein Unterschied bezüglich der Natur; vgl. dazu *Martina Conticelli*, Il Procedimento Europeo di Registrazione delle Denominazioni di Origine Protetta, Rivista Trimestriale di Diritto Pubblico 2004, S. 317 (324).

[130] Vgl. dazu *Alberto Alemanno*, Regulating Organic Farming in the European Union, R.E.D.C. 2009, S. 83 (86 ff.); vgl. auch den *European Action Plan for Organic Food and Farming – KOM*, Mitteilung der Kommission an den Rat und das Europäische Parlament, Europäischer Aktionsplan für ökologische Landwirtschaft und ökologisch erzeugte Lebensmittel, SEC (2004) 739, KOM (2004) 415 endg., 10. 06. 2004; *KOM*, Mitteilung der Kommission an das Europäische Parlament, den Rat, den Europäischen Wirtschafts- und Sozialausschuss und den Ausschuss der Regionen über die Qualitätspolitik für Agrarerzeugnisse, SEC (2009) 670, SEC (2009) 671, KOM (2009) 234 endg., 28. 5. 2009.
Das Erfordernis einer doppelten Bezeichnung entstammt der Übersetzung des mehrdeutigen englischen Begriffes *organic* und betrifft nicht nur die deutsche Bezeichnung, sondern alle anderen EU-Sprachen außer Englisch.

Kombination von Produktionsregeln mit einem objektiven Kontrollsystem dar,[131] ähnlich zum System der Produktsicherheit. Im EU-Recht zur ökologischen/biologischen Produktion hat die Akkreditierung denselben Inhalt wie im Rahmen des EU-Produktsicherheitsrechts, wobei die Akkreditierung auf der Grundlage von Verordnung 765/2008 durchgeführt wird. Im Unterschied zum EU-Produktsicherheitsrecht und zur bisherigen Rechtslage sieht Art. 27 Abs. 5 *lit.* c) Verordnung 834/2007 eine Pflicht der Öko-Kontrollstellen zur Akkreditierung auf der Grundlage der europäischen und internationalen Normen vor.

c) Die Governance der Justiz

Das Hauptanliegen der 2010 gegründeten Generaldirektion Justiz der Europäischen Kommission ist die „Schaffung eines Europäischen Rechtsraumes"[132]. Um dieses Ziel zu erfüllen, unternimmt diese Generaldirektion in den letzten Jahren unterschiedliche Initiativen. Hauptbereiche ihrer Tätigkeiten sind unter anderem die „Ziviljustiz", die „Strafjustiz" sowie „wirksame justizielle Rechte" (*effective justice*).

Zur Verfolgung dieses Zwecks benutzt die Kommission die Erfahrungen von Institutionen außerhalb der EU wie die Europäische Kommission für die Effizienz der Justiz (CEPEJ) des Europarates. Am 15. Januar 2013 präsentierte die Kommission eine Studie, die in Zusammenarbeit mit der CEPEJ vorbereitet worden ist,[133] die die Effizienz mitgliedstaatlicher Justizsysteme bewertet.[134] Außerdem hat die Europäische Kommission am 1. 1. 2013 eine neue Einheit, die „General justice policies and judicial systems Unit", in der Generaldirektion Justiz eingeführt, die eine ähnliche Funktion wie die CEPEJ erfüllen soll. Das neue „EU Justice Scoreboard" vom

---

[131] *Alberto Alemanno*, Regulating Organic Farming in the European Union, R.E.D.C. 2009, S. 83 (87). Verordnung (EG) Nr. 834/2007 des Rates vom 28. Juni 2007 über die ökologische/biologische Produktion und die Kennzeichnung von ökologischen/biologischen Erzeugnissen und zur Aufhebung der Verordnung (EWG) Nr. 2092/91, ABl. EU Nr. L 189/1, 20. 7. 2007; zuletzt geändert durch Verordnung (EG) Nr. 967/2008 des Rates vom 29. September 2008 zur Änderung der Verordnung (EG) Nr. 834/2007 über die ökologische/biologische Produktion und die Kennzeichnung von ökologischen/biologischen Erzeugnissen, ABl. EU Nr. L 264/1, 3. 10. 2008. Die Verordnung 834/2007 ersetzt die Verordnung (EWG) Nr. 2092/91 des Rates vom 24. Juni 1991 über den ökologischen Landbau und die entsprechende Kennzeichnung der landwirtschaftlichen Erzeugnisse und Lebensmittel, ABl. EG Nr. L 198, 22. 07. 1991; vgl. zur alten Verordnung *Kurt-Dietrich Rathke/Britta Weitbrecht/Heinz-Joachim Kopp*, Ökologischer Landbau und Bioprodukte, München 2002.

[132] Siehe http://ec.europa.eu/justice/mission/vision/index_de.htm (alle Internet-Adressen wurden zuletzt am 31. 8. 2013 abgerufen).

[133] *Eric Dubois/Christel Schurrer/Marco Velicogna*, The Functioning of Judicial Systems and the Situation of the Economy in the European Union Member States. Report prepared for the European Commission (Directorate General JUSTICE), Strasbourg, 15 January 2013.

[134] Siehe *Adriani Dori*, The EU Justice Scoveboard-Judicial Evaluation as a New Governance Tool, MPILux Working Paper 2 (2015).

März 2013 folgt genau der Logik der Bewertung der CEPEJ und enthält CEPEJ-Daten.[135]

Ähnliche Tendenzen sind in unterschiedlichen Initiativen zu finden, die teilweise von der Europäischen Kommission unterstützt werden.[136] Die Europäische Kommission fördert zum Beispiel die Entwicklung von Netzwerken von Richtern und Gerichten. 2004 wurde die Etablierung eines Netzwerks der Richter der Obersten Gerichte der Mitgliedstaaten der EU mit dem Titel „Network of the Presidents of the Supreme Judicial Courts of the European Union" von der Europäischen Kommission initiiert.[137] Es handelt sich um ein informelles Forum, im Rahmen dessen die europäischen Institutionen die Chance haben, die Meinungen der Repräsentanten der Obersten Gerichte Europas zu erfahren, gemeinsame Probleme zu diskutieren und Ideen auszutauschen. Die Präsidenten des EuGH und des Europäischen Gerichts für Menschenrechte sind ebenfalls präsent. Seit 2006 entwickelt dieses Netzwerk mit der finanziellen Unterstützung der Kommission ein gemeinsames Portal, das den Mitgliedern Zugang zu den Rechtsprechungsdatenbanken gewährt. Eine ähnliche Funktion erfüllt das *Justice Sector Peer-Assisted Learning (JUSTPAL) Network*, das die Arbeit der Weltbank und der Europäischen Kommission im Bereich Justiz durch die Schaffung von sechs „Communities of Practice" (COPs) mit Richtern aus den ganzen Welt unterstützt.[138]

Die Tätigkeit der Kommission im Bereich der „wirksamen Justiz" sowie die Entstehung von Netzwerken von Gerichten und Richtern zeigt die horizontale Dimension der Governance der Justiz in Europa. Governance findet durch die Verbreitung von *best practices* in den europäischen Ländern und nicht durch den Versuch einer Harmonisierung der nationalen Systeme im traditionellen Sinne statt. Der Vergleich der Systeme sowie die Verbreitung der *best practices* soll zu einem gegenseitigen Lernen der Organisationen und Personen in der Justiz und somit zur schrittweisen Verbesserung der Leistungen der nationalen Justizinstanzen sowie der Kompatibilität nationaler Justizsysteme führen.

---

[135] Siehe zuletzt *European Commission,* The 2015 EU Justice Scoreboard, Communication from the Commission to the European Parliament, the Council, the European Central Bank, the European Economic and Social Committee and the Committee of the Regions, COM (2015), 116 final.

[136] Siehe auch *Burkhard Hess/Georgios Dimitropoulos,* Judicial Reforms in Luxembourg and Europe: International and Comparative Perspectives, in: Burkhard Hess (Hrsg.), Judicial Reforms in Luxembourg and Europe, Baden-Baden 2014, S. 1 ff.

[137] Siehe http://www.network-presidents.eu/.

[138] Es handelt sich um Gemeinschaften in folgenden Bereichen: Justice Sector Budget Professionals; Information Systems Professionals; Physical Infrastructure of Court; Court Managers and Administrators; Prosecution and Anti-Corruption Agencies und Civil and Commercial Courts.

III. Supranationale Reform durch nationale Reformen

1. Reform und Reformtypen

Die in der Soziologie häufig verwendete Analogie zwischen sozialen und biologischen Organismen verdeutlicht, dass sich Staaten den veränderten Umständen anpassen müssen, um weiterleben zu können. Der Mangel einer Anpassung kann gefährlich sein.[139] Aus diesem Grund sind kontinuierliche Reformen erforderlich, insbesondere in Krisenzeiten. Eine Krise selbst kann das Ergebnis einer Nichtanpassung eines Staates an die veränderten Umstände, also verpasster Reformen, sein.

Die Ausformung von horizontalen Governance-Strukturen zeigt, dass sich die Reformen in den Mitgliedstaaten und die Reform der europäischen Institutionen gegenseitig bedingen. Wenn die Governance-Strukturen der EU Horizontalisierungstendenzen aufweisen, müssen zunächst die Mitgliedstaaten reformiert werden, wenn die europäischen Institutionen und die EU als Ganzes reformiert werden sollen. Die Reform der EU geht – zumindest in dieser Phase der historischen Entwicklung der EU – über die Reform der Mitgliedstaaten. Was für Reformen sind aber für die Mitgliedstaaten erforderlich? Die Globalisierung und die Europäisierung haben tatsächlich bislang zu großen Reformen auf der staatlichen Ebene geführt.[140] Zwei gegensätzliche Reformtrends waren in dieser geschichtlichen Entwicklung zu erkennen: eine Spezialisierung von staatlichen Organen und ein Erfordernis ihrer Koordinierung.[141] Die meisten Reformen haben auch daran mitgewirkt, den traditionellen Regierungs- und Verwaltungsstrukturen Flexibilität einzuflößen.[142] Außerdem war

---

[139] Siehe *Oliver Diggelmann*, The Aaland Case and the Sociological Approach to International Law, European Journal of International Law 18 (2007), 135 (140) mit Verweis auf *Max Huber*; siehe ebenfalls zur Anpassung des Rechts an die Anforderungen des überstaatlichen Rechts *Lawrence M. Friedman*, Borders: On the Emerging Sociology of Transnational Law, Stanford Journal of International Law 32 (1996), S. 65–90: „The global economy is the engine driving convergence, and is what stimulates jurists to draft model laws and to worry about harmonization. In fact, harmonization and model laws are, in an important sense, merely responses to processes that have already taken place".

[140] *Alaisdair Roberts*, The Logic of Discipline. Global Capitalism and the Architecture of Government, Oxford 2010, S. 3: „Governmental reform that spanned thirty years ... call it the era of globalization"; zur entsprechenden Transformation des Verwaltungsrechts siehe zusammenfassend *Peer Zumbansen*, Review of Cassese, Sabino/Carotti, Bruno/Casini, Lorenzo/Cavalieri, Eleonora/MacDonald, Euan (eds. with the collaboration of Macchia, Marco/Savino, Mario), Global Administrative Law. The Casebook, Rome, New York 3rd ed. 2012: Administrative Law's Global Dream: Path Dependencies and Political Economies, Global Law Books, (elektronische Veröffentlichung, online verfügbar unter: http://www.globallawbooks.org/reviews/detail.asp?id=773, 2012).

[141] *Philippe Bezes/Anne Lise Fimreite/Patrick Le Lidec/Per Lægreid*, Understanding Organizational Reforms in the Modern State: Specialization and Integration in Norway and France, Governance 26 (2013), S. 147 (inbes. 149 ff.). Im Rahmen der Reform der Governance-Strukturen der EU nimmt Spezialisierung sowohl die Form einer vertikalen als auch einer horizontalen Spezialisierung an.

[142] Siehe *Jon Pierre*, Governance and Institutional Flexibility, in: David Levi-Faur (Hrsg.), The Oxford Handbook of Governance, Oxford 2012, S. 187 ff.

die Frage der Reform der Regulierungsmethoden nie eine Frage der Wahl zwischen Markt und Staat, sondern eine Frage der Gestaltung des Zusammenspiels von öffentlichen und privaten Elementen.[143] Diese Reformtrends werden mit der Horizontalisierung der EU-Governance-Strukturen intensiviert.

Es kann zwischen verschiedenen Typen von Reformen unterschieden werden, die für die EU-Mitgliedstaaten relevant sein können.[144] Erstens kann auf der Grundlage der Unterscheidung zwischen symbolischen und praktischen Änderungen von Rechtslagen zwischen „symbolischen Reformen" und „praktischen Reformen" differenziert werden.[145] Diese Abgrenzung spielt eine sehr wichtige Rolle für die gegenwärtige Reformdebatte. Für die Europäische Union war hauptsächlich die Anpassung der Mitgliedstaaten der EU – sowie der Kandidatenländer und der potentiellen Kandidatenländer – an den *acquis communautaire* immer wichtig gewesen. Auch die klassische Rechtswissenschaft neigte dazu, symbolische Reformen zu untersuchen. Die zunehmende Tendenz ist aber, den Fokus auf die praktischen Reformen zu legen.[146] Die Fokussierung auf die praktischen Reformen bedeutet gleichzeitig eine Refokussierung auf Rechtsimplementation statt auf Regelsetzung. Nicht nur die Änderung einer Rechtslage ist wichtig, sondern die Änderung der tatsächlichen Situation.

Die Unterscheidung zwischen Maßnahmen fiskalischer Konsolidierung (*fiscal consolidation*) und strukturellen Reformen (*structural reforms*) wird ebenfalls sehr häufig getroffen. Diese beiden Reformtypen sind auch in den internationalen Rechtstexten zu finden.[147] Die Reformmaßnahmen fiskalischer Konsolidierung sind Sparmaßnahmen, wie z. B. Gehaltsminderungen im öffentlichen Sektor, und haben die Reduzierung der staatlichen Ausgaben als direktes Ziel. In Ländern, in denen Reformprogramme der EU und des Internationalen Währungsfonds implementiert werden – oder implementiert worden sind –, haben sich meistens die Regierungen auf die Konsolidierung der staatlichen Finanzen wegen deren einfacher Umsetzung konzentriert. Die strukturellen Reformen werden ebenfalls von den interna-

---

[143] *Marc Allen Eisner*, Beyond the Logic of the Market: Toward an Institutional Analysis of Regulatory Reforms, in: David Levi-Faur (Hrsg.), Handbook on the Politics of Regulation, Cheltenham 2011, S. 129 ff.

[144] In der verwaltungswissenschaftlichen Reformdebatte finden sich weitere Typen von Reformen wie z. B. die „Governance-Reformen" und die „New Public Management-Reformen" als Unterkategorien der Verwaltungsreformen; siehe *Jon Pierre*, Governance and Institutional Flexibility, in: David Levi-Faur (Hrgs.), The Oxford Handbook of Governance, Oxford 2012, S. 187 (190).

[145] Zur Unterscheidung zwischen *symbolic* und *practical legal change* siehe *Gregory Shaffer*, Transnational Legal Process and State Change, Law and Social Inquiry 37 (2012), S. 229 (237).

[146] Vgl. Auch *Gregory Shaffer*, Transnational Legal Process and State Change, Law and Social Inquiry 37 (2012), S. 229 (237).

[147] Siehe z. B. *Internationaler Währungsfonds*, Greece: Letter of Intent, Memorandum of Economic and Financial Policies, and Technical Memorandum of Understanding, December 21, 2012, S. 1 f., 6 ff., 70 f., 71 ff.

tionalen Reformprogrammen verlangt. Bei den strukturellen Reformen könnte es sich um Restrukturierungen des öffentlichen Sektors, um die Einführung von neuen Management-Systemen für den öffentlichen Sektor, um Privatisierungen öffentlicher Unternehmen sowie um Reformen im Arbeitsrecht handeln.[148] Strukturelle Reformen sind die wichtigsten Reformen für jeden Staat, gleichzeitig ist aber ihre Implementation sehr schwierig. Sie berühren lange Zeit beschützte Interessen, wobei ihre Ergebnisse nur längerfristig zur Geltung kommen.[149] Nach einer langen Phase der Einführung von Maßnahmen fiskalischer Konsolidierung legen jetzt die meisten europäischen Mitgliedstaaten, und insbesondere die „Memorandum-Länder", besonderen Wert auf die strukturellen Reformen. Das Bedürfnis einer Refokussierung auch in dieser Hinsicht betrifft nicht nur die Memorandum-Länder, sondern alle EU-Mitgliedstaaten. Das beweist die Dynamik der asiatischen und südamerikanischen Staaten im Vergleich zu den EU-Mitgliedstaaten, aber auch die Geschwindigkeit, mit der die USA eine „US made" globale Krise im Vergleich zu Europa überwinden.

Insgesamt ist also in Zukunft für die Reformtätigkeit der Mitgliedstaaten der EU auf die praktischen strukturellen Reformen Wert zu legen.

2. Die Implementation von praktischen strukturellen Reformen

a) Mehr Zeit für Design und Implementation

Die gegenwärtigen Reformbestrebungen in den Mitgliedstaaten sind international induzierte Reformen. Nach dem berühmten amerikanischen Völkerrechtler *Louis Henkin*, „almost all nations observe almost all principles of international law and almost all of their obligations almost all of the time".[150] Das ist jedoch nicht immer der Fall hinsichtlich der praktischen strukturellen Reformen in der EU – und zwar in einem sehr stark rechtlich geprägten supranationalen Milieu. Die Unfähigkeit von Ländern wie Griechenland und Portugal, aber auch von anderen europäischen Ländern, praktische strukturelle Reformen zu implementieren, muss einige Gründe haben. Warum werden diese Reformen nicht implementiert und wie kann ihre Implementierung verbessert werden? Die Implementation und die Durchsetzung von internationalem Recht erfolgen nach einem transnationalen Rechtsprozess (*transnational legal process*), der ein sehr kompliziertes Verfahren darstellt, dessen Verwirklichung die Existenz und Kumulation von unterschiedlichen rechtlichen und außerrechtli-

---

[148] Siehe zur Privatisierung als „Reformkonzept" *Athanasios Gromitsaris*, in diesem Band.

[149] Vgl. auch *European Network of Councils for the Judiciary (ENCJ)*, Judicial Reform in Europe. Report 2011–2012, S. 25: „Fundamental reforms take time, and their costs precede the benefits".

[150] *Louis Henkin*, How Nations Behave: Law and Foreign Policy, Columbia, 2. Aufl., S. 25–26; siehe auch *Harold Hongju Koh*, Why do Nations Obey International Law? Yale Law Journal 106 (1997), S. 2599 ff.; vgl. auch *Oona Hathaway*, Between Power and Principle: An Integrated Theory of International Law, University of Chicago Law Review 71 (2005), S. 469 (481 ff.).

chen Elementen verlangt.[151] Außerdem kostet es Zeit und Geld, fundamentale Reformen, wie die praktischen strukturellen Reformen, zu implementieren.[152] Die Interaktion der international induzierten Reformen mit den nationalen institutionellen, politischen und kulturellen Kontexten bewirkt, dass die durch die Reformen induzierten Änderungen sehr oft nur evolutionär und inkrementell im Verlauf der Zeit entstehen.[153] Ein großes Problem der Reformprogramme in Europa, wie z. B. derjenigen, die in den sog. Memoranda vorgesehen sind, ist, dass sie die Änderungen der Rechtslagen direkt verlangt haben. Sowohl das Design als auch die Implementation einer Reform brauchen in der Regel viel Zeit.[154]

Jenseits des Faktors „Zeit" zeigen unterschiedliche Theorien, wie z. B. die Theorien der *New Governance*,[155] sowohl die Gründe für die Nichteinführung als auch den Weg für die Verbesserung der Implementationschancen von Reformrecht. Dieses Recht sollte bestimmten Anforderungen entsprechen. Vor allem soll das Design erfolgreicher Reformen die gegenwärtige Tendenz der Horizontalisierung respektieren. Die Europäische Union verwendet die Instrumente von *New Governance* zur Förderung der Implementation ihrer Regeln, wie z. B. im Bereich der OMC. *New-Governance*-Strukturen haben den Vorteil, dass sich die Regelsetzung von der Implementationspraxis in einem *Learning-by-doing*-Prozess inspirieren lässt. Auf der Grundlage dieses Verfahrens der Wissensgenerierung durch Implementationserfahrung soll Regelsetzung auf einem *Bottom-up*-Weg umgeformt werden. Mögliches Versagen auf der Implementationsebene soll zu einer Reevaluation des Designs der Reformregeln führen. Somit wird sich ebenfalls die Implementierung der Regeln verbessern.

b) Partizipation

Ein gemeinsamer Punkt aller modernen Governance-Theorien ist das Bedürfnis der Partizipation aller interessierten Akteure an dem *policymaking*, der Regelsetzung

---

[151] Siehe *Harold Hongju Koh*, Transnational Legal Process, Nebraska Law Review 75 (1996), 181 (194): „In short, international law is enforced by a transnational legal process, which is triggered not just by the United States and Russia, but also by the Security Council, the GATT, Exxon, Greenpeace, the Paris Club, Amnesty International, and the Lowenstein International Human Rights Clinic at Yale Law School".

[152] Siehe für den Bereich der Justiz *European Network of Councils for the Judiciary (ENCJ)*, Judicial Reform in Europe. Report 2011–2012, S. 25.

[153] *Philippe Bezes/Anne Lise Fimreite/Patrick Le Lidec/Per Lægreid*, Understanding Organizational Reforms in the Modern State: Specialization and Integration in Norway and France, Governance 26 (2013), S. 147 (167): „Because transnational law interacts with domestic institutional, political and cultural contexts, changes are often evolutionary and incremental over time"; vgl. auch *Kai-Peter Sommermann*, in diesem Band.

[154] Vgl. *Philippe Bezes/Anne Lise Fimreite/Patrick Le Lidec/Per Lægreid*, Understanding Organizational Reforms in the Modern State: Specialization and Integration in Norway and France, Governance 26 (2013), S. 147 (167), auf der Grundlage der Erfahrungen in Norwegen.

[155] Siehe dazu nur *Charles F. Sabel/J. Zeitlin* (Hrsg.), Experimentalist Governance in the European Union: Towards a New Architecture, Oxford, 2010; *Gráinne de Búrca*, New Governance and Experimentalism: An Introduction, Wisconsin Law Review (2010), S. 227 ff.

und der Implementierung.[156] Bisher fehlt es in den Reformprogrammen an einer Strategie für eine partizipative Teilnahme aller *stakeholders* bei Design und Implementation der Reformen. Das ist ein bekanntes Problem des Entwicklungsrechts,[157] das auch bei dem Design und der Implementation der Reformprogramme in Europa erneut festgestellt werden kann. Weder bei dem Design noch bei der Implementation der Reformen haben die nationalen und die internationalen Institutionen systematischen und institutionalisierten Kontakt mit den betroffenen und interessierten Akteuren. Die Teilnahme dieser Akteure könnte sowohl den Inhalt als auch die Legitimation der Reformen verbessern.

Das nicht partizipative Vorgehen der internationalen Institutionen behindert ebenfalls die Ausbildung von Netzwerken von Reformagenten. Reformorientierte Akteure im öffentlichen Sektor und in der Zivilgesellschaft sollten bei der Implementation der Programme aktiv mitwirken.

c) Verstärkung des *Ownership* der Reformprogramme

Nach der empirischen Studie von *James Raymond Vreeland* schließen Regierungen die Vereinbarungen mit dem Internationalen Währungsfonds aus unterschiedlichen Gründen ab.[158] Unter den Gründen ist der tatsächliche Bedarf nach Krediten, wobei ein weiterer Grund darin besteht, dass oft die Regierungen die IMF-Konditionen intern durchsetzen möchten. In diesen Fällen stellen die Konditionen keine Sanktionen dar, sondern sind hilfreiche Mechanismen für die Regierungen, intern Politiken zu ändern und ihre eigene Reformagenda zu erzwingen,[159] wobei sie dann als Glaubwürdigkeit steigernde Mechanismen wirken. Diese Haltung der Regierungen gegenüber Reformprogrammen zeigt ein weiteres Problem der Reformprogramme, das ebenfalls in Europa zu finden ist.

Die fehlende Zusammenwirkung und Kommunikation der entsprechenden Institutionen mit einem breiten Spektrum von Akteuren – insbesondere während der Phase des Designs des Programms – führt dazu, dass die Reformprogramme von der Bevölkerung der Reformländer als extern auferlegte Maßnahmen empfunden werden. Die Teilnahme aller reformorientierten Akteure am Design und an der Im-

---

[156] Siehe nur *Jon Pierre*, Governance and Institutional Flexibility, in: David Levi-Faur (Hrsg.), The Oxford Handbook of Governance, Oxford 2012, S. 187 (191–192); mit Blick auf *New Governance* in der EU siehe *Paul James Cardwell*, The Changing Nature of European Regulatory Governance, in: David Levi-Faur (Hrsg.), Handbook on the Politics of Regulation, Cheltenham 2011, S. 536 (543 ff.).

[157] Siehe *James Raymond Vreeland*, Why Do Governments and the IMF Enter into Agreements? Statistically Selected Cases, International Political Science Review 24 (2003), S. 321 (340).

[158] *James Raymond Vreeland*, Why Do Governments and the IMF Enter into Agreements? Statistically Selected Cases, International Political Science Review 24 (2003), S. 321 ff.

[159] *James Raymond Vreeland*, Why Do Governments and the IMF Enter into Agreements? Statistically Selected Cases, International Political Science Review 24 (2003), S. 321 (S. 339).

plementation der Reformprogramme sowie die Einführung von weiteren Instrumenten horizontaler Governance soll zur Entwicklung von länderspezifischen Reformprogrammen führen. Die Entwicklung eines heimischen *Ownership* der Programme wird ebenfalls ihre Qualität und die Implementationschancen der praktischen strukturellen Reformen verbessern.

d) Neue Accountability-Strukturen

Einer der Gründe für die defizitäre Anwendung von praktischen strukturellen Reformen ist die Existenz von zahlreichen *Command-and-control*-Mechanismen in den Reformprogrammen. Governance wurde traditionell als ein *top-down*, vertikales Verfahren verstanden.[160] Dieses Governance-Konzept ist ebenfalls in den Reformprogrammen zu finden. *New Governance* ist eine Antwort auf das verbreitet anerkannte Versagen der *Command-and-control*-Regulierung in einer turbulenten und sich schnell wandelnden Welt, genauso wie Theorien von *Behavioral Regulation*[161]. Governance soll als ein kontinuierliches Experimentieren beim *policymaking*, bei der Regelsetzung und der Implementierung verstanden werden.

In diesem Sinne sollen jenseits von *Principal-agent*-Modellen von *accountability* neue Formen von Rechnungslegung entwickelt werden, nämlich Strukturen horizontaler *accountability*. Horizontale *accountability* wird durch eine gegenseitige Unterstützung und rekursives Lernen der Einheiten derselben Governance-Ebene vorangetrieben. Das bedeutet, dass die Entwicklung von horizontalen Beziehungen zwischen mitgliedstaatlichen Reformeinheiten für den Erfolg von Reformen, und insbesondere von praktischen strukturellen Reformen, entscheidend ist. Die Einführung der *Task Force for Greece* ist ein Beispiel in diese Richtung. Diese sorgt für die Weiterleitung technischer Expertise von anderen Mitgliedstaaten nach Griechenland. Somit wird die Verantwortungslegung gegenüber der sog. Troika von Repräsentanten des Internationalen Währungsfonds, der Europäischen Kommission und der Europäischen Zentralbank durch die Verantwortungslegung gegenüber gleichrangigen Akteuren abgemildert.

3. Eine neue Rolle für den Staat

Im Verlauf der Entwicklung der europäischen Governance-Strukturen haben der Staat und die mitgliedstaatlichen Regierungen ihre traditionellen völkerrechtlichen

---

[160] *Jon Pierre*, Governance and Institutional Flexibility, in: David Levi-Faur (Hrsg.), The Oxford Handbook of Governance, Oxford 2012, S. 187 (194); siehe ebenfalls *Tom Christensen/Per Lægreid*, Governance and Administrative Reforms, in: David Levi-Faur (Hrsg.), The Oxford Handbook of Governance, Oxford 2012, S. 187 (256).

[161] Siehe nur *Cass R. Sunstein*, Nudges.gov: Behaviorally Informed Regulation, in: Egal Zamir/Doron Teichman (Hrsg.), The Oxford Handbook of Behavioral Economics and the Law, Oxford 2015, S. 719 ff.

Rollen verloren. Sollen Reformen erfolgreich sein, müssen neue Rollen für den Staat und für die mitgliedstaatlichen Regierungen in diesem Prozess gefunden werden.[162]

Die Regierungen sollen ihre Rolle als „Koordinationszentren" subnationaler Einheiten besser verstehen. Eine Koordinationsrolle für den Staat wurde auch durch die Reformen angestrebt, die auf der Grundlage der *New-Public-Management-* und der *New-Governance-*Theorien seit dem Ende der 1980er Jahre eingeführt worden sind.[163] Diese Koordinationsrolle der Regierung betrifft nicht mehr nur die Interaktion der staatlichen Instanzen mit Akteuren der Gesellschaft, sondern auch mit staatlichen und gesellschaftlichen Akteuren aus anderen Mitgliedstaaten sowie mit Instanzen aus europäischen und internationalen Organisationen. Die mitgliedstaatlichen Regierungen sollen also die Rolle einer „Regulierung der Regulierer" wahrnehmen.[164] In diesem Sinne werden zum Beispiel die Akkreditierungsstellen von den Mitgliedstaaten im Hinblick auf die laufende Übereinstimmung mit den Anforderungen der Verordnung 765/2008 überwacht.[165] Diese Überwachung komplementiert die Selbstkontrolle der Akkreditierungsstellen durch das horizontale System der Beurteilung unter Gleichrangigen.[166]

Die nationale Souveränität, die dem Staat in der Vergangenheit eine Allzuständigkeit verliehen hatte, verbleibt heute als eine Zuständigkeit einer letzten Instanz in allen Lebensbereichen. Der Staat bleibt ein Garant der im Staat ansässigen Akteure in kritischen Situationen.[167] Diese Rolle der Regierungen könnte auch ihre Pflicht zur Legitimation von politisch sensiblen Reformen beinhalten.

IV. Ein „Recht der Reformen":
Horizontalität, Kooperation, Messbarkeit

Die intensive Reformtätigkeit der letzten Jahre führt zur Evolution eines „Rechts der Reformen".[168] Es ist sehr schwierig und sehr früh, bestimmte Maßnahmen für

---

[162] Siehe auch *Matthias Ruffert*, in diesem Band. Moderne Völkerrechtstheorie beweist, dass starke interne Institutionen nicht nur für das nationale, sondern auch für das internationale Rechtsstaatsprinzip sehr wichtig sind; siehe *Oona Hathaway*, Betweeen Power and Principle: An Integrated Theory of International Law, University of Chicago Law Review 71 (2005), S. 469 (520 ff.).

[163] *Jon Pierre*, Governance and Institutional Flexibility, in: David Levi-Faur (Hrsg.), The Oxford Handbook of Governance, Oxford 2012, S. 187 (191–192).

[164] Vgl. auch *OECD*, Principles for the Governance of Regulators. Public Consultation Draft, Paris 2013.

[165] Art. 9 Verordnung 765/2008.

[166] Art. 10 Verordnung 765/2008.

[167] Siehe z. B. Art. 5 Abs. 3 und 4, 8 Abs. 10 Verordnung 765/2008.

[168] Vgl. auch *OECD*, Making Reform Happen. Lessons from OECD Countries, Paris 2010; vgl. allgemein zu den Herausforderungen des Öffentlichen Rechts in der EU *Herwig C. H. Hofmann*, Seven Challenges for EU Administrative Law, Review of European Administrative Law 2 (2009), S. 37 ff.; *ders.*, The European Picture: Ten Challenges Facing EU Public Law in

dieses Recht der Reformen zu definieren. Leitprinzipien eines solchen Rechts sind aber schon identifizierbar. In diesem Rahmen formen sich traditionelle Prinzipien des öffentlichen und des Europäischen Rechts um, wobei sich neue Prinzipien entwickeln.[169]

Von Hierarchie zur Horizontalität: Das Hierarchieprinzip gegenüber dem behördlichen Unterbau sowie Befehl und Zwang gegenüber dem Bürger als Koordinationsprinzipien traditioneller Exekutive sind nicht mehr als *Modi Operandi* einer modernen Exekutive geeignet. Man betrachtet eine Entwicklung von der Hierarchie als Prinzip rechtlicher und politischer Disziplinierung zu einem Prinzip der Horizontalität. Es ist abzuwarten, ob sich die Tendenz der Entwicklung horizontaler Governance-Strukturen verstärken wird. In diesem Rahmen sollen Reformen auf einem horizontalen Weg implementiert werden. Das bedeutet, dass weitere horizontale Mechanismen für das Design und die Implementation der Reformen eingeführt werden sollen.

Von command-and-control zur Kooperation: Das Regieren und Verwalten wandelt sich von einem hierarchischen zu einem kooperativen Prozess.[170] Die Implementierung und die Rechtsanwendung von Maßnahmen auf den Einzelfall erfolgen oft durch einen kooperativen Vorgang von Verhandlung und Konsultation in verschiedenen Foren.[171] Verbote und Gebote taugen nicht mehr als Governance-Instrumente und werden von neuen Governance-Instrumenten ersetzt. *Compliance* im Bereich der Reformen soll also nicht hierarchisch erzwungen, sondern durch kollegiale

---

the Coming Decade, in: ders./Russel L. Weaver (Hrsg.), Transatlantic Perspectives on Administrative Law, Brüssel 2011, S. 35 ff.

[169] Siehe *Daniel Sarmiento*, Reinforcing the (Domestic) Constitutional Protection of Primacy of EU Law. *Tribunal Constitucional* (Spanish Constitutional Court), Judgment 145/2012 of 2 July 2012, *Iberdrola* v. *Comisión Nacional de la Energía*, Common Market Law Review 50 (2013), S. 875 (891): „It is obvious that some of the instruments and doctrines of the 1970 s will eventually need to be revised. The exact scope and degree of such a revision is something that deserves serious consideration, as well as a cautious approach". Zur Meroni-Entscheidung als überkommenen Maßstab für die Beurteilung demokratischer Legitimation und des institutionellen Gleichgewichts unabhängiger Behörden siehe *Matthias Ruffert*, Die neue Unabhängigkeit: Zur demokratischen Legitimation von Agenturen im europäischen Verwaltungsrecht, in: Peter-Christian Müller-Graff/Stefanie Schmahl/Vassilios Skouris (Hrsg.), Europäisches Recht zwischen Bewährung und Wandel. Festschrift für Dieter H. Scheuing, 2011, S. 399 (403 ff.).

[170] *Gunnar Folke Schuppert*, Verwaltungsorganisation und Verwaltungsorganisationsrecht als Steuerungsfaktoren, in: Wolfgang Hoffmann-Riem/Eberhard Schmidt-Aßmann/Andreas Voßkuhle (Hrsg.), Grundlagen des Verwaltungsrechts, Band I: Methoden, Maßstäbe, Aufgaben, Organisation, München, 2. Aufl., 2012, § 16 Rn. 19. Allgemein zum Grundsatz der loyalen Zusammenarbeit in der EU siehe *Angelo Wille*, Die Pflicht der Organe der EG zur loyalen Zusammenarbeit mit den Mitgliedstaaten, Baden-Baden 2003, S. 19 ff.; *Armin Hatje*, Loyalität als Rechtsprinzip in der Europäischen Union, Baden-Baden 2001, S. 56 f.

[171] Siehe auch *Eberhard Schmidt-Aßmann*, Verwaltungslegitimation als Rechtsbegriff, AöR 116 (1991), S. 329 (364) unter dem Titel „Gesetzesanwendung, nicht Gesetzesvollzug".

und kooperative Interaktion ermutigt werden.[172] Ziel ist die Schaffung einer *peer culture* und von Vertrauensbeziehungen zwischen den beteiligten Akteuren.[173]

Nichtkonformität mit Reformmaßnahmen sollte also nicht zur Einführung von Sanktionen, sondern zur aktiven „freundlichen" Unterstützung der Reforminstitutionen mit dem Ziel ihrer Leistungsverbesserung führen. Instrumente wie *market pressure*,[174] *public pressure* und hauptsächlich *peer pressure* könnten als funktionale Äquivalente zu Sanktionen fungieren. Im Ergebnis soll die Implementation von Reformen eine kooperative Implementation sein.[175]

Von bloßer Rechtmäßigkeit zur Messbarkeit: „A leitmotif in administrative reform has been to focus on performance and to supplement input-based control with output-based measurement and management"[176]. Dieser Trend nimmt mit der Horizontalisierung der Governance-Strukturen in Europa zu, da die Entstehung von auf der gleichen Ebene situierten Akteuren ihren Vergleich und die Messung ihrer Leistungen vereinfacht.[177] Zur Stärkung der Messbarkeit nationaler Implementation von internationalen Politiken sind von internationalen Organisationen Indikatoren (*indicators*) in allen möglichen Politikbereichen ausgearbeitet und eingeführt worden, wobei auch die internationalen Reformprogramme zahlreiche Indikatoren

---

[172] Vgl. auch *Richard H. Thaler/Cass R. Sunstein*, Nudge: Improving Decision: About Health, Wealth, and Happiness, London 2008.

[173] Den reellen Hintergrund der Kooperation bildet gegenseitiges Vertrauen; vgl. *Giandomenico Majone*, Mutual Trust, Credible Commitments and the Evolution of Rules for a Single European Market, EUI Working Paper RSC 1 (95), S. 9.

[174] *Market pressure* wird hier nicht als reine Selbstkontrolle privater Akteure verstanden, sondern als Prozess der Verbreitung und Nutzung durch Wettbewerb von auf dem Markt entwickelten Instrumenten wie Standards, *best practices* und Verhaltenskodizes sowohl für private als auch für öffentliche Akteure.

[175] Da die Anwendung im Einzelfall nicht im Sinne traditionellen Vollzugsverwaltungsrechts stattfindet, ist die Rede von Implementation oder Rechtsanwendung statt von Rechtsdurchsetzung. Eher völkerrechtlich inspiriert spricht *Christian Tietje*, Internationalisiertes Verwaltungshandeln, Berlin 2001, S. 264 ff., von „kooperativer Rechtsverwirklichung im internationalen System" im Gegensatz zur „Durchsetzung" des klassischen Völkerrechts (*enforcement*) – dazu z. B. *Karl Doehring*, Vorwort, S. 1 ff., und *Jochen Abr. Frowein*, Collective Enforcement of International Obligations, S. 67 ff., beide in: ZaöRV 47 (1987); siehe schon *Christian Tietje*, Normative Grundstrukturen der Behandlung nichttarifärer Handelshemmnisse in der WTO/GATT-Rechtsordnung. Eine Untersuchung unter besonderer Berücksichtigung des Countertrade, Berlin 1998, S. 132 ff. m. w. N. Die kooperativen Rechtsverwirklichungsstrukturen fassen sich unter *compliance* zusammen (ebd., S. 265); zur *compliance* siehe *Abram Chayes/Antonia Handler Chayes*, The New Sovereignty. Compliance with International Regulatory Agreements, Cambridge, Mass. 1995, insbes. S. 109 ff.

[176] *Jon Pierre*, Governance and Institutional Flexibility, in: David Levi-Faur (Hrsg.), The Oxford Handbook of Governance, Oxford 2012, S. 187 (191).

[177] Siehe dazu *Georgios Dimitropoulos*, Global Administrative Law as „Enabling Law": How to Monitor and Evaluate Indicator-Based Performance of Global Actors, IRPA Working Paper – GAL Series No. 7/2012.

beinhalten.[178] Es könnte von einem Übergang von einer bloßen Rechtmäßigkeit zu einer messbaren *compliance* im Recht der Reformen gesprochen werden.

Diese Entwicklungen gehen mit einem Verständnis des Rechts der Reformen einher, das nicht fest oder unabänderbar ist: „Law is not a frozen cake of doctrine designed only to protect interests in status quo"[179]. Insofern ist, Reformen vorzunehmen, eine *never-ending story.*[180]

---

[178] Siehe allgemein zur Ausarbeitung und Verbreitung von Indikatoren in *global governance Kevin Davis/Angelina Fisher/Benedict Kingsbury/Sally Engle Merry* (Hrsg.), Governance by Indicators. Global Power through Quantification and Rankings, Oxford 2012.

[179] *Myres S. McDougal*, Law and Power, American Journal of International Law 46 (1952), S. 102 (111); siehe ebenfalls zum Konzept eines „ebabling law" *Georgios Dimitropoulos*, Global Administrative Law as „Enabling Law": How to Monitor and Evaluate Indicator-Based Performance of Global Actors, IRPA Working Paper – GAL Series No. 7/2012, S. 22 ff.

[180] Siehe auch *Jon Pierre*, Governance and Institutional Flexibility, in: David Levi-Faur, The Oxford Handbook of Governance, Oxford 2012, S. 187 (194): „Administrative reform is no longer a one-off event but more a continuous process"; vgl. auch *Martin Schulte*, in diesem Band.

Gemeineuropäische Verwaltungskultur als Gelingensbedingung europäischer Integration?

Von *Karl-Peter Sommermann**

I. Die Europäische Union als Rechts- und als Implementationsgemeinschaft

Das Integrationskonzept der Europäischen Gemeinschaften und später der Europäischen Union hat man einprägsam mit der Formel „integration through law" zum Ausdruck gebracht[1]. Die Rechtsgemeinschaft wird dabei nicht nur durch das im Wege des Vertragsschlusses generierte Primärrecht hergestellt, sondern auch und in besonderem Maße durch das auf seiner Grundlage erlassene und in den Mitgliedstaaten zu einem großen Teil unmittelbar wirksame Sekundärrecht sowie durch eine dynamische Rechtsprechung und Rechtsfortbildung durch einen europäischen Gerichtshof. Die Perspektive der „integration through law" prägt bis heute die Wahrnehmung der Integrationsfortschritte[2]: In den Integrationsverträgen wird der sichtbare Ausbau der institutionellen Strukturen von einer Erweiterung der Kompetenzen der Gemeinschaft begleitet, wobei diese Erweiterung hernach in dem Erlass neuen Sekundärrechts sichtbar wird. Die Umsetzung des Unionsrechts wird an dem Erlass entsprechender Rechtsvorschriften in den Mitgliedstaaten gemessen. Von der Kommission angestrengte Vertragsverletzungsverfahren konzentrieren sich vornehmlich auf die Umsetzung durch nationales Recht. Wie das Unionsrecht oder nationales Umsetzungsrecht angewendet wird, wird nicht systematisch überprüft. Die Praktikabilität eines solchen Untersuchungsansatzes wäre freilich auch problematisch, jedenfalls solange es nicht geeignete Aufsichtsstrukturen gibt, die zudem mit erheblichen Bürokratiekosten verbunden wären.

Ungeachtet der fortbestehenden Konzentration auf das Recht deutet sich jedoch eine Neuorientierung der Integrationspolitik der europäischen Institutionen, insbe-

---

* Prof. Dr. Dr. h.c. Karl-Peter Sommermann, Inhaber des Lehrstuhls für Öffentliches Recht, Staatslehre und Rechtsvergleichung an der Deutschen Universität für Verwaltungswissenschaften Speyer.

[1] *Joseph H. H. Weiler*, The Community System: The Dual Character of Supranationalism, in: Yearbook of European Law Bd. 1 (1982), S. 267–306; *M. Cappelletti/M. Seccombe/J. H. H. Weiler* (Hrsg.), Integration Through Law – Europe and the American Federal Experience, Bd. 1, Den Haag 1986.

[2] Wegen einer Bewertung des „integration through law"-Ansatzes siehe *Antoine Vauchez*, ,Integration-through-Law'. Contribution to a Socio-history of EU political Commonsense (EUI Working Papers RSCAS 2008/10), San Domenico de Fiesole 2008.

sondere der Kommission, dahingehend an, dass zunehmend die administrativen, sozialen und kulturellen Voraussetzungen einer wirksamen Implementierung in den Blick genommen werden. Aussagekräftig ist der unlängst veröffentlichte Bericht zum Thema „Rethinking Europe's ‚Rule of Law' and Enlargement Agenda: The Fundamental Dilemma", der im Auftrag der OECD und der Europäischen Kommission nach Konsultation einer Expertengruppe, der unter anderem der Europäische Bürgerbeauftragte angehörte, verfasst wurde[3]. Mit Blick auf die Kopenhagen-Kriterien[4], insbesondere die Forderung der Herstellung einer tragfähigen demokratischen und rechtsstaatlichen Ordnung betont der Bericht, dass in Beitrittsverfahren stärker auf die nachhaltige Entwicklung einer Rechtsstaatskultur, einer „culture of the ‚Rule of Law'" geachtet und generell bei der Evaluierung die Analyse der sozio-kulturellen Wirklichkeit eine größere Rolle spielen müsse[5]. Bislang musste in der Tat der Eindruck entstehen, dass die Beitrittsreife europäischer Staaten im Wesentlichen nach dem Vorliegen entsprechenden nationalen Umsetzungsrechts beurteilt wurde[6]. Die Rechtsstaatlichkeit etwa wurde neben Verfassungsgarantien an gesetzlichen Regelungen zum Verwaltungsverfahren und Verwaltungsrechtsschutz gemessen. Aus der gewiss vorhandenen Erkenntnis, dass der Erlass eines rechtsstaatlichen Standards entsprechenden Verwaltungsverfahrensgesetzes noch nicht ein effektiv rechtsstaatliches Verfahren garantiert[7], schien man bislang kaum Konsequenzen gezogen zu haben, wohl im Vertrauen auf eine sich schrittweise entfaltende Konvergenzwirkung rechtlicher Vorgaben[8].

Obwohl der Bericht in erster Linie das Vorgehen bei künftigen Beitritten im Blick hat, ist die Betonung der für ein Gelingen der europäischen Integration maßgeblichen außerrechtlichen Voraussetzungen von genereller Bedeutung. Sollen die Unionspoli-

---

[3] *Kalypso Nicolaidis/Rachel Kleinfeld*, Rethinking Europe's „Rule of Law" and Enlargement Agenda: The Fundamental Dilemma (SIGMA-Paper No. 49), Paris (OECD) 2012.

[4] Vgl. Europäischer Rat Kopenhagen, 21.–22. Juni 1993, Schlussfolgerungen des Vorsitzes, Dok. SN 180/1/93, S. 13.

[5] *Nicolaidis/Kleinfeld* (Anm. 3), S. 19 ff.

[6] Vgl. z. B. das Strategiepapier und den Bericht der Europäischen Kommission über die Fortschritte Bulgariens, Rumäniens und der Türkei auf dem Weg zum Beitritt v. 5.11.2003, Dok. COM/2003/0676 final, und die Analyse von *Heather Grabbe*, European Union Conditionality and the Acquis Communautaire, in: International Political Science Review Bd. 23 (2002), S. 249 ff.; *Milanda Anna Vachudova*, Europe Undivided. Democracy, Leverage, & Intergation After Communism, Oxford 2005, S. 120 ff.

[7] Dass es seit Längerem ein entsprechendes Problembewusstseins der Kommission gibt, zeigt etwa der Regelmäßige Bericht 2001 über die Fortschritte Bulgariens auf dem Weg zum Beitritt, Dok. SEK(2001) 1744 v. 13.11.2001, S. 18: „Obwohl also weitere Anstrengungen zur Schaffung einer modernen und offenen staatlichen Verwaltung unternommen wurden, bleibt noch viel zu tun, bis ein öffentlicher Dienst und eine neue Verwaltungskultur entstanden sind, die den Anforderungen der EU-Mitgliedschaft gewachsen sind."

[8] Zu den vom europäischen Recht ausgehenden Konvergenzimpulsen vgl. etwa *Georgios Dimitropoulos*, Zertifizierung und Akkreditierung im Internationalen Verwaltungsverbund, Tübingen 2012, S. 361 ff.; *Karl-Peter Sommermann*, Konvergenzen im Verwaltungsverfahrens- und Verwaltungsprozessrecht europäischer Staaten, in: DÖV 2002, S. 133, 136.

tiken in der gesamten Union greifen, ist eine im Wesentlichen gleichwertige Umsetzung und Anwendung des EU-Rechts unerlässlich: Die Union ist nicht nur Rechts-, sondern auch Implementationsgemeinschaft. Dies bedeutet nicht, dass die Implementierung entgegen dem Grundsatz der Durchführung des Unionsrechts durch die Mitgliedstaaten[9] durch Unionsorgane erfolgen soll. Auch ist nicht gemeint, dass eine lückenlose rechtliche Determinierung des Vollzugshandelns der nationalen Verwaltungen durch unionale Sekundärrechtsakte anzustreben wäre, wenngleich bereits eine zunehmende Steuerung des mitgliedstaatlichen Behördenhandelns durch die Union festzustellen ist[10], wie noch zu zeigen sein wird. Es geht vielmehr darum, die Konsequenzen aus dem Gebot des Art. 197 Abs. 1 AEUV zu ziehen, wonach die „für das ordnungsgemäße Funktionieren der Union entscheidende effektive Durchführung des Unionsrechts durch die Mitgliedstaaten … als Frage von gemeinsamem Interesse anzusehen" ist[11]. Daraus folgt, dass in allen Mitgliedstaaten strukturelle Implementierungsdefizite zu identifizieren, ihre Ursachen zu ermitteln und diese zu beseitigen sind. Dies kann im Einzelfall eine tiefgreifende Transformation der Verwaltungsregime, einschließlich der informellen Strukturen, erfordern. Dafür sieht Art. 197 Abs. 2 AEUV ausdrücklich die Möglichkeit einer Unterstützung durch die EU vor. Die Implementationsgemeinschaft verwirklicht sich somit gerade auch in einer Zusammenarbeit der Mitgliedstaaten untereinander sowie der Mitgliedstaaten mit der Union bei der Herstellung europafähiger nationaler Verwaltungen.

Es wäre freilich eine verkürzte Sicht, wollte man die in der Europäischen Gemeinschaft bzw. Europäischen Union bereits entwickelten Instrumente für eine Verbesserung einer gleichwertigen Implementation des EU-Recht in den Mitgliedstaaten außer Acht lassen. Im Folgenden sollen zunächst entsprechende rechtliche Ansätze zur Effektuierung eines unionskonformen Verwaltungshandelns identifiziert (II.) und sodann die durch sie sowie durch außerrechtliche Maßnahmen initiierte Transformation der nationalen Verwaltungskulturen in den Blick genommen werden (III.), bevor ein abschließendes Fazit gezogen wird (IV.).

II. Effektuierung der Implementierung durch rechtliche Steuerung

Aus der Erkenntnis heraus, dass die Festlegung materiell-rechtlicher Standards nicht automatisch zu einer gleich effektiven Anwendung und Implementierung in den Mitgliedstaaten führt, verstärkte der Gemeinschaftsgesetzgeber seit den achtziger Jahren des 20. Jahrhunderts die Intensität der Einwirkungen auf das nationale

---

[9] Art. 291 Abs. 1 AEUV.

[10] Zur zunehmenden Relativierung der „Verfahrens- und Organisationsautonomie" der Mitgliedstaaten vgl. *Diana-Urania Galetta*, Procedural Autonomy of EU Member States: Paradise Lost?, Berlin/Heidelberg 2010.

[11] Zur Bedeutung des Art. 197 AEUV für die „Verbundstruktur" der Union im Bereich der Verwaltung siehe *Matthias Ruffert*, in: C. Calliess/M. Ruffert (Hrsg.), EUV/AEUV. Kommentar, 4. Aufl., München 2011, Art. 197 EUV Rdnr. 4.

Verwaltungsverfahren[12]. Zwar hatte es früh auch punktuelle Verfahrensvorgaben, etwa bei Produktzulassungen, gegeben[13]; nunmehr wurden jedoch relativ umfassende Regelungen für größere Felder des Verwaltungshandelns getroffen. Beispiele für entsprechende Rechtsakte bilden die Richtlinie über die Umweltverträglichkeitsprüfung bei bestimmten öffentlichen und privaten Projekten[14], die Richtlinien zur Regelung bzw. Koordinierung der Verfahren zur Vergabe öffentlicher Aufträge[15] und die Verordnung zur Festlegung des Zollkodex der Gemeinschaften aus dem 1992[16]. Eine qualitativ neue Stufe der Entwicklung deuten die Beratungen über ein Verwaltungsverfahrensrecht der Europäischen Union[17] an. Diese beziehen sich zunächst, auch mangels einer umfassenden Kompetenz der Union, zwar nur auf die Unionsorgane. Die Regelungen werden aber auch Vorbildwirkung für die nationalen Verwaltungssysteme entfalten[18].

Es war nur konsequent, dass seit den 90er Jahren zunehmend auch das Verwaltungsorganisationsrecht Gegenstand der Sekundärrechtsetzung wurde[19]. Der Europäische Gerichtshof hatte bereits in seinem „Schaffleischurteil" aus dem Jahr 1990 (Prämienzahlung nur unter bestimmten, auch organisatorisch abzusichernden

---

[12] Dazu bereits *Karl-Peter Sommermann*, Veränderungen des nationalen Verwaltungsrechts unter europäischem Einfluss – Analyse aus deutscher Sicht, in: J. Schwarze (Hrsg.), Bestand und Perspektiven des Europäischen Verwaltungsrechts. Rechtsvergleichende Analysen, Baden-Baden 2008, S. 181, 184 ff.; zur konzeptionellen Einordnung im europäischen Verwaltungsverbund *Eberhard Schmidt-Aßmann*, Der Verfahrensgedanke im deutschen und europäischen Verwaltungsrecht, in: W. Hoffmann-Riem/E. Schmidt-Aßmann/A. Voßkuhle (Hrsg.), Grundlagen des Verwaltungsrechts, Bd. 2, 2. Aufl., München 2012, S. 495, 506 ff.

[13] Vgl. nur die Richtlinie 65/65/EWG des Rates vom 26.1.1965 zur Angleichung der Rechts- und Verwaltungsvorschriften über Arzneispezialitäten, ABl. Nr. L 22 v. 9.2.1965, S. 369. Art. 7 dieser Richtlinie trifft Aussagen zur Verfahrensdauer, Art. 11 zu Aussetzung und Widerruf und Art. 12 zur Begründung der behördlichen Entscheidungen.

[14] Richtlinie 85/337/EWG über die Umweltverträglichkeitsprüfung bei bestimmten öffentlichen und privaten Projekten, ABl. 1985 Nr. L 175 v. 5.7.1985, S. 40.

[15] Vgl. nur die Richtlinie 89/665/EWG des Rates vom 21.12.1989 zur Koordinierung der Rechts- und Verwaltungsvorschriften für die Anwendung der Nachprüfungsverfahren im Rahmen der Vergabe öffentlicher Liefer- und Bauaufträge, ABl. 1989 Nr. L 395 vom 30.12.1989, S. 33.

[16] Verordnung (EWG) Nr. 2913/92 des Rates vom 12. Oktober 1992 zur Festlegung des Zollkodex der Gemeinschaften, ABl. 1992 Nr. L 302 vom 19.10.1992, S. 1, zuletzt geändert durch Verordnung (EG) Nr. 1791/2006 des Rates vom 20. November 2006, ABl. 2006 Nr. L 363 vom 20.12.2006, S. 1.

[17] Vgl. den Bericht des Committee on Legal Affairs of the European Parliament of 12 November 2012 with recommendations to the Commission on a Law of Administrative Procedure of the European Union, Doc. A7–0369/2012, adopted by the EP on 15 January 2013, P7_TA-PROV(2013)0004.

[18] Vgl. auch *Annette Guckelberger/Frederic Geber*, Allgemeines Europäisches Verwaltungsverfahrensrecht vor seiner unionsrechtlichen Kodifizierung?, Baden-Baden 2013, S. 167 ff.

[19] Dazu näher *Sommermann*, Veränderungen des nationalen Verwaltungsrechts (Anm. 12), S. 188 ff.; *Thorsten Siegel*, Europäisierung des Öffentlichen Rechts, Tübingen 2012, S. 52 ff.

Voraussetzungen) zum Ausdruck gebracht, dass die Mitgliedstaaten verpflichtet sind, die zur ordnungsgemäßen Durchführung des Gemeinschaftsrechts notwendige Verwaltungsorganisation bereitzustellen[20]. Der Sekundärgesetzgeber der Europäischen Union hat vor allem im Zusammenhang mit der Ausgestaltung des Regulierungsrechts, sei es im Bereich Telekommunikation, sei es im Bereich Energie, Vorgaben getroffen, die letztlich nur im Rahmen unabhängiger Regulierungsbehörden zu implementieren sind[21].

Das letztgenannte Beispiel deutet bereits darauf hin, dass die Verfahrens- und Organisationsvorgaben ihre Wirkung nicht immer nur auf direktem Wege entfalten, sondern teilweise auch indirekt eine Europäisierung bewirken. Diese zu den dargestellten direkten Formen der Europäisierung hinzutretenden Phänomene einer Transformation der nationalen Rechtsordnungen ist von besonderem Interesse, da sie nicht immer gleich als durch das Unionsrecht induzierte Veränderungen zu erkennen sind.

Wie an anderer Stelle gezeigt[22] lassen sich vier Fallgruppen der indirekten Europäisierung der nationalen Verwaltungssysteme unterscheiden: erstens die funktionelle Anpassung, zweitens sogenannte Spill-over-Effekte, drittens wettbewerbsbedingte Anpassungen und viertens Transnationalisierungsphänomene.

Bei der *funktionellen Anpassung* induzieren Aufgaben- und Verfahrensnormen in Verbindung mit dem Kooperationsprinzip, das einen reibungslosen Austausch zwischen der Unionsebene und der nationalen Ebene fordert[23], eine Anpassung der nationalen Strukturen des Verwaltungsverfahrens- und Verwaltungsorganisationsrecht. Ein Beispiel bilden die soeben erwähnten Veränderungen im Verwaltungsorganisationsrecht.

Spill-over-Effekte[24] sind dadurch gekennzeichnet, dass die vom europäischen Gemeinschaftsrecht für bestimmte Aufgabenbereiche vorgesehenen inhaltlichen Maßstäbe, Verfahren oder Organisationsstrukturen auf benachbarte Bereiche übertragen werden oder sogar Grundstrukturen des nationalen Verwaltungsrechts dem europarechtlich geprägten Referenzgebiet angepasst werden. So löste z. B. die Umweltinformationsrichtlinie[25] in vielen Mitgliedstaaten bald die Einführung von Regelungen

---

[20] EuGH, Rs. C-8/88 (Deutschland/Kommission), Slg. 1990, S. I-2321.

[21] Näher zur Europäisierung im Regulierungsrecht *Gabriele Britz*, Vom Europäischen Verwaltungsverbund zum Regulierungsverbund?, in: EuR Bd. 2006, S. 46 ff.

[22] *Sommermann*, Veränderungen des nationalen Verwaltungsrechts (Anm. 12), S. 193 ff.

[23] Vgl. dazu *Eberhard Schmidt-Aßmann*, Strukturen des Europäischen Verwaltungsrechts, in: ders./W. Hoffmann-Riem, Strukturen des Europäischen Verwaltungsrechts, Baden-Baden 1999, S. 9, 19 f.; *Jürgen Schwarze*, Einführung, in: ders., Europäisches Verwaltungsrecht, 2. Aufl., Baden-Baden 2005, S. CVII ff.; *Wolfgang Kahl*, in: C. Calliess/M. Ruffert (Hrsg.), EUV/AEUV. Kommentar, 4. Aufl., München 2011, Art. 4 EUV Rdnr. 38 ff., 59 ff.

[24] Zum Begriff vgl. auch *Karl-Heinz Ladeur*, Supra- und transnationale Tendenzen in der Europäisierung des Verwaltungsrechts – eine Skizze, in: EuR Bd. 30 (1995), S. 227, 228.

[25] Richtlinie 90/313/EWG, über den freien Zugang zu Umweltinformationen, ABl. 1990 Nr. L 158 v. 23. 6. 1990, S. 56; an ihre Stelle ist die Richtlinie 2003/4/EG des Europäischen Parlaments und des Rates v. 28. 1. 2003 über den Zugang der Öffentlichkeit zu Umweltinfor-

zur generellen Erleichterung des Informationszugangs und zur Verbesserung in der Transparenz der öffentlichen Verwaltung aus.

Wettbewerbsbedingte Anpassungen erwachsen daraus, dass im europäischen Binnenmarkt Verwaltungsorganisation und Verwaltungsverfahren als Standortfaktoren im wirtschaftlichen Wettbewerb wahrgenommen werden. Die gemeinsamen rechtlichen und wirtschaftlichen Rahmenbedingungen in der Europäischen Union machen auch die Leistungsfähigkeit und Problemlösungskapazität der nationalen Verwaltungssysteme transparenter. Eine wettbewerbsbedingte Anpassung kann z. B. in Maßnahmen zur Beschleunigung von Genehmigungsverfahren liegen.

Transnationalisierungsphänomene bezeichnen die wechselseitige Rezeption verwaltungsrechtlicher und verwaltungskultureller Standards, wobei die jeweilige rezipierende Ordnung naturgemäß die Elemente, an denen sie sich orientiert, nicht einfach gleichförmig übernimmt (Akkulturation), sondern aufgrund ihrer eigenen verwaltungskulturellen Voraussetzungen verarbeitet (Transkulturation)[26]. Exemplarisch zu beobachten waren solche Phänomene bei der Verbreitung von Ombudsmann-Einrichtungen in Europa.

Namentlich die beiden erstgenannten Fallgruppen indirekter Europäisierung zeigen, dass die Wirkungen des Unionsrechts auf die nationalen Verwaltungssysteme häufig erheblich weiter reichen als der Anwendungsbereich der Normen.

III. Die Rolle der Verwaltungskultur

Trotz der durch Recht direkt oder indirekt bewirkten Angleichungen der prozeduralen Standards und organisationalen Strukturähnlichkeiten, die sich in entsprechenden nationalen Rechtsnormen niederschlagen, weist die Implementierung des Unionsrechts, wie eingangs erwähnt, immer noch erhebliche Unterschiede auf. Diese beruhen zum einen auf der fortbestehenden Einordnung der unionsrechtlich determinierten Regelungen in die jeweiligen Strukturen des nationalen Verwaltungsrechts und in die nationale Verwaltungsorganisation, zum anderen aber auf unterschiedlichen verwaltungskulturellen Voraussetzungen in den Mitgliedstaaten. Es gibt nach wie vor stark kontextabhängige institutionelle Identitäten und unterschiedliche korporative und individuelle Werthaltungen.

Eine im Jahr 1988 erschienene, von *Heinrich Siedentopf* und *Jacques Ziller* herausgegebene Studie „Making European Policies Work – L'Europe des Administrations?"[27], hat die naheliegende Annahme bestätigt, dass das Unionsrecht oder das in

---

mationen und zur Aufhebung der Richtlinie 90/313/EWG des Rates, ABl. 2003 Nr. L 41 v. 14. 2. 2003, S. 26, getreten.

[26] Begriff von *Fernando Ortiz Fernández*, Contrapunteo cubano del tabaco y el azúcar, La Habana 1940, Neuausgabe 1983, insbes. S. 90; vgl. dazu *Phyllis Mary Kaberry*, Einleitung zu Bronislaw Malinowski, Die Dynamik des Kulturwandels, Wien u. a. 1951, S. 9 f.

[27] *H. Siedentopf/J. Ziller* (Hrsg.), Making European Policies Work – The Implementation of Community Legislation in the Member States/L'Europe des Administrations?, Bd. 1:

seiner Umsetzung ergangene nationale Recht im Wesentlichen in gleicher Weise angewendet wird wie das originäre nationale Recht. Die Studie stützte sich auf eine Untersuchung der Implementierung von 17 ausgewählten Richtlinien zum Umweltschutz in den damals zehn Mitgliedstaaten der Europäischen Gemeinschaft. Es ist daher folgerichtig, dass sich die Unionsorgane nicht nur mit dem rechtlichen Überbau der nationalen Verwaltungen befassen, sondern zunehmend auch mit den die Rechts- und Verwaltungswirklichkeit tragenden Substrukturen, namentlich mit den verwaltungskulturellen Grundlagen. Zur „Verwaltungskultur" rechnet man im engeren Sinne die „Orientierungsmuster" (Meinungen, Einstellungen und Werthaltungen), die das Verhalten der in der Öffentlichen Verwaltung tätigen Personen bestimmen[28], in einem weiteren Sinne auch die formalen und informalen Kommunikations-, Verfahrens- und Organisationsformen, die die Verwaltung eines Landes sowohl im Binnenbereich als auch in ihrer Wechselbeziehung mit den Bürgern prägen[29]. Die Verwaltungskultur wird naturgemäß beeinflusst von der politischen Kultur und der Rechtskultur eines Landes, letztlich auch von den Werthaltungen der Gesellschaft insgesamt. Das bedeutet freilich nicht, dass es innerhalb „der Verwaltung" keine kulturelle Vielfalt gäbe. Bei einer Feinanalyse ist in der Regel je nach Verwaltungs- und Behördentyp, ja sogar zwischen einzelnen Behörden und innerhalb der Behörden gegebenenfalls zwischen den Abteilungen eine organisationskulturelle Binnendifferenzierung festzustellen[30].

Comparative Syntheses/Synthèses comparatives, Bd. 2: National Reports/Rapports nationaux, Bruxelles 1988.

[28] Vgl. *Werner Jann*, Staatliche Programme und „Verwaltungskultur". Bekämpfung des Drogenmissbrauchs und der Jugendarbeitslosigkeit in Schweden, Großbritannien und der Bundesrepublik Deutschland im Vergleich, Opladen 1983, S. 28 ff.; *Michelle Cini*, Administrative Culture in the European Commission: The Cases of Competition and Environment, in: N. Nugent (Hrsg.), At the Heart of the Union. Studies of the European Commission, 2. Aufl., Hondmills 2000, S. 73, 74; *Onkar Prasad Dwivedi*, Administrative Culture and Values: Approaches, in: J. G. Jabbra/O. P. Dwivedi (Hrsg.), Administrative Culture in a Global Context, Wgitby (ON) 2005, S. 19, 20 ("… administrative culture, understood here in its broadest sense as the modal pattern of values, beliefs, attitudes and predispositions that characterize and identify any given administrative system").

[29] Dazu *Maximilian Wallerath*, Die Änderung der Verwaltungskultur als Reformziel, in: Die Verwaltung Bd. 33 (2000), S. 351, 354 f.

[30] Vgl. *Edgar H. Schein*, Organizational Culture and Leadership. A Dynamic View, San Francisco u. a. 1985, der (Organisations-)Kultur als „a learned product of group experience" definiert (S. 7), *Klaus König*, Verwaltungskulturen und Verwaltungswissenschaften, in: K. König/C. Reichard (Hrsg.), Theoretische Aspekte einer managerialistischen Verwaltungskultur (Speyerer Forschungsberichte 254), Speyer 2007, S. 1, 2 ff., und *Keith M. Henderson*, American Administrative Culture: An Evolutionary Perspective, in: Jabbra/Dwivedi (Hrsg.), Administrative Culture in a Global Context (Anm. 28), S. 37, 51 ff. Zur Explikation von Überlagerungen und Durchmischungen auf der Grundlage einer empirischen Untersuchung siehe *Horst Damskis/Bärbel Möller*, Verwaltungskultur in den neuen Bundesländern – Werte und Einstellungen in den Ministerialverwaltungen von Brandenburg und Sachsen, Frankfurt a. M. u. a. 1997, insbesondere S. 154 ff.

Bei einer Betrachtung der Verwaltungskulturen der EU-Mitgliedstaaten sind zunächst Veränderungen in den Blick zu nehmen, die gleichsam als Nebeneffekt von Sekundärrechtsakten eingetreten sind und davon zeugen, dass die Veränderung der rechtlichen Oberflächenstrukturen durchaus Tiefenwirkungen entfalten können. Als Beispiel mögen die seit den 90er Jahren besonders dynamischen Entwicklungen im Bereich der Verbesserung der Transparenz sowie, als eines ihrer Kernelemente, des Informationszugangs dienen. Staaten, die bereits früher den Informationszugang unabhängig von individueller Betroffenheit eröffnet hatten, wie insbesondere die skandinavischen Staaten oder auch – seit den 70er Jahren – beispielsweise Frankreich[31], haben die Zugangsrechte erweitert[32]. Andere Staaten, zu denen neben dem Vereinigten Königreich[33] auch Deutschland gehört[34], haben sich vom Prinzip der begrenzten Aktenöffentlichkeit im Zuge der allgemeinen Öffnungswelle abgewandt und einen allgemeinen Anspruch auf Informationszugang eingeräumt. Der Rechtfertigungsdruck der Regierungen bzw. der Parlamente in den Staaten, die noch kein Informationsfreiheitsgesetz besitzen, ist mittlerweile erheblich. In den Reformdebatten treten neben rechtsstaatliche und managerialistische Überlegungen zunehmend demokratisch-funktionale Erwägungen, wie etwa das Beispiel Spaniens zeigt[35]. Insbesondere legt Transparenz des Staatshandelns die Verantwortlichkeiten offen[36].

Zu einer Veränderung der nationalen Verwaltungskulturen trägt indirekt auch die Zunahme europäischer Verwaltungszusammenarbeit bei. Fachspezifische Verfahrensregelungen zur Zusammenarbeit sowohl im vertikalen Verhältnis zwischen Europäischer Union und Mitgliedstaaten als auch im horizontalen Verhältnis letzterer untereinander[37] finden sich in einer Reihe von Richtlinien, etwa im Produktzulas-

---

[31] Bereits das Gesetz Nr. 78–753 vom 17.7.1978 (J.O. v. 18.7.1978) in der Fassung des Gesetzes Nr. 79–5877 vom 11.7.1979 (J.O. v. 12.7.1979) regelte ausführlich die „liberté d'accès aux documents administratifs".

[32] Vgl. für Frankreich insbesondere das Gesetz Nr. 2000–321 du 12 avril 2000 relative aux droits des citoyens dans leurs relations avec les administrations (J.O. v. 13.4.2000), insbesondere Titel I: „Dispositions relatives à l'accès aux règles de droit et à la transparence".

[33] Vgl. den Freedom of Information Act 2000 (2000 chapter 36).

[34] Vgl. auf Bundesebene das Gesetz zur Regelung des Zugangs zu Informationen des Bundes (Informationsfreiheitsgesetz – IFG) vom 5.9.2005 (BGBl. I, S. 2722) sowie die entsprechenden Landesgesetze. Weitergehende Transparenz soll das Hamburger Transparenzgesetz vom 19.6.2012 (HmbGVBl. 2012, S. 271) schaffen; dazu *Johannes Caspar*, Informationsfreiheit, Transparenz und Datenschutz, in: DÖV 2013, S. 371 ff.

[35] Vgl. die Präambel (Exposición de motivos) des am 27.7.2012 vom spanischen Ministerrat (Consejo de Ministros) angenommen Proyecto de Ley de Transparencia, Acceso a la Información Pública y Buen Gobierno.

[36] Vgl. *Karl-Peter Sommermann*, La exigencia de una administración transparente en la perspectiva de los principios de democracia y del Estado de Derecho, in: R. García Macho (Hrsg.), Derecho administrativo de la información y administración transparente, Madrid 2010, S. 11, 18 ff.

[37] Dazu die eingehende Analyse von *Gernot Sydow*, Verwaltungskooperation in der Europäischen Union: Zur horizontalen und vertikalen Zusammenarbeit der europäischen Verwaltungen am Beispiel des Produktzulassungsrechts. Verwaltungskooperation in der Europäi-

sungsrecht[38], andere Regelungen beispielsweise im europäischen Unions- und Völkerrecht der polizeilichen Zusammenarbeit[39]. Mit einem weiten Anwendungsbereich regelt die europäische Dienstleistungsrichtlinie im Einzelnen Kooperationspflichten der Mitgliedstaaten[40], die in ihrer Strukturbildung und Detailliertheit bislang beispiellos sind. Ihrer Effektuierung dient das bei der Kommission angesiedelte Binnenmarkt-Informationssystem, das freilich eine Reihe praktischer, insbesondere sprachenbezogener Fragen nicht ohne weiteres lösen kann[41]. Die meisten Staaten haben den unionsrechtlichen prozeduralen Vorgaben zur europäischen Zusammenarbeit in den allgemeinen Umsetzungsregelungen zur Dienstleistungsrichtlinie Rechnung getragen. In Deutschland wurde das geschärfte europäische Verwaltungskooperationsrecht in das Allgemeine Verwaltungsverfahrensgesetz [42] integriert (vgl. §§ 8a-8e des Gesetzes). Wenngleich das europäische Kooperationsverwaltungsrecht erst in Ansätzen Eingang in die Kodifikationen des allgemeinen Verwaltungsverfahrens gefunden hat, lässt sich doch unschwer voraussagen, dass es sich hier um einen Bereich im Moment zwar noch verhaltener, aber potentiell hoher Entwicklungsdynamik handelt, der die nationalen Verwaltungskulturen nicht unberührt lassen wird.

Mittlerweile, und dies ist hier von besonderem Interesse, wird die Veränderung der nationalen Verwaltungskulturen nicht nur als erwünschter Nebeneffekt begrüßt, sondern ergreifen die Unionsorgane auch Maßnahmen, die, ohne dass dies expliziert würde, eine Transformation der nationalen Verwaltungskulturen herbeiführen sollen[43]. Es geht dabei letztlich um die Frage der „Gestaltbarkeit von Verwaltungen"[44]

---

schen Union, Tübingen 2004; siehe auch *ders.*, Vollzug des europäischen Unionsrechts im Wege der Kooperation nationaler und europäischer Behörden, in: DÖV 2006, S. 2006 ff.; siehe auch *Thorsten Siegel*, Entscheidungsfindung im Verwaltungsverbund, Tübingen 2009, S. 320 ff.

[38] Siehe beispielsweise die Verordnung (EG) Nr. 258/97 über neuartige Lebensmittel und neuartige Lebensmittelzutaten, ABl. 1997 Nr. L 43, S. 1.

[39] Vgl. z.B. die im Beschluss des Rates vom 6.4.2009 zur Errichtung des Europäischen Polizeiamts (Europol), ABl. Nr. L 121, S. 37, geregelte Zusammenarbeit.

[40] Vgl. Art. 28 ff. der Richtlinie 2006/123/EG des Europäischen Parlaments und des Rates über Dienstleistungen im Binnenmarkt, ABl. Nr. L 376, S. 36.

[41] Vgl. *Franziska Kruse*, Das Verwaltungsverfahrensgesetz und die Jahreszeiten – Die raison d'être der Europäischen Zusammenarbeit, in: H. Hill (Hrsg.), Verwaltungsmodernisierung 2010, Baden-Baden 2010, S. 169, 187 f.; *Lorenz Prell*, Verwaltungszusammenarbeit im Binnenmarkt, in: M. Burgi/K. Schönenbroicher (Hrsg.), Die Zukunft des Verwaltungsverfahrensrechts, Baden-Baden 2010, S. 48, 55 f.

[42] Verwaltungsverfahrensgesetz (des Bundes) vom 25.6.1976 (BGBl. 1976 I, S. 1253), zuletzt geändert durch Gesetz vom 14.8.2009 (BGBl. 2009 I 2827).

[43] Zur Rolle eines „Soft Law" der Union vgl. *Daniel Sarmiento*, El *Soft Law* administrativo. Un estudio de los efectos jurídicos de las normas no vinculantes de la Administración, Cizur Menor 2008, S. 55 ff.

[44] Zur „Gestaltbarkeit von Verwaltungen" näher *Wallerath* (Anm. 29), S. 368 ff. Zur Problematik der „Gestaltbarkeit von Verwaltungskulturen" auch *Stefan Fisch*, Verwaltungskulturen – geronnene Geschichte?, in: Die Verwaltung Bd. 33 (2000), S. 303, 313 f.

durch Kontextsteuerung[45]. Eine wichtige Rolle können dabei das in Art. 41 der Europäischen Grundrechtecharta verankerte Recht auf gute Verwaltung[46] und seine rechtlichen und metarechtlichen Ausformungen spielen. Zwar gilt Art. 41 der Grundrechtecharta und der zu seiner Konkretisierung vom Europäischen Bürgerbeauftragten entwickelte Europäische Kodex für gute Verwaltungspraxis[47] zunächst nur für die Unionsorgane; die in ihnen entfalteten Standards sind indes Teil einer gesamteuropäischen Debatte, die auch im Europarat geführt wird und dort beispielsweise in der an die Mitgliedstaaten gerichteten Empfehlung des Ministerkomitees zur guten Verwaltung aus dem Jahre 2007[48] Gestalt gewonnen hat[49]. Das in Art. 41 der Grundrechtecharta verankerte Recht auf gute Verwaltung wird daher letztlich eine Annäherung der verschiedenen Verwaltungskulturen in bestimmten Kernbereichen befördern.

Sowohl im Kodex als auch in der Empfehlung stehen rechtsstaatliche und bürgerfreundliche Verfahrensweisen im Vordergrund, im Kodex werden zusätzlich persönliche Verhaltensstandards niedergelegt. Das Recht auf gute Verwaltung zielt damit in die Tiefenstrukturen des Verwaltungshandelns, die persönlichen Einstellungen und Werthaltungen der Amtswalter. Diese neue Perspektive fügt sich in einen in den Mitgliedstaaten bereits früher zu beobachtenden Trend. Die in den USA bereits vor längerer Zeit geführte Debatte über die Ethik des öffentlichen Dienstes[50] hat alle europäischen Staaten erfasst. Auffällig ist, dass *Ethic Codes* oder *Codes of Conduct*, die teilweise als außerrechtliche Verhaltensdirektiven Gegenstand der Personalführung sind, zunehmend mit dem Recht verknüpft werden, wie es in Frankreich schon länger hinsichtlich der professionellen Deontologie der Fall war[51]. Ein jüngeres Beispiel bil-

---

[45] Der Begriff der „Kontextsteuerung" wurde zunächst für die Steuerung selbstregulativer Systeme des privaten Sektors verwandt (vgl. *Matthias Schmidt Preuß*, Verwaltung und Verwaltungsrecht zwischen gesellschaftlicher Selbstregulierung und staatlicher Steuerung, in: VVDStRL Bd. 56 [1997], S. 160, 185 ff.), lässt sich aber auch für indirekte Steuerung von Verwaltungssystemen durch eine übergeordnete Ebene verwenden.

[46] Auf nationaler Ebene ausdrücklich zuerst in Art. 21 der finnischen Verfassung verankert.

[47] Vgl. zu diesem am 6.9.2001 vom Europäischen Parlament angenommenen Kodex und weiteren Kodizes *José Martínez Soria*, Die Kodizes für gute Verwaltungspraxis – ein Beitrag zur Kodifikation des Verwaltungsverfahrensrechts der EG, in: EuR Bd. 36 (2001), S. 682 ff.

[48] Recommendation CM/Rec(2007)7 of the Committee of Ministers to member states on good administration (im Vorspann Hinweis auf die früheren Empfehlungen zu Standards des Verwaltungshandelns).

[49] Zur Bedeutung der Empfehlungen des Europarats für die Herausbildung allgemeiner rechtsgrundsätz vgl. *Ulrich Stelkens*, Europäische Rechtsakte als „Fundgruben" für allgemeine Grundsätze des deutschen Verwaltungsverfahrensrechts, in: ZEuS 2004, S. 129, 133 ff.

[50] Dazu *Karl-Peter Sommermann*, Brauchen wir eine Ethik des öffentlichen Dienstes?, in: Verwaltungsarchiv Bd. 89 (1998), S. 290, 292 ff.; *Nathalie Behnke*, Ethik in Politik und Verwaltung. Entstehung und Funktionen ethischer Normen in Deutschland und den USA, Baden-Baden 2004.

[51] Vgl. *Nicole Decoopman*, Droit et déontologie: contribution à l'étude des modes de régulation, in: Centre universitaire de recherches administratives et politiques de Picardie, Les usages sociaux du droit, Paris 1989, S. 88 ff.

det das spanische Basisstatut über den öffentlichen Dienst aus dem Jahre 2007, das in einem eigenen Kapitel einen detaillierten Verhaltenskodex (*Código de conducta*) normiert[52]. Die dort niedergelegten Pflichten gehen weit über die im deutschen Beamtenrecht niedergelegten Grundpflichten der Beamten hinaus. Bemerkenswert ist auch der britische Constitutional Reform and Governance Act 2010[53], der den Erlass eines Verhaltenskodex für den öffentlichen Dienst vorschreibt. Insgesamt lässt sich feststellen, dass die aktuelle Ethikdiskussion, die rechtliche und außerrechtliche Verhaltensstandards verknüpft, zu deutlichen Veränderungen bei der Gestaltung von Verwaltungsverfahren und einer Annäherung der Verwaltungskulturen beitragen wird.

Einen wichtigen Beitrag zur Verbesserung der Implementationsbedingungen in den Mitgliedstaaten können, wie bereits erwähnt, die Zusammenarbeit zwischen den Mitgliedstaaten und eine wechselseitige bzw. von oder mittels der Union bereitgestellte Unterstützung leisten. Die am 20. Juli 2011 eingesetzte Task Force für Griechenland bietet dafür ein Beispiel[54] Insgesamt erlauben die in Art. 197 Abs. 2 AEUV vorgesehenen Maßnahmen eine effektive Unterstützung durch die Union. Voraussetzung für eine nachhaltige Wirkung der meist verengend „technische Hilfe" (technical assistance) genannten Maßnahmen ist allerdings, dass sie nicht nur die „Oberflächenstrukturen", sondern auch die Substrukturen wie die bestimmende Verwaltungskultur in den Blick nehmen. Aus- und Weiterbildungsmaßnahmen sollten in besonderer Weise für verwaltungskulturelle Eigenheiten und Unterschiede sensibilisieren, wobei die systematische Förderung eines transnationalen Austauschs der Mitglieder des Öffentlichen Dienstes der Mitgliedstaaten helfen kann. Da die Annahme von Unterstützung freiwillig ist, kann sich das Potential wechselseitigen Lernens freilich nur entfalten, wenn in den Mitgliedstaaten die Bereitschaft wächst, eine Unterstützung in Anspruch zu nehmen[55]. Insgesamt stellt die Entwicklung einer konsistenten Strategie zur Transformation von Verwaltungskulturen ein dringendes Desiderat dar.

---

[52] Siehe Art. 52 ff. des Gesetzes 7/2007 (Ley 7/2007, de 12 de abril, del Estatuto Básico del Empleado Público), B.O.E. núm. 89 v. 13.4.2007; kritisch zu dem „Código de conducta", der in weiten Teilen an den 2005 von der Regierung erlassenen „Código de Buen Gobierno" anknüpft, *José Luis Carro Fernández-Valmayor*, Ética pública y normativa administrativa, in: Revista de Administración pública 2010, núm 181, S. 9, 18 ff.

[53] 2010 Chapter 25.

[54] Mittlerweile liegen fünf Quartalsberichte vor, vgl. zuletzt European Commission, Task Force for Greece, Fifth Activity Report, October 2013 (reporting period: April-September 2013).

[55] Zur „Aufnahmebereitschaft" und weiteren Voraussetzungen für ein effektives „Veränderungsmanagement" siehe *Wallerath* (Anm. 29), S. 370 ff.

IV. Fazit

Als Ergebnis ist festzuhalten:

1. Obwohl das Sekundärrecht der Europäischen Union in wachsendem Maße neben materiellen Regelungen auch Vorgaben für das nationale Verwaltungsverfahren und die nationale Verwaltungsorganisation enthält, bestehen in den Mitgliedstaaten weiterhin große Unterschiede hinsichtlich der Effektivität der Durchführung des Unionsrechts.

2. Der Lissabonner Vertrag statuiert ausdrücklich, dass die effektive Durchführung des Unionsrechts „als Frage von gemeinsamem Interesse" anzusehen ist. Damit wird die Rechtsgemeinschaft durch die Perspektive einer Implementationsgemeinschaft ergänzt. Diese zielt allerdings nicht auf supranationale Totalsteuerung, sondern auf die Beseitigung von Implementationsdefiziten in den Verwaltungssystemen der Mitgliedstaaten durch kooperatives (vertikales und horizontales) Zusammenwirken.

3. Durch rechtliche Vorgaben für das Verwaltungsverfahren und die Verwaltungsorganisation können zwar wichtige Transformationsprozesse in den Mitgliedstaaten in Gang gesetzt werden; eine nachhaltige Veränderungsstrategie muss aber noch stärker die Substrukturen, d.h. insbesondere die jeweilige nationale Verwaltungskultur einbeziehen. Es sind nicht zuletzt die von diesem Begriff umfassten „Orientierungsmuster" (Meinungen, Einstellungen und Werthaltungen), die das Verhalten der in der Öffentlichen Verwaltung tätigen Personen bestimmen.

4. Verwaltungskulturelle Veränderungsprozesse sind eng mit der seit geraumer Zeit zunehmenden Ethikdiskussion in der öffentlichen Verwaltung verbunden. Ein wesentlicher rechtlicher Bezugspunkt ist das Recht auf gute Verwaltung, dessen Konkretisierung sich nicht nur in der Identifizierung der wesentlichen rechtsstaatlichen Verfahrenselementen erschöpft, sondern auch – namentlich vom Europäischen Bürgerbeauftragten – durch verhaltensbezogene (außerrechtliche) Maßstäben angereichert wird. Das unionale Recht auf gute Verwaltung besitzt trotz der Begrenzung seines Anwendungsbereichs auf die Unionsorgane Leitbildfunktion.

5. Eine im Wesentlichen gleichwertige Implementation des Unionsrechts durch die Mitgliedstaaten ist Voraussetzung für das Vertrauen der Bürger in die Funktionsfähigkeit der Europäischen Union. Maßnahmen der Europäischen Union zur Beseitigung von Dysfunktionalitäten müssen daher letztlich auch auf die Veränderung der nationalen Verwaltungskulturen zielen, soweit sie einer wirksamen Implementierung des Unionsrechts entgegenstehen. Ziel kann dabei nicht die Schaffung einer europäischen Einheitsverwaltungskultur sein, die ohnehin unrealistisch wäre, sondern die Entwicklung und Weiterentwicklung gemeinsamer verwaltungskultureller Mindeststandards, die einerseits Raum für verwaltungskulturelle Vielfalt lassen, andererseits verwaltungskulturelle Kohärenz vermitteln. In diesem Sinne kann die weitere Herausbildung einer gemeineuropäischen Verwaltungskultur als Gelingensbedingung europäischer Integration begriffen werden.

Transnationalisierung juristischer Methodik in Europa

Von *Antonis Chanos*

1. Der Vorgang der Europäisierung der nationalen Rechtsordnungen der Mitgliedsstaaten der EU befindet sich in vollem Gange. Die Rechtsangleichung, insbesondere auch die Auslegung, Anwendung und Fortbildung des Rechts durch den nationalen Richter am Maßstab des supranationalen Europarechts, – aber auch mittels einer vergleichenden Annäherung an andere nationale Rechtsordnungen in Europa mit dem Zweck einer kreativeren Auseinandersetzung mit Rechtslösungen, die aus Bereichen ausländischer Rechtsprechung und Rechtsdogmatik stammen –, stellen die nationalen juristischen Methodenlehren vor Herausforderungen, die von den einschlägigen Lehrbüchern bislang nur in begrenztem Maße wahrgenommen werden[1]. Gerade der mehrdimensionale und mehrstufige Vorgang der Konstituierung eines europäischen Rechtsraums ruft zu einer tiefgreifenden Reflexion über Rolle und Sinn der juristischen Methode innerhalb eines neuen, sowohl geschichtlich als auch geographisch erweiterten Rahmens auf.

Es gibt z. Z. – soweit ersichtlich – noch keinen allgemein anerkannten Begriff einer europäischen juristischen Methodenlehre. Er dient wohl eher als ein heuristischer Begriff[2] bzw. als ein Arbeitsbegriff. Inwiefern kann bzw. soll sich also eine *europäische* juristische Methodik von den (nationalen) juristischen Methodenlehren unterscheiden? Um diese Frage zu beantworten benötigt man ein umfassendes Konzept einer europäischen juristischen Methodenlehre. Es ist dabei zwischen zwei Ebenen zu unterscheiden. Der Begriff einer europäischen juristischen Methodenlehre müßte auf der ersten Ebene durch die Eigenart ihres Gegenstandes, während auf der zweiten Ebene nach Maßstab der spezifischen Methoden und Methodiken definiert werden, deren System sie ausmacht.

2. Die europäische juristische Methodenlehre kann auf einer *ersten Ebene* als Methodik mit einem distinkten Gegenstand angesehen werden. Ihn bilden zwei (Kategorien von) Rechtsordnungen, nämlich einerseits das (supranationale oder mehrstufig angelegte) Europarecht, und andererseits, das angeglichene bzw. europäisierte nationale Recht. Auf dieser Ebene ist europäische juristische Methoden-

---

[1] S. *Axel Flessner*, Juristische Methodenlehre und europäisches Privatrecht, JZ 2002, S. 14–23, 14 f.

[2] Vgl. zum Begriff des europäischen Privatrechts als einem heuristischen Begriff *Axel Metzger*, Extra legem, intra ius. Allgemeine Rechtsgrundsätze im europäischen Privatrecht, Tübingen 2009, S. 111 ff.

lehre zweierlei: (a) eine Methodenlehre des Europarechts und (b) eine Methodik der Europäisierung der nationalen Rechtsordnungen in Europa. Im ersten Fall ist es zweckmäßig, zwischen einer Methodik des Gemeinschaftsrechts bzw. des EU-Rechts[3] einerseits und einer Methodik des europäischen Privatrechts[4], des europäischen Strafrechts und des (sonstigen) europäischen öffentlichen Rechts, insbesondere des europäischen Verfassungsrechts und Verwaltungsrechts zu unterscheiden. Im zweiten Fall gehört zum Begriff der europäischen juristischen Methodenlehre sowohl die Herausbildung eines „gemeinen" europäischen Rechts (neues europäisches *ius commune*)[5] als auch die Methodik der (sonstigen) Europäisierung des nationalen Rechts[6].

Das methodische Werkzeug, in dem sowohl die vertikale als auch die horizontale Dimension der gerichtlichen Europäisierung des nationalen Rechts synthetisiert werden, ist die „europäische" Auslegung[7] des nationalen Rechts[8].

3. In der *vertikalen* Dimension nimmt die europäische Auslegung des nationalen Rechts hauptsächlich die Form der europarechtskonformen[9] (bzw. unionsrechts-

---

[3] S. etwa *Sebastian A. E. Mertens*, Methodenlehre des Unionsrechts, Tübingen 2013.

[4] *Christiane Wendehorst*, Methodenlehre und Privatrecht in Europa, in: Vom praktischen Wert der Methode. Festschrift für Heinz Mayer zum 65. Geburtstag, hrsg. von Clemens Jabloner, Gabriele Kucsko-Stadlmayer, Gerhard Muzak, Bettina Perthold-Stoitzner und Karl Stöger, Wien 2011, S. 827–837.

[5] S. etwa *Jan M. Smits*, A European Private Law as a Mixed Legal System: Towards a Ius Commune through the Free Movement of Legal Rules, Maastricht Journal of European and Comparative Law 5 (1998), S. 328 ff.; *P. Larouche*, Ius Commune Casebooks for the Common Law of Europe: Presentation, Progress, Rationale, European Review of Private Law 8 (2000), S. 101–109.

[6] S. etwa *Thomas Pfeiffer*, Methodik der Privatrechtsangleichung in der EU. Der gemeinsame Referenzrahmen zum europäischen Vertragsrecht, AcP 208 (2008), S. 227–247.

[7] *Bettina Heiderhoff*, Grundstrukturen des nationalen und europäischen Verbrauchervertragsrechts. Insbesondere zur Reichweite europäischer Auslegung, München 2004, S. 85 ff.; *dies.*, Gemeinschaftsprivatrecht, 2. Aufl., München 2008, S. 58 ff.; *Martin Gebauer*, Europäische Auslegung des Zivilrechts. Methodik – Auslegung und Direktwirkung des europäischen Rechts – Richtlinienkonforme Auslegung und Fortbildung des nationalen Rechts, in: Martin Gebauer/Thomas Wiedmann (Hrsg.), Zivilrecht unter europäischem Einfluss. Die richtlinienkonforme Auslegung des BGB und anderer Gesetze – Kommentierung der wichtigsten EU-Verordnungen, 2. Aufl., Stuttgart 2010, S. 111–140; *Bettina Heiderhoff*, Constitutional Interpretation and European Interpretation of Private Law in Germany, in: dies./ Grzegorz Żmij (Hrsg.), Interpretation in Polish, German and European Private Law, München 2011, S. 101 ff.; *Hannes Rössler*, Aufgaben einer europäischen Rechtsmethodenlehre, Rechtstheorie 43 (2012), S. 495–517, 495 ff. S. ferner *Winfried Veelken*, Die Bedeutung des EG-Rechts für die nationale Rechtsanwendung, JuS 1993, S. 265 ff.

[8] Zur Auslegung des Rechts der Europäischen Union s. *Peter Mayer*, Die Grundsätze der Auslegung im Europäischen Gemeinschaftsrecht, Jura 1994, S. 455 ff.; *Werner Schroeder*, Die Auslegung des EU-Rechts, JuS 2004, S. 180–186.

[9] *Alexander S. Metallinos*, Die europarechtskonforme Auslegung, Münster 1994.

konformen[10]) Auslegung ein. Insbesondere die sekundärrechtskonforme Auslegung[11] mit ihren Hauptformen der gemeinschaftsrechtskonformen[12], der richtlinienkonformen[13] und der rahmenbeschlußkonformen[14] (sowie die an den entspre-

---

[10] *Olivier Gänswein*, Der Grundsatz unionsrechtskonformer Auslegung nationalen Rechts. Erscheinungsformen und dogmatische Grundlagen eines Rechtsprinzips des Unionsrechts, Frankfurt am Main 2009.

[11] Zur primärrechtskonformen Auslegung (von Sekundärrecht) s. *Clemens Höpfner*, Die systemkonforme Auslegung. Zur Auflösung einfachgesetzlicher, verfassungsrechtlicher und europarechtlicher Widersprüche im Recht, Tübingen 2008, S. 220 ff.; vgl. auch *Stefan Leible/ Ronny Domröse*, Die primärrechtskonforme Auslegung, in: Karl Riesenhuber (Hrsg.), Europäische Methodenlehre, 2. Aufl., Berlin/New York 2010, § 9 (S. 250–284). S. ferner *Friedrich Rüffler*, Aspekte primärrechtskonformer und sekundärrechtskonformer Auslegung nationalen Lauterkeitsrechts, in: Reiner Schulze (Hrsg.), Auslegung europäischen Privatrechts und angeglichenen Rechts, Baden-Baden 1999, S. 97 ff.

[12] Vgl. *Ninon Colneric*, Auslegung des Gemeinschaftsrechts und gemeinschaftsrechtskonforme Auslegung, ZEuP 13 (2005), S. 225 ff.; *Kai Krieger*, Die gemeinschaftsrechtskonforme Auslegung des deutschen Rechts, Münster 2005; *Höpfner*, Die systemkonforme Auslegung, a.a.O., S. 218 f.; *Höpfner/Rüthers*, Grundlagen einer europäischen Methodenlehre, a.a.O., S. 23 ff.

[13] S. dazu etwa *Udo Di Fabio*, Richtlinienkonformität als ranghöchstes Normauslegungsprinzip?, NJW 1990, S. 947 ff.; *Hans D. Jarass*, Richtlinienkonforme bzw. EG-rechtskonforme Auslegung nationalen Rechts, EuR 1991, S. 211 ff.; *Georg Ress*, Die richtlinienkonforme „Interpretation" innerstaatlichen Rechts, DÖV 1994, S. 489 ff.; *Marek Schmidt*, Privatrechtsangleichende EU-Richtlinien und nationale Auslegungsmethoden, RabelsZ 59 (1995), S. 569 ff.; *Stefan Grundmann*, Richtlinienkonforme Auslegung im Bereich des Privatrechts – insbesondere: der Kanon der nationalen Auslegungsmethoden als Grenze?, ZEuP 1996, 399–424; *Friedrich Rüffler*, Richtlinienkonforme Auslegung nationalen Rechts, ÖJZ 1997, S. 121 ff.; *Stefan Vogenauer*, Richtlinienkonforme Auslegung nationalen Rechts, ZEuP 1997, S. 158 ff.; *Ton Heukels*, Von richtlinienkonformer zur völkerrechtskonformen Auslegung im EG-Recht: Internationale Dimensionen einer normenhierarchiegerechten Interpretationsmaxime, ZEuS 2 (1999), S. 313 ff.; *Katharina Wöhlermann*, Die richtlinienkonforme Auslegung im Europäischen Arbeitsrecht. Perspektiven und Barrieren für eine *europäische Rechtsmethodik* am Beispiel arbeitsrechtlicher Gleichbehandlungsrichtlinien, Stuttgart usw. 1998; *Markus Frisch*, Die richtlinienkonforme Auslegung nationalen Rechts, Münster 2000; *Marcus Klamert*, Die richtlinienkonforme Auslegung nationalen Rechts, Wien 2001; *Helmut Satzger*, Richtlinien und Strafrecht: Die Bedeutung von EG-Richtlinien und ihrer nationalen Transformationsakte für die Auslegung deutscher Straftatbestände, in: Gerhard Hohloch (Hrsg.), Richtlinien der EU und ihre Umsetzung in Deutschland und Frankreich. 10. „Deutsch-Französisches Juristentreffen", Baden-Baden 2001; *Robert Manger*, Richtlinienkonforme Auslegung im Privatrecht in Literatur und Rechtsprechung unter Heranziehung ausgewählter Entscheidungen des zweiten BGH-Senats in Zivilsachen und des House of Lords, Berlin 2002; *Jan Suhr*, Richtlinienkonforme Auslegung im Privatrecht und nationale Auslegungsmethodik, Baden-Baden 2012.

[14] Zur rahmenbeschlußkonformen Auslegung s. *B. R. Killmann*, Die rahmenbeschlußkonforme Auslegung im Strafrecht vor dem EuGH, JBl. 2005, S. 566 ff.; *Anne Wehnert*, Rahmenbeschlußkonforme Auslegung deutschen Strafrechts, NJW 2005, S. 3760 ff.; *Höpfner*, Die systemkonforme Auslegung, a.a.O., S. 321 ff.; *Höpfner/Rüthers*, Grundlagen einer europäischen Methodenlehre, a.a.O., S. 30 f.; *Isabel Röcker*, Die Pflicht zur rahmenbeschlußkonformen Auslegung nationalen Rechts, Heidelberg 2013.

chenden europäischen Vorgaben orientierte[15]) Auslegung und Rechtsfortbildung[16] durch den nationalen Richter kommen hier zum Zuge. Zwischen europarechtskonformer und europarechtsorientierter Auslegung besteht nun folgender Unterschied: Erstere dient der Überprüfung des (von vornherein nicht eindeutigen) normativen Inhalts der auszulegenden nationaler Gesetzesbestimmung am Maßstab europarechtlicher Vorschriften, also der Vereinbarkeit zumindest eines von mehreren Auslegungsergebnissen mit dem höherrangigen (bzw. umzusetzenden) Europarecht und damit[17] deren Geltungs„rettung" im Anwendungsbereich des letzteren (bzw. der Vermeidung von Konsequenzen im Fall der Nichterfüllung der Umsetzungspflicht) (*Inhaltskontrolle*)[18]. Während die europarechtsorientierte Auslegung auf die *Inhaltsbestimmung* der nationalen Gesetzesbestimmungen mit Hilfe europarechtli-

---

[15] S. etwa *Martin Nettesheim*, Auslegung und Fortbildung im Lichte des Gemeinschaftsrechts, AöR 119 (1994), σ. 261–293. Zur richtlinienorientierten Auslegung s. *Torsten Jäger*, Überschießende Richtlinienumsetzung im Privatrecht.: Zugleich ein Beitrag zur Dogmatik der Mindestharmonisierung, der richtlinienorientierten Auslegung und des Vorabentscheidungsverfahrens, Baden-Baden 2006, S. 104 ff.; *Höpfner*, Die systemkonforme Auslegung, a.a.O., S. 256, 285; *Martin Weber*, Grenzen EU-rechtskonformer Auslegung und Rechtsfortbildung, Baden-Baden 2010, S. 127 ff.; *Christian M. Bron*, Rechtsangleichung des Privatrechts auf Ebene der Europäischen Union. Genese, Festaltung und Vision, Baden-Baden 2011, S. 165 ff.; *Alexander Weiss*, Widersprüche im Recht – unter besonderer Berücksichtigung europarechtsbedingter Widersprüche im deutschen Zivilrecht, München 2011, S. 162 f.; *Rolf Wank*, § 2 Rangkonforme Auslegung und Europarecht, in: Ioannis K. Karakostas/Karl Riesenhuber (Hrsg.), Methoden- und Verfassungsfragen der europäischen Rechtsangleichung, Berlin/New York 2011, S. 15–35, 26; *Nicole Baldauf*, Richtlinienverstoß und Verschiebung der Contra-legem-Grenze im Privatrechtsverhältnis. Der Konflikt zwischen Richtlinie und nationalem Recht bei der Rechtsanwendung, Tübingen 2013, S. 110 ff. Zur gemeinschaftsrechtsorientierten Rechtsgewinnung s. *Carsten Herresthal*, Rechtsfortbildung im europarechtlichen Rahmen. Methoden, Kompetenzen, Grenzen dargestellt am Beispiel des Privatrechts, München 2006, S. 280 ff.

[16] *Claus-Wilhelm Canaris*, Die richtlinienkonforme Auslegung und Rechtsfortbildung im System der juristischen Methodenlehre, in: Im Dienste der Gerechtigkeit. Festschrift für Franz Bydlinski, hrsg. von Helmut Koziol und Peter Rummel, Wien 2002, S. 47–103; *Martin Gebauer*, Umsetzungsprobleme von EG-Richtlinien und ihre Lösung – Richtlinienkonforme Auslegung als Mittel der Rechtsfortbildung im Privatrecht, AnwBl 2007, S. 314–319; *Clemens Höpfner*, Voraussetzungen und Grenzen richtlinienkonformer Auslegung und Rechtsfortbildung, in: Christoph Busch/Christina Kopp/Mary R. McGuire/Martin Zimmermann (Hrsg.), Jahrbuch Junger Zivilrechtswissenschaftler 2009, S. 73–108; *Wank*, § 2 Rangkonforme Auslegung und Europarecht, a.a.O., S. 29 ff. S. ferner *E. Kohler-Gehring*, Europarecht und nationales Recht – Auslegung und Rechtsfortbildung, JA 1998, S. 807 ff.; insbesondere zur richtlinienkonformen Rechtsfortbildung s. *Jan Schürnbrand*, Die Grenzen richtlinienkonformer Rechtsfortbildung im Privatrecht, JZ 2007, S. 910–918. *Carsten Herresthal*, Voraussetzungen und Grenzen der gemeinschaftsrechtskonformen Rechtsfortbildung, EuZW 2007, S. 396–400; *Clemens Höpfner*, Über Sinn und Unsinn der sog. „richtlinienkonformen Rechtsfortbildung" – Replik auf Möllers / Möhring, JZ 2008, S. 919 ff., JZ 2009, S. 403–405.

[17] Nämlich aufgrund des Anwendungsvorrangs der unmittelbar geltenden gemeinschaftrechtlichen Vorschriften (bzw. der –meistens bei den Richtlinien bzw. Rahmenbeschlüssen bestehenden– staatlichen Umsetzungsverpflichtung).

[18] Deshalb sollte sie eigentlich nicht als Aspekt der Auslegung im klassischen Sinne betrachtet werden.

cher Vorschriften im Rahmen systematischer Argumentation abzielt.[19] In diesen Zusammenhang gehört – auf prozeduraler Ebene – auch der Vorgang der Vorlage beim EuGH seitens eines nationalen Gerichts einer Interpretationsfrage (Vorabentscheidungsverfahren)[20], vor allem im Fall der Auslegung von Generalklauseln.[21]

In der *horizontalen* Dimension der europäischen Auslegung des nationalen Rechts sind drei Erscheinungsformen zu unterscheiden: die vergleichende Interpretation, die harmonisierende Auslegung und die „international brauchbare Auslegung des nationalen Rechts".

Die vergleichende Auslegung des Gesetzes[22] durch den Richter kann in eine raumbezogene und in eine zeitbezogene unterschieden werden[23]. Die vergleichende

---

[19] *Höpfner*, Die systemkonforme Auslegung, a.a.O., S. 178 ff.; *Wank*, § 2 Rangkonforme Auslegung und Europarecht, a.a.O., S., 21, 26 f. mit weiteren bibliographischen Angaben.

[20] S. *J. Streil*, Das Vorabentscheidungsverfahren als Bindeglied zwischen europäischer und nationaler Rechtsprechung, in: Jürgen Schwarze (Hrsg.), Der Europäische Gerichtshof als Verfassungsgericht und Rechtsschutzinstanz, Baden-Baden 1983, S. 69 ff.; *Rudolf Streinz*, Auswirkungen des vom EuGH „ausgelegten" Gemeinschaftsrechts auf das deutsche Recht, Jura 1995, S. 6 ff.; *Bruno Schima*, Das Vorabentscheidungsverfahren vor dem EuGH. Unter besonderer Berücksichtigung der Rechtslage in Österreich, Wien 1997; *Bernd Heuermann*, Die Vorabentscheidung nach Art. 177 EGV und das Verhältnis von europäischem und nationalem Recht, ThVBl. 1998, S. 1 ff.; *Bruno Schima*, Zur Wirkung von Auslegungsentscheidungen des Gerichtshofes der Europäischen Gemeinschaften, in: Birgit Feldner/Nikolaus Forgó (Hrsg.), Norm und Entscheidung, Wien/New York 2000, S. 280 ff; *Waltraud Hakenberg*, Vorabentscheidungsverfahren und europäisches Privatrecht. Erfahrungen aus europäischer Sicht, RabelsZ 66 (2002), S. 367 ff.; *Burkhard Heß*, Rechtsfragen des Vorabentscheidungsverfahrens, RabelsZ 66 (2002), S. 470 ff.; *Bettina Heiderhoff*, Grundstrukturen des nationalen und europäischen Verbrauchervertragsrechts. Insbesondere zur Reichweite europäischer Auslegung, München 2004, S. 85 ff.; *dies.*, Gemeinschaftsprivatrecht, 2. Aufl., München 2008, S. 94 ff.; *Dörte Poelzig*, Ist das Vorlageverfahren gemäß Art. 234 EG noch zeitgemäß?, in: Christoph Busch/Christina Kopp/Mary R. McGuire (Hrsg.), Europäische Methodik: Konvergenz und Diskrepanz europäischen und nationalen Privatrechts, Jahrbuch Junger Zivilrechtswissenschaftler 2009, Stuttgart 2010, S. 209–232; *Verena Klappstein*, Die Bindungswirkung der Vorabentscheide des EuGH, in: Christoph Busch/Christina Kopp/Mary R. McGuire (Hrsg.), Europäische Methodik: Konvergenz und Diskrepanz europäischen und nationalen Privatrechts, Jahrbuch Junger Zivilrechtswissenschaftler 2009, Stuttgart 2010, S. 233–272; *Meinhard Schröder*, Die Vorlagepflicht zum EuGH aus europarechtlicher und nationaler Perspektive, EuR 46 (2011), S. 808–827. Zur vom EuGH entwickelten „acte clair"-Doktrin s. *Morten Broberg/Niels Fenger*, Theorie und Praxis der Acte-clair-Doktrin des EuGH, EuR 45 (2010), S. 835–853.

[21] *Christian Kohler*, Integration und Auslegung – Zur Doppelfunktion des Europäischen Gerichtshofs, in: Erik Jayme (Hrsg.), Ein internationales Zivilverfahrensrecht für Gesamteuropa. EuGVÜ Lugano-Übereinkommen, und die Rechtsentwicklungen in Mittel- und Osteuropa, Heidelberg 1992, S. 11–28; *Oliver Remien*, Die Vorlagepflicht bei Auslegung unbestimmter Rechtsbegriffe, RabelsZ 66 (2002), S. 503 ff.; *Anne Röthel*, § 12 Die Konkretisierung von Generalklauseln, in: Karl Riesenhuber (Hrsg.), Europäische Methodenlehre. Handbuch für Ausbildung und Praxis, 2. Aufl., Berlin/New York 2010, S. 349–371.

[22] *Albert Bleckmann*, Die wertende Rechtsvergleichung bei der Entwicklung europäischer Grundrechte, in: Europarecht, Energierecht, Wirtschaftsrecht. Festschrift für Bodo Börner, hrsg. von Jürgen F. Baur, Peter-Christian Müller-Graff und Manfred Zuleeg, Köln 1992,

Interpretation führt nicht unbedingt zu einer Harmonisierung oder Konvergenz. Durch die Feststellung von Unterschieden gegenüber der verglichenen Rechtsordnung und den eventuellen Ausschluß der Lösungen, die von dieser angeboten werden, kann das vorzuziehende Interpretationsergebnis bei seiner Begründung nichtsdestotrotz vollständiger ans Licht gebracht werden.[24] Zweifellos aber stellt die vergleichende Interpretation (vor allem in Bezug auf mehrere ausländische

---

S. 29 ff.; *Reiner Schulze*, Vergleichende Gesetzesauslegung und Rechtsangleichung, ZfRV 1997, S. 183 ff.; *Bettina Heiderhoff*, Grundstrukturen des nationalen und europäischen Verbrauchervertragsrechts. Insbesondere zur Reichweite europäischer Auslegung, München 2004, S. 180 ff.; *Jian Mi*, From Comparative Law to Ius Commune, in: Zivil- und Wirtschaftsrecht im Europäischen und Globalen Kontext. Festschrift für Norbert Horn zum 70. Geburtstag am 18. August 2006, hrsg. von Klaus Peter Berger, Georg Borges, Harald Herrmann, Andreas Schlüter, Berlin 2006, S. 1215–1226; *Franz C. Mayer*, Rechtsvergleichung und Verfassungsvergleichung im Europarecht, in: Christian Calliess (Hrsg.), Verfassungswandel im europäischen Staaten- und Verfassungsverbund, Tübingen: Mohr Siebeck 2007, S. 167–185; *Antonios Emmanuel Platsas*, The Functional and the Dysfunctional in the Comparative Method of Law: Some Critical Remarks, Electronic Journal of Comparative Law vol. 12.3 (December 2008) (http://www.ejcl.org/123/art123-3.pdf); *Roberto Caranta*, Pleading for European Comparative Administrative Law; What is the Place for Comparative Law in Europe?, in: K. J. de Graaf/H. J. Jans/A. Prechal/R. J. G. M. Widdershoven (Hrsg.), European Administrative Law: Top-Down and Bottom-Up. Proceedings of the First *ReaLaw* Research Forum, Groningen 2010, S. 155 ff.; *Andreas Schwartze*, §4 Die Rechtsvergleichung, in: Karl Riesenhuber (Hrsg.), Europäische Methodenlehre. Handbuch für Ausbildung und Praxis, 2. Aufl., Berlin/New York 2010, S. 113–133; *Sebastian A. E. Martens*, Rechtsvergleichung und grenzüberwindende Jurisprudenz im Gemeinschaftsrecht, in: Christoph Busch/Christina Kopp/Mary R. McGuire (Hrsg.), Europäische Methodik: Konvergenz und Diskrepanz europäischen und nationalen Privatrechts, Jahrbuch Junger Zivilrechtswissenschaftler 2009, Stuttgart 2010, S. 27 ff., 31 ff.; *Thomas Coendet*, Rechtsvergleichende Argumentation. Phänomenologie der Veränderung im rechtlichen Diskurs, Tübingen 2012; *Michal Bobek*, Comparative Reasoning in European Supreme Courts, Oxford 2013. S. allgemeiner auch *Robert S. Summers/Michele Tarrufo*, Interpretation and Comparative Analysis, in: D. Neil MacCormick/Robert S. Summers (Hrsg.), Interpreting Statutes: A Comparative Study, Aldershot 1991, S. 461 ff. Zum Charakter der Rechtsvergleichung als Auslegungsmethode oder rechtswissenschaftlichen Disziplin s. *Otto Pfersmann*, Le droit comparé comme interprétation et comme théorie du droit, Revue international de droit comparé 53 (2001), S. 275–288 und ferner *Djalil Kiekbaev*, Comparative Law: Method, Science or Educational Discipline?, Electronic Journal of Comparative Law, vol 7.3 (September 2003), (http://www.ejcl.org/73/art73-2.html).

[23] Die Unterscheidung sollte eher als eine analytische verstanden werden. Vgl. *Eberhard Schmidt-Aßmann*, Administrative Law in Europe: Between Common Principles and National Traditions, in: Matthias Ruffert (Hrsg.), Administrative Law in Europe. Between Common Principles and National Traditions, Groningen 2013, S. 3 ff., 8 f., der von der zentralen Rolle einer „Historically-Informed Administrative Legal Comparison" im Rahmen von horizontalen Austauschvorgängen zwischen gemeinsamen Rechtsprinzipien und nationalen Rechtstraditionen in Europa spricht.

[24] S. aber *Clemens Höpfner/Bernd Rüthers*, Grundlagen einer europäischen Methodenlehre, AcP 209 (2009), S. 1–36, 16 f. S. ferner *Jan M. Smits*, Comparative Law and its Influence on National Legal Systems, in: Mathias Reimann/Reinhard Zimmermann (Hrsg.), The Oxford Handbook of Comparative Law, Oxford 2006, S. 477–512.

Rechtsordnungen) das nationale Gericht vor große Herausforderungen.[25] Auf der anderen Seite kann die Herausbildung von europäischen allgemeinen Rechtsgrundsätzen[26], die den nationalen Rechtsordnungen gemeinsam sind, ohne den Vergleich[27] und eine gewisse Annäherung bzw. „Konvergenz"[28] der nationalen Rechtssysteme nicht auskommen. Die Frage ist, ob das Anliegen der Vergleichs auf die Schultern des nationalen Richters geschoben werden kann, oder -was ja eher zutreffen würde- ob darin eine Aufgabe der rechtswissenschaftlichen Forschung zu erblicken ist, worauf der Richter dann sich stützen kann.[29]

Die rechtsvergleichende Auslegung wird vorausgesetzt bei, aber auch übertroffen von einer (ohne jede formelle Verpflichtung dazu stattfindenden) sogenannten harmonisierenden Auslegung der nationalen Gesetze zugunsten der Herausfindung

---

[25] *Bettina Heiderhoff*, Grundstrukturen des nationalen und europäischen Verbraucheivertragsrechts. Insbesondere zur Reichweite europäischer Auslegung, München 2004, S. 180–182.

[26] *Axel Metzger*, Extra legem, intra ius: allgemeine Rechtsgrundsätze im europäischen Privatrecht, Tübingen 2009; *ders.*, Allgemeine Rechtsgrundsätze im Europäischen Privatrecht: Ansätze für eine einheitliche Methodenlehre im europäischen Mehrebenensystem, Rechtstheorie 40 (2009), S. 313–336; *ders.*, Allgemeine Rechtsgrundsätze in Europa – dargestellt am Beispiel des Gleichbehandlungsgrundsatzes, RabelsZ 75 (2011), S. 845–881. S. am Beispiel des Privatautonomiegedankens *Gralf-Peter Calliess*, Die Zukunft der Privatautonomie. Zur neueren Entwicklung eines gemeineuropäischen Rechtsprinzips, in: Prinzipien des Privatrechts und Rechtsvereinheitlichung, Jahrbuch Junger Zivilrechtswissenschaftler 2000, Stuttgart 2001, S. 83–108. Insbesondere zum Verhältnis von allgemeinen Rechtsgrundsätzen und Gemeinschaftsprivatrecht s. *Jürgen Basedow*, Anforderungen an eine europäische Privatrechtsdogmatik, in: Reinhard Zimmermann in Zusammenarbeit mit Rolf Knütel und Jens Peter Meincke (Hrsg.), Rechtsgeschichte und Privatrechtsdogmatik, Heidelberg 1999, S. 79–100, 81 f. Vgl. im Hinblick auf das Gemeinschaftsrecht *R.-E. Papadopoulou*, Principes généraux du droit communautaire. Origines et concrétisation, Bruxelles 1996; *Xavier Groussot*, General Principles of Community Law, Groningen 2006; *Takis Tridimas*, The General Principles of EC Law, 2. Aufl., Oxford 2006.

[27] Zum Beitrag der richterlichen Rechtsvergleichung zur Herausbildung eines gemeineuropäischen Verfassungsrechts s. *Mattias Wendel*, Richterliche Rechtsvergleichung als Dialogform: Die Integrationsrechtsprechung nationaler Verfassungsgerichte in gemeineuropäischer Perspektive, Der Staat 52 (2013), S. 339–370; *ders.*, Comparative reasoning and the making of a common constitutional law. EU-related decisions of national constitutional courts in a transnational perspective, International Journal of Constitutional Law 11 (2013), S. 981–1002; *Franz C. Mayer*, Constitutional comparativism in action. The example of general principles of EU law and how they are made – a German perspective, International Journal of Constitutional Law 11 (2013), S. 1003–1020.

[28] Von einer Vermittlungsfunktion der allgemeinen Rechtsgrundsätze spricht etwa *Ilka Klöckner*, Grenzüberschreitende Bindung an zivilgerichtliche Präjudizien. Möglichkeiten und Grenzen im Europäischen Rechtsraum und bei staatsvertraglich angelegter Rechtsvereinheitlichung, Tübingen 2006, S. 218 f.

[29] *Reinhard Zimmermann*, Die Europäisierung des Privatrechts und die Rechtsvergleichung. Vortrag gehalten vor der Juristischen Gesellschaft zu Berlin am 15. Juni 2005, Berlin 2006.

einer „europaweit akzeptablen" Interpretationslösung.[30] Der Anspruch, der hierbei mancherorts erhoben wird[31], daß bei der Entscheidungsfindung (zumindest durch die nationalen Höchstgerichte) die in anderen europäischen Ländern gefundenen Lösungen unbedingt mitberücksichtigt werden sollten, ansonsten seien richterliche Urteile „methodisch inakzeptabel"[32], scheint übertrieben zu sein.[33]

Schließlich kann die „international brauchbare Auslegung des nationalen Rechts"[34] die mit praktischen Schwierigkeiten verbundene rechtsvergleichende Interpretation des Richters erleichtern, sofern er die Option hat, sich an Regel- und Prinzipienkatalogen zu orientieren, die von wissenschaftlichen Arbeitsgruppen zugunsten der Vereinheitlichung des Privatrechts in Europa bearbereitet worden sind.[35]

4. Die europäische juristische Methodenlehre hat es – und somit kommen wir zur *zweiten,* sozusagen *reflexiven Ebene* der europäischen juristischen Methodenlehre – mit dem Phänomen der Vielzahl, vor allem aber der Vielfalt von Rechtsordnungen zu tun, mit der sich der Gemeinschafts-, aber zunehmend auch der nationale Richter bei der praktischen Anwendung des geltenden Rechts im Einzelfalle konfrontiert sieht. Es handelt sich dabei um eine Vielfalt in doppeltem Sinne. Es geht nämlich auf der einen Seite (a) um eine Vielfalt von Rechtsquellen[36] und auf der anderen Seite (b) um eine Vielfalt von Rechtsmethoden und juristischen Methodologien[37].

---

[30] *Walter Odersky*, Harmonisierende Auslegung und europäische Rechtskultur, ZEuP 1994, S. 1 ff.; *Bettina Heiderhoff*, Grundstrukturen des nationalen und europäischen Verbrauchervertragsrechts. Insbesondere zur Reichweite europäischer Auslegung, München 2004, S. 147 ff.; *dies.*, Gemeinschaftsprivatrecht, 2. Aufl., München 2007, S. 58 ff.; *Ilka Klöckner*, Grenzüberschreitende Bindung an zivilgerichtliche Präjudizien. Möglichkeiten und Grenzen im Europäischen Rechtsraum und bei staatsvertraglich angelegter Rechtsvereinheitlichung, Tübingen 2006, S. 88 ff., 91 ff.

[31] *Axel Flessner*, Europäisches Privatrecht und juristische Methode, JZ 2002, S. 14–23, 17. Vgl. auch *Ilka Klöckner*, Grenzüberschreitende Bindung an zivilgerichtliche Präjudizien. Möglichkeiten und Grenzen im Europäischen Rechtsraum und bei staatsvertraglich angelegter Rechtsvereinheitlichung, Tübingen 2006, S. 98.

[32] *Axel Flessner*, Europäisches Privatrecht und juristische Methode, JZ 2002, S. 14–23, 17.

[33] S. auch *Clemens Höpfner/Bernd Rüthers*, Grundlagen einer europäischen Methodenlehre, AcP 209 (2009), S. 1–36, 17 (mit Anm. 90).

[34] *Klaus Peter Berger*, Vom praktischen Nutzen der Rechtsvergleichung: die „international brauchbare" Auslegung nationalen Rechts, in: Festschrift für Otto Sandrock zum 70. Geburtstag, hrsg. von Klaus Peter Berger, Heidelberg 2000, S. 49–64; *ders.*, Auf dem Weg zu einem europäischen Gemeinrecht der Methode, ZEuP 2001, S. 4–29, 8 ff.

[35] *Bettina Heiderhoff*, Grundstrukturen des nationalen und europäischen Verbrauchervertragsrechts. Insbesondere zur Reichweite europäischer Auslegung, München 2004, S. 184 f., 216.

[36] S. *Peter Häberle*, Pluralismus der Rechtsquellen in Europa – nach Maastricht: Ein Pluralismus von Geschriebenem und Ungeschriebenem vieler Stufen und Räume, von Staatlichem und Transstaatlichem, JöR 47 (1999), S. 79–98; *Jan M. Smits*, The Europeanisation of national legal systems: some consequences for legal thinking in civil law countries, in: Mark Van Hoecke (Hrsg.), Epistemology and Methodology of Comparative Law, Oxford 2004,

So entsteht allmählich auf europäischer Ebene einerseits eine Methodik, die die Vielfalt[38] und sogar Fragmentierung[39] ihres Gegenstandes, nämlich des „geltenden

S. 229–245, 235 f.; *ders.*, The Complexity of Transnational Law: Coherence and Fragmentation of Private Law, Electronic Journal of Comparative Law vol. 14.3 (December 2010) (http://www.ejcl.org/143/art143-14.pdf); *ders.*, Plurality of Sources in European Private Law, or: How to Live With Legal Diversity?, in: Roger Brownsword/Hans W. Micklitz/Leone Niglia/Stephen Weatherill (Hrsg.), The Foundations of European Private Law, Oxford 2011, S. 323–335; *Johannes Köndgen*, § 7 Die Rechtsquellen des Europäischen Privatrechts, in: Karl Riesenhuber (Hrsg.), Europäische Methodenlehre. Handbuch für Ausbildung und Praxis, 2. Aufl., Berlin 2010, S. 191–224; *Holger Fleischer*, Europäische Methodenlehre: Stand und Perspektiven, RabelsZ 75 (2011), S. 700–729, 722 f.; *Tobias Kruis*, Der Anwendungsvorrang des EU-Rechts in Theorie und Praxis. Seine Durchsetzung in Deutschland. Eine theoretische und empirische Untersuchung anhand der Finanz- und Verwaltungsgerichte und Behörden, Tübingen 2013, S. 10 ff. Von der Rechtsquellenlehre als einem „polyzentrischen Gefüge" spricht *Eberhard Schmidt-Aßmann*, Verwaltungsrechtliche Dogmatik: Eine Zwischenbilanz zu Entwicklung, Reform und künftigen Aufgaben, Tübingen 2013, S. 34 ff. Mit Blick auf die europäische Rechtsquellenlehre: *Johannes Köndgen*, Die Rechtsquellen des Europäischen Privatrechts, in: Karl Riesenhuber (Hrsg.), Europäische Methodenlehre: Handbuch für Ausbildung und Praxis, 2. Aufl., Berlin/New York 2010,S. 191 ff, insbes. 191–193; *Gunnar Folke Schuppert*, Governance und Rechtsetzung. Grundfragen einer modernen Regelungswissenschaft, Baden-Baden 2011, S. 321 ff. sowie *Sebastian A. E. Martens*, Methodenlehre des Unionsrechts, Tübingen 2013. Es kann an dieser Stelle nicht auf die Frage der (Möglichkeit bzw. Notwendigkeit einer) Neukonzeption der herkömmlichen Rechtsquellenlehre eingegangen werden; s. dazu *Matthias Ruffert*, Rechtsquellen und Rechtsschichten des Verwaltungsrechts, in: Wolfgang Hoffmann-Riem/Eberhard Schmidt-Aßmann/Andreas Voßkuhle (Hrsg.), Grundlagen des Verwaltungsrechts, Band I, München 2006, § 17 Rn. 8 ff.

[37] Vgl. *Ulrike Seif*, Methodenunterschiede in der europäischen Rechtsgemeinschaft oder Mittlerfunktion der Präjudizien, in: Freiheit und Verantwortung in schwieriger Zeit. Festschrift für Ellen Schuchter, hrsg. von Gunner Duttge, Köln 2002, S. 133 ff.; *Stephen Weatherill*, Can There Be Common Interpretation of European Private Law?; Georgia Journal of International & Comparative Law 139 (2002–2003), S. 31 ff.; *Hans-Heiner Kühne*, Europäische Methodenvielfalt und nationale Umsetzung von Entscheidungen Europäischer Gerichte, Goltdammer's Archiv für Strafrecht 152 (2005), S. 195–214.

[38] *Ernst A. Kramer*, Vielfalt und Einheit der Wertungen im Europäischen Privatrecht, in: Recht, Staat und Politik am Ende des zweiten Jahrtausends. Festschrift für Arnold Koller zum 60. Geburtstag, hrsg. von Walter Schluep, Bern/Stuttgart/Wien 1993, S. 729–750; *Otto Sandrock*, Die Europäischen Gemeinschaften und die Privatrechte ihrer Mitgliedstaaten: Einheit oder Vielfalt?, EWS 1994, S. 1–8; *Klaus Schurig*, Europäisches Zivilrecht – Vielfalt oder Einerlei?, in: Festschrift für Bernhard Großfeld, hrsg. von Ulrich Hübner, Werner F. Ebke, Heidelberg 1999, S. 1189–1111; *H. Muir-Watt*, European Integration, Legal Diversity and the Conflict of Laws, Edinburgh Law Review 9 (2004–2005), S. 6 ff.; *Johan P. Olsen*, Unity and diversity. European Style, ARENA WP 24/2005; *Gerhard Wagner*, The Virtues of Diversity in European Private Law, in: Jan Smits (Hrsg.), The Need for a European Contract Law, Groningen 2005, S. 4 ff.; *Claudio Franzius*, Europäisches Verfassungsrechtsdenken, Tübingen 2010, S. 123 ff.

[39] *Thomas Wilhelmsson*, Private Law in the EU: Harmonised or Fragmented Europeanisation?, ERPL 10 (2002), S. 77–94; *Jan M. Smits*, The Complexity of Transnational Law: Coherence and Fragmentation of Private Law, Electronic Journal of Comparative Law vol 14.3 (December 2010) (http://www.ejcl.org/143/art143-14.pdf). Zu den Ansätzen der Fragmentierungsdebatte im Bereich des *Völkerrechts* s. *M. Koskenniemi/P. Leino*, Fragmentation of International Law? Postmodern Anxieties, Leiden Journal of International Law 15 (2002),

Rechts" (regulatorischer Pluralismus)[40], zu verwalten hat. Diese Methodik sieht sich aber andererseits zusätzlich mit der Frage konfrontiert, ob die Rechtsordnungen in Europa durch einen Methodenmonismus oder vielleicht durch einen Methodenpluralismus[41] gekennzeichnet sind (bzw. werden sollen).

S. 553 ff.; *Joost Pauwelyn*, Bridging Fragmentation and Unity: International Law as a Universe of Inter-connected Islands, Michigan Journal of International Law 25 (2004), S. 903–916; *Karel Wellens*, Fragmentation of International Law and Establishing an Accountability Regime for International Organizations: The Role of the Judiciary in Closing the Gap, Michigan Journal of International Law 25 (2004), S. 1159–1181; *Martti Koskenniemi*, Fragmentation of International Law: Difficulties arising from the Diversification and Expansion of International Law, Report of the Study Group of the International Law Commission, UN A/CN.4/L.682, 3 April 2006; *T. Stephens*, Multiple International Courts and the „Fragmentation" of International Environmental Law, Australian Yearbook of International Law 25 (2006), S. 227–271; *Carmen Thiele*, Fragmentierung des Völkerrechts als Herausforderung für die Staatengemeinschaft, AVR 46 (2008), S. 1 ff.; *A.-C. Martineau*, The Rhetoric of Fragmentation: Fear and Faith in International Law, Leiden Journal of International Law 22 (2009), S. 1–28. Mit Blick auf das *Weltrecht* und das *transnationale* (Verwaltungs-, aber auch Privat-)*Recht* s. *Andreas Fischer-Lescano/Gunther Teubner*, Regime-Collisions: The Vain Search for Legal Unity in the Fragmentation of Global Law, Michigan Journal of International Law 25 (2004), S. 999–1046; *M.-S. Kuo*, Between Fragmentation and Unity: The Uneasy Relationship between Global administrative law and global constitutionalism, San Diego International Law Journal 10 (2009), S. 439–467. Mittlerweile hat sich die Debatte über Fragmentierung auf das Gebiet des *nationalen Rechts* erweitert, in dem sich Trends der Herausbildung diverser Regimes bemerkbar machen, und zwar je nach dem Grad der Europäisierung bzw. ob Bereiche desselben vom Einfluss des Gemeinschaftsrechts (noch) unberührt geblieben sind. S. dazu *Tony Weir*, Divergent Legal Systems in a Single Member State, ZEuP 1998, S. 564–585; *J. Dickson*, Directives in European Union Legal Systems: Whose Norms Are They Anyway?, European Law Journal 17 (2011), S. 190–212.

[40] S. dazu *Gabriele Bauschke* et al. (Hrsg.), Pluralität des Rechts – Regulierung im Spannungsfeld der Rechtsebenen, Stuttgart 2003; *Matthias Kötter/Gunnar Folke Schuppert* (Hrsg.), Normative Pluralität ordnen. Rechtsbegriffe, Normenkollisionen und Rule of Law in Kontexten dies- und jenseits des Staates, Baden-Baden 2009; *Ulrich Sieber*, Rechtliche Ordnung in einer globalen Welt. Die Entwicklung zu einem fragmentierten System von nationalen, internationalen und privaten Normen, Rechtstheorie 41 (2010), S. 151–198, 170 ff.; *Andreas Paulus*, From dualism to pluralism: the relationship between international law, European law and domestic law, in: P. H. F. Bekker/R. Dolzer/M. Waibel (Hrsg.), Making Transnational Law Work in the Global Economy. Essays in Honour of Detlev Vagts, Cambridge 2010, S. 132–153; *Sebastian A. E. Martens*, 27 Rechtsordnungen oder mehr? Die Regelungsvielfalt des Privatrechts in der Europäischen Union, Rechtswissenschaft – Zeitschrift für rechtswissenschaftliche Forschung 2012, S. 432–452. Zu einschlägigen Fragen des europäischen Rechtspluralismus s. allgemeiner *Massimo La Torre*, Legal Pluralism as an Evolutionary Achievement of European Community Law, in: Francis G. Snyder (Hrsg.), The Europeanisation of Law: The Legal Effects of European Integration, Antwerpen 2000, S. 125–138; *J. Tontti*, European legal pluralism as a rebirth of ius commune, Retfaerd 40 (2001), S. 40–54; *N. W. Barber*, Legal Pluralism and the European Union, ELJ 12 (2006), S. 306 ff.

[41] Vgl. *Stefan Grundmann*, Methodenpluralismus als Aufgabe. Zur Legalität von ökonomischen und rechtsethischen Argumenten in Auslegung und Rechtsanwendung, RabelsZ 61 (1997), S. 423–453 zum Privatrecht und *Claudio Franzius*, Funktionen des Verwaltungsrechts im „Steuerungsparadigma" der Neuen Verwaltungsrechtswissenschaft, Die Verwaltung 39 (2006), S. 335–371, 370 zum Verwaltungsrecht. S. ferner *Konrad Hermann Theodor Schiemann*, Should we come together? Reflections on different styles of Judicial Reasoning, Zeit-

Allenfalls ist bei der methodischen Selbststeuerung des Rechtssystems „die" juristische Methode nicht vorgegeben. Sondern es hat einerseits, wie der erst in seinen Anfängen sich befindende Methodenvergleich zwischen verschiedenen europäischen Rechtsordnungen zeigt, jede Rechtsordnung eine relativ unterschiedliche methodische (etwa Gerichts- und Verwaltungs-)Praxis[42] sowie eine dazugehörige juristische Methodenlehre[43]. Es gibt also keinen europaweit rechtsordnungsübergreifenden Methodenmonismus. Andererseits konkurrieren seit eh und je verschiedene Theorieansätze um die Vorherrschaft bei der inhaltlich-begrifflichen Besetzung des Terminus „juristische Methode".[44]

Eine so verstandene, „pluralistisch" angelegte europäische juristische Methodenlehre scheint also eine Methodik der „Verwaltung" von Divergenz zu sein, und zwar zwischen den methodischen Praktiken (und den entsprechenden juristischen Methodiken) der Rechtsordnungen[45] in Europa und nicht eine Methodik einer vollständigen methodischen bzw. methodologischen Konvergenz[46], die ohnehin nicht in Sicht für die absehbare Zukunft wäre.[47]

---

schrift für Europarechtliche Studien 9 (2006), S. 1 ff.; *Marc Amstutz, Ouroboros* – Nachbemerkungen zum pragmatischen Methodenpluralismus, in: Festschrift für Pierre Tercier, hrsg. von Peter Gauch, Franz Werro, Pascal Pichonnaz, Zürich usw. 2008, S. 19–32; *Franz Reimer,* Vielfalt und Einheit juristischer Methoden, in: Festschrift für Jan Schapp zum siebzigsten Geburtstag, hrsg. von Patrick Gödicke, Horst Hammen, Wolfgang Schur, Wolf-Dietrich Walker, Tübingen 2010, S. 431–444.

[42] Vgl. *Martin Morlok/Ralf Kölbel/Agnes Launhardt*, Recht als soziale Praxis. Eine soziologische Perspektive in der Methodenlehre, Rechtstheorie 31 (2000), S. 15–46.

[43] *Stefan Vogenauer,* Die Auslegung von Gesetzen in England und auf dem Kontinent. Eine vergleichende Untersuchung der Rechtsprechung und ihrer historischen Grundlagen, 2 Bände, Tübingen 2001; *Ulrike Seif,* Die europäische Rechtsprechung zwischen „interprétation", „Rechtsfortbildung" und „case law", in: Reiner Schulze/Ulrike Seif (Hrsg.), Richterrecht und Rechtsfortbildung in der europäischen Rechtsgemeinschaft, Tübingen 2003, S. 1–23.

[44] S. etwa *Walter Krebs*, Die juristische Methode im Verwaltungsrecht, in: Eberhard Schmidt-Aßmann/Wolfgang Hoffmann-Riem (Hrsg.), Methoden der Verwaltungsrechtswissenschaft, Baden-Baden 2004, S. 209 ff.

[45] S. dazu etwa *Uwe Diederichsen*, Juristische Methodenlehre und praktische Jurisprudenz, in: Ulrich Immenga (Hrsg.), Rechtswissenschaft und Rechtsentwicklung. Ringvorlesung von Professoren der Juristischen Fakultät der Georg-August-Universität Göttingen, Göttingen 1980, S. 17–31.

[46] Vgl. *Luke Nottage*, Convergence, Divergence, and a Middle Way in Unifying or Harmonising Private Law, EUI Working Paper LAW no 2001/1, San Domenico 2001; *Walter Van Gerven*, Needed: A method of Convergence for Private Law, in: Andreas Furrer (Hrsg.), Europäisches Privatrecht im wissenschaftlichen Diskurs, Bern 2006, S. 437 ff. und allgemeiner *Gert Brüggemeier*, Einführung: Unterschiedliche Rechtskulturen – Konvergenz des Rechtsdenkens, in: Hans-Dieter Assmann/Gert Brüggemeier (Hrsg.), Unterschiedliche Rechtskulturen – Konvergenz des Rechtsdenkens, Baden-Baden 2001, S. 1 ff.; *Ernst A. Kramer*, Konvergenz und Internationalisierung der juristischen Methode, in: Heinz-Dieter Assmann/Gert Brüggemeier/Rolf Sethe (Hrsg.), Unterschiedliche Rechtskulturen – Konvergenz des Rechtsdenkens, Baden-Baden 2001, S. 31 ff.

[47] Vgl. auch *Karl Riesenhuber*, Europäische Methodenlehre – Einführung und Übersicht, in: Karl Riesenhuber (Hrsg.), Europäische Methodenlehre. Handbuch für Ausbildung und

Man muß daher zwischen (a) einer *gemeinen europäischen Methodik des Rechts*[48] und (b) eine *Methodik des Gemeinen Europäischen Rechts* (ius commune europaeum) klar unterscheiden. Wichtigste methodische Werkzeuge, um ein zeitgenössisches gemeines europäisches Recht zu schaffen, sind die Rechtsvergleichung und die Europäische Rechtsgeschichte. Für die Schaffung einer gemeinen europäischen juristischen Methodenlehre am wichtigsten sind die historische Methodenvergleichung und die Methodenvergleichung zwischen verschiedenen Rechtsordnungen innerhalb Europas.

5. Die juristische Methodenvergleichung[49] trägt (auf der theoretischen Ebene) zu einer *„horizontalen" Europäisierung der nationalen Rechtsordnungen* bei, ebenso wie die vergleichende und harmonisierende Auslegungsmethode auf rechtspraktischer Ebene.[50] Es ist zu erwarten, daß die Methodenvergleichung zu einer „methodischen Vernetzung"[51] und zu einem Vorgang der (wohl auch) methodischen

---

Praxis, Berlin 2006, S. 1–4, 4. S. ferner: *Gunther Teubner*, Legal irritants: good faith in British law, or how unifying law ends up in new differences, in: Francis Snyder (Hrsg.), The Europeanisation of law: the legal effects of European integration, Oxford 2000, S. 243–268 [Erstveröffentlichung: Modern Law Review 61 (1998), S. 11 ff.] sowie den immer noch lesenswerten Beitrag von *Bernhard C. H. Aubin*, Europäisches Einheitsrecht oder intereuropäische Rechtsharmonie? Grundfragen einer europäischen Zusammenarbeit im Privatrecht, in: Konrad Zweigert (Hrsg.), Europäische Zusammenarbeit im Rechtswesen, Tübingen 1955, S. 45–78. A.A. scheint *Peter Raisch* (Juristische Methoden. Vom antiken Rom bis zur Gegenwart, Heidelberg 1995, S. 221) zu sein: „Mag eine Vereinheitlichung der nationalen Rechte in Europa gegenwärtig ein utopisches Fernziel sein, einheitliche Anwendungsweisen der nationalen Rechte zu erreichen, erscheint durchaus denkbar".

[48] *Stefan Vogenauer*, Eine gemeineuropäische Methodenlehre des Rechts – Plädoyer und Programm, ZEuP 2005, σ. 234–263. *Michel Reinhardt*, Konsistente Jurisdiktion. Grundlegung einer verfassungsrechtlichen Theorie der rechtsgestaltenden Rechtsprechung, Tübingen 1997, S. 225 ff. spricht von einem „methodischen ius commune europaeum".

[49] S. *Hartmut Hahn*, Nationale Auslegungsmethoden, vergleichend betrachtet – europäische Anforderungen an die Methodenlehre, ZfRV, S. 163 ff.; *Günter Hager*, Rechtsmethoden in Europa. Tübingen 2009; *Thomas Henninger*, Europäisches Privatrecht und Methode. Entwurf einer rechtsvergleichend gewonnenen juristischen Merthodenlehre, Tübingen 2009. Vgl. auch *Thomas Kadner Graziano*, Die Europäisierung der juristischen Methode und die vergleichende Methode – Fallstudien, ZVglRWiss 106 (2007), S. 248 ff. sowie *Holger Fleischer*, Rechtsvergleichende Beobachtungen zur Rolle der Gesetzesmaterialien bei der Gesetzesauslegung, AcP 2011, S. 317–351 (veröffentlicht auch in: Juristische Studiengesellschaft Karlsruhe (Hrsg.), Jahresband 2010, Heidelberg, München, Landsberg, Frechen, Hamburg 2011, S. 125–160).

[50] S. auch *Peter Raisch*, Juristische Methoden. Vom antiken Rom bis zur Gegenwart, Heidelberg 1995, S. 220, wo aber die zwei Ebenen offenbar miteinander verwechselt werden: „Wenn eine rechtsvergleichende Studie der Rechtsfindungsmethoden in Europa viele Übereinstimmungen ergäbe, wäre für eine einheitliche Auslegung, z.B. der in den Mitgliedstaaten umgesetzten Richtlinien, der Weg geebnet und damit ein wichtiges Stück europäischen Rechtsvereinheitlichung erreicht".

[51] S. *Jürgen Basedow*, Nationale Justiz und europäisches Privatrecht – eine Vernetzungsaufgabe, Karlsruhe 2003. Vgl. *Olga Arnst*, Instrumente der Rechtsprechungskoordination als judikative Netzwerke?, in: Tobias Herbst/Matthias Kötter et al. (Hrsg.), Netzwerke, Baden-Baden 2007, S. 58 ff.; *dies.*, Grenzüberschreitende Verrechtlichungsprozesse: Einige Überle-

Koordinierung[52] der nationalen Rechtsprechungen führen wird.[53] Im Rahmen der Öffnung der äußeren Souveränität und damit eihergehenden Bildung eines Mehr-ebenen-Systems der Gerichtsbarkeit[54] mit Netzstruktur ist auch schon die Rede von einer „eher netzwerkähnlichen als hierarchischen, auf gegenseitige Selbst-Koordi-nation angelegten Organisation des Rechtsprechungsverbundes", der zusammen-gesetzt wird von nationalen Verfassungsgerichten, dem Europäischen Gerichtshof und dem Europäischen Gerichtshof für Menschenrechte,[55] aber auch von den na-tionalen Fachgerichten. Das Verhältnis der unterschiedlichen Rechtsprechungssy-steme zueinander ist durch eher *heterarchische Kopplungen*, das europäische judi-zielle (wie auch das administrative) Mehrebenensystem durch *Selbstheterarchisie-rung*[56] gekennzeichnet.

---

gungen zur Konzeptualisierung, in: Friedrich Arndt/Carmen Dege/Christian Ellermann/Ma-ximilian Mayer/David Teller/Lisbeth Zimmermann (Hrsg.), Ordnungen im Wandel. Globale und lokale Wirklichkeiten im Spiegel transdisziplinärer Analysen, Bielefeld 2008, S. 155–176.

[52] Im Hinblick auf die Koordination von juristischen Methodiken s. auch *Axel Metzger*, Allgemeine Rechtsgrundsätze im Europäischen Privatrecht: Ansätze für eine einheitliche Methodenlehre im europäischen Mehrebenensystem, Rechtstheorie 40 (2009), S. 313–335, 335.

[53] *Arnst*, Instrumente der Rechtsprechungskoordination als judikative Netzwerke?, a.a.O., S. 58 ff.; *Ilka Klöckner*, Grenzüberschreitende Bindung an zivilgerichtliche Präjudizien. Möglichkeiten und Grenzen im Europäischen Rechtsraum und bei staatsvertraglich angelegter Rechtsvereinheitlichung, Tübingen 2006.

[54] S. dazu etwa *Ingolf Pernice*, Die Dritte Gewalt im europäischen Verfassungsverbund, EuR 1996, S. 27 ff. Vgl. für den Fall der Verwaltung *Thorsten Siegel*, Entscheidungsfindung im Verwaltungsverbund. Horizontale Entscheidungsvernetzung und vertikale Entscheidungs-stufung im nationalen und europäischen Verwaltungsverbund, Tübingen 2009.

[55] *Stefan Oeter*, Rechtsprechungskonkurrenz zwischen nationalen Verfassungsgerichten, Europäischem Gerichtshof und Europäischem Gerichtshof für Menschenrechte, VVDStRL 66 (2007), S. 361–391, 388.

[56] S. demgegenüber zu strukturellen Kopplungen zwischen verschiedenen Gerichten bzw. Gerichtszweigen im Rahmen der *Selbsthierarchisierung* staatlich organisierter Rechtssysteme *Andreas Schemann*, Strukturelle Kopplung. Zur Festlegung und normativen Bindung offener Möglichkeiten sozialen Handelns, in: Werner Krawietz/Michael Welker (Hrsg.), Kritik der Theorie sozialer Systeme, Frankfurt am Main 1992, S. 215–229, 227/228. Zur evolutionären Errungenschaft der *Selbsthierarchisierung* staatlich organisierter Rechtssysteme im Sinne einer Asymmetrisierung der Verhältnisse, in denen rechtserzeugende Staatsorgane bzw. Rechtsnormtexte zueinander stehen, s. *Werner Krawietz*, Reine Rechtslehre oder System-theorie? Anfragen an eine analytische Jurisprudenz, in: ders., Recht als Regelsystem, Wies-baden 1984, S. 81–143, 133 ff. [zuerst veröffentlicht unter dem Titel: Reinheit der Rechts-lehre als Ideologie?, in: ders./Ernst Topitsch/Peter Koller (Hrsg.), Ideologiekritik und Demo-kratietheorie bei Hans Kelsen. Beiträge zu dem von der österreichischen Sektion der Inter-nationalen Vereinigung für Rechts- und Sozialphilosophie (IVR) vom 15. bis 17. Mai 1981 in Retzhof bei Graz veranstalteten gleichnamigen Symposion, Berlin 1982, S. 345–421]; *ders.*, Die Lehre vom Stufenbau des Rechts – eine säkularisierte politische Theologie?, in: ders./ Helmut Schelsky (Hrsg.), Rechtssystem und gesellschaftliche Basis bei Hans Kelsen, Rechtstheorie-Beiheft 5, Berlin 1984, S. 255–271; *Athanasios Gromitsaris*, Normativität und sozialer Geltungsgrund des Rechts. Zur Revision und Reformulierung der Normentheorie Theodor Geigers, Berlin 1992, S. 13 ff.

Man kann allerdings mit Grund erwarten, daß die zunehmende Intensivierung der vertikalen und horizontalen Europäisierung der nationalen Rechtsordnungen und die damit verbundenen immer größeren Schwierigkeiten bei der Identifizierung des primären und „echten" Ursprungs einer nationalen Regelung (nationaler, internationaler oder Gemeinschaftsgesetzgeber?) sowie der rechtspolitischen und rechtsethischen Prinzipien einer nationalen Rechtsordnung (rein nationale Rechtsordnung, Gemeinschafts- bzw. EU-Recht, gemeinsame europäische Rechtskultur, internationale Rechtsquellen?) in der Zukunft zu einer „Hybridisierung"[57] der Methodik des nationalen Rechts der Mitgliedsstaaten führen wird sowie zu internen Spannungen im Hinblick auf die Frage nach Homogenität.

Aus diesen Gründen wäre vielleicht besser von einem durchaus dezentralen „Netzwerk"[58] juristischer Methoden und Methodiken zu sprechen. Dieser im Begriff des Netzwerks innewohnende nicht statische, sondern durchaus dynamische Vorgangscharakter deutet gewissermaßen auf eine *Transnationalisierung juristischer Methodik*[59] im europäischen Rechtsraum hin. So gesehen wäre es m. E. nicht verfehlt, von der allmählichen Emergenz eines europäischen „*juristischen Methodenverbunds*"[60] zu sprechen. Es dürfte klar sein, dass die europäische juristische Methodenlehre nicht mit der Methodik des supranationalen Gemeinschafts- bzw. Unionsrechts zusammenfällt.[61] Die europäische juristische Methodenlehre sieht sich allerdings mit einem „rechtsmethodologischen Nationalismus"[62] und einem

---

[57] Zur Hybridisierung des Rechts s. *Andreas Fischer-Lescano/Lars Viellechner*, Globaler Rechtspluralismus, Aus Politik und Zeitgeschichte 34–35/2010 (http://www.bpb.de/apuz/ 32564/globaler-rechtspluralismus?p=all#fr-footnode42). S. auch *V. Heyvaert*, Hybrid Norms in International Law, London School of Economics, Law, Society and Economy Working Paper 6/2009.

[58] S. dazu etwa *Ino Augsberg*, Das „Gespinst des Rechts". Zur Relevanz von Netzwerkmodellen im juristischen Diskurs, Rechtstheorie 39 (2007), S. 479 ff.

[59] *Anne Peters*, Transnational law comprises constitutional, administrative, criminal and quasi-private law, in: Making Transnational Law Work in the Global Economy. Essays in Honor of Detlev Vagts, hrsg. von Pieter H.F. Bekker, Rudolf Dolzer, Michael Waibel, Cambridge 2010, S. 154–173 (https://ius.unibas.ch/uploads/publics/6919/20101124152339_4ced1 feb3ee74.pdf).

[60] Zum Begriff des Verbundes s. *Ingolf Pernice*, Theorie und Praxis des Europäischen Verfassungsverbundes, in: C. Calliess (Hrsg.), Verfassungswandel im europäischen Staaten- und Verfassungsverbund, 2007, S. 61 ff. S. auch *Armin von Bogdandy/Stephan Schill*, Die Achtung der nationalen Identität unter dem reformierten Unionsvertrag, ZaöRV 70 (2010), S. 701 ff., 705, nach derer Ansicht die Ordnungsidee des Verbundes „die Eigenständigkeit der Akteure und gleichzeitig ihr gegenseitiges Aufeinander-Angewiesen-Sein, das Rücksichtnahme und die Fähigkeit zu gemeinsamem Handeln" verdeutliche.

[61] Vgl. *Johannes Köndgen*, Editorial: Europäische Methodenlehre: zu wichtig, um sie nur den Europarechtlern zu überlassen, GPR 2005, S. 105. Zur Methodik des EuGH s. neuerdings etwa *Suvi Sankari*, European Court of Justice Legal Reasoning in Context, Groningen 2013.

[62] Vgl. etwa *Paul Kirchhof*, Verkehrspolitik im Lichte des deutschen Verfassungsrechts, DRiZ 1995, S. 253 ff., 259; *ders.*, Die Gewaltbalance zwischen staatlichen und europäischen Organen, JZ 1998, S. 965–974; *ders.*, Der europäische Staatenverbund, in: Armin von Bogdandy/Jürgen Bast (Hrsg.), Europäisches Verfassungsrecht. Theoretische und dogmatische

„rechtsmethodologischen Eurozentrismus"[63] konfrontiert und muß ihren Weg zwischen diesen beiden Polen finden.[64]

6. Aus der obigen Ausführungen folgt, dass die europäische juristische Methodik eine dominante Koordinationsrolle zu spielen hat bei der parallelen Koexistenz und der dynamischen Wechselwirkung zwischen nationalen, supra- und internationalen methodischen bzw. methodologischen Referenzsystemen in Europa. Dies scheint auch die epistemologische Aufgabe einer europäischen juristischen Methodenlehre als eigenständiger Disziplin (europäischer) Rechtswissenschaft zu sein – nicht mehr aber auch nicht weniger als dies. Diese Koordinierung darf allerdings auf keinen Fall im Sinne einer zentralen Steuerung mißverstanden werden. Es handelt sich hier um die interaktive wechselseitige Anpassung der oben genannten Systeme durch Vorgänge der Selbststeuerung und der gleichzeitig und parallel zueinander vor sich gehenden Koevolution derselben.[65]

Eine wirksame europäische juristische Methodenlehre sollte nicht einfach die bereits genannten methodischen bzw. methodologischen Subsysteme umfassen, sondern vor allem zwischen ihnen vermitteln, damit innerhalb des europäischen Rechtsraums „normative Kompatibilitäten"[66] und somit auch methodisch gültige

---

Grundzüge, 2. Aufl., Berlin/Heidelberg/New York 2009, S. 1009–1044. Zum Begriff des methodologischen Nationalismus s. *Christian Joerges*, Europäisierung als Prozess: Überlegungen zur Vergemeinschaftung des Privatrechts, in: Festschrift für Andreas Heldrich, hrsg. von Horst Eidenmüller, Stephan Lorenz, Alexander Trunk, Christiane Wendehorst, Johannes Adolff, München 2005, S. 205–224; *Jan M. Smits*, The Draft Common Frame of Reference. Methodological Nationalism and the Way Forward, European Review of Contract Law 4 (2009), S. 270–280; *Lucinda Miller*, The Emergence of EU Contract Law: Exploring Europeanization, Oxford 2011, S. 166 ff. [Es ist manchmal allgemeiner von „juristischem Nationalismus" (s. etwa *Jean-Louis Halpérin*, Entre nationalisme juridique et communauté de droit, Paris 1999), von „rechtsphilosophischem Etatismus" (s. *Lorenz Kähler*, Abschied vom rechtsphilosophischen Etatismus. Besteht ein notwendiger Zusammenhang zwischen Recht und Staat?, in: Gralf-Peter Calliess/Matthias Mahlmann (Hrsg.), Der Staat der Zukunft: Vorträge der 9. Tagung des Jungen Forum Rechtsphilosophie in der IVR, 27–29 April 2001 an der Freien Universität Berlin, Stuttgart 2002, S. 69–83) sowie von „epistemischem Nationalismus" (s. *Anne Peters*, Die Zukunft der Völkerrechtswissenschaft. Wider den epistemischen Nationalismus, ZaöRV 67 (2007), S. 721–776) die Rede]. Es sei nebenbei bemerkt, dass der Terminus „methodologischer Nationalismus" aus der Sozialtheorie stammt, s. *Herminio Martins*, Time and Theory in Sociology, in: J. Rex (Hrsg.), Approaches to Sociology: an introduction to major trends in British sociology, London 1974, S. 276 sowie *Daniel Chernilo*, Social Theory's Methodological Nationalism: Myth and Reality, European Journal of Social Theory 9 (2006), S. 5 ff. mit weiteren bibliografischen Angaben.

[63] Vgl. *E. Jayme/C. Kohler*, Europäisches Kollisionsrecht 2006: Eurozentrismus ohne Kodifikationsidee?, IPRax 2006, S. 537 ff.

[64] S. auch *Holger Fleischer*, Europäische Methodenlehre: Stand und Perspektiven, RabelsZ 75 (2011), S. 700–729, 706.

[65] Vgl. auch *Oliver Remien*, Einheit, Mehrstufigkeit und Flexibilität im europäischen Privat- und Wirtschaftsrecht, RabelsZ 62 (1998), S. 627 ff.

[66] *Marc Amstutz*, Normative Kompatibilitäten. Zum Begriff der Europakompatibilität und seiner Funktion im Schweizer Privatrecht, in: Astrid Epiney/Florence Rivière/Sarah Theuerkauf/Markus Wyssling (Hrsg.), Schweizerisches Jahrbuch für Europarecht 2004/2005, Bern

Interlegalität geschaffen werden kann. Ob eine derartige Vermittlung auch eine institutionelle Empathie[67] (fordern und) fördern wird, mag offen bleiben. Mancherorts ist von der Notwendigkeit der Bildung eines europäischen, transnationalen[68] Vertrauens die Rede, welche als ein sozialer Mechanismus der Ebenenverkopplung[69] zu rekonstruieren sei.[70] „Die Legitimation der Europäischen Union" – so heißt es – „speist sich ... aus dem wechselseitigen *Vertrauen* als Verschiedene, gerichtet auf den Erhalt von Differenz"[71]. Ob auch mit Blick auf die sich intensivierende methodische Vernetzung im europäischen Rechtsraum Vertrauen als Kategorie horizontaler Legitimation[72], – ganz gleich ob im Sinne eines sogenannten „regelorientierten" oder eher im Sinne eines „prinzipiengeleiteten" Vertrauens[73] – zu konzipieren ist, oder aber eher Mechanismen eines *institutionalisierten Mißtrauens*[74], also einer auf Dauer angelegten, wie auch immer (von gerichtlicher oder wissenschaftlicher Seite) organisierten, (womöglich) letztlich *vertrauens*konstituierenden, normativen Konsistenz- und Kompatibilitäts*kontrolle* vonnöten wären, mag dahin stehen und letztlich der Evolution des Rechtssystems überlassen bleiben.

Der Grad der „Autonomie" der europäischen juristischen Methodenlehre wird allerdings unter Berücksichtigung von zwei wesentlichen, höchst eigenwilligen, Merkmalen relativiert[75]: Erstens, der europäischen juristischen Methodenlehre kann

---

2005, S. 235–251. Vgl. *Kramer*, Konvergenz und Internationalisierung der juristischen Methode, a.a.O.

[67] *Marc Amstutz/Ramon Mabillard*, Fusionsgesetz (FusG) Kommentar zum Bundesgesetz über Fusion, Spaltung, Umwandlung und Vermögensübertragung vom 3. Oktober 2003, Basel 2008, S. 175 f. Zur „sympathetic consideration" durch einen transnationalen „Dialog der Gerichte" s. *Neil Walker*, Beyond boundary disputes and basic grids: Mapping the global disorder of normative orders, International Journal of Constitutional Law 6 (2008), S. 373–396.

[68] *Jan Delhey*, Nationales und transnationales Vertrauen in Europa, Leviathan 32 (2004), S. 15–45.

[69] Zu den Geboten der völkerrechts-, insbesondere der EMRK-konformen Auslegung und der gemeinschaftskonformen Auslegung als den zentralen methodischen Instrumenten der Verkopplung der (komplementären) Organe der Verfassungsgerichtsbarkeit im europäischen Verfassungsverbund s. *Stefan Oeter*, Rechtsprechungskonkurrenz zwischen nationalen Verfassungsgerichten, Europäischem Gerichtshof und Europäischem Gerichtshof für Menschenrechte, VVDStRL 66 (2007), S. 361–391, 378 ff., 390.

[70] *Claudio Franzius*, Europäisches Vertrauen? Eine Skizze, Humboldt Forum Recht 12/2010, S. 15 (http://www.humboldt-forum-recht.de/deutsch/12-2010/beitrag.html#41).

[71] *Claudio Franzius*, Europäisches Verfassungsrechtsdenken, Tübingen 2010, S. 85.

[72] *Franzius*, Europäisches Verfassungsrechtsdenken, a.a.O., S. 80.

[73] *Claudio Franzius*, Gewährleistung im Recht. Grundlagen eines europäischen Regelungsmodells öffentlicher Dienstleistungen, Tübingen 2009, S. 202 ff., 208 ff.

[74] Vgl. am Beispiel der Wirtschaftsprüfung *Torsten Strulik*, Nichtwissen und Vertrauen in der Wissensökonomie, Frankfurt/New York 2004, S. 153 ff.

[75] Vgl. *Thomas Henninger*, Europäisches Privatrecht und Methode. Entwurf einer rechtsvergleichend gewonnenen juristischen Methodenlehre, Tübingen 2009, S. 333: „... das europäische Privatrecht [befindet sich] im Schnittpunkt von autonomem Gemeinschaftsrecht und von nationalen Rechtsordnungen. Die zu entwickelnde Methode muß auf einem Konsens der einzelnen nationalen europäischen Methoden und der Besonderheiten des europäischen Pri-

nicht ein unmittelbar präskriptiver Inhalt zugesprochen werden, als ob sie eine traditionelle „Lehre über die Methode" wäre, wie es bei den herkömmlichen, etwa den nationalen, juristischen Methodenlehren der Fall ist[76]. Was diese Inhalte (also vor allem Anweisungen über die „richtige" Anwendung und Fortbildung des geltenden Rechts im Einzelfalle unter Miteinbeziehung der dazugehörigen Begründung und Argumentation) angeht, „verweist" die europäische juristische Methodenlehre auf die einzelnen methodologischen Referenzsysteme als ihre Komponenten. Diese Referenzsysteme bilden Methodiken *erster Ordnung*, während die europäische juristische Methodenlehre eine solche *zweiter Ordnung* darstellt.[77]

In unmittelbarem Zusammenhang mit dem ersten Merkmal steht ein zweiter Punkt: europäische juristische Methodenlehre *besteht* letztendlich *in* der dynamischen Ko-Evolution[78] der einzelnen juristischen Methoden und Methodiken (und zwar auf nationaler, internationaler, supranationaler Ebene) und in der Interaktion zwischen ihnen. Diese Eigenschaft verleiht der europäischen juristischen Metho-

---

vatrechts beruhen. Die Autonomie der europäischen Methodenlehre ist folglich durch die jeweiligen nationalen und gemeinschaftsrechtlichen Methoden beschränkt".

[76] Siehe allgemeiner *Axel Adrian*, Wie wisenschaftlich ist die Rechtswissenschaft? Gibt es eine bindende Methodenlehre?, Rechtstheorie 41 (2010), S. 521–548.

[77] Zur Frage nach der Möglichkeit eines wirklich autonomen europäischen Rechtsdenkens s. allgemeiner *Sjef van Erp*, Editorial: The Methodological Impossibility to Create Autonomous European Law, European Journal of Comparative Law Vol. 14.2., October 2010: „Autonomous legal thinking is simply impossible. What we should do when developing European concepts (...) is, realising the existing diversity, analyse the various aspects and elements of that diversity and from there on build a European concept. In this way, European concepts will not be totally disconnected from the laws of the Member States and at the same time Member States will not be able to claim the concept as their own for originating in their national legal tradition. Proceeding in this way, Europe could (and in my view: will) develop into a mixed legal system, or to be more precise: a mixed system *sui generis*".

[78] Vgl. mit Blick auf die Ko-Evolution von Gemeinschaftsrecht und nationalen Rechtsordnungen: *Ralph Christensen/Markus Böhme*, Europas Auslegungsgrenzen. Das Zusammenspiel von Europarecht und nationalem Recht, Rechtstheorie 40 (2009), S. 285–311, 285 ff. – Interessant in diesem Zusammenhang ist auch der Begriff der Ungleichzeitigkeit [vgl. etwa im Bereich des europäischen Verfassungsrechts: *Daniel Thym*, Ungleichzeitigkeit und europäisches Verfassungsrecht. Die Einbettung der verstärkten Zusammenarbeit des Schengener Rechts und anderer Formen von Ungleichzeitigkeit in den einheitlichen rechtlichen institutionellen Rahmen der Europäischen Union, Baden-Baden 2004; *Jürgen Bast/Philipp Dann*, European *Ungleichzeitigkeit:* Introductory Remarks on a Binational Discussion about Unity in the European Union, in: Philipp Dann/Michał Rynkowski (Hrsg.), The Unity of the European Constitution, Berlin/Heidelberg/New York 2006, S. 1–9], sowie der Begriff der Koordination (siehe z.B. für den Bereich des europäischen Verwaltungsrechts *Karl-Peter Sommermann*, Verwaltungskontrolle im Europäischen Verwaltungsraum: zur Synchronisierung der Entwicklung von Verwaltungsrecht und Verwaltungskontrolle, in: Verwaltungswissenschaft und Verwaltungspraxis in nationaler und transnationaler Perspektive. Festschrift für Heinrich Siedentopf zum 70. Geburtstag, hrsg. von Siegfried Magiera, Karl-Peter Sommermann, Jacques Ziller, Berlin 2008, S. 117–129).

denlehre den Charakter eines *Mehr-Ebenen-Systems*.[79] In der Tat könnte die europäische juristische Methodenlehre –verstanden in dem oben geschilderten Sinne als ein „System von Systemen"– als ein Mehr-Ebenen-System bezeichnet werden, wenn man in den nationalen, supra- und internationalen methodischen bzw. methodologischen (Sub-)Systemen zumindest analytisch getrennte „Ebenen"[80] erblicken würde. In diesem Fall sollte die Beziehung zwischen den Ebenen nicht als eine hierarchische betrachtet werden, sondern als deutlich heterarchisch. Letztendlich kann eins sicher sein, nämlich dass die europäische juristische Methodenlehre sich erst am Anfang eines langen und faszinierenden Entwicklungsprozesses befindet, da sie einen integralen Bestandteil jeglicher Bemühung um die Errichtung eines mehrdimensionalen europäischen Rechtsraums darstellt.

---

[79] *Udo Di Fabio*, Recht im Mehrebenensystem, in: Ines Härtel (Hrsg.), Handbuch Föderalismus – Föderalismus als demokratische Rechtsordnung und Rechtskultur in Deutschland, Europa und der Welt, Berlin/Heidelberg 2012, S. 981 ff. S. auch allgemeiner *Thomas König/ Elmar Rieger/Hermann Schmitt* (Hrsg.), Das europäische Mehrebenensystem, Frankfurt am Main/New York 1996.

[80] Zum Begriff der Ebene s. *Franz Mayer*, The European Constitution and the Courts. Adjudicating European constitutional law in a multilevel system, European Integration: The New German Scholarship, Jean Monnet Working Paper 9/03, S. 55 ff. (http://centers.law.nyu. edu/jeanmonnet/archive/papers/03/030901–03.pdf). S. ferner *Franz C. Mayer*, Multi-Layered and multi-levelled? Public law architectures for the 21st century. Review Essay on N. Bamforth und P. Leyland (Hrsg.), Public Law in a Multi-Layered Constitution, Oxford: Hart Publishing, 2003, Walter Hallstein-Institut für Europäisches Verfassungsrecht Paper 5/06 (2006) (http://www.whi-berlin.eu/documents/whi-paper0506.pdf).

A Weberian Moment for Europe?*

By *Massimo La Torre*

I.

Our age is no longer a quiet one. European integration cannot now be assumed as a matter of course. The "ever closer union" among European States is challenged. Such challenge should be taken seriously and dealt with. For this task it might be useful, I believe, to render more explicit the relevance of Max Weber's work in the present European predicament.

As a matter of fact, we are back to a Weberian moment in Europe, and the world. Weber had to face a fundamental theoretical and historical dilemma. On the one side, on the ground of philosophical self-identification of reality, there was Nietzsche's challenge launched by a reappraisal of truth conditions. Reality was seen as only disposable through interpretive acts and existential commitments, and these were conceptualized as irremediably concerned with life styles and power relations. Science neutrality was very much put into question. Weber constructively reacted to that sceptical attitude, which is not very dissimilar from the contemporary post-modernist challenge to social sciences. His strategy was to integrate some kind of perspectivist categorial framework within social studies, through the adoption of "ideal types", while however considering strong normativity a domain irremediably driven by pluralist forms of life and value *Weltanschauungen*. The contemporary debate in the political philosophy and sociology is again not very far from this sort of pluralist landscape.

Weber's "clash of Titans" may be seen as the metaphor that renders justice to contemporary value conflicts. Weber reconnected this constellation to the issue of secularization. The relationship between religion and politics (and law) was a central theme around which the modern State had to be analysed and explained. We are now back to this very *problématique*, given that migration has made of our society a multicultural compact and that consequently religious discourses have become again central when not dominant in public spheres.

The secular age is not just to be taken for granted as a past achievement, but as a task or a problem, even and perhaps especially in liberal societies. Such tension

---

* A previous version of this paper has been given at the Conference "State Reform for a Better Europe", organised by the *European Public Law Organisation* together with the *Alexander von Humboldt Foundation*, Athens, 30–31 May 2013. Many thanks to Patrick Birkinshaw and Agustin Menendez for suggestion and advice.

should in my view be assumed as one of the thematical areas around which a fruitful research programme in legal and social theory deserves to be developed. We need a public sphere that is at the same time inclusive and liberal, and a political culture that takes seriously both religion and a common space of deliberation and identity. This is not easily done. There is necessity indeed to devote much energy to such an issue.

II.

The other Max Weber's great question was the State. Weber saw how much the Nineteenth liberal model was eroded through social pluralism. National identity – he believed – could be considered a solution to pluralism and an integrating factor in the process of building up, consolidating and reproducing a stable and effective State structure. However, he was not confronted with the enormous pressure that we are now experiencing due to the massive migratory movements from poor countries. National identity becomes therefore a more controversial status.

On the other side, national identity feeds a sense of belonging that is sometimes intractable through constitutional provisions, in so far as membership is not considered in terms of a self-defining citizenship, but rather as given through prepolitical commitments. Democracy could thus be rendered a fight for groups whose characters could be neither reshaped nor accomodated through constitutional rules. The commonality of the political space would either be equivalent to nationality or it would become just a prudential calculus of cost and benefits in an contingent and fully unstable arena of trade-off and compromise. The European Union has faced and keeps facing a rather similar problem.

The principle of respect of national identity has been concretised in the Treaty of Lisbon (article 4.2) as a safeguard of national *constitutional* identities. That article is dense in normative content. Among the many norms that could be said to be comprised in it, perhaps two are the most fundamental: the principle of equality of Member States; the mandate to the European Union, and all its institutions, to regard the constitutional and political structure of the Member States as part of the wider unity that is the European Union. The latter mandate reflects the implicit premise that the European Union is legally and politically built on the basis of the collective of national constitutions and political systems. Nationality is here a supportive principle of constitutionalism and democracy in Weberian terms.

Respect of national constitutional identities implies the assumption that there is a European constitutional law, and that such law is built upon national constitutional laws. The beginning of the process of integration is indeed to be found in the national constitutional clauses that opened up and mandated for integration. That transformed the identity of the constitutional States of post-war Europe from autarchic to open States, to States that accepted the basic principle that a Social and Democratic *Rechtsstaat* could not be realised in a national autarchic fashion. Openness required being ready not only to share one's own competences, but also to consider as relevant how other Member States implemented fundamental rights and organised their democratic welfare.

European integration was a means of creating the proper breadth and scope of public power to protect the Social and Democratic *Rechtsstaat,* and in doing so defending the normative project of each and every Member State's national constitution. Common rules meant at the same time adapting the concrete means of giving force to the national constitutional project to what the other democratically grounded legal and political systems did. The recognition of national constitutional identity in the Treaty of Maastricht, later expanded in the Treaty of Lisbon, cannot but be regarded as reflecting this very same principle.

National constitutional identity offers a shield with which to protect national constitutions against self-generated integrative pressures. The principle of equality of Member States implies that European integration should be so structured as to avoid that the will of one or a very few Member States can be translated into the general will of the Communities. Moreover, the principle of respect of national constitutional identity might be read as containing the normative justification for national resistance to supranational decisions, not in the name of idiosyncratic components of national constitutional law, but appealing to the collective of national constitutions that European law is called to reflect and preserve. This task however should be able to deal with migration in a liberal way. Otherwise, national identity preservation could assume an antipluralist sense that would then backfire against the European integration project.

III.

The fact of value pluralism and the tension between European integration, national constitutions, and migratory phenomena: these are the two main areas around which European constitutionalism is now challenged. A few most recent decisions of both the Luxembourg European Court of Justice and of European constitutional courts force us to ask whether a Weberian approach based on the figure of nation State could still offer a perspective to European integration. The latter has recently been driven by a move that tries to reach a "closer union" and a quasi-federal supranational structure by downplaying the identity-producing character of National constitutionalism.

Constitutionalism is then reinterpreted just in terms of principles that are better disposed through European jurisdiction. This might remind us of some views adopted by Weber when discussing the prospect of a republican constitution for Germany. He – we remember – was committed to a strong executive and a more homogeneous federal structure.

However, Max Weber was radically sceptical about the objectivity of normative principles and values. His noncognitivism is well known and it was extreme. In his perspective therefore a legitimacy based only on substantive principles, on justice, could not be independent from the subject vindicating and producing the principles in question. *Werte*, values, in Weberian (and Nietzschean) terms are unavoidably *Wertungen*, evaluations, something that is the outcome of positive deliberation and volition. We should then conclude, if we believe that principles are not free-standing entities, and they need at least to be endorsed, especially by those that are going to be affected by them, that "the content of justice is simply too controversial to be identified other than through democratic means"[1].

But how much executive and jurisdictional federalism is compatible with the cultural and value pluralism that is nonetheless a defining feature of a European polity? The propelling energy that was produced through a long lasting juridical coup d'état (a ECJ jurisprudence indeed changing meaning and purport of the EC Treaty of Rome) can no longer fuel an integration process whose constitutional collateral damages for member States seem increasingly severe. Is there not a danger that the clash of titans till now filtered and civilised through the compromise of national constitutions will be reopened through an over strong supranational managerialism? Could supranational constitutional "principles" be an appropriate or better alternative to a constitutional polity as a sphere disposable by national legislatures? Is deliberation to be disconnected from representation?

Weber, as is well known, singled out three main sources for legitimacy in a political system. These are tradition, charisma, and legality. To the European Union tradition as a legitimacy ground seems to be precluded. A supra-national order, beyond national cultures, is a too novel an experiment in European history to be backed through a meaningful tradition. Charisma needs to be transmitted and shared as something like a common background of symbols and myths. In the present situation of pluralism and post-modern social dissipation such symbols and myths, however, are not really available beyond national frontiers (as its made evident by the anodyne European Union flag). Legality would seem to be the only reference left.

As a matter of fact, the stress several scholars put on the EU as *Rechtsgemeinschaft*, a "community of law", is but a development of a Weberian motive, especially in so far as legality is thought by Weber to be the specific source of legitimacy under modern conditions. Here legality means procedural rationality, "Legitimation durch Verfahren" (in Niklas Luhmann's wording), formal *Rechtsstaat,* and as such does not need immediately an additional democratic resource. The reference to "Amt" as feeding justification demands in the European Union takes the same route and could be easily equated with Weberian legitimacy.

However, Max Weber is aware that legality is not substantive enough as a standard to meet the need of a polity, of a State, that is now far from just being a night watchman: it has to deal with a strong demand for social rights and support. Legality is too "thin" for this task; it's not instrumental, or purposive enough. It cannot without contradicting itself take the route of a *Zweckprogramm* (again using Luhmann's cat-

---

[1] *D. Nicol*, "Can Justice Dethrone Democracy in the European Union? A Reply to Jürgen Neyer", Journal of Common Market Studies, 2012, p. 2.

egories). Legality as achitectural legitiming resource could be working only once the present (though very much weakened) Welfare State could be put back into the anachronic form of a Nineteenth century liberal State machine. But even the regulatory State that so often has been assimilitated to the EU machinery is not driven by a "conditional programe". It remains powerfully "purposive", "material", not "formal", though under different, economic priorities.

The question in any case remains whether the European Union legal may be considered a self-sufficient constitutional system. The Kadi ruling (case C-404/05 and C-415/05) of the European Court of Justice lavishly grants a self-contained dignity to the EU legal order before International law in terms that are denied to any domestic law. Fundamental rights as guaranteed in the European Charter later entrenched in the Lisbon Treaty have been once again proclaimed as derogative of member Statess' basic rights protection. The Melloni ruling (case C-399/12) is a renewed and vocal vindication of EU law primacy over the normative core off national constitutional orders. There is no national basic rights' *Wesensgehalt* that could resist the risk of compromising "the primacy, unity and effectiveness of EU law". National law-making is down-played to a sort of administrative function; its main task is just implementing primary and secondary EU law and regulatory measures. In this mood directives are boldly declared to have direct effect even before the end of the tranposition period granted to national legislations (case C-144/04, *Werner Mangold v. Rüdiger Helm*)[2].

Could European nation States that have usually been framed according to a dense catalogue of fundamental and social rights still be able to expand such rights to an increasing number of subjects? Actually, in the present crisis of the EMU whereby fiscal stability is prescribed to prevail on welfare rights, could we still honestly speak of a social agenda for EU member States? They do not seem any longer capable to meet citizens' expectations of a decent, widespread standard of well-being. How could then non-citizens, or migrants, be considered an opportunity and a resource for European integration? The future of European democracy and the moral quality of its society indeed depend on which answers we are able and willing to give to such questions.

IV.

Now, a response seems to be available through a generous enlargement of the very idea of constitutionalism. This enlargement is attempted in two more or less converging directions. On the one side, constitutionalism is diluted as concept and practice. It is now thought as a basic legal regulation or regularity within a certain scope. In this way whenever we have a normative practice or a social institution or even a social fact we should find a correspondent "constitution". For instance, since we face globali-

---

[2] Cf. *Alexander Somek*, The Emancipation of Legal Dissonance, in: F. Carbonell et al. (eds.), Hope, Reluctance or Fear? The Democratic Consequences of the Case Law of the European Court of Justice, ARENA, Oslo 2011, p. 87.

zation, and this takes the shape of some thick net of interactions, according to this view we should be able to single out an underlying constitutional basis. It is no longer important to assess the nature or quality of normative or social relationships.

There is no need to separate "public" from "private". As a matter of fact we do have a *lex mercatoria* acting as a kind of *Grundnorm* in international business, ergo we do have there a constitution. This is what some scholars call "societal coinstitutionalism". Or, according to a somewhat different perspective, we have a converging practice in civil or private law in Europe. There is a trend for a homogeneous regulation as far as contracts or consumers are concerned. This now could be done through non-public actors, and nonetheless be considered as the basic economic constitution of an emerging European polity.

In both these exercises the issue of legitimacy (a central one indeed for constitutionalism) is not raised. Or, if it is at all raised, it is solved as a question of output, of efficiency. A constitution is a set of regulations "for the people". Whether it is derivable "by the people" becomes a minor point, not really decisive for the quality of that practice. It will be in any case a constitution, if it can be used as a constitution by officers and reconstructed as such by scholars. The norm-user is now just a passive consumer, without access to the definition of the norm itself. If you like, all you are allowed to do is picking up and "sniffing" a norm for your private, personal use, but you cannot have the ambition to "cook" or sell it yourself.

A similar path is taken by what is now a little pompously called "global constitutionalism". The starting point here is not unsound. It is an intuition that the fact of globalisation is instilling in all of us. The arena for relevant social and political action reaches now much further beyond the precinct of a nation State. The second intuition following this first one and feeding "global constitutionalism" is that a public sphere could be possible even at a supranational level. Thus, a constitution that is a specific practice of shaping public spaces should also be admissible in a supranational dimension.

There is not anything conceptual, there is not any necessary connection, between a constitution and nation State. It's true, until now constitutions have been artifacts and practices taking place in the context of nation States. But this was matter of contingency, something appropriate to and required only by a specific historical stage of political evolution. We enter now into a different era. Global constitutionalism conceptually is no contradiction. This train of argument is plausible and might be agreed. However, a conceptual possibility does not immediately imply a practical chance of implementation.

There are two further features of a constitution that are equally relevant as the that of offering the basic rule for a social institution. A constitution is the basic rule for the "polity", meaning a scheme and a fact of mutual acknowledgment whereby people find a sense for their public life. This also means that the polity in question in principle is the one that makes it possible for the actor to perform the whole of her fundamental actions and furthermore to be protected in her fundamental needs. A polity is a space of social intercourse that makes a difference and that requires a special commitment.

A constitution makes it possible to articulate this special commitment as an exercise of autonomy and self-consciousnesss, in the sense that actors by a constitution are given the capacity of defining themselves the rules they will be going to abide by. This is the "constitutional moment", a special foundational practice common to the whole of social actors engaged and committed to the particular scheme of community.

But a "constitutional moment" is not just a historical moment. It can be conceptualised and also practised once there is an institutional path for channelling a formed public opinion and a system of political representation by which rule users are given voice and the capacity of effectively contributing to the making and applying of rules, of laws. This means that a constitution is not given and practised in an empty space or in a thin context of relationships where no "walls", no institutions, or representative structures are able to act properly.

We should somehow have a "people", not in the sense of an ethnic or national entity, or of a unified compact body, but of a concrete historical collective actor. It could also be "peoples" in the plural, that decide to undertake a common scheme of govermnent. But they should be given the capacity of trace back and assess this decision and to ascribe it to concrete subjects and their representatives.

Unfortunately, the necessity of such "constitutional moment" is not seriously taken into account by most global constitutionalists. The accent is given on the one side on the fact of a global net of rules, of a global "governance", that as such would imply the existence of a "global constitution". On the other side, the idea is that a constitution is the outcome of "constitutionalism", and that constitutionalism is a body of principles that could be implemented from above by agencies, administrators, "decisors" and judges. Constitutionalism is conceived in terms of a theory of adjudication, a special doctrine of how law should be used by courts, and of which substance those principle should be. Once judges (and "decisors") conform the requirements of such doctrine, then we shall have a constitution. Or it is equated with legal "pluralism", a system of now basically only vertical division of powers, with institutional bodies that check or refer the one the other in a circular way, while the balance between them is striken by a proportionality rule administered by courts.

The democratic deficit, that is the impossibile imputation of representation to supranational agencies that we are experiencing in the European Union, seems to be solved through the quality of the deliberation and expertise we find in such agencies. Procedural fairness, openess, publicity and adversarial fact-finding may all be guaranteed. In a different but not distant mood EU legitimacy is based on "office" *(Amt)* and "public good". That is, EU agencies are considered as already constrained by their being held by civil servants, or by their being engineered as a "public office", and institutional constraints on national sovereignty find their justification in the architectural purpose of the public good. Public power – it is claimed – is above all founded on the realisation of public good. However, this, "public good", is quickly equated with the "highly competitive social market" of the neo-liberal newspeech we are ministered in article 3 of the Treaty on European Union. "Price stability" as a special value to pursue is also attached to that wording. That is, public good at the end of the day is reconstructed as mostly private (the one that is produced through accelerated market competition) and it is connected to a particular substantive (and perhaps even idiosyncratic) economic doctrine. And all this would offer a sustainable substantive ground for the legitimacy of European Union governance, which is again an output-oriented legitimacy strategy.

Constitutionalism is thus once more seen not as a practise of self-definition of a comprehensive social project, based on the inclusion of the people affected. It is rather a dispute-settlement or management technique, that as such should be better put in the hands of an impartial Aristotelian *spoudaios, "the man of good character"*(1113a), possibly of a wise and more or less senior judge, or – why not? – of a Prussian *Beamte*.

Now, we can and do have a "global", or supranational judiciary, or disputes settlement agencies, for instance the European Court of Justice or the WTO. If these are wise enough to move along the path of constitutionalism (as a body of interpretive principles and procedural fundamental rights), well, gobal constitutionalists would say, it will not be an exaggeration to claim for this to be equivalent to the establishment of a "global constitutional" regime. International law, while assuming on the one side the shape of imperial rule, is increasingly formed not through treaties or intergovernmental conventions and agreements. There is a quickly developing number of supranational agencies, networks, NGOs, that is active in the interstices of international relations and deals with issues that have a strong technical purport. Here it is a kind of international administrative law that is growing, which could, in so far it is not imputable to any specific sovereign act, be envisaged as the promising ground for a next evolutionary step, an *international constitutional law*.

V.

What is now happening in Europe should teach us about the dangers of an over-stretched conceptual strategy. The economic and fiscal crisis after 2008 has severely hit European Union member States and especially Eurozone members. The narrative we were used to tell about a progressive movement of European integration cannot any longer be recounted. The grand, nearly Hegelian dialectics of an "ever closer Union" has been falsified.

Do have Greek, or Spanish, or Portuguese citizens more rights and more welfare now than in 1999? Is European Union membership offering a bonus of welfare and dignity to them? Constitutions of European member States have been quickly (and more or less silently) revised to include the principle of fiscal stability, indeed a requirement that, being connected to a specific economic policy frameork, should not be received in a constitution, that is in a context of basic rules that intend just to determine the most fundamental procedural and substantive criteria of a peaceful living together. Economic policies are contigency dependent; therefore they cannot find a room and should not be enshrined in a document that has the ambition of being durable and more or less permanent in time. The timing of a constitution is not the same of business management.

Policies that decide about the destiny of citizens are now dictated by agencies and actors that remain outside the territory and the cycle of their political representation, sometimes even in violation of explicit constitutional norms of the country affected. A first dramatic shift has been the change of the hierarchy and lexical priority between fundamental rights operated by the European Court of Justice. "Viking"(C-438/05) and "Laval"(C-341/05) rulings are a case in point, where social and political rights (the right to strike or to collective bargaining in labours relations) have been downgraded to the profit of the "four freedoms" that constitute the ideological core of European Treaties and the content of what is demanded as national legislation "rationality".

Actually – we should sadly confess – labour law has been dismantled by lawyers and "decisors". This especially happened in those countries where the European democratic deficit has assumed shrilling tones, that is, in member States that to cover their dramatic sovereign debt had to appeal to European solidarity, a European Financial Stabilty Fund (EFSF), that, under the present post-modern conditions, has taken the shape of a Luxemburger "société anonyme"[3]. Thanks to the novel constitutional amendments fiscal stability is to prevail over the once fundamental rights to education or health care. Public services are thus dismantled too. A crass sample of such brutal trend is the closing of the Greek public television last July. A robust welfare State seems to be no longer compatible with a strong European integration, certainly not with a strong common European currency.

In long years of European enthusiasm the EC principle forbidding discrimination on the basis of nationality has been reinterpreted in terms of a general market freedom, here indeed in partial violation of the originary spirit of the Treaty of Rome. European commission has been given powers of regulative "surveillance" that go beyond any sensible possible representative ascription. Policies to face the sovereign debts are competence of an agency, the Troika, an *Amt* that is clearly outside the cycle of political representation[4]. European Parliament, a gigantic, babelian body of professionals of national politics, has only co-decision powers, and not – as is

---

[3] Cf. *A. J. Menéndez*, De la crisis económica a la crisis constitucional de la Unión Europea, Eolas Ediciones, León 2012, pp. 96 ss.

[4] Actually there is a general crisis of political representation in European States that EU memberhip has only rendered acute. For general view, with special attention to the Italian case, cf. *F. Bilancia*, La crisi dell'ordinamento giuridico dello Stato rappresentativo, CEDAM, Padova 2000.

well known – in all the matters they are handled through European regulations. Legislative initiative is a strong privilege of the European Commission.

The European Council unanimity rule makes the Luxemburg court de facto immune or irresponsible to whatever representative body within the Union, since there is no practicable way to counteract its decisions. It is inconceivable to change primary and even secondary EU law to stop a jurisprudential line or position taken by the ECJ. It is, on the contrary, EU primary and secondary law, and national constitutions, that are amended in order to comply with ECJ case law. It has never been done.

Now, we find scholars that try to depict the European Union institutional mess and democratic immaturity (or senility?) as still a form of "multilevel" constitutionalism, or a sample of "global constitutionalism". Sometimes, this technocratic, baroque institutional building is even conceptualised as an "evolution" from the obsolete State form that has finally reached its own institutional "Aufhebung", "sublation". It is a parlance that is just dodging or downplayng the dramatic proportion of our political crisis.

We are quickly driving towards a form of "polity" ("republic"?), or "State", or "Bund", it doesn't matter very much which of them, where rules are just a matter of happy "few", holding a special "office", well entrenched beyond national borders in a park, a kind of Elysium, whose shining fields normal citizens are not permitted to enter; and they cannot let hear their voice. Albert Hirschmann taught us that an alternative strategy to "voice" could be "exit". But it seems that this is not an option either for those poor, increasingly impoverished and disempowered Europeans trapped (for ever?) in the European Monetary Union.

In Max Weber's spirit, should we again, to recover a viable public space and a sense for collective action, hope in the resurrection of nation State? Or, perhaps again in Weber's or better in Friedrich Naumann's spirit, should we wait for the epiphany of a new (though "unwilling") benevolent European hegemon, to rule a great political space that marks the definitive demise of the old State form?

A Short Bibliography

Aristotle, Ethics, English translation by J. A. K. Thomson, London, 1976.

Avbelj, M. / *Komárek*, J., Constitutionalism Pluralism and Beyond, Oxford, 2012.

Azzariti, G., Il costituzionalismo moderno può sopravvivere? Roma, 2013.

Beck, U., German Europe, London, 2013.

Calhoun, C. / *Mendieta*, E. / *Van Antwerpen*, J. (eds.), Habermas and Religion, London, 2013.

Carbonell, F. / *Menéndez*, A. J. / *Fossum*, J. E. (eds.), Hope, Reluctance or Fear? The Democratic Consequences of the Case Law of the European Court of Justice, Oslo, 2011.

Couch, C., Post-democarcy, London, 2004.

Dobner, P. / *Loughlin*, M., The Twilight of Constitutionaalism. Demise or Transmutation? Oxford, 2010.

Fossum, J. E. / *Menéndez*, A. J., The Constitution's Gift. A Constitutional Theory For a Democratic European Union, London, 2011.

Foucault, M., The Essential Works, 3 vols., London, 2002.

Goulard, S. / *Monti*, M., La democrazia in Europa. Guardare lontano, Milano, 2012.

Habermas, J., Nachmetaphysisches Denken II, Frankfurt am Main, 2012.

– The Crisis of European Union. A Response, London, 2012.

– Im Sog der Technokratie, Frankfurt am Main, 2013.

Hirschmann, A. O., Exit, Voice and Loyalty: Response to Decline in Firms, Organisations, and States, Cambridge, Mass., 1990.

Krisch, N., Beyond Constitutionalism. The Pluralist Structure of Post-National Law, Oxford, 2012.

Luhmann, N., Legitimation durch Verfahren, Frankfurt am Main, 1973.

Menéndez, A. J., De la crisis económica a la crisis constitucional de la Unión Europea, León, 2012.

Naumann, F., Mitteleuropa, Berlin, 1915.

Nicol, D., The Constitutional Protection of Capitalism, Oxford, 2010.

Niglia, L. (ed.), Pluralism and European Private Law, Oxford, 2013.

Piris, J.-C., The Future of Europe: Towards a Two-Speed EU? Cambridge, 2011.

Poiares Maduro, M. / *Azoulai*, L. (eds.), The Past and Future of EU Law. The Classics of EU Law Revisited on the 50th Anniversary of the Rome Treaty, Oxford and Portland, Oregon, 2009.

Schönberger, Dh., "Hegemon wider Willen. Zur Stellung Deutschlands in der Europäischen Union", Merkur, 1/2012.

Somek, A., Individualism, Oxford, 2008.

Somek, A. / *Wydra*, D. (eds.), Is There a European Common Good?, Baden-Baden, 2013.

Streeck, W., Gekaufte Zeit. Die vertagte Krise des demokratischen Kapitalismus, Frankfurt am Main, 2013.

Taylor, Ch., A Secular Age, Cambridge, Mass., 2007.

Tsagourias, N. (ed.), Transnational Constitutionalism, Cambridge, 2007.

Walker, N. / *Shaw*, J. / *Tierney*, St. (eds.), Europe's Constitutional Mosaic, Oxford, 2011.

Watkins, S., "The European Impasse", The London Review of Books, Vol. 35, No. 16, 2013.

Weber, M., Gesammelte Politische Schriften, Tübingen, 1988.

– Wirtschaft und Gesellschaft, Tübingen, 1980.

Zweiter Teil

**Krisenbewältigung und Gegenstand der Reform:
Zur Reform als Krisenausweg /
Crisis Management and Reform Agenda:
On Reform as a Way Out of the Crisis**

Res Publica semper reformanda est

Zur Funktion des Rechts im Rahmen einer Staatsreform

Eine Skizze in 15 Thesen

Von *Martin Schulte*

> Die heute prominenten Reformer sind, …,
> nicht mehr Zielstreber, sondern Defektflüchter.
> (*Niklas Luhmann*, Organisation und Entscheidung, 2000, S. 344
> unter Bezugnahme auf Odo Marquard)

I. (Staats)Reform:
Begriffsgeschichte – Begriffskonnotationen – Begriffsbildung

1. Reformbedarf für Organisationen gesellschaftlicher Funktionssysteme ist offensichtlich nicht rechtfertigungsbedürftig. Ecclesia semper reformanda ist längst zum geflügelten Wort geworden. Jede Generation von Lehrern und Schülern weiß aus eigener Anschauung von Schulreformen oder gar „Reformschulen" zu berichten. Und das Thema „Staatsreform" ist so alt, dass es im Verlaufe einer nun bald ein Jahrzehnt währenden globalen Finanzkrise wohl bloß sein déjà vu erlebt.

2. Begriffsgeschichtlich[1] entstammt der Reformbegriff dem französischen Sprachkreis und findet erst im 18. Jahrhundert Eingang in die deutsche Sprache. Begriffsgegenständlich erstreckt er sich zunächst vor allem auf den kirchlichen, aber auch auf den militärischen Bereich. Von Anfang an formuliert Reform eine Beziehung zum Staat und seinen Institutionen. Dabei geschieht dies insbesondere in Abgrenzung zum Begriff der „Revolution", wonach Reform als „nicht-revolutionäre, die Substanz des bisherigen Zustands bewahrende Veränderung" begriffen wird. Insgesamt erfährt der Reformbegriff im 18. Jahrhundert jedoch eine eher zurückhaltende Verwendung. Dies ändert sich erst im Verlaufe des 19. Jahrhunderts, in dem sein Gebrauch selbstverständlich wird. Reform sei das „gesunde, wohlgeordnete Staatsleben" selbst, während ihr Ausbleiben zur Revolution führe. Allerdings fächert sich der Reformbegriff von der Mitte des 19. Jahrhunderts (im Nachgang zur gescheiterten Deutschen Revolution von 1848) dann immer stärker auf, wird zunehmend konturlos und erleidet schließlich in der zweiten Hälfte des 20. Jahrhunderts das Schicksal völliger inhaltlicher Beliebigkeit.

---

[1] Siehe zum Folgenden ausführlich *Wolgast*, Reform, Reformation, in: Brunner/Conze/Koselleck (Hrsg.), Geschichtliche Grundbegriffe, Bd. 5, 1994, S. 313, 339 ff.

3. Mit dem Begriff der Reform wird nicht selten die Konnotation verbunden, dass es dabei um etwas Neues gehe. Etwas anspruchsvoller formuliert werden Reform und Innovation miteinander in Verbindung gebracht. Insoweit ist zunächst anzumerken, dass Reform in begriffsgeschichtlicher Perspektive keineswegs immer Innovation bedeutet hat. Im Mittelalter ging es vielmehr um die „Reaktualisierung eines bewährten Vorbilds aus der Vergangenheit", z. B. eines Idealbilds des Reichs oder der Kirche.[2] Darüber hinaus gilt es, das Neue als besonders „zerbrechlich" und „flüchtig" zu begreifen. Definiert sich das Neue doch nur über die „Negation des Überkommenen". Und wie sehr wohnt dem Neuen doch die Tendenz inne, alt zu werden; das Schicksal der sog. „Postmoderne" mahnt zur Vorsicht. Schließlich fast paradoxal wird der Bezug auf das Neue, wenn mit dem Begriff der Reform die Vorstellung einer „Planung der Neuheit" einhergeht.[3]

4. Auch die Konnotation, dass mit der Reform alles besser werde – erneut anspruchsvoll formuliert in der Verbindung von Reform und Fortschritt – ist begriffsgeschichtlich nicht zu belegen. So war mit Fortschritt im Mittelalter ein Prozess gemeint, „durch den etwas im Inneren heranwächst", was aber nicht notwendigerweise hieß, „dass es eine Veränderung im Sinne einer Umwandlung in etwas Anderes – und noch weniger in etwas Besseres – gab."[4] Darüber hinaus befindet sich der Fortschrittsgedanke in einer unheiligen Allianz mit dem historischen Entwicklungsdenken. Ihm hat er als Fortschrittsglaube lange Zeit Pate gestanden.[5] Wer aber in Entwicklungslinien denkt[6] und damit Fortschritt verbindet, dessen deterministisches Weltbild kennt keine unerwarteten „jumps".

5. Lässt man deshalb solche Begriffskonnotationen mit Grund beiseite, so hat sich die Begriffsbildung aus der Perspektive einer soziologischen Theorie des Rechts, die sich der Systemtheorie Niklas Luhmanns verpflichtet weiß, zunächst einmal auf das System zu beziehen, in dem die Reformen umgesetzt werden sollen. Das ist in unserem Untersuchungskontext das politische System. Des Weiteren ist zu beachten, dass man nicht das System selbst, also die Politik, die Religion oder die Erziehung reformiert, sondern dass die Reformversuche die in diesen wirkenden Organisationen, sprich Staat, Kirche oder Schule, zum Gegenstand haben.[7] Hintergrund dafür ist ein Verständnis von Reform, das diese als beobachtete und auf Entscheidungen

---

[2] Siehe dazu insb. *Esposito*, Geplante Neuheit: die Normalität der Reform, in: Corsi/dies. (Hrsg.), Reform und Innovation in einer unstabilen Gesellschaft, 2005, S. 51.

[3] Siehe dazu *dies.*, ebd., S. 51 f.

[4] *Dies.*, ebd.

[5] *Koselleck*, Fortschritt, in: Brunner/Conze/Koselleck (Hrsg.), Geschichtliche Grundbegriffe, Bd. 2, 1975, S. 351 ff.; *ders.*, ‚Fortschritt' und ‚Niedergang' – Nachtrag zur Geschichte zweier Begriffe, in: ders., Begriffsgeschichten, 2006, S. 159 ff.; *Ritter*, Fortschritt, in: ders. (Hrsg.), Historisches Wörterbuch der Philosophie, Bd. 2, 1972, Sp. 1032 ff.

[6] Siehe nur *Wahl*, Entwicklungspfade im Recht, JZ 2013, 369 ff.

[7] Ebenso *Baecker*, Die Reform der Gesellschaft, in: Corsi/Esposito (Hrsg.), Reform und Innovation in einer unstabilen Gesellschaft, 2005, S. 61, 65 ff.; *Corsi*, Reform – zwischen Organisation und Gesellschaft, ebd., S. 79 ff.

zurückzuführende Veränderung begreift. Und es ist eben gerade dieses Merkmal der Entscheidung, welches Organisationen kennzeichnet.[8]

II. Funktionsverlust des Rechtssystems: Krise und Reform

6. Auf dieser Grundlage eröffnet Recht – funktional betrachtet – eine zeitliche Dimension, indem Kommunikation „in zeitlicher Extension ihres Sinnes" an Erwartungen orientiert wird und zwar in dem Sinne, sich „auf der Ebene der Erwartungen auf eine noch unbekannte, genuin unsichere Zukunft einzustellen".[9] Recht hat es folglich primär mit dem „Aufbau von Erwartungserwartungen" zu tun.[10]

7. Die zeitstabile Erwartungssicherung durch das Recht erzeugt Anlass für die Unterscheidung von Konsens und Dissens, an der sich soziale Spannungen im Sinne einer Bifurkation entzünden. Das Problem dieser Spannung von Zeit- und Sozialdimension wird vom Recht erfasst und in der Kombination der Unterscheidungen kognitiv/normativ des Erwartens sowie Recht/Unrecht der Codierung verarbeitet. Dadurch ermöglicht es, gesellschaftliche Komplexität auch unter den Bedingungen evolutionärer Steigerung auszuhalten.[11]

8. Wo immer von der Funktion sozialer Systeme die Rede ist, wird nicht selten zugleich ihr Funktionsverlust thematisiert. So gehe die klassische, Generationen verbindende Großfamilie im Zeichen der modernen „Patchwork-Family" mehr und mehr ihrer angestammten Funktion verlustig. Auch die Religion beklagt ihren Funktionsverlust in einer zunehmend säkularisierten Gesellschaft, die sich immer mehr an kurzlebigen „events" und immer weniger an christlichen Grundwerten orientiere. Für das Rechtssystem gilt nichts anderes, wie die aktuellen Diskussionen um das Steuer- und das Steuerstrafrecht anschaulich belegen. Es fertigt dabei eine Selbstbeschreibung von sich an, die durch zahlreiche Stereotype gekennzeichnet ist. Das geläufigste ist regelmäßig, dass sich alles in der „Krise" befinde.[12] Unabweisbar sei eine „Krise des (regulativen) Rechts".[13] Und wem das nicht reicht, der sieht gar den gesamten

---

[8] *Luhmann*, Organisation und Entscheidung, 2000, passim; siehe aber auch *ders.*, Die Religion der Gesellschaft, 2000, S. 244 ff.

[9] *Ders.*, Das Recht der Gesellschaft, 1993, S. 130.

[10] *Gephart*, Gesellschaftstheorie und Recht, 1993, S. 98 f.; vgl. insb. *Chanos*, Erwartungsstruktur der Norm und rechtliche Modalisierung des Erwartens als Vorgaben sozialen Handelns und Entscheidens, in: Krawietz/Welker (Hrsg.), Kritik der Theorie sozialer Systeme, 1992, S. 230 ff.

[11] *Luhmann*, Das Recht der Gesellschaft, S. 126, 130 f.

[12] Zum Status von Krisen siehe insb. *Di Fabio*, Das Recht offener Staaten, 1998, S. 9 f.; vgl. auch *Merkel*, Krise?, Krise!, FAZ Nr. 104 v. 6.5.2013, S. 7; *Schümer*, Die endlose Krise ist ein Machtinstrument. Ein Gespräch mit Giorgio Agamben, FAZ Nr. 119 v. 25.5.2013, S. 44.

[13] *Günther*, Der Wandel der Staatsaufgaben und die Krise des regulativen Rechts, in: Grimm (Hrsg.), Wachsende Staatsaufgaben – sinkende Steuerungsfähigkeit des Rechts, 1990, S. 51 ff.

„Verwaltungsstaat", noch weiterreichend den „Rechtsstaat" oder sogar die „Repräsentative Demokratie" in der Krise.[14]

9. Man wird nun aber andererseits auch nicht so weit gehen müssen, den vermeintlichen Funktionsverlust sozialer Systeme und die damit einhergehenden Krisenszenarien als „optische Täuschung" zu diskreditieren.[15] Das Krisengerede beansprucht nämlich zumindest Aufmerksamkeit im Rechtssystem, die sich nicht selten im Ruf nach „dringend notwendigen Reformen" niederschlägt. Rechtspraxis und Rechtsdogmatik sehen sich dann aufgerüttelt und alarmiert, ihre bisher eingenommenen Positionen erneut zu reflektieren und sich des eigenen Standorts zu vergewissern. Damit leisten sie einen nicht zu unterschätzenden Beitrag zur Identitätsbildung im Rechtssystem. Aus der Perspektive einer soziologischen Theorie des Rechts ist insoweit allerdings Zurückhaltung geboten. Denn nicht jedes Krisengerede oder noch so dramatisch gezeichnete Krisenszenario ist bereits Ausdruck einer Krise. Vielmehr gilt es, sich der Kontingenz wahrheitsbeanspruchender Beschreibungen bewusst zu sein und deshalb einen bloßen Wandel des Gegenstandes, des Beobachters oder gar nur der Begrifflichkeit für zumindest ebenso wahrscheinlich zu halten.[16]

10. Für das Rechtssystem ist sein vermeintlicher Funktionsverlust aber zumeist Anlass für den Versuch, im Rahmen von Reformbemühungen die Steuerungsfähigkeit des Rechts wieder zu erlangen. Beispielhaft sei auch an dieser Stelle nur die Diskussion um die Abschaffung oder zumindest auf eindeutige Bagatellfälle begrenzte Möglichkeit der steuerstrafbefreienden Selbstanzeige des Steuerschuldners genannt. Dem Ansatz liegt die Annahme zugrunde, dass sich die Rechtswissenschaft nicht darauf beschränken dürfe, „Rechtsregeln, Figuren, Institute und Lehrsätze dogmatisch auszuformen", sondern sich zugleich mit den Wirksamkeitsbedingungen des Rechts[17] zu beschäftigen habe.[18] Allerdings erweist sich das dahinter stehende handlungstheoretische, akteurbezogene Steuerungskonzept[19] als rechts- und gesellschaftstheoretisch unterkomplex, weil verkannt wird, dass Steuerung nur als Vergrö-

---

[14] *Pitschas*, Verwaltungsverantwortung und Verwaltungsverfahren, 1990, S. 48; *Grimm*, Der Wandel der Staatsaufgaben und die Krise des Rechtsstaats, in: ders. (Hrsg.), ebd., S. 291 ff.; VVDStRL 72 (2013): Repräsentative Demokratie in der Krise?

[15] So aber *Luhmann*, Das Recht der Gesellschaft, S. 154.

[16] *Di Fabio*, Das Recht offener Staaten, S. 9 f.

[17] Siehe nur *Hof/Lübbe-Wolff* (Hrsg.), Wirkungsforschung zum Recht I. Wirkungen und Erfolgsbedingungen von Gesetzen, 1999, passim.

[18] *Voßkuhle*, „Schlüsselbegriffe" der Verwaltungsrechtsreform, VerwArch 92 (2001), 184, 194 f.

[19] Erfreulich differenzierend *Mayntz*, Politische Steuerung: Aufstieg, Niedergang und Transformation einer Theorie, in: dies., Soziale Dynamik und politische Steuerung, 1997, S. 263, 286

ßerung oder Verringerung spezifischer Differenzen durch Selbststeuerung zu begreifen ist.[20]

III. Die Poesie einer Staatsreform

11. All dies mag für die „Verfechter" und für den „Erfolg" von Reformen auf den ersten Blick nicht gerade ermutigend klingen, soll aber andererseits keineswegs bedeuten, auf Reformen etwa ganz und gar verzichten zu können. Plädiert wird vielmehr für eine Beobachtung und Beschreibung von „Reform", die bei aller mit ihr verbundenen Planung und Steuerung ihre Einbettung in die Realität der Evolution nicht unberücksichtigt lässt. Reform und Planung sind eine „Komponente der Evolution des Systems".[21]

12. Reformen sind ressourcenabhängig.[22] Sie sind Ausdruck einer Veränderungsplanung, die sich zwischen Vergangenheit und Zukunft bewegt. Ihre „strukturelle Dynamik" gewinnen sie aus einer Kombination von „verschwiegenem Vergessen" und „gezieltem Unterlassen". Verschwiegenes Vergessen meint dabei, dass der Ruf nach Reformen voraussetzt, die Gründe zu vergessen, aus denen frühere Reformen gescheitert sind. Die Entstehungsgeschichte der abgabenrechtlichen Vorschrift, die der Selbstanzeige des Steuerschuldners strafbefreiende Wirkung beimisst, kann dafür ein weiteres Mal als Beispiel dienen. Mit gezieltem Unterlassen lässt sich demgegenüber der Umstand beschreiben, dass zu den wichtigsten Ressourcen von Reformen zählt, die Ergebnisse einer Reform nie zu evaluieren. Auch dafür ein Beispiel, diesmal aus dem Bereich des Erziehungssystems: Die neunjährige gymnasiale Schulausbildung wurde in Deutschland vor einigen Jahren nahezu flächendeckend durch das sog. „Turboabitur" mit acht Jahren gymnasialer Verweildauer ersetzt, um nunmehr fast ebenso flächendeckend und ohne die Wirkungen der sog. G8-Reform auch nur abzuwarten, vor allem aber selbstredend ohne jede Evaluation der Reform, wieder zur neunjährigen gymnasialen Schulausbildung zurückzukehren.

13. Reformen sind leicht anzustoßen. Ihr Ausgangspunkt ist in aller Regel ein gemeinhin konstatierter, häufig als „Krise" deklarierter Missstand, der in den Zeitkontext von (schlechter) Vergangenheit und (besserer) Zukunft eingeordnet wird.[23] Inhaltlich lassen sich Reformen dann entweder als „bessere Anpassung an Ideen" oder als „bessere Anpassung an Realitäten" kennzeichnen.[24] Natürlich darf die „Realität" dabei nicht ontologisch, sondern nur konstruktivistisch als das verstanden werden, was das System als solche wahrnimmt. So geht das Rechtssystem gegenwärtig

---

[20] *Luhmann*, Das Recht der Gesellschaft, S. 154; *ders.*, Steuerung durch Recht? Einige klarstellende Bemerkungen, ZRSoz 12 (1991), 142, 143 f.; *ders.*, Politische Steuerung: ein Diskussionsbeitrag, PVS 30 (1989), 4 ff.

[21] *Ders.*, Organisation und Entscheidung, S. 356.

[22] Dazu und zum Folgenden eingehend *ders.*, ebd., S. 338 ff.; *ders.*, Das Erziehungssystem der Gesellschaft, 2002, S. 166 f.

[23] Siehe dazu auch *Männle*, Verwaltung (in) der Gesellschaft, 2011, S. 338.

[24] *Luhmann*, Organisation und Entscheidung, S. 336.

von schwindender Steuerehrlichkeit und gleichzeitigen Ungerechtigkeiten im Steuerstrafrecht aus, um es deshalb im Wege der Reform an die „Realität" anzupassen.[25]
Zur Beglaubigung der Reform wird dabei übrigens ein nicht unbeträchtlicher seman-
tischer Apparat, „bestehend aus Prinzipien, Normen, evaluativen Standards, Statistiken, Bilanzen", mitgeschleppt.[26] Wem nimmt man eine Reform des Steuerstraf-
rechts schon ohne umfängliche Statistiken zur Kapitalabwanderung ins Ausland,
zum Umfang steuerlicher Veranlagung entzogenen Kapitals, zur Entwicklung steuerlicher Selbstanzeigen usw. usw. ab?

14. Reformen sollen Erfolg haben. Dies hängt damit zusammen, dass Organisationen, die Gegenstand von Reformen sind, als Systeme rationaler Problemlösung
begriffen werden.[27] Und dennoch scheitern Reformen – ungeachtet aller „mechanisms of hope"[28] – in aller Regel. Das muss allerdings kein Grund zur Besorgnis
sein, wenn man ihre Funktion nur dahingehend beschreibt, dass sie Interessenunter-
schiede sichtbar machen, die anderenfalls latent geblieben wären. Reformen ermöglichen damit eine kontroverse Selbstbeschreibung des Systems und einen Widerstand
desselben gegen sich selbst, der im Gegensatz zur Differenz von Problem und Problemlösung zu einem „besseren Verständnis von Realität" beiträgt.[29] Und dies ist
wahrlich kein kleiner Beitrag zur Systemrationalität.

15. Reformen gehört die Zukunft. So paradox dies klingen mag, so deutlich sei
noch einmal hervorgehoben, dass es nicht darum geht, für die Zukunft einen Reform-
verzicht vorzuschlagen. Reform ist, wenn sie vorkommt, ein Moment von Evolution.
Allerdings muss Reform, und das gilt auch für eine Staatsreform, in Kauf nehmen,
dass unbekannt ist und bleibt, was künftige Entscheidungen aus ihr machen. Im
Zweifel wartet die „Gegenreform" immer schon ante portas. Und was aus diesem
„Mysterium der ‚permanenten Reform'"[30] wird, stellt sich einzig und allein durch
Evolution heraus.[31]

---

[25] Zu weiteren Beispielen aus dem Bereich der Verwaltung siehe *Männle*, Verwaltung (in)
der Gesellschaft, S. 338.

[26] *Luhmann*, Organisation und Entscheidung, S. 339.

[27] *Ders.*, ebd., S. 336 f.

[28] *Baecker*, Die Reform der Gesellschaft, in: Corsi/Esposito (Hrsg.), Reform und Innovation in einer unstabilen Gesellschaft, S. 61, 65 f.

[29] *Luhmann*, Organisation und Entscheidung, S. 337; vgl. auch *Baecker*, ebd., S. 69, 71, 78,
der nicht zuletzt die Vergrößerung kommunikativer Optionsspielräume in Organisationen als
Reformerfolg begreift.

[30] *Corsi/Esposito*, Einleitung, in: dies., Reform und Innovation in einer unstabilen Gesellschaft, S. 1, 5; vgl. auch *Brunsson*, Reform als Routine, ebd., S. 9, 19.

[31] *Luhmann*, Die Gesellschaft der Gesellschaft, 1997, S. 347, 354, 430 mit Blick auf den
Gedanken der Planung.

Administrative Reform in Greece:
Public administration evolves through self-reflection – not borrowed identities

By *Panagiotis Karkatsoulis*

Introduction

The polymorphic crisis has poised a central question to every country enduring it: Which administration, what kind of State and what quality of institutions are apt to respond to a new economy? In other words, what kind of institutions do we need, so that to strengthen the societal capacity to avoid the repetition of such disastrous phenomena. The search finds us far from ready. The first almost spontaneous reaction is that if the proposed reforms would have been implemented there would have been no crisis (*OECD*, 2009). But such a cyclic argument is not enough, since it underestimates the social character of the reforms and perceives them as technocratic endeavors cut off their context.

We estimate that there is a much deeper problem in regard to our own way of thinking about the issue and the toolkit we use to deal with it. Have the very means of our thought gown too old and we need new ones, which are, at first glance, much more complicate, but would prove to be much simpler in the end?

In this study, these considerations are tackled with a focus on the "perfect" case study: Greece. The Greek economy and public administration have been at the center of interest of states, experts, journalists etc. All possible reform idea has been proposed and some of them tested with no prior analysis or applicability test. Most of them have already failed, but both local and international decision makers are not willing to learn by their mistakes. So, we are phasing a situation where a monetaristic, procroustian policy is being implemented, while theories are retrieving from the old dust theories about the wild capitalism, along with any sort of conspiracy theory. This way they create a mostly welcome populist comfort which, on the other hand, does not offer any solution. It is equally worrying, of course, the fact that the administrative theory and practice were in no way able to contribute to the exit from the crisis. The economic Armageddon dragged and overcome the logic of gradual reforms, of private-public partnerships, consultation, social cohesion and the rest of the new public management imperatives learnt during the previous 30 years.

After four (4) years of experimentation Greece is still located on the edge of the cliff having lost 25 % of GDP, with 60 % youth unemployment and broken public services. It is a country that presents after 3 rescue programs and several millions injected to it, a situation that is no better than it was in the beginning of the crisis. That's why we must review the policy models used. This applies to the design and implementation of both national and international public policies. This is, because failure lies not only with national governments, but the international community as well which not only proved that has had no plan for the restoration of public administration but marched to the opposite direction of what should have been done.

In this study we focus on the reform of public administration in order to highlight the dual dimension of the problem mentioned above: a) Why in Greece reforms that could support a different model of economic and social development never took place and are still not planned and b) Whatever is planned to happen from now on is doomed to fail if it is based on the current epistemological and methodological paradigm of public administration reform.

To illustrate the above, the study will show in its first part the inadequacy of existing epistemological and methodological tools of the administrative science and practice to deal with the issue. In the second part, we will show through the case study the correct diagnosis, the wrong treatment and the (systemic) failure to implement reforms in Greece. Furthermore, in the third part, we will mention the necessary methodological innovations that must be agreed upon, in order to be able to overcome the devastating "one size fits all" way of thinking, and be able to reach, in a globalized social order, different legal and administrative systems, with differentiated understanding and management policies.

I. Public Administration and Administrative Reform

Current administrative theory and practice have been developed around a working hypothesis, according to which reforms/changes can take place in an environment of external serenity; otherwise, in a state of equilibrium between the administrative system undergoing reform and its environment. In fact, previous approaches to the administrative phenomenon considered all unrest or differentiation as pathology and proposed measures and methods to confront them. The idea that reforms can succeed in an environment of crisis is relatively recent and is linked to the development of theorems for risk management (*Tompson*, 2009).

The view that fiscal constraints and, often, the inadequate management of public finances create fertile ground for the development of reform teachings and actions, which was established in the 1990s, is of particular interest to this study. Many European administrations, following the Anglo-Saxon model, reorganized their structure and operation by limiting superfluous units, competences, procedures and, finally, transaction costs. Theoretical documentation of change and also practical examples of re-orientation of reformed public organizations refer repeatedly to the relevant "New Public Management" manuals (*Barzelay*, 1999). It is still, however, disputed whether the services provided after the implementation of reforms really are of a better or at least equal quality compared to those provided prior to the reforms (*Copus*, 2006).

1. New Public Management

Focusing on the exploitation of operational and structural reforms in the private sector, which led businesses to prosperity and progress (prior to the appearance of the global economic crisis of the past few years), New Public Management (NPM) established the following priorities:

A. The constitutive structure of each organization is not particularly important. A common way of understanding problems is more important. There can be an exchange of information and learning.

B. The extroverted character of reforms is important for their evaluation. Reforms are not evaluated on the basis of the process followed to pursue the desired result, but on the basis of the result itself.

C. Reforms are evaluated using criteria that may contradict the criteria of traditional legality. Among them quality, effectiveness, performance and cost-efficiency are included.

NPM reforms do not constitute an exclusive list. Many sub-reforms can be included, and their relationship can be defined according to the particular culture of each public organization. The main sub-reforms include:

– The management of results;

– Quality management for services provided;

– E-government and simplification of administrative procedures;

– Regulatory reform/Better Regulation;

– Performance-based budgeting;

– Human capital development (through personalization, accountability and networking).

The relationship between NPM reforms and their enactment differs from country to country, the existing organizational culture being the main factor determining success or failure. In a general classification, it is possible to distinguish between the reforms implemented in Anglo-Saxon countries, where reforms preceded their regulatory establishment, and those taking place in Central European countries, which, by contrast, created the regulatory framework first and then proceeded to the operational changes required for implementation of the reforms. Today, this distinction appears to have receded significantly, and it is clear that the success of reforms does not depend on the time parts of the implementation procedure are applied but, much more, on the degree to which these have been internalized by the citizens and social partners concerned by such reforms, thus making them sustainable.

Despite objections as to the transparency and clarity of its proposals, NPM has been prevalent for more than thirty years, leaving a definite footprint on the public organizations in which it has been applied and a major legacy: That the public and private sectors of the economy and administration are not two parallel universes, but interconnected qualities with a relevant autonomy that are not (and must not be) alienated in favour of one or the other.

2. Good Governance

Good Governance, which constitutes the succession of the NPM doctrine – without, however, possessing the breadth of its practical applications – sought to cover the latter's greatest weakness: the de facto equalization of public and private organizations, resulting in the creation of a quasi-private public sector. The economization of the public sector provoked reactions from all those who perceived its problems as problems which, apart from the economy, were inexorably interwoven with politics. Consequently, it was reasonable to reinstate the "political economy of reforms", which is being developed, especially during the years of the crisis. The trend in the economic science pertains to neo-institutional economics, whereby the role of institutions is pivotal both in overcoming crises and in developing a successful strategy. Therefore, the introduction of reforms which improve efficiency and effectiveness should be combined with supporting the institutions and the traditional achievements of the rule of law, as well as ensuring broader involvement of civil society in state/administrative action (*Walzer*, 1980).

The following operational proposals put forward by Good Governance are considered the most significant:

– Fostering broader consultation between the state and stakeholders.

– Encouraging participative decision-making.

– Promoting networks as a suitable governance structure for complicated social problems.

– Highlighting the significance of accountability and responsibility along all the network elements (organizational/individual).

Many of the experimentations attempted with the aim of corroborating the theory of good Governance did not yield the expected results. For instance, "Europeanization" (*Radaelli*, 2004), which constituted one of the most significant experimentations, remained unfulfilled or, in any case, was approached in an entirely different manner and moved towards different directions to those that had originally been defined (*Ladrech*, 2007).

Nonetheless, two significant and unforeseen developments radicalized the theory of Governance, leading the conundrums of experts to the current paths of administrative theory and practice. The first was the outbreak of the combined fiscal, economic and social crisis, while the second was the promotion of the concept of the system in place of the network.

The crisis and the system

Crisis, in its many interpretations, continues to be defined based on its traditional medical/ biological denotation, i. e. as a stressful condition, which eventually leads a body to its absolute tolerance limits. A different understanding of crisis, the functional one, treats it as a process whereby the elements of a system are rearranged, so that it may adjust to one or more external strains. Few share this understanding of crisis, while even fewer understand that crisis is a necessity for redirecting the main values of a social system's identity. According to the latter view, which is supported by the theory of self-referential social systems, identity is defined in a manner that is essentially different to its ontological and functional conceptualizations.

According to this definition, identity neither constitutes an invariable quality nor a homogenous unique and integral quantity inherent to a system. More so, it is a binary opposition which is made up of two parallel and unconnected qualities, based on which the "element of difference" is established (*Derrida*, 1982). This forms the foundation where concepts and communications that compose each specific social system are recorded, classified and understood.

The concept of identity in the theory of self-referential social systems rather constitutes a paradox. This is because, by veering from its traditional conception as a stable quality that remains unchanged over time, identity becomes a dynamic quantity, which is shaped by the environment within the continuous differentiation of the system (*Simon, B.*, 2004).

Identity determines the extent and quality of organizational contemplation and, by extension, knowledge. Organizational knowledge and the binary code, whereby this is articulated, reflect the individual local and other features of the organization in question.

In all events, public organizations define themselves (*Kieserling*, 1999). This means that the organizations themselves are the ones that define their objectives and directions based on the values that compose their identity. This is achieved via continuous mutual infiltration in other systems, thus remaining open to and in constant interaction with their external environment, while they are closed to their internal endeavors (*Parsons*, 1964). This new systemic rationality, as Luhmann first called it, comes to replace a deterministic and teleological rationality, offering a much broader field of correlations, causes and results (*Luhmann, N.*, 1968).

The history of successful reforms confirms the previous cognitive approach. The reforms that were actually successful were those which managed to express, on the one hand, the need for organization (and, in a way, they possessed *knowledge*) and, on the other, the strength and assimilation ability of systems consisting their environment. Clearly, missing linkages between an organization and its environment lead to failed reforms.

II. Functional Review of the Greek Public Administration

The functional review of the Greek central public administration was the most clearly distinct action of the first Memorandum of Understanding between the Troika[1] and the Greek Governments in 2010, with regard to the administrative reform of the Greek state. The unprecedented survey that followed led to a fully documented mapping of the issues faced by the Greek public sector, something that was attempted for the first time in the Greek state.

The functional review has already been heralded as a methodological innovation, since it significantly deviated from the standards of similar analyses. Specifically, a systemic approach towards public administration, which differs from a simple deterministic or teleological approach, was adopted by the functional review. The problems and the proposed solutions are interdependent and the challenge is to determine the central, linked notions that are reflected in each part of the administrative system. For example, the initial idea was not described by the question "What problems are associated with the human resources or the budget?" but rather by the question "What links the human resources problems to the ones of the budget?" There are some common underlying realities that manifest themselves as different problems. What are the fundamental conceptualizations that require each part of the administrative system to share the same notion and variety of practices?

Further documentation of the systemic methodology for functional review should be sought in the principles and implementation of the self-referential social systems. These became known around the world through the work of the German Sociologist Niklas Luhmann (*Luhmann,* N., 1994); His main principles and parameters have led us to the following conceptualization concerning the functional review:

– Functional review should aim to identify and encode the similarities/"parallel worlds" (appearing in the form of "functionally equivalent"[2] options), which can be either collective actions or individual ventures and views/attitudes, in relation to a given reference problem. In effect, each one of the functionally equivalent alternatives can indeed meet a given requirement or condition for the generation of a system under a given conjuncture.

– Consequently, a "function" can no longer be defined as a means for achieving a certain purpose. A function represents a (communicative) notion, which develops so as to contribute an alternative solution, with the aim of reducing internal and external complexity.

– Meaning (and functions) develop in conjunction with a binary code, which constitutes the main prerequisite for determining the identity of a system (*Spencer-Brown,* 1969). This implies that meanings are developed based on a binary code (i.e. both in their positive as well as negative core-values of a system/organisation) and this constitutes a certain condition of their identity (*White,* 2008).

---

[1] Troika consists of representatives from the International Monetary Fund, the European Commission and the European Central Bank.

[2] A functionally equivalent object/idea/meaning/action is one that differs from another, yet, can still perform the same functions within the same timeframe. Two functionally equivalent objects need not necessarily be two tangible entities. Ideas and methods can also be functionally equivalent.

– Therefore, a functional review reflects/illustrates a set of specific meanings which allow an administrative system to act within a given social environment. In other words, a functional review, literally, provides crucial information on the main social structure of any system in question, since said system is merely a sub-system of the social system. Consequently, the system in question shares common values, notions and communication with other social sub-systems (*Teubner*, 1990). So far, several processes have been put forward regarding the extent of the autonomy of the system elements (*Simon, H. A.*, 1962) and their interconnection mechanism[3].

– A significant difference between systemic and non-systemic functional reviews is that according to the systemic logic, certain deviations/dysfunctions/discrepancies within a given administrative system should not be perceived as a determined cause-effect relationship (and, consequently, the recommendations for resolving/reorganizing them cannot follow the same deterministic way of thinking and acting). Structural priorities, or even ontological interpretations (i. e. interpretations that link administrative dysfunctions to features or attributes of a particular actor), are also excluded.

– When it comes to the different perspectives of a subjective and a systemic point of view, the theory of self-referential systems defines "meaning" as the difference between the understanding of the meaning by the actor and its systemic perception. Therefore, if a functional review leads to specific recommendations for action, then they should be perceived in a way that satisfies both systemic rationality and personal understanding.

However, a functional review is not just limited to its theoretical justification. It is primarily a guide for action, which requires an operational plan, based on the transaction among the following five subsystems of the administrative system:

1. Regulations

2. Competences and Administrative Procedures

3. Structures Infrastructures

4. Human Resources

5. Budgeting.

Each of the aforementioned subsystems was selected in accordance with the following working hypothesis, which reflects key priorities of administrative theory and practice.

Regulations

– The more regulations are in force, the more bureaucracy, delays, confusion and economic stagnation will ensue.

---

[3] See the discourse on the notion of "Interpenetration" developed by T. Parsons (*Parsons*, 1951) to the notion of "Interference" developed by Teubner (*Teubner*, 1990).

- Planning and implementation of policies for better regulation ensure an efficient tool for treating overregulation, legalism and formalism.

- The greater the dispersion of competencies is, the more administrative silos, non-communication, formalism and low productivity will increase.

Competences and Administrative Procedures

- Lack of standardization of procedures leads to deadlocks, increases complexity and corruption.

- Policies for the reduction of administrative burdens (internal/external) and net costs are welcome.

- Planning and implementation of policies that integrate local specificities is recommended.

- One-stop services, e-government applications and policies that aim to upgrade the quality of the services rendered have also proved to be useful.

Structures / Infrastructures

- The greater the dispersion of structures, the more limited and inadequate their co-ordination.

- Less supervision on any type of structure propagates administrative costs and enhances isolation.

- Supportive competences are better offered by the private sector[4].

---

[4] Finally, we proceeded in our functional review with one more horizontal distinction between the so-called "executive" and "supportive" competences. We were led to this horizontal distinction due to multiple reports on the existence of numerous competences circumscribed in law provisions, which, however, do not necessarily imply a strategic state. Competences of a strategic nature can be found, especially under the following titles:
  - Strategic planning.
  - Better Regulation (impact analysis, simplification of administrative procedures, codification of legislation).
  - Organization and management of HR.
  - Goal setting/Performance indicators.
  - Structure and policy coordination.
  - Internal and external communication and management of organizational knowledge.
  - Monitoring of policy outcomes (Controlling/Auditing).   The supportive competences are mainly encountered in the following topics:
  - Daily financial management.
  - Daily human resource administration.
  - IT and electronic applications support.
  - Licenses (businesses/citizens).
  - Approvals/Certifications (businesses/citizens).
  - Information and Communication.
  - Administrative inspections/reviews.
  - Disciplinary controls.

Human capital development

– The more rationally designed the duties and tasks of civil servants, the greater their effectiveness.

– The integrated development of human capital requires adequate diversification and integration of the different categories of civil servants.

– The informal administrative attitudes and practices have an important role in the overall performance of public organisations.

Budgeting

– The greater the dispersion of budget lines, the lower the capacity of a budget to serve as a tool for growth.

– The efficiency of public organization increases when the existing competences, procedures and structures are replaced by broader policy fields[5] (CoFoG), results and performance indicators.

– More and better results are increasingly achieved when the role of the ministries of finance is not limited to legality checks and budgetary ceilings observance but is extended to substantial efficiency monitoring.

a) Quantitative and qualitative approach during data collection and analysis

The credibility of the functional review lied in the combination of quantitative and qualitative data, which provided the necessary documentation to the working hypothesis. The data collected has been evaluated by the steering committee of the project, comprised by high level administrators and academics with significant experience in social research.

With respect to the qualitative part of the analysis, we attempted to capture the subjective views of the civil servants using both an attitude/perception questionnaire and focus groups in organized debates.

The questionnaire has been structured according to variables (and sub-variables) which reflect the aforementioned working hypothesis. The selection of the sample which answered the questionnaire, its completion, the support offered to the respondents and the collection of the questionnaires were conducted in accordance with the apt knowledge standards for quantitative surveys, under the auspices of the OECD.

The focus groups transferred pieces of knowledge referring to the informal organization and culture, closing the gap of addressing between the formal and informal administrative reality.

---

[5] The policy fields based on OECD's Classification of Functions of Government (CoFoG) are frequently used.

Finally, a database was designed in a way to allow maximum flexibility when combining different organizational, operational or fiscal data. The data were extracted using all the convenient methods available (XML, CSV, Excel, Tab Delimited files etc). The database would preferably allow access from any computer or mobile device using a web browser. The database also produced pre-designed reports, while, at the same time, it allowed an a-la-carte reference, a fact that multiplied our informational and interpretive capacity.

b) Administrative structure of the project

The administrative structure of the functional review was extremely simple: Two hundred high profiled civil servants were split into 16 working groups reporting to and coordinated by a small team, which undertook the project management.

The researchers of the reporting groups have had access to any data related to the aforementioned issues. They had adequate managerial skills, which allowed them to co-operate with and co-ordinate with the other researchers during the activity, albeit the fact that they originated from different Ministries (and ministerial cultures, subsequently).

During data collection, the impartiality of the groups was also ensured due to their mixed composition: Some of the members of a reporting group came from the ministry in question, and usually not the majority.

As mentioned above, a high-level steering committee, undertook to guide and coordinate the mapping teams. Another purely political group, consisting of political figures (General Secretaries) was never actually required to convene.

1. Legal flood and overregulation

The functional review underlined the fact that the existing overregulation is a major problem of the Greek public administration. Hundreds of thousands of regulations have disastrous results for citizens and businesses, delay the dispensation of justice, hamper the operation of institutions, and, ultimately, have a negative effect on the economy of the country.

Although one of the reasons for the legal flood originates in the EU acquis, there are some features that lead to a differentiation of Greece from other EU member states. Among them, the dispersion of regulations, the lack of standardization and recasting mechanisms are remarkable. Surprisingly enough, the constitution insists on a particularly tight conceptualization of the "discretionary power", feeding in fact the pathologies that a better regulation policy is trying to constrain.

Furthermore, the Greek particularities that significantly burden the Greek legislature are the malpractice of adding irrelevant provisions to laws, alienated from the main subject of the law. The same goes to the transposition of the *acquis* as well as international treaties and conventions, where the original provisions are burdened with extra requirements (goldplating).

Although this problem has been pointed out as a repeatedly major dysfunction of the legislative practice, the current government intensified the malpractice by issuing "Government Decrees"[6] in order to speed up the implementation of the MoU. This kind of legislation has been heavily criticized as a marginally legitimate law making process (*Chrysogonos*, 2010).

a) Past failures – Future challenges

The enactment of Law 4048/2012 on better regulation was the only considerable effort to limit the legal flood and overregulation. Unfortunately, this law still remains inactive, because the government has not included Better Regulation in its priorities. Even codification, which used to be an effective approach to halt excessive overregulation in the Greek legal system, has also been abused by the failing experimentations of new structures of codification. Through volatile schemes by committees and counter-committees, which never actually worked, the Central Codification Committee, emaciated and working with part-time members, never managed to affect in the slightest the sewer of overregulation and bad laws with its few codifications. As far as it concerns the "Raptarhis" Project[7], although there has been an effort to modernize it, remained unfinished. Emphasis should be given to the completion of the unfinished project as well as to the promotion of the thematic codification by making best use of the IT.

No reform that can curbe the enforcement deficit has been attempted for decades. Public opinion and many experts in the relevant fields consider that this is due to the lack of political will. The underlying statement behind such an approach is a passive behavior: "If the politicians do not want to act, citizens will just have to wait for

---

[6] Article 44§1 of the Hellenic Constitution authorizes the President of the Hellenic Republic to issue a regulation, which must have been proposed by the Council of Ministers in order to address emergencies. Governmental decrees must be submitted to Parliament for ratification within forty days from their issuance or within forty days from the convening of the parliamentary session. In case they are not submitted to Parliament within the above time limits, or if they are not approved by the Parliament within three months since their submission, they are no more into force. The practice of regulating through Governmental Decrees has not been used, up to the crisis, but in certain and very few extraordinary circumstances. Much critique has been addressed towards the regulatory delegation foreseen in article 44§1 of the Hellenic Constitution, as it blurs the boundaries between the legislative (parliament) and the executive power.

[7] Raptarchis is the official system for collecting all regulations on a subject matter under certain chapters. It is a system that originated in the early efforts of a civil servant working at the National Gazette to collect and systematize all regulations relevant to a subject matter into thematic dossiers. Raptarchis is now managed by the Ministry of Administrative Reform and has taken the form of an electronic database of regulations. However, the database is not up to date, which leads professionals to address their queries on some regulatory matter to privately owned databases.

them". In this case, invoking political will has exactly the same effect as invoking "clientelism", another widely used term. Both terms may be used to target the political system but in fact they support it as the analysis doesn't go any further than just the use of these terms.

Law enforcement could become part of the better regulation policy, since the ex-post evaluation of enforced laws might provide us with specific information about the sources of lawlessness (anomy).

It should be stressed that political reluctance with respect to the controls and law enforcement is directly linked to invested, private interests within the political system and the state mechanism, in other words, corruption. Thus, solving the problem of corruption (which is wrongly presented by many as a standalone problem) requires a systemic approach, namely a combination of parallel reforms in different policy fields, aiming to the modernization of the Greek Public Administration. While that kind of proposals are not in place, then they are replaced by ethic crusades, such as the currently popular perjury, which, beyond the controversial results, brutally infringe fundamental rights (presumption of innocence, prior hearing of accused person) of civil servants, who even have to claim their capacity as citizens[8].

b) The informalities of reality

Several departments codify the dispersed provisions that affect them using their own means and only for internal use. The informal networks both within the public administration as well as between the administration and the judges participating in the law making process compensate for the lack of formal communication lines by assisting in avoiding errors, duplication or overlapping.

The Greek courts and judges pay excessive effort in issuing their decisions and produce high quality decisions.

2. Detailed and overlapping competences

The thousands of detailed competences[9] consist the regulatory environment of the Greek Ministries. The problems that arise from this fact have been repeatedly noted (*Karkatsoulis*, 2004). However, the functional review has provided us with the evidence on this issue. The picture that emerges is rather confusing: Thousands of com-

---

[8] In the beginning of the crusade against the perjuries in the public sector, their population has been announced that it was 7000 (see. Article in the newspaper "TO VIMA" published on 6/3/2013, http://www.tovima.gr/society/article/?aid=501521) in a total of 650.000 civil servants. Seven months later, their population has been carefully studied and they are no more than 600 as the Minister of Administrative Reform and e-Government said during the parliamentary discussion on Tuesday October the 22nd.

[9] By the term "competences" we refer hereafter to the regulated tasks of the Greek Public Administration.

petences, randomly arranged, create a mixed canvas (or, rather, a patchwork) which leads an already faltering public administration to the labyrinths of bureaucracy, to silos and to legalistic shells. The entrenchment of public administration leads to a detriment of efficiency, administrative quality and cost effectiveness.

Although Ministries are supposed to be the strategists of public administration, this is not at all the case: 48 % of the mapped competences are not of a strategic character (42 % of them have a supportive character, 4 % lead to service delivery although this is a competence normally carried out at local level and 6 % are of a control nature). But even the strategic competences, if examined thoroughly are not so strategic: They are too many, very detailed and in many cases they seem to have been invented in order to justify the existence of the supportive competencies.

The tradition of legalism and formalism, burdened with corporatistic pressures and clientelistic networks, has led to an extremely poor quality of governance, which runs through all levels of public administration. Having an administrative system established on legalism and formalism leads to a negative self-reference, with more competences continuously asked by the public organisations in order to deliver their mandate. They neglect the fact that the existing thousands of competences have not increased efficiency. In fact, their substitution by informal practices leads to an administrative reality, where rational administrative actions become redundant. The Greek public administration uses the plethora of its competences as an internal mechanism to justify its existence. Being "responsible" for something means that one can handle some issue, but cannot decide or act. The normative power has a practical benefit for bureaucrats: That is to assign the decision-making to someone else! The implementation of the decision is being pushed forward to the higher level, which on the other hand is supposed to be responsible for taking and not implementing the decision. Therefore there is a constant enforcement deficit.

This never ending appetite of public agencies for more competencies is evident when one looks at the normative means by which the competences are assigned to the agencies: For new competencies to be assigned to the agency, a presidential decree should be issued. The issuance of presidential decrees ensures an ex ante control by the Court of the State, and it is generally a procedure that goes through some intense scrutiny. Nevertheless, only 64 % of the existing competencies were assigned to the Ministries by presidential decrees. There is an extensive use of laws and even ministerial decisions for this purpose: That means that Ministers assign to themselves some competencies with no prior control.

One of the findings of the functional review that confirms the previous statement is the fact that the Greek public administration does not deliver results but notes and memos. In order to collect the information supporting the above mentioned argument, a questionnaire was circulated to all General Directors, who were leading agencies with strategic competencies exceeding the 50 % of their total competencies. The findings are presented in the following figure 2.

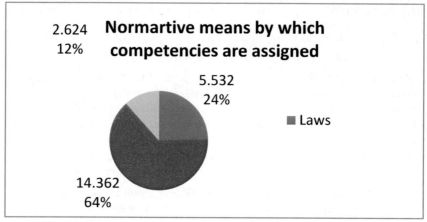

Fig. 1: Normative means by which competencies are assigned

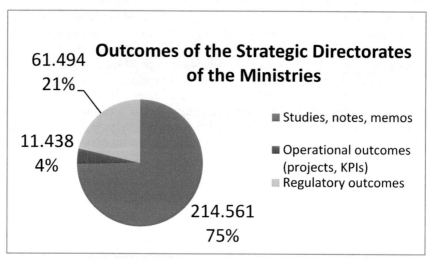

Fig. 2: The production of the strategic directorates of the ministries (2009–2010)

It should be noted that the completion of the said questionnaire proved to be the most difficult task of the entire functional review, since General Directors were unwilling to complete it.

a) Past failures – Future challenges

As far as it concerns the linkage of the competences to concrete results, it should be mentioned that it consists one of the more rigorous reforms needed in Greece. The management by objectives and results has met fierce resistance from politicians, bureaucrats and trade unions. A Law (3032/04) on goal setting allows administrative departments\agencies to set goals and to evaluate the results of their actions. But all other activities complementary to goal setting (i. e. job profiles, standardization of procedures, appraisal) have not been established. A decisive step to solve this problem is to broaden the fragmented and dispersed competences by introducing the notion of "policy areas"[10].

An attempt to connect budgetary expenditures to policy areas has taken place, with the OECD's support, between 2007–2010 (*Emery/Bergvall/Hawkesworth/ Wehner*, 2008), but was finally abandoned just after the outburst of the crisis, as it met the fierce opposition from almost all members of the cabinet. The reconstruction of existing competences, their settlement into policy areas and their allocation to the appropriate administrative level is a top priority. A large part of the supportive competences could be delegated to the private sector; following some good practices. This would result to some decongestion of the public sector and would also boost employment. Furthermore the 939 service delivery competences, along with the 1672 ministerial competences to give information to the public could either be abolished or partially transferred to the local government.

Special reference should be made to the controlling competences. Thousands of competences, described as controlling competences, have accumulated over the past decades by governments in order to develop a symbolic policy of fighting against corruption. In the last twenty years, every minister of public administration has added his own amendments to the patchwork of regulations that define the controlling function. From a normative point of view, Greece with over 1,500 controlling competences and dozens of controlling bodies, should be have been a champion of the fight against corruption. This is not though the case, since the international classifications[11] rank Greece at the bottom of EU countries, and place it among the developing ones. The current practice of the extremely narrow disciplinary control, which is supposed to eliminate the administrative arbitrariness, hinders in effect the undertaking of initiatives in order to achieve results and undermines responsibility and accountability. To that end, disciplinary control should be steered towards results.

b) The informalities of reality

Personal relationships between employees, very often, counterbalance the lack of institutional communication between administrative structures. Much of the confusion relating to given competences is resolved informally, after dialogue between civil servants from different administrative units and ad hoc developed practices. To the same issue, it has been registered that when citizens' networks are established, ad hoc solutions are invented resulting to a significant reduction of bureaucracy.

---

[10] A policy area is a functional classification of governmental actions which can be further specified to certain actors and/or activities. (*OECD*, 2011).

[11] Transparency International, Global Integrity Report.

The same (ad hoc solutions) applies when local leaders are involved, to solve administrative problems. Due to their knowledge of the administrative reality, they can manage better the situation and develop initiatives, in order to fill gaps and counterbalance administrative inefficiencies. There are many such examples especially from the health or the environmental policy areas.

3. Complicated procedures

Subsequent but equally important to the overregulation problem is the vast and cumbersome bureaucracy created by the not-standardized administrative procedures which derive from the already described plethora of competences. The announcement some years ago[12], that the greek bureaucracy consumes 14bn euros (6.8% GDP) from the Greek economy in order for businesses to comply with the existing regulations, didn't generate any reaction both in the administration as well as in the business community or civil society. The complexity and uncertainty of the administrative procedures poses costs not only on the economy but within the administration as well.

a) Past failures – Future challenges

A recent law (Law 3853/2010) on the simplification of the licensing procedure of businesses provoked confusion and uncertainty to the stakeholders. The government had been unable to resist the various pressures from interested groups affected by the simplification of procedures retreaded disorderly. Instead of a point of single contact that was initially planned to be established for licensing a business, many points of "single" contact were created. Parties involved either institutionally or as facilitators in the licensing process claimed a single point status, and they got it: 3.330 notaries, 54 Citizens' Service Centers and 59 chambers of commerce have been established a point of "single" contact. The General Commercial Register (GEMI[13]), which is a step towards resolving the weaknesses of the regulatory environment for businesses, is still in a pilot phase.

The perplexity that occurred because of the existence of many different points of single contact can only be remedied by using the well branded and known Citizens' Service Centers (KEP[14]s) as the only points of single contact. GEMI is also important and when it will be fully operational many problems will be solved. To that end, there is room for improvement: GEMI, local databases and applications, developed either regionally or for specific categories of business activities, must be connected to lead to end solutions to chronic problems.

---

[12] Newspaper "TO VIMA", 25/11/2007 (http://www.tovima.gr/relatedarticles/article/?aid=185186).

[13] http://www.businessportal.gr/english/index.html.

[14] http://www.kep.gov.gr/portal/page/portal/kep.

The effort that began with the development of a methodology for identifying administrative burdens, adapted to the Greek reality, encountered an orchestrated resistance from domestic and foreign anti-reformers. Their rationale has been organized around a pseudo-argument according to which launching major projects for the detailed recording, analyzing and reducing of administrative burdens was far too costly and time consuming. All that pressure bear fruits and finally, instead of the initially proposed approach, some projects of low budget and symbolic character have been selected. It should be also underlined that programmes to drastically reduce the intra-administrative workload must be launched an articulation to the simplification projects, if the simplification is to be sustainable (*Hood/James/Jones/Travers*, 1999).

Furthermore, the e-government policy, failed to achieve significant results in incorporating the ICT to the quest for the reduction of bureaucracy. Having used four Community Support Frameworks (two of which contained a considerable amount of activities and money for developing e-government apps) the Greek public administration is still lacking behind the results expected to have through such assistance.

The most significant items of administrative organization and operation, such as the Civil Service Code or the Code of Administrative Procedures, have not been standardized yet and their proper implementation lies in the will and understanding of every single implementation officer. Furthermore, technological applications that could decongest the intra-administrative workload are not used to their full potential to simplify the procedures but they rather copy the paperwork to the ICTs systems resulting into further burdening for the civil service departments. Some positive measures such as the online submission and retrieval of certain official document as well as the self-appointed search for documents by the public administration in order to avoid repeated submission of the same information by the citizen are in place, but not enough for decisively reducing bureaucracy. Positive results arising from such simplification initiatives are often neutralized by the regulatory inflation along with the constant control mechanisms weaknesses. Moreover, the absence of a policy which leads to the ex-ante check of administrative burdens, makes it very hard to identify them afterwards. If the Better Regulation law (4048/2012) had been activated and enforced, those dysfunctions could have been significantly reduced, but as already mentioned this is not the case.

b) The informalities of reality

As a counterbalance of the non-existence of a formal better regulation policy, public organizations/agencies often systemize the required supporting documents and simplify in practice the activities to be performed in order to complete a procedure. There are also cases, when structures involved in complicated procedures may interpret the requirements of the regulatory framework either in favor of the citizens or more rigidly by imposing even more burdens. A common practice, for example, is to facilitate the registration process. Nevertheless, this or similar informalities may function as safety valves of a bureaucratic administration. They exist due to formal procedures and they cannot be replaced by them (*Francis*, 1995).

4. Isolated, dispersed structures

The thousands of competences and endless administrative procedures require just as many intricate structures so they can be performed. The 15 Greek Ministries have 149 General Directorates, 886 Directorates and 3,720 Departments. Personnel staffing all those structures is divided in to 1445 different "branches", staff categories. Under these circumstances the administration's capacity to organize its tasks and run specific projects is very weak. It is worth noting that the increase and expansion of structures seems to be a constant feature of the Greek administrative formation. The Greek administrative system seems to be a typical case of the "Parkinson's Law" (*Parkinson*, 1986).

The Ministry of Labour, for example, has not only being changing its statutory regulation once or more often every year, but more structural units were added with every change. Between 1990 and 2009 the following changes took place:

1. In 1990 the presidential decree 337 established three general directorates and a strategic planning unit.

2. In 1991, the presidential decree 152 established four more directorates

3. In 1991 again, the presidential decree 436 abolished one directorate

4. In 1992, the presidential decree 293 established one more directorate.

5. In 1993, the presidential decree 475 established a general secretariat

6. In 1994, law 2224 established 5 new directorates

7. In 1995, the presidential decree 372 established one new general secretariat

8. In 1995 again, the ministerial decision 95445 established a new administrative domain

9. In 1998, the presidential decree 65 "re-allocated" eight directorates under different general directorates.

10. In 1998, law 2639 established a new control body.

11. In 2000, the common ministerial decision 92880 an administrative domain.

12. In 2000 again, the ministerial decision 118627, established a special unit for the implementation of programmes.

13. In 2000, law 2874 established two more additional special units related to EU co-funded projects.

14. In 2001, the common ministerial decision 180691 established one more special unit.

15. In 2001, the common ministerial decision 80056 abolished three directorates.

16. In 2003, law 3144 established one more directorate

17. In 2004, law 3277 established two new directorates

18. In 2005, the presidential decree 194 established another directorate and an office

19. In 2006, law 3458 established a special secretariat

20. In 2008, the common ministerial decision 25255 established another special unit

21. In 2009 the presidential decree 189 abolished a special unit.

22. In the two snapshots below, one can see the structure of the Ministry in 1991 and then again in 2009.

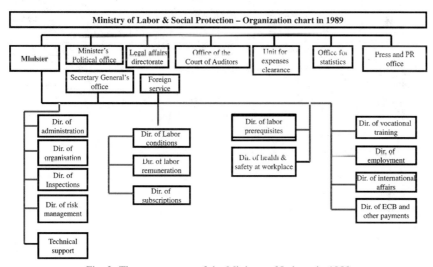

Fig. 3: The organogram of the Ministry of Labour in 1989

Another metric that the functional review studies is the span of control at different administrative levels of the central administration. Although there is not an arguably optimal span of control, one could easily spot that there are some substantial differentiation among the spans of control in different administrative levels. There are on average

- 5 General Secretariats per Ministry

- 2 General Directorates per General Secretariat

- 6 Directorates per General Directorate

- 4 Departments per Directorate.

This is a rather narrow span of control especially the fact that every Secretary General in a Ministry has on average just two persons reporting to him/her from the next hierarchy level (General Directors). A logical assumption would be that the span of

Ministry of Labor & Social Protection – Organization chart in 2009

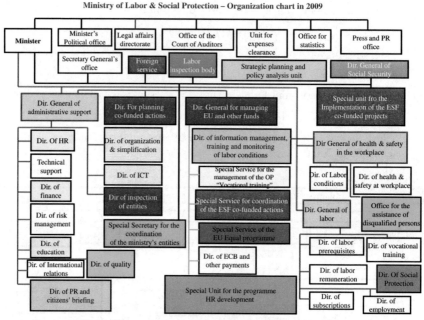

Fig. 4: The organogram of the Ministry of Labour in 2009

control gets narrower as one reaches to the top of the hierarchy ladder, because the difficulty of the issues and the responsibilities assigned to that level are usually more burdensome compared to those at the lower hierarchical levels. But as the span of control at the lowest level (Departments per Directorate) is just 4, there is no much room for following such a rule. The narrow span of control is a result of the over-fragmentation of structures especially at the top levels, which does not depict the real needs of the public organisations but is rather the creation of highly esteemed positions for politically friendly affiliates. This argument is made obvious if one looks at the personnel staffing all those structures:

- 21% of the departments of the central administration have no employees

- 14% of the departments of the central administration have one employee

- 55% of the departments of the central administration have up to 3 employees

The phenomenon of understaffed departments is not a new one in the Greek Public Administration. A similar research carried out in 1994 in 1085 departments in 18 different ministries showed that (*Karkatsoulis*, 1997):

- 113 departments had 1 employee.

- 135 departments had 2 employees.

- 47 departments had no head and no employees at all.

– 69 departments had a head but no employee.
– 124 departments had employees but no heads.

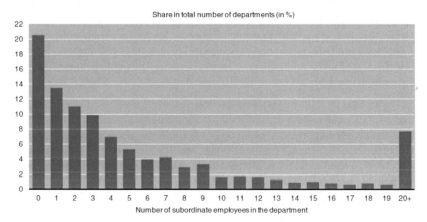

Fig. 5: Number of employees per department as measured in 2011[15]

Indeed, the structural inflation causes a series of major distortions; inability to co-ordinate the administrative work and excessive administrative burdens being the major ones. It is quite evident that these under-staffed structures are either obsolete but are still there – burdening the state budget – or they fail to respond to the tasks assigned to them. In each case the number of structures is greater than that required for the smooth and efficient functioning of the administration. The fragmentation of the administrative tasks to segmented structures constitutes an obstacle for the coor-dination of the administrative activities while, at the same time, it is impossible to effectively monitor and evaluate the structures.

The question, then, is why structural inflation continues to exist, or else, why ra-tionalization efforts fail. The answer comes precisely from the fact that the nature of the problem is systemic, while the attempts to solve it were one-dimensional and fragmented. Apart from the 'oversupply' of bureaucratic structures due to the incen-tives deriving from political rent-seeking and administrative appetite for more high ranked positions, there are certain institutional and organizational problems that have further reinforced the trend of structural inflation, or at least failed to limit it. The most important ones are:

a) The inability to connect the structures with the budget and the level of expend-iture, so there is no incentive to merge / delete non-productive structures.

b) The absence of assessment tools and control systems of operational outputs, necessary in order to identify the non-effective or non-productive structures.

---

[15] *OECD*, 2011, Greece: Review of the central administration.

c) The dispersion of the organizational structures into many buildings; a fact that increases the need for support structures. This need of course, is a consequence of the prevailing integrated organizational culture (silo based approach), which creates silos and leads services to operate as closed systems.

d) In direct correlation with the above is the fact that the introduction of information technology was done in a fragmented manner, without significantly affecting the way public administration has been operating. There were cases where new structures were created just for the management of specialized technological applications, without ultimately improve the administrative functions.

e) The institutional framework and the organizational regulations describing the structures in particular, did not rapidly adapt to any changing conditions. Changes in regulations have been retro-active, and no flexible and efficient mechanism has been established. Thus, the effort to respond through reallocation of responsibilities results in a disorderly break-up and bonding of structures which increases continuously the organizational size, creates overlaps and increase administrative burdens.

The structures dealing with the co-ordination of public policies fall within the same rule: Too many structures have been created; the lines of command and communication are not clear and overlapping competencies result in a problematic situation as shown in figure 6.

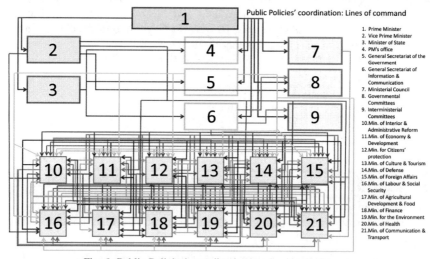

Fig. 6: Public Policies' coordination mechanism in Greece

With such an uncontrolled functional and organizational inflation, no one expects a rational political structure: 1686[16] advisors, along with their political supervisors,

---

[16] Data according to the official registry of civil servants and advisors as presented in http://apografi.yap.gov.gr/apografi/Flows_2013.htm. Site visited on November 12, 2013.

create an intermediate layer, a pseudo-structure, which, following a self-preservation attitude, burdens even further the already malfunctioning bureaucracy.

But the structural inflation is not confined within the ministerial departments. Many agencies and public entities were created and were mostly used to accommodate partisan affiliates. Those entities operate under private law or public law, regardless the need to have such entities in place, their specific mission or the policy area in which they operate. There is no single registry of these entities and the Greek government (including the General Accounting Office) is not in a position to figure the total amount of public money all these entities cost. That's the reason why the expenses of some of them are written in the state budget, while for some others, money is given to the supervisory ministry which then allocates the resources to the public entity.

We mapped 1646 different public entities among which:

– 728 are public entities that operate under public law.

    758 are public entities that operate under private law.

– 75 are companies owned by the state.

– 119 are supervised by the Ministry of Development.

– 441 are supervised by the Ministry of Agriculture.

– 146 are supervised by the Ministry of Education.

– 39 are supervised by the Ministry of Health.

– 19 are supervised by the Ministry of Justice.

– 8 are supervised by the Ministry of Defense.

– 5 are supervised by the Ministry of Labour and Social Protection.

a) Past failures – Future challenges

While the functional review's suggestions to the Greek government were to deal with the organizational inflation through re-conceptualization of competences and their replacement with policy areas along with the subsequent job descriptions/positions and programme based budgeting based on output/results, the government never put these reforms in the agenda. On the contrary it adopted some anti-reform positions by promoting a quasi-reform agenda. An example is the so called restructuring of central public organisations and public legal entities. The heavily advertised restructuring has remained only in paper so far, while the reduction/merge of the legal entities has been frozen due to a reluctance of not only the Greek Ministry[17,18] but of the Task Force[19] as well.

---

[17] "By the end of 2012 the new organograms of the central government will have been delivered, instead of 2013, announced the Minister of Administrative Reform after his meeting with the Troika", at skai.tv news, 31/7/2012, http://bit.ly/186gE8k.

A lege artis reconstruction requires a distinction of competencies into executive/ strategic, supportive, controlling and service delivery ones. The ministries should be confined to the executive/strategic competences, assigning the supportive ones to the private sector and the controlling ones to other administrative levels. Above all, what is needed is as already mentioned above the replacement of the detailed, fragmented competences with wider policy areas.

It also requires the establishment of coordination mechanisms, either in the form of hyper-structures inside the ministries ("Coordination Units") or in the form of a horizontal coordination network. The option chosen was that of the establishment of a central coordination body – the General Secretariat for Coordination which was established by Law 4109/2013. Almost one year after its establishment, the co-ordination is still weak. However, even these poor results are getting poorer, since the aforementioned reforms are being deployed separately: the lack of coordination/syn-ergies between the Ministers/Ministries on the goals of an administrative reform strategy makes it impossible for the Minister of Public Administration to push the reform agenda forward.

To conclude on restructuring, it should be mentioned that no re-organisation will be feasible without measures to contain the overgrown political part of the adminis-tration. Among them, it should be the selection of General/Special Secretaries of Ministries from non-political figures, as well as the abolition of all revocable employ-ees and the reduction of the number of members of parliament. The abolition of the permanent positions of civil servants should also be decided, but such a decision can only take place in a wider reform framework which includes constitutional changes as well.

b) The informalities of reality

The structural rigidities and inefficiencies are often bypassed by collateral cooper-ation activities, which mainly develop on an ad hoc basis. Beyond the interpersonal relationships that allow outflanking of structural defects, informal working groups often invent solutions that would be impossible with respect to the internal or external hierarchies and structures. Of course, informality leads "often" to additional bureau-cratic burdens, instead of solving problems. Sectors/ people involved in informalities often multiply bureaucratic burdens, since they may invent ad hoc solutions for them in order to feel safe. On a larger scale, it becomes a huge patchwork without orien-tation or any performance added value.

---

[18] "The Greek Minister of Administrative Reform, Mr. A. Manitakis visits the President of the Hellenic Republic and announces that the Administrative reform is proceeding vigorous-ly", newspaper Naftemporiki at 15/01/2013, http://www.naftemporiki.gr/story/514511.

[19] The Task Force for Greece (TFGR) was launched in July 2011 to provide technical assistance to the Greek authorities. It coordinates technical assistance in order to implement structural reforms as part of the economic adjustment programme.

5. Scattered, non-interoperable infrastructures

Dispersion, lack of interconnection and silos are traits found not only in competences and structures, but also extend to infrastructures.

The functional review registered the following: 263 leased, 271 owned and 70 consigned central government's buildings, the majority of which violate the main principles of town planning, safety and working areas quality standards, stacking the civil servants under their roof. Obviously, information technology and communications cannot offer much help in such a building infrastructure. They can, however, be used as an excuse to increase the demand of ICT equipment in order to ensure some quick profit to technology resellers: 54,927 terminals, 2,983 servers, but only 332 Integrated Information Systems/Databases and only 25 % of civil servants with an official governmental email account (13,343), are the evidence of such a claim. While there are plenty of buildings and digital infrastructures, a deficit in spatial rationality and e governance is obvious.

a) Past failures – Future challenges

The vision of Doxiadis[20] and Kandylis to create a governmental park have not met their implementer yet. The lack of a clear-cut policy on public buildings, especially in the times of austerity and financial crisis, resulted to a without any criteria abandonment of public buildings on the grounds of financial savings, which, consequently, lead to the stacking of people and equipment into places that fulfill none of the hygiene and safety in the workplace standards.

An example of this ineffective policy is the relocation/merging of tax offices, which resulted not only in the deterioration of the heavily inhabited buildings but to the decrease of the quality of the services provided after all. The issue of the public buildings although it is related to the issue of restructuring of public organisations was never put into the agenda. It would be a challenge, especially in view of the downgrading of the center of Athens, to undertake the endeavour for the relocation of the public services: Such a project would not only answer to the financial aspect of the problem but would be of added value for the city identity.

With respect to electronic infrastructure and applications, twenty years after the establishment of the "IT Development Department" and "Information Society SA", there is still no strategic development plan for IT, while there are numerous and expensive projects that can hardly be maintained. The biggest achievement of the previous decade is the enhancement of the awareness that many of the administrative problems can be solved using technology. But there are only few who would commit that IT is not just a tool for a given purpose, but a new way of thinking which redefines objectives and actions. The successful planning and the correct implementation of

---

[20] *Constantinos A. Doxiades:* Texts, designs, settlements, Edited by Alexandros Kyrtsis, Ikaros publications 2006.

Table 1

ICT infrastructures mapped in the functional review

Ministry	No of Servers	No of terminals	No of laptops/ notebooks	No of databases that are not a vertical integrated ICT solution	No of vertical ICT solutions	No of staff with a governmental email account	% supportive competences over the total of the ministries' competences	No of staff	% of staff with a governmental email account	% of staff with a terminal	Databases/ total number of vertical ICT solutions
Min. of administrative reform	206	1811	46	33	11	1852	56%	2111	88%	88%	75%
Min. Finance	1137	16890	2512	2	15	1225	34%	20931	6%	93%	12%
Min. of Foreign affairs	357	3211	51	0	11	55	40%	1285	2%	110%	0%
Min. of Defense	316	4314	481	35	26	1388	37%	8206	58%	202%	57%
Min. of Development	218	1303	76	9	8	1562	32%	1824	85%	75%	53%
Min. of Environment	65	1070	23	19	0	1070	37%	990	92%	94%	100%
Min. of Education	161	1820	19	30	14	1314	37%	1568	83%	116%	68%
Min. of transport	18	430	55	5	0	380	37%	3122	7%	8%	100%
Min. of Labour	67	1565	22	29	1	686	30%	1629	44%	103%	97%

Table 1 (Continued)

Ministry	No of Servers	No of terminals	No of laptops/notebooks	No of databases that are not a vertical integrated ICT solution	No of vertical ICT solutions	No of staff with a governmental email account	% supportive competences over the total of the ministries' competences	No of staff	% of staff with a governmental email account	% of staff with a terminal	Databases/total number of vertical ICT solutions
Min. of Health	32	543	15	3	0	613	47%	1760	38%	35%	100%
Min. of Agriculture	80	1857	49	34	6	1088	37%	2014	49%	85%	85%
Min. of Justice	113	1000	10	5	28	279	4C%	159	92%	105%	15%
Min. of public order	133	12477	340	2	2	668	44%	428	100%	100%	50%
Min. of culture & tourism	163	2650	30	7	1	1200	37%	8979	16%	35%	88%
Min. of Maritime Affairs	12	125	16	5	1	119	31%	1413	15%	18%	83%
General secretariat of the PM and General secretariat of the Government	6	40	1	0	0	40	34%	94	33%	33%	0%
Total	3084	51106	3746	218	124	13539	42%	56513	51%	81%	61%

e-Government projects do not require "hardware", "wires" and "experts" but public participation, transparency and openness. Therefore, "electronic governance" and "digital future" are elements of good governance par excellence. Open software, distributed experience and web production refer to the socialization of information – and also of information technology- promoting it from tool to central concept in a demystified society. The "platforms" that are the object of the current discussion do not require consortia or traders of information technology (sub)products. They require the largest possible participation, originality and imagination and they promote a way of wide redistribution of social goods and in this aspect they contribute to "open governance". The question that remains unsolved in the Greek case is the following: How much openness, how much democracy and social participation does the digital vision of the governments in crisis, take?

b) The informalities of reality

Civil servants solve many of the problems caused by the lack of a practical framework for IT projects. In many cases, they develop applications within existing sources in order to support their work and be able to respond to pressing needs. The fact that systems are non-interoperable is often overcome by creating ad hoc interfaces. The lack of qualified personnel also often creates the need for additional efforts by the civil servants themselves to support the entire IT process (from equipment maintenance to software development).

6. Disengaged and neglected human capital

The fragmentation of functions and structures and the resulting confusion has also been reflected in human capital development. When it comes to the Greek Public Administration, it's well known that all governments from the 1980s onwards resorted to the strategic option of systematically expanding the public sector through a peculiar definition of it: The notion of the narrow and wider public sector has been invented. The narrow public sector includes the Ministries, local governments and all entities that operate under public law, while the wider public sector includes all entities that are supervised by the state but operate under private law. Making use of the different employment contracts that were possible under the private law, these public entities were used as hiring hubs for the partisan clientele. In that way, many people entered the wider public sector under differentiated employment statuses in the early 1980s.

The public sector staff, almost doubled during the 1980s compared to the previous thirty-year period (1950–1980), when the civil service population remained stable at approx. 230,000 people. The population was re-doubled once more in the subsequent twenty-year period. It's though a remarkable fact that the size of the Greek public administration remained after all, rather on the average of OECD countries.

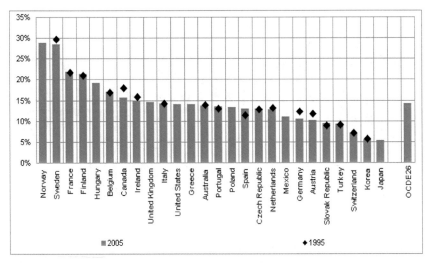

Fig. 7: Percentage of civil servants over the total workforce in OECD countries

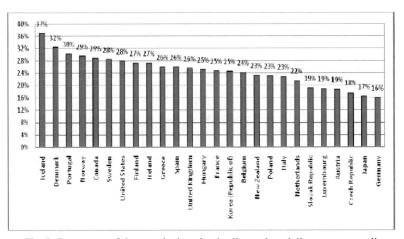

Fig. 8: Percentage of the state budget that is allocated to civil servants payroll
in the OECD countries

As it is shown in figures 7, 8 and 9 the civil servants payroll expenses did not exceed the OECD's countries' average regardless the remarkable increase of their population.

The fact that most of the civil servants were hired during the '80s / early '90s has led to a disproportionate age distribution of the civil servants currently in force. The population is ageing and there are specific ministries were the ageing problem is endangering their sustainability:

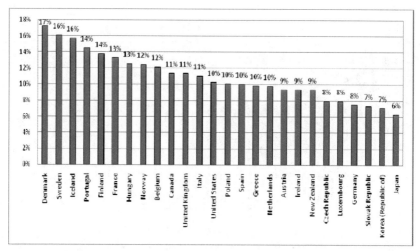

Fig. 9: Civil servants payroll expenses as a percentage of GDP in OECD countries

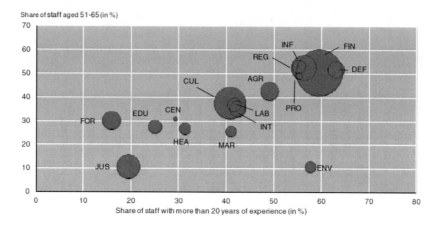

Fig. 10: Age and experience trends in Ministries[21]

As shown in figure 12[22], the civil servants' population increased sharply in the beginning of the '80s. This increase is mainly due to the establishment of many different public entities rather than hiring excessively in the central government. The most rapid and voluminous hirings took place in public entities that operate under private law. This is because these entities, do not have to follow the hiring process through ASEP (Supreme Council for Civil Personnel Selection) and were in many cases used as hiring hubs to serve partisan clienteles.

---

[21] The size of bubbles is proportionate to each ministry's staff numbers (central and decentralized services).

[22] The year 1996 was left out of the diagramme because data for 1996 was not available.

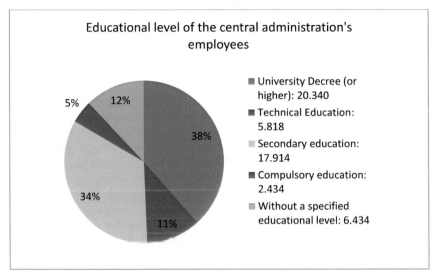

Fig. 11: Educational level of the central administration's employees

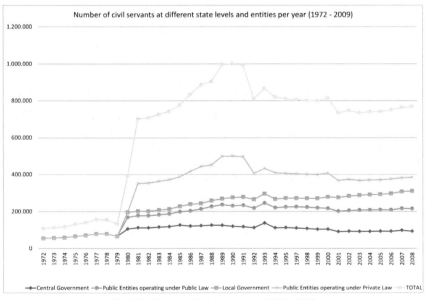

Fig. 12: Number of civil servants 1972–2009

a) Past failures – Future challenges

The generalized austerity policy of the Memorandum between the Troika and the Greek Governments since 2010, had a dramatic impact on human capital in public administration. Without any preparatory work on the establishment of a minimum social safety net for the civil servants who are going to be laid off, a consequent social problem will emerge and be added to the already existing financial and social problems. In any case, many skilled executives rushed towards any available pension scheme as the salaries almost halfed. Even those qualified civil servants that are still in the public service workforce, have been demoralized by the ongoing public discourse that stigmatizes civil servants as the root of all evil and have lost most of their motivation. Even young civil servants, relatively new to the public service workforce, are discouraged because of the limited possibilities for a fulfilling career path in the public sector. Unfinished reforms, such as the performance assessment of agencies and persons, the restructuring towards better efficiency and the enhancement of the strategic character of the Ministries were stuck at the initiatives steps of their implementation and were finally abandoned, while other reforms which were rather useful, such as the decentralization, the programme based budgeting etc. are still pending. However, moral crusades and punitive policies along with quasi reforms, such as the nominal restructuring of the ministerial units, compose the puzzling current situation.

The combination of the ongoing public accusations of civil servants as being the cause of the crisis, the austerity measures disproportionately imposed on civil servants along with the reforms that were only announced but never happened, broke all trust bonds between public administration and the political system of the country. Without such trust linkages, any amelioration seems very difficult if not impossible.

For a meaningful human capital development in the Greek public administration to take place and deliver results, one should start from scratch: A vision for the Greek state is needed, its role in society and economy and the significance of the people working for it, shall be declared. Such a vision should reflect the deeply rooted in the Greek public administration principles and values of patriotism, devotion to duty and social solidarity which are prevailing although not often recognized throughout the history of the Greek state.

Nevertheless, the self-fulfilled prophecy about the lazy civil servants has been overturned by the findings of the functional review. The Greek civil servants explicitly declared[23] that they strongly support the reforms and believe that it is the only way to guarantee public sector sustainability.

It is worth noting that their attitude is not reflected in the programs (and especially the practice) of political parties. The official discourse is based on a manipulating negative concept which alienates civil servants from their core values and beliefs. All this negativism is embedded in civil servants consciousness through the back

---

[23] See next figure.

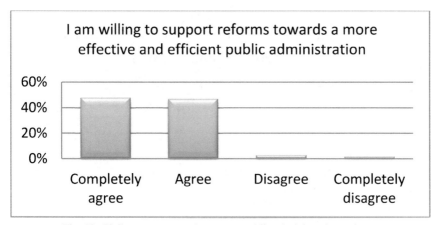

Fig. 13: Civil servants strongly support public administration reforms

door: The clientelistic system forces them to adopt for themselves the view of their political masters. But in their deep structure and when a crisis emerges they don't identify themselves with the negative qualities attributed to civil servants by the mainstream stereotypes. It's a fact mirrored in the answers civil servants gave when asked to describe themselves: They consider themselves as being diligent, hardworking, often working overtime to finish the job, monitoring ongoing issues and willing to offer their services.

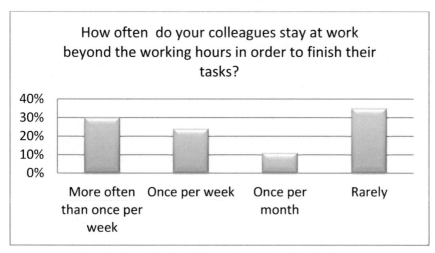

Fig. 14: How often do civil servants work overtime in Greece

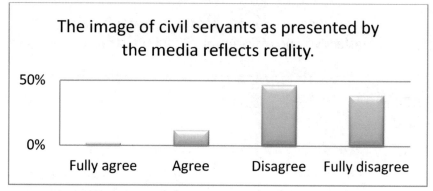

Fig. 15: Civil servants believe that the negative stereotypes
about them do not depict the reality

The deviation between the discourse about civil servants and their self-identity leads to a lack of trust which is ongoing and has been recorded several times (*Karkatsoulis*, 2004).

b) The informalities of reality

The unofficial networking and communication bridges built among civil servants in order to achieve results overpassing the obstacles set by official regulations, statements and hierarchies have already been reported. Civil servants outweigh shortcomings and weaknesses in organization and operation, by summoning up knowledge, sensitivity and appreciation for both citizens and entrepreneurs. Despite repeated attacks on the public sector (or just because of that), unity and commitment lead to the development of an administrative solidarity (*Crozier*, 1964). Administrative solidarity may manifest itself either positively or negatively, when a defensive mechanism entrenches civil servants within the borders of their silos creating the so-called "ministerial patriotism"[24].

7. Detailed, incremental budgeting

Such a system could only be financed via a budget that shows exactly the same features as the other parts of the administrative system: large dispersion of codes, lack of their connection to specific results (since it is impossible for them to be calculated due to large dispersion of structures and diverse employment relationships, which do not allow either categorizations or comparisons) and weakness of the supervisory role of the Ministry of Finance. The financial services of the ministries – let

---

[24] Negative solidarity in the Greek public administration has an introvert character: There are few civil servants interacting with outsiders. Most of them deal on a daily basis with colleagues from the same department, while mobility is not applied in their carrier path. Note that 66% of them said that their daily tasks have not been changed in the previous five years. (*Karkatsoulis*, 2004).

alone the legal and decentralized entities – are underperforming or they operate in a totally outdated way, failing to abide by the modern accounting standards. The Greek budgeting system is based on a credit-debit base: It only records expenses and revenues, without any connection to targets, outcomes or results. It is mainly a resource management system instead of being a system for managing results. On one hand, there is no connection between the expenses in a public entity and the results it achieved, and on the other hand there is a very rigid system in place which does not allow the head of a public entity to transfer unused funds from a budget line to another that is to set its priorities. Such a situation creates a sense of alienation between the manager and the budget as a management tool, and lifts responsibility of resource allocation from the public entity's manager to the minister of finance.

The funding of the Greek public entities follows a structural criterion and not a functional one: The budget is broken down to accounts per "public body" and not per function (i. e. education, health etc.). But public bodies may be ministries, general secretariats or the hundreds of public entities already mentioned. When a ministerial restructuring takes place – the quite often[25] phenomenon of merging or separating ministerial departments, then the budget needs to be accordingly formulated, and this creates discontinuities which make the follow up of the budget and the extraction of any useful conclusion on budgetary performance almost impossible.

When, for example, the general secretariat for the consumers' protection was transferred in 2011 from the ministry of development to the ministry of labor, the expenses for the salaries of the secretariat's personnel continued to be allocated as expenses of the Development Ministry's budget. A major breakdown of the ministerial expenses from 2007 to 2010 in two categories, salaries and operational expenses, that was carried out during the functional review showed that per average 75 % of a ministries' expenses are spent in salaries and the rest 25 % is operational costs.

a) Past failures – Future challenges

An effort was initiated in mid-2010 to move towards programme based budgeting by introducing a mid-term planning along with a three years budget. This is a progress towards moving away from the incremental budgeting which had no connection to the expected results and which ultimately led to the country's deficit. Nevertheless, even though the effort towards a more results oriented budget is technically correct, it lacks legitimacy: Priorities are set, the budget is formulated and, more importantly, it is implemented with limited stakeholders' involvement and no motivating vision for the society.

Furthermore, the prevalence of an austerity policy to the detriment of a growth plan has led to a one-way effort for controlling public expenditure, through horizontal reduction of wages, other social expenditure (pensions, benefits), investment funds

---

[25] From October 2009 to February 2012 two such ministerial restructurings took place.

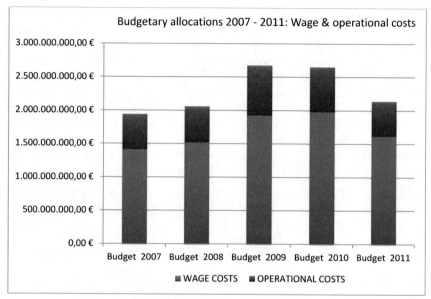

Fig. 16: Budgetary allocations 2007–2011

and consumer spending. At the same time, the reasons for the unjustified expenses that continue to be included in the budgets of the ministries are not being scrutinized. More importantly, the structural weaknesses of the fiscal system, caused by the structure and the function of the state in general, and which give rise to waste and lack of transparency in government spending, are also not being examined.

The goal to create a modern framework for financial management and control, which will lead to savings and will be described by rationalization and accountability of everyone that manages public money, can be only achieved if fiscal discipline and cost reduction is combined with the maximum returns and value added to the target group of each public policy. Making the state budget work for some measurable good of the society is not a purely technical issue: An organizational shift towards results is needed. But, it requires a huge effort to influence existing organizational behavior; a fact that is doing the whole task extremely complicated and difficult. Despite the efforts for rationalization, there are still many different financial means, used in a way that does not meet transparency and accountability standards: direct funding, transfers, payments, subsidies, etc. which are not clearly used for certain, known in advance, cases. Decentralizing accountability is the way to change behavioral patterns and practices that neglect the financial efficiency aspect of any decision taken.

In terms of changes to the financial administration regulatory framework and structures involved, some significant changes should be undertaken; the financial services should be organized in the form of a modern accounting office, with suitable IT systems and skilled personnel. The state-finances system should be updated and upgraded according to a reform vision: any accounting, presentation and auditing of public expenditure shall abide by appropriate international accounting standards and be supported by proper IT means (e. g. double entry accounting, cost accounting, and new way of presenting the budget and other accounting and fiscal statements).

Specifically, as far as it concerns the internal and external auditing processes (e. g. certified/chartered accountants, auditing committee) they should be standardized and integrated according to modern auditing methods (e. g. risk based audits), which will not only focus on ensuring legality and regularity of expenditure, but also on achieving economy, efficiency and effectiveness (e. g. by establishing specific financial or other indicators for the public sector). The integration of relevant standards and methods from other countries or international standardization organizations (e. g. European System of Accounts/ESA 95, Public Sector Accounting Standards) would help to upgrade the accounting and coherence of fiscal operation and information for the public sector as a whole (central administration and wider public sector.)

III. Lessons Learned from the Functional Review

The functional review of the Greek central public administration demonstrated that all parts of the administrative system suffer from legal formalism, lack of management practices, fragmentation of structures, people and resources and lack of co-ordination. These distortions of the administrative system serve the political system which mainly operates under clientelistic rules and seeks to redistribute public wealth to its own and its clientele's benefit. That means that the rhetoric about a monstrous bureaucratic state, shock therapies needed to make it operate efficiently and the rest, should be abandoned. Focus is needed on a comprehensive problem solving that deals with public administration as a system with several elements to be taken care off. It should be stressed that such an action plan, of a systemic character, for the implementation of the functional review's recommendations, prepared by the administration, has been sabotaged by consequent ministers. At the same time, oversimplified austerity measures (wages and budget cuts, pension reductions and heavy taxation) have been implemented. All these recipes have been proved quite unproductive.

Three years on, after the recommendations of the functional review have been submitted but not taken into account, the view that public administration's problems are of a technocratic nature is not as prevailing as it used to be in the outburst of the crisis. Furthermore, those who, due to ignorance or voluntarism, attempt to diagnose a unique fundamental cause of the problem that can be treated with a drastic solution, simply cloud the dimensions of the problem, creating further complications.

That might be the most recognizable byproduct of the crisis: The fact that the problems are of a systemic character has started to take on a meaning in the greek context. That means that complex solutions for complex problems should be invented. For such solutions to be put forward, there is a sine qua non prerequisite: Strategy. The strategy for public administration reform encompasses the social perceptions and values, and creates a wider orientation and targeting framework for society in general and the administrative subsystem in particular. Neither a credible budgeting nor an efficient human capital policy, not even a renewed competences framework outlining the boundaries of state action, can exist without a wider reference point, without a strategy. Without it, many of the valiant efforts for reform are cancelled either by contradicting efforts or by the lack of them. A strategy presupposes either wider social consensus or enlightened leadership, which can motivate, organize and drive the society forward. The notions and meanings to be used in such an endeavor can only be formulated under the self-referential systems perspective.

A strategy for Greek public administration cannot but be based on a one dimensional Greek identity. Developing a Greek strategy is by no means an easy task. It dictates and requires the need for universal reflection that will showcase and redefine those values of Hellenism that were degraded, scoffed and eventually transformed into a parasite of the Greek identity. Abolishing and distorting one side of the Greek identity that of patriotism, solidarity, tolerance and honor, has led to the emergence of deception, trickery and exorbitant individualism; the development of informal networks; the alienation from work; and eventually a deep discord and a loss of orientation.

Taking stock of the most successful public administration reform ever happened in the Greek state, the creation of KEPs (citizens' service centers) one can identify eleven (11) myths that were falsified while implementing reforms in the Greek context:

1. Reforms are common to all and globalized (One size fits all)

A reform cannot be copied from country to country. Greek reforms should reflect the greek problems and values, but for such a reflection to take place it takes that Greeks manage to picture themselves and their administration in the globalized world, "Glocalization", to recall Manuel Castells (*Manuel*, 2005). Rediscovering the Greek identity may be the fundamental convention that would permit us to survive and, possibly, render us competitive!

2. Reforms happen when there is the political will

The political will is fundamental for the reforms to be launched; however it is not so important for their overall success. A critical parameter affecting the viability and sustainability of reforms is their bye-inn by the citizens and other stakeholders.

3. It is the administration and the bureaucracy that kills the reforms

If the reforms are in their initial stage left to bureaucrats, there is a failure risk. If, however, the administration is involved in the next stage, when the policy has been established, it may offer real life solutions to every-day problems and support the sustainability of the reform.

4. Planning is very important (especially strategic one)

Sophisticated reports and studies are not necessarily a prerequisite for successful reforms. What it certainly takes for a reform to take place is its osmosis with the society and the passionate involvement of policy makers, stakeholders and bureau-crats[26].

5. Administrative structures are omnipotent

A reform may only be successful if it's existence criterion is functional: Not structural, nor regulatory neither even ontological. These are mainly means towards the attainment of the reform's objective.

6. Competence (regulated administrative task) is a prerequisite for administrative action

Dislocating competence from administrative structures and creating a more flexible framework which is service oriented and assigns responsibility (along with credit) to the service provider proved to be more efficient during the establishment of KEPs.

7. Reforms require elaborate and sophisticated IT infrastructure fully interoperable

ICT systems and other resources do need to be very expensive or elaborated in advance, in order to be able to host the reform. Technology is not just a host; it must co-evolve along with the reform notions and development. The same goes for personnel training: Then people within the administration to bring any reform to life, need to have their hands on the job and not just be "well trained" in a sterilized environment away from where the reform happens.

8. Reforms are costly

The KEPs reform was the cheapest reform ever happened: Apart from a computer, the salary of an employee and the initial cost for building the required database, the expansion of KEPs was mainly undertaken by the local societies.

9. Reforms must be based on a robust ideology and a concrete set of principles

The reforms reflect and are reflected in beliefs, culture and organizational identity of the people creating as well as the people using them. Reforms do not follow prescribed patterns – they rather create new ethos. The KEPs, for example, highlighted the Greek ethos of transparency and participation.

So, who will undertake such a difficult endeavor as it is the reform of the Greek administrative system? There is – and could not have been because of the systemic nature of the problem – a single answer to that. Will they be the "thinkers" who shall dare become exposed, the management executives who shall cease fearing losing their tattings, the low-ranking politicians who shall dare resist party privileges and the private sector which shall realize that the drivel that wanted it to be competitive towards the public sector is good enough for the Orient, but none of the powerful nations has adopted it? Even in the womb of capitalism, the USA, the powerful private sector is in step with a strong public sector.

---

[26] See Hayek on "muddling through" (*Hayek*, 1973).

Change will eventually come from society itself, through reflection and redefinition. Greek public administration shall succeed in claiming its future from the same place it always has, its people – whom it owes its existence to – if they ever decide to do so.

1. Re-examining the cognitive and methodological foundation of public administration reforms

As the previous analysis has shown the specific solutions and suggestions which have been proposed to solve the Greek public administration's problems did not work. This might have happened either because the proposed solutions were not applied at all, or because the initial assumptions upon which they were based, were wrong. The reforms continue, even today, to remain directed towards a metaphysical hyper-rational subject or a hyper-rational entity, which is able to unmistakably distinguish what is right and what is wrong every time in every different context. And this happens despite the proven (*Ostrom*, 1991) fact that the complexity arising upon implementing reforms is much greater that what could have been estimated when said reforms were being planned (*Elster*, 1989). Nonetheless, many of the misconceptions, overestimations and erroneous actions might have been avoided if the analysis had been based on the self-referential rationality of the social systems involved (*Brans/Rossbach*, 1997). What follows is a rough re-conceptualization of the central parts of the administrative system, based on the theoretical premises of administrative self-reference (*Esmark*, 2009) and the experience of public administration reforms in a European country in a crisis environment.

a) Competences/Decision-making system

As per the central European tradition, each administrative action must be based on one or more legal competences. The onset of competence can be traced back to its connection with a nebulous "common good" or "volonté general" which is difficult to identify in each given administrative action. Bridging the notion of common good to the legal competence of the administration, the proof of evidence justifying an administrative action moved to another genus: invoking a procedure or structure for verifying that legality was being observed would suffice (*Killion*, 2010). However, even though this reasoning could have proven analytically useful, in practice it proved useless or detrimental, since it acted as an alibi for justifying failures and omissions. Competences and their legality check often function to the detriment of efficiency, effectiveness, and economy.

Based on the rationale of self-referential systems, competence could be defined as a normative entry (distinction) (*Spenser-Brown*, 1969) in the life-world (*Habermas*, The theory of communicative action, 1984). The need for an entry in the life-world arises from a new social problem which calls for state intervention. State intervention can only be substantialized by means of a regulation, which is ultimately the result of the osmosis between the social issue that arised and the state's norms and attitudes.

Based on this definition of competence, the state competences should be reviewed both in terms of what the societal problem they tackle is, as well as in terms of the adequacy of the regulatory instrument adopted. The regulatory instrument is not evaluated only by evaluating its content: the legal form, its flexibility to adopt to reality, the process by which it was introduced, its enforceability and the governance of the regulatory apparatus are among the aspects that influence the regulatory quality of a given competence. Administrative self-reference accepts neither the top-down specification of the social issues that need to be regulated nor the ex-ante determination of its content by some hierarchical center of power. Both the problem definition and the content of the regulation are to be defined through a deliberative process that takes place between the social sub-system that is need of intervention and the administrative sub-system (*Luhmann*, N., Zweckbegriff und Systemrationalität: Über die Funktion von Zwecken in sozialen Systemen, 1968). That means that the regulations should be quite abstract in order to be able to host the evolving social contexts into which the regulation aspires to operate (*Teubner*, 1987) (*Wietholter*, 1982).

b) Structures

The self-referential perspective shifts the argument about organizational effectiveness away from the NPM and good Governance imperative of lean and flat structures that need a strong accountability framework to back them up. After all, the recent financial crisis has proven that lean structures and business-like accountability in the public sector, are not enough to safeguard effectiveness and efficiency in the era of a networked economy and society. In this perspective, the simplistic approach of the lean structures/state is wrong. Its abandonment has led to the appearance of some more qualitative, value based and less quantitative indicators used to evaluate administrative structures. The quite frequent use of "smart" instead of "lean" – indifferently if it goes to a structure or a regulation, testifies the changes to the orientation of the public administration reformers when it comes to the quality of structures, formal or informal. Nevertheless, it is clear that the prevailing administrative culture, which reflects the values of the social system, is the one that furnishes structures with content regardless if they are lean or not. It also gives meaning to the existing informal structures which often function effectively bypassing the official ones.

The micro-sociological approach of organizations (*Giddens*, 2011) has demonstrated the significance of informal structures, liberating them from their negatively clustering to the pathologies of the administration. An informal structure opens up a wealth of new possibilities, interconnections, references and controls, but it also gives rise to a fertile discourse on self-referential systems which leads to their definition in a way that their selectively encompasses its external environment. This is the result of a process of creating "distinctions and forms[27]", with regard to both the external environment of the organization and its internal binary code.

In this sense, the concept of "multi-level governance" may also be enriched: It can no longer be a way to organize a state which is difficult to establish, implement, and follow up because of the coordination and communication problems caused by the predefined and inflexible structures. Multi-level governance can be seen as a more open and network like way of organizing the state according to the problems arising each time and the functions needed to face them. For example, central government, whose powers were redeemed in favor of networks and the autonomy of agencies (agencification) and stakeholders, dynamically re-entered the limelight, with the crisis playing a major role in this. Privatizations did not lead to a sustainable solution either: Public entities and local-government organizations may have been privatized but the connecting thread that would establish a whole of government approach was still missing. That's why the observed re-centralization is not a self-defensive reaction of the state after the crisis but rather a re-conceptualization of the accountability dynamics that the crisis made emerge. The mutual, hyper-cyclical (*Eigen/Schuster*, 1979) coupling of different organizations and concepts offers a possibility to create common organizational meanings and communications, thus reinstating, a well-functioning multi-level governance, which is not based on the existence of convergences but on the creation of distinctions.

c) Human capital development

The decisive significance of social conceptualizations and assessments is evident in no other category of administrative reforms as much as it is in human resources management. The administrative science and practice has tested several approaches for developing human capital: Some more operational ones, like those which were imitating the industrial production lines or the management of multinational companies. The economization of participants in public organization was also a major trend along with approaches that considered leadership to be a top priority. The contemporary (*Billet*, 2009) debate on human capital focuses on understanding the learning process and transforming the participant/cognitive subject into a social partner (*Berger/Luckman*, 1967). The administrative subject who undertakes action ("civil servant") is elevated into a significant center of interest, which, in a constant interaction with the administrative system itself establishes the binary code of the public organization (*Willke*, 2004).

The concepts according to which the actor equals to a "psychic system" (*Simon*, F. B., 1997) (*Habermas/Luhmann*, 1971), had been misconstrued as shrinking the breadth and importance of the actor in a social system. These misinterpretations are no more prevailing: The interaction of the administrative system with the social

---

[27] Distinction is the creation of a threshold between different parts (and space) which when created takes the shape of a form (*Spencer-Brown*, 1969).

systems, and their subsequent interaction with their psychic systems, has led to the members of organizations being seen as having the same significance as the organization itself; and, in this sense, human capital is today being upgraded as a necessary environment of the social/administrative system (*Luhmann*, N., 1987).

Therefore, it is impossible to formulate a policy for human capital development in public administration without civil servants being a part of it. As a matter of fact, such a policy can only be determined with civil servants' values, culture and stances towards the public administration be taken into account and reflected in the policy itself. Thus, a human capital policy cannot arise from another administrative subsystem, i. e. structures, procedures, but from the human capital itself. Human capital development literature (*Schein*, 1996) has been also pointing to that direction since the classic "Culture's Consequences" (*Hofstede*, 1980).

d) Budgeting

After the developments in understanding of the function of the budget, brought along by the PPBS (Programming, Planning and Budgeting System) theory (*Schick*, 1996), which demonstrated that only when a budget is connected to the administrative functions of an organization can it constitute a tool for its development (*Boorsma*, 1999), the current conundrum focuses on the mechanisms and methods for such a transformation of the budget to be achieved (*Thompson/Gates*, 2007). As budget refers to the future and because people with clairvoyant abilities are a rare occurrence, interest has shifted to forecasts and risk assessments, often using sophisticated mathematical and statistical models (*Caiden*, 1988). Using budget as a forecasting tool, implies an underlying "one-size-fits-all" approach, as observations on situations of the past are hold to be "true" in assumptions about unknown, future situations. Future forecasting is but an extension of the present. In this light, time is continuous and, consequently, changes do not wait for a point in time to occur, but rather take place constantly. If we accept this approach, i. e. changes (must) occur constantly, then the nature of the budget changes and it is transformed from a forecasting tool into a leveraging tool for the changes and reforms that are already taking place (*Strauch/Hallerberg/von Hagen*, 2004).

That's why the budgeting reform is not only about replacing the detailed expenditure codes of the current incremental budget with groups of programs and interrelated actions. For this reform to be successful, what is required is not just instrumental knowledge, which leads to homogenization of the technical details that determine the relationship between actions and expenditures for each public organization, but also substantial knowledge of the public policy each organization deals with is needed. This knowledge may only be acquired as a product of the reflections on the actions, programs, prospects, trends and risks that correspond to and are determined by the organizational identity.

2. Addendum

"Se vogliamo che tutto rimanga come è, bisogna che tutto cambi[28].

This paradox applies both for individuals and organizations. The rationale of this statement is grounded on the fact that identity building of an organization is a dynamic process of constant change, whereby it is redefined and differentiated from other organizations. Consequently, the changes attempted by an organization are not only related to itself (and any of its possible internal needs), but also to its environment. The ways that an organization is differentiated from its environment, as well as the "re-entry"[29] mechanism according to which each element that has already been subjected to the basic binary code of the system re-enters the system, has adequately been described in the literature on autopoetic systems. According to this theory, an organization must continuously evolve, since changing constitutes an immanent trait thereof (*Simon*, F., 2007), (*Baecker*, 1999). Even the organizations which seemingly remain unchangeable develop self-referential reproductive mechanisms, which are evidently activated in crisis situations. That is when the organization decides which of the changes occurring in its environment (in other organizations) pertain to it and rearranges its internal forces in order to either reject or adopt some of them.

An organization is faced with a trilemma during this transitional stage:

1. Become integrated with another organization and shunt its identity

2. Integrate selected elements of its environment and maintain its autonomy

3. Fully absorb external pressures, weakening/eradicating them.

Which of the three options an organization might select, depends on the level of its self-referential evolution. On the specific topic of this study, public administration reforms can be seen as the operational tools an administrative system may use in order to undertake one of the three above mentioned options. Consequently, the programs and reform actions may contribute towards exiting the crisis only when they are suited to and reflect the administrative identity. The case study herewith described, relating to the Greek public administration, could be used as a benchmark for the verification or the falsification of the theory of the self-referential social systems.

---

[28] "If we want things to stay as they are, things will have to change", Il Gattopardo, 1958, Giuseppe Tomasi di Lampedusa.

[29] The re-entry mechanism is a process which safeguards the continuity of the binary code of a system as described by Spencer Brown (*Spencer-Brown*, 1969). It is through the "re-entry" process that the difference upon which a system is built becomes element of the system, so whatever has already been distinguished according to the basic distinction of the system, re-enters the distinction criteria (i.e. is it wright or wrong to distinguish between wright and wrong?). The outcome of such a re-entry of the distinction establishing a system into itself is another form (i.e. another organization) which is the same as the previous one, but yet different.

Bibliography

Baecker, D. (1999): Organisation als System. Frankfurt am Main.

Barzelay, M. (1999): How to argue about the new public management. International Public Management Journal, 2(2), 183–216.

Berger, P./*Luckman*, T. (1967): The social construction of reality. Harmondsworth.

Billet, S. (2009): Conceptualizing Learning Experiences: Contributions and Mediations of the Social, Personal, and Brute. Mind, Culture, and Activity, Volume 16, Issue 1, pages 32–47.

Boorsma, P. (1999): Measuring performance and quality is a sign that PPBS is alive and well! In: H. Arie, Performance and quality measurement in Government (pp. p.vii-xiii).

Brans, M./*Rossbach*, S. (1997): The Autopoiesis of Administrative Systems: Niklas Luhmann on Public Administration and Public Policy. Public Administration, Volume 75, Issue 3, pages 417–439.

Caiden, N. (1988): Shaping thing to come. In I. Rubin, New Directions in Budget Theory (pp. 43–58). Albany.

Chang, Y.-F. (2013): Structure-Function-Result Mode in Sociology, Hypercycle and Knowledge Economic Theory. International Journal of Modern Social Sciences, Vol.2, No 3, pp 155–168.

Chrysogonos, K. H. (2010): The lost honour of the Hellenic Democracy (in Greek). Nomiko Vima (The Legal Rostrum).

Copus, C. (2006): British Local government: A Case for a New Constitutional Settlement. Public Policy and Administration, 21:4–21.

Crozier, M. (1964): The bureaucratic phenomenon. Chicago.

Derrida, J. (1982): Margins of philosophy. Chicago.

Eigen, M./*Schuster*, P. (1979): The Hypercycle: A principle of Natural Self-organization. Berlin.

Elster, J. (1989): Solomoni judgements: Studies in the limitations of rationality. New York.

Emery, R./*Bergvall*, D./*Hawkesworth*, I./*Wehner*, J. (2008): Budgeting in Greece. Paris.

Esmark, A. (2009): The functional differentiation of governance: Public governance beyond hierarchy, market and networks. Public Administration, Volume 87, Issue 2, pages 351–370.

Francis, F. (1995): Trust – The social virtues and the creation of prosperity. London.

Giddens, A. (2011): An introduction to sociology. Polity.

Habermas, J. (1984): The theory of communicative action. Boston.

Habermas, J./*Luhmann*, N. (1971): Theorie der Gesellschaft oder Sozialtechnologie. Frankfurt am Main.

Hayek, F. (1973): Law, legislation and liberty. Chicago.

Hofstede, G. (1980): Culture's Consequences: International Differences in Work-related Values. Newbury Park/CA.

Hood, C./*James*, O./*Jones*, G./*Travers*, T. (1999): Regulation Inside Government. Waste-Watchers, Quality Police, and Sleazebusters. Oxford.

Karkatsoulis, P. (1997): Qualitative characterisitics of the Greek Civil Service (in Greek). Administrative Reform, 28–40.

Karkatsoulis, P. (2004): The State in Transition (in Greek). Athens.

Kieserling, A. (1999): Kommunikation unter Anwesenden. Studien über Interaktionssysteme. Frankfurt a. M.

Killion, U. M. (2010): The Function of Law in Habermas' Modern Society. Global Jurist, Volume 10, Issue 2.

Ladrech, R. (2007): National Political Parties and European Governance: The Consequences of 'Missing in Action'. West European Politics.

Luhmann, N. (1968): Zweckbegriff und Systemrationalität: Über die Funktion von Zwecken in sozialen Systemen. Tübingen.

Luhmann, N. (1987): Die Autopoiesis des Bewusstseins. In A. Hahn/V. Kapp, Selbstthematisierung und Selbstzeugnis: Bekenntnis und Geständnis (pp. 25–94). Frankfurt a. M.

Luhmann, N. (1994). Soziale System. Frankfurt a. M.

Manuel, C. (2005): Transnationalism, Cosmopolitanism and Glocalization. Current Sociology, 53: 113–135.

OECD (2009): The political Economy of Reform. Paris.

OECD (2011): Classification of the Functions of Government (COFOG). In OECD, Government at a Glance 2011 (pp. doi: 10.1787/gov_glance-2011–68-en). Paris.

Ostrom, E. (1991): Rational Choice Theory and Institutional Analysis: Toward Complementarity. The American Political Science Review, Vol. 85, No. 1 (Mar., 1991), pp. 237–243.

Parkinson, N. C. (1986): Parkinson's Law or the Pursuit of Progress. Penguin Books Ltd, 1986.

Parsons, T. (1951): The social system. Illinois.

Parsons, T. (1964): Evolutionary Universals in Society. American Sociological Review, Vol. 29, No. 3, pp. 339–357.

Radaelli, C. (2004): Europeanisation: Solution or problem? European Integration online Papers (EIoP), Vol. 8 (2004) N° 16; http://eiop.or.at/eiop/texte/2004–016a.htm.

Schein, E. H. (1996): Three Cultures of Management: The Key to Organizational Learning. Sloan Management Review, Fall, 9–20.

Schick, A. (1996): The Road to PPB: The Stages of Budget Reform. Public Administration Review, 26 (4), 243–258.

Simon, B. (2004): Identity in Modern Society: A social psychological perspective. Blackwell publishing Ltd.

Simon, F. (2007): Einführung in die systemische Organisationstheorie. Heidelberg.

Simon, F. B. (1997): Lebende Systeme: Wirklichkeitskonstruktionen in der systemischen Therapie. Frankfurt a.M.

Simon, H. A. (1962): The Architecture of Complexity. Proceedings of the American Philosophical Society, Vol. 106, No. 6, pp. 467–482.

Spencer-Brown, G. (1969): The Laws of Form. London.

Strauch, R./*Hallerberg*, M./*von Hagen*, J. (2004): Budgetary forecasts in Europe – The track record of stability and convergence programmes. Europan Central Bank, Working Paper Series, No 307.

Teubner, G. (1987): Autopoietic Law: A New Approach to Law and Society. Berlin.

Teubner, G. (1990): Social regulation through reflexive law. In: G. Teubner, Law as an Autopoietic System. Oxfrord.

Thompson, F./*Gates*, B. L. (2007): Betting on the Future with a Cloudy Crystal Ball? How Financial Theory Can Improve Revenue Forecasting and Budgets in the States. Public Administration Review, Volume 67, Issue 5, pages 825–836.

Tompson, W. (2009): The political economy of reform: Lessons from Pensions, Product Markets and Labour Markets in ten OECD countries. Paris.

Walzer, M. (1980): The Moral Standing of States: A Response to four Critics. Philosophy & Public Affairs, Vol.9, No. 3, pp. 209–229.

White, H. (2008): Identity and Control: How Social Formations Emerge. Princeton.

Wietholter, R. (1982): Entwicklung des Rechtsbegriffs. In V. Gessner/G. Winter, Jahrbuch für Rechtssoziologie und Rechtstheorie. Rechtsformen der Verflechtung von Staat und Wirtschaft. Opladen.

Willke, H. (2004): Einführung in das systemische Wissensmanagement. Heidelberg.

Die Gesetzesqualität als Faktor der Rechts(un)sicherheit insbesondere in Krisenzeiten

Von *Spyridon Vlachopoulos*

I. Einleitung

Im Rechtsstaat ist es selbstverständlich, dass die qualitative Gesetzgebung die wichtigste Voraussetzung – eine conditio sine qua non – der Rechtssicherheit ist. Es ist auch selbstverständlich, dass die überflüssige und, *a fortiori*, die schlechte Gesetzgebung eine wichtige Gefahr für die Rechtssicherheit und fur den Rechtsstaat darstellt. Diese Feststellungen sind allgemein anerkannt[1] und deswegen an dieser Stelle nicht weiter erläutert.

Es wird aber untersucht, ob der griechische einfache Gesetzgeber die Pflicht der guten Gesetzgebung[2] beachtet, insbesondere während der Krise. Ich bin optimistisch – und viele werden diese Meinung teilen –, dass Griechenland die finanzielle Krise überwinden wird. Auf der anderen Seite, ist Griechenland seit ungefähr zwei Jahren gezwungen, unter einem unvorstellbar großen Zeitdruck, eine Menge von unterschiedlichen Vorschriften zu Lasten der Rechtssicherheit in Kraft zu setzen. Der Schaden für die griechische Rechtsordnung ist so groß, dass er auch nach der Überwindung der ökonomischen Krise und für einige Jahrzehnte wahrscheinlich noch präsent sein wird.

II. Die maßgeblichen Verfassungsvorschriften und ihre Verletzung

Die griechische Verfassung 1975/1986/2001/2008 ist von einer sehr hohen normativen Qualität.[3] Das größte Problem der griechischen Rechtsordnung ist, dass

---

[1] Siehe statt vieler *Tsoukas*, Panagiotis: Merkmale und Praxis des schlechten (griechischen) Gesetzgebers, in: (Bürgerbewegung für eine offene Gesellschaft), Polynomia, Kakonomia, Anomia (auf Griechisch), 2011, S. 45 ff.

[2] Diese Pflicht ist auch gesetzlich festgelegt; siehe Gesetz 4048/2012 „Regulative Regierung: Grundsätze, Verfahren und Mittel der guten Gesetzgebung" (Gesetzesblatt, Band A, 34/23–2–2012).

[3] Es ist charakteristisch für ihre Qualität, dass die griechische Verfassung schon im Jahr 1975 den Umweltschutz als Grundrecht verankert hat (Art. 24). Auf der anderen Seite, liegt ihr wichtigster Nachteil darin, dass sie viele Einzelheiten beinhaltet, die ihre Anpassung an die wechselnden gesellschaftlichen Verhältnisse schwierig machen und mit ihrem Charakter als eine unter sehr strengen Voraussetzungen (siehe Art. 110) abänderbare Verfassung unvereinbar sind.

viele Vorschriften der Verfassung nicht geachtet werden. Das gilt auch für die Verfassungsvorschriften, die sich auf die gute Gesetzgebung beziehen.

Im Folgenden werden drei charakteristische Beispiele erläutert:[4]

1. a) Erstes Beispiel: Art. 74 Abs. 5 der griechischen Verfassung heißt wie folgt: „Gesetzesentwürfe oder Gesetzesvorschläge, die Vorschriften enthalten, die nicht im Zusammenhang mit dem Hauptgegenstand des Gesetzesentwurfes oder des Gesetzesvorschlages stehen, werden nicht zur Beratung vorgelegt". Dasselbe Verbot gilt auch für Zusatz- und Änderungsanträge, die nicht im Zusammenhang mit dem Hauptgegenstand des Gesetzesentwurfes oder des Gesetzesvorschlages stehen.

Diese Verfassungsverbote haben ein ziemlich klares Ziel und sind sehr eng mit dem Konzept der Rechtssicherheit verbunden. In einer rechtsstaatlichen Rechtsordnung sollte es nur *ein* Hauptgesetz für jedes Sachgebiet geben (z. B. *ein* Gesetz über die Universitäten, *ein* Gesetz über die Einwanderung von Ausländern usw.), so dass sowohl den Staatsorganen ihre Befugnisse als auch den Bürgern ihre Rechte und Pflichten jederzeit klar sind. Das gilt insbesondere für Rechtsordnungen – wie die griechische – wo die Gesetzesunwissenheit nicht erlaubt ist.

b) Was ist aber die Praxis? Art. 74 Abs. 5 wird systematisch verletzt, wobei diese Verfassungswidrigkeit gar nicht gerichtlich kontrolliert und sanktioniert wird und werden kann, weil diese Rechtslage – nach h.M. – als *interna corporis* des Parlaments eingestuft wird.[5] Das ist kein neues Phänomen, aber hat in den letzten Jahren seinen Höhepunkt erreicht. In den letzten ungefähr drei Jahren werden fast alle Gesetzesentwürfe als „Multigesetzesentwürfe" (*Polinomosxedia*) oder als „Staubsaugergesetzesentwürfe" (*Nomosxedia–skoupa*) bezeichnet. In 2011, wurden im griechischen Parlament 128 Gesetzen abgestimmt. Die meisten von ihnen – 85 – waren Ratifizierungen von internationalen Verträgen, Verkörperung von EU Recht usw. Wie schon ihr Titel „Gesetz über ... und andere Vorschriften" beweist, von

---

[4] Weitere Beispiele könnten genannt werden. Nach Art. 76 Abs. 4 und 5 der griechischen Verfassung: „4. Ein von der Regierung als sehr dringlich bezeichneter Gesetzesentwurf oder Gesetzesvorschlag wird nach beschränkter Beratung in einer einzigen Sitzung im Plenum oder in der Abteilung gemäß Artikel 71, zur Abstimmung gebracht, wie die Geschäftsordnung des Parlaments dies vorsieht. 5. Die Regierung kann verlangen, dass ein Gesetzesentwurf oder Gesetzesvorschlag von dringendem Charakter in einer bestimmten Anzahl von Sitzungen beraten wird, wie die Geschäftsordnung des Parlaments dies vorsieht". In den letzten Jahren wurden die meisten Gesetzesentwürfe mit besonderer haushaltlicher Bedeutung von der Regierung als sehr dringlich bezeichnet und unter beschränkter Beratung nach Art. 76 Abs. 4 und 5 griechischer Verfassung abgestimmt. Es ist selbstverständlich, dass der Zeitdruck bei der Gesetzgebung ihre Qualität auf eine negative Weise beeinflusst.

[5] Siehe z. B. *Symvoulio tis Epikratias* (oberster Verwaltungsgericht Griechenlands), Entscheidungen 1721/1991, 1686/2003, 2927/2004, 309/2010, 3086/2011. Siehe auch die Minderheitsmeinung des Richters *Vassilios Aravantinos* in der Entscheidung *Symvoulio tis Epikratias* 3086/2011, nach der in Extremfällen die Einhaltung der Verfassungsvorschriften über das Gesetzgebungsverfahren ausnahmsweise gerichtlich kontrolliert werden kann.

den übrigen 43 Gesetzen mit original normativem Charakter war kein einziges Gesetz mit Art. 74 Abs. 5 der griechischen Verfassung vereinbar.[6]

c) Die Situation ist nicht sehr viel besser hinsichtlich der Zusatz- und Änderungsanträge zu den Gesetzesentwürfen. Diese Anträge haben im Regelfall nichts mit dem Hauptgegenstand des Gesetzesentwurfes zu tun. Zum Beispiel vom 5. bis zum 19. März 2012 – d. h. innerhalb von nur zwei Wochen – wurden ungefähr 150 Zusatz- und Änderungsanträge von Ministern und Mitgliedern des Parlaments in verschiedene Gesetzesentwürfe und zu allen möglichen Themen eingeführt. Regelungsgegenstände waren, *inter allia*, der Status der Gemeindeparteien, der Gehalt der Berater der Bürgermeister, die Ansiedlungsplanung, die Arbeitsprobleme in einem bestimmten Unternehmen, der Eintrittspreis zu Casinos, die Legalisierung von Häusern ohne Baugenehmigung, der Bau eines Friedhofs in einem Vorort von Athen usw.[7]

2. a) Zweites Beispiel: Nach Art. 76 Abs. 1 der griechischen Verfassung heißt, dass „über jeden Gesetzesentwurf und jeden Gesetzesvorschlag nur einmal dem Grundsatz nach, über die einzelnen Artikel und in seiner Gänze beraten und abgestimmt [wird]".

Diese Vorschrift, und insbesondere das Gebot der Abstimmung über die einzelnen Artikel, setzt voraus, dass ein Gesetzesentwurf mehrere Artikel beinhaltet. Mit anderen Worten, ist es verboten einen Gesetzesentwurf mit nur einem Artikel abzustimmen. Auch diese Verfassungsvorschrift ist sehr eng mit der Rechtssicherheit verbunden. Ein Gesetz mit allen möglichen Vorschriften in einem Artikel ist mit dem Rechtssicherheitsprinzip unvereinbar. Ein solches Gesetz ist nicht klar, es hat keine sinnvolle Strukturierung und seine einzelnen Vorschriften sind selbst nicht zitierbar.

b) Art. 76 Abs. 1 der griechischen Verfassung wurde bis vor kurzem gefolgt. Der griechische Gesetzgeber hat aber in den letzten Jahren selbst diese Vorschrift verletzt. Das Gesetz 4093/2012 – das sog. ‚Mittelfristige ökonomische Programm' – ist ein ziemlich charakteristischer Fall einer solchen Verletzung. Es hat theoretisch drei, praktisch aber nur einen Artikel.[8] Der erste Artikel beträgt ungefähr hundert Seiten im Gesetzesblatt[9] und befasst sich mit jedem möglichen Sachgebiet. Es gibt fast kein einzelnes Gebiet des staatlichen Handelns, das von diesem Artikel nicht geregelt wird. Nach diesen ungefähr hundert Seiten des ersten Artikels, folgt ein Artikel

---

[6] Diese Daten finden sich bei *Gerapetritis*, Giorgos: Die wirtschaftliche Krise als Element der Deregulierung der Rechtsquellenhierarchie (auf Griechisch), Nomiko Vima 2012, S. 2754 [2758].

[7] Siehe *Gerapetritis*, Giorgos: Verfassung und Parlament. Autonomie und Unkontrollierbarkeit von interna corporis (auf Griechisch), Athen, 2012, S. 223, Fn. 774.

[8] Dasselbe gilt für das Gesetz 4152/2013 ‚Eilige Maßnahmen über die Anwendung der Gesetze 4046/2012, 4093/2012 und 4127/2013' (Gesetzesblatt, Band A, 107/9 – 5 – 2013). Sein erster Artikel zählt ungefähr fünfzig Seiten und sein zweiter und letzter Artikel bezieht sich lediglich auf die Zeit der Inkraftsetzung des Gesetzes.

[9] Siehe Gesetzesblatt, Band A, 222/12 – 11 – 2012, S. 5525 ff.

von nur zwei Seiten über die griechische Lotterie „OPAP" („Organismos Prognostikon Agonon Podosferou") und ein dritter Artikel über die Zeit der Inkraftsetzung des Gesetzes. Dieses Gesetz ist tatsächlich überhaupt nicht zitierbar. Der griechische Gesetzgeber hat in einem neueren Gesetz[10] versucht, die Vorschriften des Gesetzes 4093/2012 wie folgt zu zitieren: „Der Satz c des inneren Absatzes 1 des Falls 1 des Unterabsatzes Z.3 des Absatzes Z des ersten Artikels des Gesetzes 4093/2012, wird wie im Folgendem ersetzt : ...".

3. a) Drittes Beispiel: Art. 44 Abs. 1 der griechischen Verfassung bestimmt: „In Ausnahmefällen eines außerordentlich dringenden und unvorhergesehenen Notstandes kann der Präsident der Republik auf Vorschlag des Ministerrates gesetzgeberische Akte [auf Griechisch: Praxis Nomothetikou Periechomenou] erlassen. Diese werden nach der Bestimmumgen des Artikels 72 Absatz 1 [d. h. im Parlamentsplenum] innerhalb von vierzig Tagen nach ihrem Erlaß oder innerhalb von vierzig Tagen nach Einberufung des Parlaments zu einer Sitzungsperiode dem Parlament zur Genehmigung vorgelegt. Werden sie dem Parlament innerhalb dieser Frist nicht vorgelegt oder vom Parlament innerhalb von drei Monaten nach ihrer Vorlage nicht genehmigt, treten sie für die Zukunft außer Kraft".

b) Auch diese Vorschrift wird nicht geachtet. Obwohl die gesetzgeberischen Akte nach dem Willen des Verfassungsgebers die absolute Ausnahme bleiben sollten, nahm ihre Zahl in den letzten Jahren wesentlich zu und die gesetzgeberischen Akte werden immer öfter von der Exekutive benutzt. Diese Praxis ist eine Verletzung des Demokratiegebots: Demokratie heißt vor allem dass alle wesentlichen Entscheidungen von den Volksvertretern getroffen werden und dass das Parlament sich nicht auf die Rolle der Ratifizierung der Regierungsentscheidungen beschränkt.

c) Die nur in Ausnahmefällen Benutzung der gesetzgeberischen Akte ist auch aus der Sicht der guten Gesetzgebung geboten. Das formale Gesetz – das heißt das vom Parlament abgestimmten Gesetz – ist mit Verfahrensvorkehrungen verbunden, die auf einen qualitativen Gesetzesinhalt zielen: Begründungsbericht, Bericht über die ökonomischen Konsequenzen der Gesetzesanwendung, Beratung des Gesetzesvorschlages im zuständigen Parlamentsausschuss, Beratung im Parlamentsplenum im Regelfall in mehreren Sitzungen, Änderungsanträge zum ursprünglichen Gesetzesvorschlag usw. Alle diese – mit der qualitativen Gesetzgebung sehr eng verbundenen – Möglichkeiten gibt es bei den gesetzgeberischen Akten einfach nicht.

---

[10] Art. 1 des Gesetzgeberischen Aktes (Praxi Nomothetikou Periechomenou nach Art. 44 Abs. 1 griechischer Verfassung) vom 9. 11. 2012 (Gesetzesblatt, Band A, 224/12–11–2012). Sehr charakteristisch für die schlechte Gesetzgebungsqualität ist auch die Tatsache, dass dieser Gesetzgeberische Akt das Gesetz 4093/2012 ändert, das am selben Tag (9–11–2012) abgestimmt worden ist.

III. Schlussbemerkung

Rechtssicherheit ist ein wesentlicher Bestandteil des Rechtsstaates. Die Überwindung der ökonomischen Krise und der inländische und ausländische Druck zur Einführung der damit verbundenen Vorschriften dürfen nicht zur Verletzung der Verfassungsvorschriften führen, die zum Schutz der Rechtssicherheit dienen. Aus diesen Gründen ist heute noch aktuell der Gedanke eines der größten deutschen Verfassungsrechtslehrer, Konrad Hesse. Er hat betont, dass eine Verfassung, der in Krisenzeiten nicht gefolgt wird, ihre Bedeutung verliert.[11]

---

[11] *Hesse*, Konrad: Grundfragen einer verfassungsmäßigen Normierung des Ausnahmezustandes, JZ 1960, S. 105 [108].

The Role of Private Arbitral Tribunals in State Reform: Can we trust Private Justice?

By *Stavros Brekoulakis**

Introduction

The paper argues that a critical shift from State to private justice may operate as an effective vehicle for State reform, by increasing efficiency in the administration of justice and eventually by enhancing the rule of law.[1]

The need for reform in the State judicial system makes comes from a commonplace yet crucial observation: State courts, and Greek courts in particular, are drowning under an excessive backlog of cases, which has critically undermined the delivery of justice, as well as public's confidence in the role of State judiciary. In some regional courts of Athens, the first available date for a hearing of a commercial dispute is in 6 years time, even more. Further, inefficiency of the Greek national justice system has been highlighted recently in the European Commission's Semester Report (issued in March 2013). The Report publishes a EU Justice Scoreboard for justice systems in all Member States, where Greece scores poorly in many areas, such as the time needed to resolve civil and commercial cases, the rate of resolving civil and commercial cases, the perception of independence of Greek civil justice and the lack of electronic systems to manage cases. This is despite the fact that the Greek government scores highly with regard to money invested in national civil justice (it is ranked 8th among EU Member States), and with regard to the ratio of judges to inhabitants (Greece is raked 9th with approx. 30 judges per 100.000), and the ratio of lawyers to inhabitants (Greece is ranked 1st alongside Luxemburg with approx. 360 lawyers per 100.000 inhabitants).[2]

Of course, it is not only Greek courts and the Greek judicial system that is faced with such grave challenges calling for radical reforms. Similar issues trouble almost all national judicial systems, including those in common law jurisdictions, which

---

[*] Professor in International Arbitration and Commercial Law, School of Law, Queen Mary University of London.

[1] I use the term private justice to refer to any type of alternative to national courts dispute resolution. This includes mainly arbitration, whereby the decision rendered in the form of an arbitral award is final, binding and mandatory for the parties, just like a court judgement. But it also includes other non-adjudicatory methods, such as mediation, conciliation or assisted negotiation.

[2] See in more detail: http://ec.europa.eu/justice/effective-justice/files/justice_scoreboard_communication_en.pdf.

normally enjoy an excellent reputation of efficiency in the delivery of justice. However, the Greek case for reform becomes more complicated because of the strong aversion, which often takes the form of an ideological resistance, of large parts in the Greek state and society against any attempt for change.

Now, if we agree that state justice systems face existential challenges today, and fail to deliver efficient and timely services, the question is whether alternative dispute resolution methods may be more efficient? There are a number of studies that have demonstrated that the answer to the above question is an unequivocal yes. Arbitration is not without problems, but it has proved to be, if not less costly, certainly quicker, with the average time for the resolution of a commercial dispute being 18 months from the time the Claimant initiates arbitral proceedings.

But, if private justice can deliver, at least in some areas of law, faster and more efficient justice what is the main stumbling block that hinders the transition from public to private litigation? Why do we show a remarkable resistance in allowing a wide range of commercial, and I would dare to think some types of non-commercial, disputes to be determined by private tribunals? Why do we still argue, for example, whether anti-trust disputes, tax disputes, labour disputes, administrative disputes, insolvency disputes, let alone family disputes, can be submitted to tribunals? The answer to all the above questions is because of perceptions, which are often misplaced about the role of public policy and private justice. Again, the criticism against arbitration is not exclusively associated with the project of reforms in the Greek state judiciary. Rather, it has wider implications for state judiciaries in many other jurisdictions where critics question the authority of private tribunals to deal with disputes involving state-sensitive matters, such as anti-trust disputes, or disputes involving parties with presumably weak negotiation power, such as employees, franchisees and consumers.[3]

The paper examines the criticism against private justice and attempts to restore some truths about it. Debunking misplaced myths about the role of private justice and international arbitral tribunals is a necessary condition for a well-informed and unbiased discussion on state court reforms.

Main Part

Critics of the arbitration paradigm take issue with a number of typical features of the arbitration procedure, such as the evidentiary process,[4] the private and confiden-

---

[3] *Linda Silberman*, 'International Arbitration: Comments from a Critic' 13 Am Rev Int'l Arb (2002) 17 "My quarrel with these various dispute resolution mechanisms has more to do with the basic underlying decision to entrust matters of great public significance to decision-making by supranational institutions than it does with arbitration *per se*. But the process of arbitration exacerbates the concern."

[4] It is pointed out that the evidentiary process in arbitration is less rigorous than that followed by national courts. For example, the U.S. Supreme court has noted in *Alexander v.*

tial nature of arbitration proceedings,[5] or the lack of appeal process in arbitration.[6] Eventually, accusations against the conduct of arbitration lead to an unwarranted debate on policy preferences.[7] This debate has been the subject matter of extensive discussion and there is little scope in revising it here.[8]

Gardner-Denver: "[T]he fact-finding process in arbitration usually is not equivalent to judicial fact-finding. The record of the arbitration proceedings is not as complete; the usual rules of evidence do not apply; and rights and procedures common to civil trials, such as discovery, compulsory process, cross-examination, and testimony under oath, are often severely limited or unavailable".

[5] *Choudhury,* supra note 13, at 784, 788, who refers to the lack of transparency and democratic process in arbitration: "A final difference that raises democratic concerns is that, despite parallels between the functions of investment arbitral tribunals and administrative agencies, certain democratic restraints on administrative agencies do not apply to investment arbitral tribunals." Cf also the decision of the US Supreme Court in *Merrill Lynch, Pierce, Fenner & Smith, Inc. v. Ware,* 414 U.S. 117, 136, 94 S Ct 383, 394, 38 L.Ed.2d 348 (1973). Here the Court in rebutting an argument forwarded by Merrill Lynch that the public adjudication of disputes may jeopardise the confidence of the investors and the market in general, noted at 136: "There is no explanation of why a judicial proceeding, even though public, would prevent lessening of investor confidence. It is difficult to understand why muffling a grievance in the cloakroom of arbitration would undermine confidence in the market. To the contrary, for the generally sophisticated investing public, market confidence may tend to be restored in the light of impartial public court adjudication."

[6] See Justice Stevens, dissenting in *Mitsubishi Motors Corp. v. Soler Chrysler-Plymouth 473 U.S. 614 S Ct 3346 (1985) (U.S. Supreme Court, 2 July 1985)* at 657–658: "Arbitration awards are only reviewable for manifest disregard of the law [...] and the rudimentary procedures which make arbitration so desirable in the context of a private dispute often mean that the record is so inadequate that the arbitrator's decision is virtually unreviewable. Despotic decisionmaking of this kind is fine for parties who are willing to agree in advance to settle for a best approximation of the correct result in order to resolve quickly and inexpensively any contractual dispute that may arise in an ongoing commercial relationship. Such informality, however, is simply unacceptable when every error may have devastating consequences for important businesses in our national economy and may undermine their ability to compete in world markets." See also *Silberman,* supra note, at 11 "the lack of a genuine appeal means there is no meaningful oversight with respect to rulings of the arbitrators." See further Van Harten, *supra* note 19, at 435 "unlike other decisions or awards in public law, awards under investment treaties are internationally enforceable in courts around the world with limited opportunity for judicial review, in particular for alleged errors of law (other than jurisdictional or gross procedural errors). As a result, investment treaty arbitrators have a comprehensive jurisdiction to decide what the state is, what it is allowed to do under the law, and what happens when it is found to have done something unlawful, without the prospect of review and correction of their decisions by a court, whether domestic or international."

[7] See for example *Jean Sternlight,* Rethinking the Constitutionality of the Supreme Court's Preference for Binding Arbitration: A Fresh Assessment of Jury Trial, Separation of Powers, and Due Process Concerns, 72 Tul. L. Rev. 1 (1997) who argues that private dispute system violates US constitutional rights because it allows for no jury trial or for US style discovery process or appeal process or even the fact that arbitrators selected need not be lawyers, or other of the typical features found in the US litigation system.

[8] For a more detailed discussion of all of these points see *Thomas Carbonneau,* 'Arbitracide': The Story of Anti-Arbitration Sentiment in the US Congress, 18 Am. Rev. Int'l

There is, though, one pervasive accusation of the arbitration paradigm, which arbitration scholars have been unable to convincingly respond to so far. This accusation concerns *arbitrators* as decision-makers, rather than the conduct of arbitration. Here the critique is that arbitrators are – at worst – biased in favour of a particular group of interests, represented by investors or private corporations,[9] and – at best – not able to take the public interests into account when deciding an investment treaty dispute or a commercial dispute that implicates public policy. It is this accusation that is the main focus of this essay.

The view that arbitrators are predisposed or unfit to deal with public policy disputes is often explained by reference to some fundamental differences between national courts and arbitration, such as the difference in the status of arbitrators and judges, and the difference in the process for their selection. Judges are selected and promoted on the basis of a rigorous system of review of their skills and competences in law. By contrast, anyone can theoretically be selected and appointed as an arbitrator, even if he or she is not a lawyer.[10] Tenured judges are public servants and financially dependent on the state. By contrast, arbitrators are private adjudicators who have a contractual duty toward the parties that selected them, and they have no allegiance to a public institution or society.[11] Thus, the party-selection process

---

Arb. 233 (2007), who reviews addresses many of the criticisms raised in a number of recent US legislative initiatives, attempting to curtail the material scope of arbitration.

[9] See in more detail the collection of essays in *Michael Waibel/Asha Kaushal* et al. (eds.), The Backlash against Investment Arbitration (Kluwer 2010), and in particular the essay of *Gus Van Harten*, Perceived bias in Investment Treaty Arbitration, at 434, arguing that the arbitration paradigm is not appropriate for investment treaty disputes, because the latter "concern the exercise of general regulatory powers that are typically subject to judicial review under constitutional or administrative law", and also at 432, arguing that "Investment treaty arbitration is characterized by an apparent bias in favor of claimants and against respondent states. This perception is reasonably held in light of structural features of the system, especially its use of arbitration to decide public law."

[10] In *University Life Insurance Co. v. Unimarc Ltd.,* Judge Posner wrote: "[Federal antitrust issues] are considered to be at once too difficult to be decided competently by arbitrators – who are not judges, and often not even lawyers – and too important to be decided otherwise than by competent tribunals".

See also the 8 May 2012 Open Letter (Petition) From Lawyers to the Negotiators of the Trans-Pacific Partnership Urging the Rejection of Investor-State Dispute Settlement (available at: http://tpplegal.wordpress.com/open-letter/?pagename=open-letter&like=1&_wpnonce=eae4429cd0&wpl_rand=5697917af3). "Moreover, the design of the Investor-State system tribunals allows lawyers to rotate between roles as arbitrators and advocates for investors in a manner that would be unethical for judges."

[11] *Van Harten*, supra note, at 444, notes "Arbitrators, unlike judges, operate in a market where each supplier of the symbolic capital underlying individual reputations has an interest to further his or her own status and that of the industry as a whole". Also *Choudhury*, supra note, at 787 argues "A second difference is the lack of independence of the adjudicative body. Whereas in many judicial systems, the hallmarks of an independent judiciary are tenure and financial security, investment arbitration has neither".

is viewed as giving arbitrators an incentive to favour repeat arbitration players, which are largely assumed to be the big corporations or investors.[12]

Arbitration scholars have attempted to respond to these criticisms, which are often overplayed and seem to be based more on entrenched perceptions than empirical observations. For example, it has been noted that empirical evidence is inconclusive on whether arbitrators are biased in favour of repeat players in arbitration.[13] In any case, it is wrong to assume that investors and big corporations are the only possible repeat-players in arbitration. Investment disputes tend to implicate a small number of states, which therefore appear repeatedly as respondents in investment treaty arbitrations.[14] Furthermore, the fact that arbitrators are chosen by the parties may actually create a market competition among arbitrators that should give arbitrators an incentive to improve their decision-making skills and quality of their judgment, and build an inde-

---

[12] See further relevant discussion among US scholars, Rau, Alan Scott Rau, 'Integrity in Private Judging' (1997) 38 S Tex L Rev 485, at 521 "Repeat business for the arbitrator is likely only if he is able to retain the future goodwill of both union and management; the desire to do so may give him an incentive (in the hallowed phrase) to 'split the baby'."; *Chris Drahozal*, A Behavioral Analysis of Private Judging, 67 L. & Contemporary Problems 105, 127 (2004), "competition among arbitrators also gives rise to the possibility of 'repeat player' bias, in which arbitrators have an incentive to favor parties who are more likely to provide future business. To date, however, the evidence is inconclusive on whether such bias exists"; *Sternlight*, supra note, at 4 "claims brought in federal court were required to be heard by a judge who, having been appointed for life and ensured no diminution in compensation, [are] more insulated from bias than an elected decision maker" and p. 6 "The arbitrators selected need not be lawyers nor need they follow the law. They may even be affiliated with the company's line of business."
Similar concerns have been raised by scholars in relation to investment treaty arbitration. See for example *Choudhury*, supra note, at 787 "the market for appointments as an arbitrator is highly competitive and arbitral fees are very lucrative, heightening the need for arbitrators to be concerned about their reputations in order to ensure reappointment"; *Van Harten*, supra note , at 152–53 "as merchants of adjudicative services, arbitrators have a financial stake in furthering [arbitration's] appeal to claimants", which leads to an "apprehension of bias in favor of allowing claims and awarding damages against governments".

[13] *William Park*, Arbitrator Integrity, in: Waibel/Kaushal, supra note, at 208: "Much can be said on behalf of the 'professional arbitrator' who serves repeatedly, albeit in different types of cases. There may be some truth to the oft-repeated assertion that arbitrators want to see cases decided in favor of the parties which appointed them. Usually, however, an even stronger incentive exists to safeguard professional status, particularly with peers. Individuals who serve as arbitrators care deeply about the respect of their colleagues, for reasons both personal and professional. Doing a good job builds a positive reputation. Few enticements to good behavior are stronger for those who sit regularly as arbitrators than a colleague's appreciation of one's ability and integrity."

[14] For example, 51 cases have been filed against Argentina and 25 against Venezuela (Latest Developments in Investor-State Dispute Settlement, UNCTAD, April 2012, http://unctad.org/en/PublicationsLibrary/webdiaeia2012d10_en.pdf). Cf *Park*, idem, at .216: "no evidence supports the proposition that the arbitration system operates as an assembly line of decisions that favors the investor. Host states seem to win their share of cases; however, a win might be measured" referring to a long list of investment decisions favoring host states at fns 96 and 96.

pendent and impartial profile as an arbitrator.[15] Finally, it has been pointed out that existing provisions in institutional rules, national laws and codes of best practices require arbitrators to meticulously disclose any potential conflict of interest and refuse appointments in cases that may give rise to appearance of bias.[16]

All these responses are well known in arbitration discourse. However, they tend to focus on how arbitration deals with *individual biases*.[17] These responses aim to explain, for example, why an individual arbitrator has a market incentive to improve his personal decision-making skills and try to abandon his personal predilections, or when an individual arbitrator must disclose any potential conflict he may have with one of the parties or the subject matter of the dispute. They say little about whether the system of arbitration is designed to foster or eschew *collective biases*, which may also explain why accusations of bias still persist in arbitration.

By collective biases I refer to the case where a *strong majority* of the people who act as arbitrators share the same view on fundamental legal, social, economic and of course political matters, which naturally leads all of them to systematically favour

---

[15] See *Richard A. Posner*, An Economic Approach to the Law of Evidence, 51 Stan. L. Rev. 1477, 1491, 1501 (1999); but cf *Drahozal*, supra note 210, at 128 who states that there is no conclusive answer to this point "While there is reason to believe that market forces may reduce the effect of cognitive illusions on arbitral decisionmaking, the results of existing studies are far from conclusive." *Park*, supra note 146, at 206: "no evidence supports the proposition that the arbitral system as it now exists provides incentives to produce inaccurate decisions that favor either claimants or respondents or even that such incentives actually exist. Common sense tells us that the big losers would be none other than professional arbitrators themselves if the process did not inspire general confidence."

Of course one could point out here that competition among arbitrators may indeed provide market incentives for arbitrators to improve their decision-making skills, but it can equally provide them with incentives to develop a specific decision-making profile, for example by awards or scholarly writing, leaning towards one or another side of crucial arbitration debates in order to be more attractive to specific types of repeat arbitration users.

[16] See 2012 UNCITRAL Arbitration Rules Art.11 "When a person is approached in connection with his or her possible appointment as an arbitrator, he or she shall disclose any circumstances likely to give rise to justifiable doubts as to his or her impartiality or independence. An arbitrator, from the time of his or her appointment and throughout the arbitral proceedings, shall without delay disclose any such circumstances to the parties and the other arbitrators unless they have already been informed by him or her of these circumstances". Similar provisions can be found in ICC Art.11, LCIA Art. 5.3 and in the rules of all major arbitration institutions. Cf the IBA Guidelines on Conflicts of Interests in International Arbitration provided for detailed guidelines on disclosure. Further, on this point see in general the discussion *Carbonneau*, supra note, at 269; and *Rau*, supra note, at 485.

[17] Risking stating the obvious, I should note here that I am not referring to explicit biases, namely any conscious decision of an arbitrator to choose one outcome that he knows it is the "wrong" one, even in his own eyes. This kind of behaviour is sanctioned by all arbitration law that provide for the removal of a biased arbitrator (see for example EAA s.24). I am here talking about unconscious, semi-conscious biases (to use Laski's term *Harold Joseph Laski*, Studies in Law and Politics 164–80 (1968)) cognitive limitations, natural inclinations and predilections that may Inadvertently influence the judgment of an arbitrator.

certain legal interpretations and outcomes when they are performing their decision-making task.

This work accepts as a working hypothesis that individual biases abound in arbitration as in every other decision-making body.[18] It may even be futile to attempt to deal with individual biases. For example, the International Bar Association Guidelines on Conflicts of Interest in International Arbitration set out a number of typical factual scenarios that are only *proxies* of impartiality, and they are naturally unable to capture cognitive biases, natural inclinations and or unconscious and semi-conscious predilections. The International Bar Association Guidelines on Conflicts of Interests in International Arbitration for example refer to cases where "the arbitrator is a manager, director or member of the supervisory board, or has a similar controlling influence in one of the parties"[19] or the case where "the arbitrator is a lawyer in the same law firm as the counsel to one of the parties."[20]

Individual biases should be acceptable in arbitration,[21] as long as the system ensures that an assortment of individual biases and prejudices exists among arbitrators. Instead of looking for individual biases, the focus of our inquiry should turn on whether the system of arbitration eschews or nurtures *collective* biases among arbitrators.

Irrespective of whether one takes the hard-line view of legal realists that law is so indeterminate that it is effectively reduced to politics,[22] or a more moderate view of qualified indeterminacy,[23] it is nowadays generally accepted that law allows for a great deal of decision-making discretion. If substantive law, even under a qualified theory on indeterminacy, allows for more than one possible construction and outcome, an adjudication system that espouses collective biases will produce decisions

---

[18] *Rau*, supra note, at 488 "An abundant literature continues to remind us that decisionmakers who have lived in the world at all will invariably come to a case with perspectives and beliefs and preconceptions that bear the stamp of their past experiences. This is unavoidable-nor would we prevent it if we could."

[19] IBA Guidelines on Conflicts of Interests in International Arbitration non-waivable red list.

[20] IBA Guidelines on Conflicts of Interests in International Arbitration waivable red list.

[21] *Rau*, supra note, at 495: "arbitrators … are particularly likely … when not sitting as arbitrators, to be actively engaged in professions whose members cross each other's paths daily and this suggests that it may be unrealistic to insist on any degree of isolation that approaches the judicial. In the abstract, perhaps, such an intensity of worldly connection might seem to justify an even greater concern and vigilance in review, especially when it is coupled with the norm-free, unreviewable nature of arbitral discretion. But after all, arbitrators are likely to be valued at least in part precisely for the background and interests they share with the parties themselves."

[22] See for example *Brian Leiter*, Legal Indeterminacy, in Legal Theory, 481 (1995).

[23] The issue of indeterminacy in law has been the subject of extensive debate; see *Catherine Rogers*, 'The Vocation of the International Arbitrator' (2005) 20 Am UJ I'l L 988, at 988 who refers to a "bounded discretion" that decision-makers enjoy, and also provides a brief overvies of the relevant literature on indeterminacy.

that largely favour a certain outcome. How can we assess whether an adjudication system, and arbitration in particular, is institutionally biased? There are different possible methodological approaches to this inquiry.

One is to conduct behavioural studies to examine whether arbitrators are more susceptible to biases than judges. Alternatively, we may conduct statistical and empirical surveys in order to find out whether a significant percentage of awards typically favour one particular party, for example the investors or states in investment treaty arbitrations. This type of empirical survey actually exists. However, the findings of these surveys provide us with inconclusive evidence on whether the decision-making behaviour of arbitrators differs from that of judges,[24] or whether international tribunals statistically favour a certain party over another.[25]

Another way to deal with collective biases is to perform a doctrinal analysis, looking into whether the jurisprudence of arbitral tribunals has developed legal norms and principles that systematically favour a certain party over another. This type of analysis abounds, in arbitration literature, but its findings are equally inconclusive, with scholars taking differing views.[26]

---

[24] *Drahozal*, supra note, refers to the findings of a number of experimental studies on bias in decision making, which then applies to arbitrators to tentatively conclude that "like judges, arbitrators may be less susceptible to at least some cognitive illusions than jurors".

[25] See study of *Susan Franck,* International Investment Arbitration: Winning, Losing and Why, 7 Columbia FDI Perspectives (2009), who has found that in investment treaty arbitration States tend to be more successful (58 %) than investors (39 %). She further shows that investors even when successful tend to receive a relatively small portion of the damages claimed, namely US$10 million on average, with the average amount of claim being at US$ 343 million. For commercial arbitration cf *Drahozal*, supra note 210, who notes that although there have been suggestions that one possible collective cognitive bias of arbitrators is their tendency to compromise (or split the baby), there is no empirical evidence to that effect. In fact Drahozal points out "Two published studies of commercial arbitration (one domestic and one international) have found no evidence that arbitrators make compromise awards." Referring to *Soia Mentschikoff*, Commercial Arbitration, 61 Colum. L. Rev. 846 (1961), and *Stephanie E. Keer/Richard W. Naimark*, Arbitrators Do Not "Split the Baby" – Empirical Evidence from International Business Arbitration, 18 J. Int'l Arb. 573, 573–74 (2001) who have showed "emphatically that arbitrators do not engage in the practice of 'splitting the baby'."

[26] On the one hand see for example *Brower/Schill*, supra note, at. 476 who argue that "investment treaties and investment-treaty arbitration do not unilaterally favor investors' interests over competing public policy choices and do not institutionalize a pro-investor bias. To the contrary, investment law and arbitration … aim at anchoring good governance standards that lock states into a policymaking framework that is open towards the functioning of markets in a global economic system, without losing sight of the state's legitimate regulatory interests."

On the other hand see for example *M. Sornarajah*, BIICL Annual Conference, described in Tolga Yalkin, International Investment Arbitration: Poisoned at the Root, Jun. 24, 2009, http:// papers.ssrn.com/s013/papers.cfm?abstract_id=1438634, arguing that the arbitration paradigm is biased in favour business interests and capital exporting states. At the same time, scholars who argue that jurisprudence has developed norms that favour investors at the expense of human rights, have been working on doctrinal solutions that would allow for a more balanced approach in investment arbitration. For example, an increasing number of scholars have been arguing that investment treaty tribunals should adopt the principle of proportionality as the

By contrast, I intend to discuss collective biases by looking into the procedural design arbitration and focusing on some basic structural features such as the method for the constitution of arbitral tribunals and the lack of tenured arbitrators. As was briefly mentioned above, these typical features of the arbitration model have been the subject of examination and criticism on the basis that they compromise arbitration's integrity and legitimacy.[27] However, I intend to discuss them from a different position, which is informed by the findings of studies on adjudication and politics, and come to a different conclusion, arguing that they actually constitute important safeguards that ensure that collective biases in arbitration are eschewed.

Seminal scholarly works have shown that the paradigm of state judiciary is highly politicized and conducive to collective biases. Griffiths has illustrated this point with regard to the judiciary in the United Kingdom using empirical data and doctrinal analysis of the jurisprudence of Court of Appeal and House of Lords.[28] Duncan Kennedy has shown the same for the United States adopting a critical legal theory approach and relying on analytical and even linguistic constructs.[29] Other scholars have come to similar conclusions for other types of adjudication[30] and adjudication

---

default method of adjudication in order to judicially balance competing policies, such as economic law and human rights, and eschew one-sided awards; see for example *Jasper Krommendijk/John Morijn*, 'Proportional' by What Meaure(s)? Balancing Investor Inteterests and Human Rights by Way of Applying the proportionality Principle in Investor-State Arbitration, in: Pierre-Marie Dupuy/Francesco Francioni/Ernst-Ulrich Petersmann, Human Rights in International Investment Law and Arbitration 422 (2009); see also in the same collection of essays Part III. Judicial 'Balancing' or Economic Law and Human Rights in Regional Courts.

[27] It is argued for example, that the system of *ad hoc* arbitral panels where arbitrators are selected by the parties, rather than a 'neutral' and central authority, raises concerns about bias and conflicts of interests; see *Silberman*, supra note, p 17 discussing the constitution of WTO, NAFTA and ICSID arbitral panels in particular noting that "A lack of transparency and accountability exists at both the 'panel' and Appellate Body level. The competence and neutrality of the decisionmakers is critical to the success of the system, but a system of *ad hoc* panels leaves open concerns about expertise, bias, and conflicts of interest."; see further *Van Harten*, supra note, at 437 who argues that "security of tenure, remuneration, and administrative independence – are critical safeguards of judicial independence" and further at 445 "Security of tenure serves the additional purpose of insulating adjudicators from powerful private interests and of ensuring that no one can reasonably claim that a judge decided a dispute, or interpreted the law, in order to further his or her own career. In this respect, the public law character of the adjudicative mechanism becomes critical".

[28] *John Griffith*, The Politics of the Judiciary (4th ed. 1991), see also *Adam Gearey/Wayne Morrison/Robert Jago*, The Politics of the Common Law: Perspectives Rights, Processes, Institutions (2009) Chapters 3 and 4, which provide an excellent interdisciplinary account of the politics of English common law and judiciary.

[29] *Duncan Kennedy*, A Critique of Adjudication (Harvard 1997).

[30] See for example Cf *Max M. Schanzenbach/Emerson H. Tiller*, Reviewing the Sentencing Guidelines: Judicial Politics, Empirical Evidence, and Reform, 75 U. Chi. L. Rev. 715 (2008) illustrating how political ideology matters in criminal sentencing and *Thomas J. Miles/Cass R. Sunstein*, The Real World of Arbitrariness Review, 75 U. Chi. L. Rev. 761 (2008) who has presented empirical data suggesting that the political preferences of judges influence their review of agency decisions.

bodies, including regional courts such as the Court Justice of the European Union,[31] and international courts, such as the International Court of Justice and the International Criminal Court.[32]

A common finding of all these works is that judiciary systems with a structured hierarchy and a central authority, either the state or intergovernmental political bodies, that exercises political control over the appointment, promotion and financial remuneration of the judges are conducive to collective biases. In many of these works it is further demonstrated that the process of the selection, appointment and promotion of the judges within such a structured judiciary system is *actually* informed and governed by clear political considerations.[33]

Equally interesting, albeit hardly surprising, is the finding that the development of collective biases in national judiciaries begins much earlier than the time that a judge is first appointed in the judiciary office. Education, social background and the early professional life of potential judges are crucial factors that are heavily influenced by the class structure of a state and further contribute to the homogeneity of national judiciaries. As Griffiths notes, UK "judges are the product of a class and have the characteristics of that class. Typically coming from middleclass professional families, independent schools, Oxford or Cambridge, they spend twenty to twenty-five years in successful practice at the bar, mostly in London."[34] Griffiths was of course writing these lines in the 1990's.[35] Since then a range of policies was developed to

---

[31] See *Karen Alter*, Who are the 'Masters of the Treaty'?: European Governments and the European Court of Justice, 52 International Organisation 121 (1998).

[32] See *Ruth Mackenzie/Kate Malleson/Penny Martin/Philippe Sands*, Selecting International Judges: Principles, Process, and Politics (2010) who have found that "Evidence of politicization is apparent at both the nomination and election states... it is not unusual for individuals to be selected as a result of overtly political considerations or even nepotism. Whatever form of nomination process is adopted, all nominated candidates must work their way through a highly politicized selection process"; see also *Phillippe Sands*, Global Governance and the International Judiciary: Choosing Our Judges, 56 Current Legal Problems 481 (2003); The Politics of Establishing an International Criminal Court, 6 Duke J. Comp. & Int'l L. 167 (1995) 167.

[33] *Erik Voeten*, The Politics of International Judicial Appointments, 9 Chi. J. Int'l L. 387, 389 (2009) who refers to a number of political factors "including party affiliation and political connections".

[34] *Griffith*, supra note refers to a number of surveys which show that a notable majority of the judges come from certain classes, schools and universities, see pp. 31 et seq. "Occasionally the brilliant lower-middle-class or working-class boy or girl has won their place in this distinguished gathering. With very few exceptions, judges are required to be selected from amongst practicing barristers and it is difficult for anyone without a private income to survive the first years of practice. To become a successful barrister, therefore, it is necessary to have financial support and so the background has to be that of the reasonably well-to-do family which, as a matter of course, sends its sons or daughters to public schools and then to Oxford or Cambridge."

[35] The first edition was in the 1970's; but the Oxbridge reference has not changed in later editions. Cf also *Rau*, supra note, fn 113 "Of all federal district judges appointed in the Nixon through Clinton administrations (through 1994), 88% were male, and 86.4% were white. Of

reform the judicial appointment process and promote diversity.[36] Yet, as is generally acknowledged, the deep-seated problem of lack of diversity in the judiciary of the United Kingdom is still persisting.[37]

Moreover, the privileges of a tenured judiciary post accords national judges a status of established authority that further informs their attitude towards the law. They enjoy absolute immunity and they are often appointed to preside over commissions, committees and tribunals of all kinds. These privileges reinforce the perception of them, as well as their self-perception, *as guardians of the state interests and order.*

The result of these processes is a judiciary that is an institutionally cohesive group of adjudicators, the great majority of whom share "a unifying attitude of mind, a political position, which is primarily concerned to protect and conserve certain values and institutions".[38]

For example, Griffiths shows that in England for over a century the attitude of the senior judiciary has been consistently favouring the interests of *status quo* in a number of legal matters, including that of law and order, political and economic conflict, sexual and social mores, personal liberty and property rights, race relationships, protest and governmental confidentiality.

Judges are therefore collectively part of the state apparatus that generally favours a certain construction of a piece of legislation or a certain outcome of a legal inquiry, which are unlikely to be progressive at any rate.

I should qualify the above observations with two clarifications. First, when I am referring to political biases, I am not referring to political *partisanship.* Even within the homogeneous ideological context of national judiciaries, there are genuine differences among judges on a number of legal and political matters. The political division is most obvious in the Supreme Court of the United States, for example, where judges tend to take differing approaches to law on the basis of their general political stance as conservative or liberal. Rather, I am here referring to the critical state function that judges perform, as well as the perception of themselves as guardians of the *status quo* and the existing political structure.[39] Individually, judges may support the Republicans or the Democrats in the US, or they may vote for the Conservative or the Labour or the Liberal party in the UK. Collectively, though in their role and function, they are neither political partisans nor radicals. They are "protectors and conservators of what

---

all federal court of appeals judges appointed during this time, 89 % were male, and 90.2 % were white" citing *Kathleen Maguire/Ann L. Pastore*, Sourcebook Of Criminal Justice Statistics – 1994 68–69 (1995), as his source.

[36] See *Kate Malleson*, Diversity in the Judiciary: The Case for Positive Action, 36 J. Law & Soc. 376 (2009). The most radical of these policies has been the creation of a new Judicial Appointments Commission in 2006.

[37] See *Lizzie Barmes/Kate Malleson*, The Legal Profession as Gatekeeper to the Judiciary: Design Faults in Measures to Enhance Diversity, 74 Modern L. Rev. 245 (2011).

[38] *Griffith*, supra note, at 19.

[39] Idem, at 272–73.

has been, of the relationships and interests on which, *in their view*, our society is founded".[40]

Secondly and more importantly, I am not at all suggesting – nor do the studies I refer to suggest – that national judges are deliberately or in bad faith making decisions in order to serve the interests of the government or the central authority that has appointed them. I do not for a moment question their moral integrity, and I readily accept that they decide on the basis of what they consider to be the best course of action for the whole society and public interests. I am simply arguing that what they consider to be in the interest of the state and the society is heavily informed by their unconscious and semi-unconscious cognitive biases and prejudices, which have been taken into account for their appointment in the first place. The judiciary performs with integrity the function that it was originally created to perform.

The appointing processes and structure of judiciaries, which shape its political function and ideology, should be contrasted with those of arbitral tribunals. The lack of tenured arbitrators and the selection of the members of the tribunal by the parties make international arbitration an adjudication paradigm of diffused biases. As is well known, in international arbitration each party will typically appoint one arbitrator, with the presiding arbitrator being appointed by the two party-appointed arbitrators and very often with the agreement of the parties.[41] Normally, there is no central authority in international arbitration that collectively selects and appoints all members of a tribunal on the basis of a single set of political criteria and influences.[42] It is the parties that determine *ad hoc* the synthesis of the tribunal on the basis of self-interested and therefore often conflicting considerations.

In fact, the right of the parties to participate in the constitution of arbitral tribunals is a constitutional feature of arbitration.[43] An arbitration clause that provided, for example, that "if a dispute arises, one party will appoint all members of the tribunal"

---

[40] Idem, at 20 and at 328: "this does not mean that no judges are capable of moving with the times, of adjusting to changed circumstances. But *their function in our society is to do so belatedly*" (emphasis added).

[41] This is the case when a tribunal consists of three members, which is often the case in large disputes, see for example the ICSID Convention Art. 37 and the UNCITRAL Arbitration Rules Art. 9. However, even when a tribunal consists of one member (cf LCIA Rules Art.5.4 ("A sole arbitrator shall be appointed unless the parties have agreed in writing otherwise or unless the LCIA Court determines that in view of all the circumstances of the case a three-member tribunal is appropriate"), parties will equally participate in the constitution of the tribunal, by agreeing to jointly appoint the arbitrator.

[42] *Park*, supra note, at 191 "In contrast to national legal communities, which tend to adopt relatively formalized paths for appointing judges, the fragmented framework of international arbitration relies on more fluid processes for selecting decision-makers and vetting their integrity.

[43] *Rau*, supra note, at 506: "In international practice, the tripartite model is in fact a norm which will be surrendered only with difficulty to many, indeed, the right to choose one member of the panel is the very 'essence of arbitration.'"

would most likely be an invalid arbitration clause.[44] This unique forum design of arbitration makes it likely that tribunals will represent the biases of all the parties in a dispute.[45] Thus, individual cognitive biases and prejudices of the members of a tribunal are expected to cancel each other out, or at least lead to a balanced and moderate approach.[46]

As was noted above, despite the lack of diversity in national judiciaries, judges may still have their personal ideological preferences that will naturally inform their legal decisions on particular matters.[47] Judiciaries may lack partisans or radical decision-makers in their rankings, but they have certain judges leaning toward conservative ideas or toward liberal ideas. As Duncan Kennedy notes, a conservative judge will normally favour the principle of freedom of contract and the efficiency of free markets, whereas a liberal judge will favour the application of mandatory rules on a number of issues from minimum wage and product liability. When parties submit their dispute to national courts, they are normally left at the mercy of the ideological biases of the judge or judges that happen to be called to determine the case. Whether the judge or judges, reviewing a dispute, will take a conservative or a liberal approach thereto is a matter of good or bad fortune for a party, and there is nothing that a party can do to ensure that the ideological premise of his position is shared with at least one of the judges that will determine the issue. Therefore, it is likely that a

---

[44] See here the *Dutco v BKMI and Siemens*, decision of the Cour de Cassation, 7 January 1991, Journal de Droit International 707 (1992) with note Ch. Jarrosson. In a consortium dispute Dutco brought a claim before an ICC tribunal against BKMI and Siemens. The two co-defendants requested the ICC Court to appoint one arbitrator each, claiming that they have divergent interests, but the ICC Court rejected their request and asked them to jointly appoint a single arbitrator; otherwise, the ICC Court threatened them to appoint a single arbitrator on their behalf. Eventually, the two co-defendants appointed a single arbitration but they subsequently challenged the ensuing award before the French courts on the basis of violation of due process. The Cour de Cassation found that by threatening the two co-defendants to appoint a single arbitrator on their behalf when the claimant had already exercised its right to appoint its own arbitrator, the ICC Court had violated due process and "equality of the parties in the appointment of arbitrators [which] is a matter of public policy which can be waived only after the disputes has arisen".

[45] *Rau*, supra note, at 495 "arbitrators are likely to be valued at least in part precisely for the background and interests they share with the parties themselves. And so the parties'can ask no more impartiality than inheres in the method they have chosen'. Where they bargain with their eyes open for such a process of dispute resolution, there is much in the way of 'interests' and 'relationships' that such a bargain can legitimate. The result is in any case likely to come closer to their original expectations and to their sense of justice than could any result mandated by the law of judicial disqualification."

[46] Cf *Esposito/Martire*, supra note, at 327, "International arbitration has to be considered neutral because it is *de facto* capable of neutralizing the cultural-clash so often present in international disputes."

[47] Cf *Duncan Kennedy*, supra note, at 149 "if we imagine that the judge is asked to choose between two rules strictly on the basis of the ideologically polarised policy arguments that are standard in legal discourse it is hard to see how her choice can be uninfluenced by ideology."

party may lose the ideological battle and therefore the case before the trial even begins.

By contrast, in arbitration both parties will always have at least the opportunity to shape the biases of the arbitration panel. This observation moves the focus of inquiry beyond the debate on adjudication between liberal and critical legal scholars. The former argue that although there are ideological stakes in adjudication, the discursive process of decision-making by national judges is or ought to be ideologically neutral by pointing to institutional constraints such as judicial review that arguably eschew personal biases.[48] By contrast the latter argue that that adjudication and decision-making is always and by definition ideologically biased.[49] This debate does not really matter in arbitration – what matters here is that both parties in a dispute have the opportunity to shape the biases of the decision-making panel.

More generally, the right of the parties to participate in the constitution of the tribunal is a unique design feature of arbitration. As is rightly pointed out, "[p]articipation brings together social and legal elements in allowing confidence in the accuracy of procedures that have made use of the 'best' sources of information. In this way, participation makes for the legitimacy of legal procedures."[50] While participation in many legal, and political fields, is usually limited to the opportunity of a party to present its case, give evidence and respond to questions relevant to the dispute,[51] in arbitration participation extends to its full democratic meaning, allowing the parties to engage in the process of the constitution of the tribunal. This special feature of the arbitral process therefore provides a powerful account of democracy and legitimacy in the institution of arbitration.[52]

Of course, it would be naïve to deny the fact that in practice those who appoint arbitrators tend to rely on a relatively small pool of practitioners and academics who – although not necessarily – tend to have a similar approach to some aspects of arbitration. Yet, there can be no comparison between the cohesive ideological structure of national judiciaries, and the loose and dynamic ideological spectrum of international tribunals. There is indeed a danger that as arbitration becomes more successful, and profitable, it may develop in the future a more solid and homogeneous substratum, which can lead to the development of collective biases. Currently, though, international arbitration remains a system that is fairly open to legal and cultural diversity; as system where an English barrister who has graduated from Ox-

---

[48] See *David Shapiro*, Courts, Legislature, and Paternalism, 74 Va. L. Rev. 519 (1988); *Dworkin*, supra note 81, and *Neil McCormick*, Reconstruction after Deconstruction: A Response to CLS, 10 Oxford J. Leg. Stud. 539 (1990).

[49] See *Duncan Kennedy*, supra note, p. 23.

[50] *Gearey/Morrison/Jago*, supra note, at 9.

[51] *Gearey/Morrison/Jago*, idem.

[52] *Park*, supra note, at 201 "party participation democratizes the process, serving to foster trust that at least one person on the tribunal (the party's nominee) will monitor the procedural integrity of the arbitration".

bridge, a Greek lawyer with a middle class background and a South-American state officer can equally be (and indeed *are*) appointed as arbitrators.

It is for this reason that the arbitration community should resist attempts to institutionalise the selection and appointment processes of arbitrators. Recently, there have been proposals, advocated by very eminent and highly influential arbitration practitioners and scholars, arguing that the party-appointed system in arbitration should be abolished.[53] Instead, it has been suggested that all members of an arbitral tribunal should be appointed by arbitral institutions. According to this view, a system of institutionally selected arbitrators would allow for more transparency in the appointing process and better control of the quality of the appointed arbitrators.

For all the reasons that have been discussed above, this is a misguided view that would bring arbitration closer to the institutional structures of national judiciaries, and would take away one the most distinctive, as well as ingenious, features of forum design, which safeguards diversity and increases the legitimacy of arbitration.

If anything, arbitration needs to promote institutional changes that enhance ideological pluralism and prevent homogeneity. For example, we may consider increasing the number of arbitrators sitting in a case from one or three to five.[54] More crucially, we should find ways to enlarge the pool and increase the diversity of potential arbitrators. An increasing number of arbitration programmes are now offered by universities around the world, which should provide for a larger pool of lawyers from more countries who will be familiar with the necessary expert knowledge of the mechanics of arbitration proceedings.[55] Still, costs involved in special arbitration courses may be prohibitive for many unprivileged students and lawyers, and therefore the arbitration community should further look into initiating capacity-building projects on arbitration in developing countries.[56]

---

[53] *Jan Paulsson*, Moral Hazard in International Dispute Resolution, 25 ICSID Rev. 339 (2010); *Albert Jan van den Berg*, Dissenting Opinions by Party-Appointed Arbitrators in Investment Arbitration, in: Mahnoush Arsanjani et al. (eds.), Looking to the Future: Essays on International Law in Honor of W. Michael Reisman 821 (2011). See also *Van Harten*, supra note 19, at 175–84 who suggests a system of tenured international judges in the "public law" model.

[54] *Toby Landau*, supra note.

[55] A good indication of the wide-range of education in arbitration is the fact that almost 300 universities from around the world participation in the Willem Vis Moot arbitration competition.

[56] See for example the capacity-building project, including teach-in workshops, scholarships for LLM studies in arbitration, initiated by Professor Catherine Rogers and supported by a number of arbitration-related institutions and organizations, such as the ICC, the Peen State University, the Queen Mary University of London, which aims at the strengthening of the Palestinian legal profession, judiciary and business professionals in order to enable them to participate more effectively in international arbitration.

Conclusion

In conclusion and to put the discussion on private justice and public policy in a wider context, I should briefly refer to two interesting developments from the common law world. The first is a very recent decision of the High Court in London,[57] which allowed a family dispute to be resolved by private arbitration. The wife and husband were observant Orthodox Jews – they had two children, and the family was living in England. Their marriage was concluded before a NY Rabi under the Jewish tradition. When they faced insurmountable difficulties in their marriage, they sought permission from English courts to submit their family dispute to private arbitral tribunals (the Beth Din Jewish Arbitral tribunal in NY), which would have the authority to dissolve their marriage and determine the issue of the custody of their children as ell as all financial matters arising from the divorce.

The English High Court gave them permission, making a very interesting observation on arbitration and the role of public policy and state. It observed that: "Arbitration is in line with the principle that primary responsibility for children rests with their parents who should be entitled to raise their children without the intrusion of the state save where the children are suffering, or likely to suffer, significant harm. That principle in turn is in line with Article 8 of the European Convention for the Protection of Human Rights and Fundamental Freedoms, the right to respect for private and family life, and the concept of personal autonomy which underpins that right. In short, it is up to parents to agree how their children should be brought up and, if they cannot agree, they should be entitled to choose how their disagreement should be resolved without state intervention, unless either (a) one or both parents invoke the help of the court or (b) the children are suffering or likely to suffer significant harm as a result of their parents' actions."

The second development also indicates that litigation and justice should be seen as another form of service providing, which is amenable to private interests and market forces, rather than a sacrosanct notion exclusively related to state and public policy. I am referring here to third-party funding litigation which in the last decade has become increasingly more acceptable in the UK. By third-party funding litigation I mean the case where a party, who is not the Claimant to an action, agrees to cover all or some of the costs of the litigation, in return for a share of the proceeds if the litigation is successful. If the litigation is not successful, the third-party funder bears the costs it has agreed to fund. This type of commercialization of justice was originally resisted, but a series of cases of the English CA[58] and the 2010 Jackson Review of Civil Litigation Costs in the UK have effectively endorsed private litigation funding.

The above observations of course do not mean that we should do away with public justice altogether. Private arbitration, of course, is all well and good, and it enjoys a

---

[57] *Re AI and MT* [2013] EWHC 100 (Fam).

[58] See for example *Arkin v Borchard Lines Ltd,* EWCA Civ 655.

place in society's dispute-resolution processes. But, if we continue to believe that a democracy requires its public courts to play the primary role in adjudicating civil disputes and in driving the development of civil jurisprudence, then those involved in the public court system – judges and administrators alike – must work hard, and must work creatively, to preserve the role of public courts.

But to achieve that, certain radical changes need happen in the state civil justice so that public courts provide timely, cost-effective and fair access to justice to civil litigants. For example, in Canada in 2010 there was a major cultural revolution Rules of Civil Procedure with the introduction of the principle and concept of proportionality in the civil litigation, which mandates that any procedural decision taken by courts, e. g. decisions on evidence or interim measure, must be proportionate to the importance and complexity of the issue and the amount involved in the proceedings. Such cultural evolution was thought necessary when they realised that it taken five month to nine months to schedule a summary judgment motion before a judge (time-frames that are one must note significantly shorter than Greek counsel experience every day – yet, they called for a radical changes in the way that state justice should operate). There are similar efforts at European Level, where Commission has suggested introduction of electronic systems for registering and managing cases and for communication between courts and parties, improve judicial efficiency and quality.

More importantly, we need to radically change our notion of justice and accept that state judiciary has a significant role to play in the administration of justice not as monopoly forum for the resolution of disputes, even disputes involving public policy, but as part of a wider competition in the administration of justice between private and state justice.

Dritter Teil

Der Staat im Spannungsfeld von Politisierung, Wirtschaftlichkeit und Stabilität / Facing the Challenges of the Public Sector: Party-Political Influence, Cost-Effectiveness and Stability

Souveränität und Solidarität in der EU-Finanzkrise – der Fall Griechenland

Von *Werner Meng*

I. Die EURO-Schuldenkrise, insbesondere in Griechenland[*]

Als im Jahre 2009 die Finanz- und Schuldenkrise im EURO-Raum ausbrach, zunächst in Griechenland, dann aber sukzessive auch in Irland, Portugal, Spanien und Zypern, begannen auch mehr oder minder hektische Interaktionen zwischen den betroffenen Mitgliedstaaten untereinander und mit der Europäischen Union. Durch die Notwendigkeit, Rettungspakete unter Beteiligung von möglichst vielen Mitgliedstaaten schnüren zu müssen, waren bald mehr oder minder alle Mitgliedstaaten betroffen und nahmen an dem nun anschwellenden Austausch von Fragen, Schuldzuweisungen, Vorwürfen, Ratschlägen, Hilfeforderungen und Hilfsbedingungen aktiv teil. In der Hauptsache ging es dabei darum, ob und unter welchen Konditionen den Schuldnerländern geholfen werden sollte. Es war klar, dass, wenn geholfen werden sollte, dies nur unter strikten Bedingungen und Auflagen geschehen sollte. Die Tatsache, dass man bei der dann folgenden Rettungsaktion den Internationalen Währungsfonds ins Boot genommen hatte[1], der eine lange, im Laufe der Zeit modifizierte, aber immer auch heftig kritisierte Praxis der Kreditvergabe unter Konditionalität hatte, machte bereits deutlich, dass den Schuldnerländern schwer belastenden Bedingungen im Rahmen von Rettungsprogrammen auferlegt würden.

Am schwerwiegendsten waren sie im Falle Griechenlands, von dem bis jetzt radikale Veränderungen der Finanz- und Wirtschaftspolitik sowie schmerzhafte Reduzierungen im Staatssektor verlangt werden. Auch heute noch kommt periodisch die „Troika"[2] als Kontroll- und Evaluationsgremium regelmäßig nach Griechenland, um den Fortgang der versprochenen Reformschritte zu kontrollieren und daraufhin die nächste Tranche der Hilfszahlungen freizugeben.

Der historische Ablauf zeigt, dass die zugesagten politischen Veränderungen, häufig nur mit Schwierigkeiten und Druck, mit der Drohung mit dem „Staatsbank-

---

[*] Die faktischen Darstellungen in Abschnitt I. entsprechen der Zeit vor der Ergreifung der Regierung durch SIRIZA, die alle angesprochenen Probleme noch schwieriger gemacht hat. Allerdings haben diese Entwicklungen keinerlei Einfluss auf die völkerrechtlichen Erwägungen ab Abschnitt II.

[1] Was sicherlich auch deswegen geschah, weil der IMF ein Garant dafür war, dass die Konditionalität nicht durch allzu viele politische Rücksichten relativiert werden sollte.

[2] Vertreter der EU Kommission, der EZB und des IMF.

rott"[3] dem griechischen Parlament von der Regierung schmackhaft gemacht werden konnten. Auch hat die Regierung immer wieder bei bestimmten unwillkommenen Reformmaßnahmen das Parlament und die Bevölkerung wissen lassen, dass sie diese nicht aus eigenem Antrieb treffen würde. Und schließlich sind bis heute etwa 600 versprochene Veränderungen immer noch nicht erfolgt. Im Laufe der Zeit haben diese Troika-Besuche, während denen harte Verhandlungen stattfinden, in Griechenland eine so negative Publizität erlangt, dass man diese Verhandlungen jedenfalls zum Teil ab dem Herbst 2014 nach Paris verlegt, damit der unmittelbare Interventionscharakter nicht mehr so offen zu Tage liegt[4].

Ohne äußeren Druck wäre vieles wahrscheinlich anders gelaufen, jedenfalls in den vier Mittelmeer-Schuldnerstaaten. Hier drängt sich dann natürlich die Frage auf, ob es sich dabei um eine Einmischung der Geldgeber in die inneren Angelegenheiten der Nehmer-(Schuldner-)Staaten handelt, ob also damit das völkerrechtliche Interventionsverbot verletzt wird.

Damit ist dieses Problem aber noch nicht erschöpft. Denn einerseits führte die gerade geschilderte Entwicklung zu heftiger Kritik an der Konditionalität in den Parteien und Zeitungen der Schuldnerstaaten. Andererseits entstanden heftige Diskussionen in den anderen Mitgliedstaaten, ob man überhaupt und, wenn ja, zu welchen Bedingungen den Schuldnerstaaten einen finanziellen Rettungsring reichen sollte.

Dies führte dazu, dass nicht nur bei den betroffenen Regierungen der Staaten, die sich unter den „Rettungsschirm" begeben mussten, die „Nerven blank lagen", insbesondere in den Staaten, die sich wegen ihrer Schuldensituation unter den „Rettungsschirm" begeben mussten[5]. Vielmehr begann auch langsam die Diskussion in den Presseorganen ebenso wie in den gesellschaftlichen Gruppen aller betroffenen Staaten zu entgleisen. Dass dem so war, zeigte sich etwa eklatant im Umgangston zwischen Deutschen und Griechen in den Jahren 2011 und 2012. Man rang damals um die Bedingungen für die Hilfeleistung der europäischen Partner an Griechenland, und angesichts seiner dominanten Beteiligung daran stand Deutschland im Mittelpunkt der Diskussionen. Man diskutierte verschiedene Optionen, die für Griechenland harte und fremdbestimmte Eingriffe in die Finanz- und Wirtschaftspolitik bedeute-

---

[3] Angesichts des mangelnden Staaten-Insolvenzrechts ist dieser Begriff natürlich untechnisch zu verstehen.

[4] eKathimierini vom 23. 8. 2014.

[5] Zur historischen Entwicklung und rechtlichen Problematik vgl. *Thym*, D., Euro-Rettungsschirm zwischenstaatliche Rechtskonstruktion und verfassungsgerichtliche Kontrolle, in: Europäische Zeitschrift für Wirtschaftsrecht 2011, 167–171, *Wieland*, J., Der Rettungsschirm für Irland, in: Neue Zeitschrift für Verwaltungsrecht 2011, 340–343, *id.*, Unter dem Rettungsschirm der Euro, die PIIGS und das Recht, in: Öffentliches Recht im offenen Staat 2011, 851–866; *Baumgart*, J.-K., Die Zurückweisung der Verfassungsbeschwerden gegen Maßnahmen zur Griechenlandhilfe und zum Euro-Rettungsschirm, in: Neue Justiz 2011, 450–454; *Ruffert*, M., The European debt crisis and European Union law, in: Common market law review 2011, 1777–1805; *Gregorio Merino*, A.d., Legal developments in the Economic and Monetary Union during the debt crisis: The mechanisms of financial assistance, in: Common market law review 2012, 1613–1646.

ten. Im Rahmen dieser Überlegungen wurden auch kritische Bemerkungen des deutschen Finanzministers Schäuble an Neuwahlplänen der griechischen Regierung kolportiert, welche den griechischen Staatspräsidenten Papoulias zu einem öffentlichen Ausbruch gegen Schäuble verleiteten: wer Schäuble überhaupt sei und wie er dazu komme, Griechenland zu beleidigen[6]. Dies wurde dann garniert mit Erinnerungen an den griechischen Freiheitskampf gegen die deutschen Besatzer im zweiten Weltkrieg.

Auch die frühere griechische Außenministerin Bakoianni monierte, dass solche Äußerungen aus dem Ausland zu den griechischen Wahlen das griechische Volk[7], das ein stolzes Volk sei, beleidigten. Mitte 2012 hatte Deutschland angeboten, 165 Finanzbeamte zu entsenden, welche den griechischen Steuerbehörden bei der Effektivierung und Aufarbeitung der riesigen Rückstände der Steuerfälle helfen sollten. Griechenland wies dies zurück, weil es eine Einmischung in griechische Hoheitsaufgaben sei[8]. Als die griechische Regierung im Juni 2013 unter heftigen Protesten im Inland die bisherige staatliche Rundfunk- und Fernsehanstalt ERT schloss und Ihre Restrukturierung begann konnte man auch Kritik aus dem Ausland dazu hören. Der Präsident des europäischen Parlaments, Martin Schulz, forderte öffentlich Premierminister Samaras auf, diese Maßnahme weitgehend rückgängig zu machen[9].

Im übrigen ist es umgekehrt nicht verwunderlich, dass in der griechischen Bevölkerung durchaus einer Auffassung existierte, wonach alle diese Ingerenzen bis hin zur periodischen Kontrolle durch die Troika wünschenswert seien, damit es in Griechenland zu einem bitter notwendigen Politikwechsel komme. In einem Interview verlautbarte der ehemalige griechische Außenminister Droutsas[10], zwar sei er nicht für Einmischungen der Europäischen Union in welchem Mitgliedstaat auch immer. Bezogen auf Griechenland hätte er sich aber gewünscht, das solche Einflussnahme nicht nur gezielt auf die Umsetzung des Sparprogramms ausgerichtet sei, sondern auch die Umsetzung von allgemeinen politischen Reformen befördert hätte.

Schließlich bleibt noch nachzutragen, dass dieses Problem nicht nur zwischen der Europäischen Union, ihren Mitgliedstaaten und Griechenland existiert, sondern auch im Hinblick auf andere Schuldner-Staaten. Als Zypern seine Umstrukturierungsmaßnahmen beschloss, lehnte es Frau Merkel ab, dem Land zu helfen, wenn es seine Pensionskassen zur Schuldenrückzahlung verwenden wolle[11]. Als es um Politikänderungen zur Verbesserung des Schuldenstandes von Frankreich ging, wies Präsident Hollande Reformvorschläge der EU-Kommission entrüstet zurück mit der Bemerkung, über den richtigen Weg aus der Krise entscheide allein der Elysee-Palast[12].

---

[6] Siehe *Gerd Höhler* in DIE ZEIT online vom 16.2.2012.
[7] Finanzen 100 vom 16.2.2012.
[8] Bild Online vom 6.7.2012.
[9] eKathimerini vom 15.6.2013.
[10] Deutschlandradio Kultur vom 15.4.2014.
[11] Focus Online Money vom 22.3.2013.
[12] Spiegel Online vom 30.5.2013.

Gleichwohl waren solche öffentlichen Konfrontationen relativ selten, aber in der journalistischen und parteipolitischen Diskussion in Deutschland und in Griechenland überschritt der Ton zuweilen das Maß des Erträglichen. Die Bundeskanzlerin Merkel wurde mit den Nazis in Verbindung gebracht, weil sie plane, einen „Gauleiter" nach Griechenland zu entsenden. Umgekehrt zweckentfremdete die deutsche Zeitschrift „Focus" die zeitlose Schönheit der Venus von Milo mit dem deplatzierten Attribut eines „Stinkefingers", um den Griechen so bildlich unseriösen Betrug vorzuwerfen.

Alle diese Entgleisungen auf beiden Seiten geschahen im Rahmen der Diskussion über ein hartes „Memorandum of Understanding", welches die Griechen dann auch im Verhältnis zum Internationalen Währungsfonds und der Europäischen Union bzw. ihren Mitgliedstaaten unterzeichnen mussten. Dem folgte bis heute ein zweites Memorandum nach. Beide – und ihre politischen Folgen – sind seit ihrem Abschluss Gegenstand heftigen Streits zwischen der Regierung und der Opposition in Griechenland. Letztere verspricht dem Volk, die dort übernommenen Verpflichtungen nicht mehr zu erfüllen, weil sie den griechischen Staat und die griechische Bevölkerung immer mehr in die wirtschaftliche Armut führten.

Dass es so kommen würde, war bereits 2011/2012 vorauszusehen und dies führte dann in mehr oder weniger populistischer Form zu einer Souveränitätsdiskussion unter Politikern und Journalisten. „Griechenland bezahlt mit seiner Souveränität" und „Athens Premier heißt Merkel" war bereits im November 2011[13] in der Süddeutschen Zeitung zu lesen. Im Focus hieß es im Februar 2012[14], Griechenland habe seine europäischen Nachbarn immer betrogen und damit sein „Recht auf Souveränität verwirkt". Wie bei einem Entwicklungsland werde Griechenland jetzt gezwungen, sein gesamtes Staatswesen von Grund auf neu zu konzipieren.

Bereits im Juli 2011 hatte der damalige Vorsitzende der Eurogruppe, Jean-Claude Juncker, den Ton dieser Debatte angegeben, als er erklärte, die Souveränität der Griechen werde von nun an bis zur Behebung der Krise eingeschränkt[15]. Sie hätten sich bereit erklärt, „eine Expertise-Zufuhr" aus der Euro-Zone anzunehmen. Maximale Solidität auf der einen Seite müsse zusammengehen mit maximaler Solidarität auf der anderen. Auf der anderen Seite gelobte die griechische Oppositionspartei SYRIZA, die Souveränität des Landes gegen die „neokoloniale" Politik der Troika zu verteidigen[16].

Diese Diskussion ist im Übrigen nicht auf Griechenland beschränkt. Bei allen Staaten, welche nacheinander unter den europäischen Rettungsschirm schlüpften (Griechenland, Irland, Spanien, Portugal und Zypern), wurde eine Souveränitätsbeschränkung behauptet. Im Dezember 2013 meldete zum Beispiel die deutsche Tages-

---

[13] 7.11.2011.
[14] 28.2.2012.
[15] Focus vom 3.7.2011.
[16] The Guardian vom 3.6.2014.

schau, Irland verlasse den Rettungsschirm und gewinne damit seine Souveränität wieder[17].

Im Übrigen wurden solche Behauptungen auch für die andere Seite aufgestellt, wenn nämlich geltend gemacht wurde, dass durch die Mit-Bereitstellung des Rettungsschirms die Bundesrepublik Deutschland ihrerseits ihre Souveränität opfere[18]. Die Frage eines Souveränitätsverlusts und seiner Grenzen aufgrund der Mitgliedschaft in der Europäischen Union spielte im Übrigen in mehreren Verfahren vor dem deutschen Bundesverfassungsgericht, angefangen mit demjenigen, welches den Vertrag von Lissabon betraf, eine nicht unerhebliche Rolle. Darauf wird nachstehend noch einzugehen sein.

Dieses faktische Geschehen soll nachfolgend unter drei Aspekten völkerrechtlich evaluiert und gewürdigt werden. Die erste Frage stellt sich hinsichtlich der Konditionalität der Hilfe von Weltbank und europäischer Union, die teilweise als Souveränitätsverletzung angesehen wurde. Dabei wird auch zu berücksichtigen sein, dass auch in den Geberländern das Souveränitätsproblem aufgeworfen wurde. In zweiter Hinsicht geht es um die Frage einer Souveränitätsverletzung durch Einmischung in die inneren Angelegenheiten Griechenlands durch die vielen mehr oder minder gut gemeinten politischen Ratschläge bzw. Attacken. Schließlich geht es drittens darum zu überlegen, ob es eine direkte Korrelation zwischen einer Reduzierung der Souveränität und einem rechtlichen Erstarken von Solidarität innerhalb der Europäischen Union gibt.

II. Souveränität und Interventionsverbot im Völkerrecht

1. Allgemeiner Stand des Völkerrechts

Das Interventionsverbot[19] ist ein Korrelat staatlicher Souveränität[20]. Die Souveränität und insbesondere die souveräne Gleichheit der Staaten wurde im westfälischen Frieden des Jahres 1648 zu einem der Grundprinzipien der Völkerrechtsordnung gemacht, hat sich aber seitdem erheblich gewandelt. Durch den Einfluss des Denkens von Jacques Rousseau und die Verfassungsentwicklung seit der französischen Revolution wird der Staat als Träger der inneren und äußeren Souveränität nicht mehr als ein Abstractum angesehen. Er ist vielmehr eine Organisation des Staatsvolkes. Es geht also bei der Souveränität heute hauptsächlich um die Sicherung von Freiheit und Unabhängigkeit der Staatsvölker, aber auch um deren Bindung gegenüber ande-

---

[17] 13.12.2013.

[18] So der Finanzwissenschaftler Kerber in http://www.handelsblatt.com/politik/deutschland/gastbeitrag-zur-euro-debatte-deutsche-republik-im-freien-fall-seite-all/4427706-all.html vom 25.7.2011. Vgl. auch *Schachtschneider*, K. A., Die Souveränität Deutschlands. Souverän ist, wer frei ist (1. Aufl. 2012).

[19] Übersicht m.w.N. bei *Kunig*, Ph., Intervention, Prohibition of, MPEPIL (2008).

[20] Übersicht m.w.N. bei *Besson*, S., Sovereignty, MPEPIL (2013).

ren Staatsvölkern. Die Souveränität hat also heute einen personalen Aspekt, und zwar in innerer wie in äußerer Hinsicht.

Man kann heute immer wieder in der völkerrechtlichen Literatur eine Geringschätzung der Bedeutung oder gar die Behauptung des Nicht-Fortbestandes der Souveränität feststellen[21]. Dies scheint mir nicht zutreffend zu sein. Wie sich bereits in der Satzung der Vereinten Nationen zeigt, gehört sowohl die souveräne Gleichheit (Art. 2 Abs. 1 SVN) wie auch der Schutz der inneren Angelegenheiten (Art. 2 Abs. 7 SVN) zu den Grund-Verfassungsnormen der modernen Staatengemeinschaft. Sie spielt auch in Streitfällen insbesondere vor dem Internationalen Gerichtshof immer wieder eine erhebliche Rolle. Nur die Bedeutung dieser Schutzprinzipien hat sich erheblich gewandelt: heute steht der personale Schutz im Vordergrund und ist andererseits der Schutzumfang des Interventionsverbots in dem Maße geschrumpft, in dem das Völkerrecht mehr und mehr Angelegenheiten regelt, welche früher zu den inneren Angelegenheiten der Staaten gehörten.

Die Innere Souveränität ist gleichbedeutend mit der freien und selbsttätigen Selbstbestimmung des Staatsvolks. Sie wird durch die Verfassung des Staates konstituiert, wobei ihre Wahrnehmung bestimmten verfassungsgemäßen Institutionen zugewiesen wird. Die äußere Souveränität sichert dabei die innere ab, bindet sie aber auch in Verpflichtungen gegenüber anderen Staaten ein. Letzteres geschieht durch das Völkerrecht, das historisch ausschließlich auf dem Konsens der hierdurch koordinierten Staaten beruhte. Seit Mitte des 20. Jahrhunderts wird aber mehr und mehr die Ansicht vertreten, dass bei bestimmten grundlegenden und zwingenden Normen des Völkerrechts auch ohne die Zustimmung jedes einzelnen Staates alle Staaten gleichmäßig gebunden sein können.

Bei rechtmäßiger externer Bindung von Staaten müssen die so konstituierten Verpflichtungen eingehalten und Rechte gewährt werden. Allerdings wird man hier immer auch daran denken müssen, dass möglicherweise die nationalen Verfassungsordnungen nicht nur Ermächtigungen zu völkerrechtlichem Handeln enthalten, sondern auch solches Handeln begrenzen. Während man historisch sagte, dass das Völkerrecht normalerweise die nationalen verfassungsrechtlichen Vorgaben nicht berücksichtigt, so wird dies in neuerer Zeit noch einmal zu hinterfragen sein[22]. Wenn die nationalen Vorgaben nämlich dem Demokratieprinzip entsprechen, dann muss auch das Völkerrecht als eine Rechtsordnung, welche nicht in gleichem Umfang demokratisch kontrolliert wird, solche Vorgaben berücksichtigen.

Das Interventionsverbot soll den internen Bereich dieser Souveränität schützen. Dieser wird mit dem Begriff der „inneren Angelegenheiten"[23] umschrieben. Dies

---

[21] S. z.B. *Klabbers*, Jan, International Law, (213), Kindle eBook, Pos. 2574 von 11782.

[22] Dies kann im Rahmen dieses Themas aber nicht geschehen, weil es darüber hinausgehen würde sowie erheblichen zusätzlichen Raum und Zeit beanspruchen würde.

[23] Übersicht m.w.N. bei *Ziegler*, K.S., Domaine Reserve, MPEPIL (2013).

sind alle Angelegenheiten, die „im Wesentlichen"[24] nicht vom Völkerrecht geregelt werden[25]. Sie sind lediglich Angelegenheiten nationalen Rechts und nationaler Politik, also ausschließlich Ausdruck der inneren Souveränität. Allerdings schirmt in diesem Fall äußere Souveränität die Angelegenheiten der inneren Souveränität gegenüber Eingriffen aus dem Ausland ab. Dabei muss aber immer auch bedacht werden, dass der „domaine réservé" heute immer weiter zurückgedrängt wird in dem Maße, in dem das Völkerrecht immer mehr Sachverhalte und Handlungen in den Mitgliedstaaten erfasst.

Das Interventionsverbot als Verpflichtung der Völkerrechtssubjekte untereinander wird nicht in seinem vollen Umfang in der Satzung der Vereinten Nationen geregelt, welche in Art. 2 Abs. 4 Nummer nur das Interventionsverbot für die Vereinten Nationen gegenüber ihren Mitgliedstaaten normiert. Allerdings besteht kein Zweifel daran, dass das Interventionsverbot im weiten Sinne als Völkergewohnheitsrecht existiert. Ein Ausdruck der opinio iuris zu diesem Völkergewohnheitsrecht findet sich in Ziff. 1 der „Declaration on Principles of International Law concerning Friendly Relations and Co-operation among States in accordance with the Charter of the United Nations"[26], in der es unter anderem heißt:

No State or group of States has the right to intervene, directly or indirectly, for any reason whatever, in the internal or external affairs of any other State. Consequently, armed intervention and all other forms of interference or attempted threats against the personality of the State or against its political, economic and cultural elements, are in violation of international law.

No State may use or encourage the use of economic political or any other type of measures to coerce another State in order to obtain from it the subordination of the exercise of its sovereign rights and to secure from it advantages of any kind. Also, no State shall organize, assist, foment, finance, incite or tolerate subversive, terrorist or armed activities directed towards the violent overthrow of the regime of another State, or interfere in civil strife in another State.

The use of force to deprive peoples of their national identity constitutes a violation of their inalienable rights and of the principle of non-intervention.

Every State has an inalienable right to choose its political, economic, social and cultural systems, without interference in any form by another State.

Wenn in die inneren Angelegenheiten, also das „domaine reserve" „eingegriffen" wird, dann ist dies eine Völkerrechtsverletzung, eine Verletzung der völkerrechtlich geschützten Souveränität. Ein solcher Eingriff lage sicherlich dann vor, wenn er mit Gewaltanwendung einherginge. Wenngleich dies auch früher der Hauptanwendungsbereich des Interventionsverbots gewesen sein mag, so geht doch heute der Eingriffs-Begriff weiter: „the use of economic political or any other type of measures

---

[24] Art. 2.7 SVN.

[25] StIGH Nationality Decrees Issued in Tunis and Morocco on Nov. 8th, 1921, Advisory Opinion, 1923 P.C.I.J. (ser. B) No. 4 (Feb. 7).

[26] Resolution 2625 (XXV) der UN-Generalversammlung vom 24. 10. 1970.

to coerce another State in order to obtain from it the subordination of the exercise of its sovereign rights and to secure from it advantages of any kind". Es geht also um Zwangsmaßnahmen jedweder Art, welche zur Unterwerfung unter den Willen des Intervenierenden führen und diesem einem Vorteil bringen.

Daraus folgt zunächst einmal, dass reine Bemerkungen und Kritiken aus dem Ausland, in welch pointierter Formulierung sie auch immer vorgetragen werden, keine Einmischung in die inneren Angelegenheiten eines anderen Staates im völkerrechtlichen Sinne sein können. Sie mögen unklug, unhöflich und manchmal vielleicht auch beleidigend sein, aber das macht sie zu nicht mehr als einem unfreundlichen Akt, welcher aufgrund der Völker-Courtoisie selbstverständlich vermieden werden sollte. Auch im Zeitalter der Mediendemokratie, in dem jede fremde Äußerung über einen Politiker in einem Staat erhebliche Image-Schäden hervorrufen könnte, kann man nicht davon ausgehen, dass hierin eine verbotene Einmischung bestehe.

Speziell auf die Europäische Union gemünzt wird man sagen müssen, dass in Zukunft solche mehr oder minder höflichen Bemerkungen über Zustände in einem anderen Mitgliedstaat proliferieren werden. Denn in dem Maße, in dem die politische Verflechtung durch die fortschreitende Integration immer stärker wird, wächst natürlich das Interesse, auch das kritische Interesse an den anderen Mitgliedstaaten. Die zunehmende Verbindung politischer Parteien über die Staatsgrenzen hinweg bringt es mit sich, dass Wahlvorschläge und Wahlergebnisse in anderen Mitgliedstaaten direkt auch von regierenden Politikern in anderen Mitgliedstaaten betrachtet, kommentiert und kritisiert werden. Und die Probleme gerade der europäischen Schuldenkrise zeigen auch, dass dann, wenn zusätzliche Solidarität und Hilfe eingefordert wird, ein Mitgliedstaat auch ertragen muss, dass in anderen Mitgliedstaaten über die Gründe, welche zu seinen Schulden geführt haben, kritische Bemerkungen gemacht werden. Dieses verstärkte private und öffentliche Interesse in anderen Mitgliedstaaten ist geradezu ein positiver Ausweis von Integrationsfortschritten. Dies wird natürlich selbstverständlich auch die Maßstäbe der Courtoisie verschieben. Dass eine deutsche Bundeskanzlerin sich für die Wiederwahl eines französischen Präsidenten offen ausspricht, dass sie die Neuwahlpläne in einem anderen Mitgliedstaat kritisiert, mag für sich alleine genug Beweis dafür sein, wie stark sich die Maßstäbe – notwendigerweise – bei fortschreitender wirtschaftlicher und politischer Integration verändern.

Aus diesem Grunde sollten Politiker auch ihren reflexartigen Rückgriff auf die alte Interventionsrhetorik mehr und mehr kontrollieren. Es handelt sich um ein integrationsaverses Sprachspiel. Kommentare aus anderen EU-Mitgliedstaaten sind keine Einmischung in deren innere Angelegenheiten.

2. Konditionalität bei Krediten an Staaten

Ein spezielles Problem stellt die Konditionalität dar. Sie wird insbesondere im Zusammenhang mit der Kreditvergabe von Weltbank und Weltwährungsfonds an höher verschuldete Länder diskutiert, welche nur in Verbindung mit harten Bedingungen und Auflagen stattfindet[27]. Diese Bedingungen greifen in der Regel tief in Gesellschafts-, Wirtschafts- und Innenpolitik der Empfängerländer ein. Allerdings müssen sie von diesen Ländern akzeptiert und umgesetzt werden. Verweigern sie eine solche Umsetzung oder führen Sie sie nicht wie versprochen durch, so droht der Entzug des Kredits. Zwar ist die Umsetzung formal freiwillig, aber sie wird durch Not und die Einsicht in die Notwendigkeit aufgrund ökonomischer Überlegungen ihrerseits konditioniert.

Hier wird bereits im Völkerrecht seit langem darüber diskutiert, ob damit die Schwelle des Interventionsverbot überschritten wird. Die Kreditgewährung unter Konditionalität ist eine wirtschaftliche Maßnahme. Wenn ein Staat die negativen Folgen einer Insolvenz vermeiden möchte, bleibt ihm nichts anderes übrig, als sich den Konditionen zu unterwerfen. Wenn kein anderer Staat bereit wäre, ihm einen Kredit zu gewähren (spezifisch in einer solchen Situation) können müsste er diese Folgen ertragen. Es ist aber einfacher und komfortabler, die Hilfe anderer Staaten in Anspruch zu nehmen. Auf diese Hilfe hat aber der ersuchende Staat – außer in Ausnahmefällen – keinen Anspruch, ebenso hat der ersuchte Staat im Regelfall keine Pflicht, dem Ersuchen nachzukommen[28].

Für eine Entscheidung des Problems wird man den Begriff der „Zwangswirkung" zentral betrachten und entscheiden müssen. Hier ist entscheidend, ob man eine „Unterwerfung aufgrund der Vernunft" einer „Unterwerfung unter nackten Zwang" gleichsetzen möchte. Die sollte man aber nicht tun. Letzterer Fall dürfen nur gegeben sein, wenn etwa einem Politiker bei Verhandlungen notwendige Medikamente vorenthalten werden, ohne die er nicht überleben kann, damit er einer ungewollten Entwicklung innerer Angelegenheiten zustimmt, oder wenn ohne dringliche Hilfeleistung eine Bevölkerung zum Verhungern verdammt wäre. Dass einem aber die Akzeptierung fremder Kreditbedingungen ein komfortableres Wirtschaften ermöglicht, kreiert noch keine Zwangssituation. Dies gilt auch dann, wenn die Ablehnung des Kredits in eine unvermeidliche, aber nicht existenzbedrohende Notlage für die Bevölkerung führt. An dieser Stelle kommen wir zum ersten Male zur Frage einer Solidaritätspflicht und – konkreter – einer Pflicht zum Schutz der Menschenrechte im Völkerrecht. Dazu wird später noch etwas zu bemerken sein.

[27] *Stone*, R.W., The scope of IMF conditionality, In: International organization 2008, 589–620; *Eldar*, O., Reform of IMF conditionality. A proposal for self-imposed conditionality, 8 Journal of international economic law 2005, 509–549; IBRD, Review of World Bank conditionality (2005); *Buira*, A., An analysis of IMF conditionality (2003); *Drazen*, A., Conditionality and ownership in IMF lending. A political economy approach (2002); *Denters*, E., Law and policy of IMF conditionality (1996); *Meng*, W., Conditionality of IMF and World Bank Loans: Tutelage over Sovereign States, 21 Verfassung und Recht in Übersee 1988, 263–277; *Gold*, J., Conditionality (Repr. Aufl., 1982).

[28] Ebenso *Kunig* (Anm. 19), C.3.

Die soeben skizzierte Rechtsauffassung wird bestätigt durch die Nicaragua-Entscheidung des Internationalen Gerichtshofs[29]. Hier ging es um die Frage, ob eine plötzliche Beendigung von Wirtschaftshilfe für Nicaragua durch die USA eine systematische Verletzung des Prinzips der Nichteinmischung sein könne. Der Gerichtshof stellte zunächst im Ausgangspunkt fest, dass kein Staat verpflichtet sei, Handelsbeziehungen mit einem anderen Staat ohne eine vorherige vertragliche Bindung oder ohne eine andere rechtliche Verpflichtung einzugehen oder aufrechtzuerhalten. Nur wenn es eine solche vorherige Verpflichtung gebe, könne ein solches Verhalten ein Verstoß gegen Vertragspflichten sein. In seiner abweichenden Meinung betont Richter Oda ebenso kategorisch, es gebe keine allgemeine völkerrechtliche Pflicht von Staaten zum Handel.

Einerseits ist kein Grund ersichtlich, warum man diesen Befund nicht auch auf finanzielle Hilfe ausdehnen kann. Zum anderen aber ergibt sich aus der Rechtsauffassung des Gerichtshofs für den Fall der Finanzhilfe, dass es im Normalfall keinerlei Verpflichtung zur Leistung einer solchen Hilfe gibt, wenn dies nicht vorher in irgendeiner Form rechtlich fixiert war. Wenn es aber keine solche Pflicht gibt, dann kann auch nicht die Verbindung einer zukünftigen Hilfe mit Bedingungen für den Empfängerstaat eine Verletzung des Interventionsverbots sein unter der Voraussetzung, dass die Bedingungen vom Empfängerstaat, wenn auch nolens volens, akzeptiert werden

Man könnte dieses allgemeine Ergebnis nunmehr weiter qualifizieren unter dem Gesichtspunkt, dass aufgrund der immer engeren Rechtsbeziehungen in der modernen Völkerrechtsordnung die Staaten immer mehr gegenseitigen Verpflichtungen ex ante unterliegen, die auch bei der hier aufgeworfenen Rechtsfrage eine Rolle spielen könnten. Dies ist etwa möglich im WTO-Recht bei der Frage, inwieweit etwa Diskriminierungsverbote Auswirkungen haben auf die Verhängung von Wirtschaftssanktionen oder die Verweigerung von Handelspräferenzen.

Im vorliegenden Fall geht es aber um internationale Finanzhilfen des Internationalen Währungsfonds und, pauschal gesprochen, der Europäischen Union[30]. Deren Vergabe unterliegt dem IMF-Abkommen und dem EUV. Dem IMF obliegt unter anderem als internationalem „lender of last resort" die befristete Vergabe von Krediten an Staaten mit Defiziten und Schulden (insbes. Art. I Abs. 5 IMF Articles of Agreement, IMFA)[31]. Einen Anspruch auf eine solche Hilfe haben Mitgliedstaaten des IMF nur in der General Facility beim Ankauf fremder Währungen gegen eigene Währung im Rahmen ihrer ersten Kredit-Tranche (Art. III b IMFA). In den höheren Tranchen,

---

[29] Military and Paramilitary Activities (Nicaragua/United States of America) Merits. J. 27.6.1986 I.C.J. Reports 1986, p. 14, 126 f., 138. Diss.op. Oda 252 f.

[30] Auf der EU-Seite sind Rechtsakte des Ministerrates ergangen, die verknüpft wurden mit der Kreditvergabe seitens des EFSF/EFSM. Daneben ist an den Hilfsprogrammen noch die EZB beteiligt.

[31] Allgemein hierzu siehe *Meng*, W., Conditionality of IMF and World Bank Loans: Tutelage over Sovereign States, 21 Verfassung und Recht in Übersee 1988, 263–277.

also in der Extended Facility und den darüber hinausgehenden Kreditprogrammen, welche sich in neuerer Zeit aufgrund der immer anwachsenden Staatsschulden entwickelt haben, werden die Kredite nur in Verbindung mit einer Konditionalität vergeben, die auf der Basis des Art. V a IMFA entwickelt werden durfte. Sie wird in stand-by-agreements[32] niedergelegt bzw. in beigefügten Memoranda of Understanding, welche von den Empfängerstaaten gezeichnet sind.

Die Regeln und Bedingungen für die Konditionalität sind zur Zeit in den Guidelines on Conditionality des Jahres 2002[33] festgelegt mit gewissen erneuerten Regeln im „Operational Guidance to Staff: GRA Lending Toolkit and Conditionality: Reform Proposals" (2009)[34]. Dort heißt es unter Ziff. A 3:

> National ownership of sound economic and financial policies and an adequate administrative capacity are crucial for successful implementation of Fund-supported programs. In responding to members' requests to use Fund resources and in setting program-related conditions, the Fund will be guided by the principle that the member has primary responsibility for the selection, design, and implementation of its economic and financial policies. The Fund will encourage members to seek to broaden and deepen the base of support for sound policies in order to enhance the likelihood of successful implementation.

Hieraus ergibt sich nichts, was auf einen Zwang hinweist, welcher für eine Verletzung des Interventionsverbots notwendig ist. Auch ist nicht ersichtlich dass insoweit die Konditionalität über das hinausgeht, was zur Sicherstellung der Rückzahlung des Kredits und zur Verbesserung der Wirtschaftslage notwendig ist. Dass dies in letzter Instanz der Geldgeber entscheidet, hängt natürlicherweise damit zusammen, dass dieser die Rückzahlung des Kredits sichern muss, um seine Bonität als Bank zu erhalten.

Ownership heißt in diesem Zusammenhang, dass die Konditionalität die Ziele vorgibt, die wirtschaftspolitisch erreicht werden müssen, dass aber die konkreten Ausnahmen zu deren Erreichung durch die Staaten angeboten und dann im Memorandum festgelegt werden. Wenn diese Maßnahmen zwar nicht erwünscht, aber notwendig sein sollten und es keine geringer belastende Alternative mehr gibt, so muss der Staat zwar nolens volens zustimmen, um den Kredit zu bekommen, gezwungen werden kann er hierzu jedoch nicht.

Dies ergibt sich noch aus einer weiteren Besonderheit der konditionalen Kreditvergabe durch den IMF. In Ziff. B.9 der Guidelines (Nature of the Fund Arrangements) heißt es:

> A Fund arrangement is a decision of the Executive Board by which a member is assured that it will be able to make purchases or receive disbursements from the Fund in accordance with the terms of the decision during a specified period and up to a specified amount. Fund arrangements are not international agreements and therefore language having a contractual

---

[32] Hierzu Art. XXX b IMFA.

[33] http://www.imf.org/External/np/pdr/cond/2002/eng/guid/092302.htm am 29. 8. 2014.

[34] http://www.imf.org/external/np/pp/eng/2009/031309a.pdf am 29. 8. 2014.

connotation will be avoided in arrangements and in program documents. Appropriate consultation clauses will be incorporated in all arrangements.

Die stand-by-arrangements werden also nicht völkervertragsrechtlich verbindlich. Der IMF sichert einseitig zu, bei Einhaltung der Konditionalität den versprochenen Betrag auszuzahlen. Der Empfängerstaat bleibt aber frei, die Einhaltung zu beenden. Daraufhin wird auch der IMF nach seinem eigenen Organisationsrecht von seiner Zusage befreit. Allerdings kann dann auch der Fonds nach Art. XXIV a dem Staat weitere Mitgliedschaftsrechte entziehen:

(a) If a member fails to fulfill any of its obligations under this Agreement, the Fund may declare the member ineligible to use the general resources of the Fund.

Der Empfängerstaat bleibt frei, welche nach seiner eigenen souveränen Entscheidung sich für ihn als untragbar herausstellen. Dass er dann die vernünftigerweise erstrebte Beihilfe nicht erhält, verletzt in keinem Fall seine Souveränität.

Dem hat auch der griechische Staatsrat, das oberste Verwaltungsgericht des Staates, in seiner Entscheidung aus dem Jahre 2012[35] über die Verfassungsmäßigkeit des Memorandums of Understanding Rechnung getragen, indem er das Memorandum als rechtlich nicht verbindlich und auch nicht vollstreckbar angesehen hat. Hinsichtlich der Bindungen an den IMF ist dies völlig richtig und wir werden sehen, dass auch hinsichtlich des Rechtsverhältnisses zur EU nichts anderes gilt.

Man könnte hinsichtlich des bisher gefundenen völkerrechtlichen Rechtsergebnisses noch einmal genauer nachfragen, ob Staaten oder internationale Organisationen bei der Gewährung von Finanzhilfen jede Form von Konditionalität wählen können, etwa bezogen auf das politische System des Empfängerstaates (Demokratie!), auf das Verhalten von Repräsentanten dieser Staaten im innenpolitischen und diplomatischen Verkehr, auf Gebietsansprüche, auf politische Allianzen mit dritten Staaten oder auch auf umweltpolitische Grundentscheidungen des Empfängerstaates. Man könnte sich auch aufgrund des oben zitierten Textes der Friendly Relations Declaration fragen, ob bei wirtschaftlicher Konditionalität die Motivation und die Finalität eine Rolle spielen können[36], also die Frage, ob der Geberstaat eigene wichtige und nachvollziehbare Interessen im politischen Verhältnis zum Nehmerstaat zur Grundlage seiner Konditionalität macht oder ob er lediglich rein innere Angelegenheiten durch finanziellen Druck gestalten möchte.

Ohne hierzu endgültig Stellung nehmen zu wollen kann man aber doch feststellen, dass diese Fragestellungen im vorliegenden Fall der Schuldenkrise in der Europäischen Union keine Rolle spielen. Die Konditionen der Memoranden und der letters of intent sind ausschließlich darauf ausgerichtet, einerseits die Rückzahlung der vergebenen Darlehen zu sichern und andererseits die Fähigkeit der Nehmerstaaten wiederherzustellen, sich in Zukunft selbst am Kapitalmarkt wieder finanzieren zu können, was eine glaubwürdige wirtschaftliche Gesundung verlangt. Ob die Konditio-

---

[35] Nr. 668/201.

[36] Hierzu *Kunig* (Anm. 19), C.3.

nierung richtig oder teilweise fehlerhaft ist, spielt dabei keine Rolle. Fehler müssen politisch verändert werden, machen aber die Konditionalität nicht völkerrechtlich rechtswidrig.

In der Regel gilt also: die staatliche Souveränität als die völlige Entscheidungsfreiheit unter anderem hinsichtlich der Wirtschafts- und Gesellschaftsordnung kann durch die Staaten selbst eingeschränkt werden, durch die Eingehung rechtlicher Bindungen (wie etwa den Beitritt zur WTO), aber auch durch eine faktische Verbindung als Gegenleistung für einen Vorteil wie etwa die Vergabe eines Hilfskredits. Im letzteren Fall bleibt der Staat zwar rechtlich frei zu tun, was er für richtig hält, aber faktisch wird er doch den Konditionen folgen, um die Hilfsleistung zu erhalten. In allen diesen Fällen rechtlicher oder faktischer Bindung wird zwar die Entscheidungsfreiheit eingeschränkt, aber es handelt sich nicht um eine Einmischung in die inneren Angelegenheiten des Staates. Politische Klugheit muss aber bei konditionalen Hilfeleistungen zwei Dinge gebieten. Einerseits sollen konkrete Maßnahmen tatsächlich der „ownership" der Bevölkerung des Empfängerstaates überlassen bleiben. Das heißt, dass zu erreichende Ziele festgelegt werden, die konkreten Maßnahmen zu deren Erreichung aber der demokratischen Entscheidung im Empfängerstaat überlassen werden. Zum anderen aber sollte die Hilfeleistung nicht ein Diktat der Geberländer sein, welches über das Rückzahlungsinteresse hinausgeht. Angesichts der Härten für die Bevölkerung der Empfängerländer sind die Konditionen erträglicher, wenn die Hilfeleistung als Solidaritätsakt wahrgenommen wird.

3. Souveränität und Interventionsverbot innerhalb der EU

Den bisher herausgearbeiteten völkerrechtlichen Befund kann man allerdings nicht nahtlos auf die Rechtsverhältnisse innerhalb der Europäischen Union übertragen[37]. Hinsichtlich der Souveränität gilt dort auch heute noch der grundlegende Satz in der Entscheidung Costa v. ENEL des EuGH[38]: „Aus alledem ist zu schließen, dass die Gemeinschaften eine neue Rechtsordnung des Völkerrechts darstellten, zu deren Gunsten Staaten in begrenztem Rahmen, ihre Souveränitätsrechte eingeschränkt haben." Die Souveränität der EU-Mitgliedstaaten besteht also fort, aber in eingeschränktem Maße.

In eine ganz andere Richtung geht die Argumentation von Javier Solana im März 2012 in einem Gastbeitrag in der Zeitung „Die Welt"[39] unter der Überschrift „Die Idee der nationalen Souveränität ist antiquiert". Er zeigt auf, dass das alte Prinzip

---

[37] Vgl. insgesamt *Barbato*, Mariano: Souveränität im neuen Europa: Der Souveränitätsbegriff im Mehrebenensystem der Europäischen Union ((2003); *De Witte*, B., Sovereignty and European Integration: The Weight of Legal Tradition, 2 Maastricht J. Eur. & Comp. L. 1995, 145–173; *Schiemann*, K., Europe and the loss of sovereignty, in: The international and comparative law quarterly 2007, 475–489; *Walker*, N., Sovereignty and differentiated integration in the European Union, 4 European law journal 1998, 355–388.

[38] EUGH 5.2.63, 26/62, van Gend & Loos, Slg. 1963, 1, 25.

[39] 15.3.2012.

der Souveränität und der Inneren Angelegenheiten, welches im Westfälischen Frieden zum Grundprinzip der Staatengemeinschaft erhoben worden war, heute weder allgemein oder auch nur begrifflich geklärt ist und dass es insbesondere in der Europäischen Union veraltet ist, weil es dort um Interdependenz, nicht um Abgrenzung geht.

Allerdings ist dies ein politisches Statement, welches mit dem bisher geltenden Verfassungsrecht der EU nicht in Einklang zu bringen ist. Die Souveränität der Mitgliedstaaten ist eingeschränkt, aber nicht beseitigt. Dies betont der EuGH auch immer wieder einmal in seiner Rechtsprechung[40]. Auch die nationalen Verfassungsgerichte der Mitgliedstaaten haben die verbleibende Souveränität betont, allen voran das deutsche Bundesverfassungsgericht insbesondere in seiner Entscheidung zum Vertrag von Lissabon[41]. Hier wird die staatliche Souveränität zur Abwehrposition gegen zu viel Integration. Das deutsche Grundgesetz sichere das Selbstbestimmungsrecht des deutschen Volkes auch durch die völkerrechtliche Souveränität Deutschlands. Diese dürfe nicht unwiderruflich aufgegeben werden. Dies wäre der Fall beim Eintritt in einen europäischen Bundesstaat, der deshalb auch einer Verfassungs-Neugebung nach Art. 146 des Grundgesetzes bedürfe. Nur das gesamte Legitimationssubjekt des deutschen Staates, sein Staatsvolk, könne diesen endgültigen Übertragungsakt vollziehen. Auch dieser sei durch Art. 79 Abs. 3 GG, die sogenannte „Ewigkeitsklausel"[42] beschränkt, eine höchst fragwürdige Position, weil sie apodiktisch eine neue Verfassung an die alte, den pouvoir constituant an seinen Vorgänger (der ja nicht einmal das gesamte deutsche Volk und nicht einmal das Volk direkt war) bindet.

Immerhin wird hier eine völlige und endgültige Aufgabe der Souveränität nicht ausgeschlossen. Bis zu diesem Zeitpunkt aber bleiben nach Auffassung des Gerichts gewisse Materien von der Kompetenzübertragung sogar völlig ausgeschlossen. Bei aller Diskussionswürdigkeit dieser Entscheidung hat das Bundesverfassungsgericht kraftvoll den Fortbestand eines Kerns der Staatensouveränität in der EU, als Schutz individueller Freiheit und kollektiver Selbstbestimmung der Staatsvölker, bestätigt, der vom verfassungsrechtlichen Demokratieprinzip gefordert werde. Dem wird man zustimmen können, solange die Union ein unfertiger Staatenverbund ist, in dem fort-

---

[40] Hierzu *Roth*, G. H./*Hilpold*, P. (Hrsg.), Der EuGH und die Souveränität der Mitgliedstaaten. Eine kritische Analyse richterlicher Rechtsschöpfung auf ausgewählten Rechtsgebieten (2008); *Haltern*, U. R., Was bedeutet Souveränität? (2007), 99 ff.

[41] BVerfGE 123, 267–2 BvE 2/08, Vertrag von Lissabon. Die Entscheidung ist in ihrer fokussiert kontraktuellen Sicht der europäischen Integration höchst diskussionswürdig und -bedürftig, hierzu etwa *Terhechte*, J., Europäischer Bundesstaat, supranationale Gemeinschaft oder Vertragsunion souveräner Staaten? – Zu Verhältnis von Staat und Union nach dem Lissabon-Urteil des BVerfG, Europarecht – Beilage 2010, 135–149. Vielen der aufzuwerfenden Fragen kann jedoch hier nicht nachgegangen werden.

[42] „Eine Änderung dieses Grundgesetzes, durch welche die Gliederung des Bundes in Länder, die grundsätzliche Mitwirkung der Länder bei der Gesetzgebung oder die in den Artikeln 1 und 20 niedergelegten Grundsätze berührt werden, ist unzulässig."

bestehende nationale souveräne Rechte zusammengehen mit solchen, die auf die Union übertragen wurden[43].

Es gibt also auch in der EU fortbestehende Souveränität der Mitgliedstaaten, so wie man in jedem Fall auch davon ausgehen kann, dass der EU jedenfalls externe Souveränitätsrechte gegenüber Drittstaaten angewachsen sind. So lange den Mitgliedstaaten solche Rechte verbleiben, werden sie auch im Innenverhältnis durch das völkerrechtliche Interventionsverbot geschützt. Nur muss man auch festhalten, dass die Bereiche, in denen die Mitgliedstaaten wirklich völlig selbständig ohne irgendwelche gemeinschaftsrechtlichen Bindungen souveräne Entscheidungen treffen können, sehr stark geschrumpft sind. In gleichem Maße ist auch der Schutzbereich des Interventionsverbots kleiner geworden. Das Unionsrecht modifiziert nicht unerheblich nationales Recht, die Kommission beaufsichtigt und korrigiert die Mitgliedstaaten, die Mitgliedstaaten unterliegen einer Fülle von Berichtspflichten und die Mitgliedstaaten können untereinander die politische Opportunität und rechtliche Unbedenklichkeit ihres Verhaltens beobachten, bewerten, kritisieren und schließlich auch die Rechtmäßigkeit vor Gericht überprüfen lassen. Je enger die nationalen Politikbereiche koordiniert werden, desto mehr Reibungspunkte ergeben sich dort auch möglicherweise. Je größer das Interesse an der Politik eines Staates in der gleichen Integrationsfamilie ist, weil nämlich politisch alles mit allem zusammenhängt, desto geringer wird die gegenseitige Kritik von diplomatischer Zurückhaltung geprägt sein. Die Integrationsfamilie bringt neben Vorteilen auch Streit, und außer in ganz wenigen Bereichen, welche von der Integration noch ausgenommen sind, werden solche Streitigkeiten dann oft nicht mehr mit der Zurückhaltung von Regierungen untereinander, sondern auch mit offensiven Argumenten und offensivem Streit ausgetragen.

So kann man denn davon ausgehen, dass es innerhalb der EU noch erheblich seltener möglich ist als im allgemeinen Völkerrecht oder in Internationalen Organisationen, die nicht supranational sind, dass ein Staat vom anderen die Einhaltung des Interventionsverbots fordern kann. Diese allgemeine Erkenntnis kann man nun ohne Schwierigkeiten auf die hier zentral behandelte Problematik der Schuldenkrise innerhalb der EU übertragen, nämlich die Gewährung konditionaler Hilfsleistungen, die daran geknüpfte dauernde Überwachung und die diesbezüglichen Änderungsforderungen hinsichtlich der Politiken der Empfängerländer.

Auch hier schwebt die Kreditgewährung rechtlich nicht im ganz freien Raum. Vielmehr gibt es im Primär- und Sekundärrecht der Union diesbezügliche Regeln, die dabei zu beachten sind, teils auch solche Verpflichtungen, wie sie nunmehr allen Mitgliedstaaten, oder zumindest den EURO-Staaten, auferlegt werden (wie

---

[43] Dabei legt das BVerfG besonderen Wert auf die letztendlich integrale Bewahrung nationaler Souveränität auf Grund der Austrittsmöglichkeit, wie sie nunmehr im Art. 50 EUV verankert wird. Die Verlagerung von Hoheitsrechten geschieht also letztlich nur temporär.

etwa der „Six pack" oder der „Two pack"[44]). Auf alle diese Elemente, mit denen man neuerdings den EURO dauernd zu stabilisieren sucht, braucht man hier nicht einzugehen. Es geht hier vielmehr nur um die Frage, ob die Konditionalität der Hilfskredite an die Empfängerländer, welche mit äußerst harten Auflagen einhergingen, eine Verletzung des Interventionsverbots sein könnte[45].

Wenn man sich die Rechtsverhältnisse am Beispiel der Griechenland-Hilfe verdeutlicht wird klar, dass sie etwas anders gelagert sind als im IMF-Fall, obwohl die Hilfe des Fonds und die der EU gemeinsam verhandelt, aufeinander abgestimmt und auch gemeinsam überwacht werden. Trotzdem handelt es sich rechtlich gegenüber Griechenland um selbstständige, nämlich um unionsrechtliche Rechtsbeziehungen. Die Konditionen werden im Falle der Union in einem Ratsbeschluss festgelegt, der auf Art. 126 Abs. 9 und 136 AEUV gestützt, an Griechenland gerichtet ist.

Bereits im April 2009 hatte der Rat ein übermäßiges Defizit Griechenlands festgestellt und Reduzierungsmaßnahmen empfohlen. Als keine Abhilfe erfolgte, wurde Griechenland 2010 nach Art. 126 Abs. 9 AEUV in Verzug gesetzt. Die Entscheidung des Rates 2010/320/EU vom 10. 5. 2010[46] verlängert dann die Frist zur Korrektur bis 2012[47]. Es folgt die Diagnose, die Festlegung des Therapieziels und die Liste der anzuwendenden Therapiemethoden, voll von einschneidenden Reformverpflichtungen Griechenlands. Diese Entscheidung wurde dann anlässlich der periodischen Überprüfungen flexibel angepasst[48] und dann neu gefasst[49], ohne dass die Rechtsgrundlagen verändert worden wären.

Trotz der apodiktischen Formulierung des Art. 1 der Entscheidung „Griechenland beendet das derzeitige übermäßige Defizit so rasch wie möglich, spätestens aber im Jahr 2014" und trotz der ausgedehnten Liste von scheinbar angeordneten Abhilfemaßnahmen muss die Rechtsnatur der Entscheidung im Rahmen des Art. 126 AEUV gesehen werden. Bis zu der Entscheidung nach Abs. 9 bleibt alles in diesem Verfahren beim Empfehlungscharakter. Erst mit dieser Entscheidung tritt das Verzugsstadium ein, das die Empfehlungen zu Verpflichtungen macht. Gleichzeitig aber wird dem EuGH die Jurisdiktion über die Einhaltung dieser Verpflichtungen nach Abs. 10 entzogen. Vielmehr tritt ein eigenes Sanktionssystem nach Abs. 11

---

[44] EU-Kommission, Six-pack? Two-pack? Fiscal compact? A short guide to the new EU fiscal governance, http://ec.europa.eu/economy_finance/articles/governance/2012–03–14_six_pack_en.htm.

[45] Wobei dessen rechtliche Voraussetzungen innerhalb der EU die gleichen wären wie im allgemeinen Völkerrecht. Insoweit kann auf das oben Gesagte verwiesen werden.

[46] ABl. EU 2010, L 145, 6.

[47] Sie stützt sich wiederum auf Art. 126 Abs. 9 AEUV, diesmal aber zusätzlich noch auf Art. 136 AEUV, was erstaunlich ist, weil diese Vorschrift keine eigenen Kompetenzen beinhaltet, sondern nur auf andere, einschlägige Vorschriften verweist. Man wird diesem zweiten Bezug rechtlich keine Bedeutung zusprechen können.

[48] Entscheidung 210/486/EU, 211/57/EU, 211/257/EU.

[49] Entscheidung 2011/734/EU mit drei weiteren Anpassungen 2011/792/EU, 2012/211/EU und 2013/6/EU.

in Kraft, welches unter anderem auch die Hinterlegung einer Bareinlage oder auch die Verhängung von Strafgeldern vorsieht[50].

Weitere Sanktionen sind nicht vorgesehen, insbesondere nicht die Möglichkeit eines Ausschlusses für den Fall, dass der Staat beharrlich seine Pflichten nicht nachkommt. Dies ist eine freie Entscheidung der Mitgliedstaaten als Herren der Verträge welche selbst im Falle des Artikels 7 EUV offensichtlich einen Ausschluss nicht wollen[51]. Unweigerlich stellt sich in diesem Fall aber die Frage, ob nicht wenigstens die Vorschriften des allgemeinen Völkerrechts in besonderen Fällen Anwendung finden könnten. Zu denken wäre hier an die clausula rebus sic stantibus, welche ihren Niederschlag in Art. 62 der Wiener Vertragsrechtskonvention gefunden hat[52].

Wie auch bei der allgemeinen Frage eines möglichen Ausschlusses aus der Union wird man davon ausgehen müssen, dass die Mitgliedstaaten diesen bewusst in den Sanktionssystemen der Union nicht vorgesehen haben. Probleme an diesen entscheidenden Sollbruchstellen sollen offensichtlich politisch gelöst werden. Ebenso wenig, wie es also möglich ist, einen Start bei beharrlicher Pflichtverletzung aus der Union auszuschließen, so ist es auch unmöglich, ihn aus der Währungsunion auszuschließen, die erklärtermaßen unveränderbar sein soll.

Allerdings wird ein Mitgliedstaat, wenn er keine Hilfeleistung von anderen Mitgliedstaaten bekommt, bei erheblichen finanziellen Schwierigkeiten vernünftigerweise daran denken, die Währungsunion zu verlassen, um dann mit einem eigenen Währungskurs die Verluste reduzieren zu können[53]. Aber auch das einseitige freiwillige Verlassen der Währungsunion ist unionsrechtlich nicht vorgesehen. Soll es zugelassen werden, so müsste zuvor eine Vertragsänderung nach Art. 48 EUV erfolgen, eine einseitige politische Absprache zwischen den Regierungen würde also nicht ausreichen. Was auch heute schon möglich sein dürfte, ist das Verlassen der Währungsunion zusammen mit dem Verlassen der Europäischen Union nach Art. 50 EUV[54].

Der genannte Beschluss 2010/320/EU hat aber auch noch eine andere Funktion als Basis der Hilfeleistungen für Griechenland durch die EU und den IMF. Zunächst

---

[50] Über die Weisheit der Verhängung von Strafgeldern gegenüber einem Staat, der offensichtlich in erheblichen finanziellen Schwierigkeiten steckt, sollte man noch einmal intensiver nachdenken.

[51] Aus sachlichen Gesichtspunkten zustimmend hierzu *Athanassiou*, Phoebus, Withdrawal and Expulsion from the EU and EMU. Some reflections. ECB. Legal Working Paper Series No. 10, https://www.ecb.europa.eu/pub/pdf/scplps/ecblwp10.pdf. Gegen die Möglichkeit eines direkten Austritts oder Ausschlusses.

[52] Hierzu *Hanschel*, Dirk, Der Rechtsrahmen für den Beitritt, Austritt und Ausschluss zu bzw. aus der Europäischen Union und Währungsunion, NVwZ 2012, 995.

[53] Zu all dem *Hanschel*, a.a.O.

[54] Auch hier würden sich jedoch auf Grund der unzureichenden Regelung des Art. 50 EUV erhebliche Probleme ergeben. Ein einseitiges Verlassen der Währungsunion würde zu noch viel mehr Schwierigkeiten führen als ein einseitiges Verlassen der Union, vgl. hierzu *Athanassiou*, a.a.O.

war fraglich, ob solche Hilfeleistungen überhaupt unionsrechtlich zulässig waren wegen des bailout-Verbots in Art. 125 AEUV. Diese Bedenken hat jedoch der EuGH in der Pringle-Entscheidung[55] zerstreut mit der Unterscheidung zwischen währungspolitischen Hilfen, welche eine Schuldübernahme gegenüber den Gläubigern bedeuten (Art. 125) und die Marktkräfte außer Kraft setzen und wirtschaftspolitischen Beihilfen, welche den Bestand der gemeinsamen Währung sichern, rückzahlbar sind und die Schuld des Empfängerstaates unberührt lassen. Damit sind die Beihilfen zunächst der anderen Mitgliedstaaten und dann des EFSF an Griechenland zulässig. Nach Inkrafttreten der Vertragsergänzung des Art. 136 Abs. 3 sind sie auch primärrechtlich abgesichert und darüber hinaus die Grundlage für den ESM-Vertrag.

Im Falle Griechenland gibt es jetzt (zeitlich konsekutiv) zwei Memoranda of Understanding[56], welche den Beschluss 2010/320/EU hinsichtlich der zu treffenden Schritte und der Verwendung der Hilfsleistungen konkretisieren. Sie wurden von Griechenland und den Mitgliedstaaten bzw. der Union gegengezeichnet. Auf diesen Memoranden basieren wiederum die Loan Facilities Agreements, das erste mit den anderen EURO-Staaten[57], das zweite mit dem EFSF[58]. Trotz gewisser sonstiger Unterschiede sind sich beide Abkommen in den hier interessierenden Punkten (welche Verpflichtungen gibt es zwischen den Parteien, was folgt aus deren Nichteinhaltung oder Wegfall?) gleich. Diese Abkommen sind es, welche das konditionale Rechtsverhältnis zwischen den Parteien festlegen[59].

Die Agreements gewähren Griechenland einen Auszahlungsanspruch bei Einhaltung der Verpflichtungen, welche sich durch Verweis aus den Memoranden ergeben. Griechenland hat eine verzinste Rückzahlungspflicht. Hält es die Konditionalität nicht ein, so entfällt jede weitere Auszahlung, so lange der Verzug dauert und so weit nicht das jeweils gültige Memorandum angepasst wird[60]. Die bereits ausgezahlten Gelder verbleiben Griechenland aber weiter bis zum vereinbarten Rückzahlungstermin. Eine Kündigung durch den EFSF mit der Folge einer vollständigen sofortigen Rückzahlungsverpflichtung[61] ist dagegen nur möglich, wenn Griechenland die erhaltenen Gelder zweckentfremdet, geschuldete Rückzahlungen nicht pünktlich leistet. Nach dem zweiten Agreement besteht u.a. auch ein Kündigungsrecht des EFSF

---

[55] EuGH, 27.11.2012 – C-370/12, Pringle.

[56] Attachment II to the Economic Adjustment Programme for Greece of Mai 26, 2010 und Annex 3 to the Second Economic Adjustment Programme for Greece of March 2012.

[57] Vom 8. Mai 2010 http://www.minfin.gr/content-api/f/binaryChannel/minfin/datastore/30/ 2d/05/302d058d2ca156bc35b0e268f9446a71c92782b9/application/pdf/sn_kyrwtikoimf_2010_ 06_04_A.pdf, gesehen am 3.9.2014.

[58] Vom 12.12.2012 http://www.efsf.europa.eu/attachments/efsf_financial_assistance_facili ty_agreement_greece_bond_interest.pdf, gesehen am 3.9.2014.

[59] Daneben stehen allerdings die oben dargelegten primärrechtlichen Rechte und Pflichten der Mitgliedstaaten im Rahmen des primärrechtlichen besonderen Sanktionssystems.

[60] Dies erfolgte in der Realität ständig.

[61] Ein „Default" in der Terminologie der Verträge.

dann, wenn der IMF sein Arrangement beendet. Ein beiderseitiges Kündigungsrecht existiert, wenn Griechenland keinen Zugriff mehr auf die zugesagten zukünftigen Tranchen nehmen will.

4. Zwischenergebnis

Was wäre also rechtlich dazu zu sagen, wenn die griechische Regierung angesichts der Proteste der Bevölkerung die Erfüllung bestimmter Konditionen ohne Zustimmung der anderen Mitglieder und des EFSF verweigern würde oder wenn, wie bereits seit langem angekündigt, die aussichtsreichste Oppositionspartei SYRIZA bei einer Übernahme der Regierung die Bedingungen der Memoranden und der Loan Facilities Agreements in Bausch und Bogen ablehnen würde?

Zunächst kann sich Griechenland auf diese Weise nicht der europarechtlichen Pflicht entziehen, sein übermäßiges Defizit zu beseitigen, welche aus der Entscheidung 2010/320/EU bzw. einer nachträglichen Anpassung resultiert. Es muss grundsatzlich auch die in diesen Entscheidungen festgelegten Schritte zur Beseitigung vollziehen. Allerdings kann es bei Nichterfüllung weder von der Kommission nach Art. 258 noch von den anderen Mitgliedstaaten nach Art. 259 AEUV gerichtlich belangt werden. Es bleiben nur die besonderen Sanktionen nach Art. 126 Abs. 11 AEUV, also maximal die Verhängung von Bußgeldern. Schließlich bliebe Griechenland noch der Rückzug aus der Europäischen Union Art. 50 EUV beziehungsweise, nach einer formellen Vertragsänderung nach Art. 48 EUV, ein Rückzug aus dem europäischen Währungssystem. Die vom Rat in seiner Entscheidung angegebenen Maßnahmen für die Reduzierung des Defizits sind aufgrund von Art. 126 Abs. 9 AEUV in sein Ermessen gestellt, solange sie als notwendig erachtet werden.

Der gesamte aufgezeigte Mechanismus ist im primären Unionsrecht verankert. Insoweit haben alle Mitgliedstaaten ihre Souveränität beschränkt. Es kann sich also nicht um eine Einmischung in die inneren Angelegenheiten Griechenlands handeln. Dieser heißt natürlich nicht, dass die Eignung und Tragbarkeit der angeordneten Maßnahmen nicht immer wieder überprüft und politisch diskutiert werden sollte.

Im Rechtsverhältnis zum Internationalen Währungsfonds Griechenland keine Verhaltenspflichten. Allerdings wird es das benötigte Hilfs-Geld nur dann erhalten, wenn es die Konditionen aus dem Memorandum einhält. Das gleiche gilt auch von den Leistungen, welche Griechenland aufgrund der Loan Facilities Agreements erhält. Auch hier drohen nicht einmal vorzeitige Rückzahlungspflichten[62]. Um den Preis des Verlustes weiterer Hilfe könnte also Griechenland von der weiteren Erfüllung der Bedingungen des Memorandums Abstand nehmen. Will es dies nicht tun, so

---

[62] Daraus könnte im Übrigen die Gefahr eines moral hazard resultieren, dass nämlich bei weitgehend bereits erfolgter Auszahlung eine Versuchung existieren könnte, eine weitere Ausführung des Memorandums aufzukündigen. Dies wäre wohl aber nur dann realistisch, wenn die Restsumme gemessen an den Schwierigkeiten eines weiteren Festhaltens am Memorandum weniger gewichtig wäre. Auch im Herbst 2014 scheint dies aber (noch) nicht realistisch zu sein. Ende dieses Jahres soll vielmehr noch einmal über ein weiteres Hilfsprogramm verhandelt werden.

muss es weiterhin eine faktische Beschränkung seiner Souveränität hinnehmen, kann sich aber auch hier nicht auf eine Verletzung des Interventionsverbots berufen.

III. Juristische und politische Aspekte der Solidarität und des Sozialstaats

1. Fragestellung

Diese faktische Beschränkung der Souveränität aller Empfängerstaaten in der Euro-Schuldenkrise wirft aber noch weitere Probleme speziell innerhalb der inzwischen sehr engen Integration nicht nur der Mitgliedstaaten, sondern auch ihre Völker auf. Gibt es spezielle Solidaritätspflichten zwischen Geber- und Nehmerländern sowie der Europäischen Union selbst? Und weiter: dürfen Geberländer nur ihre eigenen finanzpolitischen Interessen (Rettung der gemeinsamen Währung und Rückzahlung der Darlehen) verfolgen, oder müssen sie hinsichtlich der von ihnen auferlegten Konditionalität auch bedenken, welche Konsequenzen diese Bedingungen für die Wirtschaft und insbesondere im sozialpolitischen Bereich für die Bevölkerung des Empfängerlandes haben. Geht also die Beschränkung wirtschafts- und sozialpolitischer Souveränität einher mit gesteigerter Verantwortung der Mitgliedstaaten füreinander beziehungsweise der Union für die Mitgliedstaaten?

Solidarität wird gefordert und versprochen. Im Juli 2013 sagte Wirtschaftsminister Hatzidakis gegenüber der Tageszeitung „Die Welt"[63]: „Wir brauchen keine Strafmaßnahmen, sondern ein Symbol der Solidarität". Und er kündigte an, was dann 2014 auch Wirklichkeit wurde, dass nämlich Griechenland einen Primärüberschuss erwirtschaften werde (also eine Einkommensüberschuss unter Außerachtlassung des Schuldendienstes, der allerdings alle Überschüsse noch lange zunichte machen wird): „Wenn wir zuverlässig sind und positiv überraschen, bin ich mir sicher, dass unsere Partner ihre Solidarität mit Griechenland zeigen werden." Jeder europäische Politiker, der Athen besucht, bekundet Solidarität mit dem Land, aber auf die konkrete Frage, wie man die Depression der griechischen Wirtschaft umkehren kann[64] und wie man mehr Investoren nach Griechenland holen kann, haben die Europäer und noch weniger – wie es scheint – die Griechen selbst keine Antwort. Es gibt in dieser Hinsicht auch Positivbeispiele wie etwa die chinesischen Investitionen im griechischen Verkehrssektor. Auch rufen die Griechen jetzt vollständiger die Mittel ab, welche ihnen in der EU aus den Regional- und Strukturfonds zustehen und werden weitere Programme speziell für Griechenland aufgelegt. Aber einerseits sind diese auf Grund der immer noch enormen Schulden eher ein Tropfen auf den heißen Stein und andererseits müsste man die Leiden der Individuen, der griechischen Bevölkerung so schnell wie möglich angehen, denn die werden sich nur vergrößern, bis

---

[63] Vom 2.7.2013.

[64] Die sich übrigens nicht in den nach wie vor hohen Preisen niederschlägt, was die Bevölkerung noch zusätzliche belastet. Über den Grund dieses Paradoxons soll hier nicht weiter spekuliert werden.

hoffentlich in ein paar Jahren eine wirtschaftliche Gesundung eintritt. Angesichts des hierzu notwendigen Reformbedarfs in Politik, Wirtschaft und Gesellschaft sollte man hierfür eher mehr als weniger Zeit veranschlagen.

Es geht hier also nicht um die Frage diplomatischer Solidarität oder der Verbesserung wirtschaftlicher Standortbedingungen, sondern um die Solidarität mit den Menschen und der Art und Weise, wie sie durch die Konditionalität der griechischen Rettungsprogramme betroffen sind. Müssen wegen deren Folgen die Konditionen geändert werden? Oder sollten sie geändert werden, aus politischer Klugheit oder besser noch: aus menschlicher Solidarität?

Zunächst wird zu klären sein, inwieweit es in der EU Rechtspflichten der Solidarität oder des sozialen Ausgleichs gibt. Die eigentliche Problematik wird aber im politisch-faktischen Bereich liegen: wie viel Austerität kann, wie viel darf ich einem anderen Volk in der EU bei Zugrundelegung politischer Vernunft und menschlichen Verständnisses verordnen? Diese Frage, welche sich jetzt nach Jahren der Austerität in Griechenland mit ihren heute bekannten Folgen stellt, sollte beantwortet werden, um für mögliche Fälle in der Zukunft heute bekannte Fehler zu vermeiden.

2. Die Folgen der Austerität in Griechenland

Zuerst ein kurzer Blick auf die verheerenden Folgen der Austerität auf Grund der Memoranden in Griechenland, welche durch Ausgabenkürzungen des Staates und permanente Steuererhöhungen, durch reduzierte und verspätete Zahlungen des Staates an seine Bediensteten (soweit sie nicht entlassen wurden) und an seine Lieferanten und Dienstleister umrissen werden kann. Hinzu kommen noch eine ganze andere Reihe von Maßnahmen, die insgesamt zu katastrophalen Folgen in der griechischen Gesellschaft geführt haben[65], welche sich noch zu verstärken drohen. Allerdings: nimmt man die sichtbar mangelnde Konsequenz der griechischen Politiker hinzu, tatsächlich eine Kehrtwende zum Besseren herbeizuführen, so kann die Kausalität wieder nur schwer zwischen externer Konditionalität und internem Politikversagen verteilt werden. Wenn man von rechtlichen Solidaritätspflichten sprechen will, müsste man aber eine solche Zuordnung vornehmen. Ansonsten bleibt alles politische Opportunität oder Caritas.

Die Konsequenzen des Sparkurses, den sich die griechische Regierung unter Druck der Troika verordnet hat, sind erschreckend[66]. Die Arbeitslosigkeit liegt bei

---

[65] Hierzu eindrucksvoll www.caritas.de vom 20. 4. 20141.

[66] Siehe eine Übersicht der deutschen Caritas „Griechenland: Ein Volk droht auszubluten" aus dem Jahre 2011, wobei gesagt werden kann, dass sich die Verhältnisse auch heute noch nicht wesentlich verbessert haben, http://www.caritas.de/neue-caritas/heftarchiv/jahrgang2013/artikel/griechenland-ein-volk-droht-auszubluten. Vgl. auch *Kontogiannis*, Excessive austerity killing Greece, eKathimerini vom 30. 9. 2012.

heute 28 %, die Jugendarbeitslosigkeit ist mehr als doppelt so hoch[67]. Die Familien-
einkommen haben sich um durchschnittlich 30 % verringert, während die Steuerlas-
ten jährlich steigen[68]. Ein Drittel der Bevölkerung hat keine Sozialversicherung mehr
und der öffentliche Gesundheitsdienst ist in desolatem Zustand[69]. Die Versorgung mit
Medikamenten und Verbandsstoffen ist notleidend. Die Selbstmordraten steigen si-
gnifikant. Gehälter werden verzögert oder gar nicht mehr bezahlt, ebenso Mieten und
Kredittilgungen. Immer mehr Familien, gerade auch solche mit Kindern, geraten in
die Nähe der Armutsgrenze. 730 000 Kfz sind ohne Versicherungsschutz, weil die
Besitzer die Pflichtversicherungsprämie nicht mehr zahlen können[70].

Auch die gesellschaftlichen und politischen Konsequenzen sind verheerend. Das
Ansteigen der Kriminalität und der Fremdenfeindlichkeit ist dabei noch eher zu erwarten, aber politisch gefährlich ist, dass die neo-nazistische Partei „Chrysi Avgi"
(Goldene Morgenröte) immer mehr Zulauf bekommt[71]. Andererseits ist auch auf
der linksradikalen Seite zu sehen, dass Terroristen wieder aktiver werden. Radikalisierung droht also am Horizont, wie dies aus der deutschen Geschichte ja durchaus in
ähnlicher Kausalität bekannt ist. Die Tendenz wird auch dadurch sichtbar, dass im
September 2014 eine Umfrage ergab, dass 30 % der Griechen der Meinung sind,
das Leben sei unter der Diktatur der 60er und 70er Jahre besser gewesen als
heute, was Präsident Papoulias veranlasste, seine Landsleute zu warnen, die Demokratie sei keine Selbstverständlichkeit[72].

Obwohl erste Anzeichen einer wirtschaftlichen Aufwärtsbewegung im Jahre 2014
zu sehen sind, scheint die griechische Regierung nicht wirklich die Kraft zu haben,
der genannten Probleme langsam Herr zu werden. Ihre Mehrheit im Parlament ist
(154 von 300 Sitzen) knapp, die sozialistische Koalitionspartei PASOK ist durch heftige Stimmverluste nur noch ein Schatten ihrer selbst und die aussichtsreichste, weit
links stehende Oppositionspartei SYRIZA[73] hat anhaltend etwa 3 Prozent Vorsprung

---

[67] Deutsche Wirtschaftsnachrichten vom 13.2.14, http://deutsche-wirtschafts-nachrichten.
de/2014/02/13/griechenland-arbeitslosigkeit-steigt-auf-rekordhoch-von-28-prozent/.

[68] Insbesondere erhöhte Grundsteuern sind ein beliebtes Mittel, Finanzlöcher gegenüber
der Troika zu stopfen, welche durch die Nicht-Durchführung anderer, wichtiger Maßnahmen
entstehen. Dies ist angesichts der hohen Eigenheimquote in Griechenland besonders ein-
schneidend auch für weniger Verdienende.

[69] Süddeutsche Zeitung vom 29.3.2013.

[70] Check24 vom 24.2.2014, http://www.check24.de/kfz-versicherung/news/griechenland-
fahrzeuge-ohne-versicherungsschutz-56829/.

[71] Bei der griechischen Parlamentswahlen 2012 erreichte sie knapp 7 Prozent, bei der
zweiten Wahl 21 Sitze im Parlament (Süddeutsche Zeitung vom 15.5.2012). Bei der Euro-
pawahl 2014 wurde die Partei in Griechenland drittstärkste Kraft mit 9,5 % der Stimmen und 3
Sitzen im Europaparlament (Crash Magazin Online vom 27.5.2014).

[72] eKathimerini vom 8.9.2014.

[73] Die schon seit längerer Zeit ankündigt, sie werde mit der Regierungsübernahme die
Erfüllung des Memorandums einstellen (so jüngst ihr Vorsitzender Tsipras: „Wir werden das
Memorandum abschaffen", Crash Magzine online vom 8.9.2014). Darüber hinaus hat der

vor der größeren Koalitionspartei Nea Demokratia. Die Regierung sieht sich dauern-
den Protesten aus der Bevölkerung gegen die Memorandums-Politik ausgesetzt, was
– unter anderem – auch der Grund dafür sein dürfte, dass etwa 600 mit der Troika
vereinbarte Reform-Maßnahmen lange Zeit überfällig sind[74]. Dazu gehören etwa
die Reduzierung des völlig überbesetzten öffentlichen Dienstes zugunsten des Privatsektors und die Privatisierung von unrentablen öffentlichen Unternehmen und Eigen-
tumspositionen des Staates, aber auch die Eintreibung umfangreicher Steuerschul-
den und die Bekämpfung der Steuerhinterziehung für die Vergangenheit. Hinsichtlich des öffentlichen Dienstes kommt hinzu, dass die Ministerien und die nachgeord-
neten Behörden weder ausreichend effizient noch kompetent sind, wie die OECD in
einem äußerst kritischen Bericht aus dem Jahre 2011 feststellte[75]. Der in den letzten
Jahrzehnten immer stärker bestimmende Klientilismus[76], sowie die immer noch gras-
sierende Korruption bremsen alle zaghaften Reformansätze.

In diesem politischen, sozialen und historischen Umfeld stellt sich nun die Frage,
ob hier Solidarität rechtlich oder tatsächlich gefordert ist. Dies betrifft vornehmlich
zwei Bereiche: die Folgen der Konditionalität auf der einen und die Hilfe zu wirtschaftlicher Entwicklung auf der anderen Seite. Vorstehend wurde bereits gesagt,
dass es hier nur um den ersten Bereich gehen soll, also konzentriert auf die Frage,
ob die erhebliche Relativierung der Souveränität durch die Memoranden wie in
einem System der kommunizierenden Röhren auch zu einer erhöhten Solidarität
für die Folgen der Konditionalität führen muss, und ob dies eine rechtliche Verpflichtung ist oder nur politischer Klugheit entspricht.

3. Solidaritätspflichten in der EU
und zwischen den EU-Mitgliedstaaten

a) Prinzipieller Rahmen im EU-Recht

Wo Menschen zu gemeinsamen Zwecken Gesellschaften gründen oder organisieren, da gibt es Solidaritäts- oder Treuepflichten. Die Treue zum gemeinsamen Ge-

---

Sekretär dieser Partei, Dimitris Vitsas, angekündigt: „We should fight, so that NATO breaks
up on its own" (eKathimerini vom 8. 9. 2014).

[74] Wie bereits berichtet hat die griechische Regierung die Entsendung von 175 Finanzbe-
amten aus Deutschland gleichwohl wegen Souveränitätsbedenken abgelehnt.

[75] OECD Governance Reviews: Greece 2011 (2012): es fehlt an Aufsicht und Kontrolle
und an Effizienz an der Spitze wie auch in allen anderen Bereichen der Verwaltung. Die Kraft
zu wirklichen Modernisierungen fehlt. Vgl. auch Heinrich Böll-Stiftung, Griechenland: Ein
Jahrzehnt Widerstand gegen Reformen fordert seinen Preis (2013), https://www.boell.de/de/
2014/05/07/griechenland-ein-jahrzehnt-widerstand-gegen-reformen-fordert-seinen-preis, gesehen am 9. 9. 2014.

[76] Der zwar seit Ende der Obristen-Herrschaft in der Politik wucherte und die Ineffizienz
und auch Korruption noch überhöhte, der aber als gesellschaftliches Aktionsmuster viel weiter
in die griechische Geschichte insbesondere bis hin zur Unterwerfung unter das Osmanische
Reich in manchen Landesteilen für fast vierhundert Jahre zurückreicht.

sellschaftszweck und gegenüber allen anderen Gesellschaftern ist eine selbstver-
ständliche Pflicht für alle. Die Bundestreue ist eine gegenseitige Pflicht für Organe
und Gebietskörperschaften in einem Bundesstaat. Die Treue- oder Solidaritätspflicht
ist eine Auffangnorm für alle Situationen, in denen das Verhalten nicht durch ausdrückliche Rechtsregeln determiniert ist. Sie ist denknotwendiges Korrelat des gemeinsamen Zwecks, der dem „Gesellschaftsvertrag" (in allen Facetten der Bedeutung dieses Begriffs) zugrunde liegt[77]. Speziell geregelte Ausprägungen dieser
Pflicht verengen nicht ihren Anwendungsbereich, sondern konkretisieren ihn punk-
tuell. Die generelle Treuepflicht bleibt dabei ungeschmälert erhalten.

Auch im Recht der EU ist die Solidarität oder Treuepflicht umfassend verankert
und als grundlegendes Verfassungs- und Rechtsprinzip anerkannt[78]. Sie findet sich
im Vertrag von Lissabon an 15 Stellen. Hier soll nur auf die wirtschafts- und wäh-
rungsrechtlich relevanten Normen eingegangen werden. Zwei allgemeine Normen
finden sich im EUV. Art. 3 Abs. 3 S. 3 spricht ganz allgemein vom wirtschaftlichen,
sozialen und territorialen Zusammenhalt und der Solidarität zwischen den Mitgliedstaaten, welche die Union fördern soll. Art. 4 Abs. 3 statuiert die Pflicht der Mitgliedstaaten und der Union, wechselseitig miteinander zusammenzuarbeiten und statuiert
die Pflicht der Mitgliedstaaten, alles zu unterlassen, was die Verwirklichung der Ziele
der Union gefährden könnte. Zu diesen Zielen gehört unter anderem nach Art. 3
Abs. 3 S.2 die Bekämpfung der sozialen Ausgrenzung, die soziale Gerechtigkeit
und der soziale Schutz. Man kann hieraus eine allgemeine Hilfspflicht gegenüber anderen Mitgliedstaaten, aber auch gegenüber den Menschen in diesen Staaten ableiten[79]. Nur ist diese Pflicht eher konturlos, wenn man sie nicht kombiniert mit anderen
Rechtsvorschriften der Union. Ein positives Beispiel hierfür findet sich im Urteil des
EuGH über die italienischen Schlachtprämien[80], in dem der Gerichtshof von einem
„Verstoß gegen die Pflicht zur Solidarität" spricht, welche die Mitgliedstaaten übernommen haben, der die „Grundfesten der Gemeinschaft erschüttert". Im Übrigen
kann man feststellen, dass durch die Hilfeleistungen der Mitgliedstaaten bilateral
sowie durch EFSM/EFSF in der hier erörterten Schuldenkrise ebenso wie auch die

---

[77] *Brink*, A. (Ton) van den / *Van Rossem*, Jan Willem Casper, Sovereignty, Stability and
Solidarity: Conflicting and Converging Principles and the Shaping of Economic Governance
in the European Union (December 6, 2013). UCD Working Papers in Law, Criminology &
Socio-Legal Studies Research Paper No. 04061213, S. 11. Available at SSRN: http://ssrn.com/
abstract=2439184 or http://dx.doi.org/10.2139/ssrn.2439184.

[78] Hierzu insbesondere *Calliess*, C. (Hrsg.), Europäische Solidarität und nationale Identität.
Überlegungen im Kontext der Krise im Euroraum (2013); *id.*, Perspektiven des Euro zwischen
Solidarität und Recht. Eine rechtliche Analyse der Griechenlandhilfe und des Rettungsschirms, in: Zeitschrift für europarechtliche Studien 2011, 213–282 und *id.*, Subsidiaritäts-
und Solidaritätsprinzip in der Europäischen Union. Vorgaben für die Anwendung von Art. 5
(ex-Art. 3b) EGV nach dem Vertrag von Amsterdam (2. Aufl., 1999). Vgl. auch *Kahl*, in:
Calliess, C./Ruffert, M. (Hrsg.), EUV, AEUV. Das Verfassungsrecht der Europäischen Union
mit Europäischer Grundrechtecharta. Kommentar (4. Aufl., 2011), Art. 4, Rn. 34.

[79] *Calliess*, Perspektiven (oben Fn. 78), 225, *Kahl* (Fn. 78), Rnr. 41.

[80] EuGH 7.2.1973–39/72, Kommission gegen Italien.

Einrichtung des ESM genau diese erforderliche Hilfsbereitschaft aktualisiert wurde, wie die Generalanwältin Kokott zu Recht im Pringle-Verfahren betonte[81].

Später wird noch zu untersuchen sein, ob nicht der Art. 3 Abs. 3 S. 2 allgemein auf ein Prinzip des sozialen Schutzes innerhalb und durch die Union verweist, den die Mitgliedstaaten nicht konterkarieren dürfen. Zuvor sollen aber noch spezielle Ausprägungen des Solidaritätsprinzips im Wirtschafts- und Währungsrecht erörtert werden. Zunächst einmal ist festzustellen, dass die Klausel des Art. 222 AEUV über die gegenseitige Unterstützung bei Terroranschlägen und Katastrophen auf Schuldenkrisen nicht anwendbar ist. Das Gleiche gilt auch von Art. 143 AEUV, welcher auf Zahlungsbilanzschwierigkeiten Anwendung findet. Art. 122 AEUV ist zwar Ausdruck der Solidarität in der Wirtschaftspolitik, aber er ist nicht auf Rettungsschirme der Mitgliedstaaten anwendbar[82]. Die Mitgliedstaaten bleiben zuständig, einen solchen Schirm zu errichten, aufgrund ihrer fortbestehenden souveränen Kompetenz, wobei dies auch dann ein Akt der Solidarität ist, wenn gleichzeitig noch andere Ziele, insbesondere die Rettung der gemeinsamen Währung verfolgt werden[83]. Die unionsrechtliche Rechtsgrundlage hierfür wurde geschaffen in Art. 136 Abs. 3 AEUV. Dieser ist nicht notwendig als Kompetenzgrundlage für die Mitgliedstaaten. Vielmehr führt er eine unionsrechtliche Begrenzung dergestalt ein, dass die Hilfe nur gegen strikte Bedingungen erfolgen darf.

Im Währungsrecht gibt es noch weitere unionsrechtliche Begrenzungen der Solidaritätsausübung durch die Union und durch die Mitgliedsstaaten. Art. 123 AEUV verbietet Kreditfazilitäten für öffentliche Einrichtungen bei der EZB und bei nationalen Zentralbanken. Art. 124 untersagt den bevorrechtigten Zugang von Organen der Union und der Mitgliedstaaten zu Finanzinstituten. Art. 125 schließlich, die no-bailout-Klausel, verbietet es, dass die Union oder die Mitgliedstaaten für Schulden eines anderen Mitgliedstaats die direkte Haftung übernehmen. Damit in Art. 136 Abs. 3 AEUV keine Umgehung dieser Vorschrift zu sehen ist, muss die solidarische Hilfeleistung aufgrund dieser Vorschrift freiwillig bleiben. Es gibt keine Pflicht anderer Mitgliedstaaten, solche Leistungen zu erbringen[84]. Es bleibt aber ihr souveränes Recht, dies gleichwohl zu tun.

---

[81] Stellungnahme vom 26.10.12 in der Rs. C-370/12, Rn. 144. Sie betonte aber dabei, dass es sich um die Möglichkeit, nicht aber um eine Pflicht zur Hilfe handele. Dies ist ebenfalls richtig, weil ansonsten das bailout-Verbot des Art. 125 AEUV umgangen würde.

[82] So der EuGH in der Pringle-Entscheidung (Fn. 55), Nr. 115–122. Es wäre auch sehr zweifelhaft, ob, gestützt auf den Abs. 1, die Union selbst einen solchen Schirm errichten könnte. Abs. 2 dürfte auf Schuldenkrisen, welche die Mitgliedstaaten zumindest mit zu verantworten haben, nicht anwendbar sein.

[83] Vgl. *Kokott* (Fn. 81).

[84] Der EuGH in Pringle (Fn. 55), Nr. 71–75 spricht deshalb nur von einer Zuständigkeit der Mitgliedstaaten, nicht von einer Pflicht. Deutlicher noch insoweit *Kokott* (Fn. 81).

b) Spezielle Grenzen für Konditionen?

Da Art. 136 Abs. 3 AEUV die Hilfeleistung der anderen Mitgliedstaaten an strikte Bedingungen knüpft, stellt sich die Frage, ob es für solche Bedingungen irgendwelche unionsrechtlichen Grenzen gibt. Diese Frage stellt sich natürlich insbesondere aufgrund der geschilderten negativen Konsequenzen der Konditionalität, wie sie sich in Griechenland gezeigt haben.

Weder im Unionsrecht noch im allgemeinen Völkerrecht gibt es rechtlich verbindliche Regeln über die Grenzen der Konditionalität bei der Vergabe internationaler Kredite. In Art. 136 Abs. 3 AEUV (der aber auf die Griechenland-Kredite noch nicht anwendbar ist), ist die Rede von strengen („strict") Konditionen. Im ESM-Vertrag[85] finden sich zweierlei Erwähnungen der Konditionalität. In Art. 12 heißt es:

> „Ist dies zur Wahrung der Finanzstabilität des Euro-Währungsgebiets insgesamt und seiner Mitgliedstaaten unabdingbar, so kann der ESM einem ESM-Mitglied unter strengen, dem gewählten Finanzhilfeinstrument angemessenen Auflagen Stabilitätshilfe gewähren. Diese Auflagen können von einem makroökonomischen Anpassungsprogramm bis zur kontinuierlichen Erfüllung zuvor festgelegter Anspruchsvoraussetzungen reichen."

Art. 13 Abs. 3 des Vertrages sagt:

> „Der Inhalt des MoU spiegelt den Schweregrad der zu behebenden Schwachpunkte und das gewählte Finanzhilfeinstrument wider".

Soziale Gesichtspunkte spielen also hierbei keine Rolle, es geht nur um wirtschafts- und finanzpolitische Gesichtspunkte.

Weiter könnte man noch die Guidelines on Conditionality des IMF[86] aus dem Jahre 2002 befragen, die zwar nicht extern verbindlich sind, aber wohl als internes Organisationsrecht des IMF dessen Organe binden. Aber auch hier ergibt sich, dass die sozialen Konsequenzen der Konditionalität überhaupt nicht angesprochen werden. Damit kann man feststellen, dass sich Grenzen der Bedingungen in dieser Hinsicht nur aus allgemeinem Recht ergeben könnten.

Bevor man hier an die Allgemeinen Menschenrechte als „Rückfallposition" denkt, sollte man zunächst das Unionsrecht daraufhin überprüfen, ob seine Schutzvorschriften eingehalten sind. Angesichts der geschilderten Konsequenzen der Konditionalität kann man sich hier auf hohe Arbeitslosigkeit und das Abrutschen breiter Bevölkerungsschichten in die Armut konzentrieren. Während die Hilfeleistungen der Mitgliedstaaten aus dem Rettungsschirm ausschließlich zur Begleichung der Kreditschulden Griechenlands verwendet werden, sind die mit der Konditionalität geforderten Anpassungsmaßnahmen dazu da, das Land möglichst schnell auf den Kurs zu einer wirtschaftlichen Gesundung zu bringen. Ob diese Bedingungen zweck-

---

[85] http://www.bundesfinanzministerium.de/Content/DE/Standardartikel/Themen/Europa/Stabilisierung_des_Euro/Finanzhilfemechanismen/2012-01-27-esm-anl.pdf?__blob=publicationFile&, gesehen am 9.9.2014.

[86] Oben Anm. 33.

gemäß sind oder nicht, kann nicht Gegenstand juristischer Beurteilung sein. Man muss aber fragen, ob ihre Konsequenzen rechtlich hingenommen werden müssen.

Ansatzpunkt könnte hier Art. 3 Abs. 3 S. 2 iVm Art. 4 Abs. 3 S. 3 EUV sein. Danach müssen die Mitgliedstaaten alles unterlassen, was die Bekämpfung der sozialen Ausgrenzung, die soziale Gerechtigkeit und den sozialen Schutz durch die Union gefährden könnte. Hieraus wird man aber nicht ableiten können, dass die Mitgliedstaaten in jedem Fall den Lebensstandard und die Arbeitsplätze in einem Mitgliedstaat, der in Not geraten ist, mit einem Mindeststandard absichern müssen. Vielmehr müssen die Mitgliedstaaten im Rahmen dessen, was ihnen möglich ist, die Union in die Lage versetzen, durch entsprechende Budgetzuweisungen Hilfsprogramme für notleidende Länder aufzulegen. Wie weit die Staaten hierzu in der Lage sind, müssen sie aufgrund ihrer eigenen wirtschaftlichen Situation beurteilen können. Ihr – wiederum souveräner – Beurteilungsspielraum wird hierbei so weit sein, dass man von rechtlichen Pflichten nicht reden kann.

Allerdings dürfte es nicht so sein, dass die Geberländer das Empfängerland dazu zwingen können, sozial untragbare Konsequenzen ohne jede Alternative durch eigene Wirtschaftslenkung zu induzieren. Hier kommt wieder die bereits früher genannte „ownership" zum Tragen. Die Geberländer können das wirtschaftliche Ziel vorgeben, um die Rückzahlung der Kredite einerseits und die wirtschaftliche Gesundung andererseits sicherzustellen und zu fördern, sie müssen es aber dem Empfängerland überlassen, durch welche konkreten Maßnahmen dies geschehen soll. Dies entspricht im Falle Griechenlands auch der historischen Realität. Nicht nur die Memoranden wurden verhandelt, sondern sie wurden auch im Laufe der Zeit bei den jeweiligen Überprüfungen durch die Troika angepasst. Dass man immer wieder Steuererhöhungen wählte, um die konkreten Ziele zu erreichen, und dass man zu sonstigen Reformen weniger bereit war, ist nicht die Schuld der Geberländer. Dass in vielen Bereichen ein Politikversagen Reformen verhinderte, ist ein Problem des Nehmerlandes. Es ist auch eine souveräne Entscheidung dieses Landes, Hilfsangebote anzunehmen oder auszuschlagen.

Hier treffen dann wieder Souveränität und Solidarität aufeinander. Will man nicht die Souveränität wirklich durchbrechen, will man nicht Staaten jedenfalls temporär entmündigen, muss man auch die potenziell negativen Konsequenzen hinnehmen. Eine solche Lösung wäre auch aus demokratischen Gründen völlig inakzeptabel. Jedes Land ist für seine Regierung ebenso verantwortlich wie die Regierung für ihr Land. Die Staatsgewalt jedes Landes ist vor allen Dingen dafür verantwortlich, dass ihre Handlungen nicht zu Menschenrechtsverletzungen führen.

c) Ein politisches Nachwort

Trotz dieses rechtlichen Befundes werden es sich die Union und ihre Mitgliedstaaten politisch sehr wohl überlegen müssen, ob man nicht mit weiteren Hilfen, nicht nur für die Rückzahlung der Schulden, sondern für eine wirtschaftliche Gesundung Griechenlands, die dunklen Wolken auflösen kann, welche sich aufgrund der geschilderten Entwicklungen im Land am Horizont zeigen. Will man wirklich soziale Unruhen in einem Mitgliedstaat der Europäischen Union, der auch der NATO angehört, in einem Staat mit exponierter Lage hin zu einem immer gefährlicheren Krisengebiet im Nahen Osten riskieren? Will man der Gefahr einer Radikalisierung, insbesondere am rechten Rand, in einem Land tatenlos zusehen, das schon jetzt in ständigen Spannungen zur Türkei und zu Mazedonien (FYROM) steht?

Die Frage zusätzlicher Hilfeleistungen zur Abwendung sozialer Unruhen in Griechenland wird sicherlich in den anderen Mitgliedstaaten zu erheblichen Diskussionen führen, denn auch dort gibt es Sozialabbau und erhebliche Schuldenprobleme. Man sollte aber in diesen Diskussionen nicht vergessen, dass die anderen Mitgliedstaaten ihrerseits nicht völlig schuldlos an der kritischen Situation sind. Immer wieder wird darauf hingewiesen, dass die Regierungen dieser Staaten beim Eintritt Griechenlands in die europäische Währungsunion um die tatsächliche Misere dieses Landes wussten[87]. Durch diesen Beitritt wurde also Griechenland erst in die Lage versetzt, im Schatten der Bonität des Euro seine Schulden anzuhäufen. Und schließlich hat man trotz der alarmierenden Kenntnisse ohne Warnung Banken und Wirtschaftsteilnehmer an Griechenland verdienen lassen und damit ebenfalls den Schaden noch vergrößert.

Wenn man sich also darüber klar wird, dass das Verschulden zwar überwiegend, aber nicht alleine bei Griechenland liegt, könnte man sich vielleicht eher entschließen, die Gefahren, die jetzt in diesem Land sichtbar werden, ohne Rücksicht auf rechtliche Verpflichtungen einzugrenzen und abzuwehren.

---

[87] Die Presse vom 16. 2. 2010: „Alle wussten, was schiefgeht".

Das öffentliche Dienstrecht
im Spannungsfeld von Politisierung,
Wirtschaftlichkeit und Stabilität

Von *Heinrich Amadeus Wolff*

I. Grundlagen

Das öffentliche Dienstrecht bildet die Summe der Normen, die die persönlichen Rechte und Pflichten der Beschäftigten des Staates im weiteren Sinne regeln.[1] Es bildet das Personalstatut derjenigen, die in einem personenrechtlichen Verhältnis, d. h. in einem Angestelltenverhältnis, zur öffentlichen Hand stehen.

Das öffentliche Dienstrecht ist zwischen den Staaten in seiner Erscheinungsform sehr unterschiedlich. Die meisten europäischen Staaten, aber nicht alle, wie die Beispiele von Großbritannien und Schweden zeigen, kennen ein spezielles öffentliches Dienstrecht, das von dem Recht der allgemeinen Beschäftigungsverhältnisse abweicht. Es sind zivilrechtliche und öffentlich-rechtliche Ausgestaltungen, inhaltlich starke oder geringfügige Abweichungen bekannt. Die Einstellung ist oftmals formalisiert, etwa durch Eignungsprüfungen oder durch wettbewerbsähnliche Einstellungswettbewerbe.[2] Es wird daher zu Recht davon gesprochen, das öffentliche Dienstrecht sei in seiner Erscheinungsform in die historische und rechtliche Entwicklung des jeweiligen konkreten Staates eingebunden.[3]

II. Unterscheidung von Rechten und Pflichten
und Amtsausführung

Die Erfüllung staatlicher Aufgaben und das öffentliche Dienstrecht sind grundsätzlich deutlich zu trennen. Ein Staat, der sich bei der Erfüllung seiner Aufgaben hervortut, d. h. der die Rechte und Pflichten seiner Bürger achtet, ihnen Rahmenbe-

---

[1] Vgl. *Fritjof Wagner/Sabine Leppek*, Beamtenrecht, 10. Aufl. 2009, § 1, Rn. 1; *Helmut Lecheler*, Der öffentliche Dienst, in: Josef Isensee/Paul Kirchhof, Handbuch des Staatsrechts, Bd. V, 2007, § 110, Rn. 1.

[2] Vgl. dazu *Andreas Voßkuhle*, in: Wolfgang Hoffmann-Riem/Eberhard Schmidt-Aßmann/ders., Grundlagen des Verwaltungsrechts, Bd. III, 2009, § 43, Rn. 55; *Ulrich Battis*, Öffentlicher Dienst, in: Hanno Kube u. a. (Hg.), Leitgedanken des Rechts, FS f. Paul Kirchhof, Bd. I, 2013, 799, 780.

[3] *Herbert Landau/Martin Steinkühler*, Zur Zukunft des Berufsbeamtentums in Deutschland, DVBl 2007, 133, 135.

dingungen für wirtschaftliche, kulturelle, religiöse und private Entfaltung gewährleistet, bürgerliche und soziale Sicherheit vermittelt, kann dennoch ein grauenhaftes
Dienstrecht besitzen. Das Dienstrecht besitzt nur eine „Beschaffungsfunktion" für
den Staat. Vereinfacht gesprochen gilt: So wie der Staat sich mittels Kauf- und Werk-
verträgen die sachlichen Mittel für seine Aufgabenerledigung beschafft, beschafft er
sich mittels des Dienstrechtes die erforderlichen menschlichen Ressourcen für die
Aufgabenerledigung. Die Aufgabenerledigung des Staates, das staatliche Handeln
einerseits und das öffentliche Dienstrecht andererseits, sind grundsätzlich zu trennen.

Die Trennung wird in Deutschland besonders deutlich, weil hier zwischen Rechten und Pflichten des Staates und den persönlichen Rechten und Pflichten des Amtswalters noch eine gedankliche Institutionalisierung eingeschoben wird: das konkrete
Amt.[4] Die Rechte und Pflichten des einzelnen, für den Staat handelnden Menschen,
die notwendig sind, damit staatliches Recht Wirklichkeit wird, werden zunächst ent-
personalisiert und dem konkreten Amt zugewiesen und der Einzelne als Amtswalter
oder Organwalter verstanden.[5]

Sind Rechte und Pflichten des Staates und das Personalstatut der Einzelnen grundsätzlich zu trennen, so besteht zwischen beiden dennoch ein enger Zusammenhang.[6]
Der Staat handelt nicht alleine, sondern durch Menschen in amtlicher Funktion. Das
Beschäftigungsrecht soll primär dem Beschäftigten eine angemessene persönliche
Rechtsstellung vermitteln, bezogen auf seine Dienst- oder Arbeitspflicht, sekundär
aber immer auch sicherstellen, dass die Beschäftigten als Amtswalter die Aufgaben
des Staates so ausführen, wie es der Staat nach außen schuldet. Ihm kommt eine unterstützende Funktion für die Erfüllung der Staatsaufgaben zu. Das Beschäftigungsrecht muss daher so gefasst sein, dass die Regelung der Rechte und Pflichten der Beschäftigten die Erfüllung der Aufgaben des Staates zumindest nicht behindert bzw.
noch besser fördert.

Eine zentrale Transformationspflicht kennen dabei alle Formen des öffentlichen
Dienstrechts und zwar die Pflicht des Beschäftigten, als Amtswalter die Pflichten des
Staates zu beachten.[7] Sieht beispielsweise eine polizeirechtliche Norm Tatbestands-
voraussetzungen für die Ingewahrsamnahme einer Person oder die Beschlagnahme
einer Sache vor, dann muss der konkrete Amtswalter, der diese Handlung vornimmt,
diese Voraussetzungen beachten, unabhängig davon, wie das öffentliche Dienstrecht
in seinem Staat ausgestaltet ist, und bezogen auf Deutschland unabhängig davon, ob
er bzw. sie beamtet ist. Die Pflicht der Beschäftigten des Staates, bei den Handlungen

---

[4] Instruktiv *Voßkuhle*, in: Hoffmann-Riem/Schmidt-Aßmann/ders., Grundlagen (Fn. 2),
Bd. III, 2009, § 43, Rn. 2.

[5] *Manfred Wichmann/Karl-Ulrich Langer,* Öffentliches Dienstrecht, 6. Aufl. 2007, Rn. 50.

[6] Zutreffend *Landau/Steinkühler* (Fn. 3), DVBl 2007, 133, 136 f.; *Ernst Forsthoff,* Verfas-
sungsrechtliche Grenzen einer Reform des öffentlichen Dienstrechts, Rechtsgutachten, in:
Studienkommission für die Reform des öffentlichen Dienstrechts, Bd. 5, 1973, 17, 47; *Herbert
Lecheler,* Das Berufsbeamtentum, in: Badura/Dreier (Hg.), FS 50 Jahre BVerfG, Bd. 2, 2001,
S. 360, 361.

[7] S. für Deutschland *Bonk*, in: Sachs, Michael (Hg.), GG, 5. Aufl. 2009, Art. 34, Rn. 63.

als Teil des Staates die Rechtsnormen zu beachten, die für das staatliche Handeln gelten, ist eine persönliche Rechtspflicht jedes Beschäftigten, unabhängig davon, in welchem Rechtsverhältnis er zum Staat steht. Unterhalb dieser allgemeinen Transformationsnorm gibt es wiederum Unterschiede.

III. Funktionale Aufgabe des öffentlichen Dienstrechts

Ob das öffentliche Dienstrecht diese unterstützende Funktion besser oder schlechter erfüllt, lässt sich nur bewerten und beurteilen, wenn man um die Besonderheiten staatlicher Aufgabenerledigung weiß. Eine Ausgestaltung des öffentlichen Dienstrechts ist dann geeignet, wenn sie die Besonderheiten der staatlichen Aufgabenerfüllung im Vergleich zu einer privaten Aufgabenerfüllung besonders gut unterstützt.

Die Besonderheiten staatlicher Handlungen können zum einen in deren Zielen liegen (die Erfüllung staatlicher Aufgaben[8]), die teilweise so nicht in der Privatwirtschaft verfolgt werden. Zum anderen liegen sie im Schwerpunkt wohl vor allem in der Art und Weise staatlichen Handelns. Der Staat kann mit Hoheitsgewalt handeln,[9] d. h. der Befugnis, den Einzelnen gegen seinen Willen rechtlich zu verpflichten und diese Pflicht notfalls auch zwangsweise durchzusetzen. Daraus folgt:

– Die Leitlinien der Handlung sind in hohem Maße Rechtsvorschriften.

– Das staatliche Handeln kann zur rechtlichen Bindung gegen den Willen Betroffener führen

– und mit erheblicher Gewaltanwendung verbunden sein,

– sowie immense Bedeutung und Auswirkungen für den Betroffenen besitzen.

– Weiter ist der Staat ist zu einem gleichheitsgerechten Handeln verpflichtet

– und muss das Gemeinwohl immer im Blick behalten.

Daran knüpfen sich bestimmte Folgerungen. Diese Besonderheiten verlangen einerseits nach demokratisch legitimierten und andererseits einer rechtlich gebundene Ausübung.[10] Das öffentliche Dienstrecht muss daher möglichst sicherstellen,

1. dass die demokratische Legitimation staatlichen Handelns tatsächlich wirksam ist;

2. dass die rechtlichen Vorgaben durch die Bediensteten beachtet werden;

3. dass ohne Ansehung der konkreten Person durch die Amtswalter gehandelt wird;

---

[8] S. zu den staatlichen Aufgaben *Erbguth*, in: Sachs, Michael (Hg.), GG, 5. Aufl. 2009, Art. 34, Rn. 31.

[9] *Heinrich Amadeus Wolff*, Ungeschriebenes Verfassungsrecht unter dem GG, 2000, S. 329 f.

[10] *Forsthoff*, in: Studienkommission (Fn. 6), 1973, 17, 24; *Udo Di Fabio*, Das Beamtenrechtliche Streikverbot, 2012, S. 50.

4. dass die Aufgabenerledigung immer gewährleistet wird (Gleichheit in der Zeit);

5. dass maßvoll gehandelt wird;

6. dass sachfremde Einflüsse möglichst ausgesperrt werden;

7. dass der Staat möglichst einheitlich auftritt;

8. dass zulässige Konkretisierungen von oben beachtet werden;

9. dass der Apparat nicht mehr kostet als unbedingt sein muss.

Zieht man diese Faktoren heran, lassen sich bestimmte Kriterien entwickeln, die ein öffentliches Dienstrecht erfüllen muss, damit es eine unterstützende Funktion ausüben kann. So sollte das Dienstrecht folgende persönliche Rechte und Pflichten sicherstellen:

zu 1. die Beachtung von Gesetzen und Regierungsbeschlüssen

zu 2. Rechtskunde und Rechtsbindung

zu 3. gleichheitsgerechte Amtsausführung

zu 4. Verantwortung für die Aufgabenerledigung

zu 5. gemäßigtes Auftreten und fehlendes Eigeninteresse

zu 6. Neutralität und Unabhängigkeit des Bediensteten und fehlendes Eigeninteresse an der Entscheidung

zu 7. Weisungsstränge und gebundenes Handeln

zu 8 Weisungsgebundenheit

zu 9. Wirtschaftlichkeit.

Wenn diese Vorgaben beachtet werden, ist es gleich, ob und falls, das öffentliche Dienstrecht vom allgemeinen Arbeitsrecht abweicht.

IV. Die Lösung der Aufgaben des öffentlichen Dienstrechts durch das deutsche öffentliche Dienstrecht

1. Prinzipien des deutschen öffentlichen Dienstrechts

Das deutsche Dienstrecht ist durch folgende Prinzipien beherrscht.

a) Zweiteilung des öffentlichen Dienstes

Die Bediensteten des Staates in Deutschland unterfallen in solche, die in einem besonderen öffentlich-rechtlichen Treueverhältnis stehen, hauptsächlich in dem sog. Beamtenverhältnis, und Beschäftigte, die in einem Angestelltenverhältnis stehen, dessen inhaltliche Ausgestaltung durch einen speziellen, für sie abgeschlossenen Tarifvertrag konkretisiert wird.[11] Das Grundgesetz geht davon aus, dass die Amtswalter, denen die Ausübung hoheitlicher Aufgaben dauerhaft anvertraut ist, grundsätzlich im Beamtenrechtsverhältnis stehen, die anderen im Angestelltenverhältnis.[12] Die Abgrenzung und die Folgen dieser Unterscheidung sind nicht immer streng und nicht immer klar voneinander zu trennen. Die Zweiteilung selbst existiert aber und fördert die unterstützende Funktion des Beamtenrechts, da es auf das Handeln des Staates beschränkt wird, indem in besonderem Maße Hoheitsgewalt eingesetzt wird.

b) Berufsbeamtentum

Das Beamtenrecht ist ausgerichtet am Idealbild der Beamtin bzw. des Beamten, der fachlich qualifiziert, seine Arbeitskraft vollständig dem Dienstherrn zum Zwecke der gemeinwohlorientierten Aufgabenerfüllung zur Verfügung stellt und dafür von diesem zusammen mit seiner Familie lebenslang alimentiert wird. Einstellung und Veränderungen, sowie die Grundlage der Bezahlung beruhen dabei nicht auf Vertrag sondern auf Gesetz. Die Auswahl und das Fortkommen der Beamtinnen und Beamten beruht grundsätzlich auf dem Leistungsprinzip und einer Bestenauslese. Das Rechtsverhältnis ist an den Prinzipien der Vollzeit und der Lebenslänglichkeit ausgerichtet. Nebentätigkeiten sind beschränkbar und rechtfertigungsbedürftig. Vorzeitiges Ausscheiden darf zu Verlusten in der Altersversorgung führen. Pflichtverstöße, wie etwa Trunkenheitsfahrten, auch privater Natur, unterliegen besonderen disziplinarrechtlichen Folgen. Geschuldet wird allgemeine Treue, die mit besonderer Fürsorge vergolten wird.[13]

2. Die Eignung des Berufsbeamtentums zur Absicherung der Besonderheiten des öffentlichen Dienstes

Die Abweichungen des deutschen Beamtenrechts vom Angestelltenrecht beruhen im Wesentlichen aber darauf, dass die besondere demokratische und rechtsstaatliche Bindung bei der Ausübung von Hoheitsgewalt gut unterstützt wird.[14] Bezieht man sich auf die oben genannten Kriterien, so sollen sie im deutschen Beamtenrecht wie folgt erfüllt werden:

---

[11] *Ingo von Münch*, Verfassungsrechtliche Grenzen einer Reform des öffentlichen Dienstrechts, Rechtsgutachten, in: Studienkommission (Fn. 6), 1973, 71, 132 ff.

[12] *Battis*, in: Sachs, Michael (Hg.), GG, 5. Aufl. 2009, Art. 33, Rn. 45 ff.

[13] *Klaus Stern*, Staatsrecht der Bundesrepublik Deutschland, 2. Auflage 1984, § 11, IV, S. 363, 370; *Lecheler* (Fn. 1), in: Isensee/Kirchhof, HStR V, 2007, § 110, Rn. 39 ff.; *Werner Thieme*, Verfassungsrechtliche Grenzen einer Reform des öffentlichen Dienstrechts, Rechtsgutachten, in: Studienkommission (Fn. 6), 1973, 303, 132 ff.

[14] S. dazu *Voßkuhle*, in: Hoffmann-Riem/Schmidt-Aßmann/ders., Grundlagen (Fn. 2), Bd. III, 2009, § 43, Rn. 20 f.

zu 1. Verfassungstreue und Treuepflicht[15]

zu 2. und 3. Gesetzesbindung als Dienstpflicht[16]

zu 4. Streikverbot,[17] gebundens Handeln, Überstundenpflicht[18] und Überlastungs-anzeige,[19] Vollzeitprinzip[20] und Unabhängigkeit[21]

zu 5. Mäßigungsgebot[22] und Disziplinarrecht[23]

zu 6. Lebenszeitprinzip,[24] Gesetzesbindung, Befangenheitsregelung,[25] Nebentä-tigkeitsverbot[26] und Alimentationsprinzip[27]

zu 7. Treuepflicht und Gesetzmäßigkeitsgebot

zu 8. Treuepflicht

zu 9. keine individuell ausgeprägte Pflicht.

3. Der Kern der gleichmäßigen und sachlichen Aufgabenerledigung

Das Gewaltmonopol und die Subordination der Hoheitsgewalt verlangen vor allem nach einer gleichmäßigen und sachlichen Handhabung der Hoheitsgewalt.[28] Die Erhebung der Steuer, die Verhängung von Freiheitsstrafen und die Vergabe von staatlichen Genehmigungen müssen in allen vergleichbaren Konstellationen identisch sein, insbesondere unabhängig sein von persönlichen Bindungen, persön-

---

[15] S. dazu BVerwGE 12, 273; *Ulrich Battis*, BBG, 4. Aufl. 2009, § 4, Rn. 4; *Lecheler* (Fn. 1), in: Isensee/ Kirchhof, HStR V, 2007, § 110, Rn. 67 ff.

[16] § 62 BBG; s. dazu *Battis* (Fn.15), BBG, 2009, § 62 BBG, Rn. 62, Rn. 3; *Günther*, Fol-gepflicht, Remonstration und Verantwortlichkeit der Beamten, ZBR 1988, 297 ff.; *Lecheler*, in: Badura/Dreier (Hg.), BVerfG (Fn. 6), 2001, S. 360, 369.

[17] S. dazu ausführlich OVG Münster, Urt. v. 7.3. 2012, 3 d A 317/11.O, juris = NVwZ 2012, 890; *Fabio*, Streikverbot (Fn. 10), 2012, S. 55 ff.

[18] *Battis* (Fn.15), BBG, 2009, § 62 BBG, Rn .87, Rn. 3.

[19] VG Oldenburg (Oldenburg), Urt. v. 29.03.2000, 6 A 2138/99, juris, Rn. 16.

[20] *Lucia Budjarek*, Das Recht des öffentlichen Dienstes und Fortentwicklungsklausel, 2009, 94 ff.

[21] *Landau/Steinkühler* (Fn. 3), DVBl 2007, 133, 137.

[22] § 60 BBG; *Battis* (Fn.15), BBG, 2009, § 60 BBG, Rn. 62, Rn. 17; *Lecheler* (Fn. 1), in: Isensee/Kirchhof, HStR V, 2007, § 110, Rn. 78.

[23] *Lecheler* (Fn. 1), in: Isensee/Kirchhof, HStR V, 2007, § 110, Rn. 65.

[24] *Forsthoff*, in: Studienkommission (Fn. 6) 17, 67 ff.; *Budjarek* (Fn. 20), Recht, 2009, 90 ff.

[25] § 65 BBG; *Battis* (Fn. 15), BBG, 2009, § 62 BBG, Rn. 65, Rn. 2; vgl. allgemein *Bonk/ Schmitz,* in: Paul Stelkens/Heinz Joachim Bonk/Michael Sachs, VwVfG, 7. Aufl. 2008, § 20, Rn. 1.

[26] §§ 97 ff. BBG; *Baßlsperger*, Nebentätigkeiten von Beamten, ZBR 2004, 369 ff.

[27] *Budjarek* (Fn. 20), Recht, 2009, 96 ff.

[28] *Landau/Steinkühler* (Fn. 3), DVBl 2007, 133, 137 f.

lichen Zuwendungen oder persönlichen Prioritäten.[29] Das Beamtenrecht begegnet dieser Herausforderung, indem es die Betroffenen grundsätzlich lebenslang anstellt, amtsbezogen alimentiert und eine Pflichtverletzung besonders im Wege des Disziplinarrechts sanktioniert. Das Beamtenverhältnis ist auf den Gemeinzweck, Sicherung der Amtswaltung, ausgerichtet.[30] Auf diese Weise gelingt es dem Beamtenrecht, eine verhältnismäßig hohe Sachlichkeit und Neutralität des staatlichen Handelns zu ermöglichen.[31]

4. Der Preis: Charakter des geschlossenen Personalkörpers

Das deutsche Beamtenrecht erreicht dieses Ziel, indem es in dreifacher Hinsicht einen hohen Preis zahlt.

Erstens: Es ist strukturell von einem gewissen Ganz-oder-gar-nicht-Prinzip geprägt. Beamter sein heißt, eine Lebensaufgabe zu bewältigen. Es wird über das Personalrechtsstatut ein einheitlicher Personalkörper gebildet, der zu einem soziologisch abgeschlossenen Gebilde führt.[32] Insofern hat das Beamtenrecht die aus der Monarchie des 19. Jahrhunderts kommende Vorstellung, der Beamtenkörper werde sachlich den Monarchen zugerechnet und sei ein Teil von diesen, überdauert. Die Funktion der Exekutive als selbstständige Gewalt wird – grob vereinfacht – in einen selbstständigen Personalkörper verlängert.[33]

Diese Abgeschlossenheit führt zu einer gewissen Professionalisierung der besonderen Fähigkeiten, aber auch der negativen Folgen, die mit der Hoheitsausübung verbunden sind.

Weiter führt dies zu einer erheblichen Unabhängigkeit der Sachentscheidung von äußeren Einflüssen. Die deutsche Beamtenschaft ist relativ autonom und auch gegenüber gezielter Agitation Dritter verhältnismäßig immun. Sie kann aber auch immun gegenüber berechtigten Anliegen sein.

Darüber hinaus bildet der Personalkörper auf diese Weise ein Gegengewicht zu der politisch und zugleich zeitlich begrenzt legitimierten und auf Änderung hinwirkenden Führungsebene.[34] Das Spannungsverhältnis zwischen der zu Wertungen berechtigten, mit Weisungsrecht ausgestatteten, politischen Führungsebene einerseits und der weisungsabhängigen, lebenszeitberufenen und persönlich abgesicherten Beamtenschaft andererseits prägt den deutschen öffentlichen Personalkörper in allen

---

[29] *Lecheler* (Fn. 1), in: Isensee/Kirchhof, HStR V, 2007, § 110, Rn. 59.

[30] *Lecheler* (Fn. 1), in: Isensee/Kirchhof, HStR V, 2007, § 110, Rn. 59.

[31] *Klaus Stern*, Staatsrecht der Bundesrepublik Deutschland, 2. Auflage 1984, § 11, IV, S. 363 f.

[32] *Lecheler* (Fn. 1), in: Isensee/Kirchhof, HStR V, 2007, § 110, Rn. 60, 65.

[33] *Forsthoff*, in: Studienkommission (Fn. 6), 17, 48.

[34] S. dazu *Voßkuhle*, in: Hoffmann-Riem/Schmidt-Aßmann/ders., Grundlagen (Fn. 2), Bd. III, 2009, § 43, Rn. 64; *Lecheler*, in: Badura/Dreier (Hg.), BVerfG (Fn. 6), 2001, S. 360, 365.

Bereichen. Das Spannungsverhältnis ist aber in seiner Intensität sehr unterschiedlich, je nach Organisationseinheit. Auf der Ministerialebene und auf der Kommunalebene ist dieser Konflikt stärker ausgeprägt als im mittleren Verwaltungsorganisationsbereich.

Das Aufeinanderprallen der dynamischen, demokratisch legitimierten und gestaltungswilligen Führungsebene und des eher schwerfälligen Personalkörpers ermöglicht eine Symbiose von Flexibilität und Stabilität („Gegenstromprinzip"[35]). Der Beamtenkörper bewirkt, dass flüchtige politische Ideen, vom Charakter einer Eintagsfliege, gar nicht erst zur Umsetzung gelangen und gar zu revolutionäre Neuerungen vor ihrer praktischen Umsetzung abgemildert werden, währenddessen die politische Führungsebene jeweils neue Schwünge hineinbringt und das Verharren in alten, lieb gewonnenen Verhaltensmustern unmöglich macht. Demgegenüber verleiht die Seriosität des Beamtenkörpers tragbaren, neuen politischen Ideen eine erheblich größere Durchschlagskraft im Vergleich zu einer Umsetzung durch die politische Führungsebene selbst.

5. Abkopplung vom Verwaltungserfolg

Die zweite Kehrseite liegt in einer relativ starken Abkopplung des Eigeninteresses des Amtsinhabers von dem Erfolg seines Handelns, die durch die abgeschlossene und abgesicherte Rechtsstellung des einzelnen Amtsdieners herbeigeführt wird. Die sachlich richtige und unangreifbare Verwaltungsentscheidung besitzt einen höheren Stellenwert als die Anzahl der Entscheidungen und das Ausmaß der Bedeutung der Verwaltungsentscheidung für die Allgemeinheit. Eine Kosten-Nutzen-Analyse der Handlung des einzelnen Amtswalters wird nicht in das Dienstrecht hineingetragen. Eine fehlerfreie Amtsführung wird vom Dienstrecht verlangt und nahegelegt, während eine Honorierung eines problemorientierten, managementorientierten, interessengerichteten, einzelfallbezogenen Handelns auch mit innovativem Charakter keine positiven Folgen für den Betroffenen nach sich zieht. Die Wirtschaftlichkeit des Handelns steht weniger im Fokus des Beamtenrechts als die Gesetzmäßigkeit des Handelns.[36]

6. Kosten des Personalkörpers

Drittens: Der fachlich gut ausgebildete Personalkörper, dessen Ergebnisse nach rechtlichen Kriterien hohen Standards genügen, kostet. Er kostet meist Zeit und Nerven derjenigen, die mit der Verwaltung in Berührung kommen. Er kostet vor allem staatliches Geld.[37] Das Berufsbeamtenrecht ist die personenrechtliche Umsetzung des Prinzips der Nachhaltigkeit. Wie immer bei der Pflege des Prinzips der Nachhal-

---

[35] *Franz Mayer,* Verfassungsrechtliche Grenzen einer Reform des öffentlichen Dienstrechts, Rechtsgutachten, in: Studienkommission (Fn. 6), 1973, 557, 583.

[36] *Voßkuhle,* in: Hoffmann-Riem/Schmidt-Aßmann/ders., Grundlagen (Fn. 2), Bd. III, 2009, § 43, Rn. 60; *Landau/Steinkühler* (Fn. 3), DVBl 2007, 133, 143.

[37] *Voßkuhle,* in: Hoffmann-Riem/Schmidt-Aßmann/ders., Grundlagen (Fn. 2), Bd. III, 2009, § 43, Rn. 56 ff.

tigkeit hofft man, mit relativ hohen Kosten heute, Aufgabenminderungen von morgen zu erzielen. Ob diese Überlegung im Bereich des deutschen Beamtenrechts zutrifft, ist umstritten und ungewiss.

V. Strukturelle Folgerungen

1. Nachteile des Beamtenrechts

Die Funktion des Beamtenrechts, die sachgerechte staatliche Aufgabenerledigung zu erfüllen, führt zu Folgerungen, die auch als nachteilig bewertet werden. Üblicherweise werden als Nachteile des Beamtenrechtsverhältnisses genannt:[38]

– Die Besoldung sei zu wenig leistungsorientiert.

– Besoldungs- und Versorgungslasten seien zu hoch.

– Der Austausch zwischen dem öffentlichen Sektor und der Wirtschaft sei zu schwerfällig.

– Das Beamtenrechtsverhältnis sei zu statusorientiert.

– Das Lebenszeitprinzip, die Vollzeitbeschäftigung, das Alimentationsprinzip verhindern eine direkte Rückkopplung zwischen Aufwand und Ertrag eines konkreten Verwaltungshandelns.

– Es bestünden zu viele interne Mobilitätsbarrieren.

– Der Ausbildung käme eine zu große Bedeutung zu.

– Durch die Veränderung der Gesetzgebungskompetenz in der Föderalismusreform werde der Wechsel zwischen den Verwaltungsträgern erschwert.

– Das Beförderungs- und Bewertungssystem fördere nicht ein zeitgemäßes problem- und interessengerichtetes Aufgabenmanagement.

– Das Berufsbeamtentum werde auf zu viele öffentliche Funktionen erstreckt.

– Die Teilzeitbeschäftigung werde zu sehr erschwert.

– Die zeitweise Überweisung von Führungspositionen werde erschwert.

– Ein Leistungsabfall führe nicht zu angemessenen Konsequenzen.

Diese Nachteile müssen nicht eintreten, können teilweise durch Gegenmaßnahmen abgemildert werden und sind zudem in ihrer Bewertung umstritten, sie sind aber strukturell im Beamtenrecht angelegt.

---

[38] S. dazu *Voßkuhle*, in: Hoffmann-Riem/Schmidt-Aßmann/ders., Grundlagen (Fn. 2), Bd. III, 2009, § 43, Rn. 20 f.; 35 ff., 60, 94 ff.

2. Gefährdungen

Die Eigentümlichkeiten des Beamtenrechts sind in seinem Gelingen wie bei jedem rechtlichen Institut von Bedingungen abhängig, die es nicht selbst garantieren kann. Der Wegfall dieser Bedingungen stellt zugleich Gefährdungen des Beamtenrechtsverhältnisses dar. Zu diesen Gefährdungen gehören folgende Probleme.

a) Die Umgehung der Garantie des Art. 33 Abs. 2 GG

Gemäß Art. 33 Abs. 2 GG hat jedermann Zugang zum öffentlichen Dienst gemäß seiner Eignung, Leistung und Befähigung. Art. 33 Abs. 2 GG soll das fachliche Niveau und die rechtliche Integrität des öffentlichen Dienstes sichern und den Einzelnen vor Willkür schützen. Art. 33 Abs. 2 GG soll dabei nicht nur dem einzelnen Bewerber eine Chance auf Einstellung geben, sondern das Beamtenrecht von innen heraus stärken. Dieses Prinzip gerät erheblich unter Druck durch die Erscheinung der Ämterpatronage.[39]

Unter Ämterpatronage versteht man die Begünstigung bestimmter Bewerber bei der Regulierungsbeförderung von Personal der öffentlichen Hand.[40] Es lassen sich verschiedene Formen der unsachlichen Ämtervergabe unterscheiden, wie etwa die Besetzung von Schlüsselpositionen mit eigenen Vertrauensleuten, die Besetzung von Ämtern zur wirtschaftlichen Absicherung der Begünstigten und die Aufteilung von Sitzen bei Kollegialorganen entsprechend den parteipolitischen Proporzverhältnissen.[41]

Die Ämterpatronage ist nicht primär ein Problem der rechtlichen Normierung der Besetzung der Stellen, sondern eine Frage der Verwaltungspraxis. Eine strikte Anwendung des Leistungsprinzips mitsamt der Verfahrensvorschriften bzw. eine Verschärfung der relevanten Normen, wie etwa Stellenausschreibung, Beurteilungswesen, Einschaltung unabhängiger Dritter, Dokumentationspflichten, kann hier helfen.

b) Amtsethos

Zu einer der Voraussetzungen des Berufsbeamtentums gehört das so genannte Amtsethos.[42] Das Ethos ist gekennzeichnet, durch ein die Gesamtpersönlichkeit prägendes Maß an Verantwortungsbewusstsein sowie durch ein aktives Eintreten für den Rechtsstaat, die Zurücknahme privater Bedürfnisse sowie einem würdevollen Auftreten. Das Amtsethos bildet eine Voraussetzung des Berufsbeamtentums, ohne

---

[39] *Lecheler* (Fn. 1), in: Isensee/Kirchhof, HStR V, 2007, § 110, Rn. 80 ff.; *Lecheler*, in: Badura/Dreier (Hg.), BVerfG (Fn. 6), 2001, S. 360, 372.

[40] *Lecheler* (Fn. 1), in: Isensee/Kirchhof, HStR V, 2007, § 110, Rn. 10.

[41] *Voßkuhle*, in: Hoffmann-Riem/Schmidt-Aßmann/ders., Grundlagen (Fn. 2), Bd. III, 2009, § 43, Rn. 65.

[42] Ausführlich *Landau/Steinkühler* (Fn. 3), DVBl 2007, 133, 138.

selbst ein verfassungsrechtliches Gebot zu sein. Die Prinzipien der Lebenslänglichkeit, der Treuepflicht, der Alimentation und das Verbot der Nebentätigkeit sollen die Entstehung des Amtsethos erleichtern, können es aber nicht garantieren.

Die Existenz des Amtsethos ist schwer nachweisbar, jedoch lassen sich in der Wirklichkeit gewisse Anzeichen der tatsächlichen Existenz bemerken. Geringere Krankenstände der Beamten im Vergleich zu den Angestellten, das gemäßigte Auftreten nach außen und unterdurchschnittliche Zugehörigkeit zu extremen politischen Positionen wären hier zu nennen.

VI. Resümee

Die besonderen Anforderungen, die an die staatliche Aufgabenerledigung, insbesondere durch die Mittel der Aufgabenerledigung (Gewaltmonopol und Subordination) gestellt werden, können durch ein eigenes öffentliches Dienstrecht unterstützt werden. Das deutsche Beamtenrecht fördert in hohem Maße die Gesetzesgebundenheit, Gleichmaßigkeit, Objektivität und Unabhängigkeit des Handelns, erkauft dies aber mit einer relativ hohen Abkopplung des Personalkörpers, hohen Personalkosten und weitgehender Ausblendung der Wirtschaftlichkeit als Handlungsmaßstab.

Auf dem Weg zu einer semi-autonomen Steuerverwaltung?

Bestandsaufnahme und Perspektiven aus verfassungsrechtlicher Sicht

Von *Stylianos-Ioannis G. Koutnatzis**

I. Einführung

Im Zuge der Finanzkrise und der sukzessiven Rettungspakete ist die griechische politische und rechtliche Wirklichkeit der letzten Jahre häufig von Steuerangelegenheiten überschattet. Dabei konzentriert sich die diesbezügliche Diskussion einerseits aus politischer Sicht auf das Ausmaß und die Mischung der Steuerbelastungen, andererseits aus rechtlicher Sicht auf Fragen der Verfassungsmäßigkeit etwa mit Blick auf außergewöhnliche Steuermaßnahmen oder Immobiliensteuern.[1] Häufig im Hintergrund bleiben dabei Reformbemühungen, die weitgehend auch von den internationalen Geldgebern vorgegeben sind, das Potential allerdings aufweisen, fest etablierte Grundlagen und Strukturen von Staat, Wirtschaft und Verwaltung in Frage zu stellen und damit langjährige Defizite zu überwinden. Im Fokus dieser Reformbemühungen steht nicht selten die Steuerverwaltung. Grundpfeiler der Reform ist die Differenzierung zwischen *Steuerpolitik*, für die gemäß der griechischen Verfassung die Regierung die alleinige Verantwortung behält und *Steuerverwaltung*, die ohne politische Einflüsse möglichst nach technokratischen Maßstäben vollzogen werden muss. Während die Steuerverwaltung nach wie vor in der öffentlichen Verwaltung eingegliedert ist, stellt sich dabei eine Reihe von besonderen öffentlich-rechtlichen Fragestellungen.

---

* Als Rechtsberater des Vizeministers für Finanzen der Hellenischen Republik Herrn Dr. Georgios Mavraganis (2012–2015) hat der Verfasser an der Ausarbeitung des gesetzlichen Rahmens der semi-autonomen Steuerverwaltung in Griechenland mitgewirkt. Der Beitrag gibt ausschließlich seine persönliche Auffassung wieder.

[1] Dazu etwa *X. Contiades/I. Tassopoulos*, The Impact of the Financial Crisis on the Greek Constitution, in: X. Contiades (Hrsg.), Constitutions in the Global Economic Crisis. A Comparative Analysis, Ashgate 2013, S. 195–218 (208); *K. Chryssogonos/S.-I. Koutnatzis*, Demokratie und Verfassung in der Zeit der Krise: Überblick zu Ursachen und Implikationen aus der Sicht Griechenlands, in: D. Kübler/N. Stojanovic (Hrsg.), Demokratie in der Europäischen Union/Democracy in the European Union, Schulthess 2014, S. 31–51 (35–36) m.w.N. auf die Rechtsprechung.

Vor diesem Hintergrund werden im Folgenden nach einem rechtsvergleichenden Überblick (II.) zunächst die gesetzlichen Schritte der letzten Jahre zur Selbstständigkeit der Steuerverwaltung vorgestellt (III.), um sodann die verfassungsrechtlichen Grenzen dieser Selbstständigkeit zu identifizieren und ihr Verhältnis zu den verfassungsrechtlich vorgesehenen „unabhängigen Behörden" zu skizzieren (IV.).

II. Rechtsvergleichender Überblick

Vor dem deutschen Publikum muss anfangs darauf hingewiesen werden, dass die Steuerverwaltung in der Bundesrepublik, die vor allem auf der Länderebene mithilfe der Finanzämter als eigene Angelegenheit oder im Auftrag des Bundes angesiedelt ist,[2] international nunmehr als eine Ausnahme qualifiziert werden kann. Insgesamt gliedert sich nämlich die Organisation der Steuerverwaltung auf der Grundlage von vier verschiedenen Modellen: Zum einen als eine vereinheitlichte organische Einheit der Finanzministeriums; zum zweiten in der Form von mehreren organischen Einheiten des Finanzministeriums; zum dritten als semi-autonome Einheit, dessen Vorgesetzter dem zuständigen Minister unterstellt ist und schließlich als semi-autonome Einheit, dessen Vorgesetzter sowohl dem zuständigen Minister als auch einem dritten Kontrollgremium, an dem auswärtige Mitglieder teilnehmen, unterstellt ist.[3] Dabei bewegt sich die internationale Tendenz in den letzten Jahren zunehmend dahingehend, ein besonderes vereinheitlichtes Organ für die Steuerverwaltung einzurichten, das außer der formellen hierarchischen Struktur des Finanzministeriums liegt und einen besonderen Grad der Selbstständigkeit genießt. Dabei handelt es sich um das Modell der semi-autonomen Einheit, das darauf abzielt, die Effektivität der Steuerverwaltung zu stärken.[4] Unter diesen Gegebenheiten ist die Steuerverwaltung vermutlich besser in der Lage, ihre Angelegenheiten frei von politischen Einflüssen und von den immanenten Einschränkungen des öffentlichen Sektors nach privatwirtschaftlichen Maßstäben zu regeln, um ihr Personal einzustellen, zu behalten (oder zu entlassen), ebenso angemessene Anreize zu setzen, damit ihre Effektivität gesteigert werden kann. Diese Tendenz konkretisiert auf der Ebene der Steuerverwaltung die allgemeine internationale Tendenz, Bereiche der öffentlichen Verwaltung auf der Grundlage von Institutionen zu organisieren, die über Garantien technischer

---

[2] Vgl. Bundesministerium der Finanzen, Die Steuerverwaltung in Deutschland, verfügbar unter www.bundesfinanzministerium.de/Content/DE/Downloads/Broschueren_Bestellservice/ 2014-09-10-die-steuerverwaltung-in-deutschland.pdf?__blob=publicationFile&v=3 (zuletzt abgerufen am 15. November 2015).

[3] Zahlreiche Beispiele und Vertiefung bei OECD, Tax Administration 2013, Comparative Information on OECD and Other Advanced and Emerging Economies, verfügbar unter www. keepeek.com/Digital-Asset-Management/oecd/taxation/tax-administration-2013_ 9789264200814-en, S. 19–56 (zuletzt abgerufen am 15. November 2015).

[4] Vgl. W. Crandall, Revenue Administration: Autonomy in Tax Administration and the Revenue Authority Model, International Monetary Fund 2010, S. 6.

Spezialisierung und politischer Unabhängigkeit verfügen.[5] Dabei geht es um ein beträchtliches Misstrauen gegenüber aller politischen Gewalt, die in Griechenland die verfassungsrechtliche Verankerung der sog. unabhängigen Behörden mit der Verfassungsrevision von 2001 veranlasst hat.[6]

Ob und inwieweit dieses Modell zur Stärkung der Effektivität der Steuerverwaltung führt, steht noch offen. Mehr als die Hälfte der Mitgliedstaaten der Organisation für wirtschaftliche Zusammenarbeit und Entwicklung (Organisation for Economic Co-operation and Development – OECD) haben sich allerdings bis dato für das Modell der semi-autonomen Einheit entschieden, während elf von diesen Staaten auch den weiteren Schritt vorgenommen haben, ein Verwaltungs- oder Beratergremium der Steuerverwaltung, das aus auswärtigen Mitgliedern zusammengesetzt ist, einzurichten.[7] Zu den Befugnissen der semi-autonomen Steuerverwaltung in der internationalen Praxis zählen etwa die *Verwaltung der Ausgaben*, die *Bestimmung der internen Organisationsstruktur, ihrer strategischen und operativen Ziele* ebenso wie *Beurteilungsmaßstäbe, die Personalentwicklung und -verwaltung* (durch die Bestimmung von Einstellungskriterien, der Entscheidungen mit Blick auf Einstellungen und Entlassungen, Bildungsprogramme und der Vergütung der Personals), die *Verwaltung der Informationssysteme*, die *Auslegung der steuerrechtlichen Vorschriften* ebenso wie die *Durchsetzungsbefugnisse* und die *Verhängung von Verwaltungssanktionen im Fall von Nichteinhaltung der Steuergesetzgebung.*[8]

III. Gesetzliche Schritte zur Selbstständigkeit der Steuerverwaltung

In Griechenland wurde ein erster großer Schritt zur Selbstständigkeit der Steuerverwaltung mit dem Gesetz 4093/2012 vollzogen.[9] Damit wurde das ehemalige Generalsekretariat für Steuer- und Zollangelegenheiten durch das Generalsekretariat für

---

[5] Eingehend und vertiefend statt vieler *St. Bredt*, Die demokratische Legitimation unabhängiger Institutionen, Mohr Siebeck 2006, S. 23 ff. sowie auch *Th. Antoniou*, The Role of Independent Admiministrative Authorities, in: H. Schäfer/J. Iliopoulos-Strangas (Hrsg.), Staatsmodernisierung in Europa, Ant. Sakkoulas/Berliner Wissenschaftsverlag/Bruylant 2007, S. 237–289.

[6] Dazu etwa *X. Contiades*, The Relationship between Political Parties and Independent Authorities: Tension and Supplementarity. Theoretical Remarks on the Basis of the Greek Example, in: D. Tsatsos/Ev. Venizelos/X. Contiades (Hrsg.), Political Parties in the 21st Century/Politische Parteien im 21. Jahrhundert, Ant. Sakkoulas/Berliner Wissenschaftsverlag/ Bruylant 2004, S. 115–137 (121–127); *N. Koulouris*, The Independent Administrative Authorities, in: E. Spiliotopoulos/A. Makrydemetres (Hrsg.), Public Administration in Greece, Ant. Sakkoulas Verlag, 2001, S. 95–117 (104); *G. Lazarakos (Γ. Λαζαράκος)*, Ανεξάρτητες αρχές (Unabhängige Behörden), Nomiki Vivliothiki 2010, S. 10 f.

[7] OECD, Tax Administration 2013, oben Fn. 3, S. 20.

[8] OECD, Tax Administration 2013, oben Fn. 3, S. 28: „Typical powers of autonomous revenue bodies".

[9] Vgl. Gesetz 4093/2012, Einziger Artikel, Unterabsatz E.2.

öffentliche Einnahmen nicht nur umbenannt, sondern wesentlich umgebaut.[10] So wurde in der Begründung des Gesetzes 4093/2012 dargestellt, dass die Kontinuität und Effektivität der öffentlichen Verwaltung im grundlegenden Gebiet der öffentlichen Einnahmen und ihre Befreiung von jedweden politischen Einflüssen mit gleichzeitiger Sicherstellung von Rechenschafts- und Transparenzmechanismen von grundlegender Bedeutung sind, um die (verfassungsrechtlichen) Grundsätze der Steuergerechtigkeit und Steuergleichheit durchzusetzen.[11] Die einzelnen Bestimmungen des Gesetzes 4093/2012 mit Blick auf die Zuständigkeiten, die Auswahlmodalitäten, die Amtsdauer und die Voraussetzungen vorzeitiger Beendigung der Amtszeit des Generalsekretärs für öffentliche Einnahmen unterscheiden sich von den allgemeinen Regelungen für Generalsekretäre und Vorgesetzte von Generalsekretariaten, um das notwendige Maß an Selbstständigkeit während der Ausübung seiner Aufgaben sicherzustellen.[12] Dem Generalsekretariat für öffentliche Einnahmen unterliegen seit 2013 überdies die Aufgaben, Personal und Ressourcen des Amts für interne Angelegenheiten des Finanzministeriums ebenso wie des Generalsekretariats für Informationssysteme, soweit sie mit der Ausübung der Steuer- und Zollverwaltung zusammenhängen und die steuer- und zollrelevanten Befugnisse des Amtes für die Bekämpfung der Wirtschaftskriminalität (SDOE).[13] Alle Aufgaben der Steuer- und Zollverwaltung konzentrieren sich auf diese Weise im Generalsekretariat für öffentliche Einnahmen.

Im Folgenden wird zunächst auf die Befugnisse des Generalsekretärs für öffentliche Einnahmen (1.), im Anschluss daran auf die Ernennungsmodalitäten (2.) und die bestehenden Kontrollmechanismen (3.) eingegangen werden. Ohne Anspruch auf Vollständigkeit werden dabei vor allem einzelne verfassungsrechtliche Gesichtspunkte thematisiert.

1. Befugnisse

Die Befugnisse des Generalsekretärs für öffentliche Einnahmen können in zwei Kategorien ausgegliedert werden. Zum einen geht es um direkt von Gesetzes wegen zugeordnete Befugnisse, zum anderen um Befugnisse, die auf der Grundlage von gesetzlichen Ermächtigungen, auf den Generalsekretär vom Finanzminister übertragen worden sind. Auch im zweiten Fall werden allerdings gesetzliche Vorkehrungen getroffen, die die Befugnis des Finanzministers einschränken, bereits übertragene Befugnisse per Rechtsverordnung zurückzubekommen.

---

[10] Vgl. auch *S. Weinzierl*, Die EU-Task-Force für Griechenland: Internationale Beratung am Beispiel der griechischen Steuerverwaltung, in: U.-D. Klemm/W. Schultheiß (Hrsg.), Die Krise in Griechenland, Campus Verlag 2015, S. 448–460 (455): „eine recht weitgehende Abkehr von überkommen Praktiken in Griechenland".

[11] Die Begründung des Gesetzes 4093/2012 ist verfügbar unter www.ydmed.gov.gr/?p=3644, S. 16 (zuletzt abgerufen am 15. November 2015).

[12] Vgl. die Begründung des Gesetzes 4093/2012, oben Fn. 11, S. 16.

[13] Vgl. die durch Gesetz 4152/2013 (Erster Artikel, Abs. B) durchgeführten Ergänzungen im Gesetz 4152/2013.

Zur *ersten* Kategorie der gesetzlich vorgesehenen Befugnisse des Generalsekretärs gehört vor allem die Festlegung, jährliche Aktualisierung sowie Überwachung der Implementierung der strategischen Planung des Generalsekretariats sowie qualitativer und quantitativer Ziele und Bewertungskriterien von seinen Eingliederungen sowie seines Personals (Einziger Artikel, Unterabs. E.2., Fall 4 a Gesetz 4093/2012).

Gesetzlich vorgesehen sind verschiedenartige Abweichungen von allgemeinen Regelungen des Verwaltungsrechts vor allem im Bereich des Rechts des öffentlichen Dienstes. Mit Blick auf die *Einstellung von Personal* beschränkt sich die Befugnis des Generalsekretärs darauf, die Einstellungsvoraussetzungen festzulegen und bei der unabhängigen Behörde zur Kontrolle der Einstellung von Beamten in den öffentlichen Bereich (Art. 103 Abs. 7 Verf.) Anträge für die diesbezüglichen Ausschreibungen einzureichen. Mit Blick auf die *Ernennung der Führungskräfte* verfügt der Generalsekretär hingegen über substanzielle Freiräume. Gemäß Gesetz 4093/2012 ist der Generalsekretär befugt, die Führungskräfte aller Organisationseinheiten des Generalsekretariats auszuwählen und auch die Entscheidung über die vorzeitige Beendigung ihrer Amtszeit wegen Nichterfüllung ihrer Ziele zu treffen. Dabei müssen zwar die Kriterien der Beamtenordnung eingehalten werden (Gesetz 3548/2007), nicht allerdings das dort vorgesehene (oder andere gesetzlich vorgesehene) Verfahren. Abgestellt wird auf diese Weise auf eine bereits seit 2011 statuierte Abweichung von den allgemeinen Regelungen der Beamtenordnung, indem die Führungskräfte von ausgewählten Organisationseinheiten der Steuerverwaltung in Abweichung vom in der Beamtenordnung vorgesehenen Verfahren vom Finanzminister ausgewählt worden waren (Artikel 55 Abs. 21 Gesetz 4002/2011). Mit Blick auf den Generalsekretär für öffentliche Einnahmen wurde diese Abweichung verallgemeinert, indem die Führungskräfte nunmehr aller Organisationseinheiten der Steuerverwaltung vom Generalsekretär für öffentliche Einnahmen ernannt werden.[14] Während die Entscheidungsfindung nach Leistungskriterien verfassungsrechtlich geschützt ist[15] und jedenfalls eine ausreichende Begründung der Ernennung von Führungskräften verlangt, sind die diesbezüglichen Entscheidungen nur einer minimalen gerichtlichen Kontrolle zugänglich;[16] die Möglichkeiten einstweiligen Rechtsschutzes sind auch extrem eingeschränkt, zumal es sich um Verwaltungsakte handelt, deren unmit-

---

[14] Auch nach dem Inkrafttreten eines neuen Systems für die Ernennung von Führungskräften im öffentlichen Dienst gemäß Gesetz 4275/2014 bleibt diese Abweichung gemäß der speziellen Vorschrift des Artikels 54 des Gesetzes 4277/2014 in Kraft.

[15] Gemäß der Rechtsprechung des Staatsrates ist das Leistungsprinzip verfassungsrechtlich in das Recht auf freie Entfaltung der Persönlichkeit (Art. 5 Abs. 1) angesiedelt; vgl. etwa aus der neuesten Rechtsprechung die Urteile 987/2014, *Νομικό Βήμα* (Juristisches Forum) [Zeitschrift] 2014, S. 970–980 (975) und 1251/2015, *Θεωρία και Πράξη Διοικητικού Δικαίου* (Theorie und Praxis des Verwaltungsrechts) [Zeitschrift] 2015, S. 355–360 (357) des Plenums des Staatsrates.

[16] So ausdrücklich das Urteil 1038/2013 des Oberverwaltungsgerichts von Athen, NOMOS [Datenbank].

telbare Vollstreckung im öffentlichen Interesse liegt.[17] Vor diesem Hintergrund entbehrt die seit Ende 2014 vorgenommene Selbstbindung des Generalsekretariats im Sinne einer umfassenden Regelung des Verfahrens, der zuständigen Beratergremien und der ausschlaggebenden Kriterien für die Auswahl der Führungskräfte[18] jeder gesetzlichen Grundlage, so dass ihre Gültigkeit rechtlich in Frage gestellt werden kann.

Ferner ist der Generalsekretär für öffentliche Einnahmen befugt, *Entscheidungen organisatorischer Natur* über die innere Struktur des Generalsekretariats bis zur Ebene der Direktion allein zu treffen, insbesondere neue Einheiten einzurichten bzw. abzuschaffen. Dabei muss lediglich eine formelle Voraussetzung vorliegen, nämlich dass der Generalsekretär für Verwaltungsreform innerhalb von vierzehn Tagen eine (unverbindliche) Meinung geäußert haben muss.[19] Erlaubt ist allerdings gemäß Artikel 43 Abs. 2 S. 2 Verf. die Ermächtigung zum Erlass von Rechtsverordnungen durch andere Verwaltungsorgane[20] – also nicht durch den Präsidenten der Republik – lediglich „zur Regelung von besonderen Fragen oder von Fragen mit örtlichem Interesse oder mit technischem, oder Detailcharakter".[21] Zwar hatten auch früher spezielle gesetzliche Vorschriften den Minister für Verwaltungsreform und den Finanzminister ermächtigt, per gemeinsamer Entscheidung die innere Struktur des Finanzministeriums bis zur Ebene der Direktion zu bestimmen und dabei Organisationseinheiten zu gründen oder abzuschaffen (Artikel 55 Abs. 5 Unterabs. C, 1. Satz Gesetz 4002/2011), so dass das Erlassen einer Präsidialverordnung gesetzlich nicht notwendig gewesen wäre. Hinzu kommt, dass sich eine Ministerialentscheidung (selbst eine gemeinsame Entscheidung zweier oder mehrerer Minister) und eine Entscheidung des Generalsekretärs aus der Sicht der griechischen Verfassung insoweit nicht unterscheiden. In beiden Fällen muss die gesetzliche Ermächtigung zur Regelung von „besonderen" Fragen auf dem Wege der Rechtsverordnung nicht nur eine sachliche Bestimmung des Gegenstandes der Ermächtigung, sondern auch – selbst in einem allgemeinen Rahmen – eine materielle Regelung dieses Gegenstandes darstellen, so dass die Verwaltung danach Regeln zu den Einzelthemen innerhalb dieses

---

[17] Vgl. in diesem Zusammenhang bereits das Urteil 69/2013 des Oberverwaltungsgerichts von Athen, NOMOS [Datenbank].

[18] Vgl. die im Amtsblatt B' 3380 (16–12–2014) veröffentlichte Entscheidung des Generalsekretärin für öffentliche Einnahmen („Bestimmung des Verfahrens, der Organe und der Auswahlkriterien" für Führungskräfte der Organisationseinheiten des Generalsekretariats für öffentliche Einnahmen).

[19] Art. 55 Abs. 5 Unterabs. c, 2. Satz Gesetz 4002/2011, die durch Artikel 35 Abs. 2 Gesetz 4141/2013 ergänzt wurde.

[20] Zur Frage der Anwendbarkeit des Art. 43 Abs. 2 S. 2 Verf. auch auf die verfassungsrechtlich vorgesehenen unabhängigen Behörden vgl. *Ph.-J. Kozyris*, The ‚Independent' Agencies in Greece, RHDI 2003, S. 263–280 (273).

[21] Überblick dazu bei *E. Spiliotopoulos*, Les délégations legislatives en Grece, RFDA 1987, S. 729–731; *S.-I. Koutnatzis*, Grundlagen und Grundzüge staatlichen Verfassungsrechts: Griechenland, in: A. v. Bogdandy/P. Cruz Villalón/P. M. Huber (Hrsg.), Handbuch Ius Publicum Europaeum, Bd. I, C.F. Müller 2007, § 3, Rn. 115.

Rahmens erlassen könnte.[22] Die Ermächtigung zur Bestimmung der inneren Struktur entweder des Finanzministeriums oder des Generalsekretariats für öffentliche Einnahmen enthält keine solche materielle Regelung, so dass ihre Verfassungsmäßigkeit als fraglich betrachtet werden könnte. Hinzu kommt, dass sich die Ermächtigungen zum Erlass von Rechtsverordnungen, die in der Steuergesetzgebung der letzten Jahre enthalten sind, in aller Regel nicht mehr auf den Finanzminister sondern auf den Generalsekretär für öffentliche Einnahmen beziehen. Aus dieser Sicht repräsentativ sind die Beispiele des neuen Einkommenssteuergesetzes (Gesetz 4172/2013) und vor allem des Steuerverfahrensgesetzes (das zum ersten Mal in Griechenland in kodifizierter Form mit dem Gesetz 4174/2013 erlassen wurde), die sich übrigens großenteils darauf beschränken, Regeln allgemeiner Natur zu enthalten und für die weitere Spezifizierung auf Entscheidungen des Generalsekretärs für öffentliche Einnahmen hinweisen. In diesem Zusammenhang kann allerdings nicht auf die Frage eingegangen werden, inwieweit dieser Ansatz des Gesetzgebers sich mit den strikten verfassungsrechtlichen Voraussetzungen für das Erlassen von Rechtsverordnungen vereinbaren lässt.

Über die gesetzlich vorgesehenen Befugnisse des Generalsekretärs für öffentliche Einnahmen hinaus wird der Finanzminister ermächtigt, weitere Zuständigkeiten an den Generalsekretär zu übertragen, soweit es sich um Zuständigkeiten handelt, die die Organisation und Ausübung der Steuerverwaltung bzw. die Anwendung der Steuer- und Zollgesetzgebung betreffen. Bemerkenswert ist dabei, dass die Delegation dieser Befugnisse nicht per Rechtsverordnung rückgängig gemacht werden darf; dazu ist nämlich ein Parlamentsgesetz erforderlich (Einziger Artikel, Unterabs. E.2., Fall 4 b Gesetz 4093/2012). Von dieser Möglichkeit wurde schon weitgehend Gebrauch gemacht: Bereits seit Januar 2013 wurde an den Generalsekretär für öffentliche Einnahmen die Zuständigkeit übertragen,[23] alle (sog. *individuelle*) Verwaltungsakte ebenso Interpretationsrundschreiben und -richtlinien zu erlassen, sowie grundsätzlich die Befugnis beim Juristischen Rat des Staates Fragen zu stellen[24] und seine Gutachten anzunehmen;[25] außerdem wurde der Generalsekretär für öffentliche Einnahmen im Dezember 2013 nach einer gründlichen Überprüfung der weit verstreuten steuerrechtlichen (materiellen ebenso wie prozeduralen) Vorschriften,

---

[22] Vgl. *K. Chryssogonos* (*Κ. Χρυσόγονος*), Συνταγματικό Δίκαιο (Verfassungsrecht), 2. Aufl. (unter Mitwirkung von S.-I. Koutnatzis), Sakkoulas 2014, S. 344 m.w.N. auf die Rechtsprechung.

[23] Insoweit unzutreffend *P. Karakatsoulis*, Die Reform der griechischen Steuerverwaltung, in: Die Krise in Griechenland, oben Fn. 10, S. 431–447 (437), wonach die Übertragung von Zuständigkeiten an den Generalsekretär erst im April 2013 begann, was auch die oben skizzierten gesetzlich vorgesehenen Befugnisse des Generalsekretärs außer Acht lässt.

[24] Gemäß Art. 100 A Verf. fallen in die Zuständigkeit des Juristischen Rates des Staates insbesondere die gerichtliche Unterstützung und Vertretung des Staates und die Anerkennung von Forderungen gegen den Staat oder die Einigung in Streitigkeiten mit diesem.

[25] Vgl. die im Amtsblatt B' 130/28.1.2013 veröffentlichte gemeinsame Entscheidung des Ministers und des Vizeministers für Finanzen.

die den Finanzminister ermächtigen, Rechtsverordnungen zu erlassen, mit der Zuständigkeit beauftragt, 172 solcher Akte zu erlassen.[26]

Außerdem wurde eine zusätzliche Ermächtigungsmöglichkeit statuiert: Der Generalsekretär für öffentliche Einnahmen kann die Vorgesetzten der ihm untergeordneten Organisationseinheiten mit den erforderlichen Befugnissen ermächtigen, damit sie ihre Ziele erreichen können (Einziger Artikel, Unterabs. E.2., Fall 4 b Gesetz 4093/2012). Im Gegensatz zur Ermächtigung des Generalsekretärs wird letztere Ermächtigung durch eine explizite Widerrufoption ergänzt und zwar unabhängig davon, ob die Ermächtigung vor oder nach der Ernennung des Generalsekretärs stattgefunden hat. Vorherrschend bei der gesetzlichen Ausgestaltung der Steuerverwaltung ist damit eine weitgehende Anerkennung von Freiräumen zugunsten des Generalsekretärs für öffentliche Einnahmen.

2. Ernennung

Erklärt werden diese Freiräume durch die anspruchsvollen materiellen Ernennungsvoraussetzungen zur Position des Generalsekretärs. Dazu zählen nicht nur ein Universitätsabschluss sowie vorzugsweise ein Aufbaustudiengang in Steuerverwaltung bzw. Steuersystem, sondern auch die „wesentliche Berufserfahrung vorzugsweise im privaten Sektor in Steuerverwaltung bzw. Steuersystem", ebenso wie wesentliche Verwaltungserfahrung in Verantwortungspositionen, Personalführung, strategischer Planung und Projektmanagement, Targeting, Überwachung und Koordination von Teams zur Erreichung von Zielen, Fremdsprachenkenntnisse, ebenso wie Nachweise zur Steuerpflichterfüllung (Einziger Artikel, Unterabs. E.2., Fall 5 a Gesetz 4093/2012).

Trotz dieser Ernennungsvoraussetzungen, ebenso trotz der weitgehenden Befugnisse, über die der Inhaber dieses Amtes verfügt, ist das Ernennungsverfahren des Generalsekretärs von der jeweiligen Regierungsmehrheit absolut abhängig. Ausgewählt wird der Generalsekretär vom Ministerrat auf Vorschlag des Finanzministers, während der Generalsekretär mit dem Finanzminister einen sog. „Leistungsvertrag" unterschreibt, der die quantitativen und qualitativen Ziele festlegt, die der Generalsekretär während seiner Amtszeit ebenso wie jährlich erreichen müsste (Einziger Artikel, Unterabs. E.2., Fall 5 b Gesetz 4093/2012). Im Gegensatz zu den verfassungsrechtlich vorgesehenen unabhängigen Behörden,[27] hängt das Auswahlverfahren des Generalsekretärs für öffentliche Einnahmen ausschließlich von der jeweiligen Regierungsmehrheit ab. Die Zweckmäßigkeit dieses Verfahrens kann angesichts der Tatsache nicht von vornherein zurückgewiesen werden, dass sich die Erreichung der Vierfünftelmehrheit innerhalb der „Konferenz der Parlamentspräsidenten", die von Art. 101 A Verf. für die verfassungsrechtlich verankerten unabhängigen Behör-

---

[26] Vgl. die im Amtsblatt B' 3317/27.12.2013 veröffentlichte gemeinsame Entscheidung des Ministers und des Vizeministers für Finanzen.

[27] Vgl. dazu unten III.

den verlangt wird, in der Praxis als besonders schwierig erwiesen hat. In Frage gestellt wurden damit von der Rechtsprechung des Staatsrates die Entscheidungen der unabhängigen Behörden, da sie von nicht mehr befugten Organen getroffen wurden.[28] Für die Steuerverwaltung hätte eine solche Konsequenz fatale Auswirkungen.

Dennoch kann angesichts der fehlenden prozeduralen Garantien angezweifelt werden, inwieweit die gesteigerten materiellen Voraussetzungen für die Auswahl des Generalsekretärs Anwendung finden werden. Während allerdings in der Praxis bei der ersten Auswahl des Generalsekretärs für öffentliche Einnahmen eine erste Vorwahl intern von den Büros des Finanzministers und -Vizeministers stattgefunden hatte, wurden die Bewerbungen bei der zweiten Auswahl im Juni 2014 von einem fünfköpfigen Expertengremium evaluiert, so dass der Finanzminister bei seinem Vorschlag und dann der Ministerrat bei seiner Entscheidungsfindung bloß das Ergebnis des Expertengremiums besiegelt haben. Gemäßigt werden jedenfalls die Zweifel an das gesetzliche Verfahren für die Auswahl des Generalsekretärs für öffentliche Einnahmen angesichts seiner fünfjährigen Amtszeit, die die Amtszeit der Regierung bzw. des Parlaments überschreitet und von diesbezüglichen politischen Entwicklungen grundsätzlich unberührt bleibt. Zum Zeitpunkt der Ernennung bleibt allerdings die Personenauswahl rechtlich gesehen der alleinigen Entscheidung der Regierung überlassen, wobei – jedenfalls unter den jetzigen Umständen Griechenlands – die Rolle der internationalen Geldgeber des Landes faktisch nicht außer Acht gelassen werden müsste. Nicht unproblematisch ist außerdem, dass die jeweilige Regierung, selbst am Ende ihrer Amtszeit, ihre Nachfolgerin gegebenenfalls für die Gesamtdauer ihrer Amtszeit daran hindern kann, den Chef der Steuerverwaltung auszuwählen. Während die gesetzliche Intention darin liegt, politische Einflüsse in der Steuerverwaltung zu minimieren, sind daher Konstellationen vorstellbar, die im Gegenteil diese Einflüsse verstärken bzw. perpetuieren.

3. Kontrolle

Den Gegenpol zu den weitgehenden Befugnissen des Generalsekretärs für öffentliche Einnahmen bilden gesetzlich vorgesehene Kontroll- und Rechenschaftsmechanismen.

Vorgesehen sind erstens grundlegende *Regeln zum Umgang mit Interessenkonflikten* (Einziger Artikel, Unterabs. E.2., Fall 7 Gesetz 4093/2012). So ist die Ausübung jeder öffentlichen Funktion ebenso wie die Beschäftigung im öffentlichen Sektor einschließlich der juristischen Personen des öffentlichen Rechts während der Amtszeit des Generalsekretärs nicht erlaubt. Damit inkompatibel ist außerdem die Ausübung jeder beruflichen Tätigkeit, wobei der Generalsekretär verpflichtet ist, vor seiner Amtsübernahme jede rechtliche Beziehung mit Unternehmen zu beenden, die einen Interessenkonflikt verursachen könnte. Als rudimentäre Form der *Parlaments-*

---

[28] Vgl. statt vieler das Urteil des Staatsrates 3515/2013 (Plenum), *Νομικό Βήμα* (Juristisches Forum) [Zeitschrift] 2014, S. 145–149 (147).

kontrolle ist überdies die Verpflichtung des Generalsekretärs gesetzlich vorgesehen, bis Ende Februar jedes Jahres an das Parlament einen ausführlichen Jahresbericht einzureichen, der auch die Planung der Aktivitäten des Generalsekretariats für das nächste Jahr einschließt. Darüber wird im Ausschuss für wirtschaftliche Angelegenheiten des Parlaments diskutiert, wobei der Bericht auch auf der Homepage des Finanzministeriums veröffentlicht wird[29] (Einziger Artikel, Unterabs. E.2., Fall 4 c Gesetz 4093/2012). Bis jetzt sind Zweifel angebracht, inwieweit sich diese jährliche Zeremonie zu einem wirksamen Kontrollmechanismus entwickeln wird. Mehr im Sinne von regelmäßigen Kontrollbefugnissen des Parlaments ist nicht vorgesehen – jedenfalls über die allgemeinen Regelungen der parlamentarischen Geschäftsordnung hinaus, die sich allerdings an die Regierung, hier an den Finanzminister richten.

Im Einklang mit dem Selbstständigkeitsziel der Steuerverwaltung fallen überdies Kontrollbefugnisse der *Exekutive* eher gering aus, jedenfalls was Wortlaut und Intention des Gesetzgebers angeht. Dazu gehört vor allem die vorzeitige Beendigung der Amtszeit des Generalsekretärs, die nur unter strengen Voraussetzungen möglich ist (Einziger Artikel, Unterabs. E.2., Fall 6 Gesetz 4093/2012). Abgesehen von den Fällen des Rücktritts und der (zwangsläufigen) Dienstenthebung gemäß Art. 103 Absatz 1 der Beamtenordnung kann die Amtszeit des Generalsekretärs durch Entscheidung des Ministerrates auf Vorschlag des Finanzministers ebenso beendet werden in den Fällen seines dauerhaften Ausfalls, seine Aufgaben durchzuführen, wegen körperlicher oder geistiger Krankheit oder Behinderung ebenso wie wenn die Voraussetzungen der (fakultativen) Dienstenthebung gemäß Art. 104 Abs. 1 der Beamtenordnung vorliegen. Ebenso kann der Finanzminister die vorzeitige Beendigung der Amtszeit des Generalsekretärs im Fall von offensichtlicher Abweichung hinsichtlich der Erreichung seiner Ziele anordnen unter der Voraussetzung allerdings, dass mindestens zwei Jahre nach seiner Ernennung vergangen worden sind. Jedenfalls für die ersten beiden Jahre nach der Ernennung des Generalsekretärs verfügen die Regierung bzw. das Parlament daher über keine Ersetzungsmöglichkeit, es sei denn, dass die Voraussetzungen der disziplinarischen Haftung vorliegen.

An die Grenzen der Normativität stößt demgegenüber der Rücktritt des Generalsekretärs, der nicht ausgeschlossen werden kann, selbst wenn Zweifel angebracht sind, inwieweit es sich immer tatsächlich um einen freiwilligen Rücktritt handelt – so etwa im Fall des Rücktritts der ersten Generalsekretärs für öffentliche Einnahmen Herrn Harris Theocharis im Juni 2014.[30] Noch bedenklicher war die vorzeitige Beendigung der Amtszeit der zweiten Generalsekretärin Frau Katerina Savvaidou, deren Amtszeit im Oktober 2015 durch Entscheidung des Ministerrates unter Beru-

---

[29] Vgl. den Tätigkeitsbericht für das Jahr 2014 unter www.publicrevenue.gr/.../ekthesi_apologismou_2014 (zuletzt abgerufen am 15. November 2015).

[30] Vgl. etwa den Bericht der griechischen Tageszeitung „Kathimerini", Greece's public revenue chief Harris Theocharis resigns, 5. Juni 2014, verfügbar unter www.ekathimerini.com/160534/article/ekathimerini/business/greeces-public-revenue-chief-haris-theocharis-resigns (zuletzt abgerufen am 15. November 2015) sowie *Weinzierl*, oben Fn. 10, S. 455–6, 459, *Karakatsoulis*, oben Fn. 23, S. 438, 447.

fung auf eine strafrechtliche Untersuchung wegen der Verlängerung einer Steuerzahlungsfrist vorzeitig beendet wurde,[31] obwohl die gesetzlichen Voraussetzungen der fakultativen Dienstenthebung (noch) nicht vorlagen. Ob zusätzliche gesetzliche – oder sogar verfassungsrechtliche – Absicherungen gegen politische Einflüsse sinnvoll bzw. notwendig wären, steht damit wieder auf der Agenda.

Jedenfalls aus rechtlicher Sicht lässt sich somit die Wirksamkeit der herkömmlichen Kontrollmechanismen der Steuerverwaltung in Grenzen halten. Dafür wurde mit dem Gesetz 4152/2013 ein *Beraterrat* statuiert, der seine Tätigkeit im September 2013 aufgenommen hat. Zusammengesetzt aus fünf Mitgliedern, von denen zwei wesentliche internationale Berufserfahrung im Bereich der öffentlichen Einnahmen vorweisen müssen,[32] besteht die Aufgabe des Rates darin, die Steuerverwaltung in den Grundfragen zu beraten, ihre Effektivität mit Blick auf die Planung und die gesetzten Ziele zu überwachen, und auch zu bestätigen, dass der Generalsekretär seine Aufgaben ordnungsgemäß durchführt (vgl. Einziger Artikel, Unterabs. E.2., Fall 5 d Gesetz 4093/2012). Statt den herkömmlichen Organen von Legislative bzw. Exekutive Kontrollbefugnisse anzuvertrauen wird damit eine externe Kontrollinstanz mit technokratischer Kompetenz und lediglich Beratungszuständigkeiten geschaffen – sicherlich ein zusätzliches Zeichen des Misstrauens gegenüber dem politischen System. Allgemein wird anerkannt, dass das Beratergremium während des ersten Jahres seiner Tätigkeit zur Kontrolle der Steuerverwaltung nicht substantiell beigetragen hat, während diese Institution seit dem Sommer 2014 offenbar in Vergessenheit geraten ist.

IV. Steuerverwaltung als unabhängige Behörde?

Nach diesem Überblick zur Institution des Generalsekretärs für öffentliche Einnahmen stellt sich die Frage, wie sich diese Institution mit anderen Formen der Verwaltungsorganisation der griechischen Rechtsordnung vergleicht, etwa mit den unabhängigen Behörden. Zu untersuchen ist dabei, inwieweit das Generalsekretariat für öffentliche Einnahmen in seiner Ausgestaltung seit 2012 schon eine solche unabhängige Behörde darstellt bzw. inwieweit sich Fragen zur Verfassungsmäßigkeit des Gesetzes 4093/2012 in diesem Zusammenhang stellen. Vor diesem Hintergrund ist auch die im neuen Rettungspaket niedergelegte Verpflichtung der Hellenischen Republik einzuschätzen, die Unabhängigkeit der Steuerverwaltung durch die Errichtung einer autonomen Einnahmenagentur zu stärken, deren gesetzlicher Rahmen bis Oktober

---

[31] Vgl. ähnlich den Zeitungsbericht, „Kathimerini", Cabinet dismisses revenue chief as bill seeks to increase oversight, 22 Oktober 2015, verfügbar unter www.ekathimerini.com/202770/article/ekathimerini/news/cabinet-dismisses-revenues-chief-as-bill-seeks-to-increase-oversight (zuletzt abgerufen am 15. November 2015).

[32] Unter den ersten Mitgliedern des Beraterrates zählten u.a. der ehemalige Chef der irischen Steuerverwaltung (2002–2008) Frank Daly und der ehemalige Chef der schwedischen Steuerverwaltung Mats Sjöstrand (1999–2009). Vgl. die im Amtsblatt B' 1749/15.7.2013 veröffentlichte Entscheidung des Finanzministers.

2015 erlassen werden musste,[33] um bis Juni 2016 völlig funktionsfähig zu werden (vgl. auch Gesetz 4336/2015, Absatz C, 2.3.).

Nach der Revision von 2001 enthält die griechische Verfassung sowohl eine allgemeine Regelung zu den verfassungsrechtlich garantierten unabhängigen Behörden (Art. 101 A) – soweit ersichtlich handelt es sich um die einzige europäische Verfassung mit einer solchen Regelung[34] – als auch fünf solche Behörden, die direkt auf der Verfassungsebene angesiedelt sind,[35] wobei andere weitere unabhängige Behörden erst auf der einfachgesetzlichen Ebene vorgesehen sind.[36] Die einzelnen Regelungen des Art. 101 A Verf. sind insbesondere die *bestimmte Amtsdauer* und die *Garantien persönlicher und funktioneller Unabhängigkeit*, die *Auswahlmodalitäten* von der „Konferenz der Parlamentspräsidenten" möglichst mit Einstimmung oder zumindest durch eine Entscheidung mit einer erhöhten Mehrheit von vier Fünfteln ihrer Mitglieder,[37] ebenso wie die sog. *parlamentarische Kontrolle* der unabhängigen Behörden.

Obwohl sich der Anwendungsbereich dieser Verfassungsbestimmung sowie auch ihres Ausführungsgesetzes explizit auf diejenigen unabhängigen Behörden beschränkt, deren Errichtung und Tätigkeit in der Verfassung vorgesehen ist (Art. 1 Abs. 1 Gesetz 3052/2002), weisen auch die gesetzlich vorgesehenen unabhängigen Behörden gemeinsame grundlegende Merkmale auf.[38] Es geht um *Behörden*, also staatliche Organe mit der Zuständigkeit der Ausübung öffentlicher Gewalt, die in der Regel entscheidender Natur ist, *Verwaltungs*behörden, also Institutionen, die

---

[33] Bis zum Redaktionsschluss dieses Beitrags (15. November 2015) liegt noch kein Gesetzentwurf offiziell vor, wobei angesichts der bisherigen Zeitungsberichte zu den laufenden Vorbereitungen die Versuchung naheliegen mag, unter dem Namen „Einnahmenagentur" sogar weniger Unabhängigkeitsgarantien im Vergleich zur bisherigen Situation vorzusehen. Vgl. etwa oben Fn. 31.

[34] Nach *J. Iliopoulos-Strangas*, Impulse aus dem griechischen Verfassungsrecht für den europäischen Grundrechtsschutz, in: P. Tettinger/K. Stern (Hrsg.), Kölner Gemeinschaftskommentar zur Europäischen Grundrechte-Charta, C. H. Beck 2006, S. 31–54 (52), enthält die griechische Verfassung „die detaillierteste Regelung der ‚unabhängigen Behörden' im europäischen Verfassungsvergleich".

[35] Dabei geht es um die unabhängigen Behörden zur Sicherstellung des Datenschutzes (Art. 9 A Verf.), des Briefgeheimnisses und des Geheimnisses jeder anderen freien Korrespondenz oder Kommunikation (Art. 19 Abs. 1 und 2 Verf.), zur Kontrolle der Einstellung von Beamten in den öffentlichen Bereich (Art. 103 Abs. 7 Verf.) sowie um den Nationalrat für Hörfunk und Fernsehen (Art. 15 Abs. 2 S. 2 Verf.) und den „Bürgerverteidiger" (Art. 103 Abs. 9 Verf.).

[36] So etwa die Wettbewerbskommission, die Nationale Kommission für Telekommunikation und Post und die Regulierungsbehörde für Energie. Vgl. etwa *Iliopoulos-Strangas*, oben Fn. 34, S. 53.

[37] Während überparteiliche Zustimmung für die Erreichung der Vierfünftelmehrheit zurzeit erforderlich ist, wird die Zusammensetzung der Konferenz erst in der Geschäftsordnung des Parlaments (Art. 13 Abs. 1) festgesetzt.

[38] Dazu und zum Folgenden vgl. den begrifflichen Überblick bei *Th. Tzonos* (Θ. Τζώνος), Οι ανεξάρτητες διοικητικές αρχές (Die unabhängigen Verwaltungsbehörden), Papazissis 2010, S. 150 ff.

sich im Bereich der vollziehenden Gewalt bewegen und dem Grundsatz der Gesetzmäßigkeit unterliegen, und *unabhängige* Behörden, die über Garantien funktioneller
und persönlicher Unabhängigkeit verfügen und Verwaltungsselbstständigkeit genie-
ßen.

Zu den notwendigen Begriffsmerkmalen der unabhängigen Behörden zählt dage-
gen ihre ausdrückliche diesbezügliche Kennzeichnung durch die Verfassung oder das
Gesetz nicht. So wird meistens anerkannt,[39] dass die Kapitalmarktkommission die
Begriffsmerkmale der unabhängigen Behörden erfüllt,[40] wobei davon auch für die
Diensträte der Verwaltung und die Bank von Griechenland ausgegangen werden
kann.[41]

Viele dieser Merkmale können auch für das Generalsekretariat für öffentliche
Einnahmen – schon nach dem bisherigen gesetzlichen Rahmen – als erfüllt angesehen werden: Nicht in Frage gestellt kann die Tatsache, dass es sich dabei um ein staatliches Organ mit der Zuständigkeit der Ausübung öffentlicher Gewalt handelt, das
sich im Bereich der Exekutive liegt. Obwohl sich die einschlägigen Vorschriften
des Gesetzes 4093/2012 auf Unabhängigkeitsgarantien nicht ausdrücklich beziehen,
enthalten sie aber diesbezügliche Normen. Aus der Sicht der *persönlichen* Unabhängigkeit wird der Generalsekretär für öffentliche Einnahmen für eine fünfjährige
Amtszeit ernannt, während ihre vorzeitige Beendigung nur unter außergewöhnlichen
Umständen möglich ist, zumal sie entweder den (nach der gesetzlichen Intention de-
finitionsgemäß freiwilligen) Rücktritt oder den dauerhaften Ausfall, seine Aufgaben
durchzuführen oder disziplinarrechtlich relevante Tatbestände voraussetzt. Während
die vorzeitige Beendigung der Amtszeit des Generalsekretärs wegen Abweichung
hinsichtlich der Erreichung seines quantitativen und qualitativen Ziels einer zweijährigen Sperre unterliegt, ist die Beendigung seiner Amtszeit aus im Gesetz nicht enthaltenen Gründen nicht erlaubt.

Mit Blick auf die *funktionelle* Unabhängigkeit enthält das Gesetz 4093/2012 demgegenüber keine relevanten Vorschriften. Sofern aber die Zuständigkeiten des Generalsekretärs direkt auf Parlamentsgesetzen beruhen oder jedenfalls ohne Parlamentsgesetz nicht rückgängig gemacht werden können und außerdem ausdrücklich die Befugnis der Auslegung und Anwendung der Steuergesetzgebung enthalten, würde eine
voraussichtliche Durchführung hierarchischer Kontrolle von der Regierung gegen
den Grundsatz der Gesetzmäßigkeit verstoßen. Zumal also die Zuständigkeit für
das Erlassen von Interpretationsrundschreiben und -richtlinien für die Anwendung

---

[39] Vgl. aber *Koulouris*, oben Fn. 6, S. 98 und dort Fn. 7 mit Bezug auf die Qualifizierung
der Kapitalmarktkommission als juristische Person des öffentlichen Rechts.

[40] Interessanterweise hat der Finanzminister Ende Oktober 2015, nur eine Woche nach der
vorzeitigen Beendigung der Amtszeit der Generalsekretärin für öffentliche Einnahmen, auch
den Präsidenten der Kapitalmarktkommission um Rücktritt ersucht; vgl. Kathimerini, Greek
gov't asks for securities watchdog chief to resign, 30 Oktober 2015, www.ekathimerini.com/
202995/article/ekathimerini/business/greek-govt-asks-for-securities-watchdog-chief-to-resign
(zuletzt abgerufen am 15. November 2015).

[41] So etwa *Tzonos*, oben Fn. 38, S. 164.

der Steuergesetzgebung beim Generalsekretär liegt (auch im Einklang mit Artikel 9 Abs. 1 des Steuerverfahrensgesetzes), ist der Finanzminister nicht befugt, unter dem Vorwand der Aufsicht oder Kontrolle diese Interpretationszuständigkeit auszuüben, die gemäß dem Gesetz einem anderen Organ anvertraut wird. Obwohl das Gesetz 4093/2012 die bei den unabhängigen Behörden übliche feierliche Proklamation nicht enthält, muss demzufolge davon ausgegangen werden, dass das Gesetz 4093/2012, auch angesichts seiner Entstehungsgeschichte, zwar nicht ausdrücklich aber jedenfalls eindeutig[42] die Akte des Generalsekretärs für öffentliche Einnahmen von der hierarchischen Befugnis des Finanzministers ausschließt. Der Sache nach vereinigt daher die Institution des Generalsekretärs für öffentliche Einnahmen viele der Begriffsmerkmale der unabhängigen Behörden, zumal sich diese Einrichtungen in der griechischen Rechtsordnung nicht auf die fünf verfassungsrechtlich vorgesehenen unabhängigen Behörden beschränken.

Angesichts dieses Zwischenbefundes stellt sich die Frage nach der verfassungsrechtlichen Einschätzung der semi-autonomen Steuerverwaltung. Tatsache ist, dass die ganz herrschende Meinung im Schrifttum und in der Rechtsprechung die Möglichkeit einfachgesetzlicher Errichtung unabhängiger Behörden außer derjenigen, die in der Verfassung ausdrücklich vorgesehen sind, nicht in Frage stellt.[43] Daraus ist aber nicht zu schließen, dass sich aus der Verfassung keine materiellen Einschränkungen mit Blick auf Bereiche des Verwaltungshandelns ergeben, die in der Form von unabhängigen Behörden organisiert werden können.[44] Denn die Errichtung unabhängiger Behörden stellt den Grundsatz der parlamentarischen Verantwortlichkeit der Regierung, die im Art. 86 Verf. verankert ist, auf die Probe.

Als parlamentarische Verantwortlichkeit definiert sich (auch) im griechischen Verfassungsrecht das Verfahren, durch das die Regierung kollektiv und jedes Regierungsmitglied individuell, ebenso wie die Vizeminister, kontrolliert werden und

---

[42] Allgemein wird anerkannt, dass alle Akte der hierarchisch untergesetzten Organe der Gesetzmäßigkeitskontrolle unterliegen, es sei denn, dass das Gegenteilige sich aus den einschlägigen Vorschriften ausdrücklich oder jedenfalls klar ergibt. Dazu etwa *E. Spiliotopoulos* *(E. Σπηλιωτόπουλος)*, Εγχειρίδιο Διοικητικού Δικαίου (Lehrbuch für Verwaltungsrecht), Bd. I, 14. Aufl., Nomiki Vivliothiki 2011, Rn. 248.

[43] Diese Auffassung wird auch auf eine verfassungsrechtliche Vorschrift im Kapitel über die Wahlhindernisse bei Abgeordneten gestützt, die sich ausdrücklich nicht auf die „Mitglieder der unabhängigen Behörden, welche sich gemäß Artikel 101a zusammensetzen und funktionieren" sondern auch auf die Behörden bezieht, „die durch Gesetz als unabhängig oder regulativ bezeichnet werden" (Art. 56 Abs. 3 Unterabs. b Verf.). In diesem Sinne etwa *Spiliotopoulos*, oben Fn. 42, S. 289, *Tzonos*, oben Fn. 38, S. 74.

[44] Vor allem rechtspolitische Bedenken gegen die Ausuferung der unabhängigen Behörden bei *N. Alivizatos (N. Αλιβιζάτος)*, Η προσφορά των Ανεξάρτητων Αρχών και οι προϋποθέσεις αποτελεσματικής λειτουργίας τους (Der Beitrag der unabhängigen Behörden und die Voraussetzungen ihrer effektiven Tätigkeit), in: N. Fragkakis (N. Φραγκάκης) (Hrsg.), Οι ανεξάρτητες αρχές στη σύγχρονη δημοκρατία (Die unabhängigen Behörden in der modernen Demokratie), Ant. Sakkoulas 2008, S. 33–37 (33 f., 36 f.); *P. Pavlopoulos (Π. Παυλόπουλος)*, Οι Ανεξάρτητες Αρχές στη σύγχρονη Δημοκρατία (Die unabhängigen Behörden in der modernen Demokratie), ebd., S. 99–102 (99 f.).

dabei Sanktionen unterliegen, die im Extremfall bis zur Entlassung der kontrollierten Personen reichen.[45] Ohne politische und rechtliche Konsequenzen ist die parlamentarische Verantwortlichkeit unfassbar.[46] Zwar bestimmt Art. 101 A Abs. 3 Verf. mit Blick auf die verfassungsrechtlich vorgesehenen unabhängigen Behörden, dass durch die Geschäftsordnung des Parlaments alles geregelt wird, was die Beziehung der unabhängigen Behörden zum Parlament und die Art der Ausübung der parlamentarischen Kontrolle angeht. Bei dieser Kontrolle geht es gemäß Art. 138 A der Geschäftsordnung des Parlaments um die Einreichung seitens jeder unabhängigen Behörde eines jährlichen Berichts, worüber in der Regel im Ausschuss für Institutionen und Transparenz des Parlaments diskutiert wird, während die Schlussfolgerungen der Diskussion beim Präsidenten des Parlaments eingereicht werden, der sie an den zuständigen Minister und die kontrollierte Behörde weiterleitet.[47] Werden aber im Rahmen dieser Verfahren Unzulänglichkeit, Unterlassen oder Überschreitung von Zuständigkeiten festgestellt, kann das Parlament gegen die unabhängige Behörde keine Sanktionen verhängen. Im Schrifttum ist lediglich von einem Verfahren institutionalisierter Kommunikation die Rede,[48] so dass die sog. parlamentarische Kontrolle der unabhängigen Behörden eine nur symbolische Bedeutung aufweist.[49] Gleichzeitig würde die Verhängung von Sanktionen gegen den zuständigen Minister darauf hinauslaufen, ihn für Angelegenheiten zu „bestrafen", die außerhalb seiner Zuständigkeiten liegen.

Auch im Fall des Generalsekretärs für öffentliche Einnahmen hängen die Einreichung eines jährlichen Berichts an das Parlament sowie seine Besprechung und sein Inhalt mit keinen Sanktionen zusammen. Andererseits wird die Ausübung der par-

---

[45] Vgl. statt vieler *Ph. Spyropoulos/Th. Fortsakis*, Constitutional Law in Greece, Ant. Sakkoulas/Wolters Kluwer 2009, S. 141 f.

[46] So etwa auch *Tzonos*, oben Fn. 38, S. 94.

[47] Die „Konferenz des Parlamentspräsidenten" wird gemäß Art. 14 Fall g der Geschäftsordnung des Parlaments mit der zusätzlichen Möglichkeit ausgestattet, die Mitglieder der unabhängigen Behörden für Angelegenheiten, die sich mit der Erfüllung ihrer Tätigkeit zusammenhängen, vorzuladen.

[48] *Ch. Papastylianos* (*Χ. Παπαστυλιανός*), Ανεξάρτητες αρχές και Κοινοβούλιο (Unabhängige Behörden und Parlament), in: Χ. Contiades/Ph. Spyropoulos (Ξ. Κοντιάδης/Φ. Σπυρόπουλος) (Hrsg.), Το μέλλον του ελληνικού Κοινοβουλίου (Die Zukunft des griechischen Parlaments), Sideris 2011, S. 331–343 (342).

[49] Vgl. etwa *A. Benaki-Psarouda* (*Α. Μπενάκη-Ψαρούδα*), Οι Ανεξάρτητες Αρχές στο πολιτειακό σύστημα (Die unabhängigen Behörden im Regierungssystem), in: Fragkakis, oben Fn. 44, S. 13–19 (17 f.); *G. Papadimitriou* (*Γ. Παπαδημητρίου*), Ανεξάρτητες αρχές. Η αργόσυρτη πορεία προς την ωρίμανση (Unabhängige Behörden. Auf dem langsamen Weg zur Fälligkeit), ebd., S. 45–51 (48), *I. Kamtsidou* (*Ι. Καμτσίδου*), Σκέψεις σχετικά με τις θεσμικές και πολιτικές διαστάσεις της ανεξαρτησίας των ανεξάρτητων διοικητικών αρχών (Überlegungen zu den institutionellen und politischen Dimensionen der Unabhängigkeit der unabhängigen Verwaltungsbehörden), in: Ph. Kozyris/S. Megglidou (Φ. Κοζύρης/Σ. Μεγγλίδου) (Hrsg.), Η „ανεξαρτησία" των ανεξάρτητων αρχών (Die „Unabhängigkeit" der unabhängigen Behörden), Ant. Sakkoulas 2003, S. 141–147 (145); *K. Chryssogonos* (*Κ. Χρυσόγονος*), Συμπερασματικές παρατηρήσεις (Schlussbemerkungen), ebd., S. 233–236 (234 f.).

lamentarischen Kontrolle gegen den zuständigen Minister zwar häufig in der Praxis ausgeübt,[50] sie läuft aber meistens auf eine Zeremonie hinaus, die jeglichen materiellen Inhalts entbehrt, zumal der Minister in die Lage versetzt ist, für Sachfragen Rechenschaft ablegen zu müssen, die außerhalb seiner gesetzlichen Zuständigkeiten und Einflussmöglichkeiten liegen.

Angesichts der zwangsweise lückenhaften parlamentarischen Kontrolle unabhängiger Verwaltungseinrichtungen – davon abgesehen ob sie ausdrücklich als unabhängige Behörden qualifiziert werden oder nicht – muss davon ausgegangen werden, dass die Errichtung von Verwaltungsbehörden, die der Aufsicht der zuständigen Minister kaum unterliegen, nicht uneingeschränkt möglich ist. In der deutschen Verfassungsordnung wurde auf diese Problematik bereits seit den ersten Nachkriegsjahrzehnten intensiv eingegangen. Überwiegend wird anerkannt, dass die Errichtung von ministerialfreien Räumen innerhalb der Verwaltung nicht uneingeschränkt möglich ist, obgleich keine Übereinstimmung mit Blick auf die Wesensmerkmale dieses Begriffs besteht. Nach der Rechtsprechung des Bundesverfassungsgerichts „gibt es Regierungsaufgaben, die wegen ihrer politischen Tragweite nicht generell der Regierungsverantwortung entzogen und auf Stellen übertragen werden dürfen, die von Regierung und Parlament unabhängig sind; andernfalls würde es der Regierung unmöglich gemacht, die von ihr geforderte Verantwortung zu tragen, da auf diese Weise unkontrollierte und niemand verantwortliche Stellen Einfluß auf die Staatsverwaltung gewinnen würden".[51] Zwar wird im Schrifttum der vom Bundesverfassungsgericht herangezogene Maßstab der politischen Tragweite deswegen kritisiert, weil er keine klaren Abgrenzungskriterien bietet, auf welchen Bereichen unabhängige Institutionen verfassungsrechtlich bedenklich sind. Weitere Ansätze konkretisieren die Ausnahmetatbestände, unter denen die Errichtung unabhängiger Institutionen gerechtfertigt werden kann, mit Blick auf das rechtsstaatliche Rationalitätsgebot, den Grundrechtsschutz, die partizipative Demokratie und die Grenzen des Mehrheitsprinzips.[52] In der griechischen Verfassungsordnung wird sogar allgemeiner die Auffassung vertreten, dass das Vorhandensein staatlicher Organe und die Ausübung staatlicher Funktion, die der allgemeinen Anleitung, der Koordinierung und der Aufsicht der Regierung nicht unterliegen, die Kette demokratischer Legitimation und Legitimität brechen und damit gegen die Verfassung verstoßen würden.[53]

---

[50] Zur grundsätzlichen Zulässigkeit parlamentarischer Kontrolle gegen den zuständigen Minister auch mit Blick auf die verfassungsrechtlich vorgesehenen unabhängigen Behörden vgl. auch E. Venizelos (Ε. Βενιζέλος), Οι Ανεξάρτητες Αρχές μετά την Αναθεώρηση του Ελληνικού Συντάγματος του 1975/1986/2001 (Die unabhängigen Behörden nach der Revision der griechischen Verfassung von 1975/1986/2001), in: Kozyris/Megglidou, oben Fn. 49, S. 13–23 (21 f.).

[51] BVerfGE 9, 268 (282).

[52] Eingehend dazu *Bredt*, oben Fn. 5, S. 59 ff. m.w.N.

[53] *G. Kassimatis (Γ. Κασιμάτης)*, Art. 1, in: G. Kassimatis/K. Mavrias (Γ. Κασιμάτης/ Κ. Μαυριάς) (Hrsg.), Η ερμηνεία του Συντάγματος (Die Auslegung der Verfassung) [Kommentar], 2. Aufl., Ant. Sakkoulas 2003, Rn. 354.

Im vorliegenden Beitrag kann auf die allgemeine Diskussion über die verfassungsrechtlichen Fragestellungen der unabhängigen Behörden nicht im Detail eigegangen werden; es genügt darauf hinzuweisen, dass die strikte Einhaltung der parlamentarischen Kontrolle als ein mit Sanktionen belegtes Verfahren verfassungsrechtlich angebracht ist, jedenfalls in Bereichen, die dem harten Kern der vollziehenden Gewalt angehören, wie und gerade die Steuerverwaltung. Die bloße Verpflichtung des Generalsekretärs für öffentliche Einnahmen, an das Parlament einen jährlichen Bericht einzureichen, müsste daher mit regelmäßigen Kontrollmechanismen in der Geschäftsordnung des Parlaments ergänzt werden, die die Verpflichtung enthalten, regelmäßige Erklärungen abzugeben, Zugang zu Dokumenten zu gewährleisten oder spezielle Kommissionen einzuberufen – die bereits vorgesehenen Mechanismen der parlamentarischen Kontrolle der Regierung könnten hier dementsprechend angepasst werden.[54]

Angesichts der schwerwiegenden Sanktion der vorzeitigen Beendigung der Amtszeit des Generalsekretärs ist die Situation delikater: Angesichts der regelmäßigen Kohärenz zwischen Parlamentsmehrheit und Regierung in der heutigen Verfassungswirklichkeit würde eine eventuelle Beauftragung eines parlamentarischen Ausschusses mit entscheidenden Befugnissen bei die Beendigung der Amtszeit des Generalsekretärs für öffentliche Einnahmen die eigentliche Zielsetzung der Trennung zwischen den politischen Auseinandersetzungen und die Steuerverwaltung untergraben. Insoweit sind wir allerdings auf die Grenzen der verfassungsrechtlich erlaubten Selbstständigkeit der Steuerverwaltung gestoßen: Nur sofern die Möglichkeit des Parlaments anerkannt wird, die schwerwiegende Sanktion der Entlassung gegen den Generalsekretär für öffentliche Einnahmen zu verhängen, bleiben wir innerhalb des Rahmens des parlamentarischen Systems,[55] das selbst einer Verfassungsände-

---

[54] In ähnlichem Sinne für die unabhängigen Behörden insgesamt *Antoniou*, oben Fn. 5, S. 253–4: „… regardless of the Minister, Parliament would be able to control the public administration, which in turn should be regulated by the Constitution in an autonomous way, outside the scope of political leadership".

[55] In diesem Sinne selbst für die unabhängigen Behörden der griechischen Verfassung *T. Vidalis (Τ. Βιδάλης)*, Τυπική ή ουσιαστική διάκριση των λειτουργιών; Το θεμέλιο των ανεξαρτήτων αρχών στο πολίτευμα (Formelle oder materielle Gewaltenteilung? Die Grundlage der unabhängigen Behörden im Regierungssystem), *Το Σύνταγμα* (Die Verfassung) [Zeitschrift] 2003, S. 825–838 (837); a.A. *G. Kaminis (Γ. Καμίνης)*, Οι ανεξάρτητες αρχές μεταξύ ανεξαρτησίας και κοινοβουλευτικού ελέγχου (Die unabhängigen Behörden zwischen Unabhängigkeit und parlamentarischer Kontrolle), *Νομικό Βήμα* (Juristisches Forum) [Zeitschrift] 2002, S. 95–103 (101 f.); *Lazarakos*, oben Fn. 6, S. 99; *I. Mavromoustakou (Η. Μαυρομούστακου)*, Οι διαδρομές από την αμφισβήτηση στην καθολική αποδοχή μιας νέας μορφής διοίκησης: οι ελληνικές ανεξάρτητες αρχές (Der Weg von der Infragestellung zur universellen Akzeptanz einer neuen Verwaltungsform: Die griechischen unabhängigen Behörden), *Εφημερίδα Διοικητικού Δικαίου* (Zeitschrift für Verwaltungsrecht) 2012, S. 236–249 (243).

rung entzogen ist.[56] Dabei wäre eine Reihe von möglichen Garantien denkbar, um einen Missbrauch dieser Zuständigkeit zu vermeiden, wie etwa eine erhöhte Mehrheit oder eine vorherige Äußerung des Beraterrates des Generalsekretariats, während die diesbezügliche Zuständigkeit auch vom Parlamentsplenum ausgeübt werden könnte. Weder aber kann die Steuerverwaltung außerhalb des verfassungsrechtlichen Systems politischer Verantwortung bleiben noch können die Beziehungen zwischen Steuerverwaltung und den Verfassungsorganen ausschließlich von zweifelhaften Vermutungen[57] oder außerrechtlichen Regeln von Verfassungskorrektheit[58] geregelt werden.

V. Fazit und Ausblick

Die semi-autonome Steuerverwaltung, wie sie sich in Griechenland in den letzten Jahren gesetzlich ausgestaltet worden ist, bringt mit sich Chancen aber auch Risiken. Das Model des Generalsekretärs für öffentliche Einnahmen, der in der Struktur des Finanzministeriums eingegliedert ist, allerdings weitgehende Freiräume im Vergleich zu den sonstigen Generalsekretären genießt, verwirklicht die Zäsur zwischen Steuerpolitik und Steuerverwaltung. Vor dem Hintergrund langjähriger und weitgehender parteipolitischer Einflüsse in der Steuerverwaltung muss ihre Entpolitisierung als eine fundamentale Reform für den griechischen Staat begrüßt werden, die übrigens mit den internationalen Tendenzen auf diesem Bereich vereinbar ist. Überdies werden auf diese Weise die Voraussetzungen für die praktische Durchsetzung des verfassungsrechtlichen Grundsatzes der gleichen Teilnahme aller Staatsbürger an den öffentlichen Lasten (Art. 4 Abs. 5 Verf.) besser erfüllt.

Die gesetzliche Ausgestaltung der semi-autonomen Steuerverwaltung führt zu Abweichungen von etablierten Grundstrukturen des öffentlichen Rechts mit Blick sowohl auf die weitgehenden Befugnisse des Generalsekretärs für öffentliche Einnahmen als auch auf die eingeschränkten Kontrollmöglichkeiten anderer Organe. Verfassungsrechtlich geboten ist in dieser Hinsicht vor allem die Anwendung des Grundsatzes parlamentarischer Verantwortlichkeit. Angebracht ist insoweit die Ausgestaltung in der Geschäftsordnung des Parlaments effektiver, also mit Sanktionen ausgestatteter Möglichkeiten parlamentarischer Kontrolle, die von der Einladung des Generalsekretärs, um Erklärungen abzugeben und dem Zugang zu Dokumenten bis zur vorzeitigen Beendigung seiner Amtszeit hinausreichen. Auch vor dem Hin-

---

[56] Gemäß Art. 110 Abs. 1 Verf. können die Bestimmungen der Verfassung über die Staatsgrundlage und die Staatsform als parlamentarische Republik – ebenso die in diesem Artikel ausdrücklich aufgezählten Bestimmungen – nicht geändert werden.

[57] In diesem Sinne auch *Contiades*, oben Fn. 6, S. 134. Vgl. aber *A. Iliadou (A. Ηλιάδου)*, Η „ανεξαρτησία" των ανεξαρτήτων αρχών και η άσκηση ελέγχου επί των πράξεών τους (Die „Unabhängigkeit" der unabhängigen Behörden und die Ausübung von Kontrolle über ihre Handlungen), in: Kozyris/Megglidou, oben Fn. 49, S. 149–155 (151), die von der Bereitschaft der politisch ausgesetzten Mitglieder der unabhängigen Behörden ausgeht, „freiwillig" zurückzutreten.

[58] So für die unabhängigen Behörden *Papastylianos*, oben Fn. 48, S. 337.

tergrund der bisherigen Umgehung der einfachgesetzlichen Garantien der semi-autonomen Steuerverwaltung könnte überdies die Möglichkeit ihrer verfassungsrechtlichen Verankerung durch Verfassungsrevision in Betracht gezogen werden, um die Unabhängigkeit der Steuerverwaltung sicherzustellen als auch institutionelle und demokratisch vertretbare Gegengewichte zu schaffen.

Renewable Energy:
Structural Challenges for Administrative and Constitutional Law

By *Ekkehard Hofmann*

I. Introduction

For quite some years now, these have been and still are times of crisis, in particular for Greece. A considerable number of European states are in the process of reform and have to accomplish enormous tasks. While saving money, restructuring public spending, and reorganizing public administration are important and crucial goals, it is at the same time of essential value to identify areas in which there is a strong potential for development. For Greece one of these areas is – alongside with agriculture, pharmaceutical industry and tourism – the expansion of renewable energy sources for power generation, which would render both the private sector and the public sector more independent of fossil fuels and would contribute to the reduction of greenhouse gas emissions.

It is a field in which Greece may learn from mistakes of other European Countries including Germany. Germany is under great pressure to substitute its energy sources by renewable ones since the Federal Government has committed itself to shut down nuclear power plants until the year 2022. To reach this goal without the need to buy electricity from abroad represents already a significant challenge. The decrease of power consumption, by increasing for instance energy efficiency, is itself not sufficient. German power generation will have to get swiftly and massively reorganized. Moreover, the current power line grid will have to get adjusted, since it is designed to fit the old energy generation approach, rather than the new one that focuses on renewable energy sources.

In order to assess the potential of increasing renewable power sources and explain the factual background as regards energy generation in Europe as well as the potential of renewable energy, the article first outlines the mandatory and other political targets that European countries have committed themselves to (II.). It then proceeds to an overview of the European and Greek wind energy potential (III.). The third and main part of the paper addresses three different areas in which Germany's energy politics had to be corrected or is still deficient (IV.).

II. Mandatory and Other Political Targets

Currently in Europe, the production and consumption of energy mostly stems from fossil fuels and nuclear power. Nuclear power accounted in the year 2010 for 13.4%, fossil fuels (oil, coal and lignite, natural and derived gas combined) for 78%,[1] While only 8.4% come from other sources including biomass and hydro power (s. figure 1).

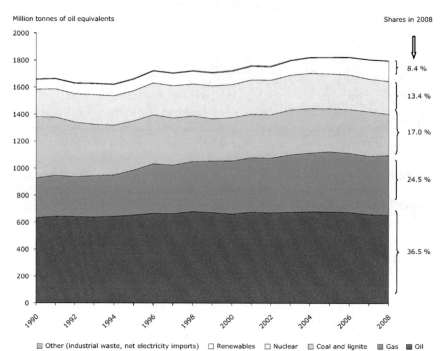

Fig. 1: Source: Primary energy consumption by fuel in the EU-27, 1990–2008 http://www.eea.europa.eu/data-and-maps/figures/primary-energy-consumption-by-fuel-1/ener26_-fig_01/image_original

Since this article focuses on electricity generation, the picture changes slightly as energy used in transport, which still relies almost completely on fossil fuels, is not considered. Even so, electricity generation shares show the domination of nuclear power and fossil fuels as well – in the year 2010, 20.9% renewable sources versus 50.9% fossil fuels (s. figure 2).

Given the current prevalence of fossil fuels, their replacement virtually requires to revolutionize the energy sector. Since Germany committed itself to terminate the use

---

[1] See http://www.eea.europa.eu/data-and-maps/figures/share-of-total-energy-consumption-1.

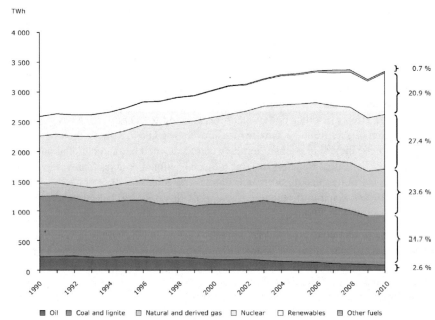

TWh

■ Oil ■ Coal and lignite ☐ Natural and derived gas ☐ Nuclear ☐ Renewables ■ Other fuels

Fig. 2: Source: Gross electricity production by fuel, EU-27, http://www.eea.europa.eu/data-and-maps/figures/gross-electricity-production-by-fuel-5

of nuclear power until 2022, it will have to replace around 29 % in less than 10 years from now. The European Union has also decided to aim for a 20 % percent share of renewable energy sources by 2020.[2] For the period from 2020 to 2030, the European Commission has presented a Communication that strives to continue the European Union's commitment to the substantial reduction of greenhouse gas emissions. However, the Commission's proposal places emphasis on member states' flexibility in the process of achieving reduction targets. Hence, the Communication does not comprise specific national targets for greenhouse gas emissions, renewable energy and energy savings. Instead, it relies upon a procedural approach during which national plans for competitive, secure and sustainable energy are subject to revision by the Commission.[3] This has been skeptically received by many observers since on the one hand it prudently allows for leeway in choosing the most cost efficient way to achieve the reduction targets, but on the other hand it grants Member States the opportunity to undermine the Union's ambition to achieve a domestic EU 40 % reduction of greenhouse gas emissions in 2030 as compared to emissions in 1990, and to replace carbon based energy production by nuclear power generation.[4]

---

[2] Cf. http://ec.europa.eu/clima/policies/package/index_en.htm (21.2.2014).

[3] European Commission, A policy framework for climate and energy in the period from 2020 to 2030, Communication of 22.1.2014, EU COM (2014) 15 final, pp. 12 and seq.

[4] European Commission, EU COM (2014) 15 final, p. 5.

In the framework of the currently applicable regime towards 2020, all European Union Member States have to rearrange their power generation and distribution. Directive 2009/28/EC calls for considerable efforts in the field of renewable energy; pursuant to article 4 of this Directive, each Member State shall adopt a national renewable energy action plan. These 'National Renewable Energy Action Plans' "shall set out Member States' national targets for the share of energy from renewable sources consumed in transport, electricity and heating and cooling in 2020, taking into account the effects of other policy measures relating to energy efficiency on final consumption of energy, and adequate measures to be taken to achieve those national overall targets, including cooperation between local, regional and national authorities, planned statistical transfers or joint projects, national policies to develop existing biomass resources and mobilise new biomass resources for different uses, and the measures to be taken to fulfil the requirements of Articles 13 to 19" (Article 1 para 1 of Directive 2009/28/EC).

Article 3 of Directive 2009/28/EC requires each Member State to ensure that the share of energy from renewable sources in gross final consumption of energy in 2020 reaches at least its national overall target for the share of energy from renewable sources in that year, which is set out in Annex I to the directive. Annex I stipulates shares of renewable energy in 2020, varying from 10 % for Malta to 40 % for Latvia. Germany and Greece both have mandatory targets of an 18 % share, meaning that renewable energy sources shall amount in 2020 to 18 % of the gross final consumption, and not just to 18 % of electricity generation. Given that Greece's share of energy from renewable sources in gross final consumption of energy accounted for 6.9 % in 2005, Greece is required to almost triple its renewable power consumption by 2020.[5]

In order to achieve these goals, the resubmitted Greek National Renewable Energy Action Plan (NREAP) of 2011 sets out a coherent concept of measures, comprising an array of different instruments, reaching from administrative procedures, spatial planning, and biogas integration into the natural gas network to district heating and cooling infrastructure development. All these measures mentioned in the Greek NREAP are supposed to contribute to the overall target of reaching a renewable energy share in final energy consumption of 20 %. Greek parliamentary law 3851/2010, which came into effect on June 4, 2010, renders this goal mandatory, and allows, inter alia, for the installation of wind farms for the production of electrical energy within the national sea territory.[6] Offshore and onshore wind energy play a major role in Greece in achieving the overall goals. Both in terms of installed capacity and gross electricity generation, Greece expects wind energy to be the greatest source of RES in the 2020 in Greece.[7] However, the Greek NREAP fails to quantify the ex-

---

[5] Directive 2009/28/EC, Annex I.

[6] Law 3851/2010, Art. 1 sec. 3 a); Art. 6 sec. 1.

[7] Greek NREAP, no year, table 10b.

pected respective shares of the included measures, making the plan somewhat less convincing.

The same applies, unfortunately, to the German NREAP. In contrast to other NREAPs (including the Greek NREAP[8]), the German NREAP aims to *reduce* the gross final energy consumption.[9] According to the plan, wind energy and photovoltaics shall account for the majority of RES generation as regards electric power (104 GWh/a resp. 41 GWh/a).[10] In the heating and cooling sector, biomass energy is dominating, complemented by a much smaller share of different kinds of heat pumps.[11]

III. Renewable Energy: European and Greek Potential

In Europe, the potential share of wind energy in the future mix of energy sources highly depends on the geographical location of wind energy sites. Wind power potential relies on wind speeds and the persistence of wind. Looking at Europe as a whole, there is no doubt that the greatest technical potential for onshore and offshore wind energy can be found in the North, mostly in agricultural and industrial northwestern areas.[12] The largest offshore-potential is situated in the North Sea, the Baltic Seas and the Atlantic Ocean. However, the European Energy Agency recognizes considerable potential in the Mediterranean Sea. Specifically for Greece, the Agency predicts a generation potential in the year 2030 of 566 TWh in total.[13] The largest share of which is deemed competitive (372 TWh).[14] These numbers even take into account constraints such as environmental protection and social factors that limit the unrestricted technical potential.

IV. Lessons Learned: the German Experience

In order to seize the potential to meet the political targets regarding the reduction of greenhouse gas emissions and the substitution of fossil and nuclear fuels, effective measures have to be planned and executed swiftly.

One of the presuppositions that call for attention is the potential bottleneck of adequate adjustment of the distribution grid to the specific demands of renewable energy, taking into consideration the features of wind energy generation, and especially

---

[8] Greek NREAP, no year, figure 3 – increase in estimated electricity generation.

[9] German Federal Government, NREAP Germany, no year, table 1.

[10] German Federal Government, NREAP Germany, no year, table 10a/b; cf. Greek NREAP, table 10a (Estimation of total contribution (installed capacity, gross electricity generation) expected from each renewable energy technology in Greece).

[11] German Federal Government, NREAP Germany, no year, table 11.

[12] EEA Technical Report 6/2009, Europe's onshore and offshore wind energy potential, An assessment of environmental and economic constraints, 2009, p. 24.

[13] EEA Technical Report 6/2009, p. 48, Table 6.8.

[14] EEA Technical Report 6/2009, p. 48, Table 6.8.

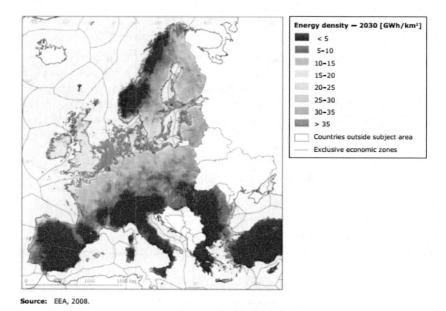

Source: EEA, 2008.

Fig. 3: Distribution of wind energy density (GWh/km²) in Europe for 2030
(80 m hub height onshore, 120 m hub height offshore)

the location of the power generation as well as the volatility of many renewable energy sources including wind power. In Germany, the current distribution grid reflects the needs of the "old" power generation structure, as most power plants are situated where the sources of energy is found and/or needed. In the West of Germany, this is mainly coal, in the East lignite, and in the South Nuclear Power. In the foreseeable future, a huge portion of power will be generated at places where no demand for electricity is, namely in the North (Sea). That entails the restructuring of the grid, and of course, construction of connections to and from the offshore wind farms, since a wind farm without a connecting line to the main distribution net does not make any sense, and vice versa. Greece may have to face similar problems concerning the connection to and from off-grid islands. How the specific adjustment of the distribution net is to be managed, depends on the structure of the relevant actors.

In Germany, there are four different distribution net operators (DNO) that are regional monopolists (TENNet, Elia, Amprion, EnBW). Of these four DNOs, two are responsible for offshore wind energy (TENNet for the North Sea; Elia for the Baltic Sea). TENNet and Elia are legally required to provide for a connection line between the general distribution net and the offshore wind farms that are to be built, which are owned and operated by other companies. That is why both actors, the DNOs on the one hand side and offshore wind farm operators (OWP) on the other, have to coordinate their tasks in order to make sure that the offshore-wind farms will be operational at the same time that the connection to the onshore distribution grid will be built (see below 2.). Time lags may heavily affect the economic soundness of these projects. The incurred planning processes are nothing like trivial, and many mistakes have been made in the recent past. In remaining part of the article, I elaborate three German conceptual shortcomings and their remedies.

1. Public Participation

The realization of large infrastructure projects such as airports, railway stations, or high voltage power lines takes a long time, and requires public decision makers to arrange a sequence of decisions on different levels. During that process, public opinion can change both in attitude and magnitude. Most types of large infrastructure projects, including energy generation and distribution, call for spatial planning at an early stage. The legislative process that sets the legal framework for these projects and precedes concrete planning acts on lower levels is political in nature and therefore mostly parliamentary, rather than administrative. With regard to the interest of the general public, spatial planning considerations are typically carried out without mandatory public participation. Final approval decisions, however, require the authorities to follow a four-tier-process. First, within a month after receiving the planning proposal, authorities shall gather the opinions of those authorities whose spheres of competence are affected by the project and shall make the plan available for inspection to the public, and more concretely to those communities the project is likely to have an impact on (Sec. 73 par. 2, 3 Administrative Procedure Act (APA), *Verwaltungsverfahrensgesetz*). Secondly, any person whose interests are affected by the project may place objections within two weeks starting at the end of the inspection period (Art. 73 par. 4 APA). Thirdly, authorities are required to execute a hearing, open to all persons who submitted objections, though not to the general public.

It is a specific feature of administrative procedure that the public – everyone – has the right to be informed at the beginning of planning procedures. However, the hearing that takes place before the final decision only includes persons whose rights might be affected by the project. The same applies to trials before administrative courts. Members of the public have no right to take actively part in the court proceedings, but shall only participate as observers.

This model represents the basic procedural structure to all final administrative approval decisions and their judicial review. With regard to offshore wind energy facilities, a whole sequence of public decisions needs to be followed before a wind turbine can be erected. This path of preparatory planning, necessary permits, and environmental impact assessments involves quite an array of public authorities. To initiate the planning process, the DNO is supposed to submit a scenario framework. A scenario is understood as a projection of likely developments (Section 12a par. 1 sentence 2 EnWG – *Energiewirtschaftsgesetz*, Energy Management Act), while the scenario framework is the basis for the so called net development plan and the offshore net development plan (Sections 12b, 17b EnWG), also provided by the DNOs. After official confirmation of the plan by the regulation authority, the federal requirements plan (*Bundesbedarfsplan*) is enacted by the federal legislator, i. e. federal parliament. The federal requirements plan defines which projects can be legally realized, but it does not determine the chronological order in which the offshore wind farms shall be erected. For almost every step along the way, some form of public participation is mandatory. Given that it is not only the turbines that need to be build, but also the subsea cable network that collects the electrical power generated, an impressive number of hearings and environmental impact assessment studies need to be carried out.

The fact that such a multifold of public decisions is subject to public participation can be attributed to the experience with other infrastructure projects that suffered from a lack of public acceptance in recent years. In particular, the conversion of a regional train terminus to a subterranean railway station in the South West of Germany, Stuttgart, gave rise to a heated political debate that might have even influenced, if not decided, the outcome of parliamentary elections. In the aftermath of the elections in Baden-Württemberg, lawmakers on state and federal level have enforced mandatory public participation, hoping to avoid such events in the future.[15]

2. Offshore-Grid-Connections

As to offshore-grid-connections, it is vital that the subsea cable, the grid connection as well as the wind turbines are completed and made ready for service at the same time. As mentioned above, the interdependence of the functioning of turbines and the grid connection is of eminent economic impact. Since it is so costly to build both, and given that the failure to provide a wind park with an operational connection to the grid may even render turbine erection projects economically unsound, the coordination of the two processes is imperative.

Before the amendment of the legal framework in December 2012,[16] the pacemaker function of the coordination was assigned to the OWP. Specifically, the OWP was entitled to a working power connection to the grid in the very moment it was ready to operate. To realize that entitlement in practice, the regulation agency and the DNO could ask the offshore wind park operator when the wind park would be expected to be up and running. From that starting point, the regulation agency and the DNO counted backwards 30 months because they assumed that the construction of the connection would take about 30 months. That coincided, luckily, with another interesting point of the chronological order of the whole process, namely with the purchase of the turbines by the OWP.

Unfortunately, after a while it turned out that the construction is more likely to take 45 to 50 months. Hence, a planning gap of roughly 18 months would result if the system still started counting when the turbines were purchased. Such a planning gap

---

[15] For the debate of these issues in legal scholarship, s. *Groß,* DÖV 2011, 510, 512; *Burgi,* NVwZ 2012, 277; *Durner,* ZUR 2011, 354; *Guckelberger,* NuR 2010, 835; *Gärditz,* GewArch 2011, 273; *Hofmann,* JZ 2012, 701; JZ 2012, *Gurlit,* JZ 2012, 833.

[16] Article 1 Law of 20. 12. 2012 BGBl. I, 2730.

would jeopardize many turbine erection projects since wind farms without a connection to the main grid would lose money and thus scare investors away. As a consequence, the legal framework was completely changed: currently, it is not the offshore wind farm operators that determine the speed of the development of offshore wind energy, but the net – and thus the Distribution Net Operator, and more specifically, the net development plan written by the DNOs. That means the DNOs provide a plan featuring a timeline for the grid connections that determines when each OWP will obtain its grid connection. In order to make that process transparent and predictable, 30 months before the expected date of completion the plan becomes binding. The binding date entails a right to damages for the OWP if the completion date is not met.

To summarize, coordination of the two planning processes is key to swift and efficient offshore wind energy development. Since it is vital to provide offshore wind energy investors with a reliable legal, technical and economic background, the assignment to the OWP of a pacemaker function for the extension of wind farms seemed like a feasible option. However, the system that relied on OWP's purchase of wind turbines turned out to be an unsuitable signal for the planning of the connection to the grid. As no other point in time seemed likely to fit the requirements, the legislative reverted the system that is now focusing on the planning of the grid connections.

3. Judicial Review of Planning Decisions

With regard to judicial protection against decisions that are deemed wrongful or illegal, the German approach features only limited options that are mostly due to the aforementioned legal framework. As explained above, there are four major different regulatory requirements that need to be met before an offshore-wind power plant can start producing energy: the official confirmation of the NDP by the regulation agency, coherence with a parliamentary act (Federal Requirement Plan), coherence with the "Federal Spatial Plan Offshore", and lastly the final approval decision that needs to take into account all other requirements on the concrete level.

The official confirmation by the regulation agency cannot be challenged separately before an administrative court, nor does the 'Federal Spatial Plan Offshore' (Sec. 17a par. 5, 17c EnWG). That leaves only the Federal Requirement Plan and the final approval decisions open to judicial review. The Federal Requirement Plan is, however, an act of parliament, and is thus only subject to review by the Federal constitutional court. This raises the question whether planning decisions can be constitutionally enacted as parliamentary acts such as the Federal Requirement Plan.

a) Legality of a Plan as a Federal Parliamentary Act?

Pursuant to the German Federal Constitutional Court, the principle of effective judicial remedy through administrative courts, stipulated in Art. 19 sec. 4 of the German Constitution, does not apply to legislative acts. Thus, the German constitution does not call for a judicial review of parliamentary acts by courts other than the Federal Constitutional Court. On the contrary, Art. 100 of the German Constitution reserves the right to the Federal Constitutional Court to declare parliamentary acts unconstitutional. There are several procedural ways of bringing laws for review before the Federal Constitutional court. The practically most important option is represented by Art. 100 of the German Constitution itself, which grants every regular court the right to refer a law to the Constitutional Court if the referring court is convinced the stipulation in question is unconstitutional. Nevertheless, no constitutional issue with the principle of judicial remedy arises when a planning decision is taken in the form of a parliamentary act.[17]

Planning decisions in the form of parliamentary acts may, however, conflict with the principle of separation of powers, as concrete provisions regarding the clearance of specific wind turbine projects for further licensing, appears to be a task for the executive branch of government. The Federal Constitutional Court does accept, however, planning decisions as parliamentary acts with regard to the principle of separation of powers. Nevertheless, it assumes that a legislator who substitutes an administrative body has to follow the principles that normally guide the actions of executive planning authorities.[18] According to the court's opinion, judicial review is meant to guarantee that the legislator relied on a complete analysis of facts and made the deliberation transparent.[19] Furthermore, the Court will only reject a planning act as unconstitutional if, and only if, the decision is evidently faulty or it conflicts with constitutional principles.

One such principles may be the prohibition of single case acts (Art. 19 para 1 sentence 1 of the German Constitution). Nevertheless, single case decisions (individual and concrete) by parliament are in principle constitutional. Even takings can be performed by parliamentary acts. However, single case decisions must be the exception, not the rule, since parliaments are constitutionally supposed to enact abstract rules. Moreover, the Court argues that planning was not per se a field in which a parliament could not act; parliaments were able to come to independent and constructive decisions.[20] If and when a parliament acts as an administrative agency, the Federal Constitutional Court indeed purports to apply a higher standard of review, much like the one applied by administrative courts.[21] If this will hold for the future Federal Requirement Act for Wind energy, remains to be seen. It seems uncertain whether the constitutional court will really apply higher standards of review.

---

[17] BVerfGE 95, 1, 15.

[18] BVerfGE 95, 1, 23.

[19] BVerfGE 95, 1, 23.

[20] BVerfGE 95, 1, 17.

[21] BVerfGE 86, 90 (107 ff.); confirmed by ruling of 19. 11. 2002 (NVwZ 2003, 850–855).

b) Modified Standards of Review
due to moving planning decisions to the legislative level

"Upgrading" to a higher level, i.e, to the level of parliamentary act, requires a constitutional justification since it generally brings about a reduced judicial review, given that administrative courts do not get access to such acts. In the area of highway planning, the justification was found in an expected acceleration of planning procedures.[22] This might not apply to wind energy planning since the pace of offshore wind energy development is mostly determined by the long term timeline provided by the offshore development plan, and not by court proceedings. Nevertheless, the court argues that the lack of judicial review by administrative courts might be compensated by higher standards of review before the Federal Constitutional Court.[23]

c) Postponement of judicial review

Since there is no judicial review of neither the confirmation of the net development plan nor of the Federal spatial plan, judicial action is limited to either a constitutional review of the parliamentary acts or to an administrative court review of final approval decisions. In particular, the exclusion of the confirmation of the net development plan from judicial review is highly problematic. The review of the Federal Requirement Plan is determined mainly by constitutional standards, thereby focusing on the results, instead of on the reasoning of the decision. Judicial review of the final approval decisions by administrative courts may come too late for many investors, and therefore, correction of errors may hardly be possible. Moreover, investors may shy away from offshore wind energy projects. But most importantly: there is no sufficient justification for the postponement of judicial review since there will be no acceleration effects nor a higher level of expertise that justifies the postponement.

V. Summary and Outlook

During times of social and state expenditure crises, austerity policies alone will not bring about the desired societal change. It is, on the contrary, quite risky to excessively cut public and private expenditures since that kind of policy undermines political support for necessary, yet tough, measures and fosters political extremism. Therefore, projects which warrant a positive outlook that make the dire present more endurable are not only imperative in dealing with the crisis, but may also help building a sustainable economic and ecologic condition in the long term. One of these sectors might be identified in the field of energy generation and distribution.

Apart from considerable potential regarding the use of hydrothermal energy for hot water generation and heating purposes that may even reduce Greece's depend-

---

[22] BVerfGE 95, 1, 23.
[23] BVerfGE 95, 1, 23.

ence on fossil fuel imports, Greece features substantial possibilities with regard to the expansion of wind energy. Wind energy is supposed to play an important role in reaching Europe's greenhouse gas reduction targets as set forth by directive 2009/28/EC and its likely successors, but at the same time it entails demanding political, technical and economical tasks. Given the trial and error nature of such processes, Greece may learn from the mistakes of other countries in this area. Judging from the German experience, large infrastructure processes need to be carried out in a transparent, reliable and open manner. In particular, it seems vital to take public participation seriously into account if public agencies, private investors, and other concerned parties are to achieve convincing results in a timely manner. Offshore grid connections are laden with particular and crucial issues concerning the coordination of distribution net operators on the one hand side and offshore wind park owners on the other. Germany had practically to reverse the relevant legal framework in order to achieve a working concept, now employing a sophisticated planning scheme that determines the chronological order of expansion projects. Finally, evading judicial review of essential planning decisions is one Germany's legislator typical reaction to (perceived or true) time pressure. This approach can be confronted with skepticism, though, as it increases the likelihood of wrongful administrative choices and disregards the possibilities that court procedures bring about in terms of further deliberation on one of the biggest environmental challenges of our times.

Privatisierung als Reformkonzept

Von *Athanasios Gromitsaris*

I. Eine eigentümliche Pendelbewegung

Privatisierungen betreffen die Problematik der Natur und Abgrenzung der öffentlichen Hand. Das wird daran deutlich, dass bei wichtigen Privatisierungsprojekten in Bereichen, welche traditionell dem öffentlichen Sektor zugeordnet werden, zuvor eine Änderung der Verfassung vorgenommen werden musste. Auch mussten neue Regulierungsaufträge im Anschluss an Privatisierungen und Liberalisierungen im Bereich der Netzwirtschaften verfassungsrechtlich verankert werden. Man denke etwa an Art. 87 sowie an Art. 87e IV und Art. 87 f I des Grundgesetzes.[1] Eine eigentümliche Pendelbewegung lässt sich in Europa seit den 90er Jahren feststellen. Zu Beginn schlug das Pendel zugunsten privater Rechtsformen von Versorgungsleistungen aus. In letzter Zeit gibt es einen Trend zur Rekommunalisierung bzw. Rückverstaatlichung. Juristisch gesehen geht es um einen Prozess der „Verstaatlichung".[2] Private Betreiber erwiesen sich z. T. teurer als die öffentliche Hand, während sich die Dienstleistungsqualität nicht wie versprochen verbessern konnte. In Großbritannien und Estland wurden Teile des Eisenbahnnetzes wieder in staatlichen Besitz übernommen, in Deutschland haben eine Reihe von Kommunen in den letzten Jahren privatisierte Dienste rekommunalisiert. Paris und Berlin nahmen die Wasserversorgung in kommunale Hand zurück.[3]

Mit dieser Pendelbewegung werden finanzielle, politische und Modernisierungserwartungen verbunden. Angesichts der Staatsverschuldung spielen Erwartungen in finanzieller Hinsicht eine wichtige Rolle. Privatisierungen versprechen privates Geld ohne Staatsverschuldung. Der Staat eigne sich nicht als Unternehmer. Es bestehe ein zu hohes Risiko, dass staatlich bestimmte Betriebe politischen Vorgaben folgen und Marktkräfte ignorieren. Mit Privatisierungen könnten hingegen verschuldete Staaten auch die „Glaubwürdigkeit ihrer Programme zur Haushaltssanierung dokumentieren und damit ein wichtiges Signal für internationale Anleiheinvestoren setzen".[4] Selbst

---

[1] Gemäß Art. 87e IV GG gewährleistet der Bund dauerhaft die Sicherung eines angemessenen Verkehrsangebots, wofür er eigene Eisenbahnverkehrsunternehmen einsetzen muss, solange sich keine privaten Wettbewerber finden.

[2] *Jörn Ipsen,* Hrsg., Rekommunalisierung von Versorgungsleistungen? Göttingen 2012.

[3] Ende der neunziger Jahre wurden 49,9 Prozent der Berliner Wasserbetriebe an den französischen Versorger Veolia und den RWE-Konzern verkauft.

[4] *Dieter Bräuninger,* Privatisierung im Eurogebiet. Unterschiedlicher Umgang mit Staatsbesitz, Deutsche Bank, Research Briefing, 11. Juli 2013, S. 2.

wenn Marktversagen vorlägen, könne der Staat nicht durch eigene Wirtschaftstätigkeit, sondern durch richtige Regulierung marktähnliche Verhältnisse für private Wirtschaftstätigkeit schaffen.[5] Was die politischen Erwartungen angeht, gibt es – je nach politischer Orientierung – einen politischen Wunsch nach „mehr Privat" bzw. nach „mehr Staat/Kommune". Dies wird teilweise durch Bürgerbegehren und durch einen Hinweis auf Aufgaben unterstützt, die nicht privatisiert werden können oder sollen, z. B. Widerstand gegen Wasserprivatisierung.[6] Dies wird zum Teil auch durch geopolitische (Verschwörungs-)Theorien gegen Privatisierung unterstützt, die durch die Finanz- und Verschuldungskrise noch verstärkt werden.[7] Auch werden die „Realitäten" der Privatisierung mit ihrer „Ideologie" und insbesondere mit „Theorien über Antriebskräfte der Privatisierung" verglichen.[8] Thematisiert wird schließlich eine Output-Legitimation von Privatisierungen.[9] Rückverstaatlichungen versprechen ihrerseits, dass der Staat doch kostengünstiger und sogar adäquater als die private Wirtschaft öffentliche Aufgaben erfüllen kann. Privatisierung und Rückverstaatlichung sind allerdings keine Gegensätze, sofern an dem zu privatisierenden Objekt der Staat beteiligt bleibt oder im Falle der Verstaatlichung am verstaatlichten Objekt private Unternehmen beteiligt werden oder bleiben. Auf diese Weise entstehen verschiedene Kooperations- und Vertragsmodelle von Öffentlich-Privaten Partnerschaften.

Es steht zwar fest, dass Gemeinwohlförderung sowohl bei Privatisierung als auch bei Rückverstaatlichung durch rechtliche Vorkehrungen zu gewährleisten ist. Dies ist aber nicht der Ausgangspunkt dieses Beitrags, dem es um Privatisierungen in Griechenland geht. Die Fragestellung lautet vielmehr: Wie sind Privatisierungen in einem

---

[5] Deutsche Bank Research, Erlöse, Wettbewerb, Wachstum. Möglichkeiten der Privatisierung im Eurogebiet, 20. Oktober 2011, S. 2.

[6] EU-Dienstleistungskonzessions-Richtlinie: Michel Barnier lenkt ein: http://www.wasser-in-buergerhand.de/nachrichten/2013/eu_dienstleistungsrichtlinie_barnier_lenkt_ein.htm. Kontrolldefizite im Wasserbereich wurden früh genug festgestellt: *Cour des Comptes,* La gestion des services publics d'eau et d'assainissement, Décembre 2003; *Martin Pigeon/David A. McDonald/Olivier Hoedeman/Satoko Kishimoto* (Hrsg.), Putting Water Back Into Public Hands, Amsterdam 2012; *David Hachfeld,* The Remunicipalisation of Water. Some Reflections on the Cases of Potsdam and Grenoble, August 2008, http://www.municipal servicesproject.org/publication/remunicipalisation-water-%E2%80%93-some-reflections-cases-potsdam-and-grenoble spricht von „global struggles for the social appropriation of Water".

[7] Zu einer „Verschwörungstheorie" aus der Sicht von Joseph Stiglitz s. *Gregory Palast*, IMF's four steps to damnation. How crises, failures, and suffering finally drove a Presidential adviser to the wrong side of the barricades, in: The Observer, Sunday 29 April 2001. Siehe ferner *Greg Palast:* Why Are the Greek People Agreeing to Their Own Destruction? By Michael Nevradakis, Truthout | Interview http://www.truth-out.org/news/item/18069-why-are-the-greek-people-agreeing-to-their-own-destruction.

[8] *Tanja Pflug,* Ideology, the Politburo of Privatisation and the German Water Sector, in: Transfer: European Review of Labour and Research 2008 14: 259 http://trs.sagepub.com/content/14/2/259.

[9] Rechtsvergleichend: *Johann Wackerbauer,* The Regulation and Privatisation of the Public Water Supply and the Resulting Competitive Effects, CeSifo DICE Report 4/2006, 42–49.

hochverschuldeten, mit schwachen staatlichen Institutionen ausgestatteten Land, in dem es an einem Gewährleistungsstaat fehlt, möglich? Es wird folgende Vorgehensweise gewählt: Zunächst wird auf die Anforderungen eingegangen, die ein normalerweise unter Bedingungen der Rechtsstaatlichkeit operierender Gewährleistungsstaat an Privatisierungs- und Rückverstaatlichungsprozesse stellt. In einem zweiten Schritt werden die Besonderheiten der griechischen Verhältnisse dargelegt. Diese Vorgehensweise macht es möglich, Privatisierungshindernisse und Argumentationsschwerpunkte der juristischen Debatte herauszustellen.

II. Privatisierungsfolgenrecht
und staatlicher Regulierungsauftrag

Die Kartierung von Erwartungen und Befürchtungen mit Blick auf Privatisierung gehört nicht nur der Sphäre der Politik an, sondern sie dient auch „als Fundus für etwaige Rechtsprobleme".[10] Nationale Verfassungen ziehen der Privatisierung Grenzen: Grundsätzlich sind die Aufgaben der Ordnungs- und Abgabenverwaltung und damit der Eingriffsverwaltung nicht privatisierbar.[11] Die für Privatisierung sprechenden Gründe wurden immer wieder bei der Einführung diverser Liberalisierungspläne der EU-Kommission diskutiert. Die Legitimierung für die Entflechtungspläne im Energiebereich ist etwa spätestens seit 2007 bekannt. Bei vertikal integrierten Energieunternehmen bestand nach Ansicht der Kommission die Gefahr einer Diskriminierung Dritter bei der Ausübung des Netzbetriebs. Auch fehlte der Anreiz für die integrierten Netzeigentümer, ausreichend in ihre Netze zu investieren. Als zweitbeste Alternative zur Eigentumsentflechtung sollten die Mitgliedstaaten eine vollständige Übertragung des Netzbetriebs an einen vom bisherigen integrierten Unternehmen unabhängigen Dritten anordnen können. Hiernach könne der Konzern zwar Eigentümer des Netzes bleiben. Er verliere aber jegliche Einwirkungsmöglichkeiten.[12] Im Rahmen der hieran angeschlossenen Debatte wurde die Eigentumsrechtsdogmatik in Deutschland und Frankreich dafür mobilisiert, die Eigentumsentflechtungsmodelle am Maßstab der Erforderlichkeit und Angemessenheit einer Eigentumsentziehung scheitern zu lassen. Verneint wurde auch schon die Zuständigkeit der Gemeinschaft für die Eigentumsentflechtungsmaßnahmen, d. h. ihre Kompetenzgrundlage für Enteignungen zulasten mitgliedstaatlich konstituierter Vermögensrechtspositionen.[13]

---

[10] *Martin Burgi,* Gutachten für den 67. Deutschen Juristentag, Band I: Gutachten / Teil D: Privatisierung öffentlicher Aufgaben Erfurt 2008, S. 21.

[11] *Hartmut Maurer,* Die verfassungsrechtlichen Grenzen der Privatisierung in Deutschland, Juridica International XVI/2009, S. 1–13.

[12] BVerfG – 1 BvR 699/06 (22.2.2011) http://eur-lex.europa.eu/JOHtml.do?uri=OJ:L:2009: 211:SOM:DE:HTML.

[13] Siehe etwa aus der damaligen Veröffentlichungslawine *Schmidt-Preuß,* Der Wandel der Energiewirtschaft vor dem Hintergrund der Europäischen Eigentumsordnung, Europarecht 2006, 463; *Kahle,* Die eigentumsrechtliche Entflechtung der Energieversorgungsnetze aus europarechtlicher und verfassungsrechtlicher Sicht, Recht der Energiewirtschaft (RdE) 2007,

Die von der EU-Kommission erarbeiteten Eisenbahnpakete sind ein weiterer Anlass zur Darlegung und Darstellung der für mehr Wettbewerb sprechenden Gründe.[14] Die Eisenbahnpläne sollen den Eisenbahnverkehr den Anforderungen eines offenen Marktes anpassen, die Europäische Eisenbahnagentur als Koordinationsstelle stärken, die Mitgliedstaaten zur Öffnung der Verkehrsmärkte zwingen sowie die Verkehrs- und Infrastrukturunternehmungen voneinander trennen. Derartige Trennungen von Netzbetrieb und netzgebundener Leistungserbringung stoßen in den verschiedenen Bereichen der Netzwirtschaften auf Widerstand. Der EuGH toleriert die Umsetzung von Entflechtungsvorgaben für Unternehmensbestandteile in den Fällen, in denen sich Staaten für Holdingmodelle und damit vertikal integrierte Unternehmensstrukturen entschieden haben.[15] Die EU-Kommission will, dass bestimmte als wesentlich erachtete Funktionen[16] nicht mehr von den traditionellen Eisenbahnunternehmen der Mitgliedstaaten wahrgenommen werden, sondern unabhängigen Betreibern übertragen werden. Zu diesen Funktionen gehören die Erteilung von Genehmigungen für Eisenbahnunternehmen, die ihnen Zugang zum Eisenbahnnetz verschaffen, die Zuweisung von Zugtrassen und die Berechnung[17] des von den Eisenbahnverkehrsunternehmen für die Netznutzung zu entrichtenden Entgelts. Die Kommission will darüber hinaus generell Intransparenz und Korruption bei allen öffentlichen Vergaben bekämpfen.

1. Verfassungsrechtliche Vorgaben

Verfassungsrechtliche Vorgaben müssen von Privatisierungsmaßnahmen und Public Private Partnerships (PPP) beachtet werden. Art. 20 II GG verlangt, dass der öffentlichen Hand Steuerungsmöglichkeiten verbleiben müssen. Das Demokratieprinzip erlegt dem Staat eine Gewährleistungsverantwortung auf, die bei funktionaler Privatisierung die Sicherung angemessener Einflussrechte der öffentlichen Hand auf das private Rechtssubjekt verlangt (Ausgleich, Vermeidung von privatisierungsbedingten „Einflussknicken"[18]). Art. 28 II GG gilt überwiegend als Organisa-

---

293. Kritisch zu diesen Widerständen: *Alan Riley,* Ownership Unbundling. A Logic Outage for the Anti-Energy Liberalisers? in: CEPS Commentary/8 April 2008.

[14] Das vierte Eisenbahnpaket – Vollendung des einheitlichen europäischen Eisenbahnraums zur Steigerung von Wettbewerbsfähigkeit und Wachstum in der EU: Brüssel, den 30. 1. 2013, COM(2013) 25 final.

[15] Siehe die Urteile in den Rechtssachen vom 5. 4. 2013: C-473/10 Kommission/Ungarn, C-483/10 Kommission/Spanien, C-555/10 Kommission/Österreich und C-556/10 Kommission/Deutschland.

[16] *Leitzke/Schmitt,* Annäherung an ein semantisches Chamäleon: Der „neue" Eisenbahninfrastrukturbegriff, IR 2006, 131 ff.

[17] *Kühling/Hermeier/Heimeshoff,* Gutachten zur Klärung von Entgeltfragen nach AEG und EIBV, Bonn 2007, abrufbar unter http://www.bundesnetzagentur.de/SharedDocs/Downloads/DE/Sachgebiete/Eisenbahn/Unternehmen_Institutionen/VeroeffentlichungenGutachten/Gutach tenEntgeltfragenLangId10175pdf.pdf?__blob=publicationFile&v=3.

[18] *Peter M. Huber,* Die entfesselte Verwaltung, StWStP 8 (1997), S 423 ff., 424.

tionsnorm. Die privatwirtschaftliche Betätigung der Gemeinde gilt nur bei Verknüpfung mit einem öffentlichen Zweck, weshalb rein auf Gewinnerzielung ausgerichtete Tätigkeiten unzulässig sind. Art. 33 IV GG verlangt, dass Hoheits- und Grundrechtseingriffsbefugnisse nicht auf Dauer und umfänglich von Privaten ausgeübt werden[19], was etwa bei PPP im Bereich des Strafvollzugs[20] von Bedeutung wäre. Ausnahmen werden nicht generell und von vornherein ausgeschlossen (Formulierung: „in der Regel").[21] Ferner resultieren Grenzen für gemischtwirtschaftliche Projektgesellschaften aus Art. 86 ff. GG. Denn es gibt Reservatbereiche staatlicher Verwaltung insofern, als der Kernbereich der Regelmaterie für den Privatsektor nicht geöffnet werden kann.[22] Wie Gemeinden ihre örtlichen Aufgaben erfüllen – in Form von PPP oder nicht – steht ihnen nach Art. 28 Abs. 2 GG frei. Die kommunale Gewährleistungsverantwortung ist auch als gesamtstaatliche Verantwortung im Sozialstaatsprinzip (Art. 20 Abs. 1 GG) zu verorten. Der Grundsatz der ohne Einnahmen aus Krediten ausgeglichenen Haushalte (Art. 109 III 1 GG) bezieht sich auf finanzielle Zuflüsse, die vertragliche Rückzahlungsansprühe mit sich bringen und nicht der Umschuldung dienen. Warenkredite und Verwaltungsschulden sind nicht unter „Einnahmen aus Krediten" zu subsumieren. Ob „neuartige Finanzierungsinstrumente", zu denen Leasinggeschäfte, Forfaitierung, Rückmietverkauf, Park- oder Platzgeschäfte oder PPP-Finanzierungen gehören, als Einnahmen aus Krediten zu verstehen sind, beurteilt sich danach, ob hierdurch langfristig laufende Zahlungsverpflichtungen für die öffentliche Hand begründet werden. Der Kreditbegriff[23] erstreckt sich dann

---

[19] *Martin Burgi*, Privatisierung öffentlicher Aufgaben-Gestaltungsmöglichkeiten, Grenzen, Regelungsbedarf, Gutachten für den 67. DJT, München 2008, S. 31 ff., 37 ff.; *Rolf Stober*, Privatisierung öffentlicher Aufgaben, Phantomdiskussion oder Gestaltungsoption in einer verantwortungsgeteilten, offenen Wirtschafts-, Sozial-, und Sicherheitsverfassung?, NJW 2008, 2301 ff., 2306.

[20] *Friederike Edel/Birgit Grüb*, PPP im Bereich der Justizvollzugsanstalten, WM 2010, 42 ff.

[21] *Jürgen Kühling/Thomas Schreiner*, Grundprobleme von Public Private Partnerships, ZJS 2011, 112 ff., 113.

[22] *Michael Schäfer/Stephanie Thiersch*, Rechtliche Rahmenbedingungen, in: Weber/Schäfer/Hausmann (Hrsg.), Praxishandbuch Public Private Partnership, München 2006, 85 ff., 98 ff.

[23] Abgesehen von der Kommentierung der Art. 109 und 115 GG ist der Kreditbegriff auch aus englischer Sicht ein Problem: http://www.publications.parliament.uk/pa/cm201012/cmselect/cmtreasy/1146/1146.pdf at p. 11: „One of the written submissions to the Committee noted that ‚Greece, Spain, Portugal and Ireland have all in recent years been very active in PFI/PPP'." In 2005 for example Greece in troduced a new ‚PPP law' and two new government bodies were set up to encourage and expand the use of Public Private Partnerships. The use of other off balance sheet financing methods deployed by governments to circumvent fiscal rules have been noted. The Financial Times reported that in 2002 Goldman Sachs had helped Greece raise off balance sheet finance „by arranging a massive swaps transaction aimed at reducing the cost of financing". The press report explained: „Because it was treated as a currency trade rather than a loan, it helped Greece to meet European Union deficit limits while pushing repayments far into the future." Vgl. ferner *Sarah Levy*, Kreditrechtliche Aspekte von Public Private Partnership Hochbauprojekten am Beispiel des Kantons Bern, Bern 2008.

auch auf Endschaftszahlungen. Kommunalrechtlich sind PPP als aufsichtsrechtlich genehmigungsbedürftige „kreditähnliche Rechtsgeschäfte" einzustufen.[24] Wirtschaftlichkeitsuntersuchungen sind durchzuführen.[25]

2. Vergabe- und beihilferechtliche Vorkehrungen

Privatisierungsverfahren müssen Vergabe- und Beihilferecht beachten. Im Rahmen der Modernisierung des EU-Vergaberechts[26] hat eine Verbesserung des Zugangs für kleine und mittlere Unternehmen – was für die in Rezession befindlichen Staaten von besonderer Bedeutung ist – zu den Vergabeverfahren stattgefunden. Die allgemeine Gruppenfreistellungsverordnung und die besonderen Regelwerke zu den einzelnen Beihilfearten haben bereits Beihilfen mit erwünschtem Anreizeffekt zur Entwicklung wirtschaftlicher Tätigkeit berücksichtigt. Das Vergaberecht findet auch dann Anwendung, wenn Waren und Dienstleistungen von der öffentlichen Hand nachgefragt werden, die nach der Privatisierung vom privatisierten Unternehmen angeboten werden. Zusätzlich sind mögliche Zustandsveränderungen des Vertragspartners des Staates im Laufe des Privatisierungsprozesses in Betracht zu ziehen: Es müssen die Risiken berücksichtigt werden, die mit seiner Stellung im Erwerberkonzern zusammenhängen (etwa Ergebnisabführungsverträge, die seine finanzielle Selbständigkeit gefährden können).[27] Die Fallgruppen sind bekannt: Wichtig ist zunächst die Frage, inwieweit ein Auftraggeber im Rahmen eines Verhandlungsverfahrens Elemente (etwa das ausgeschriebene Leistungsvolumen) verändern darf.[28] Jed-

---

[24] Urteil des BGH vom 12.12.2002 – III ZR 201/01, „Oderwitz". NRW entgeht dem Risiko einer Amtspflichtverletzung dadurch, dass es lediglich eine Anzeigepflicht für kreditähnliche Rechtsgeschäfte statuiert (§ 86 IV 1 GemO NRW).

[25] *Holger Mühlenkamp,* Ökonomische Anlyse von Public Private Partnerships (PPP)-PPP als Instrument zur Steigerung der Effizien der Wahrnehmung öffentlicher Aufgaben oder als Weg zur Umgehung von Budgebeschränkungen?, in: Jan Ziekow (Hrsg.), Wandel der Staatlichkeit und wieder zurück?, 2011, S. 67 ff.

[26] Richtlinie über die Vergabe öffentlicher Aufträge Richtlinie (RL 2014/24/EU, ersetzt die bisherige Vergabekoordinierungsrichtlinie 2004/18/EG); Richtlinie über die Vergabe von Aufträgen durch Auftraggeber im Bereich der Wasser-, Energie- und Verkehrsversorgung sowie der Postdienste (Sektoren-Richtlinie, RL 2014/25/EU, ersetzt Richtlinie 2004/17/EG); Richtlinie über die Konzessionsvergabe (neue Konzessions-Richtlinie, RL 2014/23/EU).

[27] S. etwa EuGH 10.11.05, Rs. C-29/04, Slg. 2005, I-9722, Stadt Mödling; EuGH 6.4.06, Rs. C-410/04, Slg. 2006, I-3311, ANAV; *Franz-Jürgen Säcker/Maik Wolf,* Die Auswirkungen der Rechtsprechung des EuGH zu In-House-Geschäften auf PPP, WRP 2007, 282 ff.

[28] Zu „post-tender negotiations" s. *Demetris Savvides,* The Effectiveness of the Competitive Dialogue Procedure under the EU Consolidated Public Procurement Directive (2004/18/EC) as an Award Procedure for Public Private Partnerships, EPPPL 2011, 23 ff. Ferner s. die Rechtsprechungsübersicht *Christopher Bovis,* New Directions in PPP: Judicial Developments from the ECJ, EPPPL 2011, 1 ff.; *Jürgen Kühling,* Künftige vergaberechtliche Anforderungen an kommunale Immobiliengeschäfte, NVwZ 2010, 1257; *Catharina Erps,* Kommunale Kooperationshoheit und europäisches Vergaberecht, Stuttgart/München 2010, S. 210 ff.; *Rainer Burbulla,* Die Ausschreibung von PPP-Projekten, NJOZ 2008, 211 ff.; *Dietrich Drömann,*

wede Änderung darf die Chance der zurückgestellten Bieter auf Erhalt des Zuschlags nicht beeinträchtigen.[29] Auch ist eine wesentliche Vertragsänderung während der Vertragslaufzeit, die Bedingungen einführt, welche die Zulassung anderer als der ursprünglich zugelassenen Bieter erlaubt hätte, wenn sie Gegenstand des ursprünglichen Vergabeverfahrens gewesen wäre, ausschreibungspflichtig. Wenn die Anteilsveräußerung des beauftragten Dienstleistungserbringers die Eigenleistung in Fremdleistung umwandelt, ist dies eine wesentliche Änderung.

Hinzukommt, dass Privatisierungen mit einem nunmehr stärker wirtschaftsorientierten[30] Beihilferecht konform[31] sein müssen. Die Novellierung der Beihilfeverfahrensordnung gibt der Kommission mehr Ermittlungsbefugnisse und Markterkundungsinstrumente an die Hand. Ende Mai 2014 hat die EU-Kommission eine Mitteilung angenommen, mit der Transparenzanforderungen für alle kürzlich geänderten Beihilfevorschriften harmonisiert werden.[32] Subventionierungen durch nicht marktkonformen Kaufpreis oder durch nicht marktkonforme sonstige Kaufbedingungen sind unzulässig. Verstöße gegen das zwingende Beihilfeverbot haben eine Nichtigkeit des Privatisierungsdurchführungsgeschäfts zur Folge. Eine Anteilsveräußerung muss zu einem Marktpreis erfolgen, der entweder durch den Gang an die Börse oder die Durchführung eines Bieteverfahrens oder durch die gutachterliche Bestätigung eines unabhängigen Sachverständigen ermittelt werden kann. Problematisch sind ferner die für PPP wichtigen Mehrfachbeteiligungen von Unternehmen und Banken.[33] Bei Indizien oder Auffälligkeiten hat die Vergabestelle diesen nachzugehen und bei Erhärtung des Verdachts die Beteiligten auszuschließen oder das Verfahren aufzuheben.[34] Als ein sinnvolles Instrumentarium zur Sicherstellung des Geheimwettbewerbs in diesen Situationen wurde die Einholung einer Vertraulichkeitserklä-

---

Wettbewerblicher Dialog und ÖPP-Beschaffungen – Zur „besonderen Komplexität" so genannter Betreibermodelle, NZBau 2007, 7, 51 ff.

[29] OLG Düsseldorf, Beschluss vom 5. Januar 2011 – Verg 46/10. Alle für die Zuschlagsentscheidung maßgeblichen Umstände müssen den Bietern so bekannt gemacht werden, dass sie bei Anwendung der üblichen Sorgfalt deren genaue Bedeutung verstehen und in gleicher Weise auslegen können; *EPEC*, Procurement of PPP and the use of Competitive Dialogue in Europe. A review of public sector practices across the EU, 2010, p. 7.

[30] State Aid Modernisation (SAM) Modernisierung des EU-Beihilferechts, Brüssel, den 8. 5. 2012 COM(2012) 209 final.

[31] Hierzu *Christoph von Donat*, IÖPP zwischen Vergaberecht und EU Beihilferecht, EuZW 2010, 812 ff.; *Lorenz Jellinghaus*, Zum Verhältnis von Vergabe- und Beihilferecht bei ÖPP Projekten, VergabeR 2010, 574 ff.; *ders.*, Beihilfenkonform Verwirklichung von Infrastrukturvorhaben, IR 2009, 293 ff. Wenn Infrastrukturen gewerblich genutzt werden sollen, sind die Beihilfevorschriften ohnehin zu beachten: vgl. Urteil des Gerichts vom 24. März 2011 in den verbundenen Rechtssachen T-443/08 und T-455/08. Deshalb musste auch das Vorhaben der Hafenerweiterung in Piräus vorab bei der Kommission zur Genehmigung angemeldet werden.

[32] http://europa.eu/rapid/press-release_IP-12–458_de.htm?locale=en.

[33] *ÖPP Deutschland AG*, ÖPP und Mittelstand, 2011, S. 66, 78, 123.

[34] Vgl. §§ 25 Nr. 1 I lit. f VOL/A, 25 Nr. 1 I lit. c VOB/A und 26 Nr. 1 lit. c VOB/A, 26 Nr. 1 lit. d VOL/A.

rung seitens der Banken eingeschätzt.[35] Der Vorschlag für Richtlinie (RL-Vorschlag)[36] über die Konzessionsvergabe sowie die nunmehr erlassene Konzessionsvergaberichtlinie (Konzessionsvergabe-RL)[37] ließen sich von den Grundsätzen leiten, die in der Rechtsprechung des EuGH zu den Inhouse-Geschäften, zur interkommunalen Zusammenarbeit, zu den Public-Public-Partnerships und zur standardisierten Vertragsgestaltung i. R. v. PPP entwickelt wurden. Die Tatsache, dass die PPP-Vereinbarung unter statistischem Gesichtspunkt eine Konzession darstellt, heißt nicht, dass das PPP-Vorhaben auch unter vergaberechtlichem Gesichtspunkt als eine Konzession anzusehen ist.[38] Die in Art. 42 des RL-Vorschlags und in Art. 43 der Richtlinie über die Konzessionsvergabe geregelte Problematik der Änderung von Konzessionen während ihrer Laufzeit spiegelt u. a. angelsächsische Vertragsgestaltungserfahrungen hinsichtlich der Eintrittsrechte der Kreditgeber und der Austauschmöglichkeit der Projektgesellschaft aufgrund von Direktverträgen (*direct agreements*) wider.[39] Art. 17 der Konzessionsvergabe-RL will ferner sicherstellen, dass eine von ihrem Anwendungsbereich ausgenommene öffentlich-rechtliche Zusammenarbeit keine Wettbewerbsverzerrungen im Verhältnis zu privaten Unternehmungen herbeiführt.

3. Finanzierungsstruktur

Art. 16 RL-Vorschlag und Art. 18 Abs. 2 Konzessionsvergabe-RL beruhen auf der bewährten internationalen Praxis von Autobahnkonzessionen und machen die Beschränkung der Laufzeit der Konzession von dem Zeitraum abhängig, den der

---

[35] *ÖPP-Initiative NRW*, Finanzierungspraxis bei ÖPP, April 2010, S. 59–61. Ergebnispapier zum Workshop „Bankenexklusivität im Rahmen von ÖPP-Vergabeverfahren – Bestand und Reichweite eines Verbots der Mehrfachbeteiligung" http://www.ppp.nrw.de/oeffentlich keitsarbeit/veroeffentlichungen/oepp_und_bankenexklusivitaet.pdf; s. ferner *ÖPP Deutschland AG*, Auswirkungen der Finanzmarktkrise auf ÖPP, inbes. im Hochbau, 2010, 140 ff.

[36] KOM(2011) 897 endgültig, 2011/0437(COD), Brüssel, den 20.12.2011.

[37] Richtlinie 2014/23/EU des Europäischen Parlaments und des Rates vom 26. Februar 2014 über die Konzessionsvergabe L 94/1.

[38] Hierzu: *EPEC*, Risk Distribution and Balance Sheet Treatment. Practical Guide, 2011, 1.2. „Distinguishing PPPs and Concessions (according to Eurostat)". Übrigens gibt es eine Vielheit von „Konzessionsbegriffen" je nach Rechtsordnung: *SIGMA*, Brief 18. Public Procurement. Concessions and PPPs, August 2011, p. 4.

[39] Dazu aus deutscher Sicht s. *Peter Sester*, Insolvenzfeste Direktverträge in der Projektfinanzierung und bei Public-Private-Partnership-Projekten auf Basis eines Konzessionsvertrages, ZBB 2004, 283; *Guido Meyer/Heiko Fuchs,* Public Private Partnership in der Insolvenz des Auftragnehmers (Teil 1), ZfIR 2005, 529 ff.; (Teil 2). ZfIR 2005, 569 ff. *Christian Haas*, Vertragsstrukturen privatfinanzierter Infrastrukturprojekte, 2005, 202 ff; ferner: *Philip R. Wood*, Project Finance, Subordinated Debt and State Loans, London, 1995, p. 32; *Graham Vinter*, Project Finance – a Legal Guide, 2nd Ed., London, 1998, 111. Zum Nutzen eines Schuldanerkenntnisses bei der Frage, ob die forfaitierten Forderungen des Auftragnehmers gegenüber der Öffentlichen Hand insolvenzfest sind und insolvenzfest an die Bank übertragen werden können: „Insolvenzfestigkeit von Forfaitierungen bei der Finanzierung von ÖPP" am 14.7.2010 im Finanzministerium NRW http://www.ppp.nrw.de/oeffentlichkeitsarbeit/veroef fentlichungen/workshop_insolvenzfestigkeit.pdf.

Auftragnehmer braucht, um die getätigten Investitionen wieder hereinzuholen, zuzüglich einer angemessenen Rendite auf das investierte Kapital.[40] Brenzlig wird es bei den meistens unverzichtbaren Nachverhandlungen, wozu auch die nachträgliche Aushandlung einer neuen dem Auftragnehmer günstigeren Finanzierungsstruktur nach Abschluss der Finanzverträge („*refinancing*") und Überwindung der Unsicherheiten der ersten Phase gehört. Das englische Recht hat diesbezüglich eine Dogmatik entwickelt, welche nachträgliche Finanzierungsoptimierung und Gewinnteilung auch unter den Bedingungen der Finanzkrise (seit 2007) berücksichtigt.[41] Angebote können etwa zur Verdrängung der Konkurrenz dergestalt günstig gestaltet werden, dass sie stillschweigend mit einer Veränderung der Zuschlags- und Vertragsbedingungen während des Ausführungszeitraums im Rahmen von wettbewerbsfreien Nachverhandlungen von vornherein rechnen.[42] Wesentliche Änderungen erfordern aber eine neue Vergabe.[43] Der Auftragnehmer wird eine Refinanzierung vornehmen, wenn Vorteile daraus für ihn resultieren. Der Refinanzierungsanreiz hängt für den Auftragnehmer mit Reduktionen in den Kapitalkosten bei hohem Finanzierungsvolumen zusammen, z.B: das Zinsniveau in der Volkswirtschaft und der von den Kapitalgebern geforderte Risikoaufschlag für PPP-Projekte (im allgemeinen) sinken oder die projektspezifischen Risiken sinken erheblich nach der Bauphase.[44] Allerdings ist Refinanzierung auch mit Kosten verbunden. Diese betreffen die mit neuen Finanzierungsverträgen verbundenen Transaktionskosten sowie Kündigungskompensationen bei Auflösung der alten Finanzierungsverträge für Kredite und Anleihen. Die englische Erfahrung zeigt, dass bei der vorzeitigen Kündigung von Anleihen (bei denen typischerweise die Kapitalgeber das Zinsänderungsrisiko tragen)

---

[40] Zur dahinterstehenden ökonomischen Theorie s. *Eduardo Engel/Ronald D. Fischer/ Alexander Galetovic*, Least-Present-Value-of-Revenue Auctions and Highway Franchising, in: Journal of Political Economy (109) 2001, 993–1020; in Frankreich lautet der rezipierte Begriff: „concessions à durée endogène": *Yvrande-Billo*, Concurrence et délégation de services publics, in: Revue francaise d'économie, Vol. 22 No 3, 2008, 99–131.

[41] Den Anstoß gaben die „windfall gains" des Auftragnehmers im Fall Fazakerley: The Refinancing of the Fazakerley PFI Prison Contract (PDF) National Audit Office (NAO), 2000; PFI Refinancing Update (Report) National Audit Office (NAO), 2002; Refinancing of Early PFI Transactions: Code of Conduct (PDF) HM Treasury, 2002; Guidance Note on the Calculation of the Authority's Share of a Refinancing Gain Office of Government Commerce, 2002; Update on PFI Debt Refinancing and the PFI Equity Market (PDF) House of Commons Public Accounts Committee, 2007; Update on PFI Debt Refinancing and the PFI Equity Market (PDF) National Audit Office, 2006; The Refinancing of the Norfolk and Norwich PFI Hospital (PDF) Public Accounts Committee, 2006 HM TREASURY, Impact of current funding markets on in-procurement PFI transactions, Letter of the Head of PFI Policy, 30 July 2008. Zu Verteilungsschlüssel und Risikoabsicherung bei Refinanzierungen in der Krise: *ÖPP Deutschland AG*, Auswirkungen der Finanzmarktkrise auf ÖPP, insbes. im Hochbau, 2010, S. 119.

[42] Zur internationalen Erfahrung *J. Luis Guasch*, Negotiating and Renegotiating Infrastructure PPPs and Concessions: Key Issues For Policy Makers, in: Strengthening Public Investment and Managing Fiscal Risks For PPPs Seminar, Budapest, March 2007.

[43] KOM(2011)897 endgültig, RL 2011/0437(COD), Rn. 34.

[44] *Thorsten Beckers/Jirka Gehrt/Jan-Peter Klatt*, Refinanzierung bei PPP-Projekten, Februar 2009, S. 13 ff.

eine sogen. „*spens clause*" eine Kompensation vorsieht, die aufgrund einer Diskontierung der noch ausstehenden Schuldendienstzahlungen mit einem risikofreien Zinssatz ermittelt wird. In jüngeren Verträgen macht der öffentliche Auftraggeber die Refinanzierung bei Anleihen wahrscheinlicher, indem er die Kündigungsregeln von Finanzierungsverträgen modifiziert und die von der „*spens clause*" vorgesehenen hohen Kompensationszahlungen reduziert. Als Alternative bietet sich aber auch in der Praxis die Möglichkeit, eine Senkung der Finanzierungskosten nach Abschluss der Bauphase von vornherein vertraglich vorzusehen.[45] Bei vorzeitiger Beendigung des Vertrags kommt aus deutscher Sicht § 314 BGB in Betracht, wobei die Aufnahme von Regelbeispielen „wichtiger Kündigungsgründe" in die Vereinbarung erwünscht ist.[46]

4. Risikoverteilung

Vorsicht ist auch gegenüber der Risikoverteilung und den staatlichen Gewährleistungsansprüchen im PPP-Kontext angebracht. Eurostat sieht das Finanzierungsrisiko als Teil des Baurisikos an. Bei staatlicher Übernahme des Finanzierungsrisikos (Eigen- und Fremdkapitalkosten) des Auftragnehmers übernimmt der Auftraggeber aus der Sicht von Eurostat auch das Baurisiko. Die Vermögenswerte sind bilanziell vom Auftraggeber zu erfassen. Dies gilt aber nicht für staatliche Garantieversprechen oder Finanzierungsverpflichtungen, die die Finanzierungsoptimierung nach Abschluss der Finanzierungsverträge und Beendigung der Bauphase betreffen. Die Übernahme des mit der Residualgröße verbundenen Risikos ist in Grenzfällen ausschlaggebend. Wenn der Auftragnehmer das Eigentum an der Infrastruktur unabhängig von ihrem Marktwert nach Vertragsende behält, hat diese bei ihm in der Bilanz als Vermögenswert zu erscheinen. Dasselbe gilt, wenn der Auftraggeber sich die Option vorbehält, die Infrastruktur zum Marktwert zu kaufen. Verpflichtet sich der Auftraggeber zum Kauf der Infrastruktur zu einem vorherbestimmten Preis, dann gilt nach Eurostat folgendes: Wenn der Kaufpreis höher als der wirtschaftliche Wert der Infrastruktur ist, oder wenn er zwar niedriger als der wirtschaftliche Wert ist, aber der Auftraggeber bereits einen dem wirtschaftlichen Wert entsprechenden Betrag durch laufende Entgeltzahlungen während der Geltungsdauer des Vertrages entrichtet hat, dann ist die Infrastruktur beim Auftraggeber in seiner Bilanz zu erfassen. Nachverhandlungen der PPP-Verträge nach Abschluss der Finanzverträge (*Financial Close*) können eine Neuzuordnung der Vermögenswerte herbeiführen, wenn die Risikoverteilungsstruktur verändert wird. Die Risikoverteilung ist demnach von Bedeutung für

---

[45] HM TREASURY, PFI: strengthening long-term partnerships, March 2006, 111; HM TREASURY, Value for Money. Assessment Guidance, November 2006, 46; HM TREASURY, Standardisation of PFI Contracts, Version 4, March 2007, S. 291–293. Schließlich s. für Einzelheiten und Flexibilisierungsregeln: *Guidance on application of the Spens clause to PFI transactions:* HM. TREASURY, April 2006. *EPEC,* Capital markets in PPP financing. Where we were and where we are going? March 2010, S. 9.

[46] *Jürgen Kühling/Thomas Schreiner,* Grundprobleme von PPP, ZIS 2011, 112 ff., 121. Umfassend zu Kündigungs- und Rückholklauseln im Kontext einer Gewährleistungsverantwortung *Andreas Vosskuhle,* VVDStRL 62 (2003), 266, 320 ff.

Eurostat. Wie beim Finanzierungsleasing hat der öffentliche Auftragnehmer und Leasingnehmer die Infrastruktur zu Beginn der Vertragslaufzeit als Vermögenswert und die hiermit verbundenen Zahlungsverpflichtungen als Verbindlichkeiten in der Höhe des Barwerts der zukünftigen Zahlungen in seiner Bilanz zu erfassen. Das wirkt sich auf das Staatsdefizit und das Niveau der Staatsschulden aus. Wie beim Operating-Leasing bedeutet die Nicht-Bilanzierung der Infrastruktur und der damit verbundenen Verbindlichkeiten hingegen, dass der Aufwand für den öffentlichen Auftraggeber und Leasingnehmer erst später, zum Zeitpunkt der Entrichtung der Verfügbarkeitszahlungen oder Nutzungsgebühren (bzw. Nutzungsentgelte) an den privaten Auftragnehmer entsteht. Wenn der Auftraggeber das Baurisiko und das Verfügbarkeits- oder das Nachfragerisiko auf den Auftragnehmer übertragen hat, ist der Aufwand für die Infrastruktur linear über die Laufzeit des Vertrags zu erfassen, was einen hohen Aufwand zu Beginn der Vertragslaufzeit vermeidet.[47]

5. Bedürfnis nach Transparenz

Privatisierung ist mehr als nur die Aufgabe von Eigentümerpositionen des Staates. Sie tangiert das Staatskonzept selbst insofern, als sie die Begründung für staatliche Interventionen in die Wirtschaft betrifft. Das wird am französischen Konzept des „service public" besonders deutlich, das einerseits die staatliche Intervention legitimiert und andererseits zu einer langen Tradition der Kontraktualisierung im Verwaltungsrecht führte. Die Kontraktualisierung im öffentlichen Recht instrumentalisiert die unternehmerische Leistungsfähigkeit zugunsten der öffentlichen Hand und ihrer Zwecke. Ausgangspunkt ist nicht ein wirtschaftstheoretisches Konzept der Wettbewerbsfähigkeit, sondern der Staat.[48] Eigentlich führt der wettbewerbsrechtliche und marktgerechte Zugang zum Verwaltungsvertrag zu einer Banalisierung seines „außerordentlichen" Charakters.[49] Privatisierung entzieht dem Staat all die Steuerungsinstrumente, die er dank seiner aufgegebenen Eigentümerposition in der Hand hatte. Die Frage für das Recht liegt somit darin, Steuerungsinstrumente zur Verfügung zu stellen, die nicht auf Eigentümerpositionen beruhen und gleichwohl zielführend sind. Privatisierung führt zu einer grundlegenden Umstrukturierung des Verhältnisses zwischen Staat und Gesellschaft. Sie trägt somit die Beweislast, dass die Minderung staatlicher Steuerungskapazität die Gemeinwohlorientierung und die Rolle der zu deren Handhabung berufenen Parlamente legitimatorisch kompensieren kann. Von der öffentlichen Hand beherrschte gemischtwirtschaftliche Unternehmen in Privatrechtsform unterliegen ebenso wie im Alleineigentum des Staates stehende öffentliche Unternehmen, die in den Formen des Privatrechts organisiert sind, einer un-

---

[47] *EPEC*, Eurostat Treatment of Public-Private Partnerships, 2010, S. 14, 17.

[48] *Sébastien Bernard,* La recherche de la rentabilité des activités publiques et le droit administratif, Paris 2001.

[49] *Henri Courivaud,* La concession de service public „à la française" confrontée au droit européen, Revue Internationale de Droit Economique 2004–4 (t. XVIII, 4), 395–434, 395.

mittelbaren Grundrechtsbindung (keine Flucht ins Privatrecht).[50] Der Staat muss Leistungsumfang, Qualität und Kostenrahmen des privaten Auftragnehmers steuern und kontrollieren. Im Vorfeld des Privatisierungsfolgenrechts (*post-privatisation control devices*) muss der Privatisierungsprozess derart institutionell- und verfahrensrechtlich ausgestaltet sein, dass er eine ordnungsgemäße Abwicklung und Integrität des Verkaufsverfahrens gewährleistet.[51]

a) Transparenzbericht

Für PPP bedeutet dies, dass Zuverlässigkeit und Qualität von Wirtschaftlichkeitsuntersuchungen nachweisbar sein müssen. Es besteht Bedarf an einem „neuen Infrastrukturkonsens", mehr Transparenz und Klarstellung, in welchen Fällen der private Sektor bei öffentlichen Beschaffungsmaßnahmen eingebunden werden soll.[52] Unternehmen würden sich, so die Risikolage, an Steuergeldern bereichern und dem Bürger Informationen vorenthalten. Mehr noch: öffentlichen Gremien sei aufgrund von Intransparenz der Verfahren und Verträge die Kontrolle über das Projekt entzogen, was zu einem Demokratieverlust führe. Ein Ausschreibungswettbewerb ist somit nicht nur für Unternehmer, sondern auch für verwaltungsexterne Berater erforderlich, deren Neutralität zu gewährleisten ist. Das ist für die griechischen Privatisierungsverhältnisse von besonderer Bedeutung, denn die Neutralität der Privatisierungsbehörde kann durch klientelistische Beraterauswahl umgangen werden. Eine gebührenrechtliche bzw. kartellrechtliche Preismissbrauchskontrolle ist hinsichtlich der Preisentgelte für die Infrastrukturnutzung erforderlich. Auch sollten die eingegangenen finanziellen Verpflichtungen klar als Verschuldung der öffentlichen Hand transparent gemacht werden. Eine begleitende Kontrolle durch die Aufstellung eines Transparenzberichts sollte ferner während der Vertragslaufzeit möglich bleiben. Er würde aus vier Elementen bestehen: dem Risikobericht, dem Leistungsbericht (einschl. Qualitätssicherung), dem Ressourcenbericht und dem Organisationsbericht. Ergebnisse und Verantwortlichkeiten könnten dann der interessierten Öffentlichkeit zugänglich gemacht werden. Die Verpflichtung richte sich an beide Partner. Sie mache ein angemessenes Vertragscontrolling durch den öffentlichen Partner möglich.[53] Die PPP-Transparenzinitiative der deutschen Bauindustrie[54] geht in dieselbe Richtung. Sie plädiert für Einbindung der Politik und Information der Aufsichts-

---

[50] http://www.bverfg.de/entscheidungen/rs20110222_1bvr069906.html.

[51] OECD, Privatising State-Owned Enterprises. An Overview of Policies and Practices in OECD countries 2003, DOI: 10.1787/9789264104099-en, S. 65, 84, 106 ff.

[52] Mehr Transparenz im ÖPP-Verfahren – die Sicht von Transparency International: http://www.transparency.de/Transparenz-im-OEPP-Verfahren.1763.0.html.

[53] *Dietrich Budäus/Birgit Grüb*, Public Private Partnership: Theoretische Bezüge und praktische Strukturierung, in: ZögU 30. Jg. 3/2007, http://www.zoegu.nomos.de/fileadmin/zoegu/doc/Aufsatz_07_03.pdf.

[54] Die deutsche Bauindustrie, Mehr Transparenz bei ÖPP-Verfahren, Positionspapier, Dezember 2011, http://www.oepp-plattform.de/hochbau/themen-hochbau/transparenz-bei-oepp-projekten/.

und Prüfbehörden während der Bedarfsfeststellung, sie fördert die Prüfung der Finanzierbarkeit und Maßnahmenwirtschaftlichkeit, sie will die Offenlegung der Wirtschaftlichkeitsuntersuchung für Politik, Aufsichts- und Prüfbehörden erleichtern und sie optiert für eine offensive Darstellung und Erläuterung der grundlegenden Vertragsklauseln bzw. der Risikoverteilung. Schließlich befürwortet sie die Bereitstellung aller Unterlagen für die Prüfung durch die Rechnungshöfe.

Sieht man schließlich PPP als „relationale" Verträge an, die unter bestimmten Umständen Neuverhandlungen zulassen[55], kommt es darauf an, wem *ex post* die Macht[56] dazu zufällt, Quellen von Unsicherheit zu beherrschen, die *ex ante* nicht geregelt werden konnten. Aus ökonomischer Sicht werden Vertragsanpassungen (Leistungsumfangs- und Vergütungsanpassungen) im Rahmen von „Nachverhandlungen" unter Umständen für sinnvoll gehalten.[57] Wenn PPP-Verträge durch ausgehandelte Ordnungsleistungen zur Emergenz einer individuellen projektspezifischen Ordnung führen, stellt sich vor diesem Hintergrund die Frage, in wie fern dieses ad hoc geltende Regelsystem, das zu den üblichen administrativen Entscheidungsabläufen und Kompetenzen quersteht, demokratischen und rechtsstaatlichen Legitimitäts- und Transparenzanforderungen gerecht wird.

b) Grenzen von Transparenz

Die abgeschlossenen PPP-Verträge sollten, so politische Forderungen, vollständig zugänglich gemacht werden.[58] Totaltransparenz ist allerdings für PPP-Verträge ebenso wenig wie für die klassische Beschaffungsvariante durchsetzbar. PPP-Verträge sind zivilrechtliche Verträge, die mit Blick auf etwaige Geschäftsgeheimnisse der Auftragnehmer nicht öffentlich verfügbar gemacht werden.[59] Vergaberechtliche Vorschriften stehen der Veröffentlichung der Leistungsbeschreibung, aber auch des Vertragsentwurfs, der Teil der Vergabeunterlagen und Gegenstand von Verhandlungen mit den Bietern darstellt, entgegen. Es liegt im Verantwortungsbereich des Auftragnehmers, welchen Subunternehmen, finanzierenden Instituten oder Beratungsunter-

---

[55] Zu Verhandlungen s. *Arbeitsgemeinschaft/Alfen Consult, Norton Rose/CMS Hasche Sigle,* Leitfaden: Strukturiertes Verhandlungsverfahren für die Vergabe der Betreibermodelle im Bundesfernstraßenbau (A- und F-Modelle), April 2005.

[56] Zu Macht und Einfluss innerhalb von PPP aus politikwissenschaftlicher Sicht s. *Schwalb,* Public Private Partnership in der lokalpolitischen Steuerung· Relevanz, Struktur, Interessen, 2010.

[57] Die Monographie hierzu: *Jirka Gehrt,* Flexibilität in langfristigen Verträgen, 2010.

[58] 17/5258 – Antrag Bündnis 90/Die Grünen: Transparenz in Public Privat Partnerships im Verkehrswesen http://dipbt.bundestag.de/dip21/btd/17/052/1705258.pdf; 17/9726 – Antrag SPD: Für einen neuen Infrastrukturkonsens: Öffentlich-Private Partnerschaften differenziert bewerten, mit mehr Transparenz weiterentwickeln und den Fokus auf die Wirtschaftlichkeit stärken http://dip.bundestag.de/btd/17/097/1709726.pdf.

[59] Vgl. übrigens § 6 S. 2 IFG-Bund sowie die durch § 3 Nr. 6 Alt.1 IFG-Bund erfolgende Einschränkung der Informationsfreiheit, soweit fiskalische Interessen des Staates geschützt werden sollen.

nehmen er den Vertrag im Vergabeverfahren zur Kenntnis bringt. Wirtschaftlich-keitsuntersuchungen werden der Geheimschutzstelle des Deutschen Bundestages zur Einsichtnahme durch die Abgeordneten übermittelt, damit „Rückschlüsse auf wettbewerbsrelevante Daten bzw. Vorgehensweisen der öffentlichen Hand im Rah-men der Datenerhebung und Beurteilung von Sachverhalten" nicht abgeleitet werden und die „Aufrechterhaltung eines funktionierenden Wettbewerbs" nicht gefährdet wird.[60] Zur Transparenz trägt bei, dass die Methode, nach der die finale Wirtschaft-lichkeitsuntersuchung für die Vergabe der Betreibermodelle nach dem A-Modell im Bundesautobahnbau durchgeführt worden ist, in einem Leitfaden durch die Ver-kehrsinfrastrukturfinanzierungsgesellschaft mbH (VIFG) veröffentlicht worden ist.[61] Zumindest im Straßenwesen sind die meisten Projekte (es gibt drei Modelle: Fernstraßenbauprivatfinanzierungsmodell, das Ausbau- und das Verfügbarkeitsmo-dell) eher mit Wirtschaftlichkeitsunsicherheiten verbunden; es sei daher in Zukunft damit zu rechnen, dass die Mehrzahl der Fernstraßenprojekte konventionell realisiert wird.[62] Die Problematik der Transparenz in PPP geht jedoch über transaktionskosten-ökonomische Vertragsprobleme und vergaberechtliche Gesichtspunkte hinaus.[63] Im Februar 2011 stimmten bei einem Volksentscheid 27 % der Wahlberechtigten in Ber-lin für das „Gesetz für die vollständige Offenlegung von Geheimverträgen zur Teil-privatisierung der Berliner Wasserbetriebe". Nach § 4 dieses Gesetzes sind Verträge, Beschlüsse und Nebenabreden, die nicht offen gelegt werden, unwirksam.[64] Auf diese Weise wurde die Exekutive per Gesetz zur Offenlegung der von ihr geschlos-senen PPP-Verträge verpflichtet.

Der Informationsanspruch des Bürgers wird durch die Schutznotwendigkeit von Geschäfts- und Betriebsgeheimnissen eingeschränkt. Es geht hierbei um „alle auf ein Unternehmen bezogenen Tatsachen, Umstände und Vorgänge…, die nicht offenkun-dig, sondern nur einem beschränkten Personenkreis zugänglich sind und an deren Nichtverbreitung der Rechtsträger ein berechtigtes Interesse hat" (BVerfGE 115, 205 (230)). Ein Abwägungskonzept nach dem Muster von § 7 S. 1 Hs. 2 Informa-

---

[60] DBT, 17. Wahlperiode, DS 17/3330, 10. 10. 2010, Rn. 32.

[61] DBT, 17. Wahlperiode, DS 17/3330, 10. 10. 2010, Rn. 37. Zur VIGG s. das Gesetz zur Errichtung einer Verkehrsinfrastrukturfinanzierungsgesellschaft zur Finanzierung von Bun-desverkehrswegen Verkehrsinfrastrukturfinanzierungsgesellschaftsgesetz – VIFGG.

[62] *Bundesministerium für Verkehr, Bau und Stadtentwicklung*, Öffentlich-Private-Partner-schaften – Am Beispiel des Bundesfernstraßenbaus, Juli 2011, S. 31.

[63] Die Studien von *ÖPP Deutschland AG*, Öffentlich-Private-Partnerschaften im Bereich von Kindergärten und Kindertagesstätten, Schriftenreihe Bd. 3, 2011, passim, hebt vor allem Planungssicherheit und Kostentransparenz hervor. Ein globaler, die Herstellungsbedingungen eines bei allen Akteuren „gemeinsamen Verständnisses des Projekts" einbeziehender Ansatz findet sich in *ÖPP Deutschland AG*, ÖPP im IT- und Dienstleistungsbereich: Marktüberblick und kritische Erfolgsfaktoren, ÖPP Schriftenreihe, Bd. 5, 2011, S. 92.

[64] Gesetz- und Verordnungsblatt für Berlin, 67. Jahrgang, Nr. 7, 12 März 2011. Vgl. zur Forderung eines gesetzlichen Rahmens für PPP, der Staatsverschuldungsanreize vermeidet und Mindeststandards hinsichtlich Transparenz gewährleistet: http://www.toni-hofreiter.de/faltblaetter/PPP.pdf.

tionsfreiheitsgesetz Berlin, demzufolge die Offenlegung der Informationen zulässig ist, wenn das Informationsinteresse das Geheimhaltungsinteresse überwiegt, wäre nachahmenswert. Eine weitere Grenze wird dem Informationszugangsanspruch durch die Schutznotwendigkeit der fiskalischen Interessen des öffentlichen Auftraggebers gezogen. Die vom Staate errechnete Wirtschaftlichkeitsschwelle könnte durch den Informationszugang aufgedeckt und das Kosteneinsparungspotential reduziert werden.

c) Eignungsmatrix und Rechnungslegung

Es ist vor allem mittlerweile klar geworden, dass Transparenz von den PPP-Akteuren selbst ausgehen muss. Von Nichtregierungsorganisationen, Gewerkschaften und Rechnungshöfen[65] wird somit Kritik wegen vorhandener Informationsasymmetrien geäußert, auf die nunmehr die Wirtschaftsteilnehmer[66] und die öffentliche Hand[67] mit der Erarbeitung von entgegenwirkenden Transparenz-Richtlinien reagieren. Transparenz über die Höhe der Bewertung der einzelnen Kriterien (Eignungsmatrix) ermöglicht auch schon den (mittelständischen) Unternehmen eine frühzeitige Entscheidung über die Teilnahme am Vergabeverfahren.[68] Mehr Transparenz ist schließlich auch ein Argument für die Lancierung der internationalen Rechnungslegungsstandards für den öffentlichen Sektor sowie für die Entstehung von Standardisierungen im supra- und internationalen Recht gewesen. Die IPSAS-Rechnungslegung ist sicherlich intersubjektiv und zuverlässig nachprüfbar. Man muss allerdings

---

[65] Hrsg. von den Präsidentinnen und Präsidenten der Rechnungshöfe des Bundes und der Länder, Gemeinsamer Erfahrungsbericht zur Wirtschaftlichkeit von ÖPP-Projekten, 14. September 2011.

[66] Die deutsche Bauindustrie, Positionspapier vom November 2010. Mehr Transparenz bei ÖPP-Verfahren. Zwar gelten die Basisparagrafen der VOB/A und die darin enthaltenen Geheimhaltungsvorschriften sowohl für ÖPP als auch für die klassische Beschaffungsvariante, doch haben negative Erfahrungen mit der Geheimhaltung von ÖPP-Bedingungen bei Verträgen der ersten Generation für die Herstellung eines „Anscheins" von Intransparenz gesorgt. Das Projekt Skye Bridge Ltd in Schottland stellt ein Paradebeispiel dafür dar , wie ein Vorhaben an der Spannung zwischen Vertraulichkeit und Transparenz scheitern kann: „The abolition of tolls sweeps away a source of deep division and genuine injustice", http://news.bbc.co.uk/2/hi/uk_news/scotland/4112085.stm. Zu dieser Spannung s. European PPP Expertise Centre, Procurement of PPP and the use of Competitive Dialogue in Europe. A review of public sector practices across the EU, EIB–11/2 0 1 0, S. 10. Das Positionspapier vom Dezember 2011 der deutschen Bauindustrie, ÖPP-Transparenzinitiative, S. 4. empfiehlt nach Vertragsschluss folgende Dokumente offenzulegen: „Vertragsurkunden der unterzeichneten ÖPP-Einzelverträge zwischen öffentlichem und privatem Partner (z. B. Rahmenvertrag, Bauvertrag, Betreibervertrag), zugehörige Leistungsbeschreibungen für Planung, Bau- und Betrieb (z. B. die sog. BQA – Bau-, Qualitäts- und Ausstattungsbeschreibung), ergänzende Verdingungsunterlagen des Auftraggebers, die Bestandteil des ÖPP-Vertrags geworden sind."

[67] „Um den Wettbewerb nicht zu beeinflussen, werden z. B. die Ergebnisse der Wirtschaftlichkeitsuntersuchungen nicht veröffentlicht, da diese eine Orientierung für eine Auftragserteilung beinhalten können.": *BMVBS*, Öffentlich-Private-Partnerschaften – Am Beispiel des Bundesfernstraßenbaus, Stand: Juli 2011, S. 37.

[68] *ÖPP Deutschland AG*, ÖPP und Mittelstand, ÖPP-Schriftenreihe, Bd. 6, 2011, S. 33, 116, 137.

auch die mit dem beizulegenden Zeitwert zusammenhängenden Ermessensspielräume berücksichtigen, die die Verlässlichkeit verringern, und zusätzlich dem Umstand Rechnung tragen, dass die IPSAS ausschließlich der Informationsvermittlung dienen und in das Haushaltsrecht nicht eingebunden sind.[69]

Ergebnisse und Verantwortlichkeiten müssen der interessierten Öffentlichkeit zugänglich und kontrollierbar gemacht werden. Adäquate Rechnungslegungsmodelle müssen bestimmen, wem Infrastrukturprojekte zuzurechnen sind und wie die Verantwortungsverteilung strukturiert ist. Auf den privaten Partner ist die Auslegung 12 von International Financial Reporting Interpretation Committee (IFRIC) IASB 2006, auf den Staat sind die International Public Sector Accounting Standards (IPSAS) anzuwenden. Beide Instrumente ziehen das Kontroll- (oder Beherrschungs-) Kriterium heran, während Eurostat (2010) ein Risiko und Entgeltkriterium (*risks and awards*) benutzt.[70]

6. Herstellung von Kontrollierbarkeit
durch internationale Standardisierung von PPP-Verträgen

Auf internationaler Ebene ist das Recht der PPP nicht einheitlich. Nichtsdestotrotz gibt es Übereinstimmungen zwischen den nationalen Rechtsordnungen mit Blick auf die Regelung von Kernproblemen wie z. B. den Langzeitcharakter des Vertragswerks und die Vernetzung der Beziehungen unter den Projektbeteiligten innerhalb des Vertragswerks (etwa Regelungen für Subunternehmer und Angestellte der Projektgesellschaft).[71] Eine Verstärkung der global einheitlichen Merkmale von PPP-

---

[69] *Holger Wirtz*, Grundsätze ordnungsmäßiger öffentlicher Buchführung, 2. Aufl. 2010, S. 217, 227; *Norbert Vogelpoth*, Haushaltsplanung und internationale Rechnungslegung, in: FS für Budäus, 2007, 263 ff.; *Kuno Schedler/Bernhard Knechtenhofer*, IPSAS in der Praxisanwendung-Mehr Richtlinie als Standard?, in: FS für Budäus, Bern 2007, 299 ff.

[70] http://epp.eurostat.ec.europa.eu/portal/page/portal/product_details/publication?p_product_code=KS-BE-04-004.

[71] Aus den auf internationaler Ebene vorhandenen Harmonisierungstendenzen sind die UNIDO BOT-Guidelines zu erwähnen, die einen Überblick über die wichtigsten Aspekte von BOT-Projekten geben und eine Vereinheitlichung der Infrastrukturprojektstrukturen erreichen. Dazu gehören auch der UNCITRAL-Leitfaden und die Mustergesetzgebung für privatfinanzierte Infrastrukturprojekte, wo sich Empfehlungen für den Inhalt eines einschlägigen Gesetzes finden, wie z. B. das Erfordernis einer außerordentlichen neben der periodischen externen Kontrolle der Tarifanpassungsformeln, ein Recht des öffentlichen Vertragspartners zur Überprüfung und Genehmigung der Verträge der Projektgesellschaft mit ihren Gesellschaftern und die Statuierung der Rechtswahlfreiheit der Projektgesellschaft in den Rechtsverhältnissen zu anderen Projektbeteiligten. *United Nations. Economic Commission for Europe*, Governance in Public Private Partnerships for Infrastructure Development, Draft, 2005; *UNCITRAL*, Legislative Guide on Privately Financed Infrastructure Projects, United Nations New York, 2001; *United Nations Industrial Development Organization (UNIDO)*, Guidelines for Infrastructure Development through Build-Operate-Transfer (BOT) Projects, 1996; *Gregory Shaffer*, Defending Interests: PPP in WTO Litigation, in: Transnational Dispute Management 2004, 1 ff. Zu den *OECD Basic Elements of a Law on Concession Agreements* s. http://ppp.worldbank.org/public-private-partnership/library/oecd-basic-elements-law-concession-agreements; *Christian Haas*, Vertragsstrukturen privatfinanzierter Infrastrukturprojekte, Frankfurt 2005. Diese

Projekten hängt mit dem Einfluss des angelsächsischen Rechts auf die Gestaltung von Projektverträgen zusammen. Projektverträge werden meistens detailliert ausformuliert, so dass ein projekteigenes Recht geschaffen wird, dass das jeweils staatliche Recht zumindest zum Teil ersetzt. Einheitliche Vertragsgestaltungsstrukturen betreffen die Nachverhandlung von Verträgen, die Indexierung und Eskalation von Zahlungsverbindlichkeiten (Tarifanpassungsmechanismen für Projektleistungen soweit Preisangemessenheit für die Infrastrukturendnutzer), die Bestellung von Sicherheiten über Bestandteile des Projekts, die Eintrittsrechte der Kreditgeber, die Ersetzungsbefugnis der öffentlichen Hand für den Konzessionär in Übereinstimmung mit den Kreditgebern, den Ausschluss von Rechten Dritter und das Bestimmen von Konfliktlösungsmechanismen (etwa Streitschlichtung durch Schiedsgerichtsverfahren). Standardisierungen sind somit gerade auch für Krisen- und Entwicklungsländer, die über ineffiziente[72] Verwaltungsstrukturen verfügen, insofern von Vorteil, als sie den Mangel an Erfahrung mit Infrastrukturprojekten ausgleichen und eine bewährte Grundlage für Projektvergabe und Vertragsverhandlungen darstellen. Aufgrund eines Misstrauens der Projektbeteiligten (Kreditinstitute, Bau- und Betreiberunternehmen, Anwälte und Berater) gegenüber dem nationalen Recht von Krisen- und Entwicklungsländern nimmt man beim angelsächsischen Recht Zuflucht, das den vorgefertigten Vertragsmustern i. R. d. Projektfinanzierung eine einheitliche, rechtskulturelle Unterschiede neutralisierende Gestalt verleiht. Die PPP generiert in derartigen Fällen eine möglichst autonome Rechtsordnung in der Form der für das spezifische Projekt geltenden Verträge.

a) Vertrags- und Gesetzesbindungen der PPP-Beteiligten

PPP-Standardisierungen sind Ausdruck der Akzeptanz bewährter Grundsätze. Nichtsdestoweniger modifizieren PPP die Steuerungsmöglichkeiten des Staates und sie beeinflussen hierdurch staatliche Legitimität. Die positiven Werte, die mit PPP verbunden werden (Kostendeckung, Effizienzsteigerung, Rationalisierung, Synergieeffekte) beziehen sich auf die Output-Legitimität. Eine dauerhafte finanzielle Entlastung für den Staat steht allerdings nicht von vornherein fest und muss jedes Mal ad hoc nachgewiesen werden. Denn an die Stelle klassischer Kreditraten treten Leasingraten, Vergütungen oder Konzessionsgebühren (bzw. -entgelte). Die „leeren

---

Agreements enthalten neben Orientierungspunkten für die Konzessionsvertragsverhandlungen maßgebliche Vertragsklauseln, die als kommentierte Musternormen dienen und durch eine allgemeine Nachverhandlungsklausel ergänzt werden.

[72] *OECD* (2011), Greece: Review of the Central Administration, OECD Public Governance Reviews, OECD Publishing.http://dx.doi.org/10.1787/9789264102880-en passim. Mit Blick auf ÖPP bedeutet „Krise" eben die Schwierigkeit, Bindung überhaupt möglich zu machen und Opportunitätsverhalten sowohl von Auftraggebern als auch Auftragnehmern zu verhindern: *Athanasios Gromitsaris*, Öffentliches Interesse und ÖPP, in: Strangas/Chanos/Papacharalambous/Tsouka (Hrsg.), Gut, Interesse und Recht (Αγαθό, συμφέρον και δίκαιο), 2012, S. 1061–1135 (mit franz. Zusammenfassung auf S. 1117–1135).

Kassen" reichen als Legitimitätsdiskurs nicht aus.[73] Neben den Vertragsbindungen (Projektvertrag, Schiedsvereinbarungen, Projektgesellschaftsvertrag, Finanzierungs- und Nachunternehmerverträge) muss eine Vielheit rechtlicher Rahmenbedingungen beachtet werden.[74] Die Einhaltung der rechtlichen Rahmenbedigungen und eine behutsame Vertragsgestaltung, die dem Prinzip „jus vigilantibus scriptum est" entspricht, können schon eine PPP-Projekte legitimierende Gewährleistungsfunktion wahrnehmen:[75] Die Periodengerechtigkeit der Rechnungslegung kann die Zuordnung von Vermögenswerten präzisieren, das Haushaltsrecht und das Kommunalrecht können kreditähnliche Geschäfte, Risikostreuung und Nachverhandlungen kontrollieren, das Vergaberecht kann Wettbewerb sicherstellen und somit Oligopol- bzw. Monopolstrukturen von Bietern, Beratern[76] und Finanzierungspartnern verhindern. Ferner sind die Grundsätze der Gleichbehandlung und Äquivalenz für die Gebühren-(Entgelt-)Finanzierung einer PPP-Infrastruktur (insbes. bei Kalkulation ansatzfähiger Entgelte für in Anspruch genommene Fremdleistungen, Fremdkosten i. S. d. § 6 Abs. 2 S. 4 KAGNRW) zu beachten. Diese Grundsätze entfalten eine über die Anwendung konkreter Vorschriften hinausgehende Legitimität und Vorhabenakzeptanz. Wenn sie wegen einer Erosion institutionellen Vertrauens keine Wirkung erzielen, kollabiert nicht nur die Finanzierungsbasis, sondern auch die ganze Legitimitätsgrundlage für das PPP-Projekt.[77] Allerdings kann die Statuierung von Vertrags- und Legalbindungen für die Beteiligten ohne zusätzliches Mitwirken unbeteiligter Instanzen der Wissenschaft und der externen Evaluation einem PPP-Projekt keine vollständige Legitimität spenden. Dies hängt mit dem Phänomen des Intermutationscharakters des Wettbewerbs zusammen.

b) Intermutationscharakter des Wettbewerbs
und Legitimitätsleistung externer Instanzen

aa) Inter- und supranationale Ausschlusskriterien für Bieter

An PPP wird deutlich, dass moralisches Risiko und Opportunitätsverhalten sowohl auf der Seite der öffentlichen Hand als auch des Privatsektors vorkommen können. Dies betrifft die Unterlaufung des Wettbewerbs seitens der Auftraggeber durch Haushaltsdefizite, Konsultationsgeflechte, Korruptionsanfälligkeit und Protektio-

---

[73] Eine Rechnung muss, sei es auch langfristig, vom öffentlichen Sektor ohnehin gezahlt werden: *Greve/Hodge*, Public-Private Partnerships and Public Governance Challenges, pp. 149–162 in: Osborne, The New Public Governance, 2010.

[74] Vgl. *Martin Kment*, VerwArch 2011, 63 ff.

[75] Es geht darum, dass sowohl Marktversagen als auch Funktionsmängel der öffentlichen Hand überwunden werden, s. das Beispiel von *Ankush Guha*, Privatization of Ports – Singapore and JNPT, EPPPL 2011, 38 ff.

[76] *Martin Burgi/Markus Segeth*, Rechtliche und praktische Hinweise für die Vergabe von ÖPP-Beratungsleistungen, April 2009 (im Auftrag der PPP-Task Force des Landes NRW).

[77] Vgl. *Christoph Brünning* in: Driehaus (Hrsg), Kommunalabgabenrecht, § 6 KAG NRW Stand: März 2012, Rn. 49 ff., 847 f. Als Paradebeispiel fehlenden institutionellen Vertrauens s. die soziale Bewegung „ich zahle nicht" (Massenschwarzfahren) in Griechenland.

nismus sowie die Verletzung der Wettbewerbsordnung durch die Auftragnehmer. Der Wettbewerb präsentiert sich als eine ambivalente Institution. Obwohl der Auftragnehmer das Strukturprinzip des Wettbewerbs grundsätzlich auch für sich selbst anerkennt, ist er davon überzeugt, dass besondere Umstände des Einzelfalls einen Verstoß gegen dieses Ordnungsprinzip entweder als Ausnahme rechtfertigen oder doch entschuldbar machen. Und er ist als Handelnder grds. bereit, gleiche Ausnahmen auch anderen Konkurrenten zuzubilligen (sofern ähnliche, besondere Umstände vorliegen), obwohl er diese Ausnahmen in seiner Rolle als Nicht-Handelnder, also gleichsam als Repräsentant der öffentlichen Marktordnung öffentlich und grds. verurteilt.[78] Auftraggeber und Auftragnehmer können mit Blick auf ein PPP-Projekt Anderen Normen (etwa Stabilitätspakt und Wettbewerb) zumuten, obwohl sie sich selbst ad hoc daran nicht halten. Auftragnehmer sehen sich manchmal auch durch diplomatischen Druck unterstützt, der von Staaten im Rahmen der Förderung ihrer „Champions" ausgeübt wird.[79] Diesem Rollen- und Standortwechselspiel kann nur durch projektexterne nationale und supranationale Instanzen in Europa ein Riegel vorgeschoben werden. Der RL-Vorschlag über die Konzessionsvergabe trägt diesem Umstand Rechnung: Wirtschaftsteilnehmer, die Steuern oder Sozialversicherungsbeiträge nicht zahlen oder sich der Korruption schuldig gemacht haben, sollten „mit der Sanktion eines obligatorischen Ausschlusses auf Unionsebene" rechnen.[80] Zu den Ausschlusskriterien für Bieter gehört auch die Bestechung nach Maß-

---

[78] Warum sollte man die Überwindung der ohnehin landesüblichen Korruptionsbarrieren und somit auch den Zuschlag eines lukrativen Geschäfts dem Konkurrenten überlassen? Zur Intermutation eines Ordnungsprinzips s. *Eugen Buss*, Vorüberlegungen zu einem Vertragsmodell des Marktes, in: Urs Fazis/Jachen C. Nett (Hrsg.), Gesellschaftstheorie und Normentheorie, 1993, S. 111 ff. in Anlehnung an *Geiger*, Vorstudien zu einer Soziologie des Rechts, 1987, S. 36 ff. Mit Blick auf die Rechtsanwendung s. *Athanasios Gromitsaris,* Zur Unterscheidung von Aktions- und Reaktionsnormen, in: Fazis/Nett (Hrsg.), ebd. S. 123 ff.; *ders.,* Normativität und sozialer Geltungsgrund des Rechts: Zur Revision und Reformulierung der Normentheorie von Theodor Geiger, Berlin 1992.

[79] *OECD* (2014) Foreign Bribery Report. An Analysis of the Crime of Bribery of Foreign Public Officials OECD Publishing http://www.keepeek.com/Digital-Asset-Management/oecd/governance/oecd-foreign-bribery-report_9789264226616-en; *OECD* (2012), International Drivers of Corruption: A Tool for Analysis, OECD Publishing, S. 25, 28, 65, http://dx.doi.org/10.1787/9789264167513-en; *Tina Søreide,* Drivers of Corruption. A Brief Review. A World Bank Study, Washington DC 2014, S. 51 in Anlehnung an Material von Transparency International. Dies reduziere „the prospect of ending up with the outcome most beneficial to the host country's citizens"; *dies.,* Corruption in international business transaction: the perspective of Norwegian firms, in: Susan Rose-Ackerman (Hrsg.), International Handbook on the Economics of Corruption, Massachusetts USA 2006, S. 381 ff., 408.

[80] KOM(2011) 897 endgültig, Rn. 33. Hierzu www.oecd.org/daf/nocorruption (Bribery in International Business) und insbes. *OECD*, Phase 3. Report on implementing the OECD Anti-Bribery Convention in Greece, June 2012, Rn. 13: „Where appropriate, this report also refers to the Johnson & Johnson/Dougall/DePuy case, Smith & Nephew case, and Siemens case. All of these cases involved individuals or companies from other parties to the Convention bribing Greek officials." http://www.oecd.org/dataoecd/21/2/50633313.pdf. s. ferner zum außergerichtlichen Vergleich Siemens – Griechenland: Siemens sagt Sorry für die Korruption http://www.sueddeutsche.de/wirtschaft/griechisches-parlament-segnet-vergleich-mit-unternehmen-

gabe der Definition des Art. 3 Abs. 1 der gemeinsamen Maßnahme des Rates vom 22. Dezember 1998 (98/742/JI). In diesem Absatz werden verschiedene Formen strafbarer Handlungen beschrieben, die den Tatbestand der Bestechung eines Beamten erfüllen. Die Worte „wenn eine Person vorsätzlich … einen Vorteil … verspricht oder gewährt" beziehen sich auf die Person, die die Bestechung unternimmt, gleich in welcher Eigenschaft (Mitarbeiter eines Unternehmens, Angehörige des öffentlichen Dienstes usw.) sie handelt: Privatperson bzw. Person, die eine öffentliche Funktion wahrnimmt. Es muss die Absicht vorliegen, dass ein Beamter Handlungen vornimmt, die im Widerspruch zu seinen Pflichten stehen. Ob der Tatbestand in Fällen vorliegt, in denen der Vorteilgeber zwar vorsätzlich handelt, aber hinsichtlich der Befugnisse, über die der Beamte seines Erachtens verfügt, einem Irrtum unterliegt, ist nach einzelstaatlichem Recht zu entscheiden. Ein grenzüberschreitender Informationsaustausch, der Ansätze einer Entwicklung in Richtung auf eine erwünschte Steuervollzugsunion in der EU enthält, ist hier schon nicht zu übersehen.

bb) Kontrolle ex post

Die Legitimität eines individuellen PPP-Vorhabens speist sich nicht lediglich aus dem jeweils erzielten Kompromiss von Projektbeteiligten, sie betrifft auch institutionelle Kontexte und Verhaltensweisen, die über Einzelprojekte hinausgehen. Es geht bei der Legitimität von PPP nicht nur darum, den zur Überwachung der Vertragsrisiken erforderlichen Wissensbedarf der Partner zu decken, solange dieses Wissen nicht unter das Geschäftsgeheimnis fällt. Wenn einer PPP die Erweiterung[81] des Geltungsbereichs der divergenten Handlungsrationalitäten der beteiligten Akteure gelingt, ist dies nichtsdestotrotz kein ausreichender Faktor der Vertrauensbildung. Die projektbezogene PPP-„Adhockratie" bedarf vielmehr zusätzlich einer mitlaufenden Beobachtung und Kontrolle von außen als maßgebliches Element der Vertrauensbildung. Eine Verpflichtung zur Erstellung öffentlicher Berichte in regelmäßigen Abständen würde der Intranspararenz der Verhältnisse entgegenwirken. Sie könnte durch die Etablierung einer neutralen wissenschaftlichen Projekt-Begleitforschung ergänzt werden.[82] Erforderlich ist zusätzlich eine Bewertung des PPP-Projekts ex post, die durch eine unabhängige, am Vorhaben unbeteiligte Instanz durchzuführen ist.[83] Die Rechnungshöfe weisen somit auf Fiskal- und Verschuldungsrisiken, Trans-

---

ab-siemens-sagt-sorry-fuer-die-korruption-1.1327795. Darüber hinaus ist auf das Ergebnis der Ermittlungen gegen „Atlas Elektronik. A joint company of ThyssenKrupp and Airbus DS" und die Schleichwege der Zahlungen hinzuweisen. http://www.kathimerini.gr/795684/article/epik airothta/ellada/32-atoma-parapempontai-se-dikh-gia-ta-ypovryxia.

[81] *Detlef Sack,* Zwischen Usurpation und Synergie-Motive, Formen und Entwicklungsprozesse von PPP, ZSR 2009, 211 ff., 227.

[82] European PPP Expertise Centre und ÖPP Deutschland AG haben faktisch bereits diese Rolle übernommen. Vgl. *Wolfgang Gerstlberger/Michael Siegl,* Öffentlich-Private Partnerschaften. Ein Konzept für die zukünftige Gestaltung öffentlicher Aufgaben?, Dezember 2011, S. 54.

[83] *EPEC,* The Guide to Guidance. How to Prepare, Procure and Deliver PPP Projects, 2011, 1.2, 4.2.

aktions- und eigennutzorientierte Beratungskosten sowie die mangelnde Vergleichbarkeit von Leistungsangeboten und Beschaffungsvarianten hin. Insbesondere bei Insolvenz der Projektgesellschaft sei zu vermeiden, dass der Auftraggeber im Kontext einer Forfaitierung mit Einredeverzicht keine Entgeltzahlungen für Leistungen entrichtet, die von der Projektgesellschaft nicht mehr erbracht werden.[84] Wie das Phänomen des Intermutationscharakters von Normbindungen zeigt, ist man auf externe Kontrollmöglichkeiten durch unbeteiligte Instanzen angewiesen, die über den Individualrechtsschutz von Infrastrukturnutzern hinausgehen.[85] Das gilt umso mehr, als es um Vermögenswerte mit Dienstleistungspotential geht, die, selbst wenn sie keine Nettozahlungsflüsse generieren, doch einem öffentlichen Auftragszweck dienen.[86]

cc) Kontrollbedürftigkeit unabhängiger Privatisierungsagenturen

Die Legitimationsleistung externer Instanzen ist auch im Falle unabhängiger Privatisierungsagenturen unerlässlich. Die Bundesanstalt für vereinigungsbedingte Sonderaufgaben (BvS), die die mehr als 30 000 Privatisierungsverträge der Treuhandanstalt kontrollierte, war etwa nicht in der Lage, die Einhaltung von Investitionszusagen wirksam zu prüfen und dem Missbrauch von Subventionen entgegenzuwirken. Der Bundesrechnungshof stellte fest, erhebliche Investitionszusagen würden bereits als eingehalten und überprüft angesehen, wenn die schriftlichen oder telefonischen Meldungen der Vertragspartner den vertraglichen Abreden entsprächen. Er weist auch darauf hin, dass vertraglich vereinbarte Wirtschaftsprüfertestate über durchgeführte Investitionen nicht immer verlangt würden. Eine Ursache manchen Betruges gegenüber der THA sei sicher in dem Umstand begründet, dass sich die Treuhandanstalt im Regelfall am Ertrags- und nicht am Substanzwert der von ihr zu privatisierenden Unternehmen orientierte. Dieser wiederum war oftmals sehr gering, weil die Unternehmen keine Chance hatten, im Wettbewerb zu bestehen, wenn nicht ein Investor erhebliche (kostenintensive) Umstrukturierungen vornehmen würde. Betrugsfälle seien vor allem bei der Privatisierung kleinerer, mittelständischer Betriebe (wegen der hier als gering eingeschätzten Entdeckungsgefahr) zu beobachten gewesen. Hinzu kamen die „schon unter normalen Bedingungen schwierige Aufklärung von Korruption und Untreue während des Umbruchs" und die Er-

---

[84] *Präsidentinnen und Präsidenten der Rechnungshöfe des Bundes und der Länder* (Hrg.), Gemeinsamer Erfahrungsbericht zur Wirtschaftlichkeit von ÖPP-Projekten, Wiesbaden, 14. September 2011, S. 7 und passim; s. auch das Ergebnispapier Workshop „Insolvenzfestigkeit von Forfaitierungen bei der Finanzierung von ÖPP" am 14. Juli 2010 im Finanzministerium NRW.

[85] Hierzu s. das OECD-Übereinkommen über die gegenseitige Amtshilfe in Steuersachen für ein wirksames Handeln der Steuerprüfungsbehörden, für eine Verhinderung der Steuerflucht, http://www.oecd.org/dataoecd/63/49/48980598.pdf.

[86] Vgl. etwa IPSAS 1.11.

schwerung einer effektiven Kontrolle wegen des Zeitdrucks bei der Privatisierung.[87]
Das Beispiel wird für die Problematik der Kontrollbedürftigkeit und Funktionsfähigkeit einer politisch unabhängigen griechischen Privatisierungsbehörde von Bedeutung sein.

7. Wettbewerbsregeln für den Staat

Wenn der Staat in Wettbewerb zu privaten Anbietern tritt, muss er die Wettbewerbsregeln beachten. Er kann sich von der Befolgung dieser Regeln nicht deshalb
dispensieren, weil er das öffentliche Interesse vertrete und nicht auf Gewinnerzielung
angewiesen sei. Wird der Staat in Bereichen, in denen auch Private agieren, wettbe-
werblich tätig, so gelten auch für ihn alle Regeln des europäischen Wettbewerbsrechts: Transparenz der finanziellen Verhältnisse, Wirtschaftlichkeit, Verbot von
Subventionen, Diskriminierungsfreiheit. Das heißt, dass die öffentliche Hand dauerhaft unwirtschaftliche öffentliche Unternehmungen nicht finanziell unterstützen und
vor Wettbewerb abschirmen darf, um Arbeitsplätze bzw. politische Klientelnetze zu
erhalten.

Während die Privatisierung von Telekommunikationsdiensten als europaweit ge-
lungen gilt[88], stoßen Privatisierungspläne in netzgebundenen Bereichen der Energie-
versorgung sowie Wasserversorgung und -entsorgung auf Widerstände. Auch hier
gilt es, Netzbetriebsleistungen von der privaten Herstellung der durchgeleiteten
Dienste und Versorgungsgüter zu trennen. Hierbei wird das rechtliche Augenmerk
darauf gerichtet, Versorgungssicherheit angesichts Angebotsmengen, Qualitätsstan-
dards und Nutzungsentgelte bzw. -Gebühren zu gewährleisten. Ob die Privatisierung
der Daseinsvorsorge vorteilhaft ist, kann nicht prinzipiell entschieden werden. Die
Ergebnisse öffentlicher Unternehmen müssen mit Hilfe effizienter Berichtssysteme
regelmäßig beobachtet und evaluiert werden. Externe Abschlussprüfungen müssen
dazu kommen.

a) Gemeinwohlverwirklichung durch Staat und/oder Private

Abgesehen von der Vorsicht, die bei jedem Unternehmenskauf geboten ist, muss
man sich dessen bewusst sein, dass eine staatliche Gemeinwohlverwirklichung nicht
per se demokratischer und effizienter ist. Auch gegenüber öffentlichen Unternehmen
sind Informations- und Kontrollrechte sowie Rechenschaftspflichten, Kündigungs-

---

[87] *Kari-Maria Karliczek*, Strukturelle Bedingungen von Wirtschaftskriminalität. Eine empirische Untersuchung am Beispiel der Privatisierungen ausgewählter Betriebe der ehemaligen DDR. Münster 2007, S.95, 104, 158 ff. Zitiert nach Wikipedia: Treuhandanstalt. Hierzu
auch: *Andreas Middel*, BvS fehlt wirksame Kontrolle. Treuhand-Nachfolgerin auf Angaben
der Investoren angewiesen – Kritik vom Rechnungshof, in: Die Welt vom 29.02.1996.

[88] *Joachim Scherer/Caroline Heinickel*, Die Entwicklung des Telekommunikationsrechts
in den Jahren 2009–2011, in: NVwZ 2012, 142 ff. *Franz Jürgen Säcker*, Telekommunikati-
onsgesetz, Kommentar, 3. Aufl., Frankfurt a. M. 2013.

und Rückholoptionen erforderlich.[89] Auch hier stellt sich das Problem des staatlichen Einflusses in gemischtwirtschaftlichen Unternehmen, da diese sowohl aus Privatisierungs- als auch aus Rückverstaatlichungsprozessen resultieren können. Bestimmte (mit der öffentlichen Aufgabe nicht vereinbare) Entscheidungen des gemischtwirtschaftlichen Unternehmens, in dem die öffentliche Hand keinen beherrschenden Einfluss ausübt, könnten etwa durch ein Veto des Minderheitsaktionärs verhindert werden. Das müsste aber mit Gesellschafts- und Marktrecht kompatibel sein. Die Verpflichtungen des Privaten müssen zu diesem Zweck von der öffentlichen Hand überwacht und eingefordert werden. Vorkehrung einer Exit-Option für die öffentliche Hand und Einhaltungspflicht einer Halteperiode für den privaten Partner müssten ebenfalls vorgesehen werden.

Die Erfahrung in Griechenland lehrt geradezu, dass öffentliche Unternehmungen dem Gemeinwohl nicht besser dienen als privatwirtschaftliche Unternehmungen. Als staatliches Unternehmen gilt nach dem griechischen Privatisierungsgesetz 3049/2002 (Art.1) jedes Unternehmen, bei dem die öffentliche Hand imstande ist, direkt oder indirekt bestimmenden Einfluss auszuüben, und zwar aufgrund ihrer Anteils- bzw. finanziellen Beteiligung oder der Regeln, denen das Unternehmen untersteht. Auch Tochterunternehmen von Unternehmen in staatlichem Besitz oder Unternehmen, deren Zweck in der Verwertung staatlicher Vermögenswerte besteht, und Minderheitsbeteiligungen der öffentlichen Hand gehören zum Anwendungsbereich des griechischen Gesetzes.

b) Trennung von Eigentümerfunktion und anderen Funktionen der öffentlichen Hand

Unternehmungen, in denen der Staat in Besitz sämtlicher Anteile, einer Mehrheitsbeteiligung, einer Sperrminorität oder aber auch einer kleinen Kapitalbeteiligung ist, stehen vor der Aufgabe, die Eigentumsrechte der öffentlichen Hand[90] wahrzunehmen und gleichzeitig die Wettbewerbsregeln zu beachten. Es geht darum, einen Regulierungsrahmen für öffentliche Unternehmungen zu schaffen, der gewährleistet, dass auf Märkten, auf denen öffentliche und privatwirtschaftliche Unternehmen in Wettbewerb stehen, Marktverzerrungen zugunsten des Staates verhindert und gleiche Wettbewerbsbedingungen für alle Marktbeteiligten gelten können. Die Eigentümerfunktion der öffentlichen Hand muss von anderen Funktionen klar getrennt sein, die auf die Marktregulierung Einfluss haben. Gleichheit bedeutet, dass es zum Gläubigerschutz auch ein Insolvenzverfahren gegen staatseigene Unternehmen möglich sein muss.[91] Die öffentlichen Aufgaben, die von den öffentlichen Unternehmen er-

[89] *Gary Wolff/Eric Hallstein,* Beyond Privatization: Restructuring Water Systems to Improve Performance, Oakland California 2005.

[90] *Patrice Chretien,* The Property of Public Bodies, The Public-private Law Divide: Potential for Transformation? Ed. by Matthias Ruffert, Publisher London: British Institute of International and Comparative Law, 2009, 311–332.

[91] *M. Rennie/F. Lindsay,* Competitive Neutrality and State-Owned Enterprises in Australia, in: Review of Practices and their Relevance for Other Countries, OECD Corporate Govern-

füllt werden sollen, müssten in Rechtsvorschriften festgelegt sein. Soweit ein staatseigenes Unternehmen wichtige öffentliche Aufgaben wahrnimmt, sollte es über seine Beziehungen zu den Stakeholdern Bericht erstatten. Die Finanzierungsbedingungen dieser Aufgabenerfüllung sollten völlig transparent und mit dem Beihilferecht vereinbar sein. Bei der Mittelbeschaffung sollten die Beziehungen öffentlicher Unternehmungen zum Kapitalmarkt, zu Kreditinstituten oder zu Finanzinstituten in staatlichem Besitz wettbewerblichen Bedingungen unterliegen und kommerzieller Art sein.[92] Das ist der Idealtypus, den die OECD hinsichtlich öffentlicher Unternehmungen aufstellt.[93]

Die öffentliche Hand muss mit Blick auf ihr Unternehmenseigentum gewährleisten, dass Unternehmen unter staatlichem Einfluss nach den Regeln der Transparenz und Rechenschaftspflicht geführt werden. Auch dürfen die Kontrollmechanismen des Managements bei einem öffentlichen Unternehmen nicht schlechter als bei einem privaten Unternehmen funktionieren. Konzernrecht soll hier zur Anwendung kommen. Öffentliche Unternehmen sollen mit einem Mindestmaß an Transparenz, Effektivität und Effizienz geführt werden. Die Rolle der öffentlichen Hand bei der Leitung und Kontrolle sowie die Mittel zur Erfüllung klar definierter Zielsetzungen müssen kontrollierbar sein. Die Vergütungssysteme müssen derart ausgestaltet sein, dass sie qualifizierte und motivierte Fachkräfte für die Leitung öffentlicher Unternehmen abwerben und halten können. Die Trennung zwischen politischer Verantwortung und operativer Autonomie im Tagesgeschäft ist unverzichtbar. Eine Zentralisierung der Eigentümerfunktion des Staates wird ferner zur Transparenzerhöhung vorgeschlagen. Die Aufsichtsorgane öffentlicher Unternehmen sollten dem Gebot der Integrität folgen, für die Unternehmensergebnisse verantwortlich sein und für ihre Tätigkeit zur Rechenschaft gezogen werden können. Sie sollten so zusammengesetzt sein, dass personelle Verflechtungen – insbesondere eine Personalunion zwischen dem Amt des Vorsitzenden des Aufsichtsorgans und dem des Generaldirektors – vermieden werden. Soweit Arbeitnehmervertretungen an den Aufsichtsorganen mitwirken, sind Mechanismen zur Gewährleistung der Unabhängigkeit der Aufsichtsorgane und zur Vermeidung von Kollusionen erforderlich. Die Aufsichtsorgane müssten bei der Erfüllung ihrer Aufgaben durch Fachausschüsse in den Bereichen moderner Rechnungsprüfung (Doppik), Risikomanagement und Vergütung unterstützt werden.[94] Ein Beispiel sind die „Task Forces" für PPP. Die Aufsichtsorgane öffentlicher Unternehmen müssten jährlich und leistungsbezogen evaluiert und beurteilt werden.

---

ance Working Papers, No. 4, OECD Publishing 2001, http://dx.doi.org/10.1787/5 kg54cxkmx36-en.

[92] *Gary L. Sturgess*, A Fair Field and No Favours. Competitive Neutrality in UK public service markets, January 2006 www.serco.com/institute.

[93] *OECD*, Regulating Market Activities by the Public Sector, Policy Roundtables, 2004 http://www.oecd.org/regreform/sectors/34305974.pdf.

[94] *David E.M.Sappington/J.Gregory Sidak,* Competition Law for State-Owned Enterprises, Antitrust Law Journal 71 2003, S. 479 – 523.

Ein Konflikt entsteht, wenn man bedenkt, dass einerseits staatlicher Einfluss zur Erfüllung einer öffentlichen Aufgabe erforderlich ist, und andererseits die Leitungsorgane öffentlicher Unternehmen in ihrer Unabhängigkeit respektiert werden sollten. Die staatliche Einflussnahme kann nicht anders als nach Maßgabe der von der Rechtsform des jeweiligen Unternehmens vorhandenen rechtlichen Handlungsmöglichkeiten ausgeübt werden. Das betrifft die Vertretung der öffentlichen Hand bei Aktionärshauptversammlungen und Ausübung entsprechender Stimmrechte, die Bestellung von Board-Mitgliedern und die Mitwirkung bei der Bestellung sämtlicher Leitungsorgane im Rahmen von kontrollierbaren Verfahren.

c) Misstrauen gegenüber Doppelrollen der öffentlichen Hand

Erfahrungen haben gezeigt, dass Misstrauen gegenüber Doppelrollen der öffentlichen Hand gerechtfertigt ist. Die öffentliche Hand entscheidet nämlich einerseits darüber, ob eine Privatisierung fortgeführt wird oder ob eine Rückverstaatlichung stattfindet: sie ist Entscheider und Regelsetzer. Andererseits aber ist die öffentliche Hand ein in die Aufgabenerfüllung einbezogener Akteur. Die aus der Privatisierungsdebatte schon bekannten Steuerungsprobleme sind bei Rückverstaatlichungsentscheidungen ebenfalls präsent, denn die Versorgungsleistungen werden nach der Rückverstaatlichung mit Einheiten erbracht, die vielfach in den Formen des Privatrechts organisiert sind. Die Vorgaben des Unionsrechts bleiben auch hier relevant. Das betrifft das Beihilferegime (Art. 107 I AEUV) sowie die Beachtung des Grundsatzes der unionsrechtlichen „Trägerneutralität": Wer sich in wettbewerblichen Strukturen betätigt, muss alle Regeln des europäischen Wettbewerbsrechts beachten. Das Beihilfenrecht dient der Vermeidung eines missbräuchlichen Zusammenwirkens von öffentlicher Hand und öffentlichen Unternehmen zulasten privater Konkurrenten. Es handelt sich um ein Konzept „kompetitiver Neutralität", das auf internationaler Ebene Bestätigung findet.[95] Auch staatliche Betriebe müssen anhand von Leistungsindikatoren kontrollierbar bleiben.[96]

Art. 106 I AEUV verlangt Transparenz der finanziellen Beziehungen und Diskriminierungsfreiheit. Soweit Art. 106 II AEUV Privilegierungen zugunsten von Unternehmen statuiert, so werden diese nicht wegen des Rechtscharakters von Unternehmungen als öffentlichen Unternehmungen gewährt, sondern deswegen und nur dann, wenn sie mit DAWI betraut sind. Von Art. 106 II AEUV können auch Unternehmen der Privatwirtschaft profitieren. Pläne dahingehend, die kommunale Daseinsvorsorge zu stärken, müssten dies genau bedenken. Die überörtliche wirtschaftliche Betätigung von kommunalen Unternehmen scheint nämlich dazu geeignet zu sein, Inves-

---

[95] Zur Implementierung diese Konzepts in Australien s. *M. Rennie/F. Lindsay*, Competitive Neutrality and State-Owned Enterprises in Australia: Review of Practices and their Relevance for Other Countries, OECD Corporate Governance Working Papers, No. 4, OECD Publishing, 2011, http://dx.doi.org/10.1787/5 kg54cxkmx36-en.

[96] *OECD*, Implementation Guide to Ensure Accountability and Transparecny in State Ownership,

titionen im Energiebereich zu fördern, sie werde aber durch „veraltete gesetzliche Beschränkungen" behindert.[97] Dies läuft auf ein Aufweichen der „Schrankentrias" im deutschen kommunalen Wirtschaftsrecht und insbesondere den Verzicht bzw. die Erleichterung des Subsidiaritätsnachweises, die Förderung „energiewirtschaftlicher Betätigung" sowie die Erweiterung der Beteiligung an Kraftwerksprojekten im In- und Ausland durch die Landesgesetzgeber hinaus.[98]

d) Kartellrechtliche Missbrauchsaufsicht

Normalerweise dient Missbrauchsaufsicht der Kontrolle privater Unternehmungen. Im Regulierungsrecht gibt es bereichsspezifische Vorschriften, die, wie § 42 TKG auf Unternehmen Anwendung finden, für die das Vorliegen beträchtlicher Marktmacht förmlich festgestellt worden ist. Ansonsten wird auf das kartellrechtliche Missbrauchsaufsichtsverbot des § 19 GWG oder Art. 102 AEUV zurückgegriffen. Es ist aber zu befürchten, dass auch der unkontrollierte Verhaltensspielraum der öffentlichen Versorger zu einem überhöhten Entgeltniveau führt. Anzeichen dafür ergaben sich z. B. aus dem Missbrauchsverfahren des deutschen Bundeskartellamtes gegen die Berliner Wasserbetriebe.[99] Gerade weil die Wasserversorgung der Endkunden ein natürliches Monopol darstellt, bedarf die Entgeltgestaltung der Wasserversorgung einer effektiven staatlichen Kontrolle. Mehrere Kartellbehörden haben in der Tat die Wasserpreise von öffentlichen Versorgern geprüft und entsprechende Missbrauchsverfahren eingeleitet.[100] Ein Problem ist das Nebeneinander von privatrechtlich gesetzten Preisen einerseits und öffentlich-rechtlichen Gebühren andererseits. Privatrechtlich geführte Trinkwasserversorger bieten ihre Leistung zu Preisen an, öffentlich-rechtlich organisierte Versorger erheben typischerweise Gebühren. Mit der Wahl der Rechtsform durch die zuständige Kommune (Wasserbetriebe stehen unter direktem oder indirektem eigentumsrechtlichem Einfluss kommunaler Gebietskörperschaften) ergeben sich Unterschiede in den Aufsichtsmaßstäben. Die Frage, die sich stellt, ist, inwiefern ineffizient hohe Vollkosten in der Trinkwasserwirtschaft zulasten der Verbraucher deshalb hingenommen werden sollen, weil sie mit dem Äquivalenzprinzip und dem Grundsatz der Sicherstellung einer nachhaltigen Haushaltführung bei der öffentlichen Hand vereinbar sind. Während im Gebührenrecht die Kostenkontrolle vornehmlich an der Struktur des öffentlichen Versorgers ausgerichtet ist, beruht die kartellrechtliche Preismissbrauchskontrolle in erster Linie auf den Kosten von Vergleichsunternehmen (Vergleichsmarktkonzept). Es kommt

---

[97] Landtag von Baden-Württemberg, 15. Wahlperiode, Drucksache 15 / 3255, 20.03.2013, S. 1.

[98] Siehe etwa das Gesetz zur Revitalisierung des Gemeindewirtschaftsrechts NRW vom 21. Dezember 2010.

[99] Wasserversorger sollen Preise senken, Handelsblatt vom 5. Dezember 2011, http://www.handelsblatt.com/unternehmen/handel-dienstleister/wasserversorger-sollen-preise-senken/5923692.html.

[100] BGH, Beschluss vom 2. Februar 2010, KVR 66/08 „Wasserpreise Wetzlar".

nicht auf den Ist-Kostenstandard, sondern auf die Kosten der effizienten Leistungserstellung an. Wasserpreise sind hiernach missbräuchlich, wenn ein Versorgungsunternehmen ungünstigere Preise fordert als ein Vergleichsunternehmen, es sei denn das Versorgungsunternehmen weist nach, dass der Preisunterschied auf abweichenden Umständen beruht, welche dem Unternehmer nicht zuzurechnen sind. Einem funktionalen Unternehmensbegriff zufolge unterliegt zwar auch die Tätigkeit der öffentlichen Hand dem (Wettbewerbsbeziehungen zu Dritten voraussetzenden) GWB dann, wenn sie sich auf dem Markt als Anbieter wirtschaftlicher Leistungen betätigt und privaten Marktteilnehmern Konkurrenz macht. Das GWB gelte indes nicht für den satzungsrechtlich vorgesehenen Anschluss- und Benutzungszwang, der eine hoheitliche Tätigkeit darstelle und jeden Wettbewerb Dritter von vornherein ausschließe.[101] Demgegenüber ist die Refinanzierung von Infrastrukturprojekten über Nutzergebühren bei fehlendem Anschluss- und Benutzungszwang nachfrageseitig nicht abgesichert.[102] Als besonders problematisch erweist sich in diesem Zusammenhang die Doppelrolle der öffentlichen Hand: Sie ist in der Lage, sich durch eine Änderung der Rechtsform der bisher privatrechtlich organisierten Betriebe der kartellrechtlichen Missbrauchsaufsicht zu entziehen.[103] Die Generierung von Vertrauen und Rechtssicherheit durch Institutionalisierung von Misstrauen gegen die öffentliche Hand nimmt hier die Gestalt der Frage an, wie man verhindern könne, dass die öffentliche Hand das Kartellrecht aushebelt und Verbraucher nachhaltig schädigt.[104] Die Kartellbehörden sind allerdings keine Aufsichtsbehörden gegenüber anderen staatlichen Behörden. Die Schwäche der Gebührenkontrolle scheint ihren Hauptgrund eher „in der unzureichenden fachlichen und personellen Besetzung sowie in der fehlenden Unabhängigkeit der Preisbehörden bei der Anwendung des materiellen Gebührenrechts"[105] als in der mangelnden Effizienz seiner Grundsätze zu haben. Zwar orientiert sich Preismissbrauchskontrolle in erster Linie an den Kosten von Vergleichsunternehmen, während die Kostenkontrolle im Gebührenrecht primär an der Struktur des öffentlichen Versorgers ausgerichtet ist, doch sind die Kosten auch im Gebührenrecht in Abkehr von der früher herrschenden kameralistischen Kostenermittlung nach betriebswirtschaftlichen Grundsätzen zu ermitteln.

---

[101] OLG Düsseldorf, Beschluss vom 8. Dezember 2010, VI-2 Kart 1/10 (V) zitiert nach *Monopolkommission,* Sondergutachten 63: Die 8. GWB-Novelle aus wettbewerbspolitischer Sicht, Bonn, im Februar 2012, S. 44.

[102] Vgl. die Fragestellung im entsprechenden Leitfaden des Bundesministeriums für Wirtschaft und Arbeit, Public Private Partnership International. Ein Unternehmerleitfaden für PPP-Engagements im Ausland, http://www.bmwa.bund.de: „Ist die Bereitschaft der potenziellen Endnutzer bzw. -kunden vorhanden, die durch das geplante PPP angebotene Leistung überhaupt zu nutzen?" (S. 36).

[103] Zur Rekommunalisierung in Reaktion auf die BGH-Entscheidung „Wasserpreise Wetzlar" s. *Benedikt Wolfers/Burkhard Wollenschläger,* Rekommunalisierung der Wasserversorgung, in: Ipsen (Hrsg.) Osnabrück 2012, S. 97 ff., 113 ff.

[104] Monopolkommission 2012, S. 45.

[105] *Franz Jürgen Säcker,* Die kartellrechtliche Missbrauchskontrolle über Wasserpreise und Wassergebühren, NJW 2012, 1105, 1109.

III. Privatisierungen ohne Gewährleistungsstaat

Die bisher dargelegten Anforderungen, die der Gewährleistungsstaat an Privatisierungen stellt, lassen sich auf die griechischen Verhältnisse deshalb nur bedingt übertragen, weil es in Griechenland trotz geltender Gesetzgebung[106] an einem modernen Gewährleistungsstaat fehlt. Es ist daher überaus problematisch, dass bei der Formulierung von Reformvorschlägen und der Aufstellung von Privatisierungsplänen von einem funktionierenden Staat ausgegangen wird, dem es eigentlich keine Probleme bereiten sollte, die Reformen umzusetzen und Privatisierungen in verfassungsmäßiger Weise über die Bühne zu führen. Ein wirklich transparentes Vergaberecht etwa wird als Teil der Konditionalität erst unter dem Druck der Troika eingeführt. Gesetz 4281/2014 und noch zu erlassende Verordnungen sollen durch kontrollierbare Umsetzungsmaßnahmen zur Digitalisierung und Standardisierung vergaberechtlicher Verfahren samt Einführung vorgerichtlicher Überprüfungsmöglichkeiten beitragen.[107] Die politische Unabhängigkeit der 2011 gegründeten[108] „Einheitlichen Unabhängigen Vergabestelle" soll in der Praxis erst durchgesetzt werden. In Wirklichkeit muss der Staat erst durch eine selbstinduzierte Reform zu einem handlungsfähigen Reformfaktor gemacht werden. Lange hat man eine „Stabilisierungspolitik" ohne Reform betrieben, die der Reproduktionslogik vorhandener Strukturen diente.[109] Dies betrifft nicht zuletzt die immer noch fehlende Kopplung von Wissensgenerierung, Innovationsfähigkeit und unternehmerischer Tätigkeit in einer modernen Wissensgesellschaft.[110]

Das durch das Phänomen der Privatisierung angesprochene Verhältnis des privaten zum öffentlichen Sektor spielt eine wichtige Rolle im Wettbewerb der Rechtsordnungen. Griechenland entspricht den Standards einer wettbewerbsfähigen Rechtsordnung und Volkswirtschaft keineswegs.[111] Der klientelistische[112]Aspekt des grie-

---

[106] Etwa zum Vergaberecht: Gesetz 3263/2004 (Regierungsblatt 179 A′) Vergabe im Preiswettbewerb, bei der das unter allen ordnungsgemäßen und anforderungsgerechten Angeboten preisgünstigste Angebot den Zuschlag erhält.

[107] The Hellenic Republic, Report on further Activities, Seite 42: http://www.ste.gr/images/StE/content/deltia/Hardouvelis.pdf.

[108] Gesetz 4013/2011 und Präsidialverordnungen 122/2012 und 43/2013.

[109] *Panos Kazakos,* Stabilisierung ohne Reform. Konvergenz und Pfadabhängigkeit im Griechenland der 90er Jahre, Zentrum für Europäische Integrationsforschung, Universität Bonn, C 66 2000, http://www.zei.de. Zu einer Bestandsaufnahme mittlerweile erfolgter und noch ausstehender Reformen s. die Studie des griechischen Wirtschafts- und Industrieforschungsinstituts in Zusammenarbeit mit der Boston Consulting Gruppe über die Rolle von Strukturreformen und die Aussichten der griechischen Wirtschaft. http://www.iobe.gr/docs/research/RES_03_20052014_REP_GR.pdf.

[110] Siehe nur *Michael S. Mitsopoulos/Theodore Pelagidis,* State Monopoly in Higher Education as a Rent Seeking Industry, März 2006. Abrufbar in SSRN: www.ssrn.com/abstract=890541 oder http://dx.doi.org/10.2139/ssrn.890541.

[111] Für einen Vergleich s. den „Doing Business"-Bericht der Weltbank, der zumindest den Hiatus zwischen Rechtssicherheit und Wirtschaft veranschaulicht: http://www.doingbusiness.org/data/exploreeconomies/greece/enforcing-contracts/.

chischen Rechtsstaates ist mittlerweile allgemein bekannt.[113] Der klientelistische
Tauschakt enthält zwar ein Element von „Rechenschaftspflichtigkeit" insofern, als
der Anhänger und Wähler von „seinem" Politiker eine Gegenleistung erwartet,
doch ist diese von rein privatem Nutzen, da sie persönliche Vorteile gewährt (z. B.
Arbeitsstelle in der öffentlichen Verwaltung). Demgegenüber ist Korruption ein spe-
zifisches Phänomen, das der Selbstreproduktionslogik eines etablierten Patronage-
systems dient oder aber Defizite der suboptimal funktionierenden Institutionen
des Rechtsstaates ausgleicht. Gegen Klientelismus und Ämterpatronage setzt die
Rechtsordnung die Trennung von Amt und Person sowie das Gleichheitsgebot in seiner Erscheinungsform des gleichen Zugangs der Bürger zu den öffentlichen Ämtern
nach Maßgabe transparenter und kontrollierbarer Auswahlverfahren ein.[114] Gegen
Korruption gibt es zahlreiche Regelwerke, die dennoch sehr beschränkte Ergebnisse
deshalb erzielen, weil sie auf Einzelverhalten abstellen, ohne die institutionelle Ver-
wurzelung sowie den Zusammenhang des Phänomens mit dem von ihm pervertierten
Rechtsstaat anzutasten. Internationale Erfahrungen lehren, Bestechung sei enger als
Korruption und letztere sei wiederum enger als eine auf Klientel- und Patronagenetz-
werke beruhende Verflechtung von Politik, Verwaltung und Wirtschaft. Dieser weite
Zugang umfasst Phänomene wie Ausschreibungsbetrug durch verdeckte private Monopolstrukturen oder Parteienfinanzierung, die durch Geldwäsche über den Umweg
durch Steueroasen geleistet wird, obwohl derartige Erscheinungsformen vom Korruptionswahrnehmungsindex von Transparency International nicht erfasst sind.
Nach der gängigen Kurzformel von Transparency International ist Korruption der
„Missbrauch anvertrauter Macht für private Zwecke". Dieser Begriff kann zwar ex-
tensiv ausgelegt werden, er wird allerdings in der Praxis vornehmlich auf den öffentlichen Sektor beschränkt, was übrigens an der Definition der Weltbank noch deutlicher wird, wonach Korruption einen „Missbrauch von *öffentlicher* Macht zu persön-
lichem Nutzen" darstellt. Diese engen[115] begrifflichen Instrumentarien führen auch
zu einer eingeschränkten „Geographie" der Bedingungen von Korruption auf der
Liste von Transparency International.[116] Korrekturen an diesem Bild werden durch

---

[112] Zu Begriff und Beispielen s. *Gero Erdmann,* Neopatrimoniale Herrschaft,, E+Z –
Entwicklung und Zusammenarbeit Nr. 10, Oktober 2001, S. 294–297.

[113] *Maria Hatalis,* Greek Sovereign Debt and the Rocky Road to Recovery, Perspectives on
Business & Economics Volume 30, 2012, S. 103 ff, 105: „Politicians used these ‚cradle to the
grave' jobs as a means of decreasing unemployment and providing thousands of public sector
jobs to the electorate, thereby guaranteeing re-election".

[114] Hierzu s. die Beiträge von *Ruffert* und *Wolff* in diesem Band.

[115] Zur Kritik am engen Korruptionsbegriff s. *Klaus Röhl,* Rechtssoziologie-Online.de,
§ 78 Korruption III mit dem zutreffenden Hinweis darauf, dass öffentliche Aufgaben heute in
Privatrechtsform wahrgenommen werden.

[116] „(O)ver half of the countries ranked in the ‚least corrupt' quintile of the CPI are offshore
tax havens. Something is clearly badly wrong here." Tax Justice Network, Corruption and the
Offshore Interface, http://www.taxjustice.net/cms/front_content.php?idcat=100.

den „Financial Secrecy Index"[117] angebracht, der die Bedeutung der finanziellen Ge-
heimhaltungskultur in den Vordergrund stellt.[118] Es sei hier dahingestellt, inwiefern
die Komponentenauswahl und die Messungen, auf denen der Index beruht, in jeder
Hinsicht stichhaltig sind. Die Liste macht auf jeden Fall ein Transparenz- und Ver-
trauensdefizit deutlich. Diese Umstände wirken sich in ihrer Verbindung mit (inter-)
nationalen Klientelnetzwerken negativ auf die Steuermoral in einzelnen Ländern und
somit auch auf Strukturreformen aus. Die halbautonome neugegründete griechische
Steuerbehörde wird den hohen Anforderungen, die etwa an die unabhängige und sehr
erfolgreiche peruanische Steuerbehörde gestellt werden, offensichtlich nicht gerecht.[119] Erwünscht ist ein wirklich politisch unabhängiges, über einen eigenen Verwaltungsrat verfügendes Steueramt und eine Steuerfahndungsbehörde, die ähnlich
dem U.S. Internal Revenue Service eingreifen, wenn die nachgewiesenen Lebens-
führungskosten zu den steuerlichen Erklärungen nicht passen. Denn steuerrechtliche
Reformen haben eine Legitimität beschaffende Funktion, soweit sie Steuergerechtigkeit[120] zumindest ansatzweise verwirklichen: Aus der Sicht der Theorie des Steuer-
wettbewerbs und der Stärkung des Schifffahrtstandortes sind Steuerbefreiungen und

---

[117] „Secrecy jurisdictions – a term we often use as an alternative to the more widely used
term tax havens – use secrecy to attract illicit and illegitimate or abusive financial flows … In
identifying the providers of international financial secrecy, the Financial Secrecy Index reveals
that the traditional stereotype of tax havens is misconceived. The world's most important
providers of financial secrecy are not small, palm-fringed islands as many suppose, but some
of the world's biggest and wealthiest countries … The implications for global power politics
are clearly enormous, and help explain why widely heralded international efforts to crack
down on tax havens and financial secrecy have been rather ineffective, despite many fine
words from G20 and OECD countries: for it is these countries – which receive these gigantic
inflows – that set the rules of the game." http://www.financialsecrecyindex.com.

[118] So sei etwa Deutschland „trotz Rechtsstaatsstaatlichkeit und vergleichsweise niedriger
Korruption ein zentraler Zielort für illegale Finanzströme und Geldwäscheaktivitäten" *Netzwerk Steuergerechtigkeit,* Report: Schattenfinanzzentrum Deutschland, November 2013 http://
www.globalpolicy.org/images/pdfs/GPFEurope/Report_Schattenfinanzzentrum_Deutschland_
web.pdf, während die Schweiz, die den geringsten Korruptionswahrnehmungsindex aufweist,
die finanzielle Geheimhaltungskulturliste anführe, Tax justice network, Financial Secrecy
Index-2013 Results http://www.financialsecrecyindex.com/introduction/fsi-2013-results und
das auf Platz 21 liegende Großbritannien als „heimliche Nummer eins" gelte, da es ein Netz
von Steueroasen unterstütze: Tax justice network, What is the British Connection? http://
www.beta.financialsecrecyindex.com/faq/britishconnection.

[119] Zum Regelungswerk zu dieser Behörde s. den Beitrag von *Koutnatzis* in diesem Band.
Erfolgsrezepte kann man aber eher in *IMF,* Country Report No 13/155, Greece, Selected
Issues, June 2013, S. 35 http://www.imf.org/external/pubs/ft/scr/2013/cr13155.pdf nachlesen.
Immerhin werden seit zwei Jahren Beamte der Steuerfahndung wegen Erpressung und Kor-
ruption mithilfe vorgemerkter Banknoten schon verhaftet, s. www.in.gr (10.7.2013);
www.tovima.gr (12.11.2014).

[120] „(A)ggregate inequality measures can obscure important aspects of distributional
change, and they take no account of levels of income: inequality may be lower even though
many experience considerable hardship". „In Greece, for instance, although the loss of disposable income as a result of consolidation measures increased with income over the top nine
deciles, the lowest income decile experienced a particularly large reduction." International
Monetary Fund, Taxing Times, World Economic and Financial Surveys, October 2013, S. 27.

Subventionen für die griechische Seeschifffahrt durchaus erklärlich.[121] Aus der Sicht des Steuerzahlers verstärken sie die Kluft zwischen Steuerrecht und Steuerleben und sind unter dem Aspekt des nationalen Bezuges der Steuergerechtigkeit begründungs-bedürftig.[122] Einen Beitrag will die Seeschifffahrt allenfalls i. R. einer „freiwilligen Vereinbarung" leisten.[123] Darüber hinaus ist auf die besondere Funktion von soge-nannten „steuerähnlichen Abgaben zugunsten Dritter" hinzuweisen, die zur Privile-gierung und indirekten Staatsabhängigkeit einer Reihe von Berufen sowie zur mit-telbaren Finanzierung deren Kassen durch die Verbraucher führen. Paradebeispiel sind die Abgaben, die von Aktiengesellschaften und Gesellschaften mit beschränkter Haftung (bei der Gründung, der Bekanntmachung oder Änderung der Satzungen oder der Erhöhung des Gesellschaftskapitals) zugunsten des Fonds für Juristen und des Sozialfonds der Anwaltschaft erhoben wurden. Der EuGH hat entgegen der Auffas-sung Griechenlands hierin keine zulässigen „Arbeitgeberabgaben" gesehen, sondern einen Verstoß gegen Richtlinienrecht festgestellt.[124] Von den 49 ursprünglich vorhan-denen indirekten Abgaben sind mittlerweile 12 abgeschafft worden.[125] Verteilungs

---

[121] *Achim Biesenbach*, Besteuerung und Subventionierung in der Seeschifffahrt, 2011; *Volker Runtemund,* Die Besteuerung der internationalen Seeschifffahrt gem. § 5a EStG, Baden-Baden 2007.

[122] Gesetz Nr. 27/75 über die Besteuerung von Schiffen sieht eine sechsjährige Steuerbe-freiung für in Griechenland gebaute, umgebaute oder reparierte Schiffe vor, wenn sie unter griechischer Flagge registriert sind. Art. 107 Abs. 1 Griechische Verfassung bestimmt, dass die Bestimmungen der Kapitel I. bis IV. des Ersten Teils des Gesetzes Nr. 27/75 „Über die Besteuerung von Schiffen, Auferlegung eines Beitrages zur Entwicklung der Handelsmarine, über Niederlassung ausländischer Schiffahrtsunternehmen und über die Regelung damit zu-sammenhängender Fragen" gültig bleiben.

[123] Sky News HD, Greece: Wealthy Shipowners To Bail Out Economy, Friday 19 July 2013, „The deal comes after shipowners were forced to accept a tax imposed on vessels sailing under foreign flags earlier this year" abrufbar: http://news.sky.com/story/1117906/greece-weal thy-shipowners-to-bail-out-economy.

[124] Zur interessanten Subsumtion unter „Arbeitgeberabgabe" s. EuGH, C-436/98 Kom-mission/Hellenische Republik, 19. März 2002.

[125] Folgende „indirekte steuerähnliche Abgaben" sind nach wie vor vorhanden: eine Ab-gabe in Höhe von 50–150 Euro, die von den Verbrauchern für die Genehmigung von Elekt-roarbeiten in Privathaushalten zugunsten des Vereins der Elektrotechniker zu entrichten ist, Abgaben, die auf die Bezüge von Schiedsrichtern (20%) zugunsten des Fonds für die Finan-zierung von Gerichtsgebäuden erhoben werden, Abgaben, die für jede anwaltliche Vertretung zugunsten der Anwaltskammer zu entrichten sind, eine Abgabe, die auf die Stromrechnung der Verbraucher zugunsten des nationalen öffentlichen Rundfunks erhoben wird, eine Abgabe (0,5%), die auf die gerichtliche Beschwerdegebühr zugunsten der Nationalstelle für Gesund-heitsdienstleistungen erhoben wird, eine Arbeitnehmer und Arbeitgeber belastende „Barein-lage" (10% des Bruttoeinkommens) die zugunsten des Versicherungsfonds intergenerativer Solidarität entrichtet wird, ein Beitrag (1 Euro), der von Rentnern (Sozialversicherungsamt) bei jeder Arzneimittelverschreibung zugunsten der Nationalstelle für Gesundheitsdienstleis-tungen zu entrichten ist, Abgaben, die auf den kommunalen Wasserversorgungsrechnungen zugunsten von Sport- und Kulturvereinen erhoben werden, Gebühren, die zugunsten des öf-fentlichen Stromversorgungsunternehmens (DEH) zu Betrieb und Wartung der Stromnetze erhoben werden, eine indirekte Finanzierung der Stromversorgung schutzbedürftiger Gruppen von Energieabnehmern nach Maßgabe der Höhe des Stromverbrauchs, eine Sondergebühr zur

theoretisch problematisch sind schließlich frühere Pensionierungsmöglichkeiten für bestimmte Rentnergruppen, obwohl das allgemeine Rentenalter auf 65 Jahre erhöht wurde, sowie die nicht hinreichende Differenzierung zwischen Fürsorger-, Versorgungs- und Versicherungsprinzip mit Blick auf die Auswahl der aus dem öffentlichen Haushalt zu finanzierenden Leistungen.[126] Sozialer Konfliktstoff liegt auch dem Problem der Vereinbarkeit unterschiedlicher Mehrwertsteuersätze (etwa in Kykladen oder Nordgriechenland) mit dem Gebot der steuerlichen Neutralität[127] zugrunde. Schließlich ist hervorzuheben, dass die aktuelle Debatte über die Änderung der Griechischen Verfassung Probleme anspricht, die eben die Verbindung von Rechts- und

---

Reduktion von Gasemissionen, Gebühren, die in Höhe von 2 % bzw. 5 % auf den Wert der erstellten geotechnischen Studien von den Verbrauchern zugunsten der Geotechnikkammer Griechenlands erhoben werden, eine Gebühr in Höhe von 0,1 % auf die Zahlungen für öffentliche Arbeiten zugunsten der Zentralen Behörde für die öffentliche Beschaffung, eine Gebühr in Höhe von 0,1 % auf das Beteiligungskapital der Aktiengesellschaften zugunsten der Wettbewerbskommission, eine Abgabe in Höhe von 4 % auf den Wert von Kopierern, Scannern und Papier für Kopien zugunsten von Autoren- und Verlegervereinen, eine Abgabe in Höhe von 9,02 Euro bei der Wiederausstellung gestohlener Führerscheine zugunsten der Rentenkasse für Kraftfahrer, eine monatliche Abgabe in Höhe von 2 Euro zugunsten der Sozialversicherungskasse der Gesundheitsberufe für die Wohnkosten von Rentnern mit einer Rente unter der Schwelle von 30.000 Euro, eine Abgabe in Höhe von 0,99 Euro zugunsten der Gemeinde von Prevesa, eine allgemeine Abgabe in Höhe von 2 % auf das Nettoagrareinkommen zugunsten der Griechischen Agrarversicherungsanstalt, eine Gebühr, die von den Teilnehmern an Wettbewerbsverfahren des Obersten Rates für Personalausschuss zu entrichten ist, eine Sozialabgabe in Höhe von 0,2 % zugunsten der Einheitskasse der selbständig Beschäftigten und der Kasse der Ingenieure und Auftragnehmer öffentlicher Arbeiten, eine Abgabe, die zu einem Satz von 3 % auf die Einfuhr und die heimische Erzeugung von Pflanzgut zugunsten der Zentralen Kasse für Landwirtschaft und Viehzucht erhoben wird, eine Abgabe zu einem Satz von 5 % zur Unterstützung der schwächeren Genossenschaften, die das Netz der Fernbuslinien betreiben (Gemeinsame Ertragsfonds der Linienbusse), eine Sonderabgabe in Höhe von 4 % auf die Freiluftkinos zugunsten der „im Bereich des Griechischen Films Tätigen", ein Zoll zu dem Satz von 6 % auf importierte Tonwiedergabegeräte zugunsten der Griechischen Organisation für Geistiges Eigentum, eine Abgabe, die bei Waagenjustierungsüberprüfungen im Handelsbereich erhoben wird, eine Abgabe in Höhe von 30 Euro auf die Einfuhrgenehmigung für Jagdgewehre und -patronen zugunsten des Zusatzsozialversicherungsfonds der Beschäftigten in den Sicherheitskräften, eine Abgabe in Höhe von 0,50 Euro, die bei jeder Vollmachterteilung erhoben wird, wobei hiervon 0,15 Euro in den Zusatzversicherungsfonds der Sicherheitskräfte einzuzahlen sind, eine Abgabe in Höhe von 5 Euro, die für jede anwaltliche Vertretung vor Gericht in der Stadt Xanthi zugunsten des Fonds auf Gegenseitigkeit der Anwälte dieser Stadt zu zahlen ist, eine Abgabe, die auf jede wirtschaftliche Tätigkeit in der Region des Dodekanes von jedem Unternehmer zugunsten der einschlägigen Gebietskörperschaft erhoben wird, eine Abgabe, die für die Einsatzbereitschaft der Nationalen Medikamenten-Aufsichtsbehörde mit Blick auf das Inverkehrbringen von Medizinprodukten und die Erbringungsbereitschaft einschlägiger Dienstleistungen erhoben wird, schließlich ein Betrag, der bei der Abgabe einer ehrenwörtlichen Erklärung über die ordnungsgemäße Durchführung von Elektroarbeiten zugunsten des Elektroarbeitervereins entrichtet wird.

[126] Ein Beispiel ist die Diskussion über die staatliche Finanzierung und Berechtigung zum Empfang einer monatlichen Solidaritätsleistung für Rentner (EKAΣ).

[127] Zum Thema s. schon das Urteil des EuGH vom 11.09.2014, Rs. C-219/13.

Klientelstaat thematisieren: In der Diskussion stehen vor allem die Reduzierung der
Zahl der Abgeordneten von 300 auf 200, die Unvereinbarkeit der Eigenschaft des Abgeordneten mit derjenigen des Ministers, die verfassungsrechtliche Zulässigkeit privater Universitäten, die prononcierte Stärkung der politischen Unabhängigkeit der
Justiz, die Gründung eines Verfassungsgerichts, die Reduzierung der Abgeordneten-
vorrechte auf ein Minimum, die Stärkung der Zuständigkeit und Verantwortung des
Staatspräsidenten, die Abschaffung der Sonderregelung zur Verjährung von Strafta-
ten von Abgeordneten. Von besonderer Bedeutung ist der Vorschlag, dass sich das
Parlament mit der Aufhebung der strafrechtlichen Immunität eines Abgeordneten
nur noch auf dessen Antrag befasst, in allen anderen Fällen jedoch die strafrechtliche Verfolgung eines Abgeordneten ohne jegliche parlamentarische Intervention
ablaufen soll. Diese verfassungsrechtlichen Reformziele stellen eine Veranschauli-
chung des sich in der Rechtswirklichkeit abspielenden Negativfilms dar. Für das
Thema der Privatisierungen bilden diese Zusammenhänge den Kontext, der den Idealtypus von Privatisierungen unter Rechtsstaatlichkeitsbedingungen verzerrt.[128]

1. Privatisierungshindernisse und ihre Überwindung

Privatisierungs- und Liberalisierungshindernisse sind tatsächliche und juristische
Reformhindernisse. Tatsächliche Hindernisse bringen nicht nur Partikularinteressen
zum Ausdruck. Sie stellen zugleich Problemlösungen in bestimmten Wirtschaftsbe-
reichen dar, die zur Verfestigung mangelhafter Wirtschaftsstrukturen beitragen.
Diese Doppelfunktion lässt sich am Beispiel der Liberalisierung des Taxigewerbes
veranschaulichen. Der Handel mit Taxikonzessionen, die zum Gegenstand eines klientelistischen Tauschaktes und einer Renten- und Kinderversicherung der Taxieigen-
tümer und -fahrer geworden sind, hat zu einem Schwarzmarkt in diesem Bereich geführt.[129] Nun versucht ein Gesetz[130] dies zu ändern. Die höchste Zahl von Taxi-Kon-
zessionen soll sich innerhalb des Pflichtfahrgebiets aus einer mathematischen Formel ergeben (Art. 85 Abs. 2). Die Taxikonzessionen sollen allerdings durch Schenkung unter Lebenden, oder Schenkung von Todes wegen, im Wege der Erbfolge
durch Testament oder entgeltlich übertragbar bleiben. Im Falle von Schenkung
und entgeltlicher Übertragung soll eine Urkunde beweiskräftig festgestellten Datums
erforderlich sein (Art. 102 Abs. 1). Ziel des neuen Gesetzes, das auf die 2011 vorge-

---

[128] Obwohl dem Staat ein fehlender politischer Wille zur Verfolgung der Steuerhinterziehung bescheinigt wird, regelt Art. 45 des Gesetzes 4172–2013 Regierungsblatt 167 vom
23.07.2013 zur Anwendung einkommensteuerrechtlicher Regelwerke die internationale
Amtshilfe und administrative Zusammenarbeit in Steuersachen. Er unterscheidet zwischen
„Ländern, die im Zusammenhang mit der Bekämpfung von Steuerhinterziehung keine Ko-
operationsbereitschaft zeigen" und „Ländern, die vergünstigte Steuersätze zur Verfügung
stellen". Art. 46 desselben Gesetzes behandelt die steuerrechtliche Kontrolle ausländischer
Unternehmungen.

[129] http://www.kathimerini.gr/435229/article/epikairothta/politikh/otan-leme-apeley8erwsh-
thn-ennooyme.

[130] Gesetz 4070/2012 (Regierungsblatt A 82/10–04–2012).

schlagene volle Liberalisierung des Taxigewerbes und Abschaffung der Übertragbarkeit der Taxischeine verzichtet, ist neben der Gewerberegulierung die Zerschlagung des Schwarzmarktes unter Berücksichtigung der gewachsenen (auch schattenwirtschaftlichen) Strukturen mit Hilfe von Differenzierungen und Übergangsregelungen. In allen Bereichen müssen Privatisierung und Liberalisierung Verhaltensweisen und Handlungsstrategien beseitigen oder ersetzen, die sich in verschiedenen Graden im Überschneidungsbereich von Rechts- und Klientelstaat und Schattenwirtschaft bewegen. Der symbiotische Mechanismus von Klientel- und Rechtsstaat führt zu einer institutionellen Verdoppelung: Hinter den formalen Institutionen bestehen informale Strukturen, welche die Bedürfniserfüllungen der Bevölkerung bedingen. Diese Doppelgleisigkeit verursacht Transaktionskosten, Ungerechtigkeit, politische Unterwanderung von Instanzen und suboptimale ökonomische Institutionen.[131]

a) Beamtenrecht

Juristische Privatisierungshindernisse finden sich bereits auf Verfassungsebene. Während die Verfassung die Selbstbehauptung des Klientelstaates nicht verhindern kann, stellt sie ein bislang unüberwindbares Hindernis für die Entlassung von Beamten dar.[132] Gemäß Artikel 154 Abs. 1 des Beamtengesetzes (Gesetz 3528/2007) darf ein Beamter entlassen werden, wenn seine Planstelle gestrichen wird. Art. 154 Abs. 4 der Verfassung gesteht ihm allerdings das Recht, auf Antrag eine angemessene Beschäftigung in einer anderen Behörde oder in einem Staatsbetrieb zu erhalten. Die Lösung der sogenannten „Arbeitsreserve" wurde gewählt, damit das Ziel zur Entfernung 150.000 Bediensteter aus dem öffentlichen Sektor bis 2015 erreicht wird. Arbeitsreservisten sollen acht Monate lang dreiviertel ihrer letzten Bezüge erhalten und danach, sofern sich für sie keine neue Verwendung ergibt, in die Arbeitslosigkeit entlassen werden (Art. 90 Abs. 6 Gesetz 4172–2013). Umstritten ist hier-

---

[131] *Judy Rene Sims,* Globalization and the Privatization of Radio in Greece: Influences, Issues, and Consequences, in: Isaac A. Blankson/Patrick D. Murphy (eds.), Negotiating Democracy: Media Tranformations in Emerging Democracies. Global Media Studies Series. Albany State University of New York Press, 2007, S. 240; Wikipedia, Tax evasion and corruption in Greece, http://en.wikipedia.org/wiki/Tax_evasion_and_corruption_in_Greece. Zur klientelistischen Unterwanderung des Gesundheitssystems s. *Charalambos Economou,* Greece: Health System Review 2010, Health Systems in Transition 12(7):1–180, World Health Organization 2010, S. XVI: „The dominance of clientelism and party thinking instead of consensus-building has resulted in a health policy that lacks continuity and the ability to bring about change."

[132] Artikel 103 (4) Griechische Verfassung: „Staatsbeamte, die Planstellen innehaben, sind Beamte auf Lebenszeit, solange diese Stellen bestehen. Beamte auf Lebenszeit steigen besoldungsmäßig nach Maßgabe der Gesetze auf; sie dürfen mit Ausnahme der Erreichung der Altersgrenze und der Entlassung aufgrund eines gerichtlichen Urteils nicht ohne Anhörung eines Dienstrates versetzt und nicht ohne Entscheidung eines Dienstrates herabgestuft oder aus dem Dienst entlassen werden; jeder Dienstrat besteht mindestens zu zwei Dritteln aus Staatsbeamten auf Lebenszeit. Gegen die Entscheidungen der Diensträte ist die Beschwerde beim Staatsrat nach Maßgabe der Gesetze zulässig."

bei das maßgebliche Kriterium für die Auswahl der Arbeitsreservisten. Obwohl die Evaluation der Bediensteten sowie die Art ihrer Einstellung ursprünglich als maßgebliche Auswahlkriterien vorgesehen waren, wurde der Schwerpunkt nachträglich durch einen Ministerialbeschluss[133] auf das Dienstzeitalter und insbesondere auf die Einstellung im Zeitraum von 1998 bis 2003 gesetzt, was als Verstoß gegen die Beurteilungskriterien für die Zuweisung einer Note für die von den Bediensteten vorgelegten Befähigungsnachweise und damit auch gegen das die Arbeitsreserve vorgesehene Gesetz moniert wird.[134]

b) Staatlicher Grundbesitz zwischen Schwarzbau und Privatisierung

Paradebeispiel rechtsstaatlicher Defizite in Griechenland, die Verwaltung und Bevölkerung einbeziehen und ein Misstrauen gegenüber einem wohlfunktionierenden Gewährleistungsstaat begründen, ist das Privatisierungshindernis des Schwarzbaus.[135] Schwarzbauten können durch ein Verwaltungsverfahren gem. Gesetz 4014/2011, das mittlerweile 12-mal abgeändert worden ist, legalisiert werden. Die Legalisierung erfolgt durch Zahlung einer einmaligen Legalisierungsgebühr, die allerdings das einschlägige Privatisierungshindernis nicht (schnell genug) beseitigen kann.[136] Die Kosten der nachträglichen Erschließung und Umsetzung des Anschlusszwanges wurden jedenfalls nicht in Rechnung gestellt. Der Staatsrat hat schließlich die einschlägigen Regelungen für verfassungswidrig erklärt.[137] Ihnen stehe Artikel 24 Absatz 2 der Verfassung entgegen, der die Umwelt, die rationale städtebauliche Planung und das Wohnumfeld schützt. Frühere gesetzliche Legalisierungsversuche wurden vom Staatsrat als nicht vereinbar mit dem Gleichheitsgebot (Art. 4) dem Rechtsstaatsprinzip (Art. 25) und der Menschenwürde (Art. 2 Griechische Verfassung) befunden. Ein weiteres Gesetz (4137/2013)[138], das ein Verfahren der elektronischen Einreichung der Unterlagen für die nachträgliche Legalisierung von Schwarzbauten vorsieht, wurde von drei Bürgern mit der Begründung angegriffen, es verstoße gegen den Gleichheitsgrundsatz und fördere die Gleichheit im Unrecht zugunsten der Gesetzesbrecher. Angesichts der vom Phänomen angenommenen Dimension (Presseberichten zufolge liefen Legalisierungsverfahren für 780.000 Immobilienbesitzer) optierte übrigens der Gesetzgeber nur in Ausnahmefällen für die

---

[133] Gemeinsamer Ministerialbeschluss Nr.ΥΠΠΟΑ/ΓΔΔΥ/172315/25487/23.09.2013 (Regierungsblatt B′ 2408).

[134] ΕΝΑΠ, 26.11.2013 http://www.enap.gr/index.php?view=article&catid=38:anakinosis&id=7398:26-11-2013.

[135] *Paschos Mandravelis*, Die andere „Verwertung" des staatlichen Besitzes, in: Kathimerini vom 19. July 2012.

[136] Schwarzbauten stellen etwa ein Privatisierungshindernis für Yachthäfen und Anlegestellen für Kreuzfahrtschiffe dar (insbes. in Alimos im Südwesten Athens), so dass die Fristen des Ausschreibungsvefahrens immer wieder verlängert werden: http://www.hradf.com/en/portfolio/small-ports-alimos-hydra-poros-epidavros.

[137] Staatsrat 3341/2013.

[138] http://www.ypeka.gr/Default.aspx?tabid=855.

Sanktion des Abrisses und bevorzugte statt dessen die „Regulierung" von Bauverstößen und Schwarzbauten gegen Zahlung einer in Zeiten der Staatsverschuldung ohnehin willkommenen Geldbuße.[139] Die einschlägige Geldstrafe wird zu Gunsten
einer „Grünen Kasse!"[140] entrichtet. Die Regierung bietet der Troika als Konsolidie-
rungsmaßnahme die Einkünfte aus der „monetären ‚Pönalisierung' der Schwarzbauten" an, die sich auf 200 Millionen Euro beliefen.[141] Der Staatsrat befand dieses Gesetz für verfassungsmäßig. Verworfen wurde lediglich eine Bestimmung, die gegen
das Prinzip der Gewaltenteilung (Art. 26 der Verfassung) insofern verstoße, als sie
die Legalisierung von Schwarzbauten zulasse, welche aufgrund rechtskräftigen Gerichtsurteils bereits zum Abriss bestimmt seien.[142] Ferner hebt nunmehr der Staatsrat
hervor, dass ungenehmigte Immobilien, die ganz oder teilweise Küstenstreifen be-
baut haben, „unabhängig vom Zeitpunkt ihrer Errichtung", d. h. auch bei Errichtung
vor der verwaltungsrechtlichen Abgrenzung der Küstenzone, „zwingend abzureißen
sind", da die Küste nicht durch Staatsakte, die lediglich feststellenden Charakter hätten, sondern durch natürliche Phänomene gebildet werde.[143] Der Gesetzentwurf,[144]
der das wirtschaftliche Potenzial der Küstengebiete erschließen will und es Bauher-
ren erlaubt, Küstenstreifen zu bebauen, während er gleichzeitig Straferlass für bestehende rechtswidrige Bauten vorsieht und das Recht der Öffentlichkeit auf freien Zugang zur Küste einschränkt, ist auf scharfe Kritik und Ablehnung (auch von der Ver-
waltungsrichtervereinigung) gestoßen. Das Finanzministerium räumte ein, dass „die
Beteiligung und Mitwirkung der Bürger am Konsultationsprozess auf Probleme auf-
merksam gemacht hat, die weiter untersucht werden müssen".[145] Die Gesetze zur Legalisierung von Schwarzbau und Bauverstößen (4014/2014, 4178/2013) verfolgen
neben dem Fiskalziel auch das Ziel einer endgültigen Problemlösung, das allerdings,
wie die Rechtsgeschichte in diesem Gebiet vermuten lässt, die Entstehung einer
neuen Generation von Schwarzbauten nicht ohne weiteres verhindern wird, solange
es an einem Grundbuch fehlt. Das „General Secretariat of Public Property

---

[139] So die Begründung des Gesetzentwurfs (S. 2): http://www.hellenicparliament.gr/UserFi
les/2f026f42-950c-4efc-b950-340c4fb76a24/a-afthair-eis.pdf.

[140] http://www.prasinotameio.gr/index.php/el/to-prasino-tameio/poroi-prasinou-tameiou.

[141] „Please note that only 40 % of illegal buildings have entered into the scheme of Law
4014/2011 and Law 4178/2013... (P)lease mark that another discrepancy between your gap
and our budget of €200mln should definitely be removed. We have provided all the supporting
material on which our analysis is based (i. e. profile of the monthly payments, categories of
illegal buildings, average fine and administrative fee)." The Hellenic Republic. Report on
further Activities, Email an die Troika, auf Seite 10: http://www.ste.gr/images/StE/content/del
tia/Hardouvelis.pdf; http://www.tovima.gr/files/1/2014/12/02/Hardouvelis.pdf.

[142] http://www.protothema.gr/greece/article/425979/ste-sudagmatikos-o-nomos-gia-ti-nomi
mopoiisi-authaireton/.

[143] Staatsrat 3354/2014.

[144] http://www.opengov.gr/minfin/wp-content/uploads/downloads/2014/04/aigialos.pdf.

[145] Reaktion auf die öffentliche Konsultation: http://www.opengov.gr/minfin/?p=4692.
http://savethegreekseashore.wordpress.com/category/uncategorized/.

(G.S.P.P.)",[146] das durch Art. 20 des Gesetzes 3965/2011 in Zusammenhang mit der neuen Organisationsstruktur des Finanzministeriums durch die Präsidentialverordnung 111/2014 gegründet wurde, erfüllt nicht seine Rolle des zentralen Monitoring und Schutzes staatlichen Eigentums.[147] Abrisse werden überwiegend nicht vorgenommen und der Rechtswidrigkeitsstachel bleibt im Fleische der Rechtsordnung nach wie vor sichtbar, was schon auf die Staatsgründung zurückgeht.[148] Nach der Zeit des Wirkens (1833–1843) des „Stadtarchitekten" *Friedrich Stauffert*[149] und der Suspendierung aller Ausländer aus dem Staatsdienst (1843) wurden vor allem militärische sog. „Geometer" mit der Städtebauplanung betraut, die aus politischen Gründen zur Meidung von Konflikten mit der Bevölkerung das Baurecht nicht durchsetzten.[150] Praktisch wurden nur die vorgesehenen Baulinien eingehalten. Die Gesetzesverordnung vom 17.7./16.8.1923 konnte der Herausforderung einer städtebaulichen Lösung des Flüchtlingsproblems nach der militärischen Niederlage von 1922 und dem Bevölkerungsaustausch zwischen Griechenland und der Türkei nicht gerecht werden. Sie führte zu Wellen sukzessiver Legalisierungen von Bauverstößen und ungeplanten Baugebietserweiterungen. Art. 20 des Gesetzes 3714/1928 sah die Legalisierung von Baugenehmigungen vor, die von unzuständigen Behörden erlassen worden waren. Obwohl der gesetzliche Rahmen (Art. 60 ff des Gesetzes 1923) für die Bekämpfung von Schwarzbau und Bauverstößen für die damaligen Verhältnisse sehr fortschrittlich war, wurden seine differenzierten Sanktionen nicht zur Anwendung gebracht. Der Gesetzgeber hat sich zunehmend den Interessen der rechtswidrigen Eigentümer unterworfen und hat bislang „besondere" Legalisierungsgründe immer finden können: die Sonderbedingungen des neuentstandenen Griechenlands, die Flüchtlinge (1922), den zweiten Weltkrieg, die heutige Staatsverschuldung.[151] Das Grundbuch befindet sich leider immer noch im Aufbau. Die Kartierung der noch übrigen Landfläche (rund 86 Mln ha) zur Katastererstellung stößt – im Anschluss an eine Beschwerde der spanischen Unternehmung TECNOLOGÍAS Y

---

[146] Regierungsblatt A 178/29–08–2014; http://www.gspp.gr/?page_id=71&lang=en.

[147] Wie die Troika in The Economic Adjustment Programme for Greece Fifth Review – October 2011, (Draft) S. 46 bemerkte: „A new General Secretariat of Real Estate Development is established with the aim of improving management of real estate assets, clear them of encumbrances and prepare them for privatisation. [July 2011] The secretariat has been legally established (Law 3965/2011) but no terms of reference on the operational role of this Secretariat has been sent. Its exact role needs to be clearly defined."

[148] Der Bruch mit der osmanischen und der Anfang einer europäischen städtebaulichen Entwicklung wurde in der „Verordnung, Gesundheit gemäße Erbauung von Städten und Dörfern betr." (vom 3./15. April 1835) Regierungsblatt des Königreichs Griechenland, S. 133 ff. programmatisch vorgenommen.

[149] *Alexander Papageorgiou-Venetas*, Städte und Landschaften in Griechenland zur Zeit König Ottos (1833–1862) (Peleus), Wiesbaden 2009.

[150] Das erste „Legalisierungsgesetz", das Sanktionsfreiheit gegen Entgelt sichert, kommt 1855: http://arxeiomnimon.gak.gr/search/resource.html?tab=01&id=6474.

[151] Hierzu s. http://courses.arch.ntua.gr/el/proseggiseis_toy_sxediasmoy_sthn_ellada/maui mata/2013–2014/05__h_nomouesia_gia_thn_taktopoihsh_%E2%80%93_nomimopoihsh_ tvn_ayuairetvn.html.

SERVICIOS AGRARIOS, S.A. (TRAGSATEC) – auf intransparente und gleich-
heitswidrige Ausschreibungsverfahren, die für die Vergabe der 22 von den 28
noch zu vergebenden Verträgen zur Vornahme der einschlägigen geodätischen Lan-
desregistrierungsvermessungen und zur Erstellung der Katastrierungsstudien erforderlich sind.[152] Ein Gesetzentwurf (April 2014), der die Möglichkeit außergerichtlichen Vergleichs im Falle von Eigentumsstreitigkeiten zwischen Privaten und Staat
bei Rechtshängigkeit und vor dem Fällen eines erstinstanzlichen Gerichtsurteils vor-
sah, geriet in den Sog der Debatte über die rechtliche Abgrenzung der Küstenzone
und ist nie zu Gesetz geworden.[153] Erst im Oktober 2014 wurde (unter dem Druck
der Troika) eine Beschleunigungsmöglichkeit für die Statuierung eines effizienten
Räumungsverfahrens gegen Leute, die sich illegal staatliches Eigentum angeeignet
haben, durch Gesetzentwurf dem Parlament zur Abstimmung vorgelegt.[154] Zu seiner
Umsetzung müssen allerdings ohnehin Verwaltungsakte fallbezogen erlassen werden, die natürlich wieder den Gegenstand langwieriger Gerichtsverfahren darstellen
werden. Ein umstrittener Gesetzentwurf (Erschließungsbeiträge in Land und Geld –
Straßenbauliche Enteignungen und andere Vorschriften)[155] der die Deklassifizierung
von Waldgebieten erleichtern und Abholzungen, die von Landwirten vorgenommen
worden waren, faktisch legalisieren sollte, konnte jedenfalls unter öffentlichem[156]
und wissenschaftlichem Druck erst durch die Aufnahme grundlegender Änderungen
und Differenzierungen zum Gesetz[157] werden. Ein ausdrückliches Bauverbot auf ab-
geholzten Waldgebieten musste statuiert und die Bestimmung von Art. 12 Abs. 3 des
Gesetzentwurfs, der zufolge eine Anordnung zur Wiederaufforstung nach Ablauf
von fünf Jahren aufzuheben wäre, „wenn sich die Wiederaufforstung als nicht durch-
führbar erwiesen hätte“, musste gestrichen werden. Der Wissenschaftsdienst des Parlaments hatte die Vereinbarkeit der Bestimmungen von Art. 12 des Gesetzentwurfes
mit Art. 24 (der Schutz der natürlichen und kulturellen Umwelt ist Pflicht des Staates) und mit dem unmittelbar anzuwendenden[158] Art. 117 Abs. 3 (zwingende Wiederaufforstung verbrannter Wälder) der Verfassung und der einschlägigen Rechtsprechung des Staatsrates[159] verneint.[160] Die rechtliche Regelung und gerichtliche Nach-

---

[152] http://www.ktimatologio.gr/sites/en/Pages/Default.aspx; http://www.naftemporiki.gr/fi
nance/story/888922/akuroi-oi-22-apo-tous-28-diagonismous-tou-ktimatologiou.

[153] http://www.opengov.gr/minfin/wp-content/uploads/downloads/2014/04/epilyshidiokti
siwn.pdf; http://www.opengov.gr/minfin/?p=4756.

[154] http://www.tanea.gr/files/1/2014/9057039.pdf%20TAIPED.pdf.

[155] http://www.hellenicparliament.gr/Nomothetiko-Ergo/Anazitisi-Nomothetikou-Ergou?
law_id=247fa2eb-10b2-4680-aa19-a3fc00c9cf96.

[156] WWF-Griechenland 11.12.2014 „Brief an die Abgeordneten“: http://www.wwf.gr/ima
ges/pdfs/Epistoli-pros-vouleftes-gia-dasiko-nomosxedio-eisforas-se-gi-December2014.pdf.

[157] Gesetz 4315/2014 (ΦEK Α′ 269/24–12–2014).

[158] Siehe Staatsrat 952/1990.

[159] Staatsrat: ΣτΕ 3980/2011 und ΣτΕ 1599/2014, ΣτΕ 952/1990, 1517/2009, 2126, 1316/
2000,1573/2002; ΣτΕ 2694/2012, 1508/2008, 772/1992, 2770/1998.

[160] http://www.hellenicparliament.gr/UserFiles/7b24652e-78eb-4807-9d68-e9a5d4576eff/
p-ghra-epi.pdf insbes. auf S. 7–10.

prüfbarkeit einer Anordnung zur Wiederaufforstung oder einer Umwandlung von Wäldern in Bau- bzw. Ackerland werden ohne Grundbuch weiterhin mit massiven Unsicherheiten verbunden bleiben.

c) Schließung, Sanierung und Privatisierung von Staatsbetrieben

Weiteres Beispiel der Legitimationsschwierigkeiten, mit denen Privatisierungen zu kämpfen haben, sind die öffentlichen Unternehmen und Anstalten. Die Privatisierung eines Staatsbetriebs, der bereits dem privilegierten, „privaten" Zugang einer bestimmten politischen Klientel vorbehalten ist, bringt politische Kosten mit sich und muss der Öffentlichkeit gegenüber ihre Gemeinwohlorientierung nachweisen.[161] Ebenso anschaulich ist die rechtswidrige Schließung des Staatsrundfunks. Die Begründung für die Schließung ging dahin, die Rationalisierung der Art und Kosten der Dienstleistungserbringung des öffentlichen Rundfunks solle durch die Gründung und Ausgestaltung eines neuen Trägers erfolgen, der den verfassungsrechtlichen Vorgaben entspreche, mit den demokratischen, sozialen und kulturellen Anforderungen der Gesellschaft konform gehe und den Pluralismus in der Medienlandschaft wahre. Der geschlossene Staatsrundfunk (ERT) musste infolge einer einstweiligen Verfügung des höchsten Verwaltungsgerichts (Staatsrat) wieder auf Sendung gehen. Er solle so lange weiter arbeiten, bis eine rechtliche Regelung über eine Neuordnung des Rundfunks getroffen sei. Erst wenn eine neue dem öffentlichen Interesse dienende Sendeanstalt gebildet werde, könne der alte Rundfunk ersetzt werden (Prinzip der „continuité du service public").[162] In seiner späteren Entscheidung in der Hauptstreitsache wurde die Schließung für verfassungsmäßig befunden. Mit dem mittelfristigen Strukturanpassungsprogramm habe sich der Staat dazu verpflichtet, einen Plan zur Schließung, Zusammenstellung oder Sanierung „nicht erforderlicher staatlicher Verwaltungsstellen und Staatsbetriebe" aufzustellen. Art. 15 Abs.2 Griechische Verfassung bestimme, dass Hörfunk und Fernsehen unter der unmittelbaren Kontrolle des Staates stehen. Er schreibe aber nicht das Vorhandensein einer „öffentlich-rechtlichen Sendeanstalt" vor. Optiere der Gesetzgeber für die Einrichtung einer öffentlichen Sendeanstalt, müsse diese eine pluralistische Struktur haben, Einflüsse seitens der Regierung und der politischen Parteien ausschließen und nach Maßgabe der Grundsätze der Objektivität, der Unparteilichkeit und des Pluralismus operieren.

---

[161] Die Athener U-Bahn gilt als bekanntes Beispiel. Zur klientelistischen Struktur sowie mangelnden organisatorischen und finanziellen Rechenschaftspflicht s. Presseberichte: *Giorgos Papachristou*, Ta Nea vom 9. July 2013. Siehe auch: *Nick Malkoutzis*, An Underground Resistance in Athens, ekathimerini.com, Thursday Jan 24, 2013: „Decision makers are also paying the price for treating the civil service as a private club to which they could bring new members whenever they wanted. It has been well documented that the metro experienced a surge in its employee numbers, often in nontransparent circumstances, under the 2004–09 New Democracy government. The current administration is now trying to slash costs that were in some cases unnecessarily created by its predecessors." Ferner s. *Wolfgang Lieb*, NachDenkSeiten – Die kritische Website, 16. Juli 2013, http://www.nachdenkseiten.de/?p=17985.

[162] Staatsrat 236/2013, Rn. 11, 12.

Die Entscheidung hebt hervor, dass die Schließung des staatlichen Rundfunks nicht lediglich aus fiskalischen Gründen erfolgte, sondern auch das Ziel der Errichtung einer neuen Sendeanstalt nach dem Gesetz 4173/2013 verfolgte, wobei bis zur Neuerrichtung eine Übergangssendeanstalt ihre Arbeit aufnahm und ordnungsgemäß operierte. Ein Verstoß gegen Art. 10 EMRK wurde ebenfalls verneint.[163] Auch der neu gegründeten Rundfunkanstalt „NERIT" wird allerdings Misstrauen entgegengebracht. Die Europäische Rundfunk- und Fernsehunion teilte in ihrem Brief vom 12. 8. 2014 ihre „tiefe Besorgnis" über die Entscheidung des griechischen Parlaments vom 5. 8. 2014 zum Ernennungsverfahren des Aufsichtsrats des neuen staatlichen Rundfunks NERIT mit. Denn, obwohl das Gesetz 4173/2013 eine Reihe von Kautelen eingeführt habe, um dem politischen Einfluss auf den Rundfunk einen Riegel vorzuschieben und seine Unabhängigkeit und Pluralität von der Legislative und der Exekutive zu gewährleisten, seien diese Neutralitätsgarantien nunmehr „über Nacht" durch die genannte parlamentarische Entscheidung entgegen der in Europa etablierten „best practices" komplett geändert worden.[164]

Ein weiteres Privatisierungshindernis ist die politische „Kolonialisierung" der Wirtschaft durch die Selektivität der nationalen Subventionierungspolitik, die zugleich der Reproduktion des politischen Klientelsystems dient. Öffentliche Unterstützungsmaßnahmen müssen den EU-Vorschriften und den Bestimmungen über staatliche Beihilfen zur Rettung und Umstrukturierung von in Schwierigkeiten geratenen Unternehmen genügen.[165] Das ist beim Staatsbetrieb der griechischen Wehrindustrie[166] Larco nicht der Fall. Larco hat in der Vergangenheit staatliche Beihilfen von über 105 Mio. EUR erhalten. Rettungs- und Umstrukturierungsbeihilfen dürfen nur einmal innerhalb von 10 Jahren gewährt werden („Grundsatz der einmaligen Beihilfe"). Darüber hinaus müssen solche Beihilfen entweder nach Ablauf von sechs Monaten eingestellt werden oder aber zur Umsetzung eines plausiblen Umstrukturierungsplans gewährt werden. Die Europäische Kommission hat Zweifel, dass die Maßnahmen für Larco im Zusammenhang mit einem Umstrukturierungsplan gewährt und dass sie eingestellt wurden. Sie bezweifelt, dass der „Grundsatz der einmaligen Beihilfe" eingehalten wurde.[167] Larco kann zwar zu dem Zeitpunkt, als die

---

[163] Staatsrat 1901/2014.

[164] http://www.ekathimerini.com/4dcgi/_w_articles_wsite1_1_25/08/2014_542381.

[165] Mitteilung der Kommission – Leitlinien der Gemeinschaft für staatliche Beihilfen zur Rettung und Umstrukturierung von Unternehmen in Schwierigkeiten Amtsblatt Nr. 244 vom 01/10/2004 S. 0002–0017.

[166] Zum Zusammenhang von Politik, Gewerkschaften, Klientelismus, Verschwendung und Intransparenz in der griechischen Waffenindustrie s. *Nikos Chassapopoulos*, To Vima 19.09. 2013 http://www.tovima.gr/finance/article/?aid=529123. Zur internationalen „Verflechtung" am Beispiel von Krauss Maffei Wegmann (KMW) s. http://www.spiegel.de/politik/deutsch land/panzerdeals-staatsanwaltschaft-ermittelt-gegen-spd-politiker-a-970948.html; http://www. zeit.de/wirtschaft/unternehmen/2014-11/korruption-verdacht-krauss-maffei-wegmann-durchsu chung.

[167] Zur Unterstützung zählen eine Kapitalaufstockung im Jahr 2009 und mehrere staatliche Garantien für Darlehen im Zeitraum 2008–2010, der eventuelle Verzicht auf eine Rückfor-

Maßnahmen gewährt wurden, als Unternehmen in Schwierigkeiten im Sinne der Rettungs- und Umstrukturierungsleitlinien angesehen werden. Die öffentliche Hand hat jedoch keinen Umstrukturierungsplan vorgelegt, während die Maßnahmen noch nicht abgeschlossen sind. Die Kommission eröffnete das Verfahren nach Art. 108 Abs. 2 AEUV.[168]

Auf den Umstrukturierungsplan und die Wiederherstellung der langfristigen Rentabilität kommt es auch bei der „New TT Hellenic Postbank S.A." („New TT") an.[169] Die Kommission zweifelt daran, dass New TT gemäß dem Umstrukturierungsplan allein zu Rentabilitätserreichung in der Lage ist. Die vorgeschlagenen Maßnahmen zur Erwirtschaftung künftiger Gewinne schienen sehr begrenzt zu sein. Diese Zweifel beträfen insbesondere den begrenzten Personalabbau und die begrenzte Schließung von Zweigniederlassungen sowie die eingeschränkte Nutzung von Synergien. „New TT" laufe Gefahr, zu einer Brückenbank zu werden, die wiederholt staatliche Beihilfen in Anspruch nehmen müsse. Nur die Reintegration von „TT" in eine größere existenzfähige Finanzgesellschaft würde ihre Überlebenschancen erhöhen. Es sei auch nicht davon auszugehen, dass Beihilfe und Umstrukturierungskosten auf das erforderliche Minimum beschränkt seien, da „New TT" als Einzelgesellschaft umzustrukturieren sei, was die Kosten in die Höhe treibe. Zwar stammt ein Großteil der Verluste von „TT" in den letzten Jahren aus einem Schuldenerlass zugunsten des Staates, d. h. im Rahmen eines Verzichts bei Beteiligungen des privaten Sektors und einer weitgehend unter pari erfolgten Veräußerung griechischer Staatsanleihen Ende 2012, was einer Zahlung von „TT" an den griechischen Staat gleichgestellt wird und folglich eine niedrigere Vergütung der staatlichen Rekapitalisierungsbeihilfe rechtfertigen kann. Im Hinblick auf eine Wettbewerbsverzerrung wird aber von der Kommission festgehalten, dass „TT" wesentlich mehr griechische Staatsanleihen im Verhältnis zu seiner Größe hielt als andere griechische Banken; eine derart umfangreiche Investition in diese Anleihen könnte allerdings einem unangemessenen Risikoverhalten gleichkommen.[170] Staatsbetriebe, U-Bahn, Staatsrundfunk weisen beispielhaft nach, dass das Staatsvermögen bereits klientelistisch privatisiert ist.

---

derung einer ausstehenden Schuld seitens des Staates seit 2004 sowie eine Ausnahmeregelung für eine Vorauszahlung eines Steuerbußgelds im Jahr 2010. Die EU Kommission stellt fest, dass angesichts dieser Finanzdaten Larco zumindest seit 2008 in finanziellen Schwierigkeiten gewesen sein dürfte.

[168] Staatliche Beihilfen: Kommission leitet eingehende Prüfung zu möglichen griechischen Beihilfen für Larco General Mining & Metallurgical Company S.A. ein Commission Européenne – IP/13/195 06/03/2013.

[169] Am 18. Januar 2013 gründeten die griechischen Behörden das Kreditinstitut „New TT Hellenic Postbank S.A." („New TT") für eine begrenzte Dauer. New TT übernahm die soliden Geschäftszweige der ehemaligen TT Hellenic Postbank S.A. („TT"). In diesem Zusammenhang erhielt New TT eine staatliche Beihilfe in Höhe von 4,6 Mrd. EUR vom griechischen Finanzstabilisierungsfonds („Hellenic Financial Stability Fund"/„HSFS").

[170] Staatliche Beihilfe SA.31155 (2013/C) (ex 2013/NN) (ex 2010/N) – Staatliche Beihilfe für die Hellenic Postbank S.A. durch die Gründung und Kapitalisierung der Brückenbank „New Hellenic Postbank S.A.". Aufforderung zur Stellungnahme nach Artikel 108 Absatz 2 AEUV (Text von Bedeutung für den EWR) (2013/C 190/05).

d) Das Mittelstandsproblem

Der Mittelstand hätte von den Privatisierungen profitieren können, wenn die Rezession ihn nicht zum Erliegen[171] gebracht hätte und die Ausschreibungsverfahren transparent und mittelstandsfreundlicher gewesen wären, denn die Teilnahme griechischer KMU an öffentlichen – allerdings nicht elektronischen – Ausschreibungsverfahren ist viel höher als der Durchschnitt in der EU.[172] Er kommt jedoch wegen fehlender Finanzkraft und Erfahrung bei der Vergabe eines PPP-Großauftrags nicht zum Zuge. Der Grundsatz der Losvergabe (§ 97 III 1 und 2 GWB) nach Gewerbezweigen (Fachlosen) oder Räumen und Mengen (Teillosen) ist für PPP-Projekte schlichtweg ungeeignet. In solchen Fällen ist eine Gesamtvergabe erwünscht. Eine Gesamtvergabe, die eine Reduzierung der Schnittstellen zwischen Auftraggeber und Beratern, sowie eine Verringerung des Vertragsmanagementaufwandes und der Koordinierungsleistungen bedeutet, ist erlaubt, wenn wirtschaftliche oder technische Gründe es erfordern (etwa nach § 97 III 3 GWB). Das ist aber bei PPP-Projekten immer der Fall. Der Mittelstand ist also bei PPP-Projekten auf andere Art und Weise als durch Losbildung zu berücksichtigen. Der amerikanische „Small Business Act" und der Small Business Act für Europa[173] sowie die französische Lösung, welche einen bestimmten Einbindungsgrad kleiner Unternehmen zu Zuschlagsbedingung macht und die Subunternehmer nach dem Zuschlag auf Ausführungsebene besonders schützt, wären in Betracht zu ziehen.[174] Es bietet sich an, zugunsten des Mittelstandes auf Instrumente wie die öffentliche Vorinformation (§ 17a Nr. 1 VOB/A, § 17a Nr. 3 VOL/A) und die Aufwandsentschädigungsmöglichkeit (§ 20 Nr. 2 I VOB/A bzw. VOL/A) zurückzugreifen, die eine erfolgreiche Teilnahmevorbereitung von KMU und die Entscheidung über die eventuelle Bildung einer Bietergemein-

---

[171] „With real GDP in 2013 estimated to be almost 23 % below its 2008 level, Greek SMEs have borne the brunt of the economic crisis in recent years. In that period, SME employment fell by 27 % or more than 630000. Almost one in four (more than 205.000)of the SMEs that existed in 2008 closed down,reducing the total volume of business, measured in added value, by a third of its 2008 levels." 2014 SBA Fact Sheet – Greece: http://ec.europa.eu/enterprise/po licies/sme/facts-figures-analysis/performance-review/files/countries-sheets/2014/greece_en.pdf.

[172] 2014 SBA Fact Sheet – Greece, S. 11: http://ec.europa.eu/enterprise/policies/sme/facts-figures-analysis/performance-review/files/countries-sheets/2014/greece_en.pdf. Zur elektronischen Vergabe s. www.promitheus.gov.gr.

[173] http://ec.europa.eu/enterprise/policies/sme/small-business-act/sme-test/index_en.htm#h2–1.

[174] Die vertragliche Festlegung einer angemessenen Beteiligung von KMU als Nachunternehmer, ist vorgeschlagen worden, s. hierzu die Studie von *Difu u. ISFM*, PPP und Mittelstand, Januar 2008. Zur „Beteiligung an ÖPP-Projekten auf zweiter Ebene" s. *Öffentlich-Private Partnerschaften-Initiative NRW*, Kleine ÖPP-Projekte, Oktober 2008, S. 83 ff. Auf europäischer Ebene s. Evaluation of SMES' Access to Public Procurement Markets in the EU, http://ec.europa.eu/enterprise/policies/sme/business-environment/files/smes_access_to_public_procurement_final_report_executive_summary_2010_en.pdf; Der „Small Business Act" für Europa: http://eur-lex.europa.eu/LexUriServ/LexUriServ.do?uri=COM:2008:0394:FIN:DE:PDF; Circulaire du 3 août 2006 portant manuel d'application du code des marchés publics, (http://www.legifrance.gouv.fr/affichTexte.do?cidTexte=JORFTEXT000000264578&dateTexte=).

schaft erleichtern können. Nach Abschaffung des Unternehmensregisters der Vertragspartner der öffentlichen Hand und dessen (an Berufserfahrung orientierten) 7 Kategorien, die in Griechenland zur Entstehung eines Schwarzmarktes für sogenannte „Auftragsnehmererfahrungsnachweise" für Bauingenieure geführt hatte,[175] ist der Weg für neue Möglichkeiten geebnet. Die Vereinigung der Verbände der Auftragnehmer öffentlicher Bauaufträge sieht hingegen in der Abschaffung von Erfahrungskategorien und Schwellenwerten geradezu eine Förderung von Intransparenz.[176] Wie dem auch sei, müssen griechische KMU es lernen, sich verstärkt als Bewerbe- und Bietergemeinschaften im Teilnahmewettbewerb und im Vergabeverfahren zu organisieren und als Konsortien nach dem Zuschlag den Auftrag durchzuführen, wobei die politisch selektive Finanzierung durch (halbstaatliche) Banken ein Problem bleibt. Die Gründung von „one stop shops" bzw. zentralen Anlaufstellen für die Transaktionen von KMU mit der öffentlichen Hand ist auch im Kontext von Privatisierungen nützlich. Sie könnten Informationen über Ausschreibungen und die Erstellung der nationalen strategischen Rahmenpläne (NSRP), über Änderung von Steuerregelungen sowie über Investitions- Vernetzungs- und Beratungsmöglichkeiten den KMU zur Verfügung stellen.[177] Die Ausgestaltung des Eignungsnachweises (spezielle PPP-Referenzen) stellt auch in Griechenland faktisch eine Markteintrittsschranke für KMU dar. Sowohl Forfaitierungen mit Einredeverzicht als auch Projektfinanzierungen[178] sind jedenfalls mittestandsfreundlich gestaltbar: Im Rahmen der Forfaitierung sollten zu hohe Sicherheitserfordernisse in Form von Vertragserfüllungsbürgschaften und bei einer Projektfinanzierung sollten zu hohe Eigenkapitalquotenanforderungen vermieden werden. Das Morgendorfer-Modell, das eine Kommunalkreditfähigkeit schon während der Bauzeit durch Bautestate ermöglicht, erleichtert ebenfalls die Teilnahme von KMU. In Griechenland ist die Mittelstandsförderung[179] jenseits von Ausschreibungsverfahren Gegenstand eines besonderen KfW-Projektes.[180]

---

[175] http://www.kathimerini.gr/777527/article/oikonomia/ellhnikh-oikonomia/sth-die kdikhsh-dhmosiwn-ergwn-xwris-ta3eis-anwtata-kai-katwtata-oria.

[176] http://www.capital.gr/News.asp?id=2075092.

[177] Zum Bedarf früher Information s. die Ausführungen und Vorschläge im Bericht zu den griechischen KMU 23-9-2013 EKTHESI TASK FORCE MME.pdf (September 2014), S. 24, 30, 34, 36, 41, 43, 48: http://www.elanet.gr/elanet/Left%20column/Basiko%20menu% 20epilogwn/Geniki_Enhmerwsi/23-9-2013%20EKTHESI%20TASK%20FORCE%20MME. pdf.

[178] Die zwei Finanzierungshauptformen für PPP in Deutschland: *Hans-Georg Napp*, Die Finanzierung von öffentlich-privaten Partnerschaften (PPP) – Grundlagen und aktuelle Entwicklungen, Kommunalwirtschaft / Sonderausgabe 2011, 53 ff.

[179] Bericht EP 8. Januar 2013 über die Verbesserung des Zugangs von KMU zu Finanzmitteln (2012/2134(INI)) http://www.europarl.europa.eu/sides/getDoc.do?pubRef=-//EP// TEXT+REPORT+A7-2013-0001+0+DOC+XML+V0//DE.

[180] http://www.handelsblatt.com/politik/international/euro-krise-kfw-finanziert-mittelstand-in-griechenland/9922408.html. Zur Gründung eines griechischen Investment- und Wachstumsfonds s. das Gesetz Nr. 4224/2013.

e) Privatisierung im Schatten der Schuldner/Gläubiger-Differenz

aa) Vorrang für Kassenerfolge oder Reformen in der Krise?

Im Schatten der Gläubiger/Schuldner-Differenz soll Privatisierung vor allem den griechischen Schuldendienst voranbringen. Der erwartete Privatisierungserlös muss im Kontext der von der Konditionalität der Memoranda ausgeschlossenen Alternativen[181] gesehen werden. „Kassenerfolge" werden als offizielles Ziel angegeben, etwa „bis Ende des Jahres" bestimmte Summen durch Privatisierungen bzw. Verpachtungen erwirtschaftet zu haben. Vieles hängt davon ab, wie eine Regierung zu Privatisierungen steht.[182] Auf jeden Fall kann „Kassenerfolg allein einen Privatisierungsakt nicht legitimieren".[183] Dies ist ein Problem, mit dem auch verschuldete Kommunen in Deutschland zu kämpfen hatten. Früher strebten verschuldete Kommunen in erster Linie nach der Gründung von PPP, um Kapital zu beschaffen[184] und Haushaltslöcher zu stopfen. Dabei wurde in den Gesellschaftsverträgen bzw. -satzungen häufig festgeschrieben, dass das durch Veräußerung von Unternehmensanteilen erworbene Kapital ausschließlich zur Schuldentilgung verwendet werde und nur ersparte Zinsen anderweitigen kommunalen Zwecken, z. B. der Kulturförderung, Kindergärten o. ä., zukommen dürfen. Eine solche Regelung wurde meist getroffen, um die Zustimmung des Gemeinderates zur Begründung der PPP zu sichern.[185]

---

[181] „Political reluctance in Europe to start debt restructuring, the fear of potential moral hazard effects and the absence of effective mechanisms to contain its possible financial fallout made this option unappealing. The alternative, nearly-concessional lending within the framework of a large and long-lasting assistance programme, was not politically palatable either. This conundrum led the IMF and the EU to bet on the materialisation of optimistic tax revenue and privatisation assumptions. Instead of formulating a robust programme capable of withstanding adverse economic, political and financial developments, they did just the opposite. It is no surprise that these optimistic assumptions were not vindicated by events." Bruegel Blueprint Series, Volume XIX, S. 60.

[182] „(Populist governments) tend to privatize due to political and economic pressures to raise funds and escape financial pressure ... Committed governments, however, are eager to privatize because of the long-term economic benefits." So *Jared A. Blacker*, Privatization under Duress: The Privatization of the Greek Economy, in: Perspectives on Business & Economics Greece: The Epic Battle for Economic Recovery, Volume 30, http://martindale.cc.le high.edu/sites/martindale.cc.lehigh.edu/files/PrivatizationUnderDuress.pdf.

[183] „HRADF, acting solely in the public interest, implements a demanding privatisation programme with determination, consistency and transparency, contributing decisively to the growth of the Greek economy and the creation of new jobs." http://www.hradf.com/uploads/files/20130812-opap-press-en1.pdf.

[184] *Herbert Obinger/Reimut Zohlnhöfer,* Selling off the family silver: the politics of privatization in the OECD 1990–2000, TranState working papers, No. 15, 2005, http://www.econstor.eu/bitstream/10419/28265/1/497814110.PDF.

[185] Public Private Partnership, 6. Vortragsveranstaltung des Freiherr-vom-Stein-Instituts im Rahmen der Veranstaltungsreihe „Steuerung durch Organisation" am 5. 2. 2003, ein Bericht von *Sven Oliver Hoffmann*, http://www.jura.uni-muenster.de/index.cfm?objectId=F0B375B9-FAA6-6DE5-403FDAEA19629B92.

Die ganze Palette bekannter Verkaufsinstrumente ist beim Privatisierungsprogramm vorhanden: Gesamte Unternehmen oder größere Aktienpakete können direkt an einzelne Investoren verkauft und/oder Aktien einem breiten Publikum zur Zeichnung (Massenprivatisierung) angeboten werden (Kapitalprivatisierung). Auch kann die Konkursauflösung zu einem wichtigen Privatisierungsverfahren werden, wenn bei fehlender Aussicht auf jegliche Besserung eines Unternehmens nach dessen formeller Auflösung seine Bestandteile verkauft oder versteigert und die Erlöse zur Befriedigung der Gläubiger verwendet werden.[186] Es kann aber auch eine Auflösung bestehender Unternehmen und eine Überführung deren Vermögenswerte in neue Privatunternehmen erfolgen (Liquidierung). Ein der Hauptvorteile der Massenprivatisierung ist die möglichst schnelle Übertragung öffentlichen Eigentums an Private. Im Rahmen einer Privatisierung durch Aktienausgabe ist es insbesondere in Griechenland möglich, einen Prozentsatz der Aktien der zu privatisierenden öffentlichen Unternehmen an ihre Arbeitnehmer zu verkaufen, um sie für das Privatisierungsprojekt zu gewinnen.

Abgesehen von den einzusetzenden juristischen Privatisierungsinstrumenten muss aber hervorgehoben werden, dass es auf die Überwindung von Reformwiderständen ankommt. Solange die Wirtschaftslage einigermaßen gut ist, werden die Interessengruppen einschneidenden Reformmaßnahmen nie zustimmen, da sie dann auf Privilegien verzichten müssen. Und auch im Niedergang werden Privatisierungsvorschläge auf Unverständnis stoßen. Eine Umkehr kann erst erwartet werden, wenn sich die wirtschaftliche Lage derart verschlechtert hat, dass niemand mehr (unabhängig von politischer Orientierung) von der Beibehaltung der Staatsbetriebe und beste-

---

[186] Dem IWF zufolge ist im Zusammenhang mit der Privatisierung der Staatsbetriebe der griechischen Wehrindustrie nicht lediglich „restructuring", aber auch „substantial downsizing, ahead of privatization" oder „resolution of ELVO, HDS, and LARCO, both in compliance with State aid rules" in Betracht zu ziehen: International Monetary Fund, Country Report No. 13/241, Greece: Fourth Review, July 2013, S. 133. Siehe ferner die Email der Troika an die griechische Regierung, die eine Auflösung nahelegt: „You are envisaging 144 million Euro of State funds to the military activities that would result from the split between civil and military activities of HDS, additional to the already inherited liabilities from the past. The proposal is basically calling for a rather generous early retirement and exit scheme which would have implications in terms of fiscal space and the programme. Given the fiscal space constraints and the dependence of the company on domestic orders, we believe that this is not a viable solution and the company should be liquidated. If a case could be made from a national defence objective perspective, this has to involve a substantially downsized/restructured company which is domestically-oriented. It has to be seen whether at such lower scale (given lower revenues but possibly high fixed costs) it makes sense from an economic point of view to keep the company on the market or whether one should just proceed with outright liquidation." Ferner sähe sich ein potentieller Investor genötigt, rechtswidrige Beihilfen zurückzuzahlen: Gov't sends revised plan for defense firms as troika favors bankruptcy, ekathimerini.com, Tuesday November 5, 2013, http://www.ekathimerini.com/4dcgi/_w_articles_wsite1_1_04/09/2013_517243.

henden klientelabhängigen Regulierung profitiert.[187] Eine Verschlechterung der Lage bis hin zur Krise stellt sogar unter diesem Gesichtspunkt für Griechenland eine regelrechte Voraussetzung für die Durchsetzbarkeit von Deregulierung und Privatisierung dar.

bb) Privatisierungserfahrung in Transformationsländern und Privatisierungserlösparadoxon

Der Idealtypus einer Privatisierung, die hohe Privatisierungserlöse erzielt, sieht möglichst viele Nachfrager voraus, die in einem einfach und transparent gestalteten Verfahren um marktabhängig bewertete Unternehmen konkurrieren. Und der Privatisierungserlös spiegelt die abdiskontierte Summe zukünftiger Gewinne wider. Dieser Idealtypus bleibt unterkomplex. Dies zeigt sich an den Erfahrungen vieler europäischer (poststaatssozialistischer) Transformationsländer (großer Staatssektor, Budgetdefizite, öffentliche Auslandsverschuldung). Man hat etwa auf das „Privatisierungserlösparadoxon" hingewiesen, dass darin bestand, dass in dem Transformationsland, in dem die verfolgte Politik scheinbar am wenigsten auf Privatisierungserlösmaximierung ausgerichtet war, die besten Privatisierungsergebnisse erzielt werden konnten.[188] Die in der Tschechoslowakei durchgeführte Naturalrestitution (Rückgabe von Eigentum an ursprüngliche Besitzer, die in der Zeit des Kommunismus enteignet worden waren) hatte einerseits einen bewussten Verzicht auf etwaige Verkaufserlöse zur Folge, da das „Gerechtigkeitsziel" höher als fiskalische Erwägungen und die Realisierung von Privatisierungseinnahmen eingestuft wurde. Angebotsseitige Einflussfaktoren auf die Privatisierungserlöse sind die Größe, Modernität und Wettbewerbsfähigkeit des zur Privatisierung anstehenden Kapitalstocks und der Wert einschlägiger Anlagen. Dieser kann allerdings erst am Markt durch den Verkauf der Unternehmen selbst ermittelt werden. Ferner gibt es kontextabhängige politische Stockungen und Blockaden des Privatisierungsprozesses.

Am Markt der Unternehmen lassen sich ein Preisverfall, eine steigende Risikoaversion und eine sinkende Zahlungsbereitschaft der Käufer feststellen, je mehr Unternehmen privatisiert werden sollen. Auch führt die Rezession dazu, dass potentielle Käufer auf weitere Preissenkungen spekulieren und eine Wartehaltung einnehmen. Doch umfasst das Mandat des griechischen Privatisierungsfonds die Privatisierung von Vermögenswerten zu den bestehenden Marktbedingungen. Ähnlich war ein vorrangiges Ziel der deutschen Treuhandanstalt, den Privatisierungsprozess zügig und umfassend zu beenden. Diese Hierarchisierung der Privatisierungsziele schloss Möglichkeiten der Dosierung und zeitlichen Streckung des Angebots aus, die zu

---

[187] Instruktiv die Analyse von *Friedrich Schneider*, Privatisierung und Deregulierung in Österreich in den 90er Jahren: Einige Anmerkungen aus Sicht der Neuen Politischen Ökonomie, Arbeitspapier Nr. 0106, März 2001, S. 21, 22.

[188] *Dirk Süß*, Privatisierung in Polen, der Tschechischen Republik und Ungarn: Das Erlösparadoxon und seine Auflösung, Arbeitsberichte-Discussion Papers No. 15/97, Frankfurt (Oder): http://www.europa-uni.de/de/forschung/institut/institut_fit/publikationen/discussion_pa pers/1997/97-15-Suess.pdf.

einem besseren Ergebnis bei den Erlösen hätten führen können. Die Frage ist, ob man bereit ist, auf Erlös zu verzichten, um den Privatisierungsprozess schneller voranzubringen. Die Übergangskosten[189] von Privatisierung und Marktliberalisierung müssen mitberücksichtigt werden. Im Falle der deutschen Wiedervereinigung konnte dies dank der politischen Bereitschaft und Fähigkeit zu massiven Finanztransfers aus den alten Bundesländern kompensiert werden. Eine Verlangsamung des Privatisierungsprozesses kann jedenfalls positiv sein, soweit sie sich als strategisch bewusste Option für das Zurückbehalten bestimmter Anteile staatlichen Besitzes darstellt, welche nach Plan später verkauft werden: wenn etwa das Verfahren deshalb verlangsamt wird, weil die absehbaren Erlöse für wertvolle Stücke des Tafelsilbers als zu niedrig eingeschätzt werden. Sowohl gestaffelte Veräußerungen als auch ein Angebot von Vermögenswerten unter Preis kollidieren mit dem Ziel, den Anstieg der Privatisierungserlöse zu erreichen, die für die Gewährung der europäischen Finanzhilfe erforderlich sind. Die Verlangsamung wirkt sich aber auch negativ auf Privatisierungsprojekte aus, solange sie – wie im griechischen Fall – „Folge politischer Querelen" und von Reformwiderständen ist. Der Idealtypus der Privatisierung staatlichen Besitzes wird andererseits jedoch durch die andauernde politische Instabilität verzerrt. Potentielle Käufer wissen, dass Bailout-Pakete als Mechanismen der Transformation der staatlichen Verschuldung gegenüber privaten Kreditgebern in eine solche gegenüber Staaten und öffentlichen Institutionen fungieren, was eine (zusätzliche) Schuldenumstrukturierung kaum zulässt. Der politische und fiskalische Druck wird lange aufrechterhalten bleiben. Neben dem verschuldeten Zustand der Staatsbetriebe erklärt diese Lage, warum es keinen Ansturm potentieller Käufer gibt und weshalb der griechische Staat Schwierigkeiten hat, eine optimale Kombination zwischen gestaffeltem Verkauf, unter Preis Angebot von Vermögenswerten und Überwindung der Interessen des politischen Klientelsystems zu finden. Obige Problematik lässt sich am Beispiel der Privatisierung der Staatsbetriebe der griechischen Wehrindustrie veranschaulichen. Es gibt laufende Verträge, deren Kündigung die Zahlungen durch die Aktivierung vertraglicher Sanktionsklauseln auslösen wird. Ferner könnte die Entlassung aller Beschäftigten mit höheren Kosten als bei selektiven Entlassungen im Rahmen einer Betriebssanierung verbunden sein.[190] Vor dem Hintergrund dessen, dass jede Entlassung aus öffentlichen Unternehmungen politisch riskant ist, sehen nunmehr die Regelungen zum Personalabbau einen lediglich „freiwilligen Austritt" einer bestimmten Anzahl (1/3) des (Verwaltungs-)Personals aus der

---

[189] „(I)t takes time for reforms to pay off, typically at least a couple of years. This is partly because their benefits materialise through firm entry and increased hiring, both of which are gradual processes, while any reform-driven layoffs are immediate." *M. Cacciatore/R. Duval/ G. Fiori* (2012), „Short-Term Gain or Pain? A DSGE Model-Based Analysis of the Short-Term Effects of Structural Reforms in Labour and Product Markets", OECD Economics Department Working Papers, No. 948, OECD Publishing. doi: 10.1787/5k9csvkkr3xn-en.

[190] Bericht hierzu in: Kathimerini, 10.09.2013.

Hellenic Defence Systems S.A. nach Maßgabe der „funktionalen und operationellen Bedürfnissen des Betriebs" vor.[191]

f) Privatisierung als Instrument der Staatsreform

Im Kontext der Verschuldungs- und Eurokrise kommt Privatisierung eine besondere staatstheoretische und staatsrechtliche Bedeutung zu. Sie muss die Institutionen des Gewährleistungsstaates selbst schaffen, die dem ganzen Unternehmen Legitimation spenden können. Sie muss ein Gerechtigkeits-, Vertrauens- und Legitimationsdefizit[192] ausgleichen und zur Modernisierung des öffentlichen Sektors beitragen.[193] Unsichere ökonomische Aussichten und die restriktive Kreditvergabe der Banken verlangsamen die Privatisierungs-Transaktionen. Hinzu kommen politische Widerstände[194], geopolitische Überlegungen[195] und das Misstrauen der Bevölkerung gegenüber dem Privatisierungsverfahren.[196]

---

[191] Entscheidung des Wirtschafts- und Verteidigungsministers, Regierungsblatt 2708/ 10.10.2014, Art. 1 Abs. 6.

[192] „While the economy is now re-balancing apace, this is happening mainly through recessionary channels, rather than through productivity boosting reforms. Meanwhile, the mounting sense of social unfairness is undermining support for the program." IMF Country Report No. 13/20, Greece: First and Second Reviews Under the Extended Arrangement Under the Extended Fund Facility, January 2013, S. 41.

[193] Die Memoranda haben vorhandene Ungleichheiten und Steuerhinterziehung nicht zu verändern vermocht: *Silvia Avram/Francesco Figari/Chrysa Leventi/Horacio Levy/Jekaterina Navicke/Manos Matsaganis/Eva Militaru/Alari Paulus/Olga Rastrigina/Holly Sutherland*, The distributional effects of fiscal consolidation in nine countries, Euromod Working Paper 2/ 13, January 2013.

[194] Die Leute dächten, man privatisiere, um Löcher im Haushalt zu stopfen. Aber das sei nur eine der Quellen. Privatisierungen bedeuteten neue Investitionen und schafften damit neue Arbeitsplätze. Regierungen hofften, in einem besseren wirtschaftlichen Umfeld höhere Einnahmen als in der aktuellen Krise zu erzielen. „Wir verkaufen auch nicht Land, wir vergeben Konzessionen. Wo ist das Problem?" Grenzen bei der Privatisierung gebe es nicht. Die geopolitische Dimension spielt – selbst wenn dies verneint wird – politisch und in den Medienberichten ebenfalls eine wichtige Rolle: „Ich bin kein Geopolitiker. Wenn die Russen die höchsten Bieter sind – wunderbar, sie sind willkommen." So „Chefprivatisierer" Stavridis: 2,6 Mrd. als Ziel, „Privatisierungen schaffen Arbeitsplätze", in: Der Standard, 3. Mai 2013. Mit Blick auf Gasprivatisierung und Gazprom s. etwa *Art Patnaude*, EU Denies Hindering Greek Gas Privatization, The Wall Street Journal, Tuesday, June 11, 2013.

[195] *F. William Engdahl,* Die Krise in Griechenland und verborgene Ölkriege, in: Kopp Online 30.04.2013 http://info.kopp-verlag.de/hintergruende/europa/f-william-engdahl/die-krise-in-griechenland-und-verborgene-oelkriege.html.

[196] „Enthusiasm for privatisation was however dashed. Politically, the Troika was accused of pushing for the dismantling of state property. Economically, weak equity market conditions undermined potential revenues." *Jean Pisani-Ferry/André Sapir/Guntram Wolff,* EU-IMF assistance to euro-area countries: an early assessment, May 2013, S.49, abrufbar unter http:// www.bruegel.org/publications/publication-detail/publication/779-eu-imf-assistance-to-euro-area-countries-an-early-assessment/.

aa) Kontrolle durch Rechnungshof, Staatsrat und Wettbewerbsausschuss

Während Vermögenswerte in staatlichem Besitz keine nennenswerten Einkünfte erzielen, werden verlustbringende staatseigene Unternehmen aus politischen Gründen künstlich am Leben gehalten, obwohl sie Kosten für die Steuerzahler verursachen. Der Vermögensverkauf soll nicht lediglich Finanzierungszwecke verfolgen. Darüber hinaus soll er auf die Ermöglichung zusätzlicher Investitionen, die Nutzung privater Managementexpertise sowie die Erhöhung von Effizienz bei der Vermögens- und Unternehmensverwaltung zielen.[197] Alle Verfahren sind zur Erreichung dieser Zwecke von der Europäischen Kommission bezüglich staatlicher Beihilfen und Wettbewerbsfähigkeit zu prüfen und sämtliche Verträge dem Rechnungshof zur Prüfung vorzulegen. Rechnungshof, Staatsrat und Wettbewerbsausschuss müssen den Privatisierungsprozess kontrollieren und bestätigen. Die Beseitigung von Verzögerungen bei der Vergabe und der Verlängerung von Betriebsgenehmigungen darf nicht zur gleichzeitigen „automatischen" Überwindung anderer (z. B. umweltrechtlicher, archäologischer) Belange führen.

bb) Genehmigungsverfahren und Verwaltungsverhältnisse

Zu den Privatisierungshemmnissen gehören intransparente Genehmigungsverfahren und Verwaltungsverhältnisse.[198] Der griechische öffentliche Sektor ist fragmentiert mit unscharfen, sich überschneidenden Behördenzuständigkeiten, die informales Verhalten geradezu heraufbeschwören. Hinzukommt eine Vielheit von Betrieben, die formal dem privaten Sektor angehören, doch effektiv vom öffentlichen Sektor abhängig sind und den gleichen Mangel an Effizienz, Transparenz, Bilanzierungsfähigkeit (sehr eingeschränkte Anwendung doppelter Buchhaltung) sowie Rechenschaftspflichtigkeit aufweisen. Darüber hinaus wird die schlechte Nutzung des Arbeitskräftepotenzials mit einer hohen Schattenwirtschaft und einem langsamen Justizsystem kombiniert.[199] Mehr Maßnahmen zur Verringerung der regulatorischen Belastung für die Unternehmenstätigkeit müssten ergriffen werden. Eine leistungsbezogene Evaluation der öffentlichen Verwaltung müsste auf die Wege geleitet und die Überschneidung administrativer Tätigkeiten und Kompetenzen („millefeuille administratif")[200] beseitigt werden. Diese Faktoren tragen zum massiven Misstrauen der Bevölkerung gegenüber einem vom Staat durchgeführten Privatisierungsverfahren bei.

---

[197] „Additional consistent measures… are essential to build confidence among the general public that the privatisation process is aimed at maximising value for the tax payer." Rn. 31.

[198] Siehe den Beitrag von *Karkatsoulis* in diesem Band.

[199] *McKinsey&Company,* Greece 10 Years Ahead. Defining Greece's new growth model and strategy, Executive summary, November 2011, S. 20 ff. „(I)nflexible legal requirements, the cumulative effect and inflexibility frequently associated with collective labor agreements and the skewed functioning of arbitration" (S. 22).

[200] Ausdruck aus dem Bericht über Frankreich: OECD Economic Surveys: France 2013.

cc) Einführung einer unabhängigen Privatisierungsbehörde

Das Misstrauen gegenüber dem nationalen politischen und Verwaltungssystem wird hierdurch zum Ausdruck gebracht, dass das Privatisierungsverfahren politisch immunisiert wird. Um das Privatisierungsverfahren „zu beschleunigen und die Unumkehrbarkeit des Ablaufs insgesamt sicherzustellen", wurde eine Privatisierungsstelle unter der Leitung eines unabhängigen und professionellen Ausschusses eingerichtet. Sie hat die Form einer Aktiengesellschaft mit dem griechischen Staat als einzigem Anteilseigner. Die Zusammenführung des Vermögens zu einem Fonds erinnert an den von Deutschland mit der Treuhandanstalt gewählten Weg.[201] Der Fonds zur Privatisierung von Staatseigentum „TAIPED" wurde am 1. Juli 2011 (durch das Gesetz 3986/2011) gegründet.[202] Auch dem Privatisierungsfonds wird allerdings von Seiten der Politik Mistrauen entgegengebracht. Der Wissenschaftsdienst des griechischen Parlaments hat sich gegen die Statuierung einer strafrechtlichen Immunität der Mitglieder des Privatisierungsfonds bei der Ausübung ihrer Aufgaben eingesetzt. Auch sei bei Privatisierungsverträgen vom höheren Wert als 1 Million Euro keinesfalls davon auszugehen, dass eine widerlegbare Vermutung (so wie sie im Art. 9 Abs. 4 S. 2 des Gesetzes 3986/2011 statuiert wird) für die Vereinbarung einer vorteilhaften und kostengünstigen Transaktion zugunsten des öffentlichen Interesses und der öffentlichen Hand streite.[203] Das Ziel des neuen Gesetzes bestand darin, das Privatisierungsverfahren aus dem politischen Einflussbereich auszugliedern, personellen Verflechtungen im politisch-administrativen Nexus griechischer Staatsbetriebe und Behörden einen Riegel vorzuschieben (Art. 3 Abs. 14 Gesetz 3986/2011) und privaten Sachverstand zu mobilisieren. Die vom Fonds durchgeführten Privatisierungen unterliegen den Bestimmungen des Gesetzes 3986/2011 in dessen gültiger Form, während das Verfahren nach dem allgemeinen Privatisierungsgesetz 3049/2002 nur ergänzend angewendet wird. Zur „Stärkung der Glaubwürdigkeit" wurde vereinbart, „verbindliche Quartalsziele betreffend die Privatisierungserträge als Teil der Konditionalität einer aktualisierten Absichtserklärung (MoU) vorzusehen".[204] Die griechische Privatisierungsbehörde wurde für 6 Jahre eingerichtet und wird von einem Board of Directors (Aufsichts- und Verwaltungsrat) geführt. Das Parlament bestellt die Mitglieder des Board of Directors gemäß Vorschlag des Finanzministers für eine feste Amtszeit. Die EU-Kommission und die Euroländer haben das Recht, zwei Beobachter in das Board of Directors zu bestellen. Das Par-

---

[201] „Griechische Treuhandanstalt", „Großprojekte – Privatisierungen der griechischen Treuhandagentur": GTI, Wirtschaftsführer Griechenland, 2012, S. 96, 177.

[202] Dringende Maßnahmen zur Umsetzung der mittelfristigen Fiskalstrategie im Zeitraum 2012–2015. Zur Ergänzung und Abänderung s. die Gesetze 4038/2012 (A′14), 4092/2012 (A′220) und 4093/2012 (A′222).

[203] So das Gutachten des Wissenschaftsdienstes des griechischen Parlaments http://www.naftemporiki.gr/story/788237/antisuntagmatikotites-sto-polunomosxedio-briskei-i-epistimoni ki-ypiresia-tis-boulis.

[204] Hauptergebnisse der gemeinsamen Prüfung Griechenlands von Kommission, EZB und IWF (3. Mai – 2. Juni 2011).

lament genehmigt die Maßnahmen des Board of Directors und stellt dessen Mitglieder von der Haftung für im Zusammenhang mit ihren offiziellen Pflichten durchgeführte Maßnahmen frei. Ein vierteljährlich zu veröffentlichender Tätigkeitsbericht ist (samt einem geprüften Bericht über die Finanzlage und einer Darstellung des Standes eines jeden gehaltenen Vermögenswerts im Privatisierungsverfahren) dem Parlament vorzulegen.

In seinem zweijährigen Leben seit seiner Gründung ist der Privatisierungsfonds bereits viermal auf der Suche nach Führungspersonal[205] gewesen, was zumindest als Indiz für Interessenverflechtungen und Bedarf an institutionellen Vorkehrungen für Transparenz gilt. Da Privatisierungen nur schleppend vorankommen, hat es auch einen Vorstoß von Experten des Rettungsschirms des Europäischen Stabilitätsmechanismus ESM gegeben, griechische Staatsimmobilien mit einer neuen Holdinggesellschaft in Luxemburg einfacher zu privatisieren. Die Holdinggesellschaft wäre von internationalen Experten geleitet. Damit solle die Bürokratie in Griechenland, die bislang die Privatisierungspläne unterlaufe, ausgehebelt werden. Wenn allerdings nicht nur der griechischen Regierung sondern auch jeder anderen Instanz mit griechischer Beteiligung die Kontrolle über das griechische Staatsvermögen schrittweise entgleitet, macht dies zugleich eine Herstellung von „Ownership" der Reformen bei der Bevölkerung, die dann das Privatisierungsprojekt durch die Brille nationaler Semantiken verstärkt lesen wird, schlichtweg unmöglich. Hier vermag Institutionalisierung von Misstrauen Vertrauen nur noch einseitig, d. h. ausschließlich für die Gläubiger des Landes herzustellen.

Die Unwiederkehrbarkeit und Kontrollierbarkeit des Privatisierungsverfahrens soll ferner auch dadurch gewährleistet werden, dass das volle rechtliche und wirtschaftliche Eigentum an den zu privatisierenden Vermögenswerten unwiderruflich auf den Verwertungsfonds für das öffentliche Privatvermögen übertragen werden. Die öffentliche Hand trennt sich vor jedem Verkauf von ihrem Eigentum. Kein öffentlich-rechtlicher Träger darf irgendwelche verbleibenden Eigentumsrechte oder sonstigen Rechte an den Vermögenswerten behalten. Lediglich verwaltungsrechtliche Befugnisse der öffentlichen Hand bleiben unberührt. Solange die Privatisierungstransaktion nicht abgeschlossen ist, kann der Fonds keine Vermögenswerte auf die öffentliche Hand rückübertragen (Art. 2 Abs. 7 Gesetz 3986/2011). Wenn ein Vermögenswert nicht verkauft werden kann, werden seine Bestandteile verkauft, es sei denn eine Liquidierung ist eine realisierbare Option.

2. Privatisierungsprojekte

Das griechische Privatisierungsgesetz 3049/2002 erwähnt einige Beispiele von Privatisierungsformen im Art. 2: (a) Verkauf eines gesamten Unternehmens oder

---

[205] Spiegel Online, Freiflug-Affäre: Griechenlands Regierung feuert obersten Privatisierer, http://www.spiegel.de/wirtschaft/soziales/griechenland-chef-der-privatisierungsbehoerde-muss-nach-freiflug-gehen-a-917213.html, abgerufen am 21.08.2013.

von Vermögenswerten oder Zweigen des Unternehmens oder der Gesamtheit oder eines Teils der Aktien des Unternehmens mit oder ohne gleichzeitigen Abschluss einer Aktionärsvereinbarung, (b) Notierung eines Unternehmens an einer Wertpapierbörse oder einem anderen organisierten Markt, (c) Erteilen von Nutzungslizenzen oder -rechten an einem Unternehmen, (d) Übertragung der Unternehmensleitung an einen Dritten, (e) Gründung eines Unternehmens oder Unternehmensbeteiligungen mit Einbringung von Barmitteln, Vermögenswerten, Unternehmenszweigen, Rechten oder Aktien, (f) jede Form der Verpachtung eines Unternehmens als Gesamtheit oder von Teilrechten oder Vermögenswerten oder Abteilungen oder Zweigen eines Unternehmens, (g) Aktientausch (im engeren Sinne), bzw. Verkauf von Aktien mit Sondervereinbarungen, beispielsweise Rückkaufvereinbarungen, (h) Verkauf von Aktien an Kreditinstitute oder Finanzhäuser im In- und Ausland zum Zweck der weiteren Veräußerung der Aktien durch diese an Dritte, (i) Ausgabe von in Unternehmensaktien umtauschbaren Unternehmensobligationen, (j) Verkauf und Neuvermietung von Grundstücken.[206]

Für die Privatisierungen in Griechenland[207] stehen somit die üblichen Privatisierungsalternativen zur Verfügung: Veräußerung von Anteilen oder gesamten Unternehmen, Konzessionsverträge, Zusammenarbeit mit strategischen Investoren, Börsengänge und Gründung von Holdinggesellschaften. Privatisierungsmethoden wie die Errichtung von auf die Verbriefung von Vermögenswerten spezialisierten Fonds werden auch in Betracht gezogen, um Einnahmen zu erzielen. Alle verbleibenden nicht betriebsnotwendigen bzw. betrieblich genutzten Immobilien, die vor allem dem Ministerium für Landwirtschaft und dem Verteidigungsministerium zugeteilt sind, sind in einem einheitlichen Rahmen zusammenzuführen, um eine effizientere Vermögensverwaltung durch konsequente Nutzung von Größenvorteilen zu ermöglichen. Auch wird die Verwertung staatlicher Immobilien im Inland und im Ausland vorgenommen, welche den Fiskus mit erheblichen Aufwendungen belasten. Auf der Agenda stehen ebenfalls Konzessionsverträge für neue Autobahnen in Attika, auf Kreta und für die Verwaltung der Egnatia Odos (Autobahn von Igoumenitsa in der Präfektur von Thesprotia bis zu dem Ort Kipi in der Präfektur von Evros). Nicht zuletzt bestehen Pläne für eine langjährige Verpachtung von staatseigenen Flächen über

---

[206] Siehe auch Art. 2 Abs. 4, Art. 5 Abs. 1 Gesetz 3986/2011. Ferner s. GTI, Wirtschaftsführer Griechenland, 2012, S. 32. Vgl. die üblichen Unterscheidungen in der Literatur: Organisationsprivatisierung (formelle Privatisierung), Erfüllungsprivatisierung (funktionale Privatisierung), Aufgabenprivatisierung (materielle Privatisierung), Zwischengebilde (Verfahrensprivatisierung, Finanzierungsprivatisierung, gemischt-wirtschaftliche Gesellschaften, Vermögens- oder Eigentumsprivatisierung, Beleihung, d. h. öffentlich-rechtliche Betätigung eines Privaten).

[207] Auf die Privatisierungsliste kamen gleich: Athener Wasserversorgungs- und Abwassergesellschaft (EYDAP) durch Verkauf staatlicher Anteile/Aktien bzw. Betriebsrechte/Lizenzen. Wasserversorgungs- und Abwassergesellschaft von Thessaloniki (EYATH), Athener Flughafen Eleftherios Venizelos, Staatliche Glücksspielgesellschaft (OPAP), Hellenic Defense Systems (EAS), Staatliche Erdgasgesellschaft, Bergbau- und Metallhüttenwerk (LARCO), Pferderennenveranstalter (ODIE), Kasino von Parnitha, Hellenic Vehicle Industry (ELVO), Griechische Post (ELTA), Egnatia Odos, Griechische Lotterie; Hellenic Petroleum.

500 ha, die für touristische Zwecke genutzt werden sollen. Hier erstellt die *Hellenic Public Real Estate Corporation* Immobilienportfolios.[208] Die Privatisierung des Glücksspielunternehmens OPAP hatte zur Folge, dass die von der öffentlichen Hand gehaltenen 33 % am Unternehmen für 652 Mio. Euro an das tschechisch-griechische Konsortium Emma Delta Ltd verkauft wurden.[209] 622 Mio. werden sofort bezahlt, der Rest in zehn gleichen Jahresraten. OPAP muss 30 Prozent Steuern vor Gewinn auf Offlinespiele an den griechischen Staat entrichten, was das Unternehmen mit einem Schlag deutlich weniger profitabel macht.

a) Immobilieninvestmentgesellschaften

Immobilieninvestmentgesellschaften sind Vehikel, die den in vielen Ländern existierenden steuerbegünstigten Immobilienaktiengesellschaften mit börsennotierten Anteilen ähnlich sind. Sie müssen allerdings an einer europäischen Wertpapierbörse notiert sein. Sie investieren üblicherweise in gewerbliche Immobilien und schütten eine große Dividende aus. Sie kommen in den Genuss einer Reihe von Steuerbefreiungen. Sie zahlen etwa keine Gewerbesteuer, dafür aber eine jährliche Investitionssteuer nach Maßgabe ihrer Vermögenswerte und Kassenbestände berechnet als 10 % des Zinssatzes der Europäischen Zentralbank unter Hinzufügung von 1 %. Ferner sind sie von der Vermögenserwerbsteuer sowie von der Zusatzsteuer auf Mieterträge befreit und sie zahlen ermäßigte Steuersätze für jährliche Grundsteuern. Ebenso wenig sind Quellensteuern auf Dividenden vorgesehen. Kein Vermögenswert einer Immobilieninvestmentgesellschaft darf die Grenze von 25 % des von ihr gehaltenen Gesamtportfolios überschreiten. Und höchstens 25 % des Gesamtportfolios darf in Wohneigentum investiert werden. Immobilieninvestmentgesellschaften dürfen ferner Immobilienentwicklungsprojekte übernehmen, die den Wert von 80 % ihres Gesamtvermögens nicht überschreiten.[210] Diskutiert werden zwei Immobilien-Verwertungsmethoden: die Übertragung der Immobilien an Immobilieninvestmentgesellschaften, deren Aktien an der griechischen Börse notiert wären, oder der Rekurs auf die Emittierung von Schuldverschreibungen durch die Verbriefung des Einkommens, das die Immobilien künftig abwerfen werden. Es ist zweifelhaft, ob die zweite Lösung unter Rezessionsbedingungen Aussicht auf Erfolg hätte. Die Liste der Immobilien, die an den griechischen Privatisierungsfonds zunächst übertragen wurden, wird allmählich an Immobilieninvestmentgesellschaften zu Verkauf und

---

[208] http://urbact.eu/fileadmin/damwithcat/pure_value/paroysiasi%20Roma%20Urbact%20II%20Ked.pdf.

[209] http://www.hradf.com/uploads/files/20130812-opap-press-en1.pdf.

[210] Immobilieninvestmentgesellschaften unterliegen in Griechenland dem Art. 19 des Gesetzes 4141/2013 in Zusammenhang mit den Art. 21–31 des Gesetzes 2778/1999 und den Gesetzen 2892/2001, 2992/2002 und 3581/2007 sowie dem Gesetz 2190/1920. Zur Begründung der Novellierung s. http://air.euro2day.gr/cov/TR/TROPOLOGIA_2013_11_1_20_48_9.pdf.

Verwertung übertragen.[211] 28 Immobilien sind bereits unter der Kontrolle von „NBG Pangaea REIC" und „Eurobank Properties REIC"[212]. Zu den Anbietern gehörte auch Dolphin Capital Reit Ltd. Die Immobilien wurden mit dem Zweck eines Sale und Leaseback für eine Vetragslaufzeit von 20 Jahren übertragen. Auf diese Weise können auch PPP-Immobilien entstehen, die zu Anlageinstrumenten werden sollen.[213]

b) See- und Flughäfen

Die chinesische Reederei „China Ocean Shipping Company" (kurz: Cosco) hat bereits (2009) Teile des Hafens von Piräus für mehr als 30 Jahre gepachtet und beabsichtigt, den ganzen Hafen zum größten Transit-Knotenpunkt für Produkte nach Europa auszubauen. Das Management gilt als erfolgreich. Weitere Investitionen sind im Rahmen des Privatisierungsprogramms vorgesehen.[214] Der Rechnungshof hat durch seine Entscheidung zur gütlichen Einigung zwischen dem Piraeus Port Authority S.A. und dem Piraeus Container Terminal S.A. über die Errichtung (Investition von 230 Millionen) des westlichen Schiffscontainer-Terminals III den Weg zur Erweiterung geebnet.[215] Im Anschluss an die Entscheidung des Rechnungshofs soll der Mindestbetrag, dessen jährliche Zahlung ursprünglich Cosco gewährleisten sollte, durch ein gewährleistetes Mindestmaß an Containertransport und Hafenverkehr (mindeste Frachtumschlagleistung 3.087.500 TEU und jährliche gewährleistete Kapazität 4.750.000 TEU für das Jahr 2021) ersetzt werden. Eine Unterschreitung des Mindestmaßes soll Vertragsstrafen auslösen.[216] Chinesische Unternehmen haben ebenfalls Interesse an der zu privatisierenden staatlichen Eisenbahngesellschaft

---

[211] http://www.hradf.com/uploads/files/properties-lot-a-en.pdf;   http://www.hradf.com/uploads/files/properties-transferred-en.pdf.

[212] http://www.nbgpangaea.gr/English/Content_en.aspx?24; http://grivalia.com/en/portfolio/geographic-dispersion/greece/.

[213] http://www.hradf.com/uploads/files/20131019-press-release-hradf-en.pdf: Am   18.10. 2013 bemerkte die Privatisierungsagentur „the project involves the sale and leaseback of these buildings, while the investors will assume the rehabilitation of the buildings and their maintenance for the next 20 years. Investments are estimated in excess of €100 million. The total value of the financial consideration for the Hellenic Republic will amount to €261,31 million, while the privatization is expected to contribute significantly to the stimulation of the Greek real estate market."

[214] „China will expand its investment in the port of Piraeus which Premier Li described as ‚a pearl in the Mediterranean Sea'. It may also build a new airport in Crete which Li also visited." In: chinadaily.com.cn: http://usa.chinadaily.com.cn/epaper/2014–06/24/content_17612090.htm.

[215] Rechnungshof 3377/2014; http://www.olp.gr/en/press-releases/item/2297-decision-of-the-court-of-auditors-on-the-application-for-revocation-of-the-act-1912014-of-the-7th-department-of-the-court-of-auditors.

[216] http://www.theseanation.gr/images/ATTACHMENTS/27524/24.11.2014_YY_YYYYYYYY_YYYYYYYY1.pdf.

(OSE) und an der Anbindung des Containerhafens an das internationale Eisenbahnnetz.[217]

Die Privatisierungsbehörde genehmigte auch die Übertragung der Beteiligung von Hochtief am Athener internationalen Flughafen rückwirkend zum 1. Januar 2013 an den kanadischen Pensionsfonds PSP Investments. Der Flughafen von Athen wurde bis dahin in einer PPP mit dem Staat betrieben. Sieben Investoren wurden ferner zur Teilnahme an der zweiten Phase der Ausschreibung für Konzessionsvergabe, Management, Betrieb und Erhalt der in zwei Gruppen ausgeschriebenen 37 Regionalflughäfen qualifiziert.[218] Das Konsortium Fraport-Slentel Ltd hat mit 1,23 Milliarden Euro das höchste Angebot (Vorauszahlung in Höhe von € 609) für die Privatisierung von 14 Regionalflughäfen abgegeben, es erhielt den Status des „preferred bidder" und soll die Flughäfen 40 Jahre lang betreiben. Fraport ist zwar ein gemischtwirtschaftliches Unternehmen, das als Aktiengesellschaft organisiert ist, doch mehrheitlich befindet sich die Betreiberin des Flughafens Frankfurt in öffentlicher[219] Hand (Hessen, Frankfurt am Main, Streubesitz), obwohl sie selbst eine Teilprivatisierung durchgemacht hat, da der Bund seinen Anteil bereits[220] verkaufte. Das Konsortium verpflichtet sich, eine jährlich gemäß der Entwicklung des Verbraucherpreisindex anzupassende Jahreszahlung in Höhe von € 22.9 Millionen für die Lebensdauer der Konzession zu entrichten.[221]

Der alte Athener Flughafen „Hellinikon" wurde bereits der Lamda Development Real Estate Group (Latsis Gruppe) für ein Angebot in Höhe von € 915 Millionen zugeschlagen.[222] Die Ingenieurkammer Griechenlands befand hingegen in einem Gutachten (vom 31.10.2014), dass sich der Nominalwert des Geländes auf € 2.95 Milliarden und der Nettobarwert auf € 1.86 Milliarden beliefen.[223] Demgegenüber hatte das griechische Wirtschafts- und Industrieforschungsinstitut (IOBE) seinerseits in einer grundsätzlichen Studie (vom 2. April 2014) zur Privatisierung des Flughafens die positive Auswirkung der Konzession für Wachstum und Arbeitsverhältnisse her-

---

[217] „We will propose construction of a rapid land and maritime route based on the Budapest-Belgrade railroad and the Greek port of Piraeus to improve regional connectivity". So der chinesische Regierungschef *Li Keqiang*. http://uk.businessinsider.com/afp-china-steps-up-plan-for-new-export-corridor-into-europe-2014–12?r=US#ixzz3MFek2Unu.

[218] http://www.hradf.com/sites/default/files/attachments/20130910-press-release-airports-en1.pdf.

[219] BVerfG, 1 BvR 699/06 vom 22.2.2011, Absatz Nr. (1 128), http://www.bverfg.de/entscheidungen/rs20110222_1bvr069906.html.

[220] http://www.sueddeutsche.de/wirtschaft/finanznot-bund-versilbert-seinen-fraport-anteil-1.809892.

[221] http://www.hradf.com/sites/default/files/attachments/20141125-regional-airports-press-release-en.pdf.

[222] Hierzu: http://www.hradf.com/sites/default/files/attachments/20140331-press-release-hellinikon-en.pdf. Zu einem Park wird das Gelände nicht mehr werden können. Zu dieser Alternative s. The Re-development of Hellinikon. A proposal by Professor Spiros N. Pollalis http://pollalis-hellinikon.com/wp/.

[223] http://web.tee.gr/wp-content/uploads/2014/10/elliniko-TEE.pdf.

vorgehoben.[224] Die Aufhebung des Ausschreibungsverfahrens wegen Verstoßes gegen die Grundsätze der Transparenz, Diskriminierungsfreiheit und Konkurrenz aufgrund des Ausschlusses physischer Personen aus dem Verfahren konnte nicht gelingen. Die VI. Sektion des Rechnungshofes bestätigte schließlich im November 2014 die Rechtmäßigkeit des Zuschlags. Dem erhobenen Einwand gegen eine vom Auftraggeber (Privatisierungsfonds TAIPED) nachträglich vorgenommene Änderung einer „wesentlichen Ausschreibungsbedingung" (hinsichtlich der Minderheitsbeteiligung der öffentlichen Hand zu 30%) wurde vom Rechnungshof nicht stattgegeben. Chinas größtes privates Konglomerat Fosun Group wird sich im Rahmen der Global Investment Gruppe mit 200 Millionen Dollar an der Entwicklung und städtischen Erneuerung des 5, 25 Quadratkilometer großen alten Flughafens und der 0,95 Quadratkilometer großen Küstenregion beteiligen.[225] Die Staatsanwaltschaft für die Bekämpfung der Korruption hat allerdings nunmehr die Einleitung eines Ermittlungsverfahrens dahingehend für erforderlich gehalten, ob von Mitgliedern des Privatisierungsfonds Handlungen vorgenommen wurden (Missbrauch von Amtsbefugnissen, Veruntreuung), die angesichts der Bedeutung des Vermögenswertes im Verbrechensgrade strafbar sind.[226]

c) Energie

Mit dem neuen Energiegesetz (Gesetz 4001/2011, seit dem 22.08.2011 in Kraft) wurde die Richtlinie 2009/72/EG umgesetzt. Das Gesetz (Art. 61 ff) sieht unter anderem auch die Einführung eines Unabhängigen Netzbetreibers vor.[227] Das Windenergiepotenzial ist groß und kann in einer Zusammenarbeit zwischen dem Amt für Erneuerbare Energien und internationalen Investoren einen Beitrag zum Wirtschaftswachstum leisten.[228] Besonders wichtig für den Strommarkt und insbesondere für neue Spieler ist die Vereinfachung des institutionellen Rahmens für die Nutzung und den Zugang zum Netz. Mit dem Gesetz 3851/2010 (04.06.2010) wurde auch der Genehmigungsprozess für die Realisierung von Photovoltaik-Projekte teilweise neugeregelt und vereinfacht.[229] Biogasanlagen in Griechenland werden im Rahmen des

---

[224] http://www.iobe.gr/docs/research/RES_03_02042014_REP.pdf.

[225] Chinadaily.com.cn vom 21.06.2014: http://europe.chinadaily.com.cn/business/2014-06/21/content_17606598.htm.

[226] http://www.tovima.gr/society/article/?aid=660124.

[227] Mit dem Gesetz N. 4001/2011 (über „Betrieb der Energiemärkte für Elektrizität und Erdgas, Forschung, Produktion und Transportnetze für Kohlenwasserstoffe und sonstige Regelungen", ΦΕΚ 179/22–08–2011) wurden die Aktivitäten der DESMIE AG /ΔΕΣΜΗΕ ΑΕ „Verwalter des griechischen Transportsystems für elektrische Energie AG" auf die neu gegründeten Gesellschaften LAGIE AG (Betreiber des Marktes für elektrische Energie) und ADMIE AG (Unabhängiger Transportverwalter elektrischer Energie) übertragen.

[228] http://eletaen.gr/policy-position-paper-on-wind-development-in-greece/.

[229] Die für die Genehmigung oder Inbetriebnahme einer Photovoltaik-Anlage erforderlichen Schritte sind in einem Diagramm vom griechischen Fachverband der Photovoltaik-Unternehmen erläutert: Hellenic Association of Photovoltaic Companies, The authorisation

griechischen Systems für Strom aus erneuerbaren Energiequellen gefördert. Mit dem Gesetz 4093/2012 (Abschnitt I.2) wurde für alle Anlagen, die Strom aus erneuerbaren Energiequellen erzeugen, ein „besonderer Solidaritätsbeitrag" eingeführt. Aufgrund des Gesetzes 4152/2013 wurden Inhabern einer Erzeugungsgenehmigung jährliche Gebühren auferlegt, sofern die Genehmigung für einen bestimmten im Gesetz festgelegten Zeitraum erteilt und die Anlage noch nicht in Betrieb genommen wurde. Die Regulierungsverordnung zur Genehmigung der Stromerzeugung aus erneuerbaren Energiequellen (vom 15 Oktober 2011) systematisiert die Rahmenbedingungen und vereinfacht einige Genehmigungsverfahren.

Die Planung eines transparenten Privatisierungsprozesses des etablierten Betreibers im Strombereich, der staatlichen Stromgesellschaft (DEH, DEI), war Teil der Kreditvergabe-Konditionalität. Die griechische Regierung hatte sich dazu verpflichtet, im September 2013 per Gesetz eine maximale Stromerzeugungskapazität für einzelne Stromerzeugungsunternehmungen festzusetzen und eine Eigentumsentflechtung[230] des Übertragungsnetzbetreibers (griechisch: ADMHE) einzuführen. Die Privatisierungsbehörde forderte vom Bieter, dem aserbaidschanischen Staatsbetrieb State Oil Company of the Republic of Azerbaijan (SOCAR), zunächst die Beifügung einer unverbindlichen Finanzierungsbereitschaftserklärung der zu beteiligenden Banken (*letter of intent*). Verbindliche Finanzierungszusagen waren für das verbindliche Angebot erforderlich, während zur endgültigen Entscheidung über den Zuschlag sämtliche Konditionen des Bieters vorliegen mussten. Bei Feststehen der Finanzierungsrate und einer Erfüllungsgarantie erfolgte die Überprüfung durch die Finanzberater. Die Verkaufsvereinbarung von Firmenanteilen des Gasunternehmens an SOCAR wurde im Dezember 2013 unterzeichnet.[231]

Was die Spaltung und Privatisierung des griechischen öffentlichen Elektrizitätswerks angeht, sieht der einschlägige Gesetzentwurf[232] die Gründung einer neuen Gesellschaft vor, einer 100 prozentigen Tochter des staatlichen Stromversorgers (ΔEH), an die 30 % der Produktionskapazität und des Kundenstamms des staatlichen Stromversorgers (ohne Zustimmungserfordernis seitens der Kunden) sowie einige Bergwerke abgetreten werden sollen. Dieses „kleine öffentliche Elektrizitätswerk" soll dann mittels internationaler Ausschreibung an Private verkauft werden. Zweck ist die Herstellung von Wettbewerbsbedingungen in den Bereichen von Stromerzeugung, Stromübertragung, Stromlieferung und Stromhandel. Die Erwerber werden auch auf diese Weise Zugang zu dem für die Stromerzeugung zur Verfügung stehen-

---

process step by step (Stand April 2012), abrufbar unter http://www.helapco.gr/ims/file/english/the_authorisation_process(1).pdf.

[230] Die Regierung „ensures full ownership unbundling": European Commission, The Second Economic Adjustment Programme for Greece, Third Review-July 2013, Rn. 27.

[231] http://www.hradf.com/sites/default/files/attachments/20131221-press-release-desfa-el.pdf.

[232] http://www.hellenicparliament.gr/UserFiles/c8827c35-4399-4fbb-8ea6-aebdc768f4f7/8390826.pdf. Siehe nunmehr Gesetz 4273/2014 vom 11. July 2014 (FEK 146) zur „Schaffung einer neuen vertikal integrierten Elektrizitätsgesellschaft".

den Energiemix erhalten. Das „kleine Elektrizitätswerk" wird eine Produktionskapazität von 2.768 MW (aus gemischten Energiequellen: 1.380 aus Braunkohle und 903 MW aus Wasserkraft und 485 MW aus Gas) haben. Für 4 Monate wird die neue Gesellschaft ihre Kunden in den alten Bedingungen mit Strom versorgen, während die alte Muttergesellschaft für 6 Monate ihre alten Kunden durch aggressive Preispolitik nicht abwerben darf. Die alte Muttergesellschaft muss ihre Kunden binnen 3 Monaten über die Übertragung der Vermögenswerte an das „kleine Elektrizitätswerk" in Kenntnis setzen. Im Anschluss an Proteste von Gewerkschaften und Kommunen hat sich die Regierung verpflichtet, angemessene Garantien mit Blick auf Arbeitnehmer- und Sozialversicherungsschutz zu geben. Der private Erwerber des „kleinen Elektrizitätswerks" soll auch den hohen Bewässerungsbedarf der Landwirtschaft berücksichtigen: Das landwirtschaftliche Recht zur Bewässerung aus dem nunmehr privatisierten Wasserkraftwerk soll aufrechterhalten bleiben. Die Einnahmen aus dem Verkauf des „kleinen Elektrizitätswerks" an den privaten Erwerber sollen der Förderung des Investitionsprogramms der öffentlichen Stromversorgungsgesellschaft und dem Abbau ihrer Schulden dienen. Das Nutzungsentgelt, das als Vergütung für den vom Erwerber erbrachten Dienst anzusehen ist, soll politischen Forderungen zufolge auch den Kommunen zugutekommen, die von der Spaltung des öffentlichen Versorgers tangiert werden.

Der EuGH ermöglicht nunmehr den chancengleichen Zugang zu den verfügbaren Kohlevorkommen in Griechenland. Die der Öffentlichen Elektrizitätsgesellschaft auf dem Braunkohlemarkt eingeräumten Exklusivrechte beeinträchtigen den Wettbewerb auf dem Strommarkt für industrielle Großkunden. Es bedarf keiner Feststellung eines weiter gehenden Missbrauchs als desjenigen, der aus der durch die betreffende staatliche Maßnahme (die Einräumung und Aufrechterhaltung einer den Markteintritt verhindernden beherrschenden Stellung) geschaffenen Situation resultiert. Es genügt, dass das Unternehmen, dem der Staat besondere oder ausschließliche Rechte verliehen hat, zur missbräuchlichen Ausnutzung seiner beherrschenden Stellung veranlasst wird. Es muss nicht nachgewiesen werden, dass DEI ein Monopol innehat oder dass die betreffende staatliche Maßnahme der DEI ausschließliche oder besondere Rechte auf einem benachbarten und getrennten Markt einräumt oder dass DEI über eine irgendwie geartete Regulierungszuständigkeit verfügt. Ebenso wenig ist nachzuweisen, dass sich der Wettbewerbsverstoß auf die Interessen der Verbraucher auswirkt, da der Wettbewerbsschutz auch Verhaltensweisen erfasst, die dadurch einen Schaden verursachen, dass sie eine Struktur wirksamen Wettbewerbs beeinträchtigen.[233] Die Anteile der DEI an der Braunkohleproduktion müssen nun unabhängig von den vertraglichen Verpflichtungen Griechenlands i.R.d. Konditionalität schon aufgrund dieses Urteils reduziert werden. Dies geht mit dem Priva-

---

[233] EuGH, Urteil vom 17. 7. 2014 – C-553/12 P, Rn. 48 ff., 61 ff. 70 (Aufhebung des Urteils des Gerichts der Europäischen Union DEI/Kommission (T-169/08, EU: T: 2012: 448) mit dem das Gericht die Entscheidung C (2008) 824 endg. der Kommission vom 5. März 2008 zur Erteilung bzw. Aufrechterhaltung von Genehmigungen zur Braunkohlegewinnung zugunsten der DEI durch Griechenland für nichtig erklärt hatte.

tisierungsplan der Schaffung einer „kleinen DEI" konform, dem zufolge der Beteiligungsanteil der Öffentlichen Elektrizitätsgesellschaft auf 30 % beschränkt wird. Die Ausschreibung für die Vergabe des Beratervertrages zur erfolgreichen Durchführung der Spaltung und des Verkaufs der „kleinen DEI" an private Investoren wurde schließlich nicht durch die Erteilung des Zuschlags, sondern durch die Entscheidung (am 17. 12. 2014) des öffentlichen Auftraggebers (der Öffentlichen Elektrizitätsgesellschaft) beendet, das Vergabeverfahren aufzuheben. Als Gründe wurden „das nicht zufrieden stellende Ergebnis hinsichtlich des absoluten Betrags der Ausgaben und die Veränderung der Bedürfnisse des Unternehmens hinsichtlich der benötigten Dienstleistungen und des Zeitrahmens deren Erbringung" angegeben.[234] Zwei Tage (am 19. 12. 2014) später wurde allerdings die Beratungsleistung erneut (mit einem Vergütungs- und Zeitlimit) ausgeschrieben. Die Entscheidung des Staatsrates zur Verfassungswidrigkeit der Wasserprivatisierung[235] wird jedenfalls unabhängig von diesen vergaberechtlichen Schwierigkeiten bereits zur grundsätzlichen Begründung der Verfassungswidrigkeit der Schaffung der „kleinen DEI" herangezogen.[236] Aus dieser Entscheidung des Staatsrates lässt sich allerdings ebenso wenig wie aus dem Unionsrecht zu DAWI der generelle Grundsatz ableiten, dass der Staat seine Gewährleistungsaufgabe im Bereich der Daseinsvorsorge stets nur dann wirksam erfüllen kann, wenn er mit mindestens 51 % am Gesellschaftskapital beteiligt ist. Es kommt auf die konkreten Maßnahmen staatlicher Einflusssicherung an. Es wird zu prüfen sein, ob die staatlichen Einflussmöglichkeiten, die darin zum Ausdruck kommen, dass die „kleine DEI" vom Gesetzgeber als eigenständiger Betriebszweig und als Tochtergesellschaft des Öffentlichen Elektrizitätsunternehmens zunächst einmal konzipiert ist, ausreichen. Der Gewährleistungsauftrag muss auch nach dem Verkauf durch die Statuierung von Informations- und Verhaltens- bzw. Vertragsverhandlungs- und Kontrahierungspflichten erfüllt werden können.

Im Rahmen der Privatisierung im Gasbereich geht es beim Gastransportbetreiber (Hellenic Gas Transmission System Operator S.A., DESFA)[237] um eine 100 %ige Depa-Tochter („incumbent natural gas utility in Greece"),[238] welcher das griechische Gasnetz gehört. Maßgeblich für den Wettbewerb auf dem Gasmarkt wird jedenfalls sein, inwiefern die existenten geschlossenen Versorgungsgebiete und integrierte Gebietsmonopole für die drei Gaslieferanten (Gas distribution companies: EDA) und die drei Gasversorgungsunternehmen (Gas supply companies: EPA) in den Regionen Attika, Thessaloniki und Thessalien aufgehoben werden. Der staatliche Erdgaskon-

---

[234] http://www.energypress.gr/news/Poy-skontapse-o-diagwnismos-proslhpshs-symboyloygia-th-Mikrh-DEH.

[235] Staatsrat 1906/2014.

[236] *Marangopoulos Foundation for Human Rights (MFHR),* „Kleines Öffentliches Elektrizitätsunternehmen" – Große Verfassungswidrigkeit (auf griechisch), Athen, 3. 7. 2014.

[237] http://www.desfa.gr/default.asp?pid=1&la=2.

[238] http://www.depa.gr/content/article/002001001/8.html. Die DEPA-Gruppe befindet sich zu 65 % im Eigentum der Privatisierungsbehörde (HRADF/TAYPED) und zu 35 % im Eigentum von Hellenic Petroleum (HelPe).

zern DEPA hat 51 % der Geschäftsanteile an den drei gebietsgebundenen Gasversorgungsunternehmen inne, Shell ist in Besitz von 49 % der Anteile an Gasversorgungsunternehmen in Attika, die italienische multinationale Gesellschaft „Ente Nazionale
Idrocarburi" (ENI) besitzt 49 % der Geschäftsanteile an den Gasversorgungsunternehmen in Thessalien und Thessaloniki. Die Schwierigkeit liegt darin, einen Ausgleich für die beseitigten Gebietsmonopole, die bis 2030 dauern sollten, zu finden,
ohne sich Schadensersatzansprüchen auszusetzen, die Gasversorgung zu verteuern
und die Investitionsdeckungs- sowie Netzausbaupläne der Energieversorgungsunter-
nehmen zu vereiteln. Eine Entflechtung würde die im Anschluss an Ausschreibungsverfahren abgeschlossenen Verträge des Staates mit Shell und ENI zu Makulatur machen. Diese Verträge haben ausschließliche Rechte zu Aufbau, Betrieb und Ausbau
der Verteilernetze auf städtischer Ebene sowie zu Gasversorgung von Haushalts- und
Industriekunden (<100 GWh) im jeweiligen Gebiet gewährt. Ihre Nicht-Honorie-
rung könnte die Erfolgschancen einer erneuten Ausschreibung zur Privatisierung
der staatlichen und verschuldeten Gasgesellschaft DEPA, nach dem medienwirksa-
men Scheitern eines Verkaufs an Gazprom, zwar noch weiter reduzieren. Allerdings
könnten Übergangsregelungen für Verhältnismäßigkeit sorgen. Ein Gesetzentwurf[239]
geht in der Tat insofern in diese Richtung, als eine schrittweise Öffnung des Gas-
marktes und gleichzeitig die Erfüllung der vom Staat gegenüber der Troika[240] übernommenen Verpflichtung zur Gasmarktöffnung bis 2018 in Aussicht genommen
werden. Als Ausgleich für den Verlust ihrer Monopolrechte erhalten die Energiever-
sorgungsunternehmen eine 20-jährige Verlängerung mit weiterer Verlängerungs-
möglichkeit um zusätzliche 20 Jahre im Vertriebsbereich und eine Befreiung von
geographischen Beschränkungen bei der Belieferungstätigkeit. Ab dem 30. Mai
2015 soll die Trennung des Netzbetriebs von den Wettbewerbsbereichen sowohl
für DEPA als auch für die drei EPA beginnen, wobei bis zum 1. 10. 2015 die bilanzielle Entflechtung der Verteilnetzbetreiber stattgefunden haben muss. Die bereits
gebauten Netze bleiben im Eigentum von DEPA, der Netzbetrieb wird allerding
den regionalen Gasverteilern (EDA) überantwortet werden. EDA sind Verteilnetzbe-
treiberunternehmen, die nach dem hinzuzufügenden Art. 80 A des Energiemarktgesetzes zu gründen sind, um die Tätigkeit eines Unabhängigen Verteilnetzbetreibers
wahrzunehmen. Nicht alle Letztabnehmer werden sofort in der Gasversorgung unter
mehreren Lieferangeboten wählen können. Die Letztabnehmer, die ein Wahlrecht
haben werden („Erwählende Kunden" genannt) sind diejenigen, die sich außerhalb
der Versorgungsgebiete der drei EPA befinden. Dasselbe gilt für die Industriekunden
(>2,2 GWh), die sich innerhalb dieser Versorgungsgebiete befinden. Ab dem 1. 1.
2016 werden einige Letztabnehmer (Verbraucher von >2,2 GWh) und ab dem
1. 1. 2017 alle Letztabnehmer, die keine Haushaltskunden sind, unter mehreren Lieferangeboten wählen dürfen. Die Neutralität des Netzbetriebs soll durch unabhängi-

---

[239] Siehe Art. 4 des Gesetzentwurfs zur Abänderung und Ergänzung der Bestimmungen des
Energiemarktgesetzes 4001/2011: http://www.opengov.gr/minenv/?p=6369.

[240] The Second Economic Adjustment Programme for Greece, Fourth Review – April
2014, 3.6. Efficient Network Industries, S. 60 ff., 62.

ge Netzbetreiber nach dem bereits eingeführten Modell der Entflechtung im Strombereich gewährleistet werden. Ein Regelungskodex für Verwaltung, Betrieb, Wartung und Ausbau der Verteilernetze soll von der Regulierungsbehörde festgelegt werden. Bis zum 30. 5. 2015 sollen DEPA und die EPA von Attika, Thessalien und Thessaloniki die bilanzielle Entflechtung des Netzbereichs von den Wettbewerbsbereichen von der Regulierungsbehörde genehmigen lassen, die binnen drei Monaten entscheiden soll. Ab dem 1. 10. 2015 sollen DEPA und die drei EPA in ihrer internen Rechnungslegung getrennte Konten und Tätigkeitsabschlüsse für jeden einzelnen Tätigkeitsbereich (Verteilung und Belieferung) führen und bis zum 1. 1. 2017 eine operationelle und gesellschaftsrechtliche Entflechtung des Netzbereichs von den anderen Bereichen vorgenommen haben. Sie sollen sich an der Gründung neuer unabhängiger Verteilnetzbetreiber mit einer Sacheinlage beteiligen, die der Bereitstellung ihrer jeweiligen Netzanlage entspricht. Binnen 90 Tagen nach Gründung der neuen Verteilnetzbetreiber sollen die drei EPA unentgeltlich die Anteile, die sie an den relevanten Verteilnetzbetreibern innehaben werden, an die Anteilseigner der EPA entsprechend ihrer Beteiligung an dem Eigenkapital der jeweiligen EPA übertragen. Die von DEPA oder den drei EPA gebauten und genehmigten Verteilnetze bleiben im ausschließlichen Eigentum der DEPA. Die auf der Grundlage des genehmigten Netzentwicklungsplans von den EPA gebauten neuen Netze gehören hingegen diesen an.[241]

d) Eisenbahn

In zwei Phasen (Vorauswahl im Anschluss an Interessenbekundung und Zuschlag nach Unterbreitung der Angebote) soll die griechische Eisenbahngesellschaft zu 100 % privatisiert werden.[242] Das Investitionsinteresse für die Staatseisenbahn ist bei der Güterbeförderung groß, da die Anbindung der Häfen des Landes an das europäische Eisenbahnhauptnetz die Transportkosten senken wird. Ein Bündel von Richtlinien zur Liberalisierung des europäischen Eisenbahnrechts ist bereits durch Präsidialverordnungen ins griechische Recht umgesetzt worden. Vorbereitend auf die Eisenbahnprivatisierung wurden Maßnahmen zur Restrukturierung und zur Sanierung der gesamten griechischen Eisenbahngesellschaft per Gesetz (Nr. 3891/ 2010, Abschnitt 1, Art. 2) in die Wege geleitet. Vor dem Verkauf wird das staatliche Eisenbahnunternehmen ein fünfjähriges Abkommen mit dem griechischen Staat über die Bereitstellung von nicht wirtschaftlichen Personentransportdienstleistungen (*a 5-year Public Service Obligation (PSO) contract*) abschließen. Diese Dienstleistungen werden mit einer Summe bis zu € 50 Mio. pro Jahr vergütet werden. Ein Netz-

---

[241] Hierzu s. die in das Energiemarktgesetz 4001/2011 einzuführenden Art. 80 A und 80B.

[242] Invitation to submit an expression of interest for the acquisition of 100 % of the share capital of Trainose S.A. http://hradf.com/uploads/files/20130712-eoi-trainose-en1.pdf Athens, 12 July 2013. Finanztechnische Berater des griechischen Privatisierungsfonds sind die Investment Bank of Greece (Mitglied der Laiki Bank Gruppe), die Anwaltssozietäten Hogan Lovells International LLP und M & P Bernitsas Law Offices, während technischer Berater Louis Berger S.A. ist.

zugangsvertrag über die Nutzung der Schieneninfrastruktur (Schienenanschlüsse: *track access contract*) wird mit der Eisenbahngesellschaft in ihrer Eigenschaft als Infrastrukturverwalter ebenfalls geschlossen. Eine Abtrennung der Sparte der Wartung des Rollmaterials von der griechischen staatlichen Eisenbahngesellschaft und die Gründung der staatlichen Wartungsgesellschaft ROSCO (griechisch ΕΕΣΣΤΥ) die ebenfalls privatisiert (so in der Ausschreibung) werden soll, sind vorgesehen. Es geht um Verselbständigung über den Weg der Abspaltung (*spin off process*). Hauptaktivitäten der ROSCO werden die Erbringung von Leistungen für Wartung, Reparatur und Restaurierung des Roll- und sonstigen Materials der Eisenbahn und anderer schienengebundener Verkehrsmittel sowie die Verwaltung und Vermietung von Rollmaterial an Dritte sein. Ein langjähriger Leasingvertrag wird mit der Eisenbahngesellschaft in ihrer Eigenschaft als der derzeitigen Eigentümerin des Rollmaterials abgeschlossen. Ferner wird ein langjähriges Abkommen mit der noch staatlichen Wartungsgesellschaft ROSCO über die Wartung des Rollmaterials abgeschlossen. ROSCO absorbiert auf diese Weise die Sparte der Wartung des Rollmaterials der Eisenbahngesellschaft (nach der internen Betriebsordnung dieser: „Direktion für Wartung des Rollmaterials"). Die Privatisierung von ROSCO wurde am 16. 8. 2013 vom interministeriellen Ausschuss für Umstrukturierung und Privatisierung entschieden. Es erfolgte eine Übertragung aller Aktien an den Privatisierungsfonds.[243] Auch wurde eine Abtrennung der Gesellschaft für die Verwaltung des Immobilienvermögens der Eisenbahn (GAIOSE) von der Eisenbahngesellschaft vorgenommen. Schließlich wird der Abschluss langjähriger Verträge mit dem griechischen Staat über die Anmietung ausgewählter Immobilien vorgesehen, die als Logistikzentren genutzt werden sollen. In die zweite Phase des Ausschreibungsverfahrens für den 100%tigen Erwerb der TRAINOSE AG-Anteile kommen folgende Unternehmungen: Rossiyskie Zheleznye Dorogi (RZD)-GEK TERNA consortium, SNCF Participations und Grup Feroviar Roman (GFR). In die zweite Phase des Ausschreibungsverfahrens für den 100%tigen Erwerb der Anteile von ROSCO kommen die Unternehmengen RZD – GEK TERNA consortium, SIEMENS SA und Alstom Transport SA-DAMCO Energy SA consortium.[244] Da Art. 6 Abs. 3 des Gesetzes 3986/2011 die Vornahme einer Bewertung des zu privasierenden Vermögenswertes von einem unabhängigen Gutachter verlangt, ist die unabhängige Bewertung von ROSCO ausgeschrieben worden.[245]

---

[243] Regierungsblatt 2014, 16 August 2013, Beschluss-Nr. 239.

[244] Stand 31. Oktober 2013: http://www.hradf.com/sites/default/files/attachments/20131031-press-release-hradf-en.pdf.

[245] Invitation for submission of proposals to act as independent valuer to the HRADF in relation to the privatisation of the Hellenic Company for Rolling Stock Maintenance S.A. November 5, 2014: http://www.hradf.com/sites/default/files/attachments/20141105-rosco-independent-valuation-en.pdf.

e) Wasser

Der Wasserprivatisierung kommt rechtspolitisch eine anhaltende Tabuwirkung zu. Während etwa die Sonderstellung für die Strom- und Gasversorgung im Zuge der Liberalisierung der Energiewirtschaft in Deutschland durch die 6. GWB-Novelle aufgehoben wurde, blieb die Wasserwirtschaft von der Geltung des allgemeinen Kartellrechts freigestellt und im Gegenzug der verschärften Missbrauchsaufsicht unterworfen. Aufgrund der 8. GWB-Novelle (§ 31 GWB) vom 26.06.2013 (BGBl. I S. 1738) bleibt die Wasserversorgung als Ausnahmebereich teilweise von der Geltung des allgemeinen Kartellrechts ausgenommen und soll weiterhin der verschärften kartellrechtlichen Missbrauchsaufsicht unterliegen. In den meisten Mitgliedsstaaten gibt es eine breite Opposition gegen eine Privatisierung der Wasserversorgung. In Italien hat sich die Mehrheit der Bevölkerung in einem Referendum dagegen ausgesprochen. Dies hat die Verfasser der „Memoranda of Understanding" nicht daran gehindert, die Privatisierung der Wasserversorgung in den Memoranden mit Griechenland und Portugal immer wieder neu festzuschreiben. In Deutschland entschied das Bundeskartellamt 2012, dass die Wasserbetriebe die Preise für Trinkwasser „missbräuchlich überhöhten" und die Tarife zu senken seien.

Die Wasserversorgung wird in Griechenland von drei großen Dienstträgern gewährleistet: EYDAP („Gesellschaft für Wasserversorgung und Unterwasserkanalisierung der Hauptstadt") und EYATH („Gesellschaft für Wasserversorgung und Unterwasserkanalisierung von Thessaloniki"). 1999 wurde die EYDAP an die Börse gebracht. Ansonsten findet sich die Wasserversorgung in Händen von kommunalen Wasserbetrieben (DEYA). In kleinen Kommunen ist die Wasserversorgung Teil der Kommunalverwaltung oder Gegenstand interkommunaler Zusammenarbeit. Oft sind Brunnen, die am Anfang des 20. Jahrhunderts gebohrt wurden, an ein komplexes Netz von modernisierungsbedürftigen Anlagen (Wassertanks und Pumpwerken) angeschlossen, das den aktuellen Bedürfnissen und Anforderungen nicht mehr entspricht. Die Wasserversorgung sämtlicher kleinen und großen Gemeinden und Städte in Griechenland unterliegt einer zentralen Behörde für die Wasserversorgung. Es handelt sich hier um den Verein der Gemeindeunternehmen für Wasserversorgung und Unterwasserkanalisierung, der abgekürzt EDEYA genannt wird. Diese Behörde ist für die reibungslose Funktion der lokalen Dienstträger der Wasserversorgung verantwortlich und koordiniert ihre Verwaltung. Acht Kommunen von Attika haben sich bereitgefunden, den Betrieb ihrer Wasserversorgungsnetze an die an der Börse notierte öffentliche Wassergesellschaft EYDAP auf der Grundlage von Konzessionsverträgen abzutreten. Die hohen Netzwartungsanforderungen und Netzbetriebskosten veranlassen die Kommunen zu diesem Netzverkauf an den Wasserversorger EYDAP, dem sie wegen Wasserkäufe am Wassermarkt ohnehin hohe Summen schulden. Auf diese Weise könne die Kommunalverschuldung zurückgeführt und der Marktwert von EYDAP erhöht werden. Die Aufwertung von EYDAP und ein steigender Aktienkurs (Verdreifachung des Kurses innerhalb eines Jahres) machten es allerdings nicht leichter, die Privatisierungspläne umzusetzen.[246] Die an der Börse notierten Unternehmen EYDAP S.A und EYATH kaufen Rohwasser von der griechischen Regierung, welche die erforderlichen Staudämme und Wasserleitungen betreibt. Der Staat ist in Besitz der Aktienmehrheit von EYDAP und EYATH. Private Unternehmen und Einzelanteilseigner sind in Besitz von Minderheitsanteilen: etwa die Bank für Landwirtschaft (10 % von EYDAP) und das französische Unternehmen Suez (5 % von EYATH). Unter der Voraussetzung, dass ein Mehrheitsanteil von 51 % unter staatlicher Kontrolle bleibt, wird über verschiedene Möglichkeiten spekuliert. Da die Wasserversorgung ein hochbrisantes politisches Thema[247] ist, ist es umstritten, ob eine Privatisierung überhaupt legitimierbar ist und inwiefern bejahendenfalls eine Veräußerung von Aktienpaketen einem Konzessionsvertrag vorzuziehen wäre. Diskutiert wird, inwiefern ein Privater eine effiziente Überwachung und Verwaltung städtischer Wasser-, Abwasser- und Bewässerungssysteme leisten kann.

Die Wasserprivatisierung kommt in den Anwendungsbereich des Art. 106 II 1 AEUV. Diese Ausnahmevorschrift richtet sich an Unternehmen, die mit Dienstleistungen von allgemeinem wirtschaftlichem Interesse (DAWI) betraut sind. DAWI sind vom Unternehmen auch dann zu erbringen, wenn dies privatwirtschaftlichen Unternehmensinteressen widerspricht. Gemäß dem in Art. 345 AEUV verankerten Neutralitätsgrundsatz können DAWI von öffentlichen oder privaten Unternehmen erbracht werden. Anknüpfungspunkt ist nicht die institutionelle Identität des Dienstleistungserbringers, sondern die Natur der zu erfüllenden Aufgabe. Art. 14 AEUV verpflichtet Union und Mitgliedstaaten dazu, einen geeigneten Ordnungsrahmen zu schaffen, der eine funktionsfähige, dem Gleichheitsgebot und der Diskriminierungsfreiheit verpflichteten Erbringung der DAWI gewährleistet. Art. 106 II 1 AEUV verlangt, dass die Einschränkungen der Wettbewerbsregeln und der Grundfreiheiten nach Art und Ausmaß nicht über das zur Verhinderung von Gefährdungen der Gemeinwohlauftrags Erforderliche hinausgehen. Der Mitgliedstaat muss nachweisen, dass die Erfüllung von DAWI zu marktmäßigen, privatwirtschaftlichen Bedingungen gefährdet wäre. Vor diesem Hintergrund sind Demarkations- und Konzessionsverträge oder die Verweigerung eines Unternehmens, Wasser eines anderen Unternehmens durch das eigene Leitungsnetz durchzuleiten, insofern unionsrechtskonform, als sie erforderlich sind, um die Erfüllung der Gemeinwohlaufgabe der Wasserversorgung, also Gefährdungen der Erbringung einer DAWI zu verhindern. Selbst eine Monopolstruktur ist zulässig, soweit sie zur Sicherstellung der DAWI erforderlich ist, die Durchführung eines Wettbewerbs um den Markt möglich wurde und bei Ausschluss eines europaweiten Ausschreibungsverfahrens die aus den Grundfreiheiten abzuleitenden Grundsätze der Gleichbehandlung aller Bieter, der Transparenz und der wirksamen Nachprüfung beachtet wurden. Die Dauer der Gewährung von Ausschließlichkeitsrechten an einen Investor muss für die Investitionserwirtschaf-

---

[246] *Achileas Chekimoglou*, To Vima vom 1. August 2013.

[247] http://www.savegreekwater.org/?page_id=232: „Initiative for the non privatization of water in Greece" in Verbindung mit der europäischen Initiative http://www.right2water.eu/de.

tung und die damit zusammenhängende Gemeinwohlerfüllung ebenfalls erforderlich sein.[248]

Die Aktiengesellschaft EYDAP ist ausschließlich mit der Aufgabe der Wasserversorgung und Abwasserbeseitigung in der Hauptstadt betraut. Der Akt ihrer Übertragung an den Privatisierungsfonds wurde allerdings vor dem Staatsrat mit Aufhebungsantrag angefochten. Der Staatsrat stellte fest, dass die öffentliche Hand durch diese Übertragung alle ihren Beteiligungen (34,033 %) am Gesellschaftskapital der EYDAP verliert und dass die Übertragung ohne vorherige oder parallele Einrichtung einer Regulierungswasserbehörde sowie ohne die im Privatisierungsprogramm 2011 – 2015 vorgesehene Vornahme einer Trennung des Wassernetzes von „der zu übertragenden Dienstleistung" erfolgte. Der öffentlichen Hand werde durch den Übertragungsakt jede aktien- oder leitungs- und gesellschaftsrechtliche Einflussmöglichkeit auf die Wassergesellschaft, die nunmehr eine reine Gewinnerzielungsorientierung habe, genommen. Die fehlende Einflussmöglichkeit der öffentlichen Hand bedinge eine mit den Art. 5 Abs. 5[249] und 21 Abs. 3[250] der Griechischen Verfassung unvereinbaren, nicht zu beseitigende Ungewissheit hinsichtlich der Gewährleistung der Kontinuität und Qualität der Dienstleistungserbringung. Die Mindermeinung vertrat hingegen die Auffassung, dass die Beachtung der verfassungsrechtlichen Vorgaben und der Gewährleistungsauftrag durch die Ausübung staatlicher Regulierungsaufsicht durchaus sichergestellt werden könnten.[251]

IV. Generierung von Vertrauen durch Institutionalisierung von Misstrauen

Der Erfolg von Privatisierungen in Griechenland hängt nicht von der Zahl der verkauften Betriebe und der Höhe des Privatisierungserlöses, sondern von der Herstellung der Existenz- und Operationsbedingungen des Gewährleistungsstaates ab. Die Lösung dieses entwicklungspolitischen Paradoxes[252] liegt in der Herstellung institutionellen Vertrauens. Dieses kann allerdings nur mit Hilfe der rechtlichen Institutionalisierung von Misstrauen gelingen. Diese Institutionalisierungsleistung ist für die Legitimität und Kontrolle sowohl von privatisierten als auch von staatlichen Versorgungsleistungen sowie für die Bestimmung eines eigenverantwortlichen Entwicklungspfads in der griechischen Gesellschaft unverzichtbar.

---

[248] *Julia Brehme*, Privatisierung und Regulierung der öffentlichen Wasserversorgung, 2010, S. 263 – 274.

[249] „Jeder hat das Recht auf Schutz der Gesundheit und seiner genetischen Identität".

[250] „Der Staat sorgt für die Gesundheit der Bürger und trifft besondere Maßnahmen zum Schutze der Jugend, des Alters, der Versehrten und für die Pflege Unbemittelter."

[251] Staatsrat 1906/2014, Rn. 22.

[252] *Gromitsaris*, Korruption, Wirtschaftswachstum und Rechtsstaat, in: Carlos Gonzalez-Palacios/Thilo Rensmann/Otmar Seul/Manuel Tirard (Hrsg.), Democracia y Estado de derecho, S. 61 ff., Lima 2014.

1. Institutionalisierung von Misstrauen

Die Institutionalisierung von Misstrauen ist ein in Politik- und Sozialwissenschaften anerkannter Topos,[253] der im Recht durch zahlreiche Institute (etwa diverse checks und balances, externe Revisionen, Kontrollen durch Dritte), jedoch ohne explizite Erwähnung dieser sozial- und politikwissenschaftlichen Begrifflichkeit verwirklicht wird.[254] Oft wird Vertrauen als Abwesenheit von Misstrauen verstanden, wobei vor allem einem Misstrauen gegenüber dem politisch-administrativen System eine „negative Gestaltungskraft" beigemessen wird, die auf eine sich selbst bestätigende Selbstprophezeiung hinauslaufe, da Misstrauen lediglich Misstrauen erzeuge und kontraproduktiv wirke.[255] Vertrauen wird meistens im Recht unter dem Gesichtspunkt seiner Schutzwürdigkeit zum Thema. Es geht etwa um den Ersatz des negativen Interesses, das Verbot der echten Rückwirkung, den eigentumsrechtlichen Bestandsschutz, die hergebrachten und zugleich fortentwicklungsfähigen Grundsätze des Beamtentums, um dauerhafte und zugleich revidierbare gesetzliche Regelungen, administrative Bestands- und richterliche Rechtskraft oder um Anpassungsfristen und Ausnahmeregelungen vorsehende Übergangsvorschriften. Demgegenüber wird hier rechtliche Institutionalisierung von Misstrauen als eine Bedingung der Möglichkeit von Vertrauen, also als eine strukturelle Vorkehrung behandelt, die den Glauben an die Zuverlässigkeit und Berechenbarkeit staatlicher Institutionen möglich macht. Das betrifft aber auch die Regeln der Zusammenarbeit zwischen öffentlichem und privatem Sektor. Da die Verschuldungskrise die Zersetzung institutionellen Vertrauens weiter vertieft, geraten Instrumente wie PPP, die „Kommunalkreditähnlichkeit" auch für Privatinvestoren herstellen wollen und mit prognostizierten Zahlungsströmen operieren, in Schwierigkeiten. Im Zuge der Krise haben sich etwa die vielen PPP in Portugal als kaum abschätzbares Finanzrisiko herausgestellt,

---

[253] *Mark E. Warren* (ed), Democracy and Trust, Cambridge University Press 1999; *Piotr Sztompka,* Trust, distrust and the paradox of democracy, Papers//WZB, Wissenschaftszentrum Berlin für Sozialforschung, No. P 97–003 abrufbar unter http://hdl.handle.net/10419/50255; *ders.*, Does Democracy Need Trust, or Distrust, or Both? in: Stephan Jansen/Eckhard Schröter/Nico Stehr (Hrsg.), Transparenz, 2010, S. 284 ff.; *John Hart Ely,* Democracy and Distrust: A Theory of Judicial Review, Cambridge, Mass. 1980; *Pierre Rosanvallon*, La contre-démocratie, La politique à l'âge de la défiance, Paris, Le Seuil, 2006; *Jacqueline Costa-Lascoux/Lucien Jaume,* La démocratie et le déclin de la confiance, une rupture dans la culture politique, in Pascal Perrineau (dir.), Le désenchantement démocratique, Paris, Éditions de l'Aube, coll. „Monde en cours", 2003, p. 67–87.

[254] Für eine Anwendung auf Governance-Strukturen im Europäischen Verwaltungsrecht s. *Gromitsaris*, Legitimacy and Accountability: Integration and Compensation, in: Legitimacy in European Administrative Law: Reform and Reconstruction. Edited by Matthias Ruffert, European Administrative Law Series (6), Groningen 2011, pp 285–334. Zum Verhältnis von Recht und Vertrauen allgemein: Eberhard Schmidt-Aßmann/Georgios Dimitropoulos, Vertrauen in und durch Recht, in: Markus Weingardt (Hrsg.), Vertrauen in der Krise, Baden-Baden 2011, S. 129 ff. siehe auch *Christian Schilcher/Mascha Will-Zocholl/Marc Ziegler* (Hrsg.), Vertrauen und Kooperation in der Arbeitswelt, Berlin 2012.

[255] *Markus Müller,* Die Rechtsweggarantie – Chancen und Risiken, in: ZBJV 140 (2004), S. 161 ff.

weil niemand weiß, wie viel die PPP über die mehrjährigen Laufzeiten den Staat tatsächlich kosten werden.[256]

Mit Blick auf Privatisierungen nimmt die Institutionalisierung von Misstrauen spezifische Gestalt an. Sie betrifft einerseits die Herstellung von Transparenz und den Gemeinwohlschutz durch Institute des Privatisierungsfolgenrechts, die auch nach der Privatisierung wirksame Kontrollmöglichkeiten eröffnen und Rückholoptionen vorsehen. Sie bezieht sich andererseits auf Kautelen, die den Gemeinwohlschutz im Falle eventueller Rückverstaatlichungen sichern und die Beachtung der Wettbewerbsregeln durch den Staat gewährleisten, wenn dieser als Marktteilnehmer tätig wird und im Namen des öffentlichen Interesses der privaten Wirtschaft Konkurrenz macht. Denn es ist mittlerweile Universalwissen, dass erfolgversprechende Privatisierungen durch ein nicht nur formell geltendes, sondern tatsächliche Wirkung entfaltendes Regelwerk bedingt sind.[257]

Privatisierung kann, wie Befürchtungen und Diskussion bei der Wasserprivatisierung[258] zeigen, zum Problem werden, wenn eine wirkungsvolle Kontrolle unterbleibt und die Kontrolle über das Trinkwasser in die Hände globaler Konzerne gerät. Zwar besteht bei einer Privatisierung sehr wohl die Gefahr von Verteuerungen und Verschlechterungen bei der Versorgungsqualität. Allerdings wären Negativerscheinungen mit Privatinvestoren bei einer adäquaten Kartellaufsicht durchaus vermeidbar. Und die Überwachung der Entgelte ist auch bei öffentlich-rechtlichen Versorgern erforderlich. Bei einer Privatisierung wäre also zwar die Gefahr von Verteuerung und Verschlechterung von Dienstleistungen der Daseinsvorsorge abzuwenden. Denkbar ist aber auch, dass ein verschuldeter Staat sein Monopol nutzt, um etwa überhöhte Gebühren für mäßige Dienstleistungen den Bürgern abzuverlangen, während die der Marktdisziplin unterworfenen Privatunternehmungen ihre Entscheidungen nach sachlichen und nicht nach rein politischen Kriterien treffen würden. Dem kann wiederum entgegengehalten werden, dass Sparziele doch besser durch eine Verbesserung der Leistungsfähigkeit öffentlicher Unternehmungen als durch deren Privatisierung erreicht werden könnten. Es wird somit deutlich, dass weder Privatisierung noch staatliche unternehmerische Aktivität automatisch eine adäquate Gemeinwohlverwirklichung zugunsten der Bürger gewährleisten können. Bei beiden muss das Recht die Beachtung einer Reihe normativer Vorgaben überprüfen und praktische

---

[256] *Klaus Busch/Christoph Hermann/Karl Hinrichs/Thorsten Schulten,* Eurokrise, Austeritätspolitik und das Europäische Sozialmodell. Wie die Krisenpolitik in Südeuropa die soziale Dimension der EU bedroht, Friedrich Ebert-Stiftung, November 2012, S. 26.

[257] *Ernst Ulrich von Weizsäcker/Oran R. Young/Matthias Finger* (Hrsg.), Limits to Privatization. How to Avoid too Much of a Good Thing, London/New York 2005, passim.

[258] Vgl. die Aussage des EU-Binnenmarktkommissars Michel Barnier: „Zu keinem Zeitpunkt hat die Kommission vorgeschlagen, die Privatisierung öffentlicher Dienstleistungen wie der Wasserversorgung zu erzwingen oder auch nur zu fördern. Die Entscheidung darüber, wie öffentliche Dienstleistungen erbracht werden sollen, liegt ganz allein bei den Mitgliedstaaten und ihren Städten und Gemeinden. Und das wird auch so bleiben." http://ec.europa.eu/deutschland/press/pr_releases/11496_de.htm.

Herausforderungen bewältigen. Privatisierung und staatliche unternehmerische Tätigkeit müssen rechtlich gleichermaßen mit Erwartungen verbunden werden, die auf die Modernisierung der Verwaltung gerichtet sind. Man braucht eine mitlaufende Beobachtung der Reformen und Reformergebnisse (*Regulation Impact Analysis*),[259] die im Fall Griechenlands in der Konditionalität der Kreditvergabe Widerhall finden müssen. Privatisierungen hängen sowohl mit einem breiten Deregulierungsprogramm als auch mit einem neuen Privatisierungsfolgenregulierungsprogramm zusammen. Bei beiden ist ein Feedback erforderlich, der Wirkungen und Nebenwirkungen auf das Wettbewerbsklima berücksichtigt.[260]

Die Besonderheit der Privatisierungen in Griechenland ist, dass der Verkauf von Staatsbesitz eine der Bedingungen für die Kreditvergabe an ein hochverschuldetes und mit schwachen Institutionen ausgestattetes Land ist. Zentral sollte hierbei keine einseitige betriebswirtschaftliche Orientierung sein, der zufolge die Verwaltung als ein Dienstleistungsunternehmen angesehen wird. Erfolg hängt vielmehr davon ab, dass Privatisierungen mit Reformen in bestimmten Bereichen verbunden werden, die eigentlich der Durchführung von Privatisierungsprojekten vorausgehen sollten. Dies betrifft zumindest die Erleichterung der Rahmenbedingungen für geschäftliche Tätigkeiten (*ease for doing business*) sowie die Vereinfachung und Beschleunigung der Investitions- und Genehmigungsverfahren. Insofern sind Privatisierungen ein Instrument der Staatsreform. Sie verfolgen indirekte Ziele wie ökonomische Effizienz, Wachstum, Herstellung von Wettbewerbsfähigkeit sowie die Entwicklung eines nationalen funktionsfähigen Kapitalmarktes. Das impliziert, dass nationale Reformer (vor allem der öffentliche Sektor) gleichzeitig Instrument und Gegenstand von Reformen sind. Der Staat muss Troika-Programme implementieren, bei denen die Implementation die Implementationsbedingungen verändert. Aus der Sicht eines Rechts der Reformen bedeutet dies, dass man Reformen bündeln bzw. sequenzieren muss. Die Bündelung macht es möglich, dass die Verlierer einer Reform ihre Verluste durch die Gewinne, die ihnen eine weitere, hiermit zusammenhängende Reform zukommen lässt, ausgleichen und somit ihren Reformwiderstand senken können. Die Sequenzierung ist ihrerseits für die Stabilisierung von Selektionen und Ergebnissen unverzichtbar.

Aus der Sicht des Bürgers stellt sich die Frage danach, wie es zu gewährleisten ist, dass Privatisierung, die theoretisch ein Instrument von Entschuldung und Reform darstellen soll, nicht zu einem gemeinwohlwidrigen Unternehmen entartet.[261] In An-

---

[259] *OECD (Organisation for Economic Cooperation and Development)* 1995, Recommendation of the Council of the OECD on Improving the Quality of Government Regulation, OECD, Paris.

[260] „(R)egulatory impact assessment (RIA), with a particular focus on competition impact assessment of new legislation at the drafting stage, should become an integral part of the policy-making process." OECD Competition Assessment Reviews Greece, OECD 2013, 19.

[261] An Beispielen fehlt es nicht: *Emmanuelle Auriol/Aymeric Blanc,* Capture and corruption in public utilities: The cases of water and electricity in Sub-Saharan Africa, Utilities Policy 2008, 1 – 14.

lehnung an die Rechtsprechung des BVerfG zur Griechenlandhilfe und zur EFSF geht es auch im Bereich der Privatisierung von Staatsaufgaben darum, den demokratischen Willensbildungsprozess „für den Bürger offenzuhalten und ihn davor zu bewahren, zum Objekt unionalen oder staatlichen Handelns degradiert zu werden".[262] Ein glaubwürdiges Privatisierungsprogramm muss im Rahmen eines Gewährleistungsstaates, der Finanzberichterstattung und Finanzpolitik auseinanderhält, realisierbar sein und von der Gesellschaft getragen werden. Privatisierungsverfahren müssen nachweisen, dass sie privatwirtschaftliche Orientierung mit Gemeinwohl und Wettbewerbsfähigkeitsgewinnen[263] verbinden können. Hinzukommt, dass Unwägbarkeiten und Opportunitätsverhalten sowohl auf der Seite der öffentlichen Hand[264] als auch des Privatsektors vorkommen. Die Gründung eines entpolitisierten Privatisierungsfonds bringt das Misstrauen gegenüber der Fähigkeit der Politik zum Ausdruck, Privatisierungsprojekte über die Bühne zu führen. Diese Rolle des Generierens von Vertrauen übernehmen politisch unabhängige Instanzen auch im Bereich der Öffnung geschlossener Berufe und der Liberalisierung von Dienstleistungen.[265] Der Gerichtsbarkeit (vor allem dem Aufhebungsverfahren vor dem Staatsrat in einer Instanz) und dem Rechnungshof kommt auf jeden Fall im griechischen Kontext die besondere Aufgabe zu, als externe Instanzen, Privatisierungsmaßnahmen auf ihre Verfassungskonformität hin zu überprüfen und auf suboptimale Institutionen eines

---

[262] Zum Zitat und zu einem „materiellen Gehalt des Wahlrechts" bzw. einem „Recht auf Demokratie" das eben nicht nur den Bürger eines demokratischen Gläubigerstaates, sondern auch den eines demokratischen Schuldnerstaates in der EU schützen soll s. *Peter M. Huber,* Verfassungsstaat und Finanzkrise. Dresdner Vorträge zum Staatsrecht, hrsg. von A. Uhle, Bd. 7, 2014, S. 45, 73 (Zitat).

[263] „(I)n Australia, which undertook a broad programme to remove regulatory barriers to competition in the 1990 s, there have been significant benefits. In 2005 the Productivity Commission examined the effects of selected procompetitive reforms and calculated that, by enhancing productivity in particular sectors, they had boosted Australia's GDP by about 2.5 % above levels that would have otherwise prevailed." OECD Competition Assessment Reviews Greece, OECD 2013, 19.

[264] Der öffentliche Auftraggeber kann etwa im Falle des U-Bahnbaus in Thessaloniki nicht auf eine Reihe von erfolgreichen schiedsgerichtlichen Entscheidungen zurückblicken. Das Konsortium AIASA (Impregilo, Ansaldo, Seli, Ansaldobreda) hat 38–39 % des Bauwerks erstellt und dafür 385 Millionen erhalten. Im Anschluss an eine zu seinen Gunsten ergangene Schiedsgerichtsentscheidung vom 1.12.2014 wegen Verspätungen im Zeit- und Fälligkeitsplan, die es nicht zu vertreten hat, will es nun auf die weitere Durchführung des Projekts, dessen Gesamtgröße 969 Millionen umfasst, verzichten und den Vertrag auflösen. Eine Neuausschreibung für den Projektrest wäre die Folge http://www.kathimerini.gr/796318/article/epikairohta/ellada/pros-dialysh-h-symvash-gia-to-metro.

[265] Man vertraut eher in „competition authorities, rather than governments, to interpret the notion of public interest and ensure that regulations conform to the principles of non-discrimination, necessity, and proportionality. This assessment would inform amendments to sector-specific regulations. The approach taken toward services liberalization in the context of the Greece program can help illustrate the role of independent authorities and sector-specific legislation." In: *Emilio Fernández Corugedo/Esther Pérez Ruiz,* The EU Services Directive: Gains from Further Liberalization, IMF Working Paper WP/14/113, July 2014, S. 20. http://www.imf.org/external/pubs/ft/wp/2014/wp14113.pdf.

defizitären Gewährleistungsstaates hinzuweisen. Sie institutionalisieren auf diese Weise Misstrauen sowohl gegenüber einem „Ausverkauf" von Vermögenswerten „in der Not" als auch gegenüber einem ökonomisch irrationalen Aufrechterhalten von Staatsbetrieben. Sie erbringen eine Legitimationsleistung, die einen wesentlicheren Wirtschaftsfaktor als die rein fiskalisch orientierte Erzielung von Privatisierungserlösen darstellt. Die Institutionalisierung von Misstrauen hat somit einen vielfachen Richtungssinn: Sie mobilisiert verfassungsrechtliche Vorschriften, die einem abwägungsfreien Vorrang des Gläubigerschutzes durch Maximierung von Privatisierungserlösen zulasten anderer Belange entgegenstehen; sie bekämpft den politischen Klientelismus; sie setzt Staatsbetriebe, die jenseits der disziplinierenden Wirkung des Wettbewerbs operieren, unter Effizienz- und Effektivitätsdruck; sie setzt die Strukturanpassungsprogramme der Troika der wissenschaftlichen Kritik und Debatte aus. Sie allein kann eine Identifikation der Bevölkerung mit der Staatsreform herbeiführen und diffusen unwiderlegbaren Verschwörungstheorien, die jedweden Privatisierungsplan *in statu nascendi* unterminieren, den Wind aus den Segeln nehmen.

2. Generierung von Vertrauen:
Pfadabhängigkeit und europäische Integration

Kehrseite der Institutionalisierung von Misstrauen ist die Pfadabhängigkeit des institutionellen Wandels und die Ownership von Reform. Das „Theorem" der Pfadabhängigkeit suggeriert ein Mindestmaß an Kontinuität, das im Rahmen eines grundlegenden Wandels aufrechterhalten bleiben muss. Es unterstreicht auf jeden Fall die Bedeutung von Reformsequenzen. Es hat sich nämlich herausgestellt, dass sich unterschiedliche Reformsequenzen zu Beginn von Transformationsprozessen auf den späteren Transformationsverlauf eines Landes erheblich auswirken. Einen ungünstigen Verlauf der Transformationsentwicklung hat man etwa bei der Beschreibung des post-sozialistischen Transformationsprozesses europäischer Länder in einer Transformationsentwicklung gesehen, in der „die Privatisierung und insbesondere die Preisliberalisierung vor der ökonomischen Stabilisierung in Angriff genommen wurden". Ferner zeigte sich, dass eine Behinderung des Transformationsverlaufs von den „frühen Reformgewinnern" ausgehen kann, soweit diese „ihre Position durch Blockadepolitik sichern" können. Die Verschleppung von Reformen hing auch mit „korruptem *state capture* durch große privatisierte Unternehmen" zusammen.[266] Ein grundlegender Wandel institutioneller Ordnungen ist nur vor dem Hintergrund einer Mindestkontinuitätssicherung möglich, die allerdings mit der Einführung neuer Handlungsmuster kombiniert werden muss. Dies bedeutet für Akteure, die von der Vergangenheit geprägt sind, dass sie erhebliche Mühen des Umlernens und Kosten des Umstellens auf sich nehmen müssen, dass es aber auch eine neue Rolle im neuen „Geschäftsmodell" für sie geben muss. Für einen Pfadwechsel

---

[266] Siehe zitierte Stellen in *Jürgen Beyer,* Pfadabhängigkeit. Über institutionelle Kontinuität, anfällige Stabilität und fundamentalen Wandel, Frankfurt/New York, 2006, S. 173, 243, 250.

braucht man jedenfalls neues kollektives Handeln, dass tatsächlich stattfindet. Dazu braucht man reforminduzierte Alternativen, die zumindest gleich effizient sind, sonst bleiben die Hürden für neues Handeln zu hoch. Anhaltende Verfestigungen von Verhaltensstrukturen sind zwar mehr oder weniger gegen grundlegenden Wandel gefeit. Es kann aber manchmal schon ausreichen, dass einzelne Akteure von zentraler Bedeutung (etwa die Verwaltungsgerichtsbarkeit oder eine unabhängige Behörde) einen nachprüfbaren Orientierungswechsel vollziehen. Manchmal kann es wiederum notwendig sein, dass sehr viele staatliche und gesellschaftliche Akteure koordiniert den Status quo in Frage stellen. Funktionierende Problemlösungsmechanismen müssen zur Verfügung stehen, damit die Unsicherheit einer Abkehr vom Bestehenden reduziert wird. Das neue Gegenmodell muss einen größeren privaten und gesellschaftlichen, staatlichen und ökonomischen Erfolg versprechen. Akteure müssen erwarten können, dass ein Orientierungswechsel für sie im Rahmen des neuen Geschäftsmodells von Vorteil sein kann. Das ist die Problematik der „Ownership"[267] der Reform. Der Moral-Hazard-Aspekt,[268] der die Konditionalität der Strukturanpassungsprogramme mitprägt, sollte berücksichtigen, dass „die" Bevölkerung, die die Reformen unterstützen soll, in einem klientelistisch unterwanderten Rechtsstaat eine ambivalente[269] Rolle spielt: diejenigen, die vor allem die Kosten der Konsolidierungsmaßnahmen tragen, sind mit denjenigen, die von den durch Haushaltsdefizite finanzierten Staatsausgaben profitieren konnten, nicht identisch. Die Funktion des symbiotischen Mechanismus[270] „Rechts- und Klientelstaat" liegt geradezu in der Trennung von (Steuer-)Zahlern und Benefiziaren. Erstere können somit keine „Zivi-

---

[267] Hierzu s. den Beitrag von *Meng* in diesem Band.

[268] „You hear this blood-curdling moral hazard-y stuff from them (the Europeans)... ,we're going to crush them.' [That] was their basic attitude". The Telegraph, 30.11.2014, *Tim Geithner* reveals in the raw how Europe's leaders tried to commit financial suicide: http://www.telegraph.co.uk/finance/economics/11226828/Tim-Geithner-reveals-in-the-raw-how-Europes-leaders-tried-to-commit-financial-suicide.html.

[269] Ein in verschiedenen Reformkontexten bereits beobachteter Sachverhalt: „As underwriters of government indebtedness, the general public play an ambivalent role: they have to service government debt via taxation, but the benefits of borrowing may accrue to different groups of voters (both within and across generations) from those that pay." *Robert Price,* Achieving and sustaining fiscal consolidation, S. 269 ff., 270, in: Making Reform Happen. Lessons from OECD Countries, OECD 2010, http://www.sourceoecd.org/governance/9789264086289.

[270] *Generalinspektor der Öffentlichen Verwaltung,* Jahresbericht 2013, Athen, Juni 2014, S. 7: Er moniert die Rolle des Parlaments bei der positiven Diskriminierung und Deckung des Korruptionsverhaltens „prominenter" Mitglieder des Klientelsystems; *Suzanne Daley,* New Immunity Provisions Cast Doubt on Greece's Efforts to Fight Corruption, New York Times October 17, 2014, Seite A8: „Buried on page 78 (of an omnibus bill titled ,Measures of Support and Growth for the Greek Economy') was language that essentially gave retroactive immunity to thousands of workers in state-funded organizations that could shield them from future corruption prosecutions." Ein Verfassungsrechtler wird mit der Begründung zitiert: „In order to get people – in many cases Greeks who have lived and worked elsewhere – to come here and take these jobs, you have to say that they will not be held responsible. These laws are not so much to cover scandal but to allow government to function" (ebd.).

lisation" mit ihren Steuerbeiträgen „kaufen".[271] Klientelistisch induzierte Inklusion und Vollbeschäftigung im weit definierten öffentlichen Sektor sehen sich den klientelistisch exkludierten Arbeitslosen im privaten Sektor gegenüber. Nur solange Reformer für derartige Trennungen nicht blind bleiben, können sie eine echte Chance auf Akzeptanz erhalten und die Missachtung oder irreführende Verwechslung von fiskalischen bzw. Stabilisierungsmaßnahmen mit Strukturreformen vermeiden. Gefragt ist ein stabiler institutioneller Wandel, denn Investoren können politische Unsicherheit nur ertragen, wenn der institutionelle Kontext des Landes einigermaßen stabil bleibt.[272]

Durchführung und Akzeptanz von Reformen betreffen ferner die Problematik der normativen Anforderungen[273] der europäischen Integration als Wertegemeinschaft,[274] deren Leitbildfunktion in horizontalen Kooperationsstrukturen[275] und in Strukturen gegenseitigen Lernens[276] mehr Chancen hat, Vertrauen in den Strukturwandel zu generieren. Ein kulturtheoretischer Zugang zum Verwaltungsphänomen,[277] der die organisationstheoretische[278] und die juristisch-methodologische[279] Sichtweise ergänzt, gibt den Blick auf gesellschaftstheoretische Zusammenhänge und damit auch für eine Feinsteuerung des Feedbacks aus dem Reformprozess frei. Die Aufnahmebereitschaft für Reformen impliziert die Erkenntnis, dass sich rechtsstaatliche Institutionen als institutionalisierte Bedürfniserfüllungen gegen die Logik[280] eines Neo-Patrimonialstaates[281] erst durchsetzen[282] können, wenn die Problemlösungen, die sie bereitstellen, effizienter als die gemeinwohlwidrigen Bedürfniserfüllungen sind, die von klientelistischen Netzwerken zur Verfügung gestellt

---

[271] Nach dem Motto von *Oliver Wendell Holmes, Jr.* „Taxes are what we pay for civilized society, including the chance to insure." In: *Compania General De Tabacos De Filipinas v. Collector of Internal Revenue*, 275 U.S. 87, 100, dissenting opinion: http://caselaw.lp.findlaw. com/scripts/getcase.pl?court=US&vol=275&invol=87.

[272] „Our investment plans are on hold for now, since we are waiting for the result of the presidential election. If there is political stability we will increase our investments" – Independent Balkan News Agency http://www.balkaneu.com/john-paulson-freezes-investments-gre ece/#sthash.kWpxaQna.dpuf.

[273] Hierzu s. den Beitrag von *Ruffert* in diesem Band.

[274] Hierzu s. den Beitrag von *La Torre* in diesem Band.

[275] Hierzu s. den Beitrag von *Dimitropoulos* in diesem Band.

[276] Hierzu s. den Beitrag von *Hofmann* in diesem Band.

[277] Hierzu s. den Beitrag von *Sommermann* in diesem Band.

[278] Hierzu s. den Beitrag von *Koutnatzis* in diesem Band.

[279] Hierzu s. den Beitrag von *Chanos* in diesem Band.

[280] Hierzu s. den Beitrag von *Karkatsoulis* in diesem Band.

[281] Der Begriff des „Neo-Patrimonialismus" beruht auf Max Webers Begriff des „Patrimonialismus", hierzu monographisch: *Christopher Clapham,* Third World Politics. An Introduction, Madison u. a. 1985.

[282] Zur Durchsetzung von „Amt" als Begriff und Institution s. den Beitrag von *Wolff* in diesem Band.

werden.[283] So stehen am Anfang von „Reform"[284], die in einem insolventen Staat unter dem Druck des Befristeten im „verfassungsrechtlichen Ausnahmezustand"[285] stattfindet, defizitäre Institutionen des Rechtsstaates und unbewährte institutionelle Alternativen[286] im Wettbewerb. Rezession und Depression erweisen sich in diesem Kontext als reformrelevante institutionentheoretische Phänomene. Das Einbrechen der wirtschaftlichen Entwicklung treibt einen Keil in den Regelkreis zwischen Bedürfniserfüllung und Institutionenbildung derart, dass sich an die bestehenden Institutionen des Rechtsstaates und des Marktes keine neuen Verwendungsbedürfnisse lagern können, die von der Staatsabhängigkeit weg hin zur Marktabhängigkeit der Wirtschaft und zur Privatisierung führen können. Privatisierungserfolge ohne Gewährleistungsstaat tragen ihrerseits zu einer vordergründigen, lediglich fiskalischen Stabilisierung bei, die die „extraktiven Institutionen"[287] im Lande unangetastet lässt. Privatisierungen werden zu einem Katalysator für Reformen, wenn sie durch den Abbau von Marktzutrittsschranken alten und neuen Marktteilnehmern die Probe abverlangen und die korporative Abschottungsmacht fester verwurzelter Interessen unter Veränderungsdruck setzen. Sie können somit innovativen Unternehmungen den Weg ebnen, die im Stande sind, geschäftliche Entdeckungen und Erfindungen an die lokalen Verhältnisse anzupassen und diese zugleich hierdurch zu verändern.[288] Diese Unternehmungen müssen von der Rechtsform her weder privat noch öffentlich, sie müssen lediglich wettbewerbsfähig und gleichzeitig im Stande sein, erforderliche Dienstleistungspotentiale zu gewährleisten.

V. Schlussfolgerungen

1. Privatisierungen stehen in Griechenland rechtlich vor zwei Herausforderungen. Sie müssen einerseits im institutionellen Kontext eines neo-patrimonialen Rechtsstaats erfolgen, der zwar kein „failed state" ist, der doch die Gewährleistungsfunktion eines Rechtsstaates nur teilweise wahrnehmen kann. Sie müssen andererseits der Konditionalität der Strukturanpassungsprogramme der Geldge-

---

[283] *Gromitsaris*, Korruption und Wirtschaftswachstum im Rechtsstaat, in: Carlos Gonzalez-Palacios/Thilo Rensmann/Manuel Tirard (Hrsg.), Demokratie und Rechtsstaat. Deutsch-Französisch-Peruanische Sommeruniversität, Lima 2013, S. 61 ff.

[284] Zur Krise der Begriffe „Reform" und „Steuerung" s. den Beitrag von *Schulte* in diesem Band.

[285] Hierzu s. den Beitrag von *Vlachopoulos* in diesem Band.

[286] Siehe hierzu mit Blick auf die Konkurrenz von Justiz und privater Schiedsgerichtsbarkeit den Beitrag von *Brekoulakis* in diesem Band.

[287] Begriff von *Daron Acemoglu/James Robinson*, Why Nations fail. The Origins of Power, Prosperity and Poverty, New York 2012.

[288] *Edmund Phelps/Gylfi Zoega*, Entrepreneurship, culture and openness, in: David B. Audretsch/Robert Litan/Robert Strom (Hrsg.), Entrepreneurship and Openness: Theory and Evidence, Cheltenham u. a. 2009, S. 101 ff.

ber gerecht werden, aber auch deren Nebenwirkungen[289] in Rechnung stellen. Beide Aspekte verändern bzw. verzerren Kautelen, Verlauf und Wirkungen von Privatisierungen.

2. Was den ersten Aspekt angeht, ist mit Hilfe des europäischen Verwaltungsrechts die politische Neutralität und Unabhängigkeit der Privatisierungsbehörde und die Transparenz der Ausschreibungsverfahren zu gewährleisten. Der zusätzlichen Kontrolle durch Rechnungshof und Staatsrat kommt eine legitimierende Funktion zu.

3. Die Entpolitisierung des Privatisierungsfonds institutionalisiert Misstrauen gegenüber dem Klientelstaat. Der Privatisierungsfonds schützt zugleich die Gläubiger durch die Übertragung des Staatsbesitzes vor Verlust. Der Verkauf von Vermögenswerten bewirkt ferner eine Umverteilung der Ansprüche unter die einzelnen Gläubigergruppen des Landes. Unter diesem Aspekt kann Privatisierung eine de facto Seniorität etablieren.

4. Der Aspekt des Gläubigerschutzes ist reformpolitisch und rechtlich durch eine stärkere Betonung der Funktion von Privatisierung als Instrument der Herstellung von Wettbewerbsfähigkeit und der Einwerbung von Investitionen zu ergänzen. Privatisierungen sind hierbei auf flankierende Maßnahmen angewiesen, die strukturelle wettbewerbsfeindliche Blockaden beseitigen und staatsabhängige Bedürfniserfüllungen durch marktorientierte Institutionen ersetzen. Vor der Privatisierung sollten bereits Effizienz- und Profitabilitätssteigerungen ermöglicht werden, die Investitionen attraktiv machen und weitere Steigerungen nach der Privatisierung auslösen können.

5. Wenn die zu privatisierenden Vermögenswerte dem Zugriff und der Kontrolle des Schuldnerstaates völlig entgleiten, verstärkt dies zwar den Gläubigerschutz. Dies vermag allerdings ohne zusätzliche gemeinwohlorientierte Vorkehrungen keine Identifikation der Bevölkerung mit dem Privatisierungs- und Reformprogramm („Ownership") zu generieren.

6. Strukturelle Reformen, zu denen Privatisierungen auch gehören, lassen sich niemals ohne starken politischen Willen umsetzen. Im neo-patrimonialen Rechtsstaat zielt der politische Wille jedoch vor allem darauf, die Klientel der eigenen Partei zu stärken und die Gegner vom Zugang zu Machtressourcen auszuschließen. Privatisierungen können allen konkurrierenden Klientelsystemen eine wichtige Ressourcenquelle entziehen. Dies setzt allerdings voraus, dass sie selbst kein (internationaler) klientelistischer Tauschakt sind.

---

[289] Hier ist eine theoretische Zusammenfassung dieser Nebenwirkungen: „The conclusions from the large literature on structural adjustment policies suggest that the Economic Adjustment Programmes (EAPs) will: be badly implemented; be neutral or bad for growth; be bad for equity and the poor; have unpredictable policy consequences; and will allow incumbent elites to preserve their positions." *Scott Greer,* Structural adjustment comes to Europe: Lessons for the Eurozone from the conditionality debates, in: Global Social Policy 2014, Vol. 14 (1) 51–71, 51.

7. Angesichts politischer Instabilität und Vertrauenserosion haben eher krisenfeste Privatisierungsprojekte eine Aussicht auf Erfolg, bei denen Investitionen auch im Falle eines Euro-Austritts nicht an Wert verlieren. Dies lässt sich nur ändern, wenn „Grexit" kein Thema mehr ist.

8. Die Verbindung der Kredit-Konditionalität mit Privatisierungen ist insofern problematisch, als sie der Erzielung von zu hohen vorausbestimmten Privatisierungserlösbeträgen den Vorrang gewährt. Es hat sich herausgestellt, dass sich die erwarteten Kassenerfolge unter den gegebenen Krisenbedingungen nicht erzielen lassen.

9. Privatisierungen sollen nicht nur mit Ertragserwartungen verbunden werden. Sie sind darüber hinaus als strukturelle Reforminstrumente unverzichtbar. Sie müssen allerdings in dieser Funktion viel stärker als bislang in den Vordergrund gestellt werden.

10. Primärziel sollte die Entwicklung sanierungsfahiger Betriebe zu wettbewerbsfähigen Unternehmen und deren Privatisierung sein.[290] Da jedoch Privatisierungen die Strukturanpassung der Wirtschaft an die Erfordernisse des Marktes fördern sollen, müssen sie auch in eine Sequenz struktureller Reformen eingebaut werden.

11. Theoretisch gilt: Die öffentliche Hand erhält zwar durch den Verkauf von Vermögenswerten Finanzmittel zur Verringerung ihres Schulddienstlastes. Zugleich entgehen ihr dabei hierdurch zukünftige Einnahmen, denn sie wird keine Einkünfte aus den verkauften Vermögenswerten mehr erhalten können. So heben sich diese beiden Aspekte ohne Nettogewinne bzw. Nettoverluste gegenseitig auf. In Griechenland sind aber die Staatsunternehmen oft defizitär und nicht wettbewerbsfähig.

12. Wenn staatliche Betriebe weder privatisierungs- noch sanierungsfähig sind, sollten sie stillgelegt werden. Eine Überbrückungssanierung bis zur Privatisierung ist ad hoc in Betracht zu ziehen.

13. Der Privatisierungsbegriff enthält einen doppelten Auftrag: Zum einen bezieht er sich auf einen Auftrag zur Erzielung eines Verkaufserlöses und zur Erbringung einer aus Sicht eines privaten Investors marktadäquaten Rendite. Zum anderen enthält er einen Auftrag zur Errichtung einer wettbewerbsgerechten Wirtschaftsstruktur. Privatisierungsvorgänge sollten lieber nicht zur Entstehung einer Monopolposition oder einer marktbeherrschenden Stellung führen, sondern wettbewerbsfähige Strukturen fördern.

14. Folgender Zielkonflikt soll gelöst werden: Die Veräußerung lediglich staatlicher Minderheitsbeteiligungen an nicht sanierten Staatsbetrieben an den privaten Investor oder die staatliche Einhaltung von „golden shares" wirken bei der Einwerbung von Investmentkapital und der Erzielung von Effizienzgewinnen hin-

---

[290] Vgl. etwa die Formulierung § 2 VI Treuhandgesetz vom 17.6.1990.

derlich. Verbleiben demgegenüber der öffentlichen Hand keine Stimm- und Kontrollrechte, gefährdet dies die Verfassungskonformität und Legitimität des Privatisierungsvorhabens und die „Ownership" der Reform.

15. Eine Lösung dieses Konflikts kann in den PPP-Kooperationsmodellen im Bereich der Daseinsvorsorge unter zwei Voraussetzungen gefunden werden: Die öffentliche Hand soll beherrschen oder regulieren, welche Dienstleistungen der private Betreiber mit dem Vermögenswert zu erbringen hat, und an wen und zu welchem Preis diese Dienstleistungen zu erbringen sind. Die öffentliche Hand soll ferner als Eigentümerin, Nutznießerin oder anders sämtliche Residualwerte am Ende der Vertragsdauer beherrschen. Die Beherrschung der Restgrößen entzieht dem Privaten die Möglichkeit, während der Projektdauer den Vermögenswert zu veräußern, zu verpfänden, für andere Zwecke zu nutzen oder den Vertrag vorzeitig zu beenden. Die Beherrschung des Residualwertes macht insbesondere deutlich, dass kein Ausverkauf („fire sale") vorliegt.[291]

16. Privatisierungen können im griechischen Kontext einen produktiveren Einsatz von Ressourcen und Produktionsfaktoren, vor allem Kapital und Arbeit durch private Investoren mit sich bringen, sie können aber nach bisheriger Erfahrung die kurzfristige Zahlungsfähigkeit des Staates ohne Hinzutreten besserer Investitionsbedingungen kaum verbessern. Sie fungieren somit eher als ein strukturelles Reformkonzept denn als eine die Steuerlast mindernde Stabilisierungsmaßnahme.

---

[291] Hierzu: *Gromitsaris*, Zur Natur und Abgrenzung des öffentlichen Sektors nach IPSAS am Beispiel von Dienstleistungskonzessionsvereinbarungen, in: Die Verwaltung 46 (2013), S. 287–301.